Revolution and Its Discontents

The death of the Islamic Republic's revolutionary patriarch Ayatollah Khomeini, the bitter denouement of the Iran–Iraq War, and marginalisation of leading factions within the political elite, in tandem with the end of the Cold War, harboured immense intellectual and political repercussions for the Iranian state and society. It was these events which created the conditions for the emergence of Iran's post-revolutionary reform movement, as its intellectuals and political leaders sought to re-evaluate the foundations of the Islamic state's political legitimacy and religious authority. In this monograph, Sadeghi-Boroujerdi examines the rise and evolution of reformist political thought in Iran and analyses the complex network of publications, study circles, and think tanks that encompassed a range of prominent politicians and intellectuals in the 1990s. In his meticulous account of the relationships between the post-revolutionary political class and intelligentsia, he explores a panoply of political and ideological issues still vital to understanding Iran's revolutionary state, such as the ruling political theology of the 'Guardianship of the Jurist', the political elite's engagement with questions of Islamic statehood, democracy, and constitutionalism, and their critiques of revolutionary agency and social transformation.

Eskandar Sadeghi-Boroujerdi is a British Academy Postdoctoral Research Fellow in the Faculty of Oriental Studies at the University of Oxford and Postdoctoral Associate at St Cross College, Oxford. He has taught at the University of Oxford, SOAS (University of London), and the University of Exeter. Sadeghi-Boroujerdi was Associate Editor at the *British Journal of Middle Eastern Studies* from 2014 to 2017 and is Series Editor of *Radical Histories of the Middle East*. His writings on Iran have been widely published in academic journals and the international media, including the *British Journal of Middle Eastern Studies*, *Iranian Studies*, *Digest of Middle East Studies*, *Middle East Journal*, *Foreign Policy*, *Jadaliyya*, *Al Jazeera*, *Lobelog*, *Muftah*, *Jacobin*, and *The Guardian*.

The Global Middle East

The Global Middle East series seeks to broaden and deconstruct the geographical boundaries of the 'Middle East' as a concept to include North Africa, Central and South Asia, and diaspora communities in Western Europe and North America. The series features fresh scholarship that employs theoretically rigorous and innovative methodological frameworks resonating across relevant disciplines in the humanities and the social sciences. In particular, the general editors welcome approaches that focus on mobility, the erosion of nation-state structures, travelling ideas and theories, transcendental techno-politics, the decentralisation of grand narratives, and the dislocation of ideologies inspired by popular movements. The series will also consider translations of works by authors in these regions whose ideas are salient to global scholarly trends but have yet to be introduced to the Anglophone academy.

Other Books in the Series

Revolution and Its Discontents

Political Thought and Reform in Iran

ESKANDAR SADEGHI-BOROUJERDI
University of Oxford

CAMBRIDGE
UNIVERSITY PRESS

CAMBRIDGE
UNIVERSITY PRESS

University Printing House, Cambridge CB2 8BS, United Kingdom

One Liberty Plaza, 20th Floor, New York, NY 10006, USA

477 Williamstown Road, Port Melbourne, VIC 3207, Australia

314–321, 3rd Floor, Plot 3, Splendor Forum, Jasola District Centre, New Delhi – 110025, India

79 Anson Road, #06–04/06, Singapore 079906

Cambridge University Press is part of the University of Cambridge.

It furthers the University's mission by disseminating knowledge in the pursuit of education, learning, and research at the highest international levels of excellence.

www.cambridge.org
Information on this title: www.cambridge.org/9781108426343
DOI: 10.1017/9781108681834

First published 2019

Printed and bound in Great Britain by Clays Ltd, Elcograf S.p.A.

A catalogue record for this publication is available from the British Library.

Library of Congress Cataloging-in-Publication Data
Names: Sadeghi-Boroujerdi, Eskandar, 1982– author.
Title: Revolution and its discontents : political thought and reform in Iran / Eskandar Sadeghi-Boroujerdi, University of Oxford.
Description: Cambridge, United Kingdom ; New York, NY, USA : Cambridge University Press, [2019] | Includes bibliographical references and index.
Identifiers: LCCN 2018041015 | ISBN 9781108426343
Subjects: LCSH: Iran – Politics and government – 1979–1997. | Iran – Politics and government – 1997– | Political culture – Iran. | Social change – Political aspects – Iran.
Classification: LCC DS318.825 .S233 2019 | DDC 955.05/4–dc23
LC record available at https://lccn.loc.gov/2018041015

ISBN 978-1-108-42634-3 Hardback

To my parents
&
Homa Katouzian

Contents

Acknowledgements

I would first like to thank Homa Katouzian, my mentor and doctoral supervisor at the University of Oxford. He was never short of time, advice, or support and was always ready to help in any way possible. I simply cannot express sufficient gratitude for his abundant kindness, integrity, and generosity of spirit, as well as the example he has set as both a scholar and human being, all of which have indelibly left their mark.

I must profusely thank Ali Ansari and Faisal Devji, whose incisive comments and provocative questions in the course of my *viva voce* upon which this work is based were invaluable and helped me to improve this modest piece of research. Both have been a generous source of support and encouragement, indispensable to any early career scholar and their development. Nasser Mohajer is also in need of special thanks and has been a brilliant source of advice and guidance. He has spent many hours speaking with me and discussing sources, events, and historiography, very often on issues unrelated to the subject of this work. Nonetheless, I believe myself a much better researcher as a result of his positive influence and meticulous intellect, which have enabled me to understand the vicissitudes of twentieth-century Iranian history in a far deeper fashion than I might have done otherwise. He also took great care when reading the chapters I sent for his review and gave comments that were without exception insightful and thought-provoking. They always inspired me to polish and improve those points which were unclear or demanded further elucidation. Siavush Randjbar-Daemi is deserving of profuse thanks and gratitude. He has always and without fail been indefatigable in offering his help, suggestions, and constructive criticism. I feel fortunate to consider him not only a first-rate academic colleague and interlocutor but also a dear friend. Without our constant back-and-forth and intellectual dialogue I would be quite a different historian to the one I am today.

Nader Hashemi has always encouraged my research and writing and instilled confidence into me when I most doubted myself. I cannot thank him enough for all of his advice, support, and help over the years. Abdel Razzaq Takriti was a true friend, both in the good and, more importantly, in the difficult times. His friendship and intellectual camaraderie have been decisive to my personal and professional life, and I simply cannot express in words their value to me. I consider myself fortunate to know such a remarkable, passionate, and committed scholar and generous *ensan*. Arshin Adib-Moghaddam was always encouraging, and unsparing with this time and gave me crucial opportunities to teach and engage with the SOAS community for which I am immensely grateful. Ali Mirsepassi, too, has been most encouraging, and his recommendations and interjections have been vital to further improving this piece of research. Without the stellar guidance of Arshin and Ali, this book would have turned out quite differently. Hossein Kamaly was always ready with his time, kind words, and wisdom. His dignity, ethical fortitude, and learned erudition were of great inspiration. My friend and colleague Rasmus Elling kindly read the original dissertation and wrote an eloquent and insightful review as well as commenting on the draft manuscript with typical precision and insight.

Ervand Abrahamian has been an intellectual lodestar and source of inspiration since my undergraduate years. I will never forget when he generously sent this unknown and rather clueless undergraduate a photocopy of his article in the post after I emailed him out of the blue. Apart from his personal generosity, he is a scholar and a critically minded intellectual whom I have never ceased reading and learning from. I was truly humbled that he took the time, despite his many other commitments, to read an earlier draft of the manuscript and provide me with incisive feedback, which I have since incorporated. Laleh Khalil similarly read the manuscript and, as always, provoked me to thought in ways only she could. Her friendship and comradely engagement continue to stand as an exemplar. Behrooz Ghamari-Tabrizi, whose own pioneering work has always proven to be mandatory reading, was ever gracious and, despite his hectic schedule, took the time to read through an earlier draft and pose crucial questions which pushed me to refine certain key elements. Babak Rahimi provided excellent feedback leavened with humour and levity, importantly reminding me not to take myself too seriously. Another senior colleague for whom I have only admiration, Omid Safi, has never been short of encouragement, support, or advice, for which I can only express the deepest of thanks. The two anonymous reviewers should be amply thanked for their care, attention, and empathy when reading my work. It is no exaggeration to say that their input made a decisive impact on the book before you.

Edmund Herzig, Stephanie Cronin, Hamid Dabashi, Abolghasem Fanaei, Touraj Atabaki, Mohsen Kadivar, Hossein Bashiriyeh, Mehrzad Boroujerdi, Golbarg Bashi, Anoushiravan Ehteshami, Ali Rahnema, Sajjad Rizvi, Fatemeh Shams, Nazanin Shahrokni, Mazen Masri, Ariabarzan Mohammadi, Mohammadreza Jalaeipour, Reza Zia-Ebrahimi, Alam Saleh, Naghmeh Sohrabi, Yasuyuki Matsunaga, Marc Valeri, Fanar Haddad, M. Ali Kadivar, Amin Ehteshami, Janet Coleman, Amin Borzorgian, Omar Shweiki, Robert Waller, Siavash Hariri, Bahareh Zavvar, Mostafa Zavvar, Shahram Rezaei, Shahrzad Rezaei, Pankaj Santiago, Ali Rezaei, Harry Manikdiwela, and Taymour Harding all gave their precious time in a variety of ways which, directly and indirectly, contributed to this piece of research and/or my academic development, for which I cannot express enough thanks. I must heartily thank my family – Sacha Reza Sadeghi, Seyyed Morteza Tayebi-Jazayeri, Bibi Saeideh Moravej Al Ali, Ali Tayebi-Jazayeri, Shima Tayebi-Jazayeri, Sahar Tayebi-Jazayeri, Safa Tayebi-Jazayeri, Amir Ale Mohammad, and Hossein Tayebi-Jazayeri – who have sent countless books from Tehran for my research and were always ready to help in any conceivable way. My brother Sam has been invariably supportive and caring. It was in the quiet of his West London apartment that I spent many hours editing the following text.

My deepest appreciation goes to Queen's College, Oxford, for the award of bursaries and travel grants to facilitate my research. I would like to thank the British Academy, which awarded me a highly coveted postdoctoral research fellowship and thereby the opportunity to complete the final edits of this monograph before moving on to my next major project. Maria Marsh of Cambridge University Press has proven to be a terrific editor who has tirelessly stewarded the publication process from start to finish. Her assiduousness and diligent oversight made all the difference. Abigail Walkington and Natasha Whelan, also at CUP, have been incredibly helpful throughout and answered my many queries with patience and enthusiasm.

Penultimately, I would like to thank my wife, Ala, whose love, devotion, and joyfulness I could not live without. Her patience, affection, and understanding throughout the duration of working on this monograph made all the difference. Above all, I must thank my father, Mehran, without whose unconditional love and support none of this would have been possible. I alone am culpable for any of the shortcomings which follow.

Eskandar Sadeghi-Boroujerdi, April 2018, Oxford

Note on Sources and Transliteration

Part of Chapter 2 is based on a revised version of the essay 'Ali Shariati and the Ideologization of Religion', Eskandar Sadeghi-Boroujerdi, Tehran Bureau, *PBS Frontline*, 30 October 2011.

Chapter 7 is based on a revised version of the article 'From *Etelā'āti* to *Eslāhtalabi*: Sa'id Hajjarian, Political Theology and the Politics of Reform in Post-Revolutionary Iran', Eskandar Sadeghi-Boroujerdi, *Iranian Studies* 47, no. 6, 987–1009. This book uses a variation of the *Iranian Studies* journal's transliteration system, albeit dispensing with all diacritical marks reserved for long vowels.

Abbreviations

IRI	Islamic Republic of Iran (*Jomhuri-ye eslami-ye Iran*)
MRM	Association of Combatant Clerics (*Majma'-e rowhaniyun-e mobarez*)
IRGC	Islamic Revolutionary Guard Corps (*Sepah-e pasdaran-e enqelab-e eslami*)
JRM	Society of Combatant Clergy (*Jame'eh-ye rowhaniyyat-e mobarez*)
GC	Guardian Council (*Shura-ye negahban*)
IRP	Islamic Republic Party (*Hezb-e jomhuri-ye eslami*)
SMEEI	Mojahedin Organisation of the Islamic Revolution of Iran (*Sazman-e mojahedin-e enqelab-e eslami-ye Iran*)
SMEE	Mojahedin Organisation of the Islamic Revolution (*Sazman-e mojahedin-e enqelab-e eslami*)
PRG	Provisional Revolutionary Government
NAI	Freedom Movement of Iran (*Nehzat-e azadi-ye Iran*)
SFMMI	Council of National-Religious Activists of Iran (*Shura-ye fa'alan-e melli mazhabi-ye Iran*)
PFII	Participation Front for Islamic Iran (*Hezb-e jebheh-ye mosharekat-e Iran-e eslami*)
HEM	National Trust Party (*Hezb-e e'temad-e melli*)
DTV	Office for Strengthening Unity (*Daftar-e tahkim-e vahdat*)
JME	Islamic Coalition Society (*Jam'iyyat-e mo'talafeh-ye eslami*)
SQST	Society of Qom Seminary Teachers (*Jame'eh-ye modarresin-e howzeh-ye 'elmiyyeh-ye Qom*)
PMOI	People's Mojahedin Organisation of Iran (*Sazman-e mojahedin-e khalq-e Iran*)
PSRC	Presidential Strategic Research Centre
SEF	Council for Cultural Revolution (*Setad-e enqelab-e farhangi*)
OIPFG	Organisation of the Iranian People's Fada'i Guerrillas (*Sazman-e cherik-ha-ye fada'i-ye khalq-e Iran*)
FI	Devotees of Islam (*Fada'iyan-e Islam*)

Abbreviations

Introduction

All terms become new when they are transferred from their proper context to another ... When we ascend to heaven, we must speak before God in new languages ... When we are on earth, we must speak with our own languages ... For we must carefully mark this distinction, that in matters of divinity we must speak far differently than in matters of politics.[1]

Martin Luther

All significant concepts of the modern theory of the state are secularized theological concepts.[2]

Carl Schmitt

Seyyed Hashem Aqajari (b. 1957) was not a cleric but a longstanding member of the Mojahedin Organisation of the Islamic Revolution of Iran (*Sazman-e mojahedin-e enqelab-e eslami-ye Iran*, SMEEI), a prominent reform-oriented political organisation. He also happened to be a veteran of the Islamic Revolutionary Guard Corps (*Sepah-e pasdaran-e enqelab-e eslami*, IRGC), and had served on the front of the Iran–Iraq War. His commitment to one of the twentieth century's last great revolutions and his homeland were beyond reproach. As there was for thousands of others who had served in the war, there was a physical price to pay for such unwavering commitment. Aqajari lost a leg to a landmine in the course of the brutal eight-year conflict.

On 19 June 2002 [29 Khordad 1381] in commemoration of the twenty-fifth anniversary of the death of the Iranian intellectual and political activist 'Ali Shari'ati, Aqajari – now a respected history

---

[1]   Quoted in Sheldon D. Wolin, *Politics and Vision: Continuity and Innovation in Western Political Thought Expanded Edition*, 2nd ed., Kindle ed. (Princeton; Oxford: Princeton University Press, 2004), p. 152.

[2]   Carl Schmitt, *Political Theology: Four Chapters on the Concept of Sovereignty*, trans. George Schwab, foreword by Tracy B. Strong, ed. (Chicago; London: University of Chicago Press, 2005), p. 36.

professor – delivered a lecture in the mid-western city of Hamedan entitled 'Dr. Shari'ati and the Project of Islamic Protestantism'.[3] In this pugnacious lecture he lamented that, despite some 100 years having elapsed since the publication of the Qajar-era diplomat and author Mirza Yusef Khan Mostashar al-Dowleh's *Yek kalameh* (1870), and post-revolutionary reformist politicians' regular demands calling for 'the rule of law', 'law has still not come to rule'.[4] *Yek kalameh* or *One Word* was an intellectual touchstone of late-nineteenth-century reformers and Iran's Constitutional Revolution in the first decade of the twentieth century. Whatever its author's original intention, it had come to signify the struggle for the rule of law and the constraint of arbitrary power. This was the least controversial of Aqajari's comments, however. What would with great rapidity provoke enmity – not to mention a death sentence,[5] later commuted to a five-year jail term[6] – was his simple but acerbic attack on the clergy and their claims to act as intermediaries between God and the faithful. His opponents, and even some of his allies, thought he had a crossed a line.

Like many Islamic reformers before him, Aqajari distinguished between 'historical Islam' (*Islam-e tarikhi*) and 'essential Islam' (*Islam-e zati*).[7] The 'Islamic Protestants', he instructed his audience, are only concerned with the latter, while the former is little more than a human artifice manipulated to guarantee the prerogatives of a worldly caste. Just as Shari'ati had once authored searing criticisms of the much-revered Mohammad-Baqer Majlesi, the powerful Shaykh al-Islam of Isfahan during the latter stages of the Safavid dynasty,[8]

---

[3] Hashem Aqajari, 'Doktor Shari'ati va porozheh-ye porotestantism-e eslami', in *Aqajari* (Tehran: Jameh daran, 1382 [2003]), p. 13.

[4] Ibid., p. 18.

[5] Unsurprisingly, the rightist cleric Ayatollah Mesbah-Yazdi vociferously defended the death sentence against Aqajari. Reza San'ati, *Gofteman-e Mesbah: gozareshi az zendegani va mavaze'-e 'elmi-siyasi-ye Ayatollah Mesbah-Yazdi* (Tehran: Markaz-e asnad-e enqelab-e eslami, 1387 [2008]), p. 776.

[6] Nazila Fathi, 'Iran: Another Death Sentence Is Lifted', *New York Times*, February 15, 2003.

[7] Aqajari, 'Doktor Shari'ati va porozheh-ye porotestantism-e eslami', p. 28.

[8] This has become a topos of the Iranian religious reformist genre. For a recent critique of Majlesi, which even elaborates upon many of Aqajari's criticisms of the Safavid-era cleric, see Ali Rahnema, *Superstition as Ideology in Iranian Politics: From Majlesi to Ahmadinejad* (Cambridge; New York: Cambridge University Press, 2011), p. 189.

Aqajari decried Majlesi for injecting what he regarded as arbitrary beliefs, superstitions, and practices into the realm of unimpeachable sanctity – for example, wearing an agate ring on the left hand and ascribing to it salvific qualities.[9]

For Aqajari, 'Islamic Protestantism' and 'Islamic humanism' went hand in hand and ultimately entailed the clergy's obsolescence. He attributed to Luther the credo that every man can act as his own priest,[10] and it is in the Lutheran tradition that he saw the relationship between individual conscience and scriptural understanding consummated. It was in collaboration with a class of like-minded intellectuals and their supporters that he hoped to provoke something akin to a 'Puritan revolution' in the Islamic Republic.[11] The same republic he had fought to establish he would now seek to reform. The analogy was hardly new, but it proved effective, bestowing an almost historical 'objectivity' and vindication to the reformist project by proxy. Early Western observers of late-nineteenth-century Islamic reformers had been quick to invoke the 'Protestant Reformation' as a key point of comparison and analogous meta-narrative, albeit without devolving much thought to the great many differences separating these distinct historical phenomena or the diverse circumstances which had provoked their arrival on the scene.[12]

---

[9] Aqajari, 'Doktor Shari'ati va porozheh-ye porotestantism-e eslami', p. 30. Aqajari was certainly not the first to make such objections. The reform-minded cleric Shari'at-Sangelaji had uncompromisingly criticised such practices during the Reza Shah period. Ali Rahnema, *Shi'i Reformation in Iran: The Life and Theology of Shari'at Sangelaji*, Kindle ed. (London & New York: Routledge, 2016), p. 40.

[10] Aqajari, 'Doktor Shari'ati va porozheh-ye porotestantism-e eslami', p. 25.

[11] It was of course Christopher Hill who famously said that the depiction of the English Revolution as a Puritan one was a 'nineteenth-century invention'. Christopher Hill, *Puritanism and Revolution: Studies in Interpretation of the English Revolution of the 17th Century*, Kindle ed. (London: Pimlico, 2001), Loc 123. Hill was translated by Iranian reformists such as Sa'id Hajjariyan and read widely in reformist intellectual circles. See Christopher Hill and Sa'id Hajjariyan, 'Seh khoda dar enqelab-e engelestan' *Rah-e now* 1, no. 1 (5 Ordibehesht 1377 [April–May 1998]).

[12] Cemil Aydin, *The Idea of the Muslim World: A Global Intellectual History* (Cambridge, MA, & London: Harvard University Press, 2017), p. 149; Loc 2304.

Aqajari caustically mocked the clerical hierarchy and its titles of
Ayatollah, Hojjat al-Islam, and Thaqat al-Islam, remarking that
'some of their titles are so new, their lifespan doesn't exceed fifty to
sixty years'.[13] He fulminated against the clergy's putative monopoly
on the Qur'an and its claim to mastery of '101 sciences and specialisa-
tions', decrying them baseless; the office of Friday prayer leader was
an innovation, without precedent at the inception of Islam.[14] He
stressed, 'Shari'ati wanted to remove such false intermediaries (*vase-
teh-ha-ye kazeb*). In Islam, we did not have any clerical class (*tabaqeh-
ye rowhani*); the clerical class is a new class in our history.'[15] So as to
make his endgame all the more unequivocal, he categorically declared
that 'in essential Islam there is no clergy at all'.[16] Continuing his
general line of argument and remarking upon a theme that repeatedly
graced the pages of reformist intellectual periodicals,[17] he lambasts
the hierarchical relationship of master (*morad*) and disciple (*morid*)
analogous to that of *marja'* (source of emulation) and *moqalled* (one
who emulates or partakes in *taqlid*), asking rhetorically, 'are people
monkeys to imitate (*taqlid*) him [i.e., the *morad*]?'[18] The teachers of
religion (*din-shenasan*), he argues, are supposed to act as educators,
whereby the student learns, understands, matures, and is thus capable
of acting on the basis of his own reasoned conclusions. In principle, as
the student progresses he will be able to dispense with the teacher and
independently comprehend and reflect upon the sacred texts for
himself.[19] The *moqalled*, on Aqajari's understanding of Osuli Shi'i
jurisprudence, is forever bound to unthinkingly imitate and thus is
deprived of the ability to think and reason for himself, manacled and
bound in a state of interminable infancy. '*Ejtehad* does not belong to
a special group or class.'[20] These recognisable tropes of rational
deliberation and respect for the individual's moral autonomy are the
core of Aqajari's and fellow religious intellectuals' call for 'Islamic
humanism'.[21]

[13] Aqajari, 'Doktor Shari'ati va porozheh-ye porotestantism-e eslami', p. 33.
[14] Ibid., p. 31–2.   [15] Ibid., p. 33.   [16] Ibid., p. 33.
[17] Ahmad Naraqi, 'Baznegari-ye rabeteh-ye morid-moradi dar 'erfan', *Kiyan*, no. 2
(Azar 1370 [November–December 1991]).
[18] Aqajari, 'Doktor Shari'ati va porozheh-ye porotestantism-ye eslami', p. 36.
[19] Ibid., p. 36.   [20] Ibid., p. 45.
[21] Ibid., p. 37. Hassan Yusefi-Eshkevari, 'Tarhi az oumanism-e eslami', *Baztab-e
andisheh*, no. 40 (Mordad 1382 [July–August 2003]), p. 64.

Aqajari's political and intellectual trajectory were by no means unique and were shared by many of his generation. In this book I will look at a range of intellectuals and political actors who at one time had committed themselves with every fibre of their being to the last great revolution of the twentieth century, only to feel, by its second decade, that the state which subsequently emerged had lost its way and palpably failed to live up to the utopian aspirations which surfaced in the run-up to and immediate aftermath of the Pahlavi regime's demise. In this respect, Aqajari's biography speaks to the broader subject of this book and how the project for political and religious reform in post-revolutionary Iran was born and historically articulated. By elaborating the complex genealogies of political and religious reform in post-revolutionary Iran, I will not only shed light on how 'reform' was theorised and thought about by the religious and loyalist intelligentsia and part of the political class but also analyse some of the specific limitations of the way in which 'reform' was conceived and framed by these elites.

Aqajari hailed from a religious-mercantile family in Abadan, in the south-western province of Khuzestan, and his father had been a fervent supporter of Ayatollah Ruhollah Khomeini from at least the early 1960s, when the latter first came to national prominence with the uprising of June 1963 [15 Khordad 1342].[22] After his father's draper's business went bankrupt and his 'petit-bourgeois' existence was thrown into disarray, Aqajari the elder left Iran for the Persian Gulf sheikdom of Kuwait,[23] leaving his eldest son, Hashem, who was only nine years old at the time, with little choice but to help support his five brothers and sisters. During his formative years and adolescence, he did everything from selling lottery tickets to manual labour and selling fruit and vegetables on the streets of Abadan.[24] As a young teen he joined the Hojjatiyyeh Society, a religious organisation established following the 1953 coup d'état against the nationalist premier Mohammad Mosaddeq by the Mashhad-born Shaykh Mahmud Halabi. The chief

---

[22] Hashem Aqajari, Reza Khojasteh-Rahimi, and Amir-Hosayn Bala'i, 'Sharh-e zendegi-ye yek enqelabi-ye naaram: goftogu ba Hashem Aqajari', *Andisheh-ye puya* 2, no. 11 (Mehr–Aban 1392 [October–November 2013]), p. 37.

[23] Aqajari uses the term *khordeh-borzhvazi* himself to describe his class-economic background up to the age of nine years old or so, which, following his father's bankruptcy, 'reached a level beneath the proletariat'. Ibid., p. 37.

[24] Ibid., p. 37.

objective of the society was to ideologically counter Baha'i religious activism and doctrine.[25] Aqajari later left the society, unpersuaded by its 'apolitical' demeanour, and found himself spellbound by the revolutionary rhetoric and proclamations of 'Ali Shari'ati, Khomeini, and the pre-1975 People's Mojahedin Organisation.[26]

With the revolution, at the tender age of twenty-one Aqajari headed an armed intelligence-security committee in Abadan and identified 'repressive agents' of the *ancien régime* for arrest.[27] Moreover, as a committed Islamist revolutionary he joined an organisation, the Mojahedin Organisation of the Islamic Revolution (see Chapter 3), whose *raison d'être* was to act as a bulwark in defence of the newly established clerically- led order and to ensure under the threat of violence that Ayatollah Khomeini's political and religious authority remained unchallenged by ideological adversaries, both real and imagined. His specific role was one of recruiting supporters and propagating against Marxist organisations and the People's Mojahedin on Iran's university campuses.[28] Even though many of the leading lights of the Iranian left and People's Mojahedin had been killed at the hands of the former regime's security apparatus or had found themselves in exile for long stretches of time, it was believed that the ideological potency and revolutionary visions of such groups had to

---

[25] 'Emad al-Din Baqi, *Dar shenakht-e hezb-e qa'edin-e zaman* (Tehran: Nashr-e danesh-e eslami, Esfand 1362 [February–March 1984]), p. 29. It is worth noting that numerous reformist-inclined intellectuals, ideologues, and politicians were either members or sympathetic to the Hojjatiyyeh prior to the Iranian Revolution of 1978–9. These include not only Aqajari but also 'Abdolkarim Sorush, 'Emad al-Din Baqi, Mohammad-Taqi Banki, 'Ataollah Mohajerani, Mohammad-Javad Zarif, and Gholam-Hossein Karbaschi, to name but a few. Its membership was not by any means exclusive to would-be Islamic leftists/ reformists. Mohammad Quchani, 'Farzand-e maktab-e Khorasan: pazhuheshi dar risheh-ha-ye fekri-ye Anjoman-e Hojjatiyyeh: az mobarezeh ba falsafeh ta talash baraye enhelal-e hezb-e Tudeh', *Mehrnameh*, no. 25 (Mehr 1391 [September–October 2012]), p. 77.

[26] Aqajari heard Shari'ati in person when the latter gave a speech at the Oil Academy in Abadan, after which he would devour everything Shari'ati wrote (p. 37). Moreover, as a university student he would attend classes held by Ayatollahs Beheshti and Motahhari and also became familiar with 'Allameh Tabataba'i's critical engagement with Marxism in his *Osul-e falsafeh va ravesh-e re'alism* (p. 38). Aqajari, Khojasteh-Rahimi, and Bala'i, 'Sharh-e zendegi-ye yek enqelabi-ye naaram'.

[27] Ibid., p. 39.

[28] One of the SMEE 'sympathisers' under his supervision was none other than 'Emad al-Din Baqi. Ibid., p. 39.

be forcefully countered amongst the impressionable youth. The university and the wider student movement, after all, had proven time and again to be a hotbed of discontent and rebellion against the political status quo.

After factional disagreements within the Mojahedin Organisation of the Islamic Revolution came to a head, Aqajari resigned in January 1983 along with thirty-six others, many of whom would become leading proponents of reform following the 1997 presidential election. As a member of the Revolutionary Guards, Aqajari participated and witnessed first-hand one of the most brutal inter-state conflicts of the twentieth century, the Iran–Iraq War (1980–8), only to see, in the wake of Ayatollah Khomeini's death, rightist clerical rivals and their supporters seize the reins of high office to the exclusion of their erstwhile, albeit ambivalent, allies. Many of the ideals which had been championed at the outset of the revolution were perceived as having given way to despair and indifference, while the new leadership faced the unenviable task of rebuilding a ravaged nation in the absence of its inimitable founder and thus sought to redefine its mission and place in the world.

Like many others around this time, Aqajari gradually began to re-examine and critically appraise many of his most earnestly held ideological convictions. He began graduate work and research at the Presidential Strategic Research Centre as part of a quite different political trajectory to the one he formerly embodied as a young firebrand.[29] Then came May 1997 and the emergence of the 2nd Khordad Front, as well as the surprise victory of the relatively unassuming former minister of culture and Islamic guidance, Hojjat al-Islam Mohammad Khatami, which marked the return of the Islamic left to the forefront of Iranian high politics and a historic watershed in terms of the advent of what is commonly referred to as the 'epoch of reforms' (*dowran-e eslahat*).

Despite the overwhelming popular mandate enjoyed by the new administration, its success was far from assured. On the one hand, Aqajari's arrest and condemnation was one of many attempts at reversal and fierce opposition to the newly minted reformists' attempts to

---

[29] Hashem Aqajari, 'Jonbesh-e eslah-talabi, chalesh-e dow farhang-e siyasi va hamelan-e an', in *Hokumat-e dini va hokumat-e demokratik* (Tehran: Zekr, 1381 [2002]), p. 250.

realise their political programme and ambitions.[30] On the other, expectations were high that reformists would respond to persistent pressure from the burgeoning middle and lower-middle classes, which, after a decade and a half of fear, instability, and exhaustion, had returned to the assiduously managed public sphere to make their demands heard once again. This monograph examines the origins and development of the intellectual and political networks which participated in, but above all theorised, the project to reform the Islamic Republic of Iran from the mid-1990s until 2005 and which continues to cast a long shadow over the political and ideological contestations enveloping Iranian state and society in the present.

* * *

It is perhaps cautious to start any academic endeavour by beginning negatively and stating what this work is not trying to do or demonstrate. For starters, it will not provide an exposition of the collective output of Iran's post-revolutionary 'religious intellectuals' (*rowshan-fekran-e dini*) in its entirety. It would be very difficult, if not impossible, for a single volume to do justice to their voluminous writings and the disparate notions and interpretations elaborated therein, not to mention the various periods of their intellectual development over the course of four decades. Nor is this book a conventional political history which carefully and meticulously chronicles a series of events, their causes and ramifications, and the myriad carefully crafted readings which accumulate and congeal into established historiographies.

The core of this book delineates a potted intellectual history of Iran's post-revolutionary reformists (*eslahtalaban*). Specifically, it will address the political dimensions of the post-revolutionary religious intellectuals' published writings and provide a contextualised account of their political-ideological milieu and the intellectual, social, and institutional networks from which they originated. It will focus on their contribution to the various debates over the role and powers of the Shi'i clergy and the nature, modus operandi, and structure of the post-revolutionary Iranian state. It will map these intellectuals' transformation from ideological legitimators of the newly established

---

[30] In Aqajari's case even his own party organisation, the SMEEI, failed to come to his aid and publicly dissociated itself from the positions he enunciated in the Hamedan lecture. Aqajari, Khojasteh-Rahimi, and Bala'i, 'Sharh-e zendegi-ye yek enqelabi-ye naaram', p. 37.

theocratic-populist regime to internal critics whose revised vision for the politico-religious order coalesced and converged with the growing disillusionment and frustration of what will be referred to as, inter alia, the 'Islamic left' – a constellation of political forces within the political elite of the Islamic Republic, which, following the death of Ayatollah Khomeini, increasingly felt itself marginalised and on the outskirts of power. This term, along with 'Islamic *chap*', will be used interchangeably and is elaborated upon in detail in Chapter 3. For the present, let it suffice to stand for Khomeini's disciples who in the 1980s both ascribed this ideological affiliation – i.e., left (*chap*) – to themselves and for the most part advocated broadly speaking statist solutions in the domain of economic policy and social engineering. On questions of foreign policy, they also tended to be more radically inclined and willing to directly challenge the imperial hegemony of the United States and its allies within the region and beyond. In the wake of Ayatollah Khomeini's death, that would slowly start to change, and in the space of several years many of the ideological positions of the Islamic left and loyalist intelligentsia would cease to be recognisable.

In the years following Khatami's election as president in May 1997, they recast themselves as 'reformists' (*eslahtalaban*) within the political class and sought to negotiate reforms in a gradualist process from above. Sociologist Tom Bottomore distinguishes the 'political class' from the 'political elite' or 'governing elite'. The 'political class' refers to all those groups which 'exercise political power or influence and are directly engaged in struggles for political leadership'. The 'political elite' or 'governing elite' consists of those individuals who in fact 'exercise political power in a society at any given time'.[31] Antonio Gramsci, in a similar vein, contends in the *Prison Notebooks* that 'the "political class" is nothing other than the category of intellects of the dominant social group' – a conceptual formulation which goes to underline the discernible overlap and interpenetration of segments of the post-revolutionary loyalist intelligentsia and the political class.[32]

The central contentions of this book are that: 1) the political marginalisation of the Islamic left in the course of intra-elite factional

---

[31] Tom Bottomore, *Elites and Society*, Kindle; second edition (London & New York: Routledge, 1993), p. 7: Loc 148.

[32] Antonio Gramsci, *Prison Notebooks*, vol. 3 (New York: Columbia University Press, 2007), p. 252.

struggles during the early 1990s, as well as; 2) the perceived short-comings of the hierocratic-populist system which came to light in the actual process of governing and 3) failure to fulfil the grand expectations of its devoted cadres in the aftermath of the Iran–Iraq War, the death of the revolutionary patriarch, and the collapse of the Soviet Union, elicited a critical re-orientation away from the pre-revolutionary and revolutionary politico-ideological milieu which preceded it and provided the conditions under which the Islamic left, in concert with the intellectual current known as the *rowshan-fekran-e dini*, sought to partake in an elite-mediated project to redefine the central ideological categories of the post-revolutionary political order. These intersecting socio-political transformations, at both the structural and agential levels, engendered the conditions under which the politico-ideological *dispositif* of 'reform' and 'reformism' emerged onto the post-revolutionary scene in the mid-1990s.[33] In the effort to reassert their political claim on the 'regime' as a political-ideological construct and 'regime of truth',[34] in tandem with a sustained period of critical reflexivity on the margins of state power, the Islamic left and their 'religious intellectual' allies sought to accumulate symbolic power and capital in their struggle to rethink the political and religious foundations of the Islamic Republic. This process of appropriation and the project to foster a form of civil hegemony reached its apogee with the electoral victory of Mohammad Khatami on 23 May 1997 and the first three years of his presidency.[35] The book ends by examining the ideological and political challenges faced in the latter's second term as president. At a far more general level, the ambition of this book is to analyse and unravel

---

[33] Michel Foucault, *Power/Knowledge: Selected Interviews and Other Writings 1972–1977*, ed. Colin Gordon, trans. Colin Gordon et al. (New York: Pantheon Books, 1980), p. 194–5. Giorgio Agamben, *What Is an Apparatus? and Other Essays*, trans. David Kishik and David Pedatella, Kindle ed. (Stanford, CA: Stanford University Press), pp. 1–24.

[34] This notion will be addressed in further detail in Chapter 1. But it should be acknowledged that it has had different valences throughout Foucault's career. Michel Foucault, 'The Political Function of the Intellectual', *Radical Philosophy*, no. 17 (1977), p. 13. Michel Foucault, *On the Government of the Living: Lectures at the Collège de France, 1979–1980*, ed. Arnold I. Davidson, trans. Graham Burchell, Kindle ed. (Basingstoke & New York: Palgrave Macmillan, 2014), Loc 2419.

[35] Perry Anderson, 'The Antinomies of Antonio Gramsci', *New Left Review*, no. 100 (November–December 1979), p. 13.

the historical relationship between elite discourses of religious and political reform in the 1990s and early 2000s and how their conceptualisation of social change informed political practice.

This book will further illustrate how Iran's religious intellectuals have deployed, adapted, and recast the theories and critical methods of various Euro-American philosophies in their efforts to debunk and challenge clerical political supremacy during the second and third decades of the Islamic Republic's existence. The specific sources upon which Iranian reformists have drawn is itself quite telling and, as I shall demonstrate, highly significant for how 'reform' and 'political change' came to be understood. In this way, it will provide a genealogical account of the 'reformist' *dispositif* and its corresponding modes of reasoning, and how the *rowshanfekran-e dini* sought to extricate the principles and foundations of political governance and statecraft from the exclusive province of Islamic jurisprudence; concluding that the criteria and sources of legitimacy for the evaluation of political authority were ultimately extra-religious and therefore not to be adjudicated through recourse to scriptural exegesis or Islamic jurisprudential reasoning and the derivation of religiously binding legal rulings. Because of the explicit focus on the religious intellectuals' political theories, their deployment of political concepts, and their material conditions of production, many of the epistemological, hermeneutical, gender-related, and mystical problems they raise will be passed over briskly, if they are addressed at all. Many of these issues have, however, been ably dealt with by thoughtful scholars elsewhere.[36] This is not to claim that the latter are irrelevant or unimportant but merely that they are not the chief subject of this work. By contrast, my focus here will be on the political, ideological, and institutional circumstances and precedents which impelled this network of intellectuals and politicians to theorise the nature, basis, and rationality of governance and political rule in critical and provocative ways.

---

[36] Ashk P. Dahlén, *Islamic Law, Epistemology and Modernity: Legal Philosophy in Contemporary Iran*, ed. Shahrough Akhavi, Middle East Studies: History, Politics, and Law (New York & London: Routledge, 2003). Ziba Mir-Hosseini, *Islam and Gender: The Religious Debate in Contemporary Iran* (London & New York: I. B. Tauris, 2000). Hammed Shahidian, 'Feminism or Islamism?: Challenges of Feminism in Post-Revolutionary Iran', in *Women in Iran: Emerging Voices in the Women's Movement* (Westport, CT, & London: Greenwood Press).

Additionally, I will endeavour to connect Iran's reformist ideological gestalt switch and *dispositif* to a wider global history, the short-lived, albeit hotly debated, 'unipolar moment' in the aftermath of the Soviet Union's collapse. The great significance of this event, and the undulating wave of triumphalism it generated in the imperial centre and beyond, would only be compounded by the perceived 'failures' of postcolonial elites to transform their societies into paragons of stability and material affluence, often with scant attention to the reasons for these alleged failures or why they had come to pass. At this global conjuncture, collective projects of liberation and revolutionary politics found themselves discarded and supplanted by exhortations to respect the moral integrity of the individual and his inviolable God-given rights. Ideology had proven moribund and should be jettisoned, while private persons had the right to demand 'good governance' consonant with expert opinion and technocratic standards of 'development'.[37] The intrusive encroachment of the political should be rebuffed and, on the account of some, had effectively become obsolete. State power had to be constrained, minimised, and limited. As the 'end of history' was declared, it appeared to many, and not only U.S. State Department intellectuals, that Western liberalism and free-market capitalism remained the only viable models for organising human societies we might entertain in good conscience.[38] Transparency, effectiveness, accountability, and the rule of law were held up as the paramount metrics of success, distinguishing the less from the more advanced. As will be shown in subsequent chapters, this political world-view and *Lebenswelt* increasingly informed the ideological worldview of elements within the Iranian elite and was often drawn upon and deployed in the context of inter-factional competition.

Chapter Guide

Chapter 1 provides a preliminary theoretical framework for understanding the religious intellectuals' writings as political acts and

[37] The conceptual inflation of the discourse of 'good governance' has been subject to sustained criticism in recent years. Merilee S. Grindle, 'Good Governance, R.I.P.: A Critique and an Alternative', *Governance: A International Journal of Policy, Administration, and Institutions* 30, no. 1 (2016).

[38] Francis Fukuyama, 'The End of History?', *National Interest* (Summer 1989), p. 1.

interventions. It draws on the work of Quentin Skinner in the history of political thought, which attempts to explicate how authorial intentionality can be seen as embedded in texts. It also employs the insights of Pierre Bourdieu, Michel Foucault, and Antonio Gramsci in order to delineate the *rowshanfekran-e dini* and other relevant socio-political actors as a semi-institutionalised and routinised network and *dispositif* whose nodal points possess varying degrees of social capital and hegemony within the political, cultural, and intellectual fields. It is by means of this network that religious intellectuals in concert with elements of the Islamic left sought to establish moral and ideological leadership within the context of intra-elite factional struggles. Bourdieu's notions of social capital, field, and symbolic power are particularly relevant if we are to make a case with respect to the *rowshanfekran-e dini*'s relationship to the manifold institutions which comprise the 'regime' of the Islamic Republic, both institutionally and ideologically, and the numerous groups and political tendencies within the post-revolutionary political elite. The Bourdieuan concept of 'field' shares a great many points of contiguity with Foucault's explication of *dispositif* or 'apparatus', as we shall see. These concepts help us to understand the strategic import of 'reform' and 'reformism' and how it was steadily counter-posed to 'revolution' and 'utopia', harbouring its own series of distinctive rationalities and normative contours germane to the nature of socio-political change and how such change ought to be managed and enacted. Gramsci's much-fêted notion of 'hegemony' is crucial to understanding the ideological and political development of religious intellectuals and the reformist apparatus, since it clarifies how an abstract and putatively inclusive discourse, combining elements of both political and religious reform, was drawn upon to ascertain broad assent while often advancing more sectional interests, holding the universal and particular in its singular embrace. In this way, I examine the historical *specificity* of the reformist apparatus cum hegemonic formation and its many prescriptions, idealisations, objects of polemic, historical amnesias, and occlusions.

In Chapter 2 I address the ideological context preceding the emergence of the post-revolutionary *rowshanfekran-e dini* and the articulations of Shi'i Islam as a utopian political force with a radical conception of socio-political change and decided commitment to capturing the Iranian nation-state. The chapter does not try to provide an exhaustive commentary on the intellectual milieu of the

1950s through to the 1970s.[39] For instance, it does not consider at
length the crucial impact of either the People's Mojahedin
Organisation of Iran or the many variegated trends of Iranian
Marxism. Instead, it focuses on three key political figures and ideologues, their respective historical contexts, and their distinct contributions to the debate over the nature and mandate of the Islamic
state. These include: the radical Islamist group the Fada'iyan-e Islam
(Devotees of Islam) and its leader, Navvab Safavi; the future leader of
the Islamic Republic of Iran, Ayatollah Ruhollah Khomeini; and the
French-educated intellectual and activist 'Ali Shari'ati. These political
ideologues and actors, as well as several others who appear on the
margins of the chapter, were crucial to forging a new political identity and foundation for Shi'i Islam in the second half of the twentieth
century, which paradoxically saw the will of man and the artefact of
the state as integral to the realisation of the sacred law. I thought it
necessary to provide an exposition of some of these Islamic ideologues' key ideas and their political and intellectual commitments and
milieu, because the post-revolutionary *rowshanfekran-e dini* would
to a large extent be grappling with their legacies – writing both
within and against the questions they posed as well as the answers
they provided. The latter's critiques of 'jurisprudential Islam' and
what they see as the outcome of revolutionary utopian socio-
political transformation are inseparable from the ideological inheritance through which this generation of intellectuals and activists
lived.

Chapter 3 is intricately linked up with the theoretical issues and
analysis offered in Chapter 1 and traces a genealogy of the post-
revolutionary *rowshanfekran-e dini* as a social and political reality
and their historical entwinement with elements of the Islamic left.
In other words, it provides a political genealogy and account of the
historical articulation of the reformist *dispositif*. It thus details how
a politically engaged assortment of intellectuals, journalists, political

[39] The seminal contributions of Hamid Dabashi and Mehrzad Boroujerdi achieved
this formidable task many years ago. Hamid Dabashi, *Theology of Discontent:
The Ideological Foundation of the Islamic Revolution in Iran* (New Brunswick,
NJ: Transaction Publishers, 2006). Mehrzad Boroujerdi, *Iranian Intellectuals
and the West: The Tormented Triumph of Nativism*, Mohamed El-Hindi series
on Arab culture and Islamic civilization (Syracuse, NY: Syracuse University
Press, 1996).

activists, and the disparate institutions within and between which they operated came to be identified – and to identify one another – under the banner of 'religious intellectuals' (*rowshanfekran-e dini*) and 'reformists' (*eslahtalaban*), amongst others. It describes the various stages of the Islamic *chap*'s political marginalisation and how it unfolded and discusses the historical coalescence of the reformist apparatus and its routinised network of reading groups, periodicals, newspapers, research circles, and think tanks incorporating the activities of public intellectuals ascribing to the *rowshanfekr-e dini* moniker, each possessing varying degrees of social and political capital in the context of the post-revolutionary system.

In Chapter 4 I outline the historical lineage of so-called 'ideological' and 'jurisprudential Islam' (*Islam-e feqahati*) and the dismissal of 'liberalism' as merely a form of Western-imposed licentiousness, then go on to examine how such ideological formations were progressively subject to criticism and reappraisal by religious intellectuals from the late 1980s and early 1990s onwards. By the time of the revolution's second decade, the same cadre of ideologues and politicians who had formerly been on the front line in providing intellectual and political ballast for the new regime against the Marxist left and People's Mojahedin Organisation of Iran sought to 'de-ideologise' Islam and thereby dismiss 'ideology' *tout court*. This trend is epitomised in the political writings of 'Abdolkarim Sorush. To this end, several religious intellectuals drew upon the theories of a raft of European and American thinkers within the pantheon of Cold War liberalism, namely those who had become well known for their scathing criticisms of Marxist ideology, above all in its Soviet guise. The influence of Karl Popper and Raymond Aron to Arthur Koestler, Isaiah Berlin, and Friedrich Hayek, amongst others, are traced in detail, thereby linking the religious intellectuals' own distinct contributions under the Islamic Republic to the wider ideological battles of the global Cold War and its aftermath.

Following an examination of the critique of 'jurisprudential Islam' and 'Islamic ideology', in Chapter 5 I provide an exposition of Mohammad Mojtahed-Shabestari's 'critique of the official reading of religion' and explication of a more 'democratic' and 'humane' political order in its stead, as well as his articulation of an existential hermeneutics concerned with the individual believer's quest for meaning. It also looks critically at Sorush and Shabestari's defence of human rights and its concomitant shortcomings. The chapter concludes by examining

Sorush's defence of a procedural form of governance over a substantive one anchored in constituent power and popular sovereignty. Unlike Khomeini, who asked the question *who* was entitled and obliged to rule, Sorush preoccupied himself with the *how* of rule, the nature of governance and the ease with which a ruler might be deposed peacefully by the governed.

While for Iranian Islamists since at least the 1950s capturing the nation-state had been a central preoccupation, the post-revolutionary 'religious intellectuals' sought to underwrite notions of individual and democratic rights and the compatibility of faith and liberty. It was also during the course of these years that the *rowshanfekran-e dini*, playing on the Dreyfusard conception of the intellectual as a vanguard of reason, truth, and freedom, attempted to perform the role of intellectual and moral leaders. They often achieved this by explicitly challenging the very basis of the religious and political authority of those clerics who occupied high office within the constitutional and state system. The *rowshanfekran-e dini*, though hardly the post-ideological or illumined beacons of reason they often sought to cast themselves as, saw many of their more prominent representatives resolutely break with a delimited conception of political theology – to wit, the avowed derivation of political concepts and the sources of political legitimacy from religious sources, above all revealed scripture.[40] In many respects, their writings in the 1990s – foremost those published in the journal *Kiyan* (Existence) – marked a decisive shift away from a form of Shi'i Islamic political theology that had come to define the post-revolutionary 'system' (*nezam*) and 'regime', in favour of a political and ethical order which claimed to take its leave from an abstract, individual, rational, and autonomous subject. The abstract individual and human being endowed with the capacity to reason and engage in rational thought constitutes a touchstone and defining unit in their social ontology and in thinking about issues of political order, rights, and legitimacy.

It is the Catholic German jurist and one-time National Socialist Carl Schmitt who is generally credited with reviving interest in political theology in European scholarship in the first quarter of the

[40] See Victoria Kahn, 'Political Theology and Liberal Culture: Strauss, Schmitt, Spinoza, and Arendt', in *Political Theology and Early Modernity*, ed. Graham Hammill and Julia Reinhard Lupton (Chicago & London: University of Chicago Press, 2012), Loc 558.

twentieth century. In the third chapter of his slim volume *Political Theology: Four Chapters on the Concept of Sovereignty* (1922), he famously contended, 'All significant concepts of the modern theory of the state are secularized theological concepts.'[41] While several of the post-revolutionary religious intellectuals analysed herein might reject this contention and claim political concepts have an independent normative and theoretical basis irrespective of their historical origins, others would accept the proposition's veracity, self-assured that a transition to popular constitutionalism in parallel with the secularisation of Islamic jurisprudence is both an inevitable and a desirable eventuality. In such a view, divine revelation is ultimately reducible to its human interpretations and has no independent status or automatic claim on our obedience, since these renderings are subject to rational and normative criteria of evaluation. The question of the 'binding force of revelation' ceases to be a given with which we are compelled to grapple.[42] It should be acknowledged, however, that this is a hermeneutics and metaphysics which the religious intellectuals' opponents resolutely rejected and continue to reject. Rather than bow to the dictates of philosophical wisdom, these opponents continue to insist that their unwavering faith resides with the revealed word and that the challenge of revelation is not one which can easily be circumvented.

What is of even greater interest in the context of the Iranian debate is that Schmitt identified constitutionalism with deism, the idea that reason and observation suffice for the determination of God's existence. For Schmitt, just as constitutionalism endeavoured to banish the sovereign's power to decide upon exceptions to the legal order, so too did the victory of deism spell an end to the age of miracles and the supreme being's inexplicable interruption into the law-based order of nature.[43] One can concur with Schmitt on this point when considering the case of Iran's own religious intellectuals, their political allies, and the reformist apparatus more generally. In challenging the politico-theological absolutism of the Guardian Jurist, they were engaged in a struggle to constrain his

[41] Schmitt, *Political Theology*, p. 36.
[42] Heinrich Meier, *The Lesson of Carl Schmitt: Four Chapters on the Distinction between Political Theology and Political Philosophy* (Chicago & London: University of Chicago Press, 1998/2011), p. 20.
[43] I do not mean to suggest here that all of Iran's *rowshanfekran-e dini* can be categorised as deists. Schmitt, *Political Theology*, p. 36.

office within the bounds of their interpretation of the state's constitution, and thereby, in one fell swoop, both theorise and enact the dissolution of the sovereign exception and the miraculous. This project held that sovereignty should become immanent to the constitutional legal order and rendered devoid of personalism and decisionistic elements. The state and legal order should become one and the same and subject to consensual norms.[44] They thus advocated, both knowingly and unknowingly, for the inauguration and construction of a disenchanted world and regime predicated upon 'apolitical' ratiocinative-scientific administration, demystified liberal constitutionalism of which consensus-based legal norms comprise an integral part and rule-governed behaviour implementing technocratic metrics to advance a particular vision of political and economic development.[45]

Chapter 6 begins by arguing that, with the presidential electoral victory of Mohammad Khatami in May 1997, several prominent members within the semi-institutionalised network of think tanks and periodicals – the chief vehicle for the transmission, diffusion and reproduction of the religious intellectualist project – took the initiative to set up or edit national newspapers in order to reach a wider public and disseminate many of the theological and political insights of the preceding years in a more accessible and popular format. In other words, they sought to gain public support for their ideas and vision for the future by venturing out of their private-elitist discussion groups and journals to propagate them in the mass-circulation press. It is in this period that the *dispositif* of reformism can be said to have matured and find itself propounded as a distinctive form of governmentality with a view to how social change should be realised.[46] It is during this period that the ascription of 'reformists' (*eslahtalaban*) emerged as a common idiom for a segment of the political class. It investigates the issue of constitutionalism and constitutional reform through extended analysis and comparison of the political thought of Khatami and examines the synergy of post-revolutionary intellectualism and aspects of Khatami's political programme, while also

---

[44] Ibid., p. 41, 49–50.
[45] On Schmitt's rejection of Weberian disenchantment, see *Concept of the Political*, trans. George Schwab, introduction by Tracy B. Strong, ed. (Chicago & London: University of Chicago Press, 2007), Loc 310.
[46] Dean Mitchell, *Governmentality: Power and Rule in Modern Society*, 2nd ed. (Los Angeles & London: Sage, 2010), p. 20.

delineating the profound differences and heterogeneity which divided the proponents of political reform and development. It thus illustrates the genuine heterogeneity of the reformist camp and the political repercussions of theoretical disagreements within it.

In the final chapter, Chapter 7, I examine the life and thought of reformist intellectual and political strategist Saʿid Hajjariyan and the relationship of his engaged theorising to distinct forms of political organising and mobilisation which steadily burgeoned during the Khatami period. The chapter begins by analysing his highly influential interpretation of Ayatollah Khomeini's intellectual and political contributions and his contention that it may have given impetus to the disenchantment and secularisation of Iran's state and legal system. It then elaborates upon the rubric of 'political development', which became central to reformist discourse and was associated with regularised and carefully calibrated forms of political participation. Such participation would take place through electoral channels but also by means of the establishment of a mass political party, which could leverage popular demands to acquire concessions from entrenched and appointed institutions of the Iranian state. The chapter rounds off by considering the political experiment of the Islamic Mosharekat (Participation) Front of Iran and some of the reasons for its failure to bring about the sweeping change many of its supporters had anticipated.

In the course of these chapters, I will thus not only address the reasons behind the historical transformation of the Islamic Republic's political factions and elements of the loyalist intelligentsia and their advocacy of reform in the 1990s and 2000s. I will also explore in some detail their conversation with various political traditions, above all Cold War liberalism with its integral anti-communist thrust, and how it influenced the semantics of 'reform' and informed political thought and practice during a turbulent period of Iranian history. The reader should in this way acquire greater insight into the alternative politics and theology delineated by the reformists in contradistinction to the ruling doctrine of the Guardianship of the Jurist and its staunch defenders in possession of considerable institutional and state power.

1 | *Religious Intellectuals, Reform, and the Struggle for Hegemony*

[E]very contradiction is a conflict of value as well as a conflict of interest; that inside every "need" there is an affect, or "want", on its way to becoming an "ought" (and *vice versa*); that every class struggle is at the same time a struggle over values.[1]

E. P. Thompson

[A]ll political concepts, images, and terms have a polemical meaning. They are focused on a specific conflict and are bound to a concrete situation.[2]

Carl Schmitt

Introduction

'Words are deeds', declared Ludwig Wittgenstein with his inveterate pithiness.[3] I consider this direct connection between words and political praxis paramount for understanding the nature and conditions of the *rowshanfekran-e dini*'s mode of intellectual production and engagement. The medium through which they presented and put forth their ideas for consumption by political elites and the general public is crucial to understanding the religious intellectuals' role, not merely in post-revolutionary intellectual debates but also in terms of their broader political significance and how they informed political debate over the nature of political authority and the Islamic state. It also distinguishes this work's approach from that of others which have thus far sought to provide an analysis of Iran's post-revolutionary religious intellectuals' collective output within the broader sweep of Iranian intellectual history or Muslim reformist thought or a strictly

---

[1] E. P. Thompson, 'The Poverty of Theory or an Orrey of Errors', in *The Poverty of Theory & Other Essays* (London: Montly Review Press, 1978), Loc 4077.

[2] Schmitt, *Concept of the Political*, Loc 921.

[3] Ludwig Wittgenstein, *Culture and Value* (Oxford: Blackwell Publishers, 1998), p. 53e.

corpus-based study which occasionally hearkens back to the somewhat passé approach of Arthur O. Lovejoy.[4]

This chapter outlines the theoretical framework guiding the historical examination of the networks integral to the reformist project's articulation, as well as the general and interrelated features of post-revolutionary 'religious intellectual' discourse and what I call the 'reformist apparatus'. This apparatus should be thought of as the specific complex of discursive practices which frame, regulate, and govern understandings and concrete engagements with the means, nature, and ends of social change and political transformation. While making no claims to exhaust all possible ways of framing post-revolutionary religious intellectualism, it lays out some of the chief features and modus operandi of the *rowshanfekran-e dini*, their discourse, and the context and conditions of their intellectual production. It then moves to provide a sketch of the political convergence of the religious intellectuals and the Islamic left and the formation of the reformist apparatus, detailing its significance not merely for understanding Iran's recent intellectual history but its political history too. In this section, the emergence of the 'reformists' is given brief consideration since it will undergo more detailed discussion in later chapters. The 'material structures of ideology' through which the reformists sought to establish hegemony over the Iranian polity and thereby forge a national-popular will is analysed through the lens of the Gramscian notion of hegemony, Bourdieu's conceptions of field, habitus, and capital, and Foucault's understanding of an apparatus.

Performance and Political Intervention

In any hermeneutical exercise it is vital to historicise and contextualise the oeuvre in question, and Iran's post-revolutionary religious intellectuals are no exception. To provide an exposition of their ideas, one must also describe their intellectual and cultural milieu and the political history which both preceded and shaped them in turn. A basic reconstruction of the genealogy of post-revolutionary religious political thought and the variegated impulses driving its emergence will determine what compelled Iran's post-revolutionary religious intellectuals

---

[4] Arthur O. Lovejoy, *The Great Chain of Being: A Study of the History of an Idea* (Cambridge, MA & London: Harvard University Press, 1934), Introduction.

to debate and increasingly challenge the ideological foundations of the theocratic-populist state. It will also contextualise these thinkers through the years of their development and gauge how their thinking has changed in step with the social and political changes which have taken place in the course of contemporary Iranian history.

Several methodological approaches will be drawn upon in order to bring to readers' attention a defining feature of Iran's religious intellectuals' mode of intellectual production – namely, the manner in which they intervened into public debate and the public sphere and specifically shaped post-revolutionary political discourse in crucial ways. It is through such interventions that Iran's religious intellectuals, in partnership with their political allies, were able to forge a new political lexicon which profoundly changed the way segments of both the political elite and the general public thought about politics. The medium through which this was achieved was less through theoretical treatises than by means of articles, interviews, comment pieces, and public speeches, which were conceived, published, and circulated in the complex nexus of intellectual reading groups and periodicals, comprising part of a wider network of individuals and institutions linked in various ways to the political elite.

As textual criticism still grapples with notions of intertextuality and the death of the author, one must be cognisant of the dangers posed by the effort to appropriate a text and impose a determinate meaning or interlocking chain of meanings upon it.[5] Following Quentin Skinner, I consider a reconstruction of an author's intended meanings germane to understanding a particular work or oeuvre. I am not concerned merely with the truth-value of a given statement but also in what the author was doing in saying it.[6] Moreover, while an author's intention or comportment in penning a particular work by no means exhausts the entirety of the 'meaning' of a text, knowledge of such cannot but condition our response to it.[7] Dispensing altogether with authorial intentionality ignores the extent to which a 'successful act of communication' must be publicly legible and thus rely upon and invoke prevailing conventions which the contemporary audience can recognise and understand.[8]

---

[5] Graham Allen, *Intertextuality* (London; New York: Routledge, 2000), p. 4.
[6] Quentin Skinner, *Visions of Politics: Volume 1: Regarding Method* (Cambridge & New York: Cambridge University Press, 2002), p. 96.
[7] Ibid., p. 96.   [8] Ibid., p. 97.

Skinner distinguishes between intentions and motives, arguing that the former do not precede the work but can be discerned within the work itself which harbours a particular purpose in being authored. Following J. L. Austin, Skinner accepts that to issue an utterance is to speak with a certain meaning and thus illocutionary force, and to grasp the illocutionary force of an utterance is equivalent to understanding what the speaker was doing in issuing it.[9] In contradistinction to the perlocutionary force of utterances, which refers to what might be brought about *by* saying something, their illocutionary force addresses what an author may be doing *in* saying something.[10] Skinner expands this idea into the realm of the history of political thought through his examination of the nature of intention in speaking or writing with a certain force.

It is important to distinguish, according to Skinner, between an author's motives for writing, which he deems irrelevant for the interpretation of the meaning of texts, and that author's intentions in writing.[11] What Skinner means when he speaks of the effort to discern what an author is *doing* in writing in a certain way is to grasp whether, for example, he or she is attacking a particular school of thought or argument while acclaiming another. To characterise a work in terms of its intended illocutionary force is therefore to understand what the writer may have meant by writing in a particular fashion.[12] A relationship is thereby established between intentions and meaning when the author is held to have meant the text in question as, for example, an attack or defence on, or an elaboration of, a specific line of argument, political ideal, or philosophical idiom.

As alluded to above, this mode of analysis is quite fitting for an appreciation of the often-extemporaneous nature of the *rowshanfekran-e dini*'s intellectual activity and thus the sources upon which this work is based. The overwhelming majority of their 'writings' are in fact lectures, articles, or interviews which were first delivered orally in mosques, universities, or various other congregations or published in newspapers, magazines, and periodicals and then gathered together and published in a single volume, either by publishers they had a stake in, by political allies, or by publishers who were either ideologically sympathetic or saw a potential commercial opportunity. Vestiges of their historical origins are often discernible, and as a result this factor

---

[9] Ibid., p. 98.   [10] Ibid., p. 104.   [11] Ibid., p. 98.   [12] Ibid., p. 100.

will be considered in texts that will be analysed in some detail. The point is that to impose a coherent set of views or doctrines on the 'oeuvre' of individual religious intellectuals tends to occlude the scattered and diffuse nature of these texts or the disparate circumstances in which they were produced.

Though the author's own account of his or her intentions is important, it is not definitive, exhaustive, nor final, since there is every chance that authors themselves may not be entirely clear with respect to their intentions in writing the texts in question or may well be motivated to retroactively obfuscate them. It is also of far less relevance when assessing the reception of an author's work, which is tied, amongst other things, to the expectations and historical conjuncture of his or her readers.[13] This is why one must be careful to keep the 'meaning' of a particular text analytically distinct from its wider 'significance'.[14] The particular readerships with which we are concerned, and the 'uptake' of the illocutionary acts within the texts under study, are fellow public intellectuals, the Islamic Republic's political elite, and Iran's reading public. These audiences themselves too can be divided up generationally and into a number of different time frames. For J. L. Austin, 'uptake' was integral to the illocutionary act. While it does not imply that the illocutionary act in question necessarily had its desired effect, it indicates that it is crucial for the addressee to understand what has been said in a certain sense and includes acts such as warning, convincing, and persuading.[15] Bourdieu phrases it slightly differently and insists that utterances of authority need to be *recognised* as such, and this holds even when such utterances are recognised as a challenge to entrenched authority.[16] It is crucial to see how the religious intellectuals' interjections were 'taken up' and informed wider political discourse, thereby shaping the way in which political norms and ideas were discussed, understood, and justified.

---

[13]   Martyn P. Thompson, 'Reception Theory and the Interpretation of Historical Meaning', *History and Theory* 32, no. 3 (October 1993), p. 255.

[14]   Skinner, *Visions of Politics: Volume 1*, p. 74.

[15]   J. L. Austin, *How to Do Things with Words* (Oxford: Oxford University Press, 1962), p. 116.

[16]   Pierre Bourdieu, *Language and Symbolic Power*, trans. Gino Raymond and Matthew Adamson (Cambridge: Polity Press, 1991), pp. 112–13.

But, as observed by Ellen Meiksins Wood in her critique of Skinner and the Cambridge School, the 'context' of intellectual production amounts to more than the prevailing political vocabularies of the day or singular discrete events,[17] and should be linked to broader analyses of social processes and historical transformations.[18] So while assimilating many of Skinner's important insights, I regard a 'social history of political thought' in the sense advocated by Wood as essential to understanding the conditions of the religious intellectuals' and the Islamic left's intellectual engagement in postrevolutionary Iran. Just as the pantheon of great Western political philosophers were very much children of their own time and place and were immersed in the hotly debated issues of their day, it is equally the case for the Iranian intellectuals and politicians discussed in this book that '[o]ften their engagements took the form of partisan adherence to a specific and identifiable political cause, or even fairly transparent expressions of particular interests, the interests of a particular party or class', even if 'their ideological commitments could also be expressed in a larger vision of the good society and human ideals'.[19] This, by no means, demotes these thinkers to mere propagandists, since the act of theorising is not reducible to an act of persuasion but relies on 'reasoned discourse and argumentation, in a genuine search for some kind of truth'.[20] However, those issues which appear to be 'salient' and fundamentally inform debate are rarely, if ever, self-evident or cut and dried, let alone axiomatically 'perennial', but are instead shaped by 'the nature of the principal contenders, the competing social forces at work, the conflicting interests at stake'.[21]

'Fallibilism' and 'Historicity'

By the late 1990s all the members of the religious intellectual collective had become well apprised of the perils associated with the state's appropriation of religious doctrine and the divinisation of political power; namely, the notion that political power can become a vehicle for the sacred and the implementation of God's law on earth. They

---

[17] Ellen Meiksins Wood, *Citizens to Lords: A Social History of Western Political Thought From Antiquity to the Middle Ages* (London & New York: Verso, 2008), Loc 168.
[18] Ibid., Loc 187.   [19] Ibid., Loc 218.   [20] Ibid., Loc 213.   [21] Ibid., Loc 264.

also advocated and sympathised with a number of political and epistemological ideas which could be considered 'fallibilist' in that they admit the susceptibility of human knowledge of the divine to error.[22]

This admission came predominantly by means of two routes. The first was to admit the historicity or the fundamentally historical nature of human knowledge and thus human beings' knowledge of 'religion' (*din*) and religious injunctions. The historicity of religious knowledge – which became an important idea and principle, albeit in different forms, for the *rowshanfekran-e dini*[23] – was the linchpin of a whole series of other methodological and hermeneutical approaches to religious texts, including pluralistic, historically critical, and pragmatic readings of religious texts which had previously been deemed the exclusive province of the Shi'i clergy. Because human beings' knowledge of religion was deemed both 'historical' and 'fallible', the rulings and statements of the clergy were to be included under the same rubric and thus susceptible to error and criticism extraneous to the Shi'i clergy's own methodological strictures. It should be noted, however, that this could well be considered something of a straw man and that 'doubt' (*shakk*) or lack of certainty can hardly be considered alien to the history of Shi'i jurisprudence and of Osuli Shi'i jurisprudence in particular, where it was held that *zann* or the 'supposition' of his or her *mojtahed* was the best the believer could hope for.[24] Indeed, as noted by Wael B. Hallaq, 'the laws, rules, and regulations of the Shari'a are largely the result of ijtihād, a domain of interpretation that rests on

---

[22] 'Abdolkarim Sorush, 'Arkan-e farhangi-ye demokrasi,' in *Farbehtar az id'iolozhi* (Tehran: Serat, 1372 [1993]), p. 270. For Sorush, 'liberalism' and 'fallibility' are inextricably linked to one another. See ' Mabani-ye te'orik-e liberalism', in *Razdani va rowshanfekri va dindari* (Tehran: Serat, 1377 [1998]), p. 128.

[23] One of the earlier post-revolutionary uses of the term *rowshanfekran-e dini* I have come across in the oeuvre of Sorush is in his essay 'Qabz va bast-e te'orik-e shari'at' (1) (originally published in *Kayhan-e farhangi*, 5, no. 2, Ordibehesht 1367 [April–May 1988]), in *Qabz va bast-e te'orik-e shari'at: nazariyyeh-ye kamel-e ma'refat-e dini* (Tehran: Serat, 1374 [1995]), pp. 192–3. In this essay Sorush distinguishes the 'religious intellectual' from the traditional cleric or man of religious learning, by averring that the religious intellectual is aware of the historicity of his own methodological orientation towards religious knowledge.

[24] Robert Gleave, *Inevitable Doubt: Two Theories of Shi'i Jurisprudence* (Leiden & Boston: Brill, 2000).

probability'.[25] The reasons for religious intellectuals taking up this line of attack prove to be a complex mix of intellectual and political factors, which subsequent chapters will aim to unpack.

In recent years, one of Iran's pre-eminent religious intellectuals 'Abdolkarim Sorush has gone so far as to declare that the 'worldly' and 'otherworldly' are irreconcilable, a point perhaps most prominently raised by Mehdi Bazargan in one of his last, most controversial, and posthumously published texts, *Akherat va khoda: hadaf-e resalat-e anbiyya'* (*God and the Hereafter: The Objective of the Message of the Prophets*, 1998).[26] Echoing Bazargan, one of the founders of the Freedom Movement of Iran and the Islamic Republic's first prime minister of the Provisional Revolutionary Government, Sorush enacts an essential rift between the mundane and otherworldly when he says 'religion must be mundane and of this world, or otherworldly and of the next'.[27] His chief target is the clergy and what he alleges to be their confidence in religion's ability to better this world, which is posited in a relationship of continuity with the afterlife. The point is not so much whether this is an accurate representation of the Shi'i clergy and their beliefs but that his target *is* the 'clergy' in power and that he purposely frames the problematic in the language of 'Protestantism' and the 'Reformation'.[28] It is no coincidence that, in the same article, Sorush states that Protestantism's emergence in Europe has 'many great lessons to teach us Muslims' and thus held up as a model of development for the Islamic world.[29]

---

[25] Wael B. Hallaq, *The Impossible State: Islam, Politics, and Modernity's Moral Predicament* (New York: Columbia University Press, 2013), Loc 1354.

[26] Mehdi Bazargan, *Akherat va khoda: hadaf-e resalat-e anbiyya'* (Tehran: Mo'asseseh-ye khadamat-e farhangi-ye rasa, 1377 [1998]). The book was originally based on an article first published in *Kiyan*, 'Akherat va khoda: hadaf-e be'sat-e anbiya'', *Kiyan* 5, no. 28 (Azar–Bahman 1374 [November 1995–January 1996]).

[27] 'Abdolkarim Sorush, 'Shari'ati va porotestanism', *Madreseh* (Tir 1384 [June–July 2005]), p. 42.

[28] Sorush's characterisation of 'Protestantism' is really Protestantism via Max Weber's *Protestant Ethic and the Spirit of Capitalism*. The depiction is a far cry from capturing anything like the real doctrinal and historical diversity which characterised either the Reformation or Protestantism, simply taking Weber's much famed 'elective affinity' between Protestantism and capitalism as given.

[29] Sorush, 'Shari'ati va porotestanism', p. 37.

A familiar Eurocentric conception of historical development is singular and linear, where Iran, or the Islamic world more generally, is located in 'an imaginary waiting room of history'[30] and the history of Europe anticipates the image of Iran's own future. As Kamran Matin had argued in another context, in such instances we observe 'the construction of their *general* categories by reference to a *particular* European experience'.[31] In this instance, however, whether consciously or not, such Eurocentrism serves a strategic function, which I will explore further in later chapters, and is crucial to the discourse of religious intellectualism – namely, challenging clerical prerogatives and thereby widening the class of persons who can avail themselves of religious authority and the right to speak on the subject of religion. In formal terms the appeal to 'Protestant Reformation' makes strategic sense: the religious intellectuals want to undercut the Shi'i 'olama''s claims to religious and political authority and make a case for an individual's capacity to reason and argue about religion for him- or herself. As I will show, however, particularly in Chapters 4 and 5, the analogy cannot account for the *content* of the alternative political vision they provide, which is clearly informed by Cold War liberalism and the global political conjuncture in the immediate aftermath of the Soviet Union's collapse.

Perhaps most crucial of all is the anti-utopianism – another important consequence of the advocacy of fallibilism and historicity – which runs through the gamut of what Iran's religious intellectuals have produced over the last thirty years, in this instance accompanying a direct critique of the clergy. As Sorush says in his essay 'Shari'ati va porotestantism' (Shari'ati and Protestantism),

Intellectual movements that wanted to secure the world and afterlife together and intellectual movements which make the afterlife subject to this world and thus devote their primary struggle to improve the world . . . is single-minded (*tak-hadafi*) . . . [I]mproving the world and the afterlife

---

[30] One can espy considerable Eurocentrism in the oeuvre of Sorush and other religious intellectuals, who constantly read Iranian historical development in terms of an idealised European model. See Dipesh Chakrabarty, *Provincializing Europe: Postcolonial Thought and Historical Difference*, Kindle ed. (Princeton & Oxford: Princeton University Press, 2000), p. 8; Loc 500.

[31] Kamran Matin, *Recasting Iranian Modernity: International Relations and Social Change*, ed. Homa Katouzian and Mohamad Tavakoli Targhi (London & New York: Routledge, 2013), p. 2.

alongside one another by means of religion is the same thing our clergy in fact believe and until today support this view and chant slogans [in support of it] and of course such a thing in my view is impossible.[32]

Fallibilism, anti-utopianism, and the absolute Otherness of the transcendent are themes which cut across the oeuvres of many of the religious intellectuals who will be addressed in the course of this work. That is not to say that tensions and contradictions do not afflict the writings of these various intellectuals[33] but merely that these features and themes should be considered in the context of their *Kulturkampf* and critical disposition towards the political clergy's supposed monopoly on the knowledge economy of the sacred: a not-unproblematic view in light of centuries of Islamic history where there was often an acknowledged division of labour as well as, of course, considerable overlap between the intellectual and practical preoccupations of the jurists, theologians, and mystics. This is while also admitting that there are clergymen amongst their number and who concur with theses surrounding the fallibility of human knowledge of the divine order and will. These qualities and their overtly dialectical relationship with the political conditions prevailing in the country are also amongst the reasons why the discourse of the *rowshanfekran-e dini* has often been characterised as primarily 'negative' (*salbi*), rather than constructive in nature.[34]

Reformist Gradualism

The *rowshanfekran-e dini* concluded – against the background of their personal and collective experience of revolution and the Iran–Iraq War, of the arbitrary and unchecked exercise of state violence in tandem with their own political marginalisation, and alongside international developments such as the collapse of the Soviet Union – that 'revolutionary' political change (i.e., political action which seeks to rapidly overturn and replace the entirety of the existing socio-political order) is inevitably

---

[32] Sorush, 'Shari'ati va porotestanism', p. 42.

[33] Suleiman Mourad interestingly has referred to this widespread phenomenon in the history of nineteenth- and twentieth-century Islamic reformist movements as 'the Protestant trap'. Suleiman Mourad and Perry Anderson, *The Mosaic of Islam: A Conversation with Perry Anderson*, Kindle ed. (London & New York: Verso, 2016), Loc 1621.

[34] Mohammad-Javad Gholam-Reza Kashi, 'Rowshanfekran va khatar-e eqbal-e 'omumi', *Rah-e now*, no. 1 (5 Ordibehesht 1377 [25 April 1998]), p. 3.

bound for destructive, if not dystopian, failure. Their strategic readings in Euro-American philosophy and political theory were also shaped in this context and often deployed to reinforce their reservations and newly found critical comportment towards the idea of revolutionary socio-political change. This in turn has led to a striking and pronounced dichotomy on the post-revolutionary intellectual scene between notions of 'reformist' and 'revolutionary' political change. The multiple variations of this dichotomy will be explored in subsequent chapters.

The *rowshanfekran-e dini* and the Islamic left are until this day engaged in contesting the meaning and significance of the revolution, Khomeini's legacy, the Islamic Republic, and its constitution. In this respect, they were and are involved in a battle over the discursive representation of what the Islamic Republic *is*, what it *ought* to be, and the perceived disjuncture between the two. Political competition with rival groups and factions within the state apparatus and political class was thus often framed as an issue of 'fidelity' and 'commitment' to the 'real' ideals and principles of the revolution and the Islamic state. The *rowshanfekran-e dini* were of course very much involved and played a crucial part in the process of ideational contestation over the meaning of the Islamic Republic.

The emphasis on political 'reform' in contradistinction to 'revolution' is primarily the product of two factors. Firstly, Iran's religious intellectuals and the strategists of political development and reform were themselves participants in Iran's revolution. Over the last thirty years many of them developed lasting interpersonal relationships and have held official positions in state institutions such as the Council for Cultural Revolution ('Abdolkarim Sorush), the Islamic Consultative Assembly (Mohammad Mojtahed-Shabestari, Hassan Yusefi-Eshkevari, Behzad Nabavi), the Ministry of Intelligence (Sa'id Hajjariyan, 'Abbas 'Abdi),[35] the General Prosecutor's Office (Mohammad Musavi-Kho'iniha, 'Abbas 'Abdi), the presidency (Mohammad Khatami), the Ministry of the Interior (Mostafa Tajzadeh), the Ministry of Culture and Islamic Guidance (Mohammad Khatami, Mostafa Tajzadeh, Mohsen Armin, 'Ataollah Mohajerani), Islamic Republic of Iran Broadcasting (Behzad Nabavi), the Ministry of Agriculture (Mohammad Salamati), the Ministry of Heavy Industries (Behzad Nabavi, Mohsen Sazgara), and

---

[35] 'Abbas 'Abdi was of course one of the radical leaders of the Muslim Student Followers of the Imam's Line, who overran the U.S. embassy on 4 November 1979.

the Islamic Revolutionary Guard Corps (Akbar Ganji, Hashem Aqajari, Mostafa Tajzadeh, Hamid-Reza Jala'ipur, 'Ali-Reza 'Alavi-Tabar, 'Emad al-Din Baqi). It is therefore impossible to disassociate them from the history of the *nezam*, its institutions, and its purported values.[36] Taking our cue from Nicos Poulantzas, the *nezam* or 'revolutionary system' should not be regarded as an abstract and reified thing 'out there', imbued with an essence or fixed number of determinate characteristics. Rather, it can be thought of as an institutional ensemble as well as a strategic process and discursive field formed through intersecting power networks.[37] The articulatory practices through which the political order is established, and the meaning of social institutions is stabilised, are 'hegemonic practices', constituting a formation which is susceptible to challengers who in turn strive to disarticulate the existing order and install another form of hegemony in its stead.[38]

In their capacity as public intellectuals, ideologues, and politicians, they could potentially avail themselves of perquisites, accumulated social capital, and attained social mobility,[39] first in their roles as its defenders and later as internal critics of the revolutionary order. Similarly, as I will demonstrate, partially in this chapter and in greater detail in Chapter 3, their personal histories and identities were bound up with the state's establishment in a highly intricate fashion. In this sense, they were participants in the *nezam*'s revolutionary founding and consolidation, which helped shape them in turn.

Religious Intellectualism and the Circuits of Social Capital

It should be increasingly clear that Iran's *rowshanfekran-e dini* were not merely disinterested producers of theological and philosophical

---

[36] Many of these intellectuals and politicians will be fleshed out in greater detail in the course of the following chapters.

[37] Nicos Poulantzas, *State, Power, Socialism*, trans. Patrick Camiller, Kindle ed. (London & New York: Verso, 2014), p. 126. Bob Jessop, *State Power: A Strategic-Relational Approach*, Kindle ed. (Cambridge: Polity, 2008), Loc 2503.

[38] Chantal Mouffe, *On the Political* (London & New York: Routledge 2005), p. 18.

[39] Noted veteran reformist journalist Mohammad Quchani has commented upon many of these men's humble origins, hailing from the more deprived neighbourhoods of Tehran, such as Nazi-abad, 'Ali-abad, and Emamzadeh-Yahya. Mohammad Quchani, *Nazi-abadi-ha* (Tehran: Nashr-e sara'i, 1383 [2004]), p. 48.

ideas and interpretations but can be seen as embedded socio-political actors, who took and continue to take positions on a wide variety of social, cultural, legal, and political issues.[40] Nor are the texts they author straightforwardly containers of meaning but rather spaces where relations, influences, and meanings coalesce.[41] This may strike the reader as self-evident, but one dominant approach in the academic literature seriously underplays this dimension, engaging for the most part in conventional corpus study of the man, the thinker, and the ideas he expounds in his writings.[42] While I do not seek to impugn the legitimacy of such an approach, I would like to draw attention to something of a different tact. These intellectuals and the texts they author are situated in a matrix of personal and strategic relationships with political personalities, governmental and non-governmental organisations, and institutions, while implicitly or explicitly challenging the authority of other actors in the intellectual and political fields.[43] Moreover, like all public intellectuals, the *rowshanfekran-e dini* oppose and compete with intellectuals of differing political and religious persuasions and one another, in defence of the fruits of their intellectual labour.

As Edward W. Said contended, 'all intellectuals represent something to their audiences, and in so doing represent themselves to themselves'.[44] In other words, they strive to present a certain image of

---

[40] Antonio Gramsci famously offered a pointed critique of the archetype of the intellectual defended in Julien Benda's famous tract, *The Treason of the Intellectuals*. He questioned the autonomy of the intellectual and his or her relation to the state and, more generally speaking, the intelligentsia's autonomy and independence of the economic, social, and political fields. Antonio Gramsci, *Selections from the Prison Notebooks of Antonio Gramsci*, ed. Quintin Hoare and Geoffrey Nowell Smith (Midsomer Norton, Bath: Lawrence and Wishart, 1971), p. 12.

[41] Allen, *Intertextuality*, p. 12.

[42] A recent example of such an approach is Katajun Amirpur's 'The Expansion of the Prophetic Experience: 'Abdolkarim Sorush's New Approach to Qur'anic Revelation', *Die Welt des Islams*, no. 51 (2011). Forough Jahanbakhsh's monograph is arguably another example of this genre; see Forough Jahanbakhsh, *Islam, Democracy and Religious Modernism in Iran, 1953–2000: From Bazargan to Soroush*, Social, Economic, and Political Studies of the Middle East and Asia (Leiden & Boston: Brill, 2001).

[43] Loïc J. D. Wacquant, 'Sociology as Socioanalysis: Tales of "Homo Academicus" [By Pierre Bourdieu]', *Sociological Forum* 5, no. 4 (Dec. 1990), pp. 679–680.

[44] Edward W. Said, *Representations of the Intellectual: The Reith Lectures* (New York: Pantheon Books, 1994), p. xv.

themselves to the public and their opponents and thereby participate in the construction of their public persona and identity. The public space in which representation and self-representations unfold include the lecture hall, the seminar room, and of course the press, as well as academic publications, with their many disparate political leanings, norms, and expectations. Rhetoric plays an important role in this *agon* of intellectual contestation and its various fields of power. Intellectuals are not mere knowledge producers but, as Donna Haraway has argued, dexterous rhetoricians who practise the art of persuasion and endeavour to convince other social actors that their 'manufactured knowledge is a route to a desired form of very objective power'.[45] Their praxis and texts are not reducible to such a description, but it is, nevertheless, a vital part of 'what intellectuals do'.

Moreover, intellectuals in Iran, like anywhere else, fight and duke it out over the values they hold dear, and in a variety of institutional settings, spaces, and social networks, to the end of preserving and perpetuating the social and cultural capital they have accumulated.[46] The agonistic nature of such contestation thus has both a normative and a social component, the normative one being the battle and con-testation of values, which might prove incommensurable – e.g., divine rights versus popular sovereignty. Intellectual exchange between rival political and religious tendencies does of course regularly occur, and there is often sufficient overlap or a common vocabulary for exchange to take place, even if the values and world views presented therein remain irreducible to one another.[47] Violence, the logics of securitisa-tion, alongside numerous other forms of power, including the subtler absence or withdrawal of state patronage and support, have also been employed on a regular basis in order to suppress or cast aside the advocates of rival narratives, including religious ones.

The term *rowshanfekran-e dini* is not a term imposed from outside, and it is one that in recent decades has been continuously invoked but also contested by those who claim to speak on its behalf, as well as

---

[45] Donna Haraway, 'Situated Knowledges: The Science Question in Feminism and the Privilege of Partial Perspective', *Feminist Studies* 13, no. 3 (Autumn 1988), p. 577.

[46] Wacquant, 'Sociology as Socioanalysis', p. 681.

[47] Steven Lukes, *Liberals and Cannibals: The Implications of Diversity* (London & New York: Verso, 2003), p. 92. John Gray, *Two Faces of Liberalism* (Oxford Polity, 2000), chapter 4.

those claimed amongst its partisans. It is thus endogenous to the discourse of the intellectuals and political actors analysed in this book. While it is usually contrasted with the *rowhaniyyat* or clergy, the traditional guardians and propagators of religion, there is no reason why a man of the cloth cannot be considered amongst their number. At one level, a necessary, although hardly sufficient, condition is the issue of methodology and practice and the concerted effort to draw on new philosophical and critical methods in the understanding and explication of religion and its sacred texts, usually undertaken with a recognisably modern academic apparatus. This is one of the reasons why it is suggested that it ought to be in part viewed as an activity and distinctive modality of intellectual engagement in the context of the intellectual life of the Islamic Republic of Iran. The process of appropriation and the specific nature it takes, however, is thoroughly conjunctural. In other words, it is shaped by the balance of political and socio-economic forces, both domestically and geopolitically, prevailing at any one time.

Moreover, the label 'religious intellectual', in the context of a theocratic-populist state, is one that is not obviously 'subversive' or immediately threatening, since it stresses a basic preoccupation with *din* (religion) and implicitly acknowledges that intellectual activity is undertaken as a believer in defence of the faith, rather than *against* it. *Rowshanfekr* and its predecessor *monavvar al-fekr* were to an extent disburdened of their late-nineteenth-century secular connotations and association with anti-clericalism and European Enlightenment thought.[48] It has also lent its exponents' activities and positions another kind of legitimacy, since by calling themselves 'intellectuals' they were consciously emphasising their difference from 'ideologues' wedded to political interests, as they had often been portrayed by detractors in the 1980s. Instead, they regularly sought to represent themselves as independent and disinterested 'thinkers' concerned solely with the impartial search for universal 'truth'.

In this work I am not attempting to address *all* those figures who could be said to comprise part of the 'religious intellectual' family, to invoke Wittgenstein's metaphor, but to focus predominantly on those

---

[48] Hossein Bashiriyeh, *The State and Revolution in Iran, 1962–1982* (London & New York: Routledge, 1984), p. 68. Negin Nabavi, 'The Changing Concept of the "Intellectual" in Iran of the 1960s', *Iranian Studies* 32, no. 3 (1999), p. 335.

thinkers and public intellectuals who comprised part of the intellectual circle which did much of the intellectual groundwork for what came to be known as the 2nd of Khordad Front (*Jebheh-ye dovvom-e khordad*), the 2nd of Khordad (23 May 1997) marking the date of Khatami's election as president. Many of these thinkers have at various points either been affiliated with or sympathetic to the activities of what had been termed the Islamic left and its affiliated groups such as the *Majma'-e rowhaniyun-e mobarez* (Association of Combatant Clerics, henceforth MRM), the *Sazman-e mojahedin-e enqelab-e eslami-ye Iran* (Mojahedin Organisation of the Islamic Revolution of Iran, SMEEI), and, following Khatami's election, the *Jebheh-ye mosharekat-e Iran-e eslami* (Participation Front of Islamic Iran, henceforth PFII) and the *Hezb-e e'temad-e melli* (National Trust Party, HEM). These individuals not only had a shared background and experience of working for state or neo-statal institutions but emerged out of a distinct epistemic community and ethos in the intellectual and political milieu of post-revolutionary Iran. As a result of such similar backgrounds and experiences, these men also possess a comparable habitus, which Bourdieu has defined as a form of 'socialized subjectivity'.[49] The habitus is the complex and internalised series of habits, dispositions, appreciations, gestures, behaviours, and cognitive and evaluative categories which structure the agent's relations with the world. Bourdieu also refers to the habitus as an 'open system of dispositions', which, though durable, is constantly subject to new experiences which can either reinforce or change extant patterns of behaviour.[50] The *rowshanfekran-e dini* and the politicians and activists of the Islamic left under examination in this work are not merely bound together by an intellectual and political mutual sympathy but also by their embodied, and institutionalised, social, cultural and symbolic capital.

Iran's religious intellectuals, along with a slew of various other socio-political forces and institutions in the post-revolutionary milieu, occupy several 'fields', to use the terminology of Bourdieu and Foucault.[51] According to Bourdieu, a field does not have any parts or components, but it does possess its own rules and regularities

---

[49] Pierre Bourdieu and Loïc J. D. Wacquant, *Invitation to Reflexive Sociology* (Oxford: Polity, 1992), p. 126.

[50] Ibid., p. 133.   [51] Ibid., p. 76.

organised around struggles over valued resources.[52] The field is structured by relations of power and thus the production, circulation, and appropriation of goods, services, knowledge, and status. It is within manifold fields that the religious intellectual and political class's articulation of reform is constituted as a subject of historical enquiry, including the category of 'religious intellectual' itself.[53] It is a decidedly post-revolutionary accretion. While an explication of the intellectual's conceptual armoury is of considerable interest in and of itself and makes up much of this study, a prerequisite of understanding these ideas is the context and field out of which they emerged and continue to operate; in particular, the broader field of political power and capital in which these intellectuals, with their respective habitus, compete and strategise.

Bourdieu uses the analogy of the 'game' in which the agents or players have an approximate idea of the rules and norms which characterise the game, as well as of the stakes involved. The participants have to believe in the game being played, and the stakes themselves are, in part, an outcome of the competition between the players.[54] The different players in the field have varying degrees of social, cultural, economic, and symbolic capital and, in the course of their competition, accumulate and deploy their different types and amounts of capital in accordance with their habitus and the balance of forces which structure the field. Capital, as has been said, can take a number of distinct forms. Bourdieu delineates three states of cultural capital: *embodied, objectified*, and *institutionalised*.[55] Cultural capital in its embodied state overlaps with the habitus of the agent and pertains to long-standing dispositions internalised over many years during one's childhood and in later socialisation – for example, through a particular institution or social environment, such as the school, university, or seminary. In the

[52] Pierre Bourdieu, *Outline of a Theory of Practice* trans. Richard Nice, Kindle ed. (Cambridge & New York: Cambridge University Press, 1977), pp. 78–79; Loc 2024. David Swartz, *Symbolic Power, Politics, and Intellectuals: The Political Sociology of Pierre Bourdieu*, Kindle ed. (Chicago: University of Chicago Press, 2013), Loc 664.

[53] Bourdieu and Wacquant, *Invitation to Reflexive Sociology*, p. 104; Foucault, Power/Knowledge, p. 117.

[54] Bourdieu and Wacquant, *Invitation to Reflexive Sociology*, p. 98.

[55] Pierre Bourdieu, 'The Forms of Capital', in *The RoutledgeFalmer Reader in Sociology of Education*, ed. Stephen J. Ball (London; New York: RoutledgeFalmer, 2004), p. 17.

objectified state, cultural capital denotes manifest objects such as books, computers, etc., but also qualifications, permissions (*ejazeh-ha*) and certificates, and often requires economic capital for its appropriation.[56] Institutionalised cultural capital, which Bourdieu also calls social capital, refers to potential and actual resources conferred by 'membership' of a particular group or durable and semi-institutionalised relationships as part of a social network. In virtue of his or her 'membership' of the social network in question, he or she is entitled to the collective backing of the group's capital and is in this way credited by a broader web of relationships. Social capital of this kind was essential for Iran's religious intellectuals, who, as has already been intimated, initially benefited from direct state patronage and assent, or later indirect support from acquaintances, friends, allies, and relatives in positions of institutional power and authority.[57] In this way partisans of reformist politics and the religious intellectual project supported one another and wrote and acted in one other's defence when the situation demanded. This did not leave them immune to persecution or repression from political adversaries who did not accept them as part of their own social network or recognised their social capital as legitimate, but it certainly bestowed upon them a range of privileges, which other intellectuals without such institutionalised political and cultural capital palpably lacked.[58]

As Bourdieu states, 'players can play to increase or to conserve their capital, their number of tokens, in conformity with the tacit rules of the game and the prerequisites of the reproduction of the game and its stakes; but they can also get in it to transform, partially or completely, the immanent rules of the game'.[59] In addition to factoring into their intellectual considerations the unstable norms and values of the political culture, which they not only helped fashion but by which they were themselves shaped, the *rowshanfekran-e dini* operated within the

[56] Ibid., p. 20.

[57] Nodes of a social network, which could be either individuals or institutions, brought together by common norms and values enjoy what is called 'homophily'. Charles Kadushin, *Understanding Social Networks: Theories, Concepts, and Findings*, Kindle ed. (Oxford & New York: Oxford University Press, 2012), Loc 492.

[58] Bourdieu recognises that the existence of a network of social connections is not naturally given, nor does the act of its initial institution guarantee the network is constituted once and for all. Bourdieu, 'The Forms of Capital', p. 22.

[59] Bourdieu and Wacquant, *Invitation to Reflexive Sociology*, p. 99.

moving and tacit red lines of the hierocratic state, which have tightened and loosened in accordance with a wide range of factors, the political balance of forces and control of the presidency and certain ministries being a key one.[60] They have also sought to transgress what they and the authorities perceived as the 'red lines' and in this process miscommunication and misunderstanding has often occurred. This is because transgressions are frequently tacit or implied and not specifically spelt out, even in cases where the law is putatively codified. Transgressions are possible not only due to the fact that such norms are never completely internalised but because, as Bourdieu argues, intellectuals are capable of critical reflexivity and scrutinising their partisanship, and thereby transcend the immediacy of their class or subject position,[61] even when it might then entangle them in new forms of domination and symbolic violence.

Iranian intellectuals writing in venues such as *Kiyan* in the 1990s for the most part adopted the classical liberal conception of 'civil society' as a sphere of activity independent of the state, and from which the state might be criticised and held accountable.[62] They also regarded it as an important outcome of the transition from feudalism to the modern age and thus a criterion by which Iran's 'modernity' might be gauged.[63] The question of civil society and its relationship to state institutions is a pertinent one, but to understand the convergence and alliance between the religious intellectuals and the Islamic left during the 1990s and the subsequent elite-driven articulation of

---

[60] For example, the incumbent government, but especially the ministers of culture and Islamic guidance and of teaching and education, have proven of great importance on where red lines are practically drawn and recognised as hemming in intellectuals, journalists, writers, editors, etc., on what can and cannot be 'legitimately' said, argued, and announced publicly and what can and cannot be published.

[61] Charles Kurzman and Lynn Owens, 'The Sociology of Intellectuals', *Annual Review of Sociology* 28 (2002), p. 79.

[62] Majid Mohammadi, 'Mavane'-e roshd-e jame'eh-ye madani dar Iran', *Kiyan* 6, no. 33 (November–December 1996), p. 33. In this sense, much of the Iranian intelligentsia derived its understanding of civil society from the considerable literature produced on the subject by scholars and philosophers such as Jürgen Habermas, David Held, Andrew Arato, and Craig Calhoun. Craig Calhoun, 'Civil Society and the Public Sphere', in *The Oxford Handbook of Civil Society*, ed. Michael Edwards (Oxford & New York: Oxford University Press, 2011), p. 311.

[63] 'Ali Reza'i, 'Zohur va takamol-e jame'eh-ye madani', *Kiyan* 6, no. 33 (November–December 1996), p. 18, 20.

managed reform (*eslahat*), Foucault's conception of the *dispositif* or 'apparatus'can yield an incisive way of framing the process. Like the Bourdieuan field explicated above, where individuals, groups, and institutions compete over capital and partake in its exchange, an apparatus is understood as 'a thoroughly heterogeneous ensemble consisting of discourses, institutions, architectural forms, regulatory discourses, laws, administrative measures, scientific statements, philosophical, moral and philanthropic propositions – in short, the said as much as the unsaid . . . The apparatus itself is the system of relations that can be established between these elements.'[64] Despite differences, the notion of an 'apparatus' nevertheless captures an important point for our understanding of the articulation of the discourse of reform in the interstices of a variegated ensemble of discursive and non-discursive practices. That is to say, we should understand the discourse of reform, as it emerged in the 1990s, not crudely as the latest inexorable stage of the consciousness of freedom for the Iranian nation and its emancipation, a trope that runs through much liberal, civic nationalist and even Marxist-Leninist historiography.[65] Rather, reform, with its concomitant organisational, mobilising forms, mechanisms, and technologies ought to be understood as a heterogeneous assemblage of discourses, institutions, regulatory measures, and philosophical and moral propositions, constituted in power relations and serving a counter-hegemonic strategic function. As Foucault adds, 'I understand by the term "apparatus" a sort of – shall we say – formation which has as its major function at a given historical moment that of responding to an urgent need. The apparatus thus has a dominant strategic function . . . [T]here is a perpetual process of *strategic elaboration*.'[66] The strategic tenor of the 'reformist apparatus' conditioned how religious intellectuals and their audiences thought about socio-political change and the way in which such change might be brought about. Its mechanisms and regulatory

---

[64] Foucault, *Power/Knowledge*, p. 194.

[65] The work of Azimi is perhaps the most articulate and important example of such: Fakhreddin Azimi, *The Quest for Democracy in Iran : A Century of Struggle against Authoritarian Rule* (Cambridge, MA & London: Harvard University Press, 2008). An older and pre-eminent instance of Iran's liberal historiographical tradition is the work of Feridun Adamiyyat in books such as *Amir Kabir va Iran, Andisheh-ye taraqqi va hokumat-e qanun ('asr-e Sepahsalar)*, and *Fekr-e azadi va moqaddameh-ye mashrutiyyat.*

[66] Foucault, *Power/Knowledge*, p. 195.

procedures also instigated the processes of subjectification through which both the intelligentsia and citizens came to think about their agency and locate themselves in the course of such historical transformations.[67] The temporality, pace, and *telos* of social and political change, the meaning of ideology and dogmatism in contra-distinction to critique, the kinds of political reforms that were advo-cated for and the social forces that were considered to comprise part of the process were all shaped by the apparatus of reform and its concrete articulations within the political field.

Foucault argues elsewhere it is 'not a question of emancipating truth from every system of power – which would be a chimera ... but of detaching the power of truth from the forms of hegemony (social, economic, and cultural) within which it operates at the present time'.[68] In the case of the religious intellectuals, the Islamic left, and the reformist apparatus more broadly speaking, the strategic impulse was to construct a counter-hegemony by reclaiming those symbols, texts, and histories deemed sacred and contested by their political and religious antagonists, and thereby challenge and transform their dominant interpretation, meaning, and scope in the process.[69] This was achieved not only by mining the Islamic 'tradition', with its myriad philosophers, mystics, and poets, but also the strategic deployment of the ideas of Western liberal and often explicitly anti-communist thin-kers such as Popper, Hayek, Aron, and Berlin.

The Material Structures of Religious Reformism

A worthy observation in regard to the *rowshanfekran-e dini* is that their intellectual re-orientation took place less in public fora and, at

---

67 For an exposition of Foucault's conception of the *dispositif* of sexuality, see Stuart Elden, *Foucault's Last Decade*, Kindle ed. (Cambridge: Polity 2016), Loc 1691.

68 Foucault, 'The Political Function of the Intellectual', p. 14.

69 'Dominant' is meant in the same sense as it was used to great effect by Ranajit Guha in his seminal work as part of the Subaltern Studies Collective. Ranajit Guha, *Dominance without Hegemony: History and Power in Colonial India*, ed. Edward W. Said, Convergences: Inventories of the Present (Cambridge, MA; London: Harvard University Press, 1997), p. xii. 'Gramsci in India: Homage to a Teacher', in *The Small Voice of History: Collected Essays*, ed. Partha Chatterjee (Hyderabad: Permanent Black, 2012), Loc 6498–6514.

least initially, more in 'safer' and less securitised semi-private spaces. The significance of such spaces was therefore twofold. Firstly, as mentioned, it would leave them less open to the threat of violent reprisal by their ideological antagonists but also able to manage the limited audience participating in the process of critical re-evaluation, and thus eschew providing grist to the mill of the Islamic Republic's foreign adversaries and various critics abroad. It would also keep open the possibility of cooperating with sympathetic political elites in the intellectual and cultural spheres, as well as potentially provide access and resources to pursue and advance those projects most important to them. Their praxis at this stage was not one of out-and-out 'dissidence' but rather one of renegotiating within the institutional spaces and disciplinary mechanisms, norms, procedures, and boundaries to which they were subject. The 'material structure of ideology',[70] so to speak, included research units affiliated to the state, publishing houses, reading groups and private classes, elite intellectual circles, and controlled university gatherings. State-funded journals or quarterlies sponsored by religious and cultural institutions were a resource made available for religious intellectuals sympathetic to the Iranian state, and, as a result, they subsequently availed themselves of the opportunity to publish and test their theoretical mettle. The ebb and flow of disgruntlement, accession, and co-optation was ongoing. These intellectuals also served an important role insofar as they were relied upon to respond to the novel problems and issues thrown up by the realities of hierocratic-populist governance.

In the 1980s their readership was largely restricted to the country's Shiʻi-religious educated elite, and, while the Iran–Iraq War raged and Khomeini was still alive, there was little inclination or appetite to challenge the ideological foundations of the *nezam*. While ideological contestations between loose political groupings and individuals within the elite took place, they did so largely beneath Khomeini's enveloping shadow, as he was regularly called upon to step into the fray and declare his stance on issues which proved divisive among his disciples. With the inception of the 1990s in the aftermath of the war and the death of the revolutionary regime's patriarch, that segment of the intelligentsia which had

---

[70] Adam David Morton, *Unravelling Gramsci: Hegemony and Passive Revolution in the Global Political Economy*, Kindle ed. (London: Pluto, 2007), Loc 2032.

been instrumental during the 1980s in defending the new order against the ideological challenge of Marxist materialism and liberalism steadily but cautiously increased their public activity in the form of articles which were more overtly reflective and critical in demeanour. Moreover, they ceased to be directly funded by state institutions, as they had been during the 1980s. Masha Allah Shams ol-va 'ezin and Reza Tehrani's *Kiyan* (Existence)[71] and the Mojahedin Organisation of the Islamic Revolution of Iran's *'Asr-e ma* (Our Epoch) were amongst the most prominent examples of this genre, as we shall see in Chapter 3. The transition from the religious-ideological and state-sponsored defence of the newly founded clerically led system against ideological competitors – such as the Marxist Tudeh Party and the Organisation of the Iranian People's Fada'i Guerrillas (OIPFG), the liberal-nationalist National Front, the religious nationalist Freedom Movement of Iran, and the Islamist People's Mojahedin – to a financially independent, albeit internal, critic of regime elements was a delicate and incremental process of negotiation.[72]

Intellectuals and politicians, who argue and engage in public disputation, are also concerned to reproduce their values and arguments and promote them.[73] In other words, they are preoccupied with propagating their ideas in an effort to obtain and engender public assent and intellectual and moral leadership – what Antonio Gramsci famously called 'hegemony'.[74] Intellectuals' authority is thus solicited not by coercion but by means of ascertaining people's active consent and the acceptance of their intellectual and moral leadership.[75] As Laclau and Mouffe argue, hegemony's 'very condition is that a particular social force assumes the representation of a totality that is radically

---

[71] *Kiyan* can also mean 'nature', 'epicentre', and 'state of being'.

[72] Masha Allah Shams ol-va'ezin, the periodical's first editor, explains the process whereby *Kiyan* was established, and in particular he stresses the way in which he and co-founders Reza Tehrani and Mostafa Rokhsefat came 'to pursue cultural activities independently'. Masha Allah Shams ol-va'ezin, 'Gozashteh, hal, ayandeh [Originally published in *Kiyan*, no. 1, Aban 1370 (October–November 1991)],' in *Yaddasht-ha-ye sardabir* (Tehran: Jame'eh-ye Iraniyan, Bahar 1380 [Spring 2001]), p. 13.

[73] Kurzman and Owens, 'The Sociology of Intellectuals', p. 63.

[74] Joseph V. Femia, *Gramsci's Political Thought* (Oxford: Oxford University Press, 1981), p. 24.

[75] Perry Anderson, 'The Antinomies of Antonio Gramsci', *New Left Review* 1, no. 100 (November–December 1979), p. 21.

incommensurable with it'.[76] Intellectuals thus regularly speak in the name of universals and proper names, whether it be in the defence of 'liberty', 'the people', 'justice', 'Iran', or 'Islam'.

Unlike Gramsci's proletarian 'organic' intellectuals, whose social function was ultimately preoccupied with achieving hegemony through instilling class consciousness and thereby mobilising industrial workers against the ruling capitalist class,[77] Iran's religious intellectuals throughout the 1990s pursued two chief objectives. These were the propagation of a more inclusive and critical conception of religious and political authority, while also accumulating and building upon their extant capital and authority, within the possibilities and resources afforded by extant political institutions and the constitution. This effort was accompanied by means of increasing their activity in the public square, which they hoped would dovetail with their political counterparts' deeper strategies for reform. These two porous formations shared a symbiotic relationship through which the 'success' of one would prove propitious for the other. The religious intellectuals made the case for the democratic basis of political legitimacy in an avowedly religious rubric, thereby proclaiming the moral and political superiority of those state institutions open to constrained electoral contestation. The Islamic left and reformist elements in the political class would use what leverage they had in those state and quasi-statal institutions where they had managed to achieve electoral success to facilitate the expression and dissemination of the *rowshanfekran-e dini*'s ideas and accumulation of social capital. This did not entail the absence of disagreements, or that this relationship was not on occasion counterproductive following the reformists' transient capture of the executive and legislature, but was rather indicative of the symbiotic character of the overlapping projects of 'reform' and 'religious intellectualism'. This included, for instance, setting 'reform' and 'revolution' in a strict opposition and appeal to the Islamic Republic's own constitution in their struggle for greater intellectual and civic freedoms, often precluding by

---

[76] Ernesto Laclau and Chantal Mouffe, *Hegemony and Socialist Strategy: Towards a Radical Democratic Politics* (London & New York: Verso, 1985), Loc 89. Nicos Poulantzas, 'Preliminaries to the Study of Hegemony in the State', in *The Poulantzas Reader: Marxism, Law, and the State*, ed. James Martin (London & New York: Verso, 2008), p. 82. Raymond Williams, *Keywords: A Vocabulary of Culture and Society*, Kindle ed. (London & New York: HarperCollins, 1976), Loc 2615–2624.

[77] Gramsci, *Selections from the Prison Notebooks of Antonio Gramsci*, pp. 12–14.

default many social and political forces which did not come out of these bearings.

Journals such as *Kayhan-e farhangi* (Cultural Universe) in the 1980s, *Iran-e farda* (Tomorrow's Iran), *'Asr-e ma* (Our Epoch), and most prominently *Kiyan* (Existence) in the 1990s, and newspapers such as *Salam* (Peace), *Jame'eh* (Society), *Sobh-e emruz* (This Morning), *Khordad*, *Tus*, and *Neshat* (Joy) – all of which, with the exception of *Salam*, came into being after Khatami's electoral victory – played an indispensable role in not only driving debates in the public sphere and print culture but also responding to questions which had long been asked but were rarely discussed in the public domain. They also actively participated in public life by teaching in Iran's institutions of higher learning, delivering public speeches at religious and non-religious venues, undertaking and publishing research in state-funded research centres, and convening gatherings and discussion groups that would give impetus to a raft of criticism and self-reflection in the 1990s and 2000s. Such gatherings were frequented by members of the political elite as well as other political functionaries sympathetic to the issues being raised. In this sense, as already mentioned, in the first two decades following the revolution these intellectuals availed themselves of important opportunities to publish, teach, and participate in public life in a way which had been limited or denied to the overwhelming majority of their liberal, leftist, and more secularly inclined ideological competitors. This social capital facilitated the accumulation of symbolic capital – the ability to set and define the key terms of intellectual debate and establish them as the legitimate point of reference.

It is also noteworthy that while these thinkers participated in a thoroughly transformed intellectual scene and public sphere, a slew of highly consequential social and demographic changes were taking place as the number of literate and university-educated Iranians, both men and women, markedly expanded[78] – transformations that were necessary to the emergence of the religious intellectuals' 'reading public'. From 1977 to 1996 the literate population increased from

---

[78] Shams ol-va'ezin, 'Rowshanfekri-ye dini va jomhuri-ye sevvom', p. 89;
Djavad Salehi-Isfahani, 'Human Resources in Iran: Potentials and Challenges', *Iranian Studies* 38, no. 1 (2005), p. 126. Farhad Khosrokhavar and Mohammad-Amin Ghaneirad, 'Iranian Women's Participation in the Academic World', *Iranian Studies* 43, no. 2 (2010), p. 225.

47.5 per cent to 79.5 per cent, while in urban areas literacy stood at 86 per cent.[79] In 1997, the year of Khatami's election, more than 1.5 million individuals held a university qualification and 3 million in total had either passed through or were currently in the university system.[80] Women's literacy and educational attainment also exponentially increased. Again, between 1977 and 1996 women's literacy increased from 36 per cent to more than 74 per cent, reaching more than 82 per cent in urban areas. By 1997 over 51 per cent of the students granted university places were women.[81] These changes were also reflected in the number of books printed both before and after the revolution. In 1976 some 1,689 titles were printed, while in 1996 the number had reached 15,315, with as many as 80 million copies in circulation.[82] The number of those individuals who were thus able to follow and engage the work and writings of these new religious thinkers and thereby constitute a 'public' (of which there are manifold) for their writings was also considerably augmented. Many were also beneficiaries of the expansion and marketisation of education initiated in the 1980s but developed foremost in the Rafsanjani era, the so-called Islamic Azad and Payam Nur Universities, which progressively set up branches and centres across the country. While in the past children from provincial towns and villages who had performed well in the highly competitive national examinations would have to travel, sometimes great distances, to attend university in an unknown city with meagre support, the option was now available to attend a local branch of the Islamic Azad University. While not necessarily affordable or accessible to all, it provided an opportunity for many high school graduates to attend university when they might not have been able to otherwise. This stands in stark comparison to the Pahlavi period where in the mid-1970s, according to Kaveh Ehsani, almost half of the political elite held a university degree from a foreign institution but only 2 per cent of the general population had a higher degree of any kind.[83]

---

[79] Sazman-e modiriyyat va barnameh-rizi-ye keshvar, *Tahavvolat-e keshvar va 'amalkard-e dowlat; gozaresh-e ra'is-e jomhur beh mardom* (Tehran Esfand 1379 [February–March 2001]), p. 29.

[80] Ibid., p. 29.   [81] Ibid., p. 30.   [82] Ibid., p. 30.

[83] Kaveh Ehsani, 'The Urban Provincial Periphery in Iran: Revolution and War in Ramhormoz', in *Contemporary Iran: Economy, Society, Politics*, ed. Ali Gheissari (Oxford & New York: Oxford University Press, 2009), p. 43.

In the post-revolutionary Iranian milieu, the label of *rowshanfekr-e dini*, despite its retroactive application to a whole host of thinkers such as the nineteenth-century pan-Islamic political and religious reformer Seyyed Jamal al-Din Asad-Abadi (d. 1897), better known as al-Afghani, is first and foremost applicable to the group of individuals who came together in a nascent form at the journals of *Kayhan-e farhangi* (Cultural Universe) and subsequently *Kiyan* (Existence). It was the individuals at the centre of these publications, with their regular discussion groups and seminars, who came to form the so-called Kiyan circle (*halqeh-ye Kiyan*). Its most prominent intellectual, 'Abdolkarim Sorush, has said that the name 'Kiyan circle' was not consciously used by the group and only came to be spoken about much later, after the journal had been closed down.[84] Another group by the name of the Ayin circle (*halqeh-ye Ayin*) was manned by other noted intellectuals and politicians, some of whom also participated in the Kiyan circle, and operated within the fold of the Islamic left, including individuals such as Mohammad-Reza Khatami, Hadi Khaniki, Sa'id Hajjariyan, Mostafa Tajzadeh, Mohsen Aminzadeh, 'Abbas 'Abdi, and Mohsen Kadivar.[85] Rather than philosophy or theology, several of them had undertaken, or were in the process of pursuing, graduate work in political science, communications, and sociology. While less well-known than the Kiyan circle, their activities were initiated directly by none other than Mohammad Khatami, who, after his resignation as minister of culture and Islamic guidance in the Rafsanjani administration, decided to apply for a licence to publish a journal by the name of *Ayin* (Creed) as a podium and outlet for himself and like-minded individuals.[86] Even though the journal *Ayin* was not published until several years after Khatami took office as president, a small group had been engaged in intellectual collaboration and the development of an intellectual and political project in the interim.

---

[84] 'Abdolkarim Sorush and Reza Khojasteh-Rahimi, 'Dovvom-e khordad beh ziyan-e Kiyan tamam shod: halqeh-ye Kiyan dar goftogu ba doktor 'Abdolkarim Sorush', http://www.drsoroush.com/Persian/Interviews/P-INT-Kian.html

[85] Salman 'Alavi-Nik, *8 sal-e bohran afarini-ye eslahtalaban* (Tehran: Markaz-e asnad-e enqelab-e eslami, 1389 [2010]), p. 169.

[86] Mohammad-Reza Khatami and Hosayn Salimi, 'Tasavvor-e piruzi nemikardim: goftogu ba Mohammad-Reza Khatami', in *Kalbodshekafi-ye zehniyyat-e eslahgarayan* (Tehran: Gam-e now, 1384 [2005]), pp. 42–43.

The three hubs of the Kiyan circle, the Ayin circle, and the Presidential Strategic Research Centre (PSRC) – later the Center for Strategic Research (*Markaz-e tahqiqat-e esteratezhik*) under the purview of the Council for the Discernment of Regime Expediency[87] – emerged as key intellectual hubs or nodal points in which innovations in both theology and political theory unfurled and simultaneously coalesced into a more coherent, albeit differentiated, series of ideological positions that would go on to inform reformist politics and the national conversation. It also established some degree of continuity between the Muslim Student Followers of the Imam's Line (*Daneshjuyan-e mosalman payrow-ye khatt-e Imam*) – who infamously overran the U.S. embassy, taking Americans hostage for 444 days (4 November 1979 to 20 January 1981) – and the leading political supporters of Mohammad Khatami's presidential electoral bid less than twenty years later.[88] Several of the leading student activists and figures directly involved in the hostage crisis, such as 'Abbas 'Abdi, Ebrahim Asgharzadeh, Ma'sumeh Ebtekar, and Mohammad Musavi-Kho'iniha, would either take up positions in the Khatami government or come to occupy a position amongst its fiercest advocates and mobilisers, having in many ways undergone an intellectual and political metamorphosis of considerable proportions in the course of the preceding decade. A metamorphosis, which as I will demonstrate in greater detail in Chapter 3, was to a large extent the product of factional marginalisation having been shunted to the margins of state power in the early 1990s and immediate exposure to the shortcomings of a supposedly 'sacred' state, obliged to rule in the mundane world. Khatami's watershed victory would of course mark the inauguration of a new 'reformist' era in the Islamic Republic – a term not initially used by Khatami himself, as will be shown in Chapter 6. This is not to say that academics and intellectuals extraneous to this more proximate cluster of groups were not influential, or that they failed to impact these individuals' intellectual development,

---

[87] Initially affiliated to the Presidency during the Rafsanjani era, it later became attached to the Expediency Discernment Council, which was under Rafsanjani's chairmanship until his death in 2016.

[88] For example, two people who lectured in the U.S. embassy during the hostage taking were the Students' clerical mentor, Hojjat al-Islam Mohammad Musavi-Kho'iniha, the second chairman of the MRM, and political strategist Sa'id Hajjariyan.

but merely that the chief points of activity revolving around journals, publishers, intellectual circles, and research units did not have an incidental degree of contiguity.

The term 'Islamic *chap*' (left), which to a large extent overlapped with the constellation of groups and organisations that would emerge as 'reformists' in the late 1990s, are adapted from the SMEEI's famous breakdown of the Islamic Republic's elite factional composition, which was published in a series of articles in *'Asr-e ma*, the SMEEI's biweekly journal during the first half of the 1990s.[89] The articles were published from 7 Dey 1373 (28 December 1994) through to 10 Khordad 1374 (31 May 1995). In the course of the articles the group traced the history and socio-political views and make-up of the four chief factions which had developed in the course of Khomeini's lifetime as *vali-ye faqih* and following his death in June 1989. These factions consisted of the traditional right (*rast-e sonnati*), the new right (*rast-e jadid*), the left (*chap*), which we have and will continue to refer to as the Islamic left, and the new left (*chap-e jadid*), which was closer to a brand of Islamic 'neo-conservatism' today often associated with the Endurance Front of the Islamic Revolution (*Jebheh-ye paidari-ye enqelab-e eslami*) patronised by Ayatollah Mohammad-Taqi Mesbah-Yazdi.[90] The SMEEI's own analysis is not taken at face value, since, for all its analytical insight, it was itself a partisan document, indelibly marked by the ideological and political *agon* of inter-factional rivalry.[91] They are, however, a seminal series of articles on how the Islamic *chap* viewed their ideological and political rivals and the development of their world view since the first years of the Islamic Republic and in the aftermath of the Iran–Iraq War and the death of Ayatollah Khomeini.

It is important to add that, much like their counterparts on the 'right', they publicly deferred to the figure of Ayatollah Khomeini as the final arbiter and source of authority on a raft of political and

---

[89] SMEEI, 'Negahi-ye kutah beh barkhi az tayf bandi-ha-ye jadid-e fekri-siyasi-ye jame'eh', *'Asr-e ma* (7 Dey 1373 [28 December 1994] through to 10 Khordad 1374 [31 May 1995]).

[90] See Anoushiravan Ehteshami and Mahjoob Zweiri, *Iran and the Rise of Its Neoconservatives: The Politics of Tehran's Silent Revolution* (London: I. B. Tauris, 2007).

[91] This has since been admitted by Mostafa Tajzadeh, who also clarified that the articles were not the work of a single individual but rather that of the organisation as a whole. Mostafa Tajzadeh and Hosayn Dehbashi, 'Goftogu ba Mostafa Tajzadeh', *Khesht-e kham*, no. 14 (3 Bahman 1395 [22 January 2017]).

religious matters;[92] by no means an uncommon phenomenon for the founders of revolutionary states, who find themselves sacralised with the revolution's institutionalisation. How their reading of the Ayatollah's pronouncements and legacy evolved, or whether they selectively adduced his decisions, statements, and pertinent anecdotes in support of their current political ambitions or objectives, has been part and parcel of the process of political contestation since the inception of the new state's founding. As a label, the 'Islamic left' is far from ideal, since it could potentially also denote groups such as the People's Mojahedin, which had both the trappings of an 'Islamic' identity and espoused views on history, society, geopolitics, and economics influenced by Marxist thought. Nevertheless, it has been used throughout the book with this important caveat in mind. The main organised political groups which fall under this category are the MRM; the SMEEI, which was reconstituted in 1991 (1370) with a different central committee membership; and the student organisation, the Office for Strengthening Unity (*Daftar-e tahkim-e vahdat*). The history of this faction or elite political tendency and some of its leading personalities will be more fully analysed in Chapter 3, along with their ideological reconstitution as 'reformists' (*eslahtalaban*). The latter political formation will be unpacked in greater detail in Chapters 6 and 7.

---

[92] PSRC member 'Ali-Reza 'Alavi-Tabar attributed the articles to *'Asr-e ma*'s editor, Mohsen Armin. Alireza Alavi-Tabar and Ali Mirsepassi, 'Alireza Alavi-Tabar and Political Change', in *Modern Democracy in Iran: Islam, Culture, and Political Change* (New York & London: New York University Press, 2010), p. 138–139. Tajzadeh, however, a senior member of the SMEEI, has unambiguously stated that it was a group effort.

   Moslem attributes authorship to Behzad Nabavi (Mehdi Moslem, *Factional Politics in Post-Khomeini Iran* (Syracuse: Syracuse University Press, 2002), p. 92). In several instances Hajjariyan's writings were published anonymously with the initials 'S.S.', and he is even introduced as 'one of *'Asr-e ma*'s readers' who supposedly submitted an article to the editorial board, who then decided to publish it because of its 'important contents'. See, for example, S.S. [Sa'id Hajjariyan], 'Mashru'iyyat, mashrutiyyat, jomhuriyyat', *'Asr-e ma*, no. 14 (13 Ordibehesht 1374 [3 May 1995]). It was not until the publication of Hajjariyan's *'Asr-e ma* articles in, *Jomhuriyyat: afsun-zoda'i-ye qodrat* (Republicanism: The Demystification of Power) that it became publicly known that Hajjariyan was the author.

   A copy of the document was made available to me by a member of the SMEEI, but I have also cross-referenced it with the original in *'Asr-e ma*. SMEEI, 'Negahi-ye kutah beh barkhi az tayf bandi-ha-ye jadid-e fekri-siyasi-ye jame'eh', *'Asr-e ma*, no. 14 (7 Dey 1373 [28 December 1994] through to 10 Khordad 1374 [31 May 1995]), p. 13.

Figure. 1 in the Appendix is an attempt to enumerate these disparate groups and their overlapping memberships. While it does not capture the complexity of the network or the fluidity of 'membership' and 'participation', it does have some heuristic value in conveying the connections between different groups, affiliations, and their intellectual activities. Thus, we can see the overlapping memberships and intersections of the Islamic left and 'religious intellectuals', along with the various circles and hubs within which they congregated, such as the Ayin and Kiyan circles and the Presidential Strategic Research Centre (PSRC), alongside other informal channels. This is because, as has been stated above, while religious intellectualism can be defined as an activity with a method of sorts, identification on this basis alone remains vague and lacking in meaningful political content. In our analysis it is equally, if not more, important to consider the fora and relationships through which their ideas were developed and disseminated – e.g., intellectual circles, gatherings, and think tanks – which possessed varying degrees of formality and institutionalisation, namely what we have referred to as the 'material structure of ideology'. It also conveys the contribution of the Freedom Movement of Iran (NAI) and the Coalition of National Religious Activists of Iran (SFMMI) to the broader project of religious intellectualism, even if they are marginal to this study and were not permitted to take up any official positions in either the executive or legislature from the mid-1980s onwards. Another shortcoming is that it does not capture the diachrony and dynamism of membership and affiliation and the way in which one-time self-professed *rowshanfekran-e dini* and their partisans either reaffirmed the designation's continued pertinence or ceased to identify with the label over time.

Another publication, *Zanan* (Women), edited by Shahla Sherkat between 1992 and 2008, was at the forefront of debating women's issues operated in the same building as *Kiyan* and occasionally interviewed leading religious intellectuals such as Sorush and Mojtahed-Shabestari as well as the wives of prominent left and centrist politicians, such as Jamileh Kadivar, Zohreh Sadeqi, and Zahra Rahnavard – women who were all intellectuals or political figures and social activists in their own right.

In 1982, a decade prior to the establishment of *Zanan*, Sherkat joined *Zan-e ruz* (Today's Woman), published under the umbrella of the Kayhan Institute, headed by none other than Mohammad Khatami. Sherkat would resign from *Zan-e ruz* in 1991, frustrated by the conservative bent of the publication,[93] just as Seyyed Mostafa Rokhsefat, Shams ol-va'ezin, and Tehrani left *Kayhan-e farhangi* to establish a new publication which took the intellectual project of Dr. Sorush as its chief point of departure.[94] Sherkat was invited to share premises with the founders of *Kiyan*, as it lacked the sort of financial backing which the latter enjoyed. Despite there being daily interactions between the editors of the two publications, there was little obvious intellectual exchange, and issues of gender were for the most part given short shrift or were absent altogether in the theoretical and philosophical schemes the religious intellectuals drew upon. *Zanan* covered political, social, and cultural affairs through a specifically gendered lens and fostered a plethora of critical debates within Iranian society. It was a trailblazing publication. But its role and the nature of its relationship to the intellectual and political conurbation adumbrated above, so central to the production and dissemination of religious intellectual political thought, was distinct. Despite its physical proximity it was for the most part kept at arm's length. The religious intellectual-Islamic left network was overwhelmingly male-dominated, and notions of gender and feminism were marginal, if not obviated entirely, in their intellectual endeavours. Moreover, in spite of the espousal of liberal and (in the context of the period) subversive ideas and theories, such criticism and self-reflexivity did not on the whole extend to the traditional habitus of Iranian-Muslim masculinities and patriarchal authority within the family unit.[95] In other words, there was a clear disconnect between the political and the personal, as well as macro-theorising and more concrete, micro-forms of lived interpersonal engagement and exchange.

Those individuals generally considered indispensable to the 'religious intellectual' collective and project were for all intents and purposes men. It partially reflects the entrenched forms of traditional patriarchy which still characterised the social relations of the reformist intelligentsia and political class – which is not to say that these relations

[93] Hamideh Sedghi, *Women and Politics in Iran: Veiling, Unveiling, and Reveiling* (Cambridge & New York: Cambridge University Press, 2007), p. 268.
Azadeh Kian-Thiébaut, 'From Islamization to the Individualization of Women in Post-revolutionary Iran', in *Women, Religion and Culture in Iran*, ed. Sarah Ansari and Vanessa Martin (London & New York: Routledge, 2002), p. 130.
[94] Eskandar Sadeghi-Boroujerdi interview with Roza Eftekhari, 27 February 2018.
[95] Ibid.

were or are static or unchanging, nor that important developments and achievements were not realised. Despite myriad examples of women's agency and its transformative effects in the political, social, and cultural domains – for instance, one can speak of manifold grassroots women's movements, from the women's rallies of March 1979 in opposition to the imposition of compulsory hijab to the One Million Signatures Campaign in the mid-2000s – the uncomfortable fact remains that, within these circles, women were rarely seen as peers in the process of knowledge creation/production on the subject of 'religion', religious authority, and its political import. Knowledge tended towards abstraction; it was rarely seen as gendered. Nor was women's presence visible or integral to the reading groups and think tanks in which 'religious intellectualism' and 'political development' were conceived, even if the mobilisation of women in elections later came to be viewed as crucial to such. 'Women' were a subject that would occasionally be commented *upon* (see Chapter 5), but women intellectuals were rarely treated as interlocutors on par with the central figures analysed in the course of the proceeding chapters. There are, of course, counter-examples and challenges to this male-dominated terrain, but they still palpably reside with a small minority.[96] In the words of *Zanan* itself, 'the religious intellectual current has always adopted silence on issues germane to women'.[97] One could certainly offer an elaborate normative and feminist critique of the religious intellectual collective and provide an explanation for women's invisibility, but it would be something of a different task and undertaking from the work before you.

There is another issue which should be mentioned before moving to address other pertinent questions. Women, gender, and sexuality are for the most part notable for their absence in the intellectual oeuvre of the 'religious intellectuals'.[98] In contrast to the writings of ʿAli Shariʿati and Ayatollah Morteza Motahhari before the revolution, post-

---

[96] Mirjam Künkler and Roja Fazaeli, 'The Life of Two Mujtahidahs: Female Religious Authority in 20th century Iran', in *Women, Leadership, and Mosques: Changes in Contemporary Islamic Authority*, ed. Masooda Bano and Hilary E. Kalmbach (Leiden: Brill, 2013).

[97] ʿAbdolkarim Sorush, 'Qabz va bast-e hoquq-e zanan: goftogu ba doktor ʿAbdolkarim Sorush', *Zanan* 8, no. 59 (Dey 1378 [December 1999–January 2000]), p. 32.

[98] For an account of 'reformist' religious thought on questions of women's rights and gender-related issues, see Mir-Hosseini, *Islam and Gender: The Religious Debate in Contemporary Iran* .

revolutionary religious intellectuals – specifically the ones comprising the networks addressed within this work – have negligible, if any, book-length treatises or lecture series on the question of women and their political agency during the historical period under examination. There are scattered essays, but one could reasonably make the case that the 'woman question' was not at the heart of their concerns and intellectual preoccupations. Instead, and in virtue of their debt to forms of classical and Cold War liberalism they have sought to appeal to the image of 'universal humanity' (read: universal man) as a bearer of abstract rights and entitlements, which is curiously antipodal to more traditional religious discourses which have often proven to be heavily gendered, though hardly emancipatory. This degree of invisibility is, at least in part, the outcome of their heavy indebtedness to elements of the liberal tradition and the thoroughly ahistorical, disembodied, and asocial conception of human agency and subjectivity which they often uncritically reproduced.

Constructing Hegemony and the 'National-Popular Will'

In the run-up to, and following Khatami's victory in the May 1997 presidential election, the Islamic left which had hitherto represented a particular and more limited set of socio-political concerns, focusing in concerted fashion on state command of the economy and social justice, sought to appeal to a larger bloc and swathe of the population, encompassing women, students, religious and ethnic minorities, and, perhaps most decisively, the burgeoning middle class.[99] In short, it sought to construct what has been called an 'integral hegemony', where 'the relationship between leaders and led would not be contradictory or antagonistic' but rather 'organic' and continuous, 'an educative and reciprocal relationship'.[100] Khatami was himself very much part of this process, and the emphasis of his campaign on the 'rule of law', and a rights-centred discourse was indicative of his effort to

[99] For an analysis of the factors which contributed to the emergence of Iran's much spoken about, but still relatively under-theorised middle class, see Kevan Harris, 'Social Welfare Policies and the Dynamics of Elite and Popular Contention', in *Power and Change in Iran: Politics of Contention and Conciliation*, ed. Daniel Brumberg and Farideh Farhi (Bloomington, IN: Indiana University Press, 2016).

[100] Peter Ives, *Language and Hegemony in Gramsci*, Kindle ed. (London: Pluto Press, 2004), Loc 1422.

invoke issues which were less controversial but nevertheless had a broad appeal. Khatami himself was a remarkable instance of an individual who had traversed several intellectual personas and subject positions in the course of his career. As a young, politically active cleric in Qom during the 1960s, he was the model 'organic intellectual', protesting and mobilising against the Pahlavi regime, while as director of the Kayhan Institute and newspaper at the very outset of the 1980s he became one of the official voices of the newly established state in a period of fissiparousness and precarious transition. Then as minister of culture he became one of the more tolerant faces of what was on the whole seen as an environment still hostile to those writers and artists whose work did not affirm and reproduce the official ideological and cultural values of the Iranian state apparatus. Finally, as a presidential candidate and later president he combined the roles of the intellectual and statesman, where his espousal of the catchwords of liberal consti- tutionalism – e.g., 'civil society',[101] 'rule of law', 'legality and consti- tutionality' – disseminated and popularised a discourse novel to the Islamic Republic and its founding ethos in concert with sympathetic elements in the post-1997 press and intelligentsia.

As will be shown in the coming chapters, the discourse of the *row-shanfekran-e dini* bore certain similarities with the paradigmatic 'lib- eral-bourgeois' *weltanschauung* often identified with the spread of Western capitalist modernity and formal freedoms, from which it also to some extent took intellectual inspiration:[102] to wit, a discourse which valorised the rule of law and natural rights against despotic encroachment and demanded respect and security for property rights in the name of the universal and God-given rights of humanity.[103] The glaring difference was one of *topography* and conditions under which this ideology and discourse crystallised and was subsequently deployed in the process of political contestation. Rather than a revolutionary class compelled by historical necessity to overthrow the strictures of feudal absolutism because of a systemic impediment to efflorescent capitalist relations of production, a template to which few,

---

[101]   *Kiyan* dedicated a whole issue to this concept even before Khatami's election in 1997. See, 'Ezatollah Sahabi et al., 'Mizgerd-e Kiyan-e dar bareh-ye Jame'eh-ye madani', *Kiyan* 6, no. 33 (Aban va Azar 1375 [November–December 1996]).
[102]   Sorush, 'Mabani-ye te'orik-e liberalism', p. 125.
[103]   Vivek Chibber, *Postcolonial Theory and the Specter of Capital*, Kindle ed. (London & New York: Verso, 2013), p. 40.

if any revolutions have strictly approximated,[104] the 'reform move-ment' at the level of the political class was an elite-managed initiative with the desiderata of fending off attacks by the traditional and radical right through the institutionalisation of the rule of law and a mild opening-up of political competition amongst trusted religious-political forces. The appeal of abstract citizenship, legality, transpar-ency, technocratic expertise and development, and accountability, as well as their claim to embody the 'national will' and the basis of 'human dignity', went far beyond the elite and certainly resonated with the demands of a wider range of social forces. Ultimately, if only tempora-rily, it helped forge an unanticipated and unstable coalition encom-passing elements of the political class and various social and subaltern groups willing to pursue their interests through the electoral process and bequeath trust to the executive in guaranteeing their interests and security.[105]

In this sense, the Islamic left cum 'reformist' elite sought and to some extent succeeded in fashioning a 'national-popular' will and political language, in which their privileged position as mediator was largely preserved, the hallmark of a Gramscian hegemony and historical bloc.[106] In the words of Stuart Hall, such a bloc combines sections of 'the dominant class with subaltern and subordinate sec-tions of other classes, of the middle classes and the petty bourgeoisie, as well as the popular classes which have been drawn into the matrix or configuration of power ... Hegemony entails the formation of a bloc, not the appearance of a class.'[107] As alluded to above, the subject of this hegemony did not facilely map onto a socio-economically pre-constituted class but was itself politically con-structed, entailing structures of thought, feeling, and practice. In this way, the reform movement, in the words of Perry Anderson, became 'a force capable of synthesizing heteroclite demands ... [that]

---

[104] For examples of incisive critiques of the ideal-typical bourgeois revolution, see E. P. Thompson, 'The Peculiarities of the English', in *The Poverty of Theory & Other Essays* (London: Montly Review Press, 1978). Alexander Anievas and Kerem Nisancioglu, *How the West Came to Rule: The Geopolitical Origins of Capitalism*, Kindle ed. (London: Pluto Press, 2015), chapter 6.

[105] Chibber, *Postcolonial Theory and the Specter of Capital*, p. 43.

[106] Perry Anderson, 'Heirs to Gramsci', *New Left Review*, no. 100 (July–August 2016), p. 77.

[107] Stuart Hall, *Cultural Studies 1983: A Theoretical History* Kindle ed. (Durham & London: Duke University Press, 2016), Loc 3276.

could take sharply different directions, into a national-popular unity'.[108] The unity forged was always fragile and articulated in relation to pressures exerted from below and the ever-present threat of securitisation by antagonistic elements within the state apparatus itself, above all elements within the Revolutionary Guards, Judiciary, and Ministry of Intelligence. In sum, those institutions deeply resistant or wholly extraneous to the civilian government's authority and control. The reformist hegemony which thus prevailed for a time on the ideological and political planes, had negligible control over the state's institutions of organized violence and coercion. Paraphrasing Ranajit Guha, one could say that it was a hegemony devoid of the power to dominate. It is in the shadow of such multivalent pressures that the reform movement was constantly liable to fray, fracture, and find itself transformed. The question of whether the executive branch was indeed ever capable of fulfilling the expectations and demands placed upon it by manifold social forces and thus perpetuating and augmenting its hegemonic enclosure was far from clear. In reality, it had subsided, if not largely dissipated, by the time the little-known mayor of Tehran, Mahmud Ahmadi-Nezhad, had been elected to the presidency in 2005. The coalition which had brought Khatami to power arguably only visibly reconstituted itself in reaction to immense popular pressure in the summer of 2009 and the uprising known as the Green Movement and again in 2013 in the run-up to the election of Hojjat al-Islam Hassan Rowhani.

Each historical conjuncture was distinct and the forces of which they were comprised would have to be analysed on a case-by-case basis. But in the broadest of terms, one might conclude that while the *eslahtalaban* have thus far been unable to dislodge the tutelary institutions which had sought to constrain their exercise of political power, and even exclude them from it entirely, since at least the early 1990s, few would dispute that their impact on the ideological terrain fought over by the entirety of the political class and the broader public has been decisive and irrevocable.

In political terms, the strategy for reform post-1997 was most famously expressed in Sa'id Hajjariyan's call for 'pressure from below, negotiation from above' and elaborated on at length in an extended interview with the journal *Rah-e now* (New Path), published

[108]   Anderson, 'Heirs to Gramsci', p. 79.

in May 1998.[109] In that interview, published exactly one year after Khatami's triumphant victory, Hajjariyan proclaimed defiantly that 'the 2nd of Khordad was the completion of republicanism and the fulfilment of constitutionalism',[110] while at the same time advocating a gradualist and managed process of political change encapsulated in the aforementioned slogan.[111] It is also in this regard that one might argue that Iran's religious intellectuals, while themselves comprising part of the Islamic Republic's political-intellectual elite, have attempted to embark upon several 'positional' strategies[112] in order to secure hegemony and disseminate their ideas. Quoting Gramsci himself, we might say that the Islamic left and religious intellectual networks made effective use of 'a centre of formation, of irradiation, of dissemination, of persuasion'; it was 'a group of men ... which has developed [ideas and opinions] and presented them in the political form of current reality'.[113] Furthermore, Gramsci himself might have framed this process in terms of 'passive revolution',[114] by means of which the elite try to forestall revolution or more wrenching and unpredictable political upheaval by incorporating less radical demands and co-opting subaltern groups in the process. But in addition to acknowledging this process at work, it is also important to grasp how religious intellectuals and their political allies on the Islamic left sought not only to critique the *status quo* but also to ascertain support for the dividends of their

---

[109] Sa'id Hajjariyan and 'Emad al-Din Baqi, 'Goftogu ba Sa'id Hajjariyan', in *Baraye tarikh: goftogu ba Sa'id Hajjariyan* (Tehran: Nashr-e ney, 1379 [2000]), p. 25.

[110] Sa'id Hajjariyan, 'Dovvom-e Khordad: omid-ha va bim-ha: payam-ha va cheshm andaz-ha', *Rah-e now*, no. 5 (2 Khordad 1377 [23 May 1998]), p. 16.

[111] Ali M. Ansari's classic account of the Khatami era captures well this aspect of the elite-led and managed process of reform, which those around Khatami hoped to realise. Ali M. Ansari, *Iran, Islam and Democracy: The Politics of Managing Change*, 2nd ed. (London: Chatham House: Royal Institute of International Affairs, 2006).

[112] I have refrained from using the Gramscian term of 'war of position' for reasons I lay out, but 'positionality' is helpful as a concept, because it places emphasis on the struggle over meanings and values. See Steven Jones, *Antonio Gramsci* (London and New York: Routledge, 2006), p. 31.

[113] Gramsci quoted in Kate Crehan, *Gramsci, Culture and Anthropology*, Kindle ed. (London: Pluto Press, 2002), p. 153.

[114] Gramsci, *Selections from the Prison Notebooks of Antonio Gramsci*, p. 107. Morton, *Unravelling Gramsci: Hegemony and Passive Revolution in the Global Political Economy*, Loc 1525.

own intellectual labour and thereby build on their extant capital and authority.

A final important issue which should also come through in the course of the following chapters is that during the 1990s and 2000s the *rowshanfekran-e dini* proved most successful in the battle for what Bourdieu called 'symbolic power'. More than any other species of capital and its accumulation, it was in the battle for symbolic power and capital – namely, the capacity to impose classifications and meanings as legitimate – where they most evidently succeeded.[115] 'Reform' as advocated by the Islamic left and buttressed by the religious intellectuals, though certainly still contested in terms of its ambit and priorities, managed to capture the imaginations of millions and gain a currency not enjoyed by any other political discourse since that of the revolution itself. The process of naming and classifying political and religious terms not only bestowed a carefully crafted identity to the religious intellectual current but also endowed it with the necessary symbolic power to acquire the status of moral compass, as well as considerable assent in its taking the lead in defining the terms and conceptual cartography of political and religious debate.

[115] Swartz, *Symbolic Power, Politics, and Intellectuals*, Loc 715.

2 | Constructing Behesht-e Jahan: *Islam, the Clergy, and the State*

We have a weapon, and that weapon is the truth.[1]

Ayatollah Ruhollah Khomeini (1943)

Introduction

In the aftermath of Iran's military occupation by the Allies in 1941, Iranian Islamists increasingly came to envision the modern nation-state as the chief vehicle for thinking through the realisation of an Islamic utopia on earth. In the words of Navvab Safavi, the leader of the militant Fada'iyan-e Islam, it would be through the state that Iranian Muslims might finally bask in the glories of a veritable 'heaven on earth' (*behesht-e jahan*). A new generation of Iranian Islamists slowly but surely began to partake in a concerted exercise of 'seeing like a state', to borrow a fortuitous phrase from James C. Scott.[2] They struggled to forge an idealised normative Islamic social order, structured and realised by the modern nation-state and its apparatuses of legibility and control. Its partisans thought of themselves, and would be perceived in turn, as participating in a major, perhaps unparalleled episode in modern Iran's history of social engineering on grand scale.

This chapter will provide an exposition of the thought and historical milieu of prominent Islamist ideologues and political activists spanning the Pahlavi era, and thereby illustrate the ideological lineages and terrain out of which the 'Islamic Republic' would be conceived and several of its prevailing political and religious discourses and *leitmotifs* constituted. In doing so, it will adumbrate some of the chief politico-religious thinkers and concepts that the post-revolutionary

---

[1] Ruhollah Khomeini, *Kashf al-asrar* (Tehran: 1943), p. 198.
[2] James C. Scott, *Seeing Like a State: How Certain Schemes to Improve the Human Condition Have Failed* (New Haven & London: Yale University Press, 1998), Introduction.

rowshanfekran-e dini would set out to challenge, critique and revise. These engagés and political activists include Navvab Safavi (d. 1955) and the organisation he founded, the Fada'iyan-e Islam, the revolutionary patriarch of the Islamic Republic, Ayatollah Seyyed Ruhollah Khomeini (d. 1989), and the French-educated layman, 'Ali Shari'ati (d. 1977). This selection makes no claim to be exhaustive of the religious and ideological ferment of the Pahlavi era, but such an examination proves instructive insofar as it illuminates some of the more prominent questions, issues and themes characterising the writings of Iranian Shi'i Islamists of the period. These include conceptions of radical socio-political change, the political role and responsibilities of the Shi'i clergy, the foundations of political authority and the character and purview of Islamic jurisprudence.

These issues with their various ambiguities and ambivalences are especially notable in the thought of 'Ali Shari'ati, which would constitute both an object of criticism and inspiration for members of the Islamic left and the *rowshanfekran-e dini* engrossed in their own concrete politico-ideological struggles during the 1990s and 2000s. Indeed, his legacy and contribution continue to be passionately and polemically debated through to the present in leading intellectual periodicals such as *Mehrnameh* and *Andisheh-ye puya*.[3] In short, it is helpful to analyse these ideologues and political actors and their historical conditions and development to understand the eclectic political theologies, which find themselves imbricated within the ideological self-image(s) of the Islamic Republic and the institutions of which it is comprised, as well as their many unresolved tensions. The *rowshanfekran-e dini* and their political allies would find themselves thinking and acting in the interstices of these ongoing ideational conflicts.

The establishment of an Islamic state has been amongst the key, if not been *the* key, objective of Islamic revivalists of the twentieth century.[4] The historical roots of revivalism are complex and vary from case to case, and this objective in itself does not tell us much. It is palpably lacking in content. This chapter will not dwell at length upon Iranian Islamism's historical causes, though the conditions of its emergence will be addressed in the course of an exegesis of some of the more prominent

---

[3] Mohamsmad Quchani, 'Rowshanfekr-e mosallah: pazhuheshi-ye enteqadi dar andisheh-ye siyasi-ye 'Ali Shari'ati', *Mehrnameh*, no. 52 (Tir 1396 [June–July 2017]).

[4] Ali Rahnema, *Pioneers of Islamic Revival* (New York: Zed Books, 2005), p. 4.

texts in which revivalists elaborated their vision of an Islamic polity. Such an exposition will help us to better grasp the political and ideological context out of which Iran's post-revolutionary religious intellectuals emerged, and thus the figures and archetypes, which often turn out to be the object of their pointed criticism.

The two groups focused upon specifically in this chapter – namely, the Islamist clergy and representatives of the modernist laity – testify to Iranian Islamists' own internal diversity. Moreover, within these respective groups, the signifier 'Islam' fulfilled different functions and roles in the world-views of individuals who did not necessarily share common backgrounds of class, education, and culture. While the concept of 'Islamist' is useful for the organisation of historical narrative, it is crucial to bear in mind that it is a capacious one, mediated by myriad ideological and political points of contention. Arguably, it is devoid of much analytical cogency beyond pointing to a very broad and abstract conviction that 'Islam' should inform political affairs, the ordering of political institutions, and the distribution of power and wealth.[5] The individuals and movements examined in this chapter also exhibit a great many political and ideological differences, even within the sweep of their own lifetimes during which they would experience intellectual and political transformations, shifting their focus and preoccupations accordingly. With such caveats in mind, their desire to capture state power is clearly articulated, as is their view of Islam as a political system, even if there remains much disagreement over what such a political system would entail or how it might be realised.

Ali Rahnema, in his panoramic analysis of twentieth-century Islamic revivalists, contends that they have designated four essential reasons for the decline of the Islamic world and Muslim peoples:

1) The erosion of Islamic values and governments' ignorance and inaction in enforcing Islam's socio-economic and ethical ordinances.[6]
2) Quietism and the collaboration of the clergy with non-Islamic governments.

---

[5] Ziba Mir-Hosseini and Richard Tapper, 'Islamism: *ism* or *wasm?*', in *Islamism: Contested Perspectives on Political Islam*, ed. Richard C. Martin and Abbas Barzegar (Stanford, CA: Stanford University Press, 2009), Loc 1016.

[6] This is certainly a theme which runs through the writings of Ayatollah Khomeini. Khomeini, *Kashf al-asrar*, p. 104.

3) The corruption and injustice (*zolm*) of the ruling classes.
4) The ruling classes collaboration and dependence upon non-Islamic and imperialist forces.[7]

These distilled reasons should not lead one to conclude that all Islamists are bound by an essential core, since the historical variety of their discourses and demands is not only undeniable but continues to proliferate both in the non-Western and Western worlds, changing and adapting in accord with disparate geographies, political economies, cultures and subcultures, and temporalities. Furthermore, even if one concludes that the enumerated points are common to all Islamists, something which is highly disputable, the distinct historical conditions under which they are articulated vary widely. However, in the most general of terms, complementing such diagnoses of the prevailing malaise is the proffered antidote: renewal (*tajdid*). The meaning of *tajdid* has hardly remained stable or unchanging but reflects a long-standing preoccupation of many Muslim thinkers and the perceived need for their faith's periodic revitalisation.[8] *Tajdid* is indissociable from the call for a return to the essential tenets of 'Islam' as presented in the Qur'an and Traditions (*sunnah, sonnat*) of the Prophet. In Twelver Shi'i Islam this picture is complicated greatly by the various collations of the Traditions of the twelve Holy Imams and the Twelfth Imam's Occultation, with the faithful still awaiting his promised return. Nevertheless, idyllic images of the first Muslim *ummah* (or *ommat*) of Medina chequer the writings of Iranian Shi'i Islamists and modernists as an object of emulation and recreation. There is a tradition traced back to the Prophet Mohammad himself in which he is reported as saying, 'God will send to this *ummah* [the Muslim community] at the head of each century those who will renew its faith for it.'[9] This tradition has been cited approvingly across the sectarian divide. The agent of renewal is the *mojahed*, one who strives in the path of the Almighty. Only he is able to discern and

---

[7] Rahnema, *Pioneers of Islamic Revival*, p. 5.
[8] John O. Voll, 'Renewal and Reform in Islamic History: Tajdid and Islah', in *Voices of Resurgent Islam*, ed. John L. Esposito (Oxford University Press, 1983), p. 32.
[9] Ibid., p. 33. There is also a Shi'i variant propounded by the sixth Imam, Ja'far al-Sadeq. Zackery M. Heern, *The Emergence of Modern Shi'ism: Islamic Reform in Iraq and Iran* (London: Oneworld Publications, 2015), Loc 1681.

subsequently implement the authentic spirit of the divine message, thereby fulfilling God's will.[10]

Despite the attendant problems of overzealous generalisations, these broad features are certainly visible, to an extent, in the rhetoric and political theology of modern Iranian Islamists, who burst onto the political scene as a small, albeit militant, force in the 1940s.[11] Their emergence can best be understood against the background of the steady challenge to the power and authority of the 'olama' posed by the arrival of the idea of the modern nation-state. Political Islam in Iran, as elsewhere, was thus mediated by a plethora of socio-political processes and dislocations, instigated as a direct result of the construction of the modern Iranian nation-state and the often-defensive manner in which it was undertaken to ward off the encroachment of imperial powers. For reasons of contextualising the emergence and evolution of Iranian Islamism, the present chapter will briefly turn to this process and outline some of its repercussions, which Iran's Islamists had originally set out to overturn but whose assumptions they often uncritically and unconsciously appropriated and reproduced.

Authoritarian Modernisation and the Erosion of the Foundations of 'Olama' Power

The idea of the modern nation-state found passionate advocacy in the hands of a small modernising elite, who were convinced that whole-heartedly adopting the example set by European nations was the best available route if Iran was ever to escape its lamentable state of 'backwardness' and 'stagnation'. Iran's own state was almost invariably plotted on an idealised trajectory of development *vis-à-vis* Europe – a trajectory which Europe had already traversed, as evidenced by the many appurtenances of civilisation and progress testifying to its salutary role in the advancement of human history, all while Iran palpably lagged behind. Iran's own deficiencies and successes were conceivable

---

[10] Voll, 'Renewal and Reform in Islamic History: Tajdid and Islah', p. 33.
[11] It should be noted in passing that there were important historical precedents at the beginning of the nineteenth century, which can be described as amongst Iran's earliest exponents of Islamism and a strong centralised Islamic state. See Vanessa Martin, 'Aqa Najafi, Haj Aqa Nurullah, and the Emergence of Islamism in Isfahan 1889–1908', *Iranian Studies* 41, no. 2 (2008), pp. 165–7.

only with reference to 'the West'[12] and, as a result, the modern intellectual class suffered an uneasy relationship torn between modern (read: Europeanised) cultural forms and the traditional beliefs and modes of life of their forefathers.[13] The encounter with the 'West' and its history and development were crucial, ideationally speaking, in the birth of a new breed of national consciousness amongst an emerging intellectual movement, which became the vehicle of a brand of 'romantic nationalism'. Homa Katouzian describes the ideological *weltanschauung* of this generation of romantic nationalists as follows:

It was opposed to European imperialism, but also captivated and mesmerized by modern European culture and power. It was contemptuous, sometimes even ashamed, of all the existing norms and traditions – including many a great Iranian heritage, even classical Persian poetry – but was proud, instead, of the romanticized glories of ancient Persia … [I]t was thus both Europeanist and anti-imperialist, both self-glorifying and self-denigrating.[14]

This band of 'discontented modern intellectuals', inspired by, and yet seemingly oblivious to, European nation-states' disparate roads to development, would act as a base of support for the Pahlavi state's ideological rationale.[15] Even if, later on, they would grow weary of the

[12] Alexander Anievas and Kerem Nisancioglu, among others, have fundamentally challenged such a picture and sought to show the extent to which 'the multiple geopolitical advantages that thrust Europe to global ascendancy were based on prior influences of more powerful non-European societies'. This, however, does not detract from the account elaborated in this section about how Iranian elites often internalised a Eurocentric picture of European progress and supremacy. Anievas and Nisancioglu, *How the West Came to Rule*, p. 276; Loc 6765.

[13] One of the better-known examples of an Iranian intellectual who embodies such a complex and ambivalent relationship is the scholar-statesman Hassan Taqizadeh, who during his own lifetime and posthumously has been much admired and maligned as a result of his comments exhorting Iranians to wholeheartedly embrace Europeanisation both 'inside and out'. His views and their development are far more complex than many of his supporters and antagonists have let on. For more nuanced views on Taqizadeh and his intellectual trajectory, see Ali M. Ansari, *The Politics of Nationalism in Modern Iran*, Kindle ed. (Cambridge & New York: Cambridge University Press, 2012), p. 46; Loc 1417. Homa Katouzian, 'Seyyed Hasan Taqizadeh: Three Lives in a Lifetime', *Comparative Studies of South Asia, Africa and the Middle East* 32, no. 1 (2012).

[14] *Sadeq Hedayat: The Life and Literature of an Iranian Writer* (London ; New York: I. B. Tauris, 2002), p. 69.

[15] Charles Tilly, *Coercion, Capital, and European States, AD 1990–1992* (Cambridge, MA: Blackwell, 1992), p. 224.

strongman they had once rallied behind to bring order in the midst of chaos, a Cossack officer turned king, they had already unleashed a force with which they were patently unprepared to deal. Ironically, along with the traditionalist elements they had so vehemently opposed, they found themselves victims of Reza Shah's slide into autocracy and arbitrary rule.[16]

To use Charles Tilly's term, in the absence of accumulated capital, this elite advocated a 'coercive-intensive' path to statehood.[17] The state, specifically the army and internal security forces, played a crucial role in the ongoing process of internal colonisation cum nation-construction.[18] The challenge mounted by the modernising nation-state was manifold. Most salient in setting the stage for the Islamist response were efforts to wrest away the legal, juridical and educational functions of the 'olama' in the course of the nation-building process. In breaking the clerical monopoly on these functions, which formed the basis of the 'olama''s social and political power, the modernising regime of Reza Shah sought to arrogate them to the state, which, toward the final years of his rule, became increasingly identified with his person.[19] Resistance was decisively quashed. Though the Qajar state had already initiated a number of reforms, which had undercut clerical power, such as the establishment of a new secular school system in 1851,[20] the reign of Reza Shah is generally understood

[16] Ali Gheissari, *Iranian Intellectuals in the 20th Century*, 1st ed. (Austin: University of Texas Press, 1998), p. 47.

[17] Tilly, *Coercion, Capital, and European States*, p. 199.

[18] For further details on the role of the military in the formation of the modern Iranian nation-state, see Stephanie Cronin, *The Army and the Creation of the Pahlavi State in Iran, 1910–1926* (London & New York: Tauris Academic Studies, 1997), chapters 4, 6. Elsewhere, Cronin has provided a series of rich accounts detailing Reza Khan's consolidation of central authority and merciless repression of regional popular movements and local elites during the course of the 1920s: see *Soldiers, Shahs and Subalterns in Iran: Opposition, Protest and Revolt, 1921–1941* (Basingstoke & New York: Palgrave Macmillan, 2010), chapters 2, 3. In this same vein, see Pezhmann Dailami, 'The First Congress of Peoples of the East and the Iranian Soviet Republic of Gilan, 1920–21', in *Reformers and Revolutionaries in Modern Iran: New Perspectives on the Iranian Left* ed. Stephanie Cronin (London & New York: RoutledgeCurzon, 2004).

[19] Homa Katouzian, *State and Society in Iran: The Eclipse of the Qajars and the Emergence of the Pahlavis*, Library of Modern Middle East Studies (London: I. B. Tauris, 2006), p. 315.

[20] Shahrough Akhavi, *Religion and Politics in Contemporary Iran: Clergy–State Relations in the Pahlavi Period* (Albany: State University of New York Press, 1980), p. 28.

as inaugurating a new era in state–'olama' relations.[21] A host of reforms initiated during the Reza Shah period (1925–41) encompassing the legal, judicial, and educational spheres compounded those already set in motion by the Qajars and contributed decisively toward the further erosion of 'olama' power and authority.

This latest phase in state–'olama' relations was perceived as breaking with the *status quo ante* of the last 400 years and the de facto division of authority which had existed between the two, in which issues pertaining to customary law ('*orf*) fell under the jurisdiction of the legitimate monarch (*saltanat-e mashru'*), and issues pertaining to *hisbah*, based on the Qur'anic maxim of 'enjoining the good and forbidding the evil' (*amr-e beh ma'ruf va nahy az monkar*) and the *shari'ah*, fell to the 'olama'. The historical reality, of course, was far less clear-cut, but in principle a kind of *modus vivendi* emerged between the spheres of Islamic jurisprudence and statecraft and thus the 'olama' and the ruling monarch.[22] In theory, a just monarch was expected to be an observant Muslim, defend his coreligionist subjects and the Islamic homeland from foreign intrusion and threat of depredation, and permit the clergy to supervise matters covered by the *shari'ah* ('*omur-e shar'i*).[23] While Reza Khan in the lead-up to his self-coronation had curried favour and explicitly sought out the approval of the 'olama',[24] it quickly became apparent that the new Shah had little intention of emulating the ideal Islamic monarch subscribed to by the conservative clergy.

The approval of a new Commercial Code (1925), Criminal Code (1926), and Civil Code (1928), based partially on models adopted from the French legal system (though incorporating elements of a codified *shari'ah*), and finally the abolition of *shari'ah* courts in 1939–40, which were replaced by European-style civil and penal codes, deprived many 'olama' of the fundamental bases of their livelihood.[25] Other

---

21 Ibid., p. 37.
22 Mohsen Kadivar, *Nazariyyeh-ha-ye dowlat dar feqh-e Shi'eh* (Tehran: Nashr-e ney, 1376 [1997]), p. 58.
23 Ibid., p. 59.
24 Mehdi Ha'eri-Yazdi and Ziya Sedghi, *Khaterat-e Mehdi Ha'eri-Yazdi, faqih va ostad-e falsafeh-ye eslami*, ed. Habib Lajevardi, Majmu'eh-ye tarikh-e shafahi-ye Iran (Bethesda, MD: Center for Middle Eastern Studies of Harvard University, 2001), p. 12.
25 Nikki R. Keddie and Yann Richard, *Modern Iran: Roots and Results of Revolution*, Updated ed. (New Haven, CT: Yale University Press, 2006), p. 90.

issues such as the Conscription Law (1925)[26] and the sale of *vaqf* (endowed) lands also riled segments of the 'olama' against the authoritarian, modernising regime of Reza Shah.[27] Moreover, as Cyrus Schayegh has argued, the evidence of the 'transformative' power of the state had the unintended consequence of promoting an 'image of the state as the *only* motor for progress and as *fully* separate from society'.[28] This only went to reinforce the prevailing logics of centralisation and state-led political and cultural change from above.

A readily *visible* challenge to the 'olama''s presence and prestige in Iranian society was the institution of new dress codes, modelled along European lines, what Houchang E. Chehabi has dubbed the Pahlavi state's campaign for 'sartorial westernization'.[29] The so-called Pahlavi hat, comparable to the French *képi*, became mandatory for Iranian men.[30] Though the 'olama' could still wear their traditional attire, strict criteria of eligibility were demanded by the Uniform Dress Law (December 1928) passed into law by the Seventh Majles, which had been packed with regime loyalists.[31] Perhaps most controversially of all, Reza Shah launched a campaign forcibly unveiling women as early as 1928, though it had not yet become official policy.[32] After Reza Shah's first and only state visit to Turkey in 1934 and witnessing firsthand the Westernising reforms undertaken by Mustafa Kemal Atatürk, the Shah's will-to-Europeanise took on a new lease of life.[33] It would be incorrect, however, to assume that Atatürk's example was the only impetus for the Shah's modernising drive. For instance, antecedent intellectual debates surrounding women's role in Iranian society,[34]

---

[26] Akhavi, *Religion and Politics in Contemporary Iran: Clergy–State Relations in the Pahlavi Period*, p. 37.

[27] Vanessa Martin, 'Religion and State in Khumaini's "Kashf al-asrar"', *Bulletin of the School of Oriental and African Studies, University of London 56*, no. 1 (1993), p. 44.

[28] Cyrus Schayegh, '"Seeing like a State": An Essay on the Historiography of Modern Iran', *International Journal of Middle East Studies 42* (2010), p. 39.

[29] Houchang E. Chehabi, 'Staging the Emperor's New Clothes: Dress Codes and Nation-Building under Reza Shah', *Iranian Studies 26*, no. 3/4 (1993), p. 212.

[30] Ibid., p. 212.   [31] Ibid., p. 213.   [32] Ibid., p. 214.

[33] It would be inaccurate to assume that Reza Shah merely imitated Atatürk and held an entirely derivative vision for Iran's modernisation. Ibid., p. 215.

[34] Camron Michael Amin, *The Making of the Modern Iranian Woman: Gender, State Policy, and Popular Culture 1865–1946* (Gainesville: University Press of Florida, 2002), chapter 3. Rahnema, *Shi'i Reformation in Iran*, p. 19.

and, in the more immediate term, an earlier visit by Reza Shah to Afghanistan and encounter with the reform-minded Afghan king Amanollah Khan and his 'unveiled' wife in 1928, were not without significance.[35]

In 1935 men were ordered to dispense with the Pahlavi hat and wear in its stead the *chapeau* or broad-rimmed hat. Compounding resentments over heavy taxation, Mashhad witnessed the bloody repression by state forces of peaceful protestors taking *bast* in Imam Reza's shrine during July of the same year, resulting in many arrests and the exile of some seventy clerics.[36] In his first political tract, *Kashf al-asrar* (1943), Ruhollah Khomeini, then a relatively low-ranking *mojtahed* based in Qom, would openly mock and decry Reza Shah's sartorial reforms. His blistering polemic probably captures the effrontery and trauma felt amongst a considerable swathe of Iran's urban, culturally conservative population, even if they could not quite muster the same levels of vitriol to express their disapprobation. His contempt for its executors was similarly unforgiving:

Of course, those who identify civilization and the excellence of a country with women walking naked through the streets; and as they idiotically say themselves, "with forced unveiling half the population will become workers" (perhaps a line of work you all know and we all know),[37] are not prepared to run the country in a rational way or under the law of God. We have nothing to say to those who have so little power of discernment they consider the progress of the country as bound up with a bowler hat (*kolah-e lagani*), which is amongst the dross left by the beasts of Europe ... What can we say to someone who has lost so much of his sense and intelligence when confronted with foreigners and in time will imitate (*taqlid*) them ... The day they put on the Pahlavi hat they all said the country must have national symbols and that the country's independence would be preserved in wearing it. A couple of days later they put on the bowler hat and all of a sudden, their remarks changed; they now said we have contact with foreigners and must all look the same until we become great ourselves. A country which builds its greatness on the basis of a hat or a hat which they

---

[35] Jasamin Rostam-Kolayi and Afshin Matin-asgari, 'Unveiling ambiguities: revisiting 1930s Iran's *kashf-i hijab* campaign', in *Anti-Veiling Campaigns in the Muslim World: Gender, Modernism and the Politics of Dress*, ed. Stephanie Cronin (London & New York: Routledge, 2014), p. 125, Loc 3769.

[36] Azimi, *The Quest for Democracy in Iran.*, p. 98.

[37] Khomeini seems to be implying prostitution here.

[i.e., the foreigners] make for it can be stolen any day and they will also deprive it of its majesty.[38]

Despite heated opposition from important segments of Iranian society, the anti-veiling campaign, though never formally enshrined in law, was launched in December 1935, when female teachers and students in girls' schools were mandated to 'unveil' by the Ministry of Education.[39] Its effect was not only to alienate the strong, conservative-patriarchal current of Iranian society concerned with women's 'chastity' (*namus*) but also to cause many women, in the provinces and capital alike, to agonise over their appearance in public. In some instances, the police and municipal officials even assaulted women, forcibly removing the *chador*, despite ministries' insistence to the contrary.[40] It is thus of little surprise that the policy has been subsequently interpreted as disproportionately impacting the traditional and poorer segments of Iranian society, who felt it exacerbated their exclusion from public life.[41] Such alienation, in the words of Jasamin Rostam-Kolayi and Afshin Matin-asgari, should be framed within the context of 'a broader authoritarian nationalist project of modernizing women's education, physical health, and moral cultivation.'[42] Like many other modernising regimes seeking to industrialise, impediments to women's active presence in society – but more importantly, their incorporation into the labour market and workforce – were viewed critically and as obstacles to the nation's successful transition to capitalist modernity.[43] But, as Afsaneh Najmabadi has argued, Reza Shah was less inclined to encourage Iranian women to enter the factories, expecting them instead to become teachers and enter the ministries of

---

[38] Khomeini, *Kashf al-asrar*, pp. 223–4. Though perhaps not conveyed with such venom, there is ample evidence suggesting that Khomeini's antipathy was widely shared amongst the Tehran clergy as well. 'Ali-Reza Mola'i-Tavani, *Zendegi-nameh-ye siyasi-ye Ayatollah Taleqani* (Tehran: Nashr-e ney, 1388 [2009]), p. 18.

[39] Rostam-Kolayi and Matin-asgari, 'Unveiling ambiguities', p. 124; Loc 3737. Azimi, *The Quest for Democracy in Iran*, p. 98.

[40] Rostam-Kolayi and Matin-asgari, 'Unveiling ambiguities', p. 133; Loc 3981.

[41] Mehdi 'Araqi, *Nagofteh-ha: khaterat-e Shahid Hajj Mehdi 'Araqi*, Paris-Pa'iz 1357 (Tehran: Mo'asseseh-ye khadamat-e farhang-e rasa, 1370 [1991]), p. 19.

[42] Rostam-Kolayi and Matin-asgari, 'Unveiling ambiguities', p. 126; Loc 3800.

[43] Kumari Jayawardena, *Feminism and Nationalism in the Third World*, Kindle ed. (London & New York: Verso, 2016), Loc 753.

an expanding state bureaucracy in service of the Pahlavi nation-building project.[44]

Though Reza Shah would abdicate the throne in 1941 with his sartorial regime left in tatters, the reforms of the legal system and judiciary would leave an indelible mark upon a generation of 'olama', who continued to fundamentally resent the destruction of the occupational prerogatives and socio-political power they had formerly enjoyed. The Fada'iyan-e Islam (Devotees of Islam), which was formed in 1945, ought to be read as *one* politico-ideological response to these events and deeper processes of socio-political, economic, cultural, and juridical transformation, which, in turn were a partial corollary of the Pahlavi regime's authoritarian drive to craft its image as the agent and embodiment of the modern nation-state's realisation.

The Fada'iyan, however, ought not be read as merely a reactionary response to the 'olama''s increasing irrelevance and dwindling authority as a corporate group in Iranian society. Like other revivalists of the modern era, their political vision was eclectic insofar as it incorporated elements of 'tradition' – to wit, the reactive defence of clerical prerogatives and forms of social control – *and* 'modernity', in short, utilising the modern state and its apparatuses for the propagation and enforcement of the *shari'ah* as they interpreted it. While its leader was a low-ranking cleric, with few by way of scholarly credentials, the organisation's members were a ragtag assortment of the young, the unemployed, peddlers, high school students, and craftsmen.[45] The Fada'iyan-e Islam's leader and founder Navvab Safavi – after serving two months in jail for the attempted assassination of the prominent intellectual and lawyer Ahmad Kasravi – even consciously decided to recruit local hooligans, ruffians, and street toughs for the purpose of forming combat groups in locales across the country.[46] Believing he could kill two birds with one stone, Navvab thought he could reform these one-time troublemakers and place them on the straight and narrow in the name of his cause.[47] They were hardly representative of the clerical establishment and are better understood

---

[44] Afsaneh Najmabadi, 'Hazards of Modernity and Morality: Women, State and Ideology in Contemporary Iran', in *Women, Islam and the State*, ed. Deniz Kandiyoti (Philadelphia: Temple University Press, 1991), p. 54.

[45] Sohrab Behdad, 'Islamic Utopia in Pre-Revolutionary Iran: Navvab Safavi and the Fada'ian-e Eslam', *Middle Eastern Studies* 33, no. 1 (1997), p. 45.

[46] 'Araqi, *Nagofteh-ha*, p. 26.   [47] Ibid., p. 26.

as a rebellion against the higher echelons of the clergy's acquiescence and quietism in the face of the perceived 'threat' to the sanctity of religion and its role in public life.[48] But, perhaps just as importantly, they were the result of class divisions within the clergy itself. Unlike the upper ranks of the *maraje'*, this class of seminarians and their allies disproportionately suffered as their traditional crafts, trades, and shop-keeping were destroyed as a result of industrialisation and the import of cheaper foreign commodities from markets abroad.[49] The power of the guilds which had once helped shield artisans from the vicissitudes of foreign trade found itself considerably eroded,[50] and members of the petit-bourgeoisie were increasingly proletarianised and forced to migrate to the oil fields of south-western Iran or larger cities to find work,[51] of which the Fada'iyan's own leader is a prime example (see below).

In the limited writings available which adumbrate the political ideas and program of the Fada'iyan, the recourse to jurisprudential arguments in favour of the proposed Islamic state is rare, if not entirely absent. Its leader, despite his clerical garb, only possessed a rudimentary education in the Islamic sciences. But perhaps just as importantly, because of Navvab's class position and the economic dislocation he and his followers had endured, the preference for populist slogans and anti-colonial fulminations over jurisprudential reasoning and argument is hardly surprising. The revivalists were not only angered by their modernising regime's erosion and, on occasion, outright repudiation of 'Islamic' values. The authoritarian manner in which such modernising

48 Rasul Ja'fariyan, *Jaryan-ha va sazman-ha-ye mazhabi-siyasi-e Iran: az ruy kar amadan-e Mohammad-Reza Shah ta piruzi-ye enqelab-e eslami* (Tehran: Khaneh-ye ketab, 1387 [2008]), p. 208.

49 Bizhan Jazani, *Tarh-e jame'eh shenasi va mabani-ye esteratezhi-ye jonbesh-e enqelabi-ye khalq-e Iran, bakhsh-i duvvum (tarikh-e si saleh-ye siyasi-ye Iran)* (Tehran: Entesharat-e Maziyar, 1357 [1978]), p. 64. *Capitalism and Revolution in Iran*, trans. Iran Committee (London: Zed, 1980), p. 135.

50 It should be stated, however, that Qajar Iran's nineteenth-century guilds wielded nothing like the power of their European counterparts. They did, however, come increasingly into prominence first during the Tobacco Revolt (1890–1) and then the Constitutional Revolution (1905–11). See Willem Floor, *Guilds, Merchants, & Ulama in Nineteenth-Century Iran* (Washington: Mage Publishers, 2009), p. 150.

51 Touraj Atabaki, 'From 'Amaleh (Labor) to Kargar (Worker): Recruitment, Work Discipline and Making of the Working Class in the Persian/Iranian Oil Industry', *International Labor and Working-Class History*, no. 84 (2013), p. 167.

drives were carried out along with the perception of subordination to Western imperial interests provoked deep-seated resentment.[52]

Visions of the Islamic State: The Fada'iyan-e Islam, Early Khomeini, and the Politicisation of the Seminary

The Fada'iyan-e Islam, led by the young cleric Seyyed Mojtaba Mir-Lowhi, better known as Navvab Safavi (1924–55), predominantly engaged in small-scale agitation and political assassinations. A nom de guerre, Navvab (deputy, prince), consciously chose to identify himself with the dynasty that had first instituted and enshrined Shi'i Islam as Iran's state religion at the outset of the sixteenth century.[53] This tightly-knit Islamist group, comprising a handful of individuals at its core, should not be regarded as on a par with comparable regional social or anti-colonial political movements in the region such as the Muslim Brotherhood in Egypt, whose mobilising power Safavi witnessed first-hand when he met with the organisation's leaders, as well as President Mohammad Naguib and Prime Minister Gamal 'Abdel Naser, while on a visit to Cairo in 1953.[54] Though the Fada'iyan certainly had sympathisers and affiliates beyond Qom and Tehran,[55] the failure to transform itself into a broad-based movement was arguably amongst the chief reasons for its lack of success and subsequent extirpation by the security forces of the monarchical regime. However, their world-view, agenda, and committed membership provide a crucial glimpse into the beginnings of the Islamic movement as it would develop in Iran and the seeds of a radical agenda, already burgeoning elsewhere in the Middle East.

Ayatollah Mohammad-Reza Mahdavi-Kani (1931–2014), a member of the Council of the Islamic Revolution (*Showra-ye enqelab-e eslami*), one of the most important decision-making bodies established

---

[52] Hadi Khosrowshahi, *Zendegi va mobarezeh-ye Navvab Safavi* (Tehran: Ettela'at, 1386 [2007]), p. 266.

[53] Roy Mottahedeh, *The Mantle of the Prophet: Religion and Politics in Iran* (Boston: Oneworld Publications, 1985, 2000), p. 105.

   Mehdi 'Araqi states that Safavi was the family name of his maternal uncle, a judge in the Department of Justice, who raised Mir-Lowhi after the death of his father. 'Araqi, *Nagofteh-ha*, p. 20.

[54] Khosrowshahi, *Zendegi va mobarezeh-ye Navvab Safavi*, p. 264.

[55] Nasser Mohajer, 'Kard ajin kardan-e doktor Berjis', *Baran*, no. 19–20 (1387 [2008]), p. 11. Hadi Khosrowshahi, *Fada'iyan-e Islam: tarikh, 'amalkard, andisheh* (Tehran: Ettela'at, 1379 [2000]), p. 106.

by Khomeini at the outset of the 1979 Revolution, while not a formal member of the Fada'iyan-e Islam considered himself a supporter of the organisation.[56] In his memoirs he recalls his own days as a young seminarian, stating that the *tolab* who were prepared to cooperate with the Fada'iyan-e Islam were in the minority. He credits the Fada'iyan for provoking the first political stirrings in the hearts and minds of his fellow classmates in Qom. The picture drawn by Mahdavi-Kani is quite different from the surge of political tumult enveloping Qom and the environs of the Fayziyyeh seminary in particular during the early 1960s and late 1970s. It is a portrayal which instead draws attention to a growing political consciousness amongst members of the 'olama' still in an early phase of gestation.[57] Moreover, though the Fada'iyan published newspapers such as *Manshur-e baradari* (The Fraternal Proclamation) and *Nabard-e mellat* (The Nation's Battle), the reading of newspapers was frowned upon in the seminary and, if done at all, was usually concealed from the sight of others.[58] However, even Mahdavi-Kani's relatively conservative account admits that the Fada'iyan 'were inspirational and laid the groundwork for our future activities'[59] and, along with the political activism of the out-spoken cleric and Speaker of Parliament (August 1952–March 1953) Ayatollah Seyyed Abolqasem Kashani (1882–1962), 'without doubt had a great effect on Iran's Islamic revolution'.[60] One has to be careful when assessing such statements, especially since following the consoli-dation of the Islamic Republic a state-funded cottage industry has been established to fashion an official historiography retelling Khomeini and the Islamic revolution's inevitable victory and its continuity with the multifarious 'Islamic' struggles which preceded it, all seamlessly woven together in a single triumphal narrative.[61] Nevertheless, it is safe to

---

[56] Mohammad-Reza Mahdavi-Kani and Gholam-Reza Khajeh-Sarvi, eds., *Khaterat-e Ayatollah Mahdavi-Kani* (Tehran: Markaz-e asnad-e enqelab-e eslami, 1385 [2006]), p. 91.

[57] Ibid., p. 72. [58] Ibid., p. 93. [59] Ibid., p. 93. [60] Ibid., p. 94.

[61] This has been addressed in part by Kamran Scot Aghaie, 'Islamist Historiography in Post-Revolutionary Iran', in *Iran in the 20th Century: Historiography and Political Culture*, ed. Touraj Atabaki (London & New York: I. B. Tauris, 2009), pp. 236–44. Shahram Kholdi's 2011 doctoral thesis on this subject is both systematic and comprehensive. Shahram Kholdi, 'The Politics of Memory in the Islamic Republic of Iran: Memoirs and the Historiography of the Iranian Revolution of 1979' (PhD, University of Manchester, 2011).

conclude that Navvab and his small organisation did play an important role in politicising and radicalising the younger strata of the clergy, despite the wishes of the clerical and scholastic elite.

Many of the Islamic Republic's founders were either members of the Fada'iyan or sympathisers of Navvab and his cohorts' efforts to challenge the steady erosion of Iran's Islamic identity at the hands of native collaborators, foreign capital, and menacing Western imperialists. For instance, several former Fada'iyan members and supporters such as Mehdi 'Araqi and Asadollah Lajevardi went on to found the Islamic Coalition Association (*Hay'at-ha-ye mo'talefeh-ye eslami*) in the 1960s, an organisation with strong links to the bazaar that would go on to wield great power in the post-revolutionary order and which was formed on the basis of Khomeini's explicit edict.[62] Khomeini gathered together those he regarded as sympathetic to the cause, proclaiming in a meeting at his home, 'why should you be scattered? Why don't you work together?'[63] Likewise, President Akbar Hashemi-Rafsanjani (1989–97), in his memoir covering the pre-revolutionary period, *Dowran-e mobarezeh* (The Era of Struggle), speaks candidly of his sympathies for the Fada'iyan and his admiration for Navvab Safavi, whose speeches he witnessed first-hand, participating in their meetings held in Qom.[64] Rafsanjani speaks of his and fellow seminarians' anger at Grand Ayatollah Seyyed Hosayn Tabataba'i-Borujerdi, arguably the leading religious authority of the Shi'i world at the time, due to his open dissatisfaction with the Fada'iyan's agitations against the remains of the former Shah, Reza Pahlavi, being brought to Qom from South Africa for a funeral service at the Fatemeh al-Ma'sumeh shrine, after which they would be taken to Shahr-e Ray and interred. Indeed, Grand Ayatollah Borujerdi's followers would even at one point run the Fada'iyan out of the Fayziyyeh seminary and then out of Qom entirely, meting out a fierce beating in the process.[65] Despite the stark

---

[62] Asadollah Badamchiyan, *Ashena'i ba jam'iyyat-e mo'talafeh-ye eslami* (Tehran: Andisheh-ye nab, 1385 [2006]), pp. 39–40.

[63] Habibollah 'Asgarowladi, *Khaterat-e Habibollah 'Asgarowladi* (Tehran: Markaz-e asnad-e enqelab-e eslami, 1391 [2012]), p. 79.

[64] Akbar Hashemi-Rafsanjani, *Dowran-e mobarezeh: khaterat, tasvir-ha, gah shomar*, 2 vols., vol. 1 (Tehran: Nashr-e ma'aref-e enqelab, 1386 [2007]), pp. 108–9.

[65] Gholam-Reza Karbaschi, *Tarikh-e shafahi-ye enqelab-e eslami: tarikh-e howzeh 'elmiyyeh-ye Qom* (Tehran: Markaz-e asnad-e enqelab-e eslami, 1380 [2001]), pp. 322–3.

disapproval of the upper echelons of the clergy, Rafsanjani insists that
the Fada'iyan's leader continued to be the subject of considerable
reverence from the younger generation of clergymen:

Navvab was sacred (*moqaddas*) for us, very many accepted him … I can say
that the essential makings of my political temperament were from that same
time, under the influence of the wave of the National Front movement, the
struggles of Ayatollah Kashani and more than anything else the Fada'iyan-e
Islam.[66]

Mahdavi-Kani also speaks of the Fada'iyan's fierce opposition to
the imminent arrival of Reza Shah's corpse, voiced through a flurry
of speeches delivered at the Fayziyyeh seminary.[67] In a similar vein,
Sadeq Khalkhali, the infamous 'hanging judge' appointed by
Khomeini to head the Revolutionary Court which sent many members of the *ancien régime* peremptorily to the gallows, contends that
the 'first revolutionary execution of [the Fada'iyan-e Islam] was the
assassination of Ahmad Kasravi in Tehran's Department of Justice
building'.[68] According to Khalkhali, the execution of Ahmad
Kasravi (1890–1946), the famed historian of the Constitutional
Revolution and former cleric-turned formidable critic of Shi'ism
(*tashayo'*), by followers of Navvab, was the first step along
a revolutionary and hitherto untravelled road. Finally, Ayatollah
'Ali Khameneh'i, the second Guardian Jurist and Leader of the
Islamic Republic, has also testified to meeting Navvab aged eleven
when the latter visited Mashhad, the city of Khameneh'i's birth,
and admits to an infatuation with the persona of Navvab and
political Islam developing from that time onwards.[69] During
Navvab's visit to the small seminary in Mashhad he attended at
the time, Khameneh'i describes how he sat in front of the leader of
the Fada'iyan as he delivered a fiery sermon, and how his 'entire
being was captivated by this man'.[70]

[66] Hashemi-Rafsanjani, *Dowran-e mobarezeh*, 1, p. 109.
[67] Mahdavi-Kani and Khajeh-Sarvi, *Khaterat-e Ayatollah Mahdavi-Kani*, p. 72.
[68] Sadeq Khalkhali, *Khaterat-e Ayatollah Khalkhali: az ayyam-e talabegi ta
      dowran-e hakem-e shar'-e dadgah-ha-ye enqelabi-ye eslami* (Tehran: Nashr-e
      sayeh, 1379 [2000]), p. 45.
[69] 'Abdolrahman Hassanifar, ed. *Fada'iyan-e Islam dar kalam-e yaran* (Tehran:
      Markaz-e asnad-e enqelab-e eslami, 1389 [2010]), p. 262.
[70] 'Khaterat-e Ayatollah Khameneh'i az avvalin didar ba Navvab-e Safavi',
      Khabar Online 27 Dey 1389 [17 January 2011].

Nor was the influence among Khomeini, his disciples, and Navvab unidirectional. Ayatollah Khomeini's first overtly political tract, the aforementioned *Kashf al-asrar* (Revelation of the Secrets), was published anonymously in 1943,[71] and the scholar Sohrab Behdad reckons it highly probable that Navvab had read it.[72] This appears likely given that Khomeini's *Kashf al-asrar* was allegedly written at the behest of bazaar merchants in Tehran with the explicit intent of responding to ʿAli-Akbar Hakamizadeh's polemical tract, *Asrar-e hezar saleh* (Thousand Year Old Secrets) (1943). Hakamizadeh, an erstwhile man of the cloth who also happened to be the son of a well-respected cleric,[73] like Kasravi had cast aside his clerical garb in the mid-1930s and now set about challenging his erstwhile colleagues and the enduring 'superstitions' he held them responsible for perpetuating.[74] Hakamizadeh was known in Qom as the editor of the modernist journal *Homayun* and a disciple of Kasravi, whose press published the controversial text.[75]

That Kasravi's failed assassin – Navvab shot and wounded Kasravi on 28 April 1945 – may have only recently read Khomeini's 300-page point-by-point rebuttal and indictment of Hakamizadeh's pamphlet, and by extension Kasravi's own writings criticising many of Twelver Shiʿi Islam's basic tenets, is eminently plausible. Though there is as yet no conclusive evidence that Khomeini explicitly sanctioned Kasravi's assassination beforehand, the fate of Islam's enemies was made clear by him in *Kashf al-asrar*. Designated *mofsed fil arz* (sewing corruption on earth) by the young *mojtahed*, it was stated unequivocally that 'we expect Islamic government (*dowlat-e Islam*) with its religious regulations to prevent those publications which are contrary to law and religion, and that those blathering individuals be executed before the votaries of religion. Those in pursuit of sedition (*fitneh*), spreading corruption on earth (*mofsed fil arz*) must be extirpated from the earth.'[76] Abbas Milani goes as far as to claim that

---

[71] Martin, 'Religion and State in Khumaini's "Kashf al-asrar"', p. 34.

[72] Behdad, 'Islamic Utopia in Pre-Revolutionary Iran', p. 44.

[73] Rahnema, *Shiʿi Reformation in Iran*, p. 38.

[74] Yann Richard, 'Shariʿat Sangalajī: A Reformist Theologian of the Riḍā Shāh Period', in *Authority and Political Culture in Shiʿism*, ed. Said Amir Arjomand (New York: State University of New York Press, 1988), p. 160.

[75] I am thankful to Homa Katouzian for alerting me to the point that Hakamizadeh and Kasravi had fallen out at the time of the tract's publication. Ibid., p. 160.

[76] Khomeini, *Kashf al-asrar*, p. 105.

Khomeini's tract was in effect tantamount to Kasravi's death sentence.[77] Khomeini did publish a statement in the spring of 1944 which directly, albeit belatedly, called on the clergy and the pious to rise up in reaction against the deposed Shah's policies and more specifically the writings of Kasravi. Entitled 'Read and Act' (*Bekhanid va beh kar bebandid*), the statement reads like a call to arms peppered with attacks on Reza Shah, 'the illiterate Mazandarani' with a 'desiccated brain', but also 'the rascal from Tabriz [i.e., Kasravi] who curses all of your doctrines', Imam Ja'far Sadeq and the Hidden Imam.[78] Moreover, while scholarship has often confidently distinguished the Khomeini of *Kashf* from the Khomeini of later decades on the basis of his shifting views on the monarchy and the imperative of 'bad' government over chaos (*harj-o-marj*), interesting continuities persist. One example is Khomeini's famed comparison of Mohammad-Reza Pahlavi to the despised Umayyad caliphs of Shi'i lore, Yazid and his father Mu'awiya ibn 'Abi Sufyan, following the White Revolution in the early 1960s. It turns out Khomeini had previously made just the same analogy, albeit with respect to Reza Shah and Mustafa Kemal Atatürk some twenty years previously,[79] thereby demonstrating the *mojtahed*'s enduring hostility and deeply felt anathematisation of the authoritarian modernising regime and its illegitimacy and irreligiosity.

There is additional evidence of an amicable meeting-of-minds between Khomeini and Navvab. In the post-revolutionary memoir of Safavi's widow, Nayyereh al-Sadat Ehtesham-e Razavi, it has been claimed that Navvab would regularly frequent Khomeini's home at dawn to evade state harassment.[80] Hojjat al-Islam Fazlollah Mahallati (1930–85), who was both a member of the Fada'iyan-e Islam and a student of Khomeini dating back to the 1940s and who later went on to become Khomeini's representative in the Islamic Revolutionary Guard Corps, also confirms that Navvab would visit Khomeini at his

---

[77] Abbas Milani, *Eminent Persians: The Men and Women Who Made Modern Iran, 1941–1979*, 1st ed., 2 vols. (Syracuse, NY, & New York, NY: Syracuse University Press & Persian World Press, 2008), p. 947.

[78] 'Nameh-ye Ayatollah Khomeini; "Bekhanid va beh kar bebandid"', *BBC Persian* 21 March 2012.

[79] Khomeini, *Kashf al-asrar*, p. 105.

[80] Nayyereh Sadat Ehtesham Razavi and Hojjatollah Taheri, *Khaterat-e Nayyereh Sadat Ehtesham-e Razavi* (Tehran: Markaz-e asnad-e enqelab-e eslami, 1383 [2004]), p. 144–5.

home.[81] Mahallati adds that Khomeini would on occasion relay messages to Ayatollah Borujerdi via Navvab[82] but that he never actually heard Khomeini explicitly agree or disagree with the political activism of Navvab or the Fada'iyan.[83] The far more prominent figure of Ayatollah Kashani, by contrast, publicly endorsed the group until his own falling out with them in May 1951. Given Khomeini's close relationship with Kashani, who was in fact the neighbour to his father-in-law, and despite Ayatollah Montazeri's protestations that Khomeini did not support the Fada'iyan,[84] most accounts testify to the meeting-of-minds thesis, or at the very least a degree of common ground and shared aims.

Moreover, Mehdi 'Araqi (d. August 1979),[85] a member of the Fada'iyan-e Islam who played an instrumental role in many of the group's activities, including its assassination attempts against Ahmad Kasravi and other high-ranking government officialdom,[86] contends that when Khomeini heard of Navvab's imminent execution he went to lobby for Ayatollah Borujerdi's intervention, albeit to little effect.[87] He even reports Khomeini as having left Ayatollah Borujerdi's home in tears.[88] This last-ditch attempt to save Navvab's life, along with two letters penned by Khomeini to the statesman Mohsen Sadr, known as Sadr al-Ashraf and Seyyed Mohammad Behbahani, a powerful Tehran cleric with ties to the court,[89] testifies to a deep sympathy for both Navvab and the latter's cause on the part of the future revolutionary leader. Nevertheless, given the nature of the source material at our disposal and the shadow cast by post-revolutionary official historiography, it is perhaps wise to continue to assess the relationship between the two men with a degree of caution.

---

[81] Fazlollah Mahallati, *Khaterat va mobarezat-e Shahid Mahallati* (Tehran: Markaz-e asnad-e enqelab-e eslami, 1376 [1997]); ibid., p. 37.
[82] This claim is questionable given Borujerdi's much-publicised disapproval of the Fada'iyan-e Islam's activities.
[83] Mahallati, *Khaterat va mobarezat-e Shahid Mahallati*, p. 37.
[84] Hosayn-'Ali Montazeri, *Khaterat-e faqih va marja'-e 'aliqadr hazrat Ayatollah Hosayn-'Ali Montazeri* (http://www.amontazeri.com, 1379 [2000]), p. 142.
[85] For Khomeini's acknowledgement of his own long-standing acquaintance with 'Araqi following his assassination, see Ruhollah Khomeini, *Sahifeh-ye Imam*, 21 vols., vol. 9 (Tehran: Mo'asseseh-ye tanzim va nashr-e asar-e Imam Khomeini, 1378 [1999]), p. 350.
[86] 'Araqi, *Nagofteh-ha*, p. 16.
[87] Ibid., p. 137. This story is also confirmed by Navvab's widow. Ehtesham Razavi and Taheri, *Khaterat-e Nayyereh Sadat Ehtesham-e Razavi*, p. 144.
[88] 'Araqi, *Nagofteh-ha*, p. 137.
[89] Ja'fariyan, *Jaryan-ha va sazman-ha-ye mazhabi-siyasi-e Iran*, pp. 208–9.

It would be a step too far to speak of Khomeini's patronage of the Fada'iyan-e Islam, since at the time he was a relatively junior *mojtahed*, only receiving his *ejazeh* from Shaykh 'Abdolkarim Ha'eri-Yazdi in 1936,[90] and the group had the backing of high-ranking and more prominent 'olama' such as Ayatollahs Mohammad-Taqi Khonsari, Hosayn Tabataba'i-Qomi[91], and Kashani.[92] Besides, Khomeini was far from the only individual whose ire was provoked by Kasravi and his disciples' activities, whose excommunication had already been sanctified by Qomi and Khonsari, as well as other leading clerics in Najaf.[93] Indeed, Navvab had first encountered Kasravi's writings in Najaf, Iraq, and, with the financial support of 'olama' residing there, including the future *marja'* Seyyed Abolqasem Khu'i, travelled to Tehran to confront Kasravi.[94] There has not as yet been any substantiated or direct causal connection between Khomeini's writings and the Fada'iyan-e Islam's execution of Kasravi, while the search for such a connection appears to be largely motivated by a desire to plot a political genealogy for Khomeini as always having been mired in violence and fanaticism. What does appear to be the case is that there was considerable agreement amongst a cluster of senior clergymen on the permissibility of Kasravi's assassination, and while in principle Khomeini appeared to approve, it was far from needed or decisive in what followed.[95] According to another prominent member of the

---

[90] Baqer Moin, *Khomeini: Life of the Ayatollah* (London: I. B. Tauris, 1999), p. 36.
[91] Seyyed Mohammad Vahedi and Mahnaz Mizbani, eds., *Khaterat-e Shahid Seyyed Mohammad Vahedi* (Tehran: Markaz-e asnad-e enqelab-e eslami, 1381 [2002]), p. 51.
[92] 'Ali Rahnema, *Niru-ha-ye mazhabi bar bastar-e harakat-e nehzat-e melli* (Tehran: Gam-e now, 1384 [2005]), p. 29. The Fada'iyan's alliance with Kashani began in August 1946 and ended in May 1951 with considerable acrimony in the aftermath of Prime Minister 'Ali Razmara's assassination by a member of the Fada'iyan (p. 162). This is despite the fact that Kashani reportedly issued a fatwa authorising Razmara's assassination, as revealed in the course of Navvab and his top lieutenants' trial (p. 164). Farhad Kazemi, 'The Fada'iyan-e Islam: Fanaticism, Politics and Terror', in *From Nationalism to Revolutionary Islam*, ed. Said Amir Arjomand (Albany: State University of New York, 1984).
[93] 'Araqi, *Nagofteh-ha.*, p. 22.
[94] Vahedi and Mizbani, *Khaterat-e Shahid Seyyed Mohammad Vahedi*, p. 25.
[95] Navvab Safavi's widow confirms that Navvab did order the assassination of Kasravi. Nayyereh al-Sadat Ehtesham Razavi, 'Ostureh-ye mehr: goft va shenudi ba "Nayyereh al-Sadat Navvab-e Ehtesham" Hamsar-e Shahid Navvab-e Safavi', *Shahed-e yaran*, no. 2 (Dey 1384 [December–January 2005]), p. 20.

Fada'iyan-e Islam, Mohammad-Mehdi 'Abdokhoda'i, who himself as a teenager had sought to assassinate Mosaddeq ally and confidant Hosayn Fatemi, Khomeini's much revered teacher of mysticism Ayatollah Mohammad-'Ali Shahabadi even helped procure the gun.[96] But in the Fada'iyan memoir literature and contemporary accounts available to us, there is generally little mention of Khomeini, which again is unsurprising given the fact that in this period there were far more established and senior *rowhaniyun* manoeuvring on the Iranian political scene. Nonetheless, and as will be shown in greater detail below, a *politico-ideological* affinity between the Fada'iyan and Khomeini's early writings on the nature of the Islamic state is readily apparent.

Neither Navvab nor Khomeini had yet taken the radical step of declaring monarchical rule illegitimate *in principle*,[97] and a formal deference to the 1906 Constitution is persistently adduced in the two men's writings. Articles I and II of the Supplement to the Constitution of 7 October 1907, in particular, which declared the Iranian state's official religion to be Shi'i Islam and stipulated the necessity for the establishment of a supervisory body of five religious jurists (*mojtahedin*) to determine the compatibility of parliamentary legislation with the *shari'ah* are frequently alluded to in both the Fada'iyan's *Barnameh-ye hokumati-ye Fada'iyan-e Islam* (autumn 1950) (The Governmental Programme of the Fada'iyan-e Islam), also known as *Rahnama-ye haqayeq* (The Guide to Truth[s]), and Khomeini's *Kashf al-asrar*.[98] Unlike Khomeini's tract, which was distributed anonymously, the Fada'iyan sought to disseminate their manifesto far and wide. Ten thousand copies were initially printed,[99] and a list of high-level recipients in the Pahlavi court and state apparatus was drawn up, in addition to ensuring its circulation by post throughout the provinces.[100] The formal nature of this deference to the constitution is further underscored by the exalted status reserved in their writings for the most prominent anti-constitutionalist *mojtahed* of the Constitutional Revolution, Shaykh Fazlollah Nuri, unreservedly held

---

[96] Mohammad-Mehdi 'Abdokhoda'i and Hosayn Dehbashi, 'Goftogu ba Mohammad-Mehdi 'Abdokhoda'i', *Khesht-e kham*, no. 42 (2018).
[97] Khomeini, *Kashf al-asrar*, p. 187.   [98] Ibid., p. 222.
[99] Vahedi and Mizbani, *Khaterat-e Shahid Seyyed Mohammad Vahedi*, p. 122.
[100] Khosrowshahi, *Fada'iyan-e Islam*, p. 112.

up as a 'martyr'.[101] As a young seminarian in Arak, Khomeini even studied with a close associate of Nuri, Shaykh Mohsen 'Araqi, which might help to explain Khomeini's lionisation of the famous *mojtahed* executed by the constitutionalists.[102] It is worth noting that the demand for a council of *mojtaheds* empowered to veto legislation deemed incompatible with the *shari'ah* was the brainchild of Nuri, though his initial proposal was subsequently modified.[103] Khomeini and Navvab's understandings of parliament and its legislative function not only invoke Nuri's name but also echo his apologia for royal absolutism, putatively bound by the limits set by the *shari'ah* (*mashru-teh-ye mashru'eh*). In this arrangement as conceived by Nuri, the 'just jurists' (*faqihan-e 'adel*), as general deputies of the Hidden Imam (*na'eban-e 'amm-e imam-e zaman*), would supervise all matters falling under the purview of the *shari'ah*, while matters of customary law continued to reside within the jurisdiction of the monarch.[104] According to Norman Calder, the executive functions which had conventionally been reserved for the Hidden Imam by the mid-sixteenth century had come to be recast as entitlements of the clergy during the Occultation. This was encapsulated in the terminological innovation of the Ottoman-era jurist Shahid II (d. 1559), who recognised the *faqih* as the *na'ib-e 'amm* or 'general delegate' of the Hidden Imam. On this basis, the clergy were empowered to collect *shar'i* taxes such as *zakat* and *khoms*, which to a large extent underwrote clerical revenue and a degree of institutional autonomy which accompanied it. One of the few prerogatives not bestowed to the *foqaha* was that of declaring jihad for purposes of expansion.[105]

I will now examine the Fada'iyan's *Barnameh* and Khomeini's *Kashf al-asrar* in greater detail and explore their articulations of

---

[101] Mojtaba Navvab Safavi, *Barnameh-ye hokumati-ye Fada'iyan-e Islam* (Tehran: Bonyad-e be'sat, 1386 [2007]), pp. 101, 117. Khosrowshahi, *Fada'iyan-e Islam*, p. 282.

[102] Michael M. J. Fischer, 'Imam Khomeini: Four Levels of Understanding', in *Voices of Resurgent Islam*, ed. John L. Esposito (New York & Oxford: Oxford University Press, 1983), p. 151.

[103] Said Amir Arjomand, 'The State and Khomeini's Islamic Order', *Iranian Studies* 13, no. 1 (1980)., p. 155.

[104] Kadivar, *Nazariyyeh-ha-ye dowlat dar feqh-e Shi'eh*, p. 75.

[105] Norman Calder, 'Accommodation and Revolution in Imami Shi'i Jurisprudence: Khumayni and the Classical Tradition', *Middle Eastern Studies* 18, no. 1 (1982), p. 4.

some of the central themes of revivalist literature and how their respective visions set the scene for the development of what would later come to signify 'Islamic ideology' or *Islam-e feqahati* (jurisprudential Islam) in the discursive lexicon of post-revolutionary religious intellectualism (see Chapter 4). The *Barnameh* was originally published in 1950, some five years before Navvab's execution at the hands of a summary trial convened by a military court. Navvab was arrested and tried along with a handful of his disciples, after the failed assassination attempt against Hosayn 'Ala', the minister of court, who at the time was due to assume the premiership at the behest of the Shah.[106] The *Barnameh* is a repetitious and at times erratic and meandering text. It does, however, provide a fascinating window into the Fada'iyan's unswerving focus on the state apparatus, its structure, and the laws and norms that should regulate society in turn. It hammers away at two themes in particular: firstly, the irredeemable depravity and spiritual destitution of the present age; secondly, Islamic government as a sacred nomocratic order, the one and only panacea capable of bestowing salvation in the here-and-now. Even if the proposed solution was clear for Navvab and his cohort, it should be noted that the diagnosed spiritual malaise is profoundly embedded in worldly malcontent. Anger at state corruption, bribery, poverty, addiction,[107] wanton violence, imperial hubris, and hunger abound throughout the entirety of the fiery tract.[108]

In locating the 'roots of ruinous corruption' in Iran and the world at large, Navvab's vision of human nature is decisive.[109] Invoking the Qur'anic notion of *nafs* or selfhood, which in exegetical literature is shown to be rich and layered with manifold meanings,[110] Navvab identifies *nafs, simpliciter*, with the desire (*meyl*) and inclination towards sin and sinful acts.[111] It is, moreover, often identified with man's base carnality, a quality which makes his conduct and behaviour regularly indistinguishable from that of the rambunctious play of alley dogs.[112] This intrinsic desire to commit evil and sinful acts finds its

---

[106]   Sohrab Behdad, 'Islamic Utopia in Pre-Revolutionary Iran: Navvab Safavi and the Fada'ian-e Eslam,' ibid. 33(1997), p. 51; Milani, *Eminent Persians*, p. 40.
[107]   Khosrowshahi, *Fada'iyan-e Islam*, p. 208.   [108]   Ibid., pp. 203–4.
[109]   Safavi, *Barnameh-ye hokumati-ye Fada'iyan-e Islam*, p. 25.
[110]   C. E. Bosworth et al., eds., *Encyclopaedia of Islam*, vol. 7 (Leiden & New York: E. J. Brill, 1993), p. 880.
[111]   Safavi, *Barnameh-ye hokumati-ye Fada'iyan-e Islam*, p. 25.
[112]   Ibid., p. 105.

counterpoint in reason *('aql)* – reason itself is sanctified with reference to the holy Qur'an. According to Navvab, every individual is involved in resistance and is essentially in conflict with him or herself: this conflict is waged by reason, perpetually at war with man's lascivious and pernicious desires and lust *(shahvat)*. Navvab goes so far as to compare reason to 'weaponry' *(aslaheh)*, resisting the unceasing onslaught of *nafs*.[113] In this way Navvab enacts a strict dualism of the self, one in which reason and the lustful self are in a state of perpetual war. He enters the two forces of *nafs* and reason into a dialogue, personifying and ventriloquising each one, as they encourage the faithful to pursue their respective paths. The two forces also engage in mutual recrimination. For example, Navvab has *nafs* say that 'prison, especially, the prisons of today are a good place to relax. There are also good friends [in prison]. All the better.' Reason, however, coolly replies that 'you will be killed because it's possible that while drunk you will kill someone'.[114] Later in the ongoing debate between *nafs* and *'aql*, in which the former praises money-grubbing and gambling, *nafs* continues:

Death is once and in the end [man] must die and the distress of dying is five minutes, we too have been killed, what meaning does being [killed] have.[115]

Having decreed the inevitability of death and even the transience of suffering a violent death, *nafs* believes it has conclusively defeated *'aql*.[116] But, 'all of a sudden ablaze' *(nagah bar afrukhteh)*, reason retorts:

What will you do with God and God's court and the infamous court of Truth *(haqq)* and God's perpetual, endless torture that has no end?

Thus, while a violent death may well prove transient, God's retribution for the sinful is not merely inescapable but without terminus. With this rebuttal *nafs* descends into deep thought and admits defeat. Having been bested and humbled, *nafs* replies:

[Y]es brother, the court of infamy with the greatness of Truth *(haqq)* beside the Prophets of God and the Immaculate Imams and Holy Zahra and Imam Hosayn, Lord of the Martyrs and the innocent of the world and eternal, divine torture is not a joke *(shukhi)*. I will not commit evil acts.[117]

---

[113]   Ibid., p. 25.   [114]   Ibid., p. 26.   [115]   Ibid., pp. 26–7.   [116]   Ibid., p. 27.
[117]   Ibid., p. 27.

Evil, temptation, and craven desires are integral to humanity's make-up, and such desires which are ultimately the root of all earthly 'corruption' will be renounced only under threat of condemnation to the eternal agony of hellfire.[118] 'Faith' (*iman*) in the certainty of such condemnation is the only means of curbing the roots of corruption pervading society. 'Yes, for the fundamental thwarting of the foundation of corruptions, faith alone in the truths and nurturing of Islam is necessary.'[119]

Navvab makes the extent of his ambitions readily apparent. He hopes to build a 'heaven on earth' (*behesht-e jahan*), a term he deploys repeatedly in the course of the text.[120] At the top of the agenda is the implementation of Islamic ordinances, first and foremost those pertaining to the penal code.[121] Their non-implementation is one of the main factors for the 'wretchedness' (*badbakhti*) of the Iranian people's present condition. In the new Islamic order this situation will be rectified with alacrity.

Yes, yes, the law of Islamic punishments will too be executed. The hand of the thief will be cut, so that he cannot rest in the sanatorium and the prison bordello, and the fourth time [he steals] he will be killed; with that where will thievery be? ... Fornicators will be flogged in public view and the third time killed. How will they look upon the betrayal of the people's honour (*namus-e mardom*) and after seeing chaste women one or two times trick them and ultimately take them to the whorehouse and after a time with their syphilis ridden bodies dispatch them to the graveyard.[122]

Lust and carnal appetites must be restrained under threat of punishment determined in accordance with the letter of the law. Punishment in the mundane world was not only viewed as essential to avoiding eternal punishment in the next but also to creating the ideal Islamic society in the present.

The issue of feminine sexuality proves to be a particularly sensitive one. Women's 'honour' (*namus*) and chastity, treated as though they

---

[118] Hojjat al-Islam Mahallati, who attended Ayatollah Khomeini's classes on ethics in the 1940s, explains how they focused explicitly on the *ayat* of the Qur'an, which dealt explicitly with hell and its punishments. In this way, one of the most powerful reasons justifying ethical conduct inculcated into the young seminarians was the fear of hellfire and eternal damnation. Mahallati, *Khaterat va mobarezat-e Shahid Mahallati*, p. 36.

[119] Safavi, *Barnameh-ye hokumati-ye Fada'iyan-e Islam*, p. 27.

[120] Ibid., pp. 27, 28, 103.   [121] Ibid., p. 27.   [122] Ibid., p. 30.

were public property and part of community identity and standing,[123] must be preserved at all costs. The failure to do so harbours potentially disastrous consequences for social order. In this way, social cohesion and its preservation becomes inseparable from the control and regulation of women's bodies. At one point, Navvab goes so far as to speak of the 'fire of lust from the flaming naked bodies of unchaste women burning decent women' along with them.[124] The viral contagion of feminine sexuality must be reined in, Navvab argues, otherwise society, and even the family unit as we know it, will disintegrate.[125] In emphasising the perils of unceasing lust (*fa'aliyyat-e da'em-e hess-e shahvat*) and the prospects of society-wide conflagration, exemplified and embodied in the female form, Navvab unintentionally illustrates the libidinal economy and obsessions of his own imagination.[126] It is not just 'unchaste' women who provoke men's lustful appetites: cinemas, theatres, novels, and musical compositions must all be uprooted (*bayesti barchideh shavad*) and their exponents punished for much the same reason.[127] Certain concessions are made later in the text: for example, he does accept the prospect of cinemas as long as 'the subject of all the shows and films consist in the edifying histories of Islam and the Shi'i world and history, salutary pieces on ethics and war and sections on the sensitive parts of the great history of Islam and industrial, agricultural and scientific films'.[128] He also approves of the teaching of the medical, agricultural, and industrial sciences under the proper supervision of 'pure professors and learned Muslims', who have a positive role to play in the progress and development of his envisioned Islamic state.

Ultimately, only the execution of Islamic law, as he understands it, can vanquish society's ills and forge the utopian Islamic polity envisaged by Navvab. It should of course be noted that the Fada'iyan's understanding of Islamic law was patently ahistorical, unscholastic, and one-dimensional and that Navvab's screed is less the product of hard-earned erudition than it is an irascible clarion call for the overhaul

---

[123] For an explanation of the notion of *namus*, see Afsaneh Najmabadi, *Women with Mustaches and Men without Beards: Gender and Sexual Anxieties of Iranian Modernity*, Kindle ed. (Berkeley & Los Angeles: University of California Press, 2005), Loc 79.

[124] Safavi, *Barnameh-ye hokumati-ye Fada'iyan-e Islam*, p. 32.

[125] Ibid., p. 33.   [126] Ibid., p. 32.

[127] Khosrowshahi, *Fada'iyan-e Islam*, p. 210.   [128] Ibid., p. 225.

of the political order. Devoid of historical consciousness and yet unconsciously suffocating under the weight of centuries of accumulated tradition, as a result of which the *shari'ah*, 'the path to the watering-place' and metaphor for 'the path to felicity and salvation',[129] came to be identified with punitive law, pure and simple. Islamic law was torn from its historical embeddedness in socio-cultural relations, in which reason and revelation would be drawn upon by scholars and jurists to address pressing issues and questions facing the community, when, to quote Hallaq, it was 'a socially embedded system, a mechanism, and a process, all of which were created for the social order by the order itself . . . Attributing to this law roles of control and management would be a distinctly modern misconception, a back-projection of our notions of law as an etatist instrument of social engineering and coercion.'[130] In the view of the Fada'iyan-e Islam the *shari'ah* was reduced to little more than a litany of *hudud* punishments in which the violent apparatus of the state ought to be deployed to full effect. 'The sacred ordinances of Islam and punitive laws of Islam must be executed to the letter (*mu beh mu*).'[131] Because such a conception is first and foremost preoccupied with restraining men and women's carnal selves, it can only modulate social relations by means of sanctioning transgressions of the holy writ. Its predominantly punitive character thus cannot but give rise to an austere *nomocracy*.[132] Even though the state's exercise of violence against transgressions would be swift and unforgiving, there was nevertheless a recognition that the loss of 'public trust' (*e 'temad-e 'omumi*) had to be recovered and the chasm dividing state (*dowlat*) and society (*mellat*) narrowed.[133] How this would be achieved beyond moral exhortation, religious education, and the omniscient threat of punishment is left indeterminate and vague.

Many of these leitmotifs are also evident in the section entitled 'Government' (*hokumat*) in Khomeini's *Kashf al-asrar*. There he

---

[129]   Mohammad Hashim Kamali, *Shari'ah Law: An Introduction* (Oxford: Oneworld Publications, 2008), p. 2. Chibli Mallat, *The Renewal of Islamic Law: Muhammad Baqer as-Sadr, Najaf and the Shi'i International*, Kindle ed. (Cambridge & New York: Cambridge University Press, 1993), Loc 74.

[130]   Wael B. Hallaq, *An Introduction to Islamic Law* (Cambridge & New York: Cambridge University Press, 2009), p. 165.

[131]   Khosrowshahi, *Fada'iyan-e Islam*, p. 229.

[132]   For example, see the section on the Department of Justice in the *Barnameh*. Ibid., p. 229.

[133]   Ibid., pp. 215, 226.

writes, '[I]t is manifestly true that the law of Islam (*qanun-e Islam*) is more advanced than all other laws in the civilized world and with their enactment the Perfect City (*madineh-ye fazeleh*) will be established.'[134] Only the 'government of God' (*hokumat-e khoda*)[135] is able to fulfil its 'obligations', because only the government of God is founded on the basis of justice (*'edalat*), wisdom (*kherad*), and truth (*haqq*). All existing governments, according to Khomeini, were founded on the basis of illegitimate force, or, as he repeatedly puts it in the course of his tirade against the Pahlavi state, at 'the point of a bayonet'.[136] Islamic law allows the state to be born in innocence, in lieu of the original sin and founding violence which the human legal order conspires to properly efface.[137] While Khomeini expresses his reluctance to claim the state in the name of the jurist (*faqih*), he says 'government must be administered by the divine law (*qanun-e khoda'i*) that is beneficial to the country and the people and this will not be realized without the supervision of the clergy'.[138] Khomeini then goes on to invoke the constitution, which, as was mentioned previously, codified clerical supervision of the legislative process.[139] He reiterates, 'no one except God has the right to rule over another, nor do they have the right to legislate ... the law is the same laws of Islam ... [T]his law is for all and forever.'[140]

Despite salient differences, there do already appear to be seeds of Khomeini's later political doctrine of *velayat-e faqih* in *Kashf al-asrar*. While simply stating that the clergy were in possession of *velayat* or 'guardianship', in carefully defined instances, would be uncontroversial amongst the overwhelming gamut of Osuli Shi'i clergy,[141] its scope and remit was a more contentious matter. In this early work, Khomeini explicitly juxtaposes 'guardianship' and 'government': 'during this time government (*hokumat*) and "guardianship" are with the clergy'.[142] Moreover, under the section heading of 'The Reason for Government by the Jurist in the Time of the Occultation', he relates the tradition of 'Omar ibn Hanzalah, a tradition he would also cite in his

---

[134] Khomeini, *Kashf al-asrar*, p. 222.   [135] Ibid., p. 222.   [136] Ibid., p. 221.

[137] I am alluding to Walter Benjamin's well-known essay on this score, *On the Critique of Violence*. Khomeini of course does not regard the state's enforcement of the Islamic legal order, employing its monopoly of violence *as* violent, because the *shari'ah* by definition cannot be coercive. Walter Benjamin, 'On the Critique of Violence', in *One-way Street and Other Writings* (London & New York: Penguin, 2009), p. 7; Loc 237.

[138] Khomeini, *Kashf al-asrar*, p. 222.   [139] Ibid., p. 222.   [140] Ibid., p. 184.

[141] Ibid., p. 185.   [142] Ibid., p. 185.

later and more famous tract *Velayat-e faqih, hokumat-e eslami,*[143] in defence of his theory of the 'guardianship of the jurist'. In the considerably earlier *Kashf* he goes as far as to say that 'in this tradition the *mojtahed* is made ruler (*hakem*) and its rejection is a rejection of the Imam and the rejection of the Imam is the rejection of God'.[144] This is a radical proposition on Khomeini's part, given the date of the text's publication. But, as other parts of *Kashf* attest, Khomeini still had not made the break he would publicly declare over two decades later when he repudiated altogether the institution of the monarchy.[145] At the very least, the clergy were conceived as the trustees of the *shari'ah* and its exclusive administrators. His use of the term *hakem* is not unambiguous since it can mean both 'judge' and 'ruler', but then the question poses itself why Khomeini chose to use this term instead of the far less ambivalent term for judge, namely *qazi*. That many years later, while in exile in Iraq, he would draw upon this very same tradition to legitimate his conception of Islamic government headed by the clergy makes his use of terminology at this early stage of his political career even more intriguing. At other times in *Kashf,* while preserving the role of the 'just king' (*soltan-e 'adel*) he says this king should be chosen by those *mojtaheds* who make up the parliament.[146] He does, however, begrudgingly admit that the incumbent 'rotten government' is better than no government at all and that without the prospect of establishing the 'kingdom of God' (*saltanat-e khoda'i*) unjust monarchies are worthy of respect.[147] Furthermore, he cites the example of pre-eminent 'olama' in the history of Shi'i Islam, such as Nasir al-Din al-Tusi, 'Allameh Hilli, Shaykh Baha'i, Mohaqqeq Damad, and Mohammad-Baqer Majlesi, all of whom supported and collaborated with the monarchs of their day.[148] Given that in later years Khomeini met with Mohammad-Reza Pahlavi Shah on at least two occasions in his capacity as Ayatollah Borujerdi's envoy, it appears he had, for the time being, reconciled himself to what he regarded a necessary obstacle to chaos.[149]

---

[143] References to both the Persian original and the English translation by Algar have been provided. For the most part, I have relied on my own translations of the work. *Velayat-e faqih, hukumat-e eslami* (?1357 [1978])., p. 107. 'Islamic Government', in *Islam and Revolution I : Writings and Declarations of Imam Khomeini (1941–1980),* ed. Hamid Algar (Berkeley: Mizan Press, 1981), pp. 87, 92–3.
[144] *Kashf al-asrar,* p. 188.   [145] Ibid., p. 187.   [146] Ibid., p. 185.
[147] Ibid., p. 186.   [148] Ibid., p. 187.
[149] Ha'eri-Yazdi and Sedghi, *Khaterat-e Mehdi Ha'eri-Yazdi, faqih va ostad-e falsafeh-ye eslami.,* pp. 92–3.

According to Navvab's *Barnameh*, only pious Muslims could run in parliamentary elections. Non-Muslims and the 'irreligious' are strictly prohibited from standing.[150] Moreover, and crucially, since the right of law-making belongs solely to God, parliament's activities are restricted to administering the country in accordance with the *shari'ah* – or, to be more exact, the Twelver Shi'i *madhhab*.[151] It is in this sense that Navvab states the Majles is not in fact a legislative (*qanun-gozari*) body at all.[152] Ensuring all law complies with the *shari'ah* are the 'olama' who supervise Majles activities.[153] Navvab prescribes that all laws deemed non-compliant with Islamic law be purged.[154] At the time of authoring *Kashf*, Khomeini was also steadfast in his support for this basic supposition regarding the inadmissibility of positive man-made legislation in conflict with the *shari'ah* and the highly limited powers devolved to the Majles for crafting legislation.[155] The legislation authored and approved by suitably qualified clergymen in reaction to novel and unprecedented circumstances would by definition escape this pitfall and be considered consonant with the precepts of the Divine Law. On this view, the legislation authored and approved by the *foqaha* – that is to say, Islamic jurists – by default cannot be categorised as positive legislation. From his first political tract of 1943 through to the eve of the revolution, while much else would change this basic premise would govern much of Khomeini's thinking. In an interview with noted scholar Said-Amir Arjomand on 2 January 1979 in the Parisian suburb of Neauphle-le-Château, Khomeini confirmed this position with little equivocation. After having agreed unqualifiedly with Shaykh Fazlollah Nuri that positive legislation approved by parliament is contrary to Islam, because law in Islam is synonymous with the *shari'ah*, whose interpretation falls strictly under the purview of the Shi'i 'olama', he continued:

In Islam there is no room for the institution of basic laws and if an assembly is installed it will not be a legislative assembly in that sense, but an assembly to supervise government. It will deliberate [and determine] the executive matters of the kind I mentioned [i.e., urban planning and traffic regulations] and not basic laws [which are already laid down by Islam].[156]

---

150 Safavi, *Barnameh-ye hokumati-ye Fada'iyan-e Islam*, p. 102.
151 Khosrowshahi, *Fada'iyan-e Islam*, p. 283.
152 Safavi, *Barnameh-ye hokumati-ye Fada'iyan-e Islam*, p. 103.
153 Ibid., p. 103.   154 Ibid., p. 103.   155 Khomeini, *Kashf al-asrar*, p. 191.
156 Arjomand, 'The State and Khomeini's Islamic Order', p. 156.

With time and following the revolution, Khomeini's views would find themselves complicated considerably. But, on this point and at this historical juncture, the Fada'iyan-e Islam and even Ayatollah Khomeini differ little from other prominent revivalists of the twentieth century such as Abul A'la Mawdudi[157] and Sayyid Qutb,[158] both of whom, despite being Sunnis and in all likelihood highly dismissive, if not outwardly hostile, towards aspects of Iranian Shi'ism, were read and translated with much enthusiasm by young radicals in Pahlavi Iran.[159] In this way, something along the lines of a *lingua franca* of political Islam developed across sectarian lines. Though one should be careful not to overstate their influence, they agree with their Sunni counterparts in the most uncompromising terms that political sovereignty resides with the Almighty and his Will incarnate, the *shari'ah*. Genuine differences remain in their respective conceptions of the clergy's role in the envisioned state which has submitted to divine authority, but their basic premise, on the whole, is the same. Though arguably nascent in some respects, their differences would deepen profoundly with the public appearance and popularisation of Khomeini's theorisation of *velayat-e faqih*, which locates its rationale explicitly in Shi'i history, theology, *'erfan*, and jurisprudence.

That being said, the *Barnameh* evinces a degree of porousness between the 'social imaginaries' of the Fada'iyan-e Islam and the

---

[157] John J. Donohue and John L. Esposito, *Islam in Transition: Muslim Perspectives*, 2nd ed. (New York & Oxford: Oxford University Press, 2007), p. 263.

[158] Sayyid Qutb, *Milestones* (New Delhi: Islamic Book Service, 2001), p. 36.

[159] Khomeini had certainly read Sayyid Qutb. For instance, he refers to the latter's Qur'anic commentary *Fi zilal al-Qur'an* in his televised commentary on Surat al-Fatihah, delivered and broadcast after the revolution. However, it is referred to only in passing and for the sole purpose of pointing out its inadequacy. It is fair to say that Khomeini's political convictions and temperament developed largely in the context of Reza Shah's creeping autocracy during the 1930s and as a result of the threat he perceived to the clerical establishment and thus 'Islam'. For the reference to Qutb's *Fi zilal al-Qur'an*, see Ruhollah Khomeini, 'Lectures on Surat al-Fatiha', in *Islam and Revolution I: Writings and Declarations of Imam Khomeini (1941–1980)*, ed. Hamid Algar (Berkeley: Mizan Press, 1981)., p. 365.

The influence of Sayyid Qutb on the younger generation of Iranian Islamists is worthy of further investigation. It is interesting to note that Seyyed 'Ali Khameneh'i, the incumbent Supreme Leader of Iran, translated Sayyid Qutb's *Al-Mustaqbal li-hadhal-Din* from Arabic to Persian. See Seyyed Qutb, *Ayandeh dar qalamrow-ye Islam*, trans. 'Ali Khameneh'i, 5th ed. (Tehran: Daftar-e nashr-e farhang-e eslami, 1386 [2007]), Introduction.

étatism of the Pahlavi regime.[160] For instance, thirteen consecutive chapters of the *Barnameh* bear the title of a ministry and then proceed to expound its functions and priorities.[161] Neither does Navvab shy away from speaking of the homeland (*vatan*) and its defence in the face of pernicious foreign influences.[162] Other symbols of 'statehood' are also invoked, such as flags and the nation's identity – for instance, Navvab repeatedly refers to the 'nation' or 'people' (*mellat*) as the 'children of Islam and Iran'.[163] A Fada'iyan-affiliated newspaper reiterated the organisation's role as defenders of the nation in its title, *Nabard-e mellat* (The Nation's Battle). One front page of the paper bore a male caricature ensconced in a Union Jack in the process of being stabbed by unsheathed swords, while the catch-line read, 'This wounded pig will be cut to shreds by the terrifying strikes of brave Muslim nations.'[164] 'English imperialism' was deservedly the object of incessant attack and vitriol. Another memorable caricature featured a British bulldog over a map of England, defecating on the Majles speaker's head.[165]

According to 'Araqi's at times hagiographic account, Navvab was personally incensed in his adolescence by Iran's occupation by British and Russian forces in the course of the Second World War, and on several occasions he sought to rouse his fellow classmates and compatriots into action.[166] He is reported to have worked for a brief time in the oil refineries of Abadan, witnessing the vicious abuse and institutionalised discrimination suffered by Iranians under the regime of the Anglo-Iranian Oil Company,[167] and unsuccessfully tried to rally protestors following the beating of an Iranian worker at the hands of an English technician.[168] As mentioned above, Navvab himself was

---

[160] Charles Taylor, *Modern Social Imaginaries* (Durham, NC: Duke University Press; Chesham: Combined Academic, 2004), p. 23.

[161] Hassanifar, *Fada'iyan-e Islam dar kalam-e yaran*, p. 100.

[162] Safavi, *Barnameh-ye hokumati-ye Fada'iyan-e Islam*, p. 105.

[163] Ibid., p. 132.

[164] 'Dar in surat mamlekat beh atash khahim keshid', *Nabard-e mellat* 10 Esfand 1329 [1 March 1951].

[165] 'Mellat-e Iran madfu'-e sag ra beh atash mikeshad', *Nabard-e mellat* 4 Esfand 1329 [23 February 1951].

[166] 'Araqi, *Nagofteh-ha*, p. 18.

[167] The AIOC's system of institutionalised discrimination has been amply detailed by Abrahamian, among others. Ervand Abrahamian, *The Coup: 1953, the CIA, and the Roots of Modern U.S.–Iranian Relations* (New York & London: The New Press, 2013), p. 17.

[168] 'Araqi, *Nagofteh-ha*, p. 21.

a product of economic dislocation and the socio-economic transformations which had rapidly eroded the professions and crafts of his class and detrimentally impacted many others like him. Those responsible for the many oppressions, both small and large, to which he and others had been subject were self-evident, just as the solutions were cut-and-dried. Anecdotal evidence, detailed examination of the *Barnameh*, and countless editorials in publications like *Nabard-e mellat* show the extent to which an Iran purged of foreign influence and domination and the realisation of a strong Islamic state were entwined in Navvab's and his fellow-travellers' world view. As long as Iran was weak and enfeebled by foreign forces, the creation of a truly Islamic polity would be impossible, and, without the latter's creation, Iran might never ascend the blissful heights to which the Fada'iyan righteously aspired.

It is in this way that, despite its rebellion against the *status quo* in all its ungodliness, the Fada'iyan unbeknownst to themselves ended up reproducing the Pahlavi regime's own étatiste conception of socio-political change and the means of bringing about such change. At the discursive-imaginary level, the nation-state became the only means by which political transformation could be effected, and such transformation was impossible in the absence of a political program, ideology, or world view. This is not to say the Fada'iyan's rhetoric was devoid of Pan-Islamist sentiment and proclamations of solidarity. The creation of the state of Israel and the violent expulsion of Palestinians in 1948 loomed large in their minds, with Navvab declaring in one communiqué the prospect of sending some 5,000 men to fight alongside the Palestinians.[169] However, even during such moments, the image of a powerful nation-state remained the dominant optic by which Islamic countries might sever the hand of foreign meddling in Muslim lands.

As has been shown with reference to Ayatollah Khomeini's early writings, his own intellectual contribution to Iranian Shi'i Islamism echoed much of the Fada'iyan-e Islam's political world view. His rhetorical style and flourishes are certainly comparable to much of the material found in the Fada'iyan's *Barnameh*. Khomeini was not only reputed to be sympathetic to their cause but also a potential source of inspiration. The key difference that separates Khomeini's later political project was that, given his rigorous and thorough grasp

---

[169] Khosrowshahi, *Fada'iyan-e Islam*, pp. 69–70.

of virtually all the disparate branches of the traditional Islamic sciences, including *feqh*, Islamic philosophy (*hekmat*), theology (*kalam*), and mysticism (*'erfan*), he was able to articulate and combine various philosophical and jurisprudential concepts, logical arguments, and historical precedents to construct a *theory* justifying Islamic government and, in particular, the obligation and prerogative of the Shi'i jurists (*foqaha*) to rule. Despite precedents in the work of leading Osulis such as Molla Ahmad Naraqi (d. 1829),[170] Shaykh Ja'far al-Najafi 'Kashef al-Ghita'' (d. 1812),[171] it was Khomeini who would make the case for clerical political supremacy in the most forceful and uncompromising terms and at the most politically opportune time.[172]

Khomeini and the Formalisation of *Velayat-e Faqih*

Even in historical times the transition from the prophet to the legislator is fluid … In no case did such a legislator or his labour fail to receive divine approval, at least subsequently.[173]   Max Weber

While the Fada'iyan's own political program remained heavily reliant on asserting 'Islam' and the *shari'ah* would guarantee their utopian vision's realisation, during his time in exile Khomeini radicalised his conception of Islamic government working in a concerted fashion to legitimate the rule of a specific religious-corporate group, namely the Shi'i 'olama'. Based on the Qur'an and Traditions of the Prophet and Holy Imams, Khomeini sought to justify the clerics' religiously enshrined obligation (*vazifeh*) to rule. This was initially undertaken for the benefit of the community of fellow-scholars and later communicated to a broader public by Khomeini's lieutenants.[174] However,

---

170 Hamid Dabashi, 'Mulla Ahmad Naraqi and the Question of the Guardianship of the Jurisconsult (Wilayat-e Faqih)', in *Expectation of the Millennium: Shi'ism in History*, ed. Seyyed Hossein Nasr, Hamid Dabashi, and Seyyed Vali Reza Nasr (Albany: State University of New York Press, 1989).
171 Heern, *The Emergence of Modern Shi'ism*, Loc 2159.
172 Kadivar, *Nazariyyeh-ha-ye dowlat dar feqh-e Shi'eh*, p. 17.
173 Max Weber, 'The Prophet', in *On Charisma and Institution Building*, ed. S. N. Eisenstadt (Chicago & London: University of Chicago Press, 1968), p. 256.
174 Said Saffari, 'The Legitimation of the Clergy's Right to Rule in the Iranian Constitution of 1979', *British Journal of Middle Eastern Studies* 20, no. 1 (1993), pp. 68–77.

the surmise that this idea only came to the surface of Iranian clerical debates in 1970 with the publication of *Velayat-e faqih* is undermined by a review of secretly distributed publications such as *Be'sat* and *Enteqam* authored and distributed by Khomeini's disciples.[175] It was, nevertheless, the general principles of Khomeini's theory of Islamic government that went on to inform the construction of the newly founded revolutionary state. The qualification of 'general principles' is stipulated since it would be misleading to suggest the constitutional set-up of the Islamic Republic ought to be viewed as a direct translation of what Khomeini had envisaged almost a decade earlier in his famous lectures delivered in Najaf during the initial months of 1970. An elaborate discussion of *velayat-e faqih* was first conducted in print in Khomeini's most important work in Arabic, *Kitab al-bay'* (Book of Sale) in five volumes.[176] The arguments rehearsed in the aforementioned scholarly tome would be somewhat vernacularised and reprised in Persian in the course of thirteen lectures between 21 January 1970 and 11 March 1970. These lectures were then compiled into book form by his disciples under the title *Velayat-e faqih, hokumat-e eslami* (The Guardianship of the Jurist, Islamic Government) and published in Beirut in the same year.[177] The text would be printed inside Iran under the title of *Nameh'i az Imam Musavi Kashef al-Ghita'* as a supplement to *Jihad-e akbar* in 1977.[178]

We are not here delving into the practical obstacles, internecine struggles, and constitutional wrangling which almost tore the Islamic

---

[175] See for example *Enteqam*, an underground newspaper published by the young Mohammad-Taqi Mesbah-Yazdi in Qom during the early 1960s. Mohammad-Taqi Mesbah-Yazdi, *Enteqam: nashriyyeh-ye makhfi-ye tolab-e howzeh-ye 'elmiyyeh-ye Qom, 1342–44* (Tehran: Markaz-e asnad-e enqelab-e eslami, 1389 [2010]), pp. 164–5. The views of Mesbah at this time, however, certainly did not represent those of all of Khomeini's disciples in their entirety. The claim for the clergy's pre-eminent role in politics is made in *Be'sat* but without explicit mention of *velayat-e faqih. Asnad-e nehzat-e eslami-ye Iran: Be'sat, 1342–44* (Tehran Markaz-e asnad-e enqelab-e eslami, 1389), pp. 265–6.

[176] Ruhollah Khomeini, *Kitab al-bay'*, 5 vols., vol. 2 (Tehran: Mo'assaseh-ye tanzim va nashr-i asar-i hazrat Imam Khomeini, 2001), pp. 617–719.

[177] Akbar Fallahi, *Tarikh-e shafahi-ye zendegi va mobarezat-e Imam Khomeini dar Najaf* (Tehran: Markaz-e asnad-e enqelab-e eslami, 1390 [2011]), p. 150. Mohsen Kadivar, *Hokumat-e vela'i, Andisheh-ye siyasi dar Islam (2)* (Tehran: Nashr-e ney, 1377 [1998]), p. 168.

[178] *Hokumat-e vela'i*, p. 168.

Republic apart, while teetering on the brink of civil war,[179] but rather the politico-philosophical vision, which contends sovereignty, executive and legislative, resides solely with God and the clerical class as representatives of the Hidden Imam from the time of the Lesser Occultation (*ghaybat-e soghra*) (874–939 AD).[180] This vision, as laid out in Khomeini's tract *Velayat-e faqih, hokumat-e eslami*, is explicitly acknowledged in the Introduction to the Constitution of the Islamic Republic of Iran.[181] The 'olama' as the possessors of political guardianship (*velayat* or *wilaya* in Arabic) are the only legitimate representatives and interpreters of this divinely ordained sovereignty.[182] It is this uncompromising articulation of clerical supremacy and its epistemic basis – i.e., Islamic jurisprudence (*feqh*), clerical custodianship of the *shari'ah*, and in certain instances an avowed closeness to God – that Iran's post-revolutionary intellectuals would set about challenging and subject to unremitting criticism.

I will now provide a brief exposition of Khomeini's contribution to Shi'i theories of government. One wing of this discourse sought to valorise clerical political pre-eminence as exegetes and executors of the *shari'ah*, while the other urged the mobilisation of the masses in support of this vision, exemplified in the oft-repeated dictum '*hozur-e mardom dar sahneh*' (the presence of the people on the scene). Both pieces of the puzzle arguably have essentially elitist implications, one being 'Platonic' and the other 'populist-clientelistic'. Because of issues of space, the arguments for clerical political authority will be the main focus of the following sections. It is not the ambition here to explore

---

[179] For a detailed account of these wranglings, see Behrooz Ghamari-Tabrizi, *Islam and Dissent in Postrevolutionary Iran: Abdolkarim Soroush, Religious Politics and Democratic Reform* (London & New York: I. B. Tauris, 2008), chapter 3.

[180] Khomeini, 'Islamic Government', p. 42.

[181] 'Abdollah Shams, *Qanun-e asasi: az farman-e mashrutiyyat ta emruz* (Tehran: Dark, 1386 [2007]), p. 89.

[182] Khomeini, 'Islamic Government', p. 61. In two statements issued by Ayatollah Hosayn-'Ali Montazeri on 22 June 1979 in reaction to the second draft constitution presented by the provisional revolutionary government and prior to the convening of the Assembly of Experts – which would go on to enshrine the principle of *velayat-e faqih* into the constitution of the Islamic Republic – he clearly and succinctly delineates the principle of clerical guardianship. Though Montazeri's statements go into greater detail regarding specific articles and issues of the constitution, the broad strokes are in keeping with the vision of Islamic government presented by Khomeini in *Velayat-e faqih. Majmu'eh-ye Dow Payam* in Montazeri, *Khaterat*, p. 890.

Khomeini's world view exhaustively.[183] It is, however, necessary to understand the lineaments of his philosophical and juridical arguments, which in disparate contexts and forms have contributed to the ideological-religious identity and state structures of the Islamic Republic and its constitutional order. The contours of this identity and the arguments rationalising its existence would go on to shape and determine the conditions under which future generations of intellectuals would engage and labour.

What strikes one immediately upon opening Khomeini's *Velayat-e faqih* is the conviction of his doctrine's rectitude and self-evidence. He even goes so far as to say that it 'has little need of demonstration' (*borhan*).[184] Khomeini does, however, offer a defence of his conception of Islamic government, but first he deems it necessary to assure his audience that Islam is a total and complete system. Through the Prophet Mohammad, God sent down laws and practices covering all human activities from the cradle to the grave.[185] Accordingly, there 'is no subject in human life for which Islam has not established an obligation (*taklif*) and issued a ruling (*hokm*)'.[186] Material progress was in vain if not grounded in faith and morality – his antipathy towards the authoritarian modernising regimes of the Pahlavi Shahs clearly had only intensified with time. But it was not merely restricted to the latter. He also lambasts 'the conspiracy of the British imperialist government' for importing 'Western laws' during the Constitutional Revolution (1906–11).[187] Moreover, he blames the 'propaganda of the imperialists' for disseminating the falsehood that Islam is without a specific form of government and serves, if it does at all, in a purely legislative capacity.[188] Like a number of his other revivalist counterparts, he models his desired form of government on an idealised image of the government headed by the Prophet Mohammad:[189] 'Just as Islam made laws, it established an executive power.'[190] It is nevertheless important to acknowledge that the articulation of the exemplary model of the

---

183   Abrahamian persuasively addresses the question of Khomeini's populism in his seminal work: Ervand Abrahamian, *Khomeinism: Essays on the Islamic Republic* (Berkeley & London: University of California Press, 1993), pp. 13–38.
184   Khomeini, *Velayat-e faqih*, p. 6. 'Islamic Government', p. 27.
185   *Velayat-e faqih*, p. 10.   186   Ibid., p. 11. 'Islamic Government', p. 30.
187   *Velayat-e faqih*, pp. 13, 12.   188   Ibid., p. 20. 'Islamic Government', p. 36.
189   *Velayat-e faqih*, pp. 20–1. 'Islamic Government', p. 36.
190   *Velayat-e faqih*, p. 21.

Prophet's government was always intimately connected to explicitly political grievances about worldly injustices in the present.

The Prophet 'was ... a political person', Khomeini asserts.[191] His proposition is simple. The Prophet had laid down laws for his community and those laws hold for all time. A law unimplemented ceases to be a law at all, and thus Khomeini argues that 'we want a caliph (*khalifeh*) to execute the laws. The law requires an executor (*mojri*).'[192] Therefore, law, of necessity, begets an executive power. He is making a formal argument about the very nature and substance of law, and it is a key presupposition of his argument in favour of an Islamic state. A law unexecuted is not worthy of the name – not only that, but unless this law is executed by a central authority capable of determining when the *shari'ah* should be implemented or has been transgressed, the law is also deemed superfluous. This decision cannot be left to the individual believer's discretion but must be decided upon by an authority capable of judging and evaluating the acts of men and women comprising the community over which it rules. Because it is a government predicated on law, or more accurately Islamic law, Khomeini defines it as a form of 'constitutional' government. He does, however, qualify this statement immediately and state that while certainly 'constitutional' (*mashruteh*), or more accurately 'limited', and in no way 'absolutist' (*motlaqeh*) or 'despotic' (*estebdadi*), it was not a constitutional regime as commonly understood.[193] 'Of course it is not limited (*mashruteh*) in terms of its common meaning today, where approved laws are subject to the vote (*ara'*) of the people and the majority,' he declares.[194] It is constrained merely insofar as it is constrained by the ordinances set down in the Qur'an and the Traditions as determined by the 'olama'.[195] This is, of course, because, like other Islamists of various stripes, Khomeini believes the power to legislate belongs exclusively to God.

The fundamental difference of Islamic government with the governments of a constitutional monarchy and a republic (*jomhuri*) is in this. In that the representatives of the people or the Shah in these kinds of regimes partake in legislation (*qanun-gozari*), when in fact legislative power and the *shari'ah* are assigned to God. Islam's sacred legislator (*share'-e moqaddas*) is the sole legislative power. No-one has the right to legislate, and no law except the

---

[191] Ibid., p. 25. 'Islamic Government', p. 39.
[192] *Velayat-e faqih*. 'Islamic Government', pp. 36–7.   [193] *Velayat-e faqih*, p. 52.
[194] Ibid., p. 52.   [195] Ibid., p. 52. 'Islamic Government', p. 55.

ordinance of the legislator (*share'*) can be executed. For this reason, under Islamic government instead of a legislative parliament, comprising one of the three branches of government, the parliament undertakes planning (*barna-meh-rizi*) for the different ministries, managing them under the scope of Islamic ordinances (*ahkam-e Islam*).[196]

Parliament is thus not the source of legislation but rather the site of its implementation. Khomeini argues that Muslims, by virtue of being Muslims, submit to the *shari'ah*, and it is strictly in this sense that Islamic government might be said to attach and accrue (*mota 'alleq*) to the people.[197] Legitimacy thus emanates from the divine legislator, while approval from below derives from Muslims' submission to the *shari'ah* by virtue of their being Muslims.

The question that follows on naturally from the necessity of executive power is 'who is entitled to rule?' Contrary to his earlier position, he now declares monarchy and hereditary succession as 'anti-Islamic' (*zed-e eslami*).[198] What is needed rather is 'an executor of the law', as the Prophet had been in the case of the first Medinan *ummah*. The Prophet had 'implemented the penal laws of Islam, he cut off the hand of the thief and administered lashings and stonings'.[199] In Khomeini's view, the successor to the mantle of the Prophet must be prepared to undertake the same responsibilities. The laws promulgated by the Prophet are perfect and complete, which means that his political successor need not engage in the fashioning of legislation per se but merely guarantee the *shari'ah*'s implementation.[200] The ordinances of Islam are not limited by time or place, as 'they are permanent and must be enacted until the end of time'.[201] Again, we see a largely ahistorical rendering of the *shari'ah*, with a disproportionate focus on the *hudud* punishments.

The caveat should be added that the text of *Velayat-e faqih* offers a particularly astringent and raw version of Khomeini's political vision written from the comfort of exile in Najaf, one unmediated by the political exigencies which mundane political power often imposes. After the establishment of the Islamic Republic he would exhibit a far greater degree of pragmatic discretion in dealing with the many

---

[196] *Velayat-e faqih*, p. 53. 'Islamic Government', p. 55.
[197] *Velayat-e faqih va jehad-e akbar* (Tehran: Seyyed Jamal Hedayat), p. 42.
[198] *Velayat-e faqih*, p. 12. 'Islamic Government', p. 31.
[199] *Velayat-e faqih*, p. 22. 'Islamic Government', p. 37.
[200] *Velayat-e faqih*, pp. 22, 26–7. 'Islamic Government', p. 37.
[201] *Velayat-e faqih*, p. 29. 'Islamic Government', p. 41.

unforeseen eventualities generated in the process of governing the modern state apparatus, which should not be interpreted as synonymous with 'moderation', a heavily value-laden term. While the *means* employed for realising his ambitions were often eminently flexible, the *end* towards which he strove remained essentially uncompromised. 'The state', in Khomeini's words, 'is a means for the realisation of exalted goals ... and if this means is not put to good use and the realisation of exalted goals is left unachieved, it [i.e., the state] is of no value whatsoever'.[202] Far from fetishising the state and state power as an end in itself, it was nonetheless indispensable for the realisation of the nomocratic order to which he aspired.

Rather than ask who is entitled to rule, it might prove more accurate to ask, 'who is to be the executor of the law?' Both of these questions would be subject to concerted criticism by a number of Iran's post-revolutionary intellectuals in the 1990s, but for the present it should be noted that Khomeini comes out of a distinguished tradition stipulating that the rightful Islamic ruler (*zamamdar*) must possess two qualities above all others: first and foremost, he must possess a thorough knowledge of Islamic law (*'elm-e qanun*); and, second, he must administer justice (*'edalat*).[203] These two qualities have a long-standing pedigree in Islamic intellectual history, as the qualities expected of a *mojtahed* and have been advocated by such luminaries as the Shafi'i theologian and jurist Abu Hamid Mohammad al-Ghazali.[204] The stipulation of knowledge or *'elm*, however, also has an established history in the Shi'i tradition dating back to at least the sixth Imam, Ja'far al-Sadeq, where *'elm* was held to be definitive of the Imam's claim to religious leadership and authority – and thus the Imamate.[205] The species of *'elm*, which acted as guarantor of the Imamate, was, however, essentially different to that which would later be claimed for the *mojtahed* class. In the Twelver tradition, it was a power of discernment bestowed in

[202] *Velayat-e faqih*, p. 69.   [203] Ibid., p. 58. 'Islamic Government', pp. 59–60.
[204] Ahmad Kazemi-Moussavi, *Religious Authority in Shi'ite Islam: From the Office of Mufti to the Institution of Marja'* (Kuala Lumpur: International Institute of Islamic Thought and Civilization, 1996), p. 166.
[205] Marshall G. S. Hodgson, 'How Did the Early Shi'a become Sectarian?', *Journal of the American Oriental Society* 75, no. 1 (1955), p. 11. Etan Kohlberg, 'Imam and Community in the Pre-Ghayba Period', in *Authority and Political Culture in Shi'ism*, ed. Said Amir Arjomand (Albany: State University of New York Press, 1988), p. 25.

hereditary succession from Imam to Imam and formalised by a process of designation or *nass*.[206]

In the context of *Velayat-e faqih*, knowledge and understanding of Islamic law is fundamental for obvious reasons. If, as Khomeini argues, Islamic government is a government based on Islamic law, it is necessary for the ruler to have more than merely a working knowledge of the law but to 'surpass others (*fazl bar digaran*) in knowledge'.[207] This elitist dimension of Khomeini's thought, in which a specific class or individual functions as privileged interpreter and exegete of the Sacred Law, has been occasionally linked to the Platonic 'Philosopher-King' as conceived in *The Republic*, the 'Perfect Man' (*ensan-e kamel*) of the *Shaykh al-akbar*, Ibn 'Arabi and his commentators,[208] and the political philosophy of Abu Nasr Mohammad al-Farabi.[209] Khomeini's intellectual influences, though no doubt important, need not distract us here. What is crucial to grasp is the identification of political power with the hierarchical knowledge economy of Islamic law. In this way it is determined that not only the 'olama' must rule any future Islamic state but that only the *faqih* who surpasses all others in terms of his knowledge of the law can rightfully rule the community of the faithful, the *ommat*.

As Vincent J. Cornell has argued in his historical analysis and parsing of *walaya* and *wilaya*, which he contends ought to be regarded as 'semantic fraternal twins', the notion of proximity to God and authority on earth are profoundly intertwined and inform one another. As he argues, the term *wali* or *vali Allah* has both social and metaphysical connotations, and the *vali* 'protects and intercedes for others as Allah's deputy or vicegerent.'[210] Exoteric and esoteric knowledge claims complement one another without contradiction.[211] At the esoteric level,

---

[206] Hodgson, "How Did the Early Shi'a Become Sectarian?", p. 11. Najam Haider, *Shī'ī Islam: An Introduction* (New York: Cambridge University Press, 2014), p. 41; Loc 1296.

[207] Khomeini, *Velayat-e faqih*, p. 59. 'Islamic Government', p. 59.

[208] Moin, *Khomeini: Life of the Ayatollah*, chapter 3. Alexander Knysh, 'Irfan Revisited: Khomeini and the Legacy of Islamic Mystical Philosophy', *Middle East Journal* 46, no. 4 (1992), p. 635.

[209] Vanessa Martin, *Creating an Islamic State: Khomeini and the Making of a New Iran* (London: I. B. Tauris, 2003), pp. 34–5.

[210] Vicent J. Cornell, *Realm of the Saint: Power and Authority in Moroccan Sufism* (Austin: University of Texas Press, 1998), Loc 265.

[211] Knysh, 'Irfan Revisited: Khomeini and the Legacy of Islamic Mystical Philosophy', p. 633–6.

man aspires to annihilation in God. This is achieved by the purification (*tazkiyeh*) of the self and its worldly attachments and the transcendence of one's corporeal form, achieved, in principle, by means of the renunciation of everything other than God.[212] In annihilation (*fana*) man reaches true perfection and thereby 'dies to his humanity' in the words of 'Allameh Tabataba'i, the famed philosopher and Qur'anic exegete.[213] Such proximity to God is one possible vindication of the perfect man's vicegerency as the incarnation of the divine Logos (*kalimat Allah*).[214] The perfect man as portrayed in Khomeini's *Misbah al-hidaya ila al-khilafa wa al-wilaya* (Light of Guidance Towards an Understanding of *Wilaya* and Caliphate)[215] fulfils the role of God's 'vicegerent' (*khalifa*) or 'deputy' (*na'ib*), as his representative in the created world.[216] As God's deputy on earth, he is invested with the task of ensuring it is properly guided and preserved.[217]

Khomeini's mysticism is undoubtedly crucial to a proper understanding of his philosophico-political world view[218] and can be understood to be part and parcel of the aura and habitus he had cultivated over the course of many decades[219] and subsequently incorporated into his public persona and charismatic appeal. It is, nonetheless, crucial to consider other disparate intellectual threads which have also played a significant role informing the bases of his politico-theological *weltanschauung*. These obviously demand greater elaboration because the identity of the revolutionary state is intertwined with that of its formidable founder and public representations thereof. Khomeini's legacy was undoubtedly a complex one, and different factions of the Islamic

---

[212] Sayyid Muhammad Husayn Tabataba'i, *The Return to Being: A Translation of Risalat al-Walayah*, trans. Fazel Asadi Amjad and Mahdi Dasht Bozorgi, introduced and annotated by S. K. Toussi, ed. (London: ICAS Press, 2009), p. 46.

[213] Ibid., p. 45.

[214] Knysh, 'Irfan Revisted: Khomeini and the Legacy of Islamic Mystical Philosophy', p. 645.

[215] Ruhollah Khomeini, *Misbah al-hidaya ila al-khilafa wa al-wilaya*, trans. Hosayn Mostowfi, Dual Text ed. (Tehran: Nashr-e 'aruj, 1389 [2010]).

[216] Khomeini explicitly uses the term '*khalifah fi al-arz*' in *Velayat-e faqih* when referring to the Prophet's mandate, which he goes on to argue is assumed by the clergy in its political and legal dimensions. *Velayat-e faqih*, p. 53.

[217] Knysh, 'Irfan Revisted: Khomeini and the Legacy of Islamic Mystical Philosophy', p. 645.

[218] Mahallati, *Khaterat va mobarezat-e Shahid Mahallati*, p. 39.

[219] Ata Anzali, *'Mysticism' in Iran: The Safavid Roots of a Modern Concept* (Columbia, SC: University of South Carolina Press, 2017), Introduction.

Republic's ruling elite have tried to operationalise disparate and often contradictory aspects of it. Daniel Brumberg has fittingly termed this process one of 'dissonant institutionalization', the process whereby contending visions of authority are embedded within a number of official and quasi-official arenas, such as competing ideological factions, formal constitutions, and the rhetoric of political leaders.[220] Khomeini's person and his politico-ideological legacy have often been at the very heart of this drama.

Khomeini's Osulism is just as important to understanding his arguments in favour of clerical rule as is his penchant for Sadrian philosophy and Andalusian mysticism. The Osuli school – which was revived under the aegis of Mohammad-Baqer, better known as Vahid Behbahani, in the latter half of the eighteenth century – and the development of the notion of a 'lamiyyat led to the establishment of a hierarchy in the knowledge economy of Twelver Shi'i Islam.[221] In winning a protracted battle against the rival Akhbari school, which emphasised the Qur'an and hadith of the Prophet and Imams as the sole sources of law, speculative legal reasoning (*zann*), general knowledge (*'elm-e ejmali*), and the scholarly consensus of the jurists acquired a pre-eminence unprecedented in Shi'i history.[222] It was a struggle which was not only intellectual but often violent in nature, as powerful Osuli clergymen like Behbahani partook in the practice of excommunication and sent gangs of *lutis* or toughs to route opponents.[223] The status attained by clerical rulings, which now constituted legal opinions subject to emulation by ordinary believers, simply reinforced the long-standing claim to vicegerency (*niyabat*) of the Imam and the representation of his authority during the Greater Occultation.[224]

[220] Daniel Brumberg, *Reinventing Khomeini: The Struggle for Reform in Iran* (Chicago & London: University of Chicago Press, 2001), p. 100.
[221] For Behbahani's biography and details of his anti-Akhbari activities in Karbala', see Heern, *The Emergence of Modern Shi'ism*, chapter 4. Ahmad Kazemi-Moussavi, 'The Establishment of the Position of Marja'iyyt-i Taqlid in the Twelver-Shi'i Community', *Iranian Studies* 18, no. 1 (1985), p. 37.
[222] Juan Cole, *Sacred Space and Holy War: The Politics, Culture and History of Shi'ite Islam* (London & New York: I. B. Tauris, 2002), p. 66.
[223] Meir Litvak, *Shi'i scholars of nineteenth-century Iraq: 'ulama' of Najaf and Karbala* (Cambridge: Cambridge University Press, 1998), p. 123. Heern, *The Emergence of Modern Shi'ism*, Loc 1828.
[224] Kazemi-Moussavi, *Religious Authority in Shi'ite Islam*, p. 148.

Behbahani and the Osuli school shored up two principles which could be said to have paved the way for Khomeini's own hierocratic vision of political authority, even if they by no means made it inevitable. First was the special status assigned to the juristic reasoning (*ejtehad*) of Shi'i *mojtaheds* and the religious ordinances (*ahkam*) derived therefrom.[225] The second development was the Osuli school's innovation requiring believers, who were not *mojtaheds*, to choose from among the ranking *mojtaheds* whose right to derive legal ordinances had been transmitted in a 'chain of discipleship' which found its provenance in the inner circle of the infallible Imams.[226] Despite numerous precedents, it was in the late nineteenth century that Seyyed Mohammad-Kazem Tabataba'i-Yazdi (d. 1919) clearly formulated the idea that a believer ought to choose a *mojtahed* on the basis of his learning and erudition in the Islamic sciences. Moreover, those who decide to follow his rulings should consider him to be amongst the 'most learned' (*a'lam*) of his peers.[227] As a result, the *mojtahed* in question would become the believer's *marja'* (source) and followed in matters which fell under the purview of Islamic law.[228]

There were, of course, generally a few potential *maraje'* at any one time, and, insofar as none could claim the status of *primus inter pares*, religious authority resisted concentration in any one source. The few instances in which this has occurred, as is believed in the case of Shaykh Morteza Ansari (d. 1864),[229] and in the twentieth century with Ayatollah Hosayn Tabataba'i-Borujerdi, recognition of a *mojtahed*'s *a'lamiyyat* with respect to his counterparts was not coerced or imposed from above but rather subject to the agreement of the scholastic community. In this sense, *a'lamiyyat* could be said to emerge in rare instances of scholarly consensus amongst the highest-ranking 'olama'. Even when

---

[225] 'The Establishment of the Position of Marja'iyyt-i Taqlid in the Twelver-Shi'i Community', p. 38.

[226] Roy P. Mottahedeh, 'Shi'ite Political Thought and the Destiny of the Iranian Revolution', in *Iran and the Gulf: A Search for Stability*, ed. Jamal S. Al-Suwaidi (Abu Dhabi, London, New York: The Emirates Center for Strategic Studies and Research, 1996), p. 71.

[227] Kazemi-Moussavi, 'The Establishment of the Position of Marja'iyyt-i Taqlid in the Twelver-Shi'i Community', p. 39.

[228] Mottahedeh, 'Shi'ite Political Thought and the Destiny of the Iranian Revolution', p. 71.

[229] Kazemi-Moussavi, 'The Establishment of the Position of Marja'iyyt-i Taqlid in the Twelver-Shi'i Community', p. 39.

such a convergence of opinion would occur, it continued to be a largely 'informal practice', without cut-and-dried criteria or specific legal prerogatives being designated to the office.[230] Despite its clear importance to the question of religious authority, a'*lamiyyat* can hardly be said to logically and inevitably bestow the right to political-executive power. While in the past most *mojtaheds* would eschew claiming a'*lamiyyat* for themselves, Khomeini broke with the overwhelming majority of his peers by delineating the distinct possibility by which a single *mojtahed* could claim political and legislative authority on a par with the Prophet himself.[231] Khomeini makes this claim with aplomb in *Velayat-e faqih*:

If a worthy individual possessing these two qualities arises and forms a government, he will possess the same guardianship (*velayat*) as the Most Noble Messenger concerning the administration of society, and it will be incumbent upon all people to obey (*eta'at*) him.[232]

One of the notable implications of this audacious conclusion is that in the event of a single *faqih* assuming the position of *vali-ye faqih*, his authority surpasses and is binding upon all people living under his purview, including other *mojtaheds*. While the ontological *status* of the ruling *faqih* is not equal to that of the Prophet and the Imams,[233] his authority to govern and legislate is one and the same. He enjoys *velayat-e tashri'i* rather than *velayat-e takvini*. The latter as explicated by Sajjad Rizvi signifies 'a cosmological and ontological status',[234] while the former names their political and legislative mandate. In the case of the former, and the execution of the *hudud* punishments, there is no distinction to be made between the guardianship of the *faqih* and

[230] Abbas Amanat, *Apocalyptic Islam and Iranian Shi'ism* (London: I. B. Tauris, 2009), p. 181.

[231] Mottahedeh, 'Shi'ite Political Thought and the Destiny of the Iranian Revolution', p. 72.

[232] Khomeini, *Velayat-e faqih*, p. 63. 'Islamic Government', p. 62.

[233] Amir-Moezzi provides an illuminating account of this profound cosmic significance in early Imami Shi'i thought, one which Khomeini himself explicitly acknowledges in *Velayat-e faqih* (pp. 67–8). Mohammad Ali Amir-Moezzi, *The Divine Guide in Early Shi'ism: The Sources of Esotericism in Islam*, trans. David Streight (Albany: State University of New York Press, 1994), p. 31

[234] Sajjad H. Rizvi, '"Seeking the Face of God": The Safawid Hikmat Tradition's Conceptualisation of Walāya Takwīniyya', in *The Study of Shi'i Islam: History, Theology and Law*, ed. Farhad Daftary and Gurdofarid Miskinzoda (London & New York: I. B. Tauris, 2014), Loc 9407.

that of the Prophet and Imams.[235] Khomeini often seems to be of two minds when addressing his audience of fellow clerics. Contrary to official historiography, Khomeini was not without vociferous Iranian clerical critics during his first years in Najaf, Ayatollah Seyyed Mohammad Hosayni-Rowhani being one of the better-known examples. Similarly, according to the account of Ayatollah Seyyed 'Abbas Khatam-Yazdi, Grand Ayatollah Seyyed Mohsen al-Hakim also saw Khomeini as a political cleric of modest learning and a disciple of the late Ayatollah Kashani.[236] Doubts about Khomeini's theory were also rife in Iran's provinces. For instance, Morteza Alviri, a member of Fallah (one of the seven groups that would go on to form the post-revolutionary Mojahedin Organisation of the Islamic Revolution) and a future parliamentarian and Mayor of Tehran hailing from the town of Damavand, recollects the debate and controversy surrounding the book when he was a student in the early 1970s:

> At that time, the prayer leader of Damavand mosque was the late Ayatollah Majd. We sometimes had debates with him about Imam Khomeini and the book *Velayat-e faqih*. He would say that the remarks of Mr. Khomeini under the title of "velayat-e faqih" are baseless and dubious. When we asked him which one of the exalted *maraje'* are most knowledgeable (*a'lam*), he would mention Ayatollahs Kho'i and Hakim. He wasn't on our wavelength at all.[237]

Khomeini repeatedly speaks of the *faqih* and his executive *velayat* in the singular. But he also on occasion – perhaps sensing the profound implications of his argument and the danger of riling senior 'olama' – expressly states that the authority of the *foqaha* is not so absolute that it can oblige the compliance of fellow clerics.[238] It remains an open question as to whether this was merely a rhetorical gesture by Khomeini to avoid alienating the raft of sceptics in the clerical establishment at this early date and an effort to attenuate the magnitude of his break with the dominant norms of

[235] Khomeini, *Velayat-e faqih*, p. 65.
[236] Mohsen Kadivar, *Enqelab va nezam dar buteh-ye naqd-e akhlaqi: Ayatollah Seyyed Mohammad Rowhani, mobaheteh va marja'iyyat*, vol. 3, Movajeheh-ye jomhuri-ye eslami ba 'olama-ye montaqed (www.kadivar.com: Mohsen Kadivar: Official Website, 1394 [2015]), p. 24.
[237] Morteza Alviri, *Khaterat-e Morteza Alviri* (Tehran: Daftar-e adabiyat-e enqelab-e eslami, 1375), p. 25.
[238] Khomeini, *Velayat-e faqih*, p. 66.

clerical culture and practice.[239] 'It is necessary that the jurists collectively or individually form an Islamic government (*hokumat-e shar'i*) for the execution of the penal laws (*hudud*), and the preservation of borders and the regime (*nezam*). If this is possible for a single person it is an unconditional duty (*vajeb-e 'ayni*) incumbent upon him, and if not, it falls to the clergy as a whole (*vajeb-e kefa'i*).'[240] Khomeini leaves opaque the conditions under which it would be possible to identify the individual capable of fulfilling the role of the *faqih-e 'adel*, who is obliged to form an Islamic state during the Occultation. But if that jurist should by some miraculous chain of events appear, he would have a sacred obligation to found such a state, an obligation on a par with the performance of his daily prayers, an obligation which only he could perform.

The concentration of executive authority in either the person of a single *faqih* or a council of *foqaha*, without authority to bind the religious establishment, would arguably perpetuate the same inveterate dichotomy and rival claims to authority dividing the temporal and religious powers of the past. Without the power to bind, it would emerge as an essentially dysfunctional arrangement, since other clerics could always issue legal rulings in direct contradiction to those issued by the state, undermining its authority at will. Khomeini would only fully resolve this tension with the conception of the Absolute Guardianship of the Jurisconsult (*velayat-e motlaqeh-ye faqih*), which will be analysed in the next section.

In *Velayat-e faqih*, Khomeini equates 'authority' with the administrative and executive roles of government, which finds its *raison d'être* in the necessary implementation of the *shari'ah*. The authority or guardianship (*velayat*) invested in the *faqih* is thus understood by

---

[239] Mohsen Kadivar's brilliant series of texts on senior clergymen who were marginalised and repressed in the first two decades of the revolution illustrates how the Leviathan-like dilemma faced by the *vali-ye faqih* was realised in practice. Mohsen Kadivar, *Ostad az shekashteh shodan-e namus-e enqelab: negahi beh sal-ha-ye payani-ye zendegi-ye Ayatollah Seyyed Kazem Shari'atmadari*, vol. 1, Movajeheh-ye jomhuri-ye eslami ba 'olama-ye montaqed (www.kadivar.com: Mohsen Kadivar: Official Website 1394 [2015]). *Faraz va forud-e Azari-Qomi: sayri dar tahavvol-e mabani-ye fekri-ye Ayatollah Ahmad Azari-Qomi*, vol. 2, Movajeheh-ye jomhuri-ye eslami ba 'olama-ye montaqed (www.kadivar.com: Mohsen Kadivar: Official Website 1392 [2013]). *Enqelab va nezam dar buteh-ye naqd-e akhlaqi: Ayatollah Seyyed Mohammad Rowhani, mobaheteh va marja'iyyat*, 3.

[240] Khomeini, *Velayat-e faqih*, p. 67. 'Islamic Government', p. 64.

Khomeini as 'extrinsic' or 'acquired' (*e 'tebari*), as opposed to 'intrinsic' or 'existential' (*takvini*), the latter being the exclusive possession of the Prophet and Holy Imams.[241] The *faqih*'s *velayat* is thus essentially administrative and not envisaged as a corollary of the *faqih*'s 'spiritual' or 'supra-natural' station.[242] Such authority is derived by virtue of the *faqih*'s occupancy of the office of *vali-ye amr*, an office and institution not linked intrinsically to the *faqih*'s spiritual station. Even if he is required to be the most learned and just, the powers bestowed by virtue of his occupancy are immediately divested upon his relinquishment of the office.[243] In this way, the rule of the *faqih*, he adds, exists as a type of appointment. The considerable lacuna left unaddressed by Khomeini was the procedure of appointment and the body responsible for it: he preferred instead to skip over such procedural questions to detail the *faqih*'s responsibilities, such as the enforcement of the Islamic penal code and collection of taxes.

Insofar as the rule of the *faqih* is a type of appointment, it is also highly paternalistic. At one point, Khomeini goes as far to say that 'from the perspective of duty (*vazifeh*) and position (*mowghe 'iyyat*) there is no difference between the guardian (*qayyem*) of a nation and the guardian of a minor (*saghar*)'.[244] In this way he extends the *velayat* of the 'olama' traditionally reserved for legal minors (*saghir*) and the mentally incapacitated (*mahjur*) to the polity in its entirety.[245] Most crucially, Khomeini endowed the *faqih* with executive powers to which the mainstream of the 'olama' had not previously laid claim. To paraphrase Abbas Amanat, in the absence of the Hidden Imam, few jurists propounded the 'authority to judge' (*velayat-e qaza*) beyond issuing legal rulings (*fatavi*), and even in such instances there was no corresponding power to guarantee their enforcement.[246] Khomeini's radicality vis-à-vis his clerical contemporaries was his overturning of this traditional stance and theorisation of the executive-administrative rule of the clergy in the context of the modern nation-state. Khomeini denied any plaudits for originality. Instead he tried his utmost to

---

[241] *Velayat-e faqih*, pp. 68–9.
[242] Hamid Enayat, 'Iran: Khumayni's Concept of the "Guardianship of the Jurisconsult"', in *Islam in the Political Process*, ed. James P. Piscatori (Cambridge: Press Syndicate of the University of Cambridge, 1983), p. 163.
[243] Khomeini, *Velayat-e faqih*, pp. 64–5.
[244] Ibid., p. 65. 'Islamic Government', p. 63.
[245] Amanat, *Apocalyptic Islam and Iranian Shi'ism*, p. 190.   [246] Ibid., p. 190.

naturalise the doctrine as he conceived it, seeing it as an unchanging obligation incumbent on the 'olama': 'the subject of the guardianship of the jurist is not something new that we have brought out, it has been discussed from the very beginning'.[247]

The Sanctification of *Maslahat* and the Rupture with Traditional Religious Authority

To understand some of the key issues of contention highlighted by the *rowshanfekran-e dini*, which they would set out to reinterpret and challenge during the course of the 1990s, it is necessary to consider an event following the establishment of the Islamic Republic which irrevocably transformed the nature of *velayat-e faqih* and thus Khomeini's conceptualisation of the ultimate basis of the sovereign Islamic state. This was the octogenarian Ayatollah's famous decree of 6 January 1988. The decree held that the 'expediency' (*maslahat*) – sometimes translated, not unproblematically in this instance, as 'public good' – of the regime or system (*nezam*) took precedence over the primary ordinances (*ahkam-e avvaliyyeh*) of the *shari'ah*. This was Khomeini's final and arguably most radical pronouncement in the course of his long and turbulent lifetime. In the name of the revolutionary order's preservation, even the most fundamental tenets of the *shari'ah* could be abrogated and suspended by the state. This was articulated most forcefully in his well-known rebuttal of the Friday Prayer Sermon of the incumbent president, Hojjat al-Islam Khameneh'i, who according to Khomeini had misunderstood his statement issued to the Guardian Council regarding a disputed labour law already passed by the Majles. Without getting embroiled in the minutiae of the dispute itself, its consequences for the Islamic Republic, and even the issue of religious authority as a whole in Shi'i-majority Iran, are of major consequence. Khameneh'i sought to diminish the forcefulness of Khomeini's endorsement of statist intervention and thus the Musavi government, given that tensions had been mounting between the latter and the Guardian Council over the scope of the executive's authority and powers.[248] Khameneh'i averred that the Guardian Jurist

---

247 Khomeini, *Velayat-e faqih*, p. 173. 'Islamic Government', p. 124.
248 Bahman Baktiari, *Parliamentary Politics in Revolutionary Iran: The Institutionalization of Factional Politics* (Gainesville, Tallahassee, Tampa: University Press of Florida, 1996), p. 142.

had not actually meant to insinuate that the primary ordinances of Islam could be abrogated by the state if deemed expedient. Khameneh'i's declamation went beyond factional calculation, since it was in fact the default and standard position and one which Khomeini himself had adhered to in the past. Nonetheless, Khomeini brusquely dismissed his disciple, retorting:

It appears from the honourable gentleman's statements during Friday prayers that you do not approve of government in the sense of absolute guardianship which was granted by God to the Prophet ... and more important than all divine injunctions (*ahkam-e elahi*) and having priority over all religious injunctions (*ahkam-e shar'iyyeh-ye elahiyyeh*). The interpretation of what I said as meaning that the state's powers are operative within the framework provided by the divine injunctions (*ahkam-e elahi*) was entirely contrary to my statement. If the powers of government operate in the framework of divine secondary injunctions (*ahkam-e far'iyyeh-ye elahiyyeh*) the scope of divine government and absolute guardianship (*velayat-e motlaqeh*) entrusted to the Prophet must be thought meaningless and devoid of content, the consequences of which cannot oblige anyone: for example, the building of roads which requires the destruction of a house or its environs cannot be undertaken within the framework of secondary ordinances.[249]

He then goes on to state the heart of the matter with the unflappable conviction for which he was renowned:

I must say government which is a branch of the absolute guardianship of God's Prophet, is one of the primary injunctions (*ahkam-e avvaliyyeh*) of Islam and is prior to all secondary injunctions (*ahkam-e far'iyyeh*), even prayer, fasting and hajj. The ruler can destroy a mosque or house obstructing a road and compensate the home's owner. The ruler at the necessary time can close the mosques ... [T]he state can unilaterally abrogate religiously sanctioned agreements (*qarardad-ha-ye shar'i*) it has concluded with the people, when that agreement is deemed contrary to the interests of the country and Islam. And it can prevent any matter, whether devotional ('*ebadi*) or non-devotional, when it disagrees with the interests of Islam. When the state deems it contrary to the good of the Islamic country it can temporarily suspend the hajj pilgrimage, which is amongst the most important divine obligations.[250]

---

[249] Ruhollah Khomeini, *Sahifeh-ye Imam*, 21 vols., vol. 20 (Tehran: Mo'asseseh-ye tanzim va nashr-e asar-e Imam Khomeini, 1378 [1999]), p. 451.

[250] Ibid., p. 452.

The reasons for Khomeini's decision to take this step are complex and tied to his efforts to alleviate the rampant factionalism which he believed harboured the seeds of division and potentially even the regime's dissolution. Sensing death not far around the corner, this decree was part of an effort by the revolutionary patriarch to smooth the transition for his successors but also to empower the state, unimpinged by custom, tradition, or ritual obligation, to be able to overcome the challenges thrown up by modern governance. Khomeini faced the genuine dilemma of finding a politically like-minded individual with the requisite religious credentials to succeed him, the inimitable and incomparably charismatic leader, who had come to be known singularly as the Imam, a term traditionally reserved for Shi'i Islam's Twelve Infallible Imams. While scandalising some of the leading members of the Shi'i 'olama', it also meant that, in the eyes of his followers, Khomeini was reckoned irreplaceable. This clearly created a dilemma for the revolutionary state's founder, who no doubt wished to be secure in the knowledge that the state which he had been instrumental in founding would live on into the future and carry forth his legacy.

Another reason contributing to Khomeini's decree could be postulated – namely, the bloody events which transpired between Iranian demonstrators and Saudi security forces during the annual hajj pilgrimage at the end of July 1987. Minor demonstrations by Iranian protestors had previously occurred during the pilgrimage of 1980, turning increasingly violent in 1981 and 1982. Hojjat al-Islam Musavi-Kho 'iniha was the country's official representative for the hajj at the time[251] and was deported from Saudi Arabia on 9 October 1982, having been arrested for two weeks after leading protests in Mecca.[252] Tensions, however, would reach their denouement on 31 July 1987 when another prominent cleric of the Islamic left, Hojjat al-Islam Mehdi Karrubi, was Khomeini's representative for the hajj,[253] and 402 pilgrims were killed in violent clashes with Saudi police in the vicinity of the Grand

---

[251] Toby Matthiesen, *The Other Saudis: Shiism Dissent and Sectarianism*, Kindle ed. (New York Cambridge University Press, 2015), Loc 4127.

[252] Mohammad Quchani, 'Salam; aqa-ye Kho'iniha', in *Jomhuri-ye moqaddas: boresh-ha'i az tarikh-e jomhuri-ye eslami* (Tehran: Naqsh va negar, 1381 [2002]), pp.106–7.

[253] Akbar Hashemi-Rafsanjani and 'Ali-Reza Hashemi, *Karnameh va khaterat-e 1366: defa' va siyasat* (Tehran: Daftar-e nashr-e ma'aref-e enqelab, 1389 [2010]), p. 208.

Mosque.[254] According to Karrubi, despite soliciting the Saudi authorities' agreement in advance for the demonstration in which Iranian pilgrims chanted revolutionary slogans 'Disavowing the Polytheists' (*bara'at az moshrekin*),[255] they were violently attacked on all sides, first by plain-clothed assailants and then by uniformed security forces, in what he called 'an organised plan' (*barnameh-ye tanzim shodeh*).[256] These events culminated in the Islamic Republic of Iran boycotting the hajj from 1987 to 1990, essentially suspending the performance of a sacred obligation incumbent on all Muslims. This was facilitated through a claim not only to political authority but also to religious authority. More recently, in September 2015, at a time of heightened geopolitical tensions between Iran and the Saudi kingdom, a catastrophic stampede – in which as many as 464 Iranian pilgrims lost their lives and for which poor management on the part of the Saudi authorities has been blamed – resulted in a second prohibition on Iranian pilgrims from attending the hajj.[257] The precedent set by Khomeini has thus been codified and institutionalised, finding itself invoked long after his death.

In any event, it is essential to grasp the new primacy which *maslahat* (expediency/public interest) was apportioned at the expense of religious authority per se, which had previously revolved around the concepts of *marja'iyyat* and *a'lamiyyat*. This transformation in the ruling system's sources of legitimacy and scope of authority formally codified in the constitution of the Islamic Republic with the

---

[254] James P. Piscatori, 'Religion and Realpolitik: Islamic Responses to the Gulf War', in *Islamic Fundamentalism and the Gulf Crisis*, ed. James P. Piscatori (Chicago: American Academy of Arts and Sciences, 1991), p. 8. Saud al-Sarhan, 'The Saudis as Managers of the Hajj', in *The Hajj: Pilgrimage in Islam*, ed. Eric Tagliacozzo and Shawkat M. Toorawa (New York: Cambridge University Press, 2016), p. 211.

[255] Ayatollah Khomeini explicitly told Karrubi and Khatami, among others, that the 'disavowal of the polytheists', which encompassed the United States and Israel, was a 'political obligation of the hajj'. He warned the Al Saud that if they failed to adopt this conception of the pilgrimage, they would be standing against the entire Muslim world. Ruhollah Khomeini, 'Vazayef-e siyasi-ye hajj', in *Sahifeh-ye Imam* (Tehran: Mo'asseseh-ye tanzim va nashr-e asar-e Imam Khomeini, 1378 [1999]).

[256] Hashemi-Rafsanjani and Hashemi, *Karnameh va khaterat-e 1366: defa' va siyasat*, p. 207.

[257] 'Iranian pilgrims won't attend hajj amid row with Saudi Arabia', *The Guardian*, 29 May 2016. 'Hajj stampede: Iran death toll rises to 464', *BBC News*, www.bbc.co.uk/news/world-middle-east-34410484.

amendments of 1989, Article 109 specifically marking a decisive break with the regnant understanding of religious authority within the Shi'i Osuli establishment. While the Guardian Jurist post-1989 was required to have a competent grasp of *feqh* and possess the ability to issue legal rulings (i.e., he should be a *mojtahed*), an equal emphasis was placed on the Leader's 'proper political and social insight, foresight (*tadbir*), courage, administration and sufficient power to lead' – criteria which had never been explicitly thematised by the clergy or overtly deployed in the regulation of its informal hierarchies. Moreover, in the same article, Article 109 of the constitution, 'political vision' is explicitly mentioned alongside an 'Islamic legal view' (*binesh-e feqhi*).[258] Learning and erudition were commendable but hardly sufficient. Khomeini was, of course, himself a *marja'-e taqlid*, and the constitution's pre-1989 stipulation of the criterion of *marja'iyyat* as a necessary qualification for the *vali-ye faqih* could be viewed as a conciliatory gesture towards the bastions of Shi'i religious learning in Qom and Najaf. The qualification of *marja'iyyat* meant not only that the Guardian Jurist would stand amongst the highest echelons of the 'olama' but that he would also enjoy a substantial following amongst the faithful, who would dutifully adhere to his religious rulings (*fatavi*). Moreover, the authority of the *marja'* was theoretically delimited and inscribed within the bounds of the *shari'ah*. Khomeini's historic decree in one fell swoop had effectively shunted this assemblage of legal and scholarly practices, institutional norms, and traditions aside.

More radically still, Khomeini had even discarded the idea, of which he himself had once been a proponent, that all governmental legislation had to accord with the dictates of the *shari'ah* as traditionally understood. Because of his view of guardianship as 'absolute' and undivided, and first and foremost concerned with political rule, Islamic government and its establishment emerged as an incumbent obligation superseding all others. Whereas in *Velayat-e faqih, hokumat-e eslami*, the rationale and justification of Islamic government, specifically government by the *foqaha*, derived from the obligation to execute the *shari'ah*, in January 1988, it was government, under the umbrella of absolute guardianship, which took pride of place. This was to the point of government being endowed with the right to unilaterally abrogate all previously religiously sanctioned agreements and even the devotional

---

and ritual practices incumbent upon individual believers – practices hitherto postulated in that very same tradition as intimately bound up with the believer's own personal felicity in the hereafter. As a result, post-revolutionary Iran witnessed an unparalleled and vaunted status ascribed to the notion of *maslahat* and underwritten by the state without historical precedent in Shi'i jurisprudence; it also consequently emerged as a staple of the official political idiom.

In this way, Khomeini's reasoning had come full circle. He had initially argued that government was merely a means for the realisation of otherworldly felicity, since it was necessary for the execution of Islamic law. By the end of his life, by contrast, he had reached the conclusion that the preservation of state power might demand the abrogation of those very same laws for which government had been summoned. The state, perforce, ceased to be a mere means to an end but became rather a self-grounding end in itself. As such, the sovereign exception was determined by absolute guardianship and constitutive of sovereign power *in toto*.

Shari'ati, Revolutionary Religion, and the Committed Intellectual

It is a new society that we must create, with the help of all our brother slaves, a society rich with all the productive power of modern times, warm with all the fraternity of olden days.[259]

Aimé Césaire

I will now move to analyse a specific dimension of 'Ali Shari'ati's thought which has received a great deal of attention and criticism in Iran's post-revolutionary intellectual climate: the so-called 'ideologisation of Islam'. Shari'ati is of great importance because of his considerable impact on the laymen and -women of the post-revolutionary Islamic left, who would openly revive his criticisms of clerical conservatism following Khomeini's death. The nature of this selective appropriation of Shari'ati by reformist intellectuals will be touched upon in greater detail in subsequent chapters.

Though I have predominantly focused on the disparate clerical faces of Iranian Islamism, Shari'ati was undoubtedly amongst the most important of the pre-revolutionary Islamic ideologues – particularly

---

[259] Aimé Césaire, *Discourse on Colonialism*, trans. Joan Pinkham, Kindle ed. (New York: Monthly Review, 1972, 2000), p. 51.

insofar as he made 'Islam' a politically respectable force for many young men and women in Iran's traditional middle classes, many of whom had come from provincial towns and villages to embark on a course of study at either the University of Tehran or the more recently founded Arya Mehr University of Technology (today known as Sharif University of Technology), often as the beneficiaries of government largesse. In the course of the 1960s these young Iranians would form Islamic societies in the universities and gather together in safe religious spaces such as the Hedayat Mosque, where progressive and politically active clerics such as Ayatollah Mahmud Taleqani held classes in Qur'anic exegesis.[260] It was during this time of political and socio-economic transformation and dislocation that Shari'ati, Taleqani, and others furnished an alluring rendition of Shi'i Islam for these students, many of whom were studying in the modern sciences and engineering and had been born and raised in devout Muslim households. It was a class of young men and women who were politically alienated from the Pahlavi order and the torpor of the traditionalist clergy, with its strict hierarchy of *marja'* and compliant *moqalled*. They were often both emotionally and psychologically bound to the faith within which they had grown up, while at the same time demanding that their religion respond to their contemporary needs and aspirations, which increasingly became political in nature. Attracted to the uncompromising and highly critical thrust of Shari'ati's rhetoric, alongside that of groups such as the People's Mojahedin Organisation of Iran,[261] the political struggle against the Shah's autocracy along with the restitution of socio-economic injustices were foremost in their minds. Venues such as the Hedayat Mosque and the Hosayniyyeh Ershad allowed young activists to meet, exchange their views about the latest political events in the country and abroad,[262] express solidarity with anti-colonial

---

[260] Lotfollah Maysami, *Az nehzat-e azadi ta mojahedin: khaterat-e Lotfollah Maysami*, vol. 1 (Tehran: Nashr-e samadiyyeh, 1383 [2004]), pp. 88–90.

[261] For instance, see the Mojahedin's tract *Tahlili az nehzat-e Hosayni* (An Analysis of Hosayn's Movement), which bears a number of similarities with some of the most important themes of Shari'ati's corpus, some of which will be examined in greater detail below. Ahmad Reza'i, *Tahlili az nehzat-e Hosayni* (Sazman-e mojahedin-e khalq) (Springfield, MO: 1975).

[262] Maysami, *Az nehzat-e azadi ta mojahedin: khaterat-e Lotfollah Maysami*, 1, p. 88. *Tarikh-e shafahi-ye masjed-e hedayat* (Tehran: Markaz-e asnad-e enqelab-e eslami, 1387 [2008]), p. 85.

movements elsewhere in Muslim majority world,[263] and breathe new life into cherished sacred texts, making them speak once again to the political and social realities they faced in their daily lives.[264]

During this time, the fusion of the archetypal figures, myths, and narratives of the early Islamic and, specifically, Shi'i community, with the language of revolutionary insurrection which had been in the ascendance in the late 1960s and early 1970s,[265] emerged as a formidable rival to secular ideologies such as liberalism and the varieties of Marxist doctrine once openly advocated by the Tudeh Party and, during the 1970s, the Organisation of the Iranian People's Fada'i Guerrillas. Shari'ati and other religious political activists and ideologues such as Mehdi Bazargan, Mahmud Taleqani, Morteza Motahhari,[266] Jalal al-Din Farsi, the Mojahedin's Reza'i brothers, and Mohammad-Baqer al-Sadr in Iraq, each in their own way, sought to respond to the challenge laid down by Marxism and its comprehensive explanation of class conflict, imperialism, and socio-economic exploitation. In this regard, the quest for 'Islamic ideology' went far beyond Shari'ati, even if he is perhaps its most famous advocate, and defined the intellectual milieu and political coordinates in which he was himself located. As one early Mojahedin activist, Lotfollah Maysami, would recall in his memoir, 'one of our fundamental needs at that time was the issue of ideology ... the reality was this, the Marxists had an ideological position on every issue. They had a response on art, music, different classes, history and it was clearly categorised.'[267]

Moreover, Shari'ati's timely criticisms of clerical passivity and the clergy's pretension to act as the sole legitimate 'representative' of the Hidden Imam also resonated with many pious, socially mobile, and

---

[263] *Tarikh-e shafahi-ye masjed-e hedayat*, p. 137.

[264] Mahbubeh Judaki, *Hosayniyyeh-ye ershad beh revayat-e asnad* (Tehran: Markaz-e asnad-e enqelab-e eslami, 1388 [2009]), pp. 58–9.

[265] For more on the radical intellectual and political climate among the Iranian opposition of the 1960s and 1970s, see Eskandar Sadeghi-Boroujerdi, 'The Origins of Communist Unity: Anti-colonialism and Revolution in Iran's Tri-Continental Moment', *British Journal of Middle Eastern Studies*, Vol. 45, Issue 5, 2018., pp 796–822.

[266] This engagement would become increasingly polemical after the revolution, but throughout the 1960s and 1970s the engagement was certainly sustained and serious. See, for example, the posthumously published Morteza Motahhari, *Naqdi bar Marxism* (Qum: Sadra, 1363 [1984]).

[267] Maysami, *Az nehzat-e azadi ta mojahedin: khaterat-e Lotfollah Maysami*, 1, pp. 156–7.

educated Iranian youth. They would also have considerable repercussions for his post-revolutionary legacy and its adherents. It is for this reason he ought to be viewed as a *transitional* and *divided* figure. On the one hand, he was the propagator of a new and uncompromising revolutionary and emancipatory credo, which arguably harboured a multitude of authoritarian, elitist, and potentially violent implications. On the other hand, he struggled to break the clerical monopoly on religious knowledge production by promoting the layman's capacity to engage the classical narratives of Islamic history and seminal doctrinal texts, without any of the requisite training for which the seminaries had been expressly established. This considerable break with 'tradition' allowed him to interpret Shi'i Islam in an often idiosyncratic fashion, melding it with the often-scatty insights he had gleaned from the leading lights of the French intelligentsia and the revolutionary, Third Worldist, anti-imperialist zeitgeist of the late 1960s and 1970s,[268] while earning him praise and adulation – as well as numerous enemies in clerical circles.

Prior to the revolution, Khomeini very adeptly managed to remain ambiguous on Shari'ati, not wishing to alienate a possible ally along with the many young people who had accepted him as their ideological guide and teacher.[269] Less politic clergymen, however, denounced him as a 'deviant' and 'Wahhabi' with scant reservation[270] – a curious accusation, given the plethora of sacred Shi'i personages and motifs upon which he customarily drew in his speeches, but nevertheless understandable on account of his controversial attacks on the

---

[268] This atmosphere, and the way Iranian activists connected their political struggle against the Shah with American imperialism in Vietnam and the Chinese and Cuban Revolutions, is well documented. See, for example, Quinn Slobodian, *Foreign Front: Third World Politics in Sixties West Germany* (Durham & London: Duke University Press 2012), chapter 4. Hamid Showkat, *Jonbesh-e daneshju'i: konfederasiyun-e jahani-ye mohassalin va daneshjuyan [ettehad-e melli]*, 4th ed., vol. 1 (Los Angeles: Sherkat-e ketab, 2010), pp. 196–7.

[269] Ali Rahnema, *An Islamic Utopian: A Political Biography of Ali Shari'ati* (London: I. B. Tauris, 1998), p. 275. We also know that Khomeini closely read Shari'ati while in Najaf. Ja'fariyan, *Jaryan-ha va sazman-ha-ye mazhabi-siyasi-e Iran*, pp. 603–5.

[270] Ayatollah Montazeri cites Ayatollah Golpayegani's criticism of Salehi-Najafabadi's controversial book *Shahid-e javid* as 'deviant' in the preceding lines, before sketching 'olama' reactions to the work of Shari'ati. Hosayn-'Ali Montazeri and Sa'id Montazeri, *Enteqad az khod: 'ebrat va vasiyyat* (Qom: amontazeri.com, 1387 [2008]), p. 59.

conservative 'olama'. Shari'ati himself appeared to be positively disposed towards Khomeini, passing over without comment the Ayatollah's deep-seated hostility to land reform or women's suffrage as enacted in the course of the Shah's so-called 'White Revolution'.[271] Following the turmoil of June 1963 which eventually led to Khomeini's exile, Shari'ati even resigned from the editorial team of the National Front's organ abroad, *Iran-e azad* (Free Iran), over their refusal to publish an article he had penned entitled 'Mosaddeq: The National Leader, Khomeini: The Religious Leader'.[272]

Shari'ati's ideas undoubtedly influenced a notable swathe of the younger generation of men and women who would go on to compose the Islamic Republic's political elite, both clerical and lay, even if they discarded some of his less congenial formulations.[273] In spite of his not uncommon anti-clerical sentiments, which were for the most part aimed at the traditionalist clergy who abjured political involvement entirely,[274] the future political class nonetheless imbibed a great many of his arguments and attitudes which empowered them to land blows on leftist rivals and demonstrate their familiarity with modern political ideas and philosophies. This process of osmosis, however, could not elide the competition, rivalry, and jealousy which emerged between lay-ideologues such as Shari'ati and even initially sympathetic members of the politically active clergy, especially as the former's renown and popularity overtook their own. The ambivalence of Shari'ati's discourse vis-à-vis the clergy was sensed and severely criticised by several prominent figures while Shari'ati was still alive and was exemplified in

---

[271] For an insightful analysis of the ideological basis and construction of Mohammad-Reza Pahlavi's 'White Revolution', see Ali M. Ansari, 'The Myth of the White Revolution: Mohammad Reza Shah, "Modernization" and the Consolidation of Power', *Middle Eastern Studies* 37, no. 3 (July 2001), pp. 12–16.

[272] Afshin Matin-asgari, *Iranian Student Opposition to the Shah* (Cost Mesa, CA: Mazda, 2002), p. 72–3.

[273] For instance, we know that Khameneh'i regularly participated in poetry circles along with Shari'ati and other literati in Mashhad. Rahnema, *An Islamic Utopian*, pp. 77–8. Also see Khameneh'i's speech on the anniversary of Shari'ati's death delivered in the A'zam Mosque in Qom during June 1980 and reproduced in the newspaper *Jomhuri-ye eslami*, 25 June 1980.

[274] Seyyed Hosayn Nasr and Hosayn Dehbashi, *Hekmat va siyasat: goftogu ba Doktor Seyyed Hosayn Nasr*, vol. 1, Majmu'eh-ye tarikh-e shafahi va tasviri-ye Iran-e mo'aser (Tehran: Sazman-e asnad va ketabkhaneh-ye melli-ye jomhuri-ye eslami, 1393 [2014]), p. 317.

the rift which emerged between Shari'ati and Morteza Motahhari, a leading student and disciple of Khomeini and 'Allameh Tabataba'i.[275] Motahhari, whom noted scholar Hamid Dabashi has called the 'chief ideologue of the Islamic Revolution',[276] much like Shari'ati played a redoubtable role in what has since come to be widely known as the 'ideologisation of Islam'[277] and the emergence of the 'new theology' (*kalam-e jadid*), which Iran's post-revolutionary religious intellectuals would themselves take up and develop in a number of distinct directions (see Chapter 6).

More importantly, the rift with Shari'ati expressed the deep-seated tensions between a considerable segment of the clergy and elements of the lay intellectual class, which – despite often being ignored or understated in the name of political unity in opposition and exile – proved to intensify with time. While Shari'ati certainly should not be conflated with the pre-1975 People's Mojahedin, there was nevertheless considerable ideological overlap, despite the fact that both he and his father possessed far sturdier and more durable links to the Freedom Movement of Iran. Nevertheless, the shared criticism of the clergy by both fuelled the exiled Ayatollah Khomeini's scepticism of Islamic laymen, which was in any event pronounced and real. One illustrative example is Khomeini's stern recalcitrance towards endorsing the Mojahedin while in Najaf following a slew of detailed discussions with activists Seyyed Morteza, better known as Torab Haqshenas (d. 2016), and Hosayn Ahmadi-Rowhani (executed by the post-revolutionary state in 1984), notwithstanding calls by some of his top aides and colleagues, such as Montazeri, Rafsanjani, Taleqani, Do'a'i, and even Motahhari, to do so. In short, his consistent

---

[275] Another traditionalist detractor and critic has been Seyyed Hosayn Nasr. Nasr has even gone as far as to allege that Shari'ati collaborated with SAVAK and was knowingly encouraged by the security apparatus, naming Parviz Sabeti, chief of SAVAK's domestic security operations, specifically. Sabeti is claimed to have defended Shari'ati in a meeting, arguing that he served a vital purpose in attracting Iranian youth away from the allure of communism. Communism, in the context of the Cold War, by virtually all accounts was considered the pre-eminent threat in the mind of the Shah as well as in the upper echelons of SAVAK. Ibid., pp. 313–15.

[276] Dabashi, *Theology of Discontent: The Ideological Foundation of the Islamic Revolution in Iran*, p. 147.

[277] Murtaza Mutahhari, *Fundamentals of Islamic Thought: God, Man and the Universe*, ed. Hamid Algar, trans. R. Campbell (Berkeley: Mizan Press, 1985), p. 51.

reluctance, if not hostility, can be understood as an almost visceral distrust of this class of the politically independent and engagé intelligentsia.[278] On Alviri's account, another contributing factor was Khomeini's rejection of armed struggle during this time,[279] an issue which was only fully clarified for the young activist upon meeting the exiled Ayatollah in person at his home in Najaf. The Mojahedin's feelings vis-à-vis the clergy were certainly mutual, and it was their closeted repudiation of clerical leadership which led to Alviri's own break with the organisation to which he had once been sympathetic.[280] The issue of clerical leadership was an issue that would rear its head with a vengeance as the new hierocratic populist political order led by Khomeini sought to consolidate itself. The differences between Khomeini and his partisans and the Mojahedin were certainly not forgotten, even if their public expression remained repressed till the aftermath of the revolution. In the words of Hojjat al-Islam Seyyed Mahmud Do'a'i, a member of Khomeini's entourage in Najaf who went on to become editor-in-chief of the national newspaper *Etela'at* following the revolution,

When the Imam spoke with Hosayn Rowhani and heard the goals and plans of the Organisation [i.e., the Mojahedin] he went from doubt to certitude. With sagacity and perceptiveness, he discovered a kind of eclecticism (*elteqat*) and error in their beliefs, in their exaggerated, strident and even insulting statements regarding some of the clerical (*rowhani*) and traditional religious institutions of Iran, and the severe attacks that were taking place. He even stated that they were the reason for the decline of the Islamic struggles (*mobarezat-e eslami*) and abuses of the court and Shah's regime.[281]

---

[278] According to Do'a'i, Hosayn Rowhani had some fifteen meetings with Khomeini in Najaf. Mahmud Do'a'i, *Gusheh 'i az khaterat-e Hojjat al-Islam va al-Moslamin Seyyed Mahmud Do'a'i* (Tehran: Mo'asseseh-ye tanzim va nashr-e asar-e Imam Khomeini, 1387 [2009]), pp. 111–13. For the account of one of the participants in the meetings, see 'Mosahebeh ba rafiq Torab Haqshenas piramun-e yaveh-ha-ye Shaykh Mohammad Montazeri', *Peykar* (20 Mordad 1359 [11 August 1980]), pp. 11–12. On Haqshenas's account, Khomeini rejected their views on the resurrection as 'materialist' (*madi*) and their adoption of armed struggle. This is to some extent confirmed in Do'a'i's version of events; however, as can be seen, the Mojahedin's criticisms of the clergy and other traditional Shi'i institutions was also a major factor.

[279] Alviri, *Khaterat-e Morteza Alviri*, pp. 64–5.   [280] Ibid., pp. 35–6.

[281] Do'a'i, *Gusheh 'i az khaterat-e Hojjat al-Islam va al-Moslamin Seyyed Mahmud Do'a'i*, p. 111.

'Ali's Shi'ism and Safavid Shi'ism

Shari'ati's most celebrated attempt to turn Shi'i Islam into an ideology of revolutionary agency was embodied in the fabulated dichotomy between 'Ali's Shi'ism (*tashayo'-e 'alavi*) and Safavid Shi'ism (*tashayo'-e safavi*), which he explicated in a series of seminal speeches during the autumn of 1971.[282] 'Alavi Shi'ism or the Shi'ism of 'Ali and the *ahl al-bayt* is conceived by Shari'ati as first and foremost a 'no', an act of repudiation and negation protesting the status quo (*e'teraz beh vaz'mowjud*).[283] This founding gesture of rebellion was somewhat akin to Albert Camus' depiction of the rebel and her comportment towards the world, namely one of refusal devoid of renunciation,[284] with which Shari'ati was familiar:

Islam was a religion that entered human history with the "no" of Mohammad – heir to Abraham and apotheosis of the religion of divine unity and the unity of creation. A "no" that begins with the slogan of divine unity (*towhid*), a slogan that Islam began in the face of polytheism, the religion of the aristocracy and expediency.

Shi'ism was an Islam that with the great 'Ali's "no" – heir to Mohammad and the apotheosis of the Islam of justice and truth – which made both its character and direction clear in the history of Islam ...[285]

He continues:

... in the school of 'Ali, the Shi'ah as the embodiment of the sufferings and hopes of the innocent masses and conscious and rebellious against the oppression of the ruler, obtained their most fundamental slogans:

For liberation from the guardianship of tyranny (*velayat-e jowr*)

The guardianship (*velayat*) of 'Ali!

For the branding of trash and stamping of unbelief and usurpation (*ghasb*) on the forehead of the Caliphate:
"Emamat"!

---

282   Rahnema, *An Islamic Utopian*, p. 298.
283   'Ali Shari'ati, *Tashayo'-e 'alavi va tashayo'-e safavi* (Tehran: Entesharat-e chapkhash va bonyad-e farhangi-e Doktor 'Ali Shari'ati, 1388 [2009]), p. 7.
284   'What is a rebel? A man who says no, but whose refusal does not imply a renunciation.' Albert Camus, *The Rebel: An Essay on Man in Revolt*, Foreword by Sir Herbert Read ed. (New York: Vintage, 1991), p. 13.
285   Shari'ati, *Tashayo'-e 'alavi va tashayo'-e safavi*, p. 5.

And for the overthrow of the regime of contradiction and discrimination that is ownership (*malekiyat*):
"Justice"![286]

In the view of Shari'ati, Safavid Shi'ism came to stand for order, the state, political passivity and inaction, political despotism, stasis, class exploitation, and a reactionary and ossified reading of Shi'ism.[287] 'Ali's Shi'ism provided an answer to the question 'what is to be done?' (*cheh bayad kard?*), a question posed regularly in Shari'ati's writings, no doubt cognisant of Lenin's famous tract of the same name.[288] In another text, *Shi'eh, yek hezb-e tamam* (Shi'ism, A Complete Party), Shari'ati goes so far as to assert that action takes precedence over belief.[289] 'Ali's Shi'ism was a revolutionary force in history which engaged in perpetual struggle and exertion (*jihad-e mostamer*) in both theory and practice against any and every despotic regime wedded to oppressive class systems and discriminatory hierarchies.[290] This is because 'Ali's Shi'ism is an 'armed revolutionary party', 'in possession of a very profound and clear ideology'. In this respect, the Islam that Shari'ati was advocating in the course of his lectures and speeches, with their many rhetorical flourishes, was essentially a 'this worldly' (*in jahani*) and resolutely political venture. It was a doctrine that played the role of an 'enlightener' (*agahi dahandeh*) and promoter of social responsibility, and this is why Islam for Shari'ati uniquely – and in contradistinction to other world religions – was inseparable from politics (*beguneh-ye bi naziri az siyasat tafkik napazir*).[291]

---

[286] Ibid., p. 6–7.   [287] Ibid., pp. 129, 221, 258–63.

[288] Ibid., p. 7. Shari'ati was familiar with Marx and a whole raft of major Marxist thinkers, including Lenin, from the time he spent at the Sorbonne attending the lectures of the neo-Marxist sociologist Georges Gurvitch. But his grasp of historical materialism and the Marxist theory of political economy left much to be desired. Rahnema, *An Islamic Utopian*, pp. 124, 125, 288. Shari'ati regularly invoked Lenin's writings and his deeds, and quite often favourably. 'Ali Shari'ati, 'Ommat va emamat', in *'Ali* (Tehran: Nashr-e amun, 1386 [2007]), p. 428.

[289] In this text he describes the *ommat* as a 'committed group' (*goruh-e mota'ahed*) in which action ('*amal*) takes precedence over belief ('*aqideh*) (p. 79). 'Ommat means one "believing committed group"!' (p. 80). ' Shi'eh yek hezb-e tamam', in *Shi'eh* (Tehran: Elham, 1362 [1983]).

[290] *Tashayo'-e 'alavi va tashayo'-e safavi*, p. 8.   [291] Ibid., p. 125.

This brings us to what might be called 'Shari'ati's paradox',[292] since, while Shi'ism for Shari'ati was indubitably political, with the establishment of its own governmental interests and priorities (*masaleh-ye hokumati*), it was bound to forsake its original verve and objective of bestowing an enlightened and revolutionary consciousness to the masses: 'after the seizure of power, Shi'ism becomes ruler over its destiny and society, but comes to a standstill'.[293] In this sense, Shi'ism's imbrication with state power is inexorably degenerative.[294]

While certainly a pervasive theme in Shari'ati's oeuvre, another point of focus recurs in his writings of the early 1970s: that of political organisation and mobilisation. If the overriding objective and horizon of such organisation and mobilisation was not the abolition of the existing order and its replacement with a new one free of the ills and maladies prevailing in the status quo, such activities would slide into superfluity. Shari'ati's repeated assertions of man's utopian impulses would also appear to run counter to the notion that he did not have at least a vague idea of the ideal political order he saw replacing the Pahlavi state he so vehemently opposed. Moreover, Shari'ati's 'internationalism' and 'emancipatory project' were not restricted to the territorial nation-state or even the Muslim *ommat*. Ultimately, every human being was responsible for the 'salvation' (*rastegari*) of humanity as a whole.[295]

Quite unlike Navvab Safavi, Shari'ati was flexible in his recommendations that the *shari'ah* be tailored to the circumstances of time and place and the basic needs of 'the people'.[296] On the whole, it was not something he spent a great deal of time contemplating. Despite such apparent pragmatism and laxity, determining what circumstances demand and what constitutes the people's basic needs would be stringently dictated by political considerations. Shi'ism was, in Shari'ati's mind, 'a complete party' (*yek hezb-e tamam*)[297] – a party with

---

[292] Hamid Dabashi has developed this notion in a number of interesting directions in his work. See, for example, Hamid Dabashi, *Shi'ism: A Religion of Protest* (Cambridge & London: Harvard University Press, 2011), chapter 3.

[293] Shari'ati, *Tashayo'-e 'alavi va tashayo'-e safavi*, p. 180.

[294] There are also some similarities with Ibn Khaldun's theory regarding the rise and fall of dynasties. For example, see Syed Farid Alatas, *Applying Ibn Khaldun: The Recovery of a Lost Tradition in Sociology* (London & New York: Routledge, 2014), chapter 7.

[295] Shari'ati, 'Shi'eh yek hezb-e tamam', p. 59.   [296] Ibid., p. 91.

[297] Ibid., p. 90.

a powerful ideology of its own, which he called Abrahamic ideology (idi'olozhi-e ebrahimi): 'Abrahamic ideology is that shared doctrine (maktab) of all of history's prophets and the people's guides to redemption and justice to which humankind has been invited in all times and all regimes.'[298] Moreover, 'ideology is a faith that is based firmly upon the concepts of self-awareness, guidance, redemption, fulfilment (kamal), value, ideal(s) (arman) and responsibility.'[299] Ideology engenders self-awareness and creates values: it impels one to act, while it recreates its subject in the process. He exclaims at one point, 'Ideology creates you.'[300] Echoing Marx's eleventh thesis on Feuerbach,[301] Shari'ati proclaims that while the philosopher and scientist are essentially observers of the world, ideologues, by contrast, 'command the good and prohibit evil' and have an unparalleled capacity for both destruction and creation:[302] 'Ideology says: it must be thus and philosophy and science only say thus it is.'[303] The undeniable attraction of ideology for Shari'ati was that he believed it endows men with the capacity to radically transform their society and the dominant social relations within it. Ideology in conjunction with praxis allows man to break free of his stifling bondage and liberate himself and those around him. Shari'ati claims that ideology, in its most 'exalted' ('ali-tarin) and 'progressive' (motaraqi-tarin) sense, and Islam, which is 'the most complete divine religion' (kamel-tarin din-e elahi), speak with a single voice.[304] In his view, the differences between Islam and 'progressive' ideology are barely discernible.

Ideology:
Message – Mission (resalat) – Commitment – Responsibility – Struggle – People (mardom)!

Islam:
Invitation (da'vat) – Mission (resalat) – Duty – Responsibility – Jihad – People (nass)![305]

---

[298] Ibid., p. 92.   [299] Ibid., p. 93.   [300] Ibid., p. 94.
[301] 'The philosophers have only interpreted the world, in various ways; the point is to change it.' Karl Marx, 'Theses on Feuerbach', in Karl Marx: Selected Writings, ed. David McLellan (New York: Oxford University Press, 2000), p. 173. Shari'ati paraphrases Marx's eleventh thesis in 'Ali Shari'ati, Jahatgiri-ye tabaqati-ye eslami (Tehran: Qalam, 1388 [2009]), p. 171.
[302] 'Shi'eh yek hezb-e tamam', p. 95.   [303] Ibid., p. 98.   [304] Ibid., p. 95.
[305] Ibid., p. 95.

A little further down, Shari'ati in fact unambiguously states, 'Islam is an ideology, not a culture, philosophy or science.'[306] Both 'ideology' and 'Islam' emphasise a sense of mission and committed struggle in the name of the masses. For Shari'ati, man's true nature, or his philosophical anthropology, as a 'utopian' (*otopist*) and 'rebel' (*'osiyan konandeh*),[307] is realised in the disposition cultivated by the ideological cast of mind. Man, by his lights, is a 'builder of heavens' (*behesht saz*). 'Perhaps every human being in every historical era built a utopia in his mind in accord with his own understanding and excellence.'[308] Like the writings of Navvab and Khomeini, a concerted effort to imagine an ideal society runs through Shari'ati's musings and rhetorical fulminations, an impulse connecting them to the many disparate lineages of Islamic and Western political thought and their myriad intersections. Whether their respective visions were qualitatively similar is another question, but in all of their writings a certain utopian impulse to imagine a pristine and just political order drives their engagements. One interesting difference is that Shari'ati speaks little about the state per se, while Navvab and Khomeini focus squarely on the powers and duties of the modern territorial state (*hokumat*), albeit in rather broad terms.[309] At one point in *Shi'eh, yek hezb-e tamam*, Shari'ati does speak in glowing terms of the Prophet's founding of a 'powerful centralized state' (*hokumat-e markazi-ye nirumand*) upon his migration to Medina. He continues by adding that it was necessary for the Prophet to go beyond the more limited project of 'individual reform' or more literally 'individual-building' (*fard-sazi*) to the founding of a government (*hokumat*) as a prerequisite of its identity entraining a global and universal (*jahani*) movement. But the far greater point of focus for Shari'ati's reintroduction of hierarchy and order manifests itself in the form of the party, the cadre, and the enlightened warrior intellectuals whose task is to save the masses, perhaps even in spite of themselves. Those who remain unenlightened and fail to reach self-consciousness of their political destiny are condemned to be 'imperfect' and in some sense 'paralysed' (*falaj*).[310] In demarcating a certain philosophical anthropology or conception of human nature, he is thereby

---

[306] Ibid., p. 103.
[307] 'Ali Shari'ati, 'Ta'arif-e din', in *Ensan-e bikhod* (Tehran: Qalam, 1389 [2010]), p. 21.
[308] Ibid., p. 21.   [309] Shari'ati, 'Shi'eh yek hezb-e tamam', p. 128.
[310] Shari'ati, 'Ta'arif-e din', p. 23.

able to ascribe a norm to human conduct. Those who fail to abide by this norm or behave in the manner it prescribes are deemed basically deficient or incomplete. But it is man's aspiration for utopia which is perhaps the chief feature which distinguishes him from the rest of God's creation.

Another relevant point to bear in mind is that Shari'ati was relatively novel in terms of his education and intellectual influences. Despite some post-revolutionary attempts to paint Shari'ati as a committed advocate of *velayat-e faqih*, the guides and saviours he actually had in mind were people much like himself, committed or engaged intellectuals (*rowshanfekran-e mota'ahed*).[311] This conception of the intellectual is similarly reflected in Shari'ati's correspondence with Frantz Fanon, where Fanon would comment, 'I hope that your authentic intellectuals may make good use of the immense cultural and social resources harboured in Muslim societies and minds, with the aim of emancipation and the founding of another humanity and another civilization, and breathe this spirit into the weary body of the Muslim orient. It is incumbent on you and your colleagues to accomplish this mission.'[312]

In Shari'ati these committed intellectuals were presented as explicit alternatives to the clergy, who had not only cravenly worked in the service of despotic Shahs across the ages[313] but had falsely presented themselves as the only true and legitimate mediators between God and the faithful. On numerous occasions, and in the strongest of terms, Shari'ati denounced the clergy as harbingers of reaction and despotism. For example, in the posthumously edited collection *Bazgasht* (not to be confused with *Bazgasht beh khish*, which is the subject of considerable controversy),[314] he states, 'Clerical despotism is the

---

[311] Shari'ati, 'Shi'eh yek hezb-e tamam', p. 105.

[312] Frantz Fanon, *Alienation and Freedom*, trans. Steven Corcoran (London & New York: Bloomsbury Academic, 2018), Loc 12560.

[313] Shari'ati, *Jahatgiri-ye tabaqati-ye eslami*, p. 130, 170.

[314] *Bazgasht beh khish* would be serialised in the newspaper *Kayhan* and on some accounts was written under duress while Shari'ati was detained at the Komiteh prison. The allegation was rejected by Shari'ati's wife, Puran Shari'at-Razavi, and the matter is yet to be conclusively settled. It should not be confused with an earlier lecture delivered at the University of Jondi-shapur entitled *Bazgasht beh khishtan*. But due to the considerable controversy vis-à-vis *Bazgasht beh khish*, one of the foremost authorities on Shari'ati, Ali Rahnema, advises the exercise of caution regarding this work, referring to it as 'revisionist'. Rahnema, *An Islamic Utopian*, pp. 338–40, 345.

most severe and detrimental of all forms of despotism in human history.'[315] Such explicitly anti-clerical fulminations would surface politically in the rhetoric of groups like the People's Mojahedin Organisation of Iran (post-June 1981), Forqan, and Arman-e mostaz'afin (Ideal of the Oppressed),[316] the very first political group to be proscribed after the revolution.[317] It would, as I shall demonstrate, also ironically re-emerge in the second and third decades of the revolution in the work of individuals like Sorush and Aqajari, who had contributed to the curtailment and ideological repudiation of the previously mentioned groups.

I will now examine Shari'ati's elitist conception of the intellectual vanguard or the 'warrior intellectual' (*rowshanfekr-e mojahed*). He often depicts the warrior intellectuals as a committed cadre who, having espied man's true nature and political destiny, shine light upon the darkness enveloping the toiling masses. *Mojahed* also has clear religious connotations, meaning one who strives in the name of the faith. By means of the warrior intellectuals' selfless intervention, a new self-consciousness and a form of 'this-worldly' redemption is to be imparted to the masses, without which the latter would have been left in ignorance.[318] These committed warrior intellectuals are the true successors to the Prophet and the rightful inheritors of his legacy.[319] They were more than mere armchair revolutionaries in Shari'ati's view. They were warriors prepared to fight in the name of justice and the establishment of a new 'monotheistic regime' (*nezam-e towhidi*). Shari'ati's own discourse of revolutionary insurrection was part of a broader political and intellectual shift which began to gain ground amongst political activists and the intelligentsia post-June 1963 and in the aftermath of a string of tumultuous events, including the fall of the reform-inclined Amini government

---

[315] This volume begins with the lecture entitled *Bazgasht beh khishtan* and, as indicated in the volume itself, is based on the Jondi-shapur lecture.
The provenance of the 'second notebook' which also comprises this volume is not entirely clear, even if it is claimed to be a post-prison work authored in Shari'ati's later years. 'Ali Shari'ati, *Bazgasht* (Tehran: Elham, 1384 [2005]), p. 224.

[316] See, for example, the highly critical tract Arman-e mostaz'afin, *Nazar-e shoma dar bareh-ye rowhaniyyat chist?* (Iran: Entesharat-e mostaz'afin, Summer 1355 [1976]), p. 3.

[317] Ja'fariyan, *Jaryan-ha va sazman-ha-ye mazhabi-siyasi-e Iran*, p. 677–89.

[318] Shari'ati, 'Shi'eh yek hezb-e tamam', p. 95.   [319] Ibid., pp. 101, 126–7.

(1961–2), the launch of the White Revolution and the regime's bloody repression of the ensuing protests, and ever-encroaching authoritarian consolidation.[320] This paradigm shift advocated by a number of politically active men and women, including the founders of the People's Mojahedin Organisation of Iran (PMOI), incited others like themselves to part with groups such as the Freedom Movement of Iran (NAI) and the vestiges of the National Front of Iran and to abandon the idea that peaceful political reform pursued through legal and parliamentary channels had any genuine prospect of success.[321] Young Marxist-Leninists, many of whom had formerly been sympathetic to the Tudeh Party, also reached comparable conclusions during this time.[322] Support for the idea of armed struggle as the sole remaining alternative steadily gathered supporters and was itself under the sway of international developments in the period, particularly anti-colonial flashpoints during what has been named the 'global Cold War'.[323] Intellectuals and resistance fighters like Frantz Fanon and Ernesto 'Che' Guevara – and the anti-colonial movements within which they participated, such as the Algerian War of Independence (1954–62), the Cuban Revolution of 1959, and the deleterious American imperial intervention in Vietnam – all contributed to the formation of an ideological

---

[320] *Sazman-e mojahedin-e khalq: payda'i ta farjam (1344–1386)*, vol. 1 (Tehran: Mo'asseseh-ye motale'at va pazhuhesh-ha-ye siyasi, 1388 [2009]), p. 213. The events of the June 1963 protests have been analysed in some detail by Azimi and Milani. Fakhreddin Azimi, 'Khomeini and the "White Revolution"', in *A Critical Introduction to Khomeini*, ed. Arshin Adib-Moghaddam (New York: Cambridge University Press, 2014). Abbas Milani, *The Shah*, Kindle ed. (New York: Palgrave Macmillan, 2011), chapter 15.

[321] Ervand Abrahamian, *Radical Islam: The Iranian Mojahedin* (London: I. B. Tauris, 1989), p. 85. Peyman Vahabzadeh, *A Guerrilla Odyssey: Modernization, Secularism, Democracy, and the Fadai Period of National Liberation in Iran, 1971–1979*, Kindle ed. (New York: Syracuse University Press, 2010), Loc 208.

[322] The classic tracts by Ahmadzadeh and Puyan are perhaps the pre-eminent examples of this trend on the left. Amir-Parviz Puyan and Mas'ud Ahmadzadeh, *Mobarezeh-ye mosalahaneh – ham esteratezhi, ham taktik; zarurat-e mobarezeh-ye mosalahaneh va rad-e te'uri-ye baqa'* (London: Cherik-ha-ye fada'i-ye khalq-e Iran, 1379 [2000]).

[323] See Odd Arne Westad, *The Global Cold War: Third World Interventions and the Making of Our Times*, Kindle ed. (Cambridge & New York: Cambridge University Press, 2007), Introduction.

transformation defining a generation.[324] Armed resistance to imperialist penetration and the Third World's ability to proffer just and indigenous solutions to the unjust and exploitative practices of erstwhile colonial masters had captured the imagination of a considerable section of the Iranian intelligentsia, just as it had captured the imaginations of many newly emerging groups and social classes across the Global South more broadly.

In Shari'ati's mind the warrior intellectuals were first and foremost preoccupied with action, not contemplation, and specifically with enacting justice in the here-and-now, much like the Prophet Mohammad himself when he embarked upon his own prophetic mission.[325] According to Shari'ati, there was one Islam which took the form of 'uninformed and inherited devotional rulings, ceremonies and rituals for the backward (*'aqab-mandeh*)' and another Islam requiring scientific and technical expertise or 'technical Islam' (*Islam-e fani*). The first Islam belongs to the unthinking and uncritical hereditary believer, the second to the rule-obsessed clergyman. Shari'ati dismisses both in favour of the Islam of the warrior intellectual. The Islam of the warrior intellectual 'is a light which illuminates the heart'.[326] This Islam is not a form of 'technical awareness', he tells us, but natural or innate self-consciousness (*khod agahi-ye fetri*), which he then goes on to identify with 'intellectualism' (*rowshanfekri*), 'recognising the path' (*shenakht-e rah*), and the 'science of guidance' (*'elm-e hedayat*).[327] The 'correct path' or 'just society' to which Shari'ati's committed warriors will lead the oppressed masses often remains vague and unspecified. He repeatedly describes it with adjectives such as 'just' and 'emancipated' as though they were self-explanatory. This is, of course, because they were tasked to predominantly perform a rhetorical and affective purpose rather than an explanatory one – to mobilise rather than analyse.

The warrior intellectual's role was not to excessively dwell on the content of values but to proclaim them boldly, not because he had rationalised them and could support his position with a host of valid

---

[324] The overlap and convergence of anti-war protests against U.S. military intervention in Vietnam and Iranian student resistance to the Shah abroad has been attested to in several places. For example, Slobodian, *Foreign Front: Third World Politics in Sixties West Germany*, p. 108.

[325] Shari'ati, 'Shi'eh yek hezb-e tamam', p. 100.   [326] Ibid., p. 100.

[327] Ibid., p. 100.

and epistemically justified reasons but because he felt and yearned for such values' realisation on a visceral level, at the level of his innermost nature. This attitude was exemplified best in the Prophet's companion Abu Dharr, who was often depicted by Shari'ati as a proto-socialist.[328]

Shari'ati does speak of a transitional period in which the Muslim community would choose leaders who best exemplify the community's revolutionary ideals.[329] This period of leadership would come to an end with every member of the *ommat*'s revolutionary transfiguration and avowed willingness to martyr him or herself in the name of the people. The '*ommat* chooses its martyr (*shahid*), the symbol of all its transcendent and ideal values, as leader, till it is itself able as martyr to take up that leadership role and every individual within the *ommat* can be a martyr in the cause of the people ... Every individual of Mohammad's community is a leader for the people.'[330] The procedure or mechanism for discerning the point whereby members of the community have been sufficiently empowered or revolutionised to embark upon their own martyrdom for the greater good is left unaddressed by Shari'ati. Like the Marxist-Leninist promises of the state's eventual 'withering away' along with the dissolution of proletarian dictatorship following the deracination of class society,[331] the sceptic is left wondering whether the day of transition to a truly 'liberated society' would ever indeed arrive. While the Imamate is accepted on the basis of the 'authenticity of its thought' (*esalat-e fekr*) and the 'truth of the doctrine' (*haqqaniyyat-e maktab*) with their manifest self-evidence in the course of revolutionary upheaval, there is virtually no consideration of the relinquishment of its power.[332] By contrast, the latter issue would receive considerable attention from 'Abdolkarim Sorush in the 1990s (see Chapter 5).

In his essay, *Ommat va imamat* (Community and Leadership), Shari'ati speaks candidly of the Marxist 'dictatorship of the working class' and the accompanying antipathy towards liberalism and 'Western democratic freedom' it entails.[333] He lambasts those Iranian intellectuals who continue to be enamoured of the passé assurances of nineteenth-century liberalism, and shrugs off the criticisms to which he

---

[328] Rahnema, *An Islamic Utopian*, pp. 57–61.
[329] Shari'ati, 'Shi'eh yek hezb-e tamam', p. 104.   [330] Ibid., p. 104.
[331] V. I. Lenin, *State and Revolution*, Kindle ed. (London & New York: Penguin Books, 1992), p. 15.
[332] Shari'ati, 'Ommat va emamat', p. 395.   [333] Ibid., p. 347.

has been subject for his condemnation of democracy and defence of 'ideologically committed leadership' (*rahbari-ye mota'ahed-e idi'oloz-hik*). Liberalism and 'its slogans of freedom of expression (*azadi-ye ara'*) and free elections weaken the battle front and justify undemo-cratic regimes and one-man despotisms (*estebdad-ha-ye fardi*)', he proclaims in his characteristically bombastic style.[334] The life which members of the *ummah* ought to be leading is not free and disengaged (*azad va raha*) but a committed and responsible (*mota'ahed va mas'ul*) one. Shari'ati, like a great many oppositional Iranian intellectuals of his generation, was clearly influenced by the local reception of Sartre and the heated debates devoted to the merits and shortcomings of com-mitted literature and the responsibility of critical intellectuals in society.[335]

As Shari'ati stressed on a number of occasions, the Imam is human but acts as a paragon (*osveh*) upon which the *ommat*'s members ought to be modelled,[336] and if someone considers themselves part of the community they must accept such leadership.[337] It quickly emerges that Shari'ati is arguing for a form of 'guided democracy' (*demokrasi-ye hedayat shodeh*), taking his cue from Third World anti-colonial leaders such as Indonesia's Sukarno (1957–66),[338] or what he also calls 'committed democracy' (*demokrasi-ye mota'ahed*), by means of which the society would be ruled by a small revolutionary elite or perhaps even a single man.[339] At one point he even refers to the German philosopher Friedrich Nietzsche and the theory of the *Übermensch* or 'Superman' as proof of humanity's repeated need for great men to lead the masses as 'manifestations of sacred transcen-dence' (*mazaher-e moqaddas-e mota'ali*) on earth and jolt them out of their petrified and satisfied indifference.[340] He then goes on to attribute a quote to the Victorian essayist and satirist Thomas Carlyle (d. 1881),

---

[334] Ibid., p. 347.
[335] Negin Nabavi, *Intellectuals and the State in Iran: Politics, Discourse, and the Dilemma of Authenticity* (Gainesville: University Press of Florida, 2003). For a penetrating study of the reception of Sartre and the question of commitment in the Arab world, see Yoav Di-Capua, *No Exit: Arab Existentialism, Jean-Paul Sartre, and Decolonization* (Chicago & London: University of Chicago Press, 2018).
[336] Ibid., pp. 386, 388.   [337] Ibid., pp. 348–9.
[338] Vijay Prashad, *The Darker Nations: A People's History of the Third World*, Kindle ed. (New York & London: The New Press, 2007), pp. 152–3.
[339] Shari'ati, 'Ommat va emamat', p. 426.   [340] Ibid., p. 372.

stating that 'history consists in the creation of history's heroes by means of the mediocre, and were it not for these heroes the mediocre would possess nothing except a monotonous and bestial existence'.[341] The individual counts for little in this view. The individual is mere fodder for the great men of history, who are history's real makers and final arbiters. In a similar vein, and despite having earlier in the text brazenly dismissed the mystical notion of *fana* or 'annihilation' in God, Shari'ati later on, and without regard for his preceding dismissal, invokes the figure of the *ensan-e kamel* or 'perfect man' in support of his argument for 'great men' as models of emulation.[342] Ironically, in these pages he advances a homologous argument to that of the *marja'* and *moqalled* defended by Osulism and the traditional Shi'i 'olama'; a dichotomy which, in its clerical guise, Shari'ati expended a great deal of time and effort criticising and ridiculing. In fact, one could even argue that Shari'ati's vision was far less 'democratic' than the traditional hierarchy of Osulism, since the choice of one's *mojtahed* had traditionally been left to the believer, who could in practice adopt distinct rulings from a range of *maraje'* consonant with their own personal preferences. In this sense, a degree of choice and voluntary assent remained integral to the latter arrangement, which merely regulated religious ritual practice and social transactions, whereas Shari'ati's imagined order was political through and through and to be directed unilaterally by means of a revolutionary vanguard.

Such arguments clearly attest to Shari'ati's implicit and explicit spiritual and political elitism, which sits well with his conscious defence of the revolutionary leadership's prerogative to forcefully execute its ideological program irrespective of the traditions and desiderata of the led.[343] In fact, the committed leadership, Shari'ati tells us, are not bound by the views and opinions of the majority.[344] Shari'ati's 'guided

---

[341] Ibid., p. 372. Shari'ati does not provide a reference, but the quote is most likely paraphrased from Carlyle's short book *On Heroes and Hero Worship and the Heroic in History*. Curiously enough, this slim volume by Carlyle has chapters on both the Prophet Mohammad and Luther and, unlike much heresiographical and Orientalist literature produced in the Western world up to that time, spoke with great respect about the Prophet of Islam. Thomas Carlyle, *On Heroes, Hero-Worship and the Heroic in History*, Kindle ed., Rethinking the Western Tradition (New Haven and London: Yale University Press, 2013), Loc 1175.

[342] Shari'ati, 'Ommat va emamat', p. 364.   [343] Ibid., p. 427.

[344] Ibid., p. 428.

democracy', like Tito's Yugoslavia, would be a one-party state or life-time appointment for the revolution's leader *(entekhab-e madamol'amr-e rahbar-e enqelab)*, spurning 'liberalism and Western free democracy'.[345] This is because the people, whom he self-assuredly compares to sheep, will follow wherever their stomachs lead them. Without the necessary ideological awakening, the people will be bewitched and bedazzled by the 'spell of money', 'demagogic magicians', 'puppet masters' *(kheymeh shab-bazan)*, and the clergy.[346] Because of such a serious lack of confidence in the masses' own ability to better their condition, he deems the right to vote guaranteed in Western liberal democracies as little more than a 'free vote for *abgusht*' *(ara'-e azad-e abgushti)*, *abgusht* being a traditional Iranian stew of lamb, potatoes, white beans, and chickpeas often associated with the poorer segments of Iranian society.

There are some quite superficial points of comparison with the arguments made in Lenin's *State and Revolution* (1918), with which Shari'ati had some acquaintance, such as the Bolshevik leader's contention that revolutionary leadership would have to continue for several generations to suppress counter-revolutionary forces.[347] For Shari'ati, though, this passage of time would lead to suffrage and the right to vote as more and more people progressively assimilated the leadership's revolutionary message.[348] Lenin, by contrast, believed the dictatorship of the proletariat was necessary to 'smash and destroy' the capitalist state[349] and that, once this had been achieved, it was the proletarian state that would eventually 'wither away' with the establishment of communist society.[350] Unlike Lenin, however, Shari'ati gave little theoretical attention to how the revolutionary vanguard were to be kept honest and grounded[351] or how 'the revolution from above' must be 'supplemented by a revolution from below'.[352] Moreover, while Shari'ati, like Lenin,

---

[345] Ibid., p. 433.   [346] Ibid., p. 431.
[347] Ibid., pp. 433–4. Lenin, *State and Revolution*, p. 18. Robert Service, *Lenin: A Biography*, Kindle ed. (London: Pan Books, 2002 [2000]), Loc 9118.
[348] Shari'ati, 'Ommat va emamat', p. 433.
[349] Lenin, *State and Revolution*, p. 29.   [350] Ibid., p. 17.
[351] For example, Lenin states unequivocally that the officials of the proletarian state can be instantly recalled if the constituents who elected them demand such and that they will receive no remuneration beyond that of the average worker; why the 'actual existing' Soviet state never achieved this level of accountability and 'democratic centralism' is perhaps one of the most debated questions in Marxist theory and historiography. Ibid., pp. 38–9.
[352] Ibid., p. 64.

dismissed Western liberal democracy because it stood for little more than 'democracy of the elites',[353] he focused above all else on revolutionary *leadership* as the only feasible political alternative which could break down and rebuild a 'reactionary' and 'traditional, backward society' such as Iran.[354] In this sense, Shari'ati might be thought of as very much a child of the anti-colonial nationalist and developmentalist vanguards of the Global South.

Shari'ati exudes confidence as he proclaims that, under a 'great and exalted leadership', society would be propelled towards 'absolute perfection', 'absolute knowledge' and 'absolute self-consciousness', and the discovery of 'transcendent values'.[355] 'The *ommat* is a society becoming eternal (*abadi*), towards absolute transcendence (*ta'ali-ye motlaq*)!'[356] And this 'absolute transcendence' is nothing but God himself.[357] In almost Hegelian fashion, God becomes the revolutionary process itself, which mysteriously leads to something he calls 'eternity' (*abadiyyat*) and the 'absolute' (*motlaq*), in a process of 'infinite evolution' (*takamol-e layetanahi*).[358] Those traditions and ways of thinking which promote stagnation and retard progress must be destroyed and condemned.[359] There is little elaboration on how such a process is to be evaluated and how it might go awry. Except for an allusion to Maxime Rodinson, the famous French Marxist biographer of the Prophet, Shari'ati simply asserts that 'Islam is committed government (*hokumat-e mota'ahed*), the Prophet is a committed leader (*rahbar-e mota'ahed*)'.[360] In this way, we see how Shari'ati not only advocates a conception of political leadership influenced by, but ultimately very distinct from, the Marxist-Leninist 'dictatorship of the proletariat' but also an image of the Prophet and the first Islamic government from Rodinson, the Prophet's Marxist biographer, who explicitly described Islam as a political ideology which, after Mohammad's demise, went on to conquer half the known world.[361]

---

[353] Shari'ati, 'Ommat va emamat', p. 431.   [354] Ibid., p. 430.
[355] Ibid., p. 349.   [356] Ibid., p. 350.   [357] Ibid.   [358] Ibid.
[359] This sentiment is reminiscent of some of Marx's more Eurocentric and stadial pronouncements on the question of historical development and the non-European world. Karl Marx, *Capital: A Critique of Political Economy*, trans. Ben Fowkes, Kindle ed., vol. I (London & New York: Penguin Books, 1976), Loc 1607.
[360] Shari'ati, 'Ommat va emamat', p. 428.
[361] Maxime Rodinson, *Mohammed*, trans. Anne Carter (Harmondsworth: Penguin Books, 1971), pp. 299–300.

Upon assuming power, the leadership proceeds to implement a program not on the basis of 'expediency' (*maslahat*) but on the basis of 'truth' (*haqqiqat*), *tout court*. Rhetorically asking himself which truth, Shari'ati answers it is 'a truth shown by ideology and doctrine believed by the individuals of the *ommat*'.[362] The goals of the leadership, he states, are predicated on the dictum 'that which must be' (*ancheh keh bayest bashad*).[363] His praise of conviction and revolutionary leadership dispenses with issues of dialogue and consent and instead conflates mundane political action on the part of the warrior intellectual elite who benevolently guide the *ommat* in the name of its determined 'interest', with the construction of an ideal or utopian society and even with a process of becoming God himself. In the revolutionary process the transcendent inheres and becomes immanent in socio-political relations and processes. Shari'ati's political vision, according to Farzin Vahdat, owes a great deal to his view of human existence as a theomorphic 'journey' or 'movement'; a journey whereby human beings begin as 'matter' and progressively ascend to the level of the divine spirit.[364] But how mundane human relations, political organisation, and activism partake in the traversal and actualisation of such a 'theomorphic journey', and on a macro-societal scale, remains ambivalent. 'Ideology' plays a tautological role in this equation. What is true is ideological and ideology is what is true. Moreover, there is no capacity for criticism, because to criticise is also, by default, to lack commitment.[365]

Conclusion

All the ideologues about which I have spoken have believed in political power's ability to bring a utopian society into the world. 'Heaven' can be made mundane. They believed this because they were convinced they had discerned and grasped in their respective capacities 'the truth'. How they thought about these categories sometimes drastically differed, but it is nonetheless clear that unwavering conviction in one's knowledge of an

---

[362] Shari'ati, 'Ommat va emamat', p. 347.   [363] Ibid., p. 349.
[364] Farzin Vahdat, *God and Juggernaut: Iran's Intellectual Encounter with Modernity*, 1st ed. (Syracuse: Syracuse University Press, 2002), p. 140.
[365] This double-edged sword is also reminiscent of Lenin's association of 'freedom of criticism' with 'opportunism' in *What Is to Be Done?* V. I. Lenin, *Essential Works of Lenin: "What Is to Be Done?" and Other Writings*, Kindle ed. (New York: Dover, 1987 [1966]), p. 56; Loc 913.

absolute reality – whether it goes by the name of '*shari'ah*', 'Islamic state', or 'Islamic ideology' – was intertwined with the grand utopian political scheme each thought was his mission to bestow upon the world. They were, in different respects, caught between the impulse to affirm the divine will as they saw it, which existed in an explicit relationship of obedience regarding the human subject, and, at the same time, to valorise man's revolutionary potential and self-sufficiency to shape and determine his political reality and fate. Shari'ati undoubtedly went further than any of the other Islamic ideologues considered in this chapter in affirming man's freedom and the sacred nature of human values in and of themselves.[366] His approach, too, is one of existential comportment, rather than jurisprudential affirmation. This is why, in addition to his lay status and radical critique of the clerical monopoly on interpreting and defining Shi'i Islam, he might be considered a transitional figure, challenging orthodoxy and representing a new class of laymen who would take it upon themselves to interpret tradition and combine it in novel and subversive ways with a variety of leftist and post-colonial appurtenances. Moreover, unlike his clerical counterparts, Shari'ati neglects the structure and organisation of the state, preferring to focus his energies on utopian struggle itself, the process rather than the *telos*.

The tension between God and man, the infinite and the finite, and the divine and mundane recurs throughout their writings, articulated in the flux of the grand social and political transformations and struggles that were reshaping Iranian state and society and the unfolding dialectic of the formerly colonised to their one-time colonial antagonists. It was during this period of immense dislocation, revolt, and turmoil that the quixotic invention of an Islamic utopia on earth was recast in modern Iran and forged, in some instances, by a hierocratic state and Islamic law and, in others, by an exalted class of 'warrior intellectuals' and their 'perfect monotheistic ideology'. These themes, amongst others, would have a defining role in marking the terrain of ideological contestation in the post-revolutionary order.

---

[366] For instance, at one point, Shari'ati states that the Imam is just as human as any other member of the *ummah*. He also stresses that 'human values (*arzesh-ha-ye ensani*) are superior to all metaphysical values' (Shari'ati, 'Ommat va emamat', p. 384). Such comments however are undermined at other points in the same essay. For example, earlier in *Ommat va imamat*, Shari'ati speaks of the construction of the 'absolute or transcendent human' (*sakhtan-e ensan-e motlaq ya mota'ali*). Ibid., p. 365.

3 Political Genealogies of Reform: The Rowshanfekran-e Dini *and the* Islamic Left

History functions within politics, and politics is used to calculate relations of force.[1]

Michel Foucault

With the death of Ayatollah Khomeini and the end of the Iran–Iraq War, a considerable swathe of the Islamic left and the religious intelligentsia who had supported Khomeini in the first years of the revolution and revered him as the indisputable 'Imam' found common cause and a convergence of their shared interests. As the Mojahedin of the Islamic Revolution would claim in their assessment of the factional composition of the post-revolutionary political order, it had been fragile from the outset, bound together first and foremost by allegiance to the new regime and its leader:

In a short space of time, after the fleeing of Bani-Sadr and the separation of the followers of the Imam's line (*payrow-ye khatt-e Imam*) and the religious nationalists (*melli-eslami*) from one another, a new factional alignment known as "left" and "right" appeared in the former. The creation of these factions and the emergence of the new groups was and is completely natural and predictable. The Islamic followers of the line of the Imam were not and is not a party or coherent political organisation ... Even the parties and limited organisations within this spectrum, like the rest of the parties did not have a clear and coherent ideology, strategy and organisation. The essential factor binding the different factions of the aforesaid current (*jaryan*) was the existence of the enemies of the revolution, regime (*nezam*) and leadership (*rahbari*), who were considered the joint enemies of all the factions.[2]

---

[1] Michel Foucault, *Society Must Be Defended: Lectures at the Collège de France 1975–76*, ed. Arnold I. Davidson, trans. David Macey (London & New York: Allen Lane, 2003), p. 164.

[2] SMEEI, 'Negahi-ye kutah beh barkhi az tayf bandi-ha-ye jadid-e fekri-siyasi-ye jame'eh', p. 7. Ghamari-Tabrizi has made the case that this was also widely evident at the level of society, critiquing the notion that the revolution was 'hijacked' by the Islamists as certain political organisations have previously

Khomeini's leadership under revolutionary circumstances brought many men and women together when they might otherwise have been political adversaries, as indeed many of them would become in the future. Moreover, the Islamic left and *rowshanfekran-e dini*, both of whom considered themselves *delsuzan-e nezam* (sympathisers of the system),[3] were hardly two discrete groups with widely variant ideologies, habitus, and political lineages; rather, they comprised part of fluid networks ranging across the political and bureaucratic apparatus of the state, as well as manifold official and legally sanctioned organs of ideological and cultural production. In this chapter, I will provide an historical account of the political events and conjunctures which shaped the context of the Islamic left and religious intellectuals' political and intellectual shifts and transformations. Delineating this historical genealogy is essential to understanding the intellectual and political origins of the reformists of the late 1990s and how the ouster of the Islamic left from the centres of state power in the aftermath of Khomeini's death fundamentally shaped their politics and outlook. Pushed out of many of the central institutions of the Islamic state by their factional adversaries and to some extent exposed to its capriciousness, it was this tangible shift of subject position in relation to state power, a parallax view as it were, that converged with many politicians and members of the intelligentsia's overturning of a whole host of verities they had once taken for granted. In the retrospective opinion of the prominent reformist journalist and intellectual Akbar Ganji, 'everyone has changed and changes. When in power, especially in non-democratic regimes, a person finds themselves in a position where they don't understand those who critique, disagree and oppose. Soon after a powerful individual is removed and outcast from the political structure, they find themselves in the position of those devoid of power.'[4]

---

alleged. Behrooz Ghamari-Tabrizi, *Foucault in Iran: Islamic Islamic Revolution after the Enlightenment* (Minneapolis & London: University of Minnesota Press, 2016), chapter 1.

[3] This description is used by the editor of *Kiyan*, Shams ol-va'ezin, in an article which was published in *Kiyan* in the summer of 1997 following Mohammad Khatami's presidential electoral victory. Shams ol-va'ezin, 'Rowshanfekri-ye dini va jomhuri-ye sevvom', p. 96.

[4] Akbar Ganji, 'Az "'alijenab-e sorkhpush" ta "'alijenab sabzpush"', *Radio Zamaneh* (25 Ordibehesht 1392 [15 May 2013]).

Factional Rifts in the Society of Combatant Clergy

The split within the Society of Combatant Clergy (*Jame'eh-ye rowha-niyyat-e mobarez*, henceforth JRM) – which led to the establishment of the Association of Combatant Clerics (*Majma'-e rowhaniyun-e mobarez*, henceforth MRM) by clergymen on the Islamic left in the spring of 1988 (1388) – is amongst the most important events in the evolution of elite factionalism in post-revolutionary Iran.[5] The JRM was founded just prior to the revolution with the support of Khomeini and other clerical luminaries such as Ayatollah Morteza Motahhari in 1977, but it had evolved significantly as an organisation since the establishment of the Islamic Republic. The split took place with Khomeini's approval, and the MRM's first chairman became Hojjat al-Islam Mehdi Karrubi. It became public knowledge when the two clerical groups provided separate electoral lists for the Third Majles' election convened on 8 April 1988 (19 Farvardin 1367). Following the split, members of the MRM accused the JRM of being purveyors of 'American Islam' and apologists for capitalism, with the JRM returning insults in kind.[6]

The split within the JRM and consequent founding of the MRM had been preceded by Khomeini's suggestion that Akbar Hashemi-Rafsanjani and Seyyed 'Ali Khameneh'i refrain from party politics in the form of the Islamic Republic Party (*Hezb-e jomhuri-ye eslami*, IRP), stating that they should act as 'national figures' and thus resign from the party.[7] Consequently, Rafsanjani and Khameneh'i asked Khomeini for permission to end party activities. This initial and temporary

---

[5] 'Abbas Shadlu, *Ettela'ati dar bareh-ye ahzab va jenah-ha-ye siyasi-ye Iran-e emruz* (Tehran: Nashr-e vozara', 1387 [2008]), p. 311.

[6] A major issue which proved divisive was whether mines, in accordance with Islamic jurisprudence, could be regarded as public property and thus justifiably appropriated and utilised as the state saw fit. The JRM claimed they opposed such, based on a pre-revolutionary fatwa issued by Khomeini himself. The chairman of the JRM, Ayatollah Mohammad-Reza Mahdavi-Kani, in a speech delivered before the Society of Islamic Engineers – despite expressing unqualified fidelity to the by then-deceased Khomeini – was dismayed by the Imam's more recent position in favour of statist intervention and the legislation passed by the Third Majles. 'Entekhabat-e Majles-e chaharom va e'lam-e mavaze'-e Jame'eh-ye rowhaniyyat-e mobarez', *Bayan*, no. 16 (Bahman 1370 [January–February 1992]), p. 28.

[7] 'Ali-Akbar Nateq-Nuri and Morteza Mirdar, *Khaterat-e Hojjat al-Islam 'Ali-Akbar Nateq-Nuri*, vol. 2 (Tehran: Markaz-e asnad-e enqelab-i eslami, Autumn 1384 [2005]), p. 78.

cessation of activities of the Islamic Republic Party began on 1 June 1987 (11 Khordad 1366) and led to the effective, if not actual, dissolution of the party.[8] Prior to the party's dissolution there were already profound differences within its central committee, differences which had only really been suppressed in the lifetime of its founder Ayatollah Mohammad Hosayni-Beheshti, who was killed in the devastating bombing of the IRP headquarters on 28 June 1981 by the People's Mojahedin Organisation. But in the words of Mohtashamipur, who was in factional terms very much on the left, in the aftermath of Beheshti's death 'the traditional right had effectively overrun the organs of the party'.[9] These factional tensions within the IRP, as seen above, afflicted the Society of Combatant Clergy and were the seeds of far deeper rifts to come.

Hojjat al-Islam 'Ali-Akbar Nateq-Nuri, who was interior minister from 1981 to 1985 and Parliamentary Speaker in the 1990s, claims that there were three groups within the IRP at the time and palpable tensions between Mir-Hosayn Musavi and Habibollah 'Asgarowladi of the Islamic Coalition Society[10] but also with the incumbent president and head of the IRP, Khameneh'i, who opposed Musavi's reintroduction as a candidate for a second term as premier in the autumn of 1985.[11] It was only after Khomeini unambiguously stated in a meeting with Rafsanjani, Nateq-Nuri, and Ayatollahs Ahmad Jannati, Mohammad Yazdi, and Mohammad-Reza Mahdavi-Kani that 'as an ordinary citizen I announce that the election of anyone except him [i.e., Musavi] is a betrayal of Islam' that Khameneh'i withdrew overt opposition to Musavi's candidacy, even if he continued to surreptitiously oppose the latter.[12] It is believed that Khomeini's support for Musavi stemmed from the significant popularity of the prime minister among Iran's armed forces and the

---

[8] Ibid., p. 78.
[9] 'Ali-Akbar Mohtashamipur, *Chand seda'i dar jame'eh va rowhaniyyat* (Tehran: Andisheh-ye javan, 1379 [2000]), p. 28.
[10] This factional division within the IRP is also confirmed by Mohtashamipur in his account. Ibid., p. 28.
[11] Nateq-Nuri and Mirdar, *Khaterat-e Hojjat al-Islam 'Ali-Akbar Nateq-Nuri*, 2, p. 76.
[12] According to the memoir of 'Ali-Akbar Nateq-Nuri, Khomeini told his son Ahmad to make it clear that his preference for prime minister was Mir-Hosayn Musavi. 'Any time they asked the Imam in this regard [i.e., regarding the proposed premiership of Musavi], the Imam confirmed Engineer Musavi. Little by little the Imam explicitly stated his opinion and had announced to the office that no one except Mr. Musavi is expedient (*maslahat*).' Ibid., pp. 74–5.

consideration that his removal might be detrimental to morale and thus the war effort.[13] Despite Khomeini's seemingly unequivocal support for Musavi's re-election as premier, ninety-nine MPs remained steadfast in their opposition to his candidacy and voted in the Majles accordingly, with President Khameneh'i allegedly considering himself their unofficial hundredth member.[14]

The reasons for the split within the JRM are delicate, but the immediate impetus for the break was the presentation of several potential candidates for the forthcoming Third Majles elections by the JRM's left faction, nominally headed by Mehdi Karrubi, who proved unacceptable to members of the JRM's Central Council; the proposed candidates included prominent figures such as Fakhr al-Din Hejazi, Hadi Ghaffari, and Mohammad Musavi-Kho'iniha.[15] The failure of Hojjat al-Islam Mahmud Do'a'i's unsuccessful attempt to attain a majority from the Central Council, alongside the failure of prominent figures such as Hadi Ghaffari, Fakhr al-Din Hejazi, and Musavi-Kho'iniha to obtain a place on the JRM's prospective electoral list, positively contributed to the decision to secede and found an alternative organisation.[16] According to Hojjat al-Islam 'Ali-Akbar Mohtashamipur, the actual decision to break away from the JRM and establish an alternative clerical organisation was taken during a hospital visit to Karrubi by Mohammad Khatami and Musavi-Kho'iniha.[17] Such an organisation was held to be essential to the representation and advancement of these clerics' political platform and the interests on the Islamic left, but it was entirely dependent upon Khomeini's approbation if it was to succeed. Because of Karrubi's ill-health at the time, in early 1988 Musavi-Kho'iniha discussed the issue with Khomeini alone and laid out the political and ideological differences and reasons for the desired split. Khomeini would formally recognise the formation of the new clerical organisation, the MRM, on 14 April 1988,[18] which – much to their rivals'

---

[13] Mohtashamipur, *Chand seda'i dar jame'eh va rowhaniyyat*, p. 30.
[14] Nateq-Nuri and Mirdar, *Khaterat-e Hojjat al-Islam 'Ali-Akbar Nateq-Nuri*, 2, p. 80.
[15] Mohtashamipur, *Chand seda'i dar jame'eh va rowhaniyyat*, p. 36. 'Ali Kordi, *Jame'eh-ye rowhaniyyat-e mobarez az sheklgiri ta enshe'ab* (Tehran: Markaz-e asnad-e enqelab-e eslami, 1386 [2007]), p. 190–1.
[16] *Jame'eh-ye rowhaniyyat-e mobarez az sheklgiri ta enshe'ab.*, p. 191.
[17] Mohtashamipur, *Chand seda'i dar jame'eh va rowhaniyyat.*, pp. 37–8.
[18] Ibid., p. 39.

dismay – won the majority of seats in the Third Majles election. The new left-dominated Majles held its inaugural session at the end of May.[19]

Several accounts also believe the proximity of individuals such as Kho'iniha and Khatami to Ahmad Khomeini, and the latter's support for the formation of the MRM, to have been decisive. That it was reputedly Ahmad who chose the name *Salam* for the newspaper Kho'iniha would soon edit – the same newspaper that would effectively emerge as the chief platform of the *chap*, perhaps further indication of where the younger Khomeini's true sympathies lay.[20]

One of the deeper reasons for the spilt was the respective clerical factions' views on the economic powers of the state vis-à-vis the private sector as covered in article 44 of the Islamic Republic's constitution. For those elements of the political elite which believed that privatisation and abundant foreign direct investment were indispensable to the country's ability to rebuild and prosper, article 44 was regarded as an intractable obstacle and an annoyance. The aforementioned article argued in no uncertain terms that the 'state sector is to include all large-scale and major industries, foreign trade, major mineral resources, banking, insurance, energy, dams and large-scale irrigation networks, radio and television, post, telegraphic and telephone services, aviation, shipping, roads, railroads and the like; all these will be publicly owned and administered by the state'. The religious status of the state-enforced redistribution of wealth was similarly divisive.[21] The conservative-traditionalist clergy and their allies in the regime co-opted by elements of the bazaar around the Islamic Coalition Society were cautious,[22] if not altogether hostile

---

[19] Hamid Kaviyani, *Pishgaman-e eslahat: naqsh-e sazman-e mojahedin-e enqelab-e eslami-ye Iran dar tahavvolat-e siyasi-ye daheh-ye 70* (Tehran: Salam, 1379 [2000]), p. 17.

[20] Quchani, 'Salam; aqa-ye Kho'iniha', p. 109.

[21] SMEEI, 'Negahi-ye kutah beh barkhi az tayf bandi-ha-ye jadid-e fekri-siyasi-ye jame'eh', p. 55.
    For a fairly detailed English-language account of Article 44, see Evaleila Pesaran, *Iran's Stuggle for Economic Independence: Reform and Counter-Reform in the Post-Revolutionary Era* (London & New York: Routledge, 2011), p. 43.

[22] Arang Keshavarzian, 'Regime Loyalty and Bazari Representation under the Islamic Republic of Iran: Dilemmas of the Society of Islamic Coalition', *International Journal of Middle East Studies* 41(2009), pp. 229–30.

to nationalisation, state taxation, land reform, and worker profit-sharing.[23] The economic reasons for the parting of ways between the Islamic *chap* and *rast* would steadily fade into the background by the time Khatami was elected to the presidency in 1997, replaced by the putatively 'liberal' agenda, which focused on the rule of law, civil society, and increased personal freedoms.

As quoted above, the SMEEI was willing to claim that the apparent unity which characterised Khomeini's followers during the revolution's first decade was the result of 'the existence of enemies and those opposed to the revolution, regime and leadership'.[24] With the impeachment of President Abolhasan Bani-Sadr on 21 June 1981 and the repression and effective political marginalisation of the People's Mojahedin Organisation of Iran (PMOI),[25] National Front of Iran (*Jebheh-ye melli-ye Iran*), and Freedom Movement of Iran (*Nehzat-e azadi-ye Iran*), along with the gamut of the armed Marxist and Kurdish groups, the list of common foes and threats faded, and many of the nascent tensions and ideological-religious disagreements which had been relegated to secondary importance in the revolution's first years could no longer be easily swept aside.[26] 'Abdolkarim Sorush (whose writings will be analysed in Chapters 4 and 5) also had a direct hand in debunking, debating, and attacking the ideological rivals of the

---

23 SMEEI, 'Negahi-ye kutah beh barkhi az tayf bandi-ha-ye jadid-e fekri-siyasi-ye jame'eh', pp. 8–9. 'Mosahebeh ba Hojjat al-Islam va al-Moslamin Karrubi: aksariyyat-e fe'li aksariyyat-e Majles-e ayandeh khahad bud', *Bayan*, no. 16 (Bahman 1370 [January–February 1992]), p. 24.

24 The SMEEI analysis begins with the fissures within the Followers of the Imam's Line and the SMEEI and then broadens the analysis to encompass other important political actors. 'Negahi-ye kutah beh barkhi az tayf bandi-ha-ye jadid-e fekri-siyasi-ye jame'eh', p. 7.

25 For more information, see Mohammad Ja'fari, *Taqabol-e dow khatt ya kudeta-ye Khordad 1360* (Frankfurt: Barzavand, 1386 [2007]), p. 415. For Behzad Nabavi's allegedly decisive role in Bani-Sadr's ousting, also see Abol Hassan Bani-Sadr, *My Turn to Speak: Iran, the Revolution & Secret Deals with the U.S.*, Foreword by Ambassador L. Bruce Laingen ed. (Washington & New York: Brassey's (US), Inc., A Macmillan Publishing Company, 1991), chapter 3.

26 At one point the SMEEI analysis candidly speaks of the Islamic left and right's alliance in the process of eliminating (*hazf*) what he refers to as the 'intellectual current known as liberal' (*jaryan-e fekri mowsum beh liberal*), which generally pertains, if not altogether accurately, to the Freedom Movement and the National Front. SMEEI, 'Negahi-ye kutah beh barkhi az tayf bandi-ha-ye jadid-e fekri-siyasi-ye jame'eh', p. 55.

Khomeinists, in particular the Marxist left,[27] the PMOI, and the Islamic Republic's very first president, Abolhasan Bani-Sadr.[28] In one noteworthy text, aimed squarely at the deposed president Bani-Sadr, Sorush – in the florid style for which he is famed – asserts 'the manifestation and rise of the Islamic Republic in this land are from the same merciful breeze of God'.[29] A historical irony of course was that, by the end of the 1980s and during the early 1990s, much of the theoretical arsenal Sorush had borrowed from Karl Popper, Friedrich Hayek, and a number of other Euro-American thinkers – and which he had used to critique the Islamic Republic's broadly speaking Marxist and Islamist-leftist rivals – steadily began to focus its critical gaze on the

---

[27] Sorush's televised debate on the issue of dialectics alongside Mesbah-Yazdi and against the Organisation of the Iranian People's Fada'i Guerrillas leader (Majority Faction), Farrokh Negahdar (b. 1946) and Tudeh Party ideologue, Ehsan Tabari (1917–89) from the spring of 1981 has been published in recent years by the research institute headed by Mesbah-Yazdi. Mohammad-Taqi Mesbah-Yazdi et al., *Gofteman-e rowshangar dar bareh-ye andisheh-ha-ye bonyadin: monazereh-ye aqayan-e Ehsan Tabari, 'Abdolkarim Sorush, Farrokh Negahdar, Mohammad-Taqi Mesbah-Yazdi* (Qom: Mo'asseseh-ye amuzeshi va pazhuheshi-ye Imam Khomeini, 1385 [2006]); Akbar Hashemi-Rafsanjani and Yaser Hashemi, *'Obur az bohran: karnameh va khaterat-e sal-e 1360 Hashemi-Rafsanjani* (Tehran: Daftar-e nashr-e ma'aref-e enqelab, 1378 [1999]), pp. 85–87.

[28] Sorush wrote a frontal attack on both Bani-Sadr and the People's Mojahedin Organisation of Iran (PMOI) in a pamphlet: 'Abdolkarim Sorush, *Bani-Sadr, sazman-e mojahedin va hegelism* (Rome: Markaz-e farhangi-ye eslami-ye orupa, 1362 [1983]). The only version of the pamphlet I have been able to examine is one published in 1982 (1362) by the Islamic Cultural Centre in Rome. The ambassador to the Vatican at the time was Hojjat al-Islam Hadi Khosrowshahi, a well-known clerical activist and chronicler of the Fada'iyan-e Islam. The text also repeatedly refers to the Mojahedin as the *Monafeqin* or 'Hypocrites', which has since become the standard and official state term for the PMOI.
     At the more public level, Sorush's televised debates with the Marxists, Farrokh Negahdar, of the OIPFG majority faction, and Ehsan Tabari, the leading theoretician of the Tudeh Party, alongside Hojjat al-Islam Mohammad-Taqi Mesbah-Yazdi, had a greater immediate impact. Tabari was later jailed in 1983 (1362) and under torture compelled to recant his Marxist beliefs and express his 'conversion' to Islam. Incidentally, Tabari stated in his televised confession that it was after having encountered the writings of Sorush's early mentor, Morteza Motahhari, that he was prompted to re-examine and repudiate his erstwhile and 'totally spurious' beliefs. Ervand Abrahamian, *Tortured Confessions: Prisons and Public Recantations in Modern Iran*, Kindle ed. (Berkeley: University of California Press, 1999), p. 204.

[29] Sorush, *Bani-Sadr, sazman-e mojahedin va hegelism*, p. 5.

'ideological thinking' and 'dogmatism' within the ranks of the Islamic
Republic's own political and ideological apparatuses.[30]

The Marginalisation of the Islamic Left

The increasing political marginalisation of the Islamic left's clerical and
non-clerical partisans in the Fourth Majles, whose election was held on
10 April 1992 (21 Farvardin 1371), was another important event in the
history of this faction and their ideological allies.[31] It is during this
election that the Guardian Council (*Shura-ye negahban*) most brazenly
asserted its prerogative to disqualify candidates who had been
Khomeini loyalists on the basis of its interpretation of article 99 of the
constitution.[32] It should be noted that the Guardian Council's prerogative to supervise elections more broadly had long been constitutionally codified and was even included in earlier drafts of the constitution
prior to its redrafting and finalisation by the Assembly of Experts for
the Constitution in late 1979.[33] It was not, however, until the Fourth
Majles elections that the Guardian Council unilaterally arrogated the
power of approbatory supervision (*nezarat-e estesvabi*) and struck
a severe blow to the Islamic left, since the Guardian Council, dominated by stalwarts of the traditional right, could now disqualify its
ideological rivals en masse.[34] While the Assembly of Experts' election

---

[30] It is worth noting that in the mid-1990s Sorush repeated his willingness to
debate members of the conservative JRM. 'Nazarat-e yeki az nazdikan-e
Dr. Sorush dar mored-e dargiri-ye daneshgah-ye fani-ye Daneshgah-e Tehran
[Originally published in *Salam* 29/7/74 (21/10/1995)]', in *Siyasat-nameh*
(Tehran: Serat, 1378 [1999]), p. 107.

[31] Moslem, *Factional Politics in Post-Khomeini Iran*, p. 160.

[32] Kaviyani, *Pishgaman-e eslahat*, p. 18. Mostafa Tajzadeh, *Dar defa' az entekhabat-e
azad va 'adelaneh* (Tehran: Farhang va andisheh, 1381 [2002]), p. 14.

[33] Siavush Randjbar-Daemi, 'Building the Islamic State: The Draft Constitution of
1979 Reconsidered', *Iranian Studies* 46, no. 3 (2013), p. 648.

[34] This was not always the SMEEI's position. In August 1979 the organisation
issued a critique of what Randjbar-Daemi has referred to as the June text of the
draft constitution, in which they demanded a fourth branch of government,
a 'guardianship branch' that would directly supervise the Majles and presidency.
The text was entitled *Sazman-e mojahedin-e enqelab-e eslami, matn-e
pishnahadi-ye pishnevis-e qanun-e asasi* (Tehran, 1979). It has been republished
in the following volume: Mehdi Sa'idi, *Sazman-e mojahedin-e enqelab-e eslami;
az ta'sis ta enhelal 1358–1365* (Tehran: Markaz-e asnad-e enqelab-e eslami,
1385 [2006]), pp. 258–61. See Randjbar-Daemi, 'Building the Islamic State:
The Draft Constitution of 1979 Reconsidered', p. 15. While the criticisms and
recommendations in the above text bore the seal of the entire organisation, and

of 8 October 1990 (16 Mehr 1369) saw several high-profile MRM clerics disqualified, including: Sadeq Khalkhali, the infamous head of the Islamic Revolutionary Court in the immediate aftermath of the revolution; former Attorney-General Mohammad Musavi-Kho'iniha; Asadollah Bayat; Hadi Khameneh'i, the younger brother of the incumbent Guardian Jurist; and 'Ali-Akbar Mohtashamipur, one-time interior minister (1985–9) and key player in the establishment of Lebanese Hezbollah when Iran's ambassador to Syria.[35]

The Fourth Majles election has come to be viewed as a watershed event, because the Islamic left ceased to control a single branch of government due to the strategy prosecuted by the Guardian Council. Moreover, before this election, the Guardian Council had still not 'clarified' its position on article 99, which did not take place until December 1991. The Fourth Majles elections saw forty-one incumbent MPs disqualified from running in the election and nine electoral districts voided.[36] 'Non-Muslim candidates' from the Tudeh Party had been disqualified in the course of the First Majles, not with reference to article 99 but with recourse to articles 64 and 67, which stipulated that candidates must believe in God and swear an oath on one of the holy books of the three main Abrahamic religions and Zoroastrianism.[37]

The Islamic left's lack of success in the Fourth Majles' election was also the result of its perceived intellectual and ideological sterility. In an interview with *Bayan*, a monthly affiliated with the Islamic left, a few months preceding the Fourth Majles' elections, Hojjat al-Islam Mehdi Karrubi, who was still Speaker of the Third Majles, unapologetically

thus must have had the support of all the members of the organisation's central committee, the group was dissolved due to political differences between the right- and left wings of the organisation in 1986. The organisation would then reinitiate its activities with a different central committee in 1991 (1370), which was then banned in 2009, following the controversial re-election of President Mahmud Ahmadi-Nezhad.

[35] David Crist, *The Twilight War: The Secret History of America's Thirty-Year Conflict with Iran*, Kindle ed. (New York: Penguin Press, 2012), p. 122, Loc 2396.

[36] Tajzadeh, *Dar defa' az entekhabat-e azad va 'adelaneh*, p. 16.

[37] Tajzadeh does not object to the Tudeh candidates' disqualification on the grounds of their inability to pledge allegiance to one of the religions officially recognised by the constitution of the Islamic Republic. Tajzadeh's argument is rather that the Tudeh members' disqualification did not take place under the rubric of 'supervision' or *nezarat* and thus was irrelevant to the Guardian Council and the electoral veto powers it later appropriated for itself. Ibid., p. 12.

defended Khomeini's fatwa against Salman Rushdie and his faction's inveterate hostility towards the United States and Israel. Karrubi, furthermore, explicitly identified the possibility of a faction, namely the right, using the Guardian Council to disqualify members of the Islamic left ahead of the upcoming elections. But at this point he was still convinced that the incumbent Guardian Jurist, Ayatollah Khameneh'i, and the upper echelons of the revolutionary system would prevent the Guardian Council and traditional right from prosecuting the 'political elimination' *(hazf-e siyasi)* of the Islamic left.[38] But the truth of the matter was that the *chap* had come to be seen as a hindrance to the prosperity and fortunes of a powerful coalition of pragmatic and conservative forces within the political class, and, in the latter's mind, the good fortunes of the republic itself. A dogged refusal to entertain the opening of Iran's economy to the global market and economic liberalisation at home, or a softening of relations with the country's Gulf neighbours, Europe, or even the United States, are perhaps the two more notable examples.[39]

With the death of Khomeini in 1989 the Islamic left had also lost their patriarch and the only supra-factional figure capable of mediating and intervening on their behalf. When alive Khomeini had tried to prevent the outright supremacy of either the left or right factions nestled beneath his ultimate authority as the 'charismatic leader of the revolution'.[40] The arrogation of approbatory supervision by the Guardian Council would serve as a perpetual target for the Islamic left – and with good reason. Following their Fourth Majles defeat, and ever since, it would be subject to unrelenting criticism by many politicians and intellectuals within the 'reformist' fold (See Chapter 5). The left meanwhile found itself demonised by supporters of the new president, leadership, and the traditional right. Their slogan – 'The opponent of Hashemi is the opponent of the leader, the opponent of the leadership is the enemy of the Prophet' *(mokhalef-e Hashemi [Rafsanjani] mokhalef-e rahbar*

---

[38] 'Mosahebeh ba Hojjat al-Islam va al-Moslamin Karrubi', p. 22.

[39] 'Abbas Shadlu, *Jostari-ye tarikhi piramun-e takasor gara'i dar jaryan-e eslami va paydayesh-e jenah-e rast va chap-e mazhabi* (Tehran: Vozara', 1381 [2002]), p. 219.

[40] This comes through in the famous *Manshur-e baradari* (Proclamation of Fraternity), which will be analysed in greater detail below. In the *Manshur*, Khomeini warns against the elimination of one faction *(jenah)* at the expense of others. Ruhollah Khomeini, *Sahifeh-ye Imam*, 21 vols., vol. 21 (Tehran: Mo'asseseh-ye tanzim va nashr-e asar-e Imam Khomeini, 1378 [1999]), p. 179.

ast, mokhalef-e rahbari doshman-e payghambar ast) – was an especially potent expression of such factional enmity. 'The left had become homeless' recalled Ebrahim Asgharzadeh, a leading member of the Student Followers of the Imam's Line and MP in the Third Majles. '[A]ll of the pillars of power *(arkan-e qodrat)* were in the hands of the Mr. Hashemi and the right.'[41]

Behzad Nabavi, a former minister in the cabinet of Mohammad-'Ali Raja'i and founding member of the SMEEI, who was himself disqualified from running for the Fourth Majles,[42] describes the intellectual and political re-orientation which took place amongst a considerable swathe of the Islamic *chap* as '[a] process that if we want to state precisely, after the death of the Imam and the end of the war gradually enveloped the important issues which occupied our minds'.[43] Following his disqualification Nabavi wrote his famous open letter to President Rafsanjani on 25 April 1992, insisting, 'More than any issue, I emphasise this point, that despite all the difficulties and unkindness I have endured for the last fourteen years since the victory of the Islamic Revolution, as before, and God willing as long as I am alive, I regard as obligatory *(vajeb)* the protection and preservation of the system.'[44] In their analysis, the SMEEI pinpoints the Fourth Majles as a pivotal moment that led to the 'exclusion of [the left] from rule *(hakemiyyat)*', which then decided to adopt the policies of 'silence', 'patience and expectation', and 'unity and criticism, while defending the basis of the revolution and system *(nezam)*, and critiquing the intellectual and policy positions of other factions, who had the management [of the state] in their possession'.[45]

The Mojahedin Organisation of the Islamic Revolution, one of the most important non-clerical groups of the Islamic left, was itself originally formed from seven different militant groups after the revolution, issuing its first communiqué on 27 March 1979 (7 Farvardin 1358). These groups were the Mansurun, Movaheddin, Towhidi-ye

---

[41] Hosayn Dehbashi and Ebrahim Asgharzadeh, 'Goftogu-ye Hosayn Dehbashi ba Ebrahim Asgharzadeh', *Khesht-e kham*, no. 16 (15 Bahman 1395 [3 February 2017]).

[42] Behzad Nabavi and Hosayn Salimi, 'Eslahat piruz shodeh; goftogu ba Behzad Nabavi', in *Kalbodshekafi-ye zehniyyat-e eslahgarayan* (Tehran: Gam-e now, 1384 [2005]), p. 305.

[43] Ibid., p. 309.   [44] Kaviyani, *Pishgaman-e eslahat*, p. 284.

[45] SMEEI, 'Negahi-ye kutah beh barkhi az tayf bandi-ha-ye jadid-e fekri-siyasi-ye jame'eh', p. 56.

saf, Fallah, Towhidi-ye badr, Fallaq, and Ommat-e vahedeh.[46] Upon
its formation it bore the name the Mojahedin Organisation of the
Islamic Revolution (SMEE), only adding 'Iran' when the organisation
was reconstituted at the beginning of the 1990s. In an audience with
Khomeini on 3 July 1981 (12 Tir 1360), the latter approved of the
organisation's activities and existence, and he insisted its representatives cultivate strong relations with the Islamic Republic Party, Islamic
Revolutionary Guards Corp, Basij, and the armed forces.[47] According
to Mohammad Salamati, who later became the chairman of the newly
established organisation in 1991, prior to the revolution the seven
aforementioned militant groups had little to no organisational links.[48]

Many of the groups varied geographically and included men who
would go on to play prominent roles in the post-revolutionary order
and range across the ideological spectrum. These included the first
commander-in-chief of the Revolutionary Guards, Mohsen Reza'i,
a deputy commander-in-chief of the same organisation, Mohammad-
Baqer Zowlqadr, and Secretary of the Supreme National Security
Council 'Ali Shamkhani, all of whom were members of Mansurun;
Morteza Alviri, future mayor of Tehran and leading member of the
Kargozaran, was among the founding figures of Fallah; the acclaimed
film-maker Mohsen Makhmalbaf along with Behzad Nabavi, Fayzollah
'Arabsorkhi and Salamati were members of Ommat-e vahedeh, while
Tajzadeh and Armin were a members of Fallaq and Towhidi-ye saf,
respectively. As the SMEEI itself confirms, the SMEE formed essentially

---

[46] SMEE, 'E'lam-e mowjudiyat', in *Majmu'eh-ye bayaniyyeh-ha va etela'iyyeh-ha*
(Tehran: Entesharat-e sazman-e mojahedin-e enqelab-e eslami, 7 Farvardin
1358 [27 March 1979]), p. 12.

[47] Ruhollah Khomeini, *Sahifeh-ye Imam*, 21 vols., vol. 15 (Tehran: Mo'asseseh-ye
tanzim va nashr-e asar-e Imam Khomeini, 1378 [1999]), p. 271.

[48] Mohammad Salamati, 'Didgah-ha-ye sazman-e mojahedin-e enqelab-e eslami-
ye Iran dar bareh-ye tahazob va fa'aliyat-ha-ye tashkilati', *'Asr-e ma*, no. 1 (27
Mehr 1373 [15 October 1994]), p. 3. There were, however, informal links. For
instance, Hashem Aqajari and Mohammad-Baqer Zowlqadr, who would go on
to become the Deputy Commander of the Revolutionary Guards, were
housemates prior to the revolution and, despite certain disagreements, were
linked by their deep-rooted allegiance to Khomeini (p. 39). Just as economic
disagreements had polarised the traditional right linked to the mercantile class
and represented by groups like the Islamic Coalition Association (*Hay'at-ha-ye
mo'talefeh-ye eslami*), disagreements over economic policy and ideology had
a decisive role in provoking the split between the right and left of the SMEE
(p. 41). Aqajari, Khojasteh-Rahimi, and Bala'i, 'Sharh-e zendegi-ye yek
enqelabi-ye naaram'.

a militarised bulwark against those groups regarded as dubious by Khomeini and his clerical disciples or which refused to fully submit to the authority of the latter.[49] This decision to form what would effectively become the SMEE was taken when Khomeini confirmed the necessity of the formation of a coalition of militant Islamic groups to defend the revolution to Mehdi 'Araqi, Motahhari, and Jalal al-Din Farsi.[50] The key issues which united the seven groups at this point was their commitment to Islamic ideology, the leadership of Khomeini and the doctrine of the Guardian Jurist,[51] and their antagonism towards all those groups which they deemed enemies of 'the revolution', particularly the People's Mojahedin, as illustrated by the SMEE's chosen name, and with whom many members of the SMEE had had bitter relations and complicated histories stretching back into the jails of the Pahlavi regime.[52] They were equally dismissive of, if less threatened by, 'the liberals', critiquing Mosaddeq's 'unrevolutionary spirit' and the fact that his politics 'did not emanate from Islamic ideology'.[53] While distinct, their organisational view could be said to share certain similarities with that of the Fada'iyan-e Islam and their perspective on Mosaddeq's nationalist government in the early 1950s (see Chapter 2).

Despite the apparent unity witnessed in the initial years of the revolution in 1983 (1361), thirty-seven members of the organisation's left-faction, including Behzad Nabavi, Fayzollah 'Arabsorkhi, Mohsen Armin, Hashem Aqajari, Mohammad Salamati, and Mostafa Tajzadeh, submitted their joint resignation. The reason for their decision was twofold. Firstly, despite the Imam's previous encouragement to cooperate with the IRGC, by the spring of 1982 Khomeini had issued an ultimatum to the SMEE, calling on senior members of the Islamic Revolutionary Guards Corp (IRGC) to resign their membership from all political parties. Pursuant to this ultimatum the SMEE issued a statement to its

---

[49] Hajjariyan performed a comparable role in the Intelligence Ministry and has recently recounted how he was involved in the interrogations of the so-called 'Nowzheh coup' plotters and various other activities. Sa'id Hajjariyan and Reza Khojasteh-Rahimi, 'Eslahatchi, cheriki nemishavad: sharh-e yek zendegi-ye siyasi-fekri', *Andisheh-ye puya* (Tir–Mordad 1391 [July–August 2012]), p. 41.

[50] Sa'idi, *Sazman-e mojahedin-e enqelab-e eslami*, p. 75.

[51] SMEE, 'E'lam-e mavaze'-e sazman-e mojahedin-e enqelab-e eslami', in *Majmu'eh-ye bayaniyyeh-ha va etela'iyyeh-ha* (Tehran: Entesharat-e sazman-e mojahedin-e enqelab-e eslami, 16 Farvardin 1358), p. 25.

[52] Sa'idi, *Sazman-e mojahedin-e enqelab-e eslami*, p. 78. SMEE, 'E'lam-e mavaze'-e sazman-e mojahedin-e enqelab-e eslami', pp. 23–4.

[53] Quoted in Sa'idi, *Sazman-e mojahedin-e enqelab-e eslami*, p. 93.

members on 3 April 1982 calling on them to choose between the SMEE, the IRGC, and the army.[54] With the Iran–Iraq War in full swing, a number of those men who occupied the upper echelons of the IRGC accordingly resigned from the organisation.[55] Later disagreements with Hojjat al-Islam Hosayn Rasti-Kashani, Khomeini's representative to the organisation, were at the heart of the matter, however, and the chief reason for the aforementioned individuals resigning on 20 January 1983 (30 Dey 1983), after having decided in April of the previous year to retain their membership following Khomeini's ultimatum.[56] Rasti-Kashani had from the outset been regarded as too close to the rightist faction of the SMEE. He was also criticised for abjuring consultation with the left in collective decision-making prior to January 1983. Lastly, and perhaps crucially, he was not seen as truly reflecting Khomeini's views and positions in several areas, particularly on the economy and questions of social justice.[57] In October 1986, Khomeini approved the request for the organisation's dissolution made by Rasti-Kashani.[58] As mentioned above, the SMEE was later reconstituted as the Mojahedin Organisation of the Islamic Revolution of Iran (SMEEI) with a different central committee in 1991, with Nabavi, Salamati, 'Arabsorkhi, Armin, Tajzadeh, and Aqajari being amongst its more prominent members. The organisation and its periodical *'Asr-e ma* would go on to play a pivotal role in retheorising the Islamic state's ultimate sources of legitimacy.

The Ouster of Ayatollah Hosayn-'Ali Montazeri

The removal of Ayatollah Hosayn-'Ali Montazeri as successor to Khomeini in March 1989, and the routing of his household, was another series of events which deepened the rifts and animosities afflicting the political elite of the Islamic Republic and went on to impact future alignments. Montazeri had been one of Khomeini's leading students in Qom and a prominent clerical activist preceding the revolution.[59] In the words of Rafsanjani, 'when they exiled the Imam,

---

[54] Ibid., p. 155.   [55] Ibid., p. 155.   [56] Ibid., p. 234.   [57] Ibid., p. 153.
[58] Khomeini, *Sahifeh-ye Imam*, 20, p. 139.
[59] For details of this period in English, see Ulrich Von Schwerin, *The Dissident Mullah: Ayatollah Montazeri and the Struggle for Reform in Revolutionary Iran* (London & New York: I. B. Tauris, 2015), chapter 1. Sussan Siavoshi, *Montazeri: The Life and Thought of Iran's Revolutionary Ayatollah* (Cambridge & New York: Cambridge University Press, 2017), chapter 4.

in reality the leadership of the struggle was with [Montazeri]'.[60] With the collapse of the *ancien régime* and the scramble to establish a new political order, Montazeri would emerge as one of the most prominent advocates of *velayat-e faqih* prior to the convocation of the Assembly of Experts on the Constitution (*Majles-e barrasi-ye naha'i-ye qanun-e asasi-ye jomhuri-ye eslami-ye Iran*), convened in August 1979.[61] The elected body of which Montazeri would become the chairman, with Ayatollah Beheshti, secretary general of the Islamic Republic Party, his deputy, was tasked with analysing and drafting the Islamic Republic's codified constitution. Perhaps most importantly, it was during the process of the Assembly of Expert's deliberations that the Guardianship of the Jurist was enshrined into the new state's constitution.[62]

Montazeri would lose his eldest son, Mohammad, in the bombing of the Islamic Republic Party's headquarters on 28 June 1981 as mounting tensions between the clerical order and the People's Mojahedin deteriorated into near civil war, replete with the assassination of high-ranking state officialdom and a vicious cycle of state terror marking a new phase in the revolution.[63] It was a conflict that had been in the making since at least the mid-1970s, reaching its violent denouement with the IRGC's brutal clampdown on the Mojahedin-dominated protests of 20 June 1981, against what was held to be the creeping monopolisation of power by the IRP, and the aftermath of the impeachment of the Islamic Republic's first president, Abolhasan Bani-Sadr.[64]

In 1985 Montazeri was chosen by the Assembly of Experts as Khomeini's successor, a decision he states was taken without his knowledge.[65] However, his tenure would not last long. The first issue which gave impetus to the precipitous deterioration of Khomeini and Montazeri's relationship was the arrest of his one-time student and

---

[60] Akbar Hashemi-Rafsanjani, 'Nagofteh-ha-ye Hashemi-Rafsanjani az 'azl-e Ayatollah Montazeri', *Tarikh-e Irani*, http://www.tarikhirani.ir.

[61] Montazeri, *Khaterat.*, p. 890.

[62] Saffari, 'The Legitimation of the Clergy's Right to Rule in the Iranian Constitution of 1979'. Ghamari-Tabrizi has also provided an extensive analysis of these debates. See Ghamari-Tabrizi, *Islam and Dissent in Postrevolutionary Iran: Abdolkarim Soroush, Religious Politics and Democratic Reform*, chapter 3.

[63] Shaul Bakhash, *The Reign of the Ayatollahs: Iran and the Islamic Revolution* (New York: Basic Books, 1984), p. 219.

[64] Abrahamian, *Radical Islam*, p. 218.   [65] Montazeri, *Khaterat*, p. 467.

brother to his son-in-law, Seyyed Mehdi Hashemi. These events were fundamentally entwined with the ongoing process of the new state neutralising rival sources of religious, military, and economic power, including unrelenting pro-Khomeini partisans who refused to observe emerging ministerial jurisdictions. Moreover, the governing political class was committing itself to the war effort with Iraq and assuming some of the more conventional accoutrements of statehood and international relations, where the conduct of diplomacy and statecraft required a unified centre rather than competing bases of political authority for the exercise of organised violence.

With the death of Mohammad Montazeri in June 1981, Mehdi Hashemi alongside Mohsen Reza'i assumed control of the Unit for Liberation Movements (*Vahed-e nehzat-ha-ye azadi-bakhsh*), an organisation charged with delivering support to Muslim resistance movements across the globe.[66] He was also a member of the Command Council of the IRGC (*Shura-ye farmandehi-ye sepah-e pasdaran-e enqelab-e eslami*) proper.[67] He was appointed to the latter position on the recommendation of Khameneh'i, who at the time was a member of the Revolutionary Council (*Shura-ye enqelab*).[68] This soon-to-be-controversial Unit was established within the structure of the IRGC, but over time Hashemi became embroiled in numerous disagreements with leading military personnel Mohsen Reza'i and Mohsen Rafiqdust, commander-in-chief of the IRGC and minister of the IRGC respectively.[69] By November 1982 the Majles had still not conferred official status to the Unit, a development which Evan Siegel has contended was tantamount to a call for its effective dissolution.[70] Under Hashemi's leadership it continued to maintain its own base of operations, endowed with its own caches of armaments and matériel,[71] and irked personnel in both the Ministry of Foreign Affairs and the

---

[66] Mohammad Montazeri and Reza'i were both appointed by the Revolutionary Council to head the Unit. Montazeri and Montazeri, *Enteqad az khod*, p. 70.

[67] Montazeri, *Khaterat*, p. 605.

[68] Montazeri and Montazeri, *Enteqad az khod*, p. 69.

[69] Ibid., p. 70. 'Lebanese Paper on Hashemi, McFarlane Issues, *Al-Shira'*, 3 November 1986', *FBIS* VIII, p. 12.

[70] Evan Siegel, 'The Case of Mehdi Hashemi', Iranian Studies: Evan Siegel's Personal Website, http://iran.qlineorientalist.com/Articles/MehdiHashemi/MehdiHashemi.html

[71] Mohammad Rayshahri, *Khaterat-e siyasi* (Tehran: Mo'assesseh-ye motale'at va pazhuhesh-ha-ye siyasi, 1369 [1990]), p. 231.

Ministry of Intelligence as it often worked at cross-purposes with the latter. These ministries even accused Hashemi of jeopardising Iran's relations with Syria, the country's only steadfast Arab ally in the Iran–Iraq War.[72]

As divisions and factional rivalries grew within the Khomeini loyalist camp, the prospect of Hashemi having an independent and armed base of support,[73] as well as sizeable influence in and around Isfahan,[74] was viewed with heightened suspicion.[75] Khomeini wrote to Montazeri on 10 April 1986 warning his 'close friend' to keep silent regarding an investigation against Hashemi, while recounting a sordid list of allegations against the latter, including murder and the surreptitious stockpiling of weapons.[76] In the same letter, Khomeini also stated without ambiguity that 'all the activities in the name of support to so-called liberation organisations must stop and all those involved in this matter condemned (*mahkum*)'.[77] Khomeini later formally called on Hojjat al-Islam Mohammad Rayshahri to confront Hashemi in a letter to the intelligence minister dated 27 October 1986.[78]

On a related note, Akbar Ganji has spoken of his time in the IRGC and the divisions between the left and right wings of the Mojahedin Organisation of the Islamic Revolution, which also permeated the IRGC during this period, and how the left actively opposed IRGC commander Mohsen Reza'i (who had been on the right of the SMEE upon its founding) in 1984–5. The left was convinced that Khomeini was being misled by the right and had been given false promises of

---

[72] 'Lebanese Paper on Hashemi', p. 12.

[73] According to Rayshahri, the discovery of a hidden weapons store attributed to Hashemi was the point when Khomeini was finally convinced that it was necessary for the security forces to definitively tackle the question of Hashemi and his activities. *Khaterat-e siyasi*, p. 41.

[74] Siegel addresses this matter in some detail in his extensive treatment of Hashemi's case. For example, he points to how Hashemi was accused of 'acting like an autonomous government'. Siegel, 'The Case of Mehdi Hashemi'.

[75] Montazeri, *Khaterat*, p. 605. This concern is aired directly in Rayshahri's memoirs. Rayshahri, *Khaterat-e siyasi*, p. 39.

[76] The letter is reproduced in *Khaterat-e siyasi*, p. 46. It can also be found in Ruhollah Khomeini, 'Ebraz-e 'allaqeh va ta'kid bar 'adam-e hemayat az Seyyed Mehdi Hashemi va hoshdar dar mored-e dasiseh-ha-ye ou', in *Sahifeh-ye Imam* (Tehran: Mo'asseseh-ye tanzim va nashr-e asar-e Imam Khomeini, 1999).

[77] Rayshahri, *Khaterat-e siyasi*, p. 46.

[78] Ruhollah Khomeini, 'Lozum-e barkhord-e qate' ba afrad-e zed-e enqelab va monharefin vabasteh beh Mehdi Hashemi', in *Sahifeh-ye Imam* (Tehran: Mo'asseseh-ye tanzim va nashr-e asar-e Imam Khomeini, 1378 [1999]).

imminent victory on the war front. Meanwhile, elements within the left
had kept in close contact with Montazeri prior to his ousting and asked
him to convey their misgivings regarding the conduct of the war to
Khomeini. Ganji left the IRGC in the spring of 1985 shortly after
disagreements with Reza'i had boiled over, while events with
Hashemi would subsequently reach their own deadly conclusion, con-
solidating factional alignments that were set to dominate the Islamic
Republic for the next decade. Ganji adds that they were prevented, he
speculates by Khameneh'i, from meeting with Khomeini, as the IRGC
increasingly came under the grip of a more constricted coalition of
groups at the expense of the Islamic left and their allies.[79]

Nonetheless, Hashemi's ongoing support for Islamic liberation
movements independently of the governing elite was not the only
reason it was concluded that he had to be decidedly dealt with. Land
expropriations and distribution amongst the peasantry by Montazeri
and Hashemi ally Hojjat al-Islam Fathollah Omid Najafabadi had
roiled several powerful clergymen in Isfahan, who denounced his
actions as equivalent to 'godless communism' and a fundamental threat
to the sanctity of private property.[80] As a result of these ongoing
activities, Hashemi had emerged as something of an *enfant terrible*
for much of the Islamic Republic's political class and a 'problem' in
need of urgent attention. Rafsanjani warned Montazeri about the
growing sensitivity around Hashemi, even suggesting that he should
be sent abroad to act in a diplomatic role[81] until the storm had
subsided.

The Lebanese newspaper *Ash-shira* 's publication of revelations surrounding Reagan National Security advisor Robert McFarlane's secret
visit to Iran in September 1986, and the U.S. administration's sale of
arms to the Islamic Republic with Israel acting as intermediary, in what
came to be known as the Iran–Contra Affair, brought the matter to
a head.[82] *Ash-shira* ', reflecting the views of Hashemi and his circle,

---

[79] Akbar Ganji, 'Jang-e Iran va 'araq; dorughgu'i va siyasat-bazi', *Radio Zamaneh*
24 Shahrivar 1392 [15 September 2013].
[80] Siegel, 'The Case of Mehdi Hashemi'.
[81] Montazeri, *Khaterat*, p. 605. Montazeri and Montazeri, *Enteqad az khod*, p. 75.
This is also confirmed by Rafsanjani in a revealing interview. Hashemi-
Rafsanjani, 'Nagofteh-ha-ye Hashemi-Rafsanjani az 'azl-e Ayatollah
Montazeri.'
[82] The two most exhaustive accounts of Iran–Contra to date, with particular focus
on the Reagan administration and the history of Iran–Contra on the American

memorably proclaimed at the time that 'whatever the outcome, there are now two opposing logics in Tehran: the logic of the state and the logic of the revolution'.[83] Given the regime's public rhetoric fiercely declaiming its implacable opposition to both the United States and Israel, the scale of embarrassment for Khomeini and those who had been party to the transactions, such as Ahmad Khomeini, Rafsanjani, and Prime Minister Musavi, was immense.

Hashemi's supporters hoped to bring pressure to bear against the Intelligence Ministry by means of the leak,[84] but instead it essentially sealed the controversial cleric's fate. It was also used as a pretext for a frontal assault on Montazeri's household, as many of his close associates, including his son-in-law, Seyyed Hadi, were arrested.[85] Hashemi's supporters explicitly claimed that the arrest of their leader and the curtailment of his transnational activities in support of radical movements abroad was a quid pro quo, and concession to the Reagan administration, who demanded Tehran take tangible steps to curb its support for 'terrorism' and the threat posed to the security of the Gulf states.[86] Hashemi was executed in late September 1987 after having been severely tortured and subjected to peremptory trial at the hands of the Special Court for the Clergy (*Dadgah-ye vizheh-ye rowhaniyyat*), an institution that would be summoned to great effect in punishing reformist clergy who in later years dared to challenge the authority of the *vali-ye faqih*. While Montazeri tried his utmost to save Hashemi, his efforts ultimately came to nought; in his view, the proximity of Hashemi to himself and his household were seized upon by his rivals to poison his relationship with Khomeini, who, he contends, was a victim of Ahmad and Rayshahri's manipulations. While Montazeri's reading

---

side, include Malcolm Byrne, *Iran-Contra: Reagan's Scandal and the Unchecked Abuse of Presidential Power* (Lawrence, KS: University Press of Kansas, 2014). Crist, *The Twilight War*, Chapter 10.

[83] 'Lebanese Paper on Hashemi', p. 13.

[84] The leak's origin with Mehdi Hashemi is confirmed by Montazeri. Montazeri, *Khaterat*, p. 606. Also see Mohsen Hashemi and Habibollah Hamidi, *Majara-ye Makfarlin: forush-e selah, azadi-ye gerugan-ha* (Tehran: Daftar-e nashr-e ma'aref-e enqelab, 1388 [2009]), p. 176.

[85] Montazeri, *Khaterat*, p. 607.

[86] This is confirmed by Montazeri; see Montazeri and Montazeri, *Enteqad az khod*, p. 78. 'Lebanese Paper on Hashemi', p. 13. For a detailed account of some of these activities, see Siegel, 'The Case of Mehdi Hashemi'.

might have some truth to it, it appears that regime survival and stabilisation were at the heart of Khomeini's concerns. Montazeri repeated protestations and open airing of grievances steadily eroded the one-time teacher's confidence in his student's ability to assume the mammoth task of continuing his legacy as guardian of the Islamic state in his absence.

Montazeri argued in later years that Ahmad Khomeini, Mohammad Rayshahri, and Rafsanjani doggedly pursued Hashemi's neutralisation, because they believed his proximity to Montazeri would prevent their control over the latter after Khomeini died, leaving them out in the proverbial cold.[87] In his words, the prosecution of Hashemi amounted to a 'political purge' against Montazeri's household rather than a legal investigation to hold him to account for any alleged criminal wrongdoing.[88] Nevertheless, one has to square this contention with Montazeri's own judgement that Rafsanjani, along with Khameneh'i, had previously been instrumental to his appointment as Khomeini's successor during the Assembly of Expert's deliberations.[89] Moreover, it seems improbable that such a policy would have been pursued without at least Khomeini's tacit blessing, even if Montazeri's great teacher would later claim that he did not agree with the appointment of his former student.[90] Between Montazeri's appointment in 1985 and March 1989, when he had been effectively removed as successor, a series of intervening events, of which the Mehdi Hashemi affair was an especially salient episode, compelled Khomeini to withdraw his support, provide cover for Montazeri's political adversaries, and, in the last months of his life, turn away from his former student altogether.

On Khomeini's view, Montazeri's public protestations were proving far too costly politically at a time of acute and successive crises.[91] In fact, he had warned Montazeri to carefully temper the tone and nature of his statements, since they would be under constant scrutiny by both the public and politicians the world over and therefore held

---

[87] Montazeri and Montazeri, *Enteqad az khod*, p. 75.   [88] Ibid., p. 76.
[89] Montazeri, *Khaterat*, p. 475.
[90] Khomeini, "Adam-e salahiyyat baraye tasadi-ye rahbari-ye nezam-e jomhuri-ye eslami'.
[91] This view has also been subsequently upheld by Rafsanjani, who says he also warned Montazeri against publicly airing all his criticisms of the government. Hashemi-Rafsanjani, 'Nagofteh-ha-ye Hashemi-Rafsanjani az 'azl-e Ayatollah Montazeri'.

major repercussions in their wake.[92] The heir-apparent could no longer be entrusted with the precious task of safeguarding the Islamic state's future. While Montazeri, even at the end of his life, sought to shield his erstwhile mentor from responsibility, claiming he was misled and manipulated by Seyyed Ahmad, Rayshahri, and Rafsanjani, it remains an unconvincing portrayal. Rayshahri was a relatively junior cleric of little standing independent of that bestowed upon him by the Guardian Jurist and his influential father-in-law, Ayatollah Meshkini. But it seems highly unlikely that he would act so boldly against the household of the second-highest-ranking cleric in the political hierarchy of the Islamic Republic without Khomeini's imprimatur.[93] Montazeri, however, insists that Khomeini was manipulated by Rayshahri, who, as minister of intelligence, had unparalleled access to the Guardian Jurist during this time, even bugging Montazeri's phone lines and highlighting every off-colour remark or criticism to discredit the latter in Khomeini's eyes.[94]

The growing differences between Khomeini and Montazeri came to a bitter end upon the latter's written objections to the mass execution of several thousand political prisoners which began on 19 July 1988 prior to Iran's acceptance of UNSC Resolution 598, the UN-brokered cease-fire ending the Iran–Iraq War.[95] Many of those who had been executed had already served out the majority of their sentences and were impri-soned when, in the same month, the People's Mojahedin made a calamitous military incursion into Iranian territory, believing it could topple the Islamic Republic.[96] On 26 March 1989 Khomeini penned a remarkable letter to Montazeri, conveying the depth of their estrangement, stating his successor was no longer fit to be the Islamic

---

[92] Montazeri, *Khaterat*, pp. 375–6.

[93] The record shows that it was exactly this which Rayshahri sought out on numerous occasions and was wary to act without it.

[94] Montazeri and Montazeri, *Enteqad az khod*, p. 90. This is also argued by 'Ezatollah Sahabi, but the extent to which his judgement is based on first-hand experience and information is questionable since he held no high political office at the time. 'Ezatollah Sahabi, *Nim-e qarn-e khatereh va tajrobeh: khaterat-e mohandes 'Ezatollah Sahabi; sal-ha-ye 1357 ta 1379* (Paris: Khavaran, 2013), p. 193.

[95] *Nim-e qarn-e khatereh va tajrobeh*, pp. 192–3. For a remarkable memoir by someone incarcerated during the period of mass prison executions, see Shahla Talebi, *Ghosts of Revolution: Rekindled Memories of Imprisonment in Iran*, Kindle ed. (Stanford, CA: Stanford University Press, 2011).

[96] For details by a participant in the operation, see Masoud Banisadr, *Masoud: Memoirs of an Iranian Rebel* (London: Saqi, 2004), chapter 27.

Republic's Guardian Jurist. Because of its important contents it is worth quoting at length:

It is with a bloody and broken heart that I write these few words to you ... You wrote in your recent letter that you believe my view takes religious precedence over yours. I consider God and will mention some concerns. From where it is clear that after me, you will hand over this country and the Islamic Revolution of the dear Muslim people of Iran to the liberals and from there to the Hypocrites [i.e. People's Mojahedin], you have lost the competency and legitimacy to be future leader of the system (*nezam*). You have shown in most of your letters, statements, and positions that you believe the liberals and Hypocrites must rule over the country. Your comments were dictated to such an extent by the Hypocrites that I saw no point in replying to them ...

The issue of the murderer, Mehdi Hashemi, where you thought he was more pious than all the pious, even though it had been proven to you he was a murderer and regularly sent messages that he not be killed ... Because you are simple-minded (*sadeh-lowh*) and easily provoked, do not interfere in any political matter ...

I was against your election [to the post of Guardian Jurist] from the outset, but at that time I thought you were naïve, someone who was neither a manager, nor prudent, but I believed you an educated person, who was advantageous for the seminaries. If you continued this kind of work, my duty would have certainly differed, and you know I do not shirk my duty ... I swear before God that I disagreed with the premiership of Bazargan, but I thought he was a good person, and I swear before God, I did not vote for the presidency of Bani-Sadr, and in all instances assented to the views of friends ... I have made a pact with my God ... If the whole world rises against me, I will not abandon God (*haqq*) and truth (*haqqiqat*).

I am not concerned with history and what happened. I must only perform my religious duty.[97]

The severity of Khomeini's reply was such that Rafsanjani has since claimed he pleaded with him to tone it down, fearing that such a letter could result in Montazeri's murder by vigilantes. Khomeini, however, retorted, 'If I don't do this, the sedition (*fitneh*) will not be put to bed.'[98] It is crucial to note that many clerics on the Islamic left and members of the MRM, such as Mehdi Karrubi and Hamid Rowhani-Ziyarati, not

---

[97] Khomeini, "Adam-e salahiyyat baraye tasadi-ye rahbari-ye nezam-e jomhuri-ye eslami'.

[98] Hashemi-Rafsanjani, 'Nagofteh-ha-ye Hashemi-Rafsanjani az 'azl-e Ayatollah Montazeri'.

only supported Khomeini's decision and the sidelining of Montazeri but aggressively castigated the deposed Ayatollah following his ousting.[99] The left faction of the SMEE was also not very well-disposed towards Montazeri's economic views because he was thought to favour the bazaar.[100] Many politicians on the Islamic left, Karrubi perhaps being the most notable example, only began to re-evaluate their past actions and attitudes towards Montazeri, when it appeared there was little they could do to stave off their own political marginalisation at the hands of traditional conservative forces, which strongly supported the theocratic basis of the Leader's unchecked political authority.

The transition to 'reformism' on the part of the Islamic left can to a considerable extent be framed in terms of the lived experience of political marginalisation. As their position and location progressively shifted from within the heart of the state apparatus to the outskirts of power, they enjoyed what I have referred to above as a parallax view, namely a different and experientially informed perspective on the same Islamic state which they had once been instrumental in establishing. In this vein, 'Emad al-Din Baqi, a former religious seminarian and student of Montazeri, who went on to become one of the most outspoken journalists of the reformist era, contended,

> While most of the revolutionary forces were within the power structure they looked at the issue [of reform] from the inside and were more inclined to the second method i.e. the preservation of purity and a limited circle of aides and their retinue. But when for whatever reason because of their diminished power they came out or were driven out of the power structure their interpretations and views were subject to change.[101]

Hashem Aqajari, a prominent religious intellectual of the Islamic left and a long-standing member of the SMEE and later the reconstituted SMEEI, has made the same point more recently elsewhere: 'the farther

---

[99] See Mehdi Karrubi, Hamid Rowhani, and Mehdi Imam-Jamarani, 'Nameh-ye aqayan-e Karrubi, Jamarani va Rowhani beh mo 'azam lah', in *Khaterat-e faqih va marja '-e 'aliqadr hazrat Ayatollah Hosayn-'Ali Montazeri* [1379 (2000)] (www.amontazeri.com, 29 Bahman 1367 [18 February 1989]), p. 1257, published as an appendix in Montazeri, *Khaterat*.

[100] Aqajari, Khojasteh-Rahimi, and Bala'i, 'Sharh-e zendegi-ye yek enqelabi-ye naaram', p. 42.

[101] 'Emad al-Din Baqi, 'Cheguneh nasl-e enqelabi, eslahtalab shod?', *Shahrvand-e emruz*, no. 36 (14/11/1386 [3 February 2008]), p. 63.

away the left faction became from ruling and was turned into a critical force and minority, to the same extent its democratic concerns increased. The Combatant Clerics (i.e. MRM) also had the same experience.'[102] Montazeri is perhaps one of the chief exceptions to this discernible pattern, since he essentially broke with Khomeini's politics, if not his person, on the cusp of unparalleled power. Moreover, unlike Khomeini who dismissed 'history' in favour of 'truth' – 'I am not concerned with history' – in a recently leaked voice recording dating from 15 August 1988 Montazeri denounced the officials responsible for the mass prison executions, which he called 'the biggest crime under the Islamic Republic', adding that 'history will condemn us for what you have done and they will write your name [those responsible for carrying out the executions] in the future as part of the criminals of history'.[103]

The Appointment of Seyyed 'Ali Khameneh'i as Guardian Jurist

Another development linked to the above and explicitly mentioned by *Kiyan*'s editor, Masha Allah Shams ol-va'ezin, was the review of the Islamic Republic's constitution, which Khomeini ordered prior to his death in April 1989 and which, as Mehdi Moslem concurs, restructured the state in favour of the rightist factions.[104] Shams ol-va'ezin interprets the revision of the constitution as the beginning of the second republic:

[T]he birth of the meaning of the absolute guardianship of the jurist in the constitution and the emergence of the notion of authoritarianism (*eqtedar-gara'i*) on the basis of the political philosophy of the caliphate in place of charismatic leadership and the transformation of the duality of executive power between the president and prime minister, to the duality amongst the president and leadership, are amongst the first signs of the second republic, and considered as the signs demarcating the direction of the future predicament (*vaz'iyyat*).[105]

At present, it is sufficient to acknowledge that the constitutional revisions approved on 28 July 1989, following Khomeini's death, increased

---

102 Aqajari, Khojasteh-Rahimi, and Bala'i, 'Sharh-e zendegi-ye yek enqelabi-ye naaram', p. 42.
103 The audio recording can be found here: 'Enteshar-e fayel-e sawti-ye Ayatollah Montazeri dar mored-e e'dam-ha-ye sal-e 1367', *BBC Persian* 10 August 2016.
104 Moslem, *Factional Politics in Post-Khomeini Iran*, p. 86.
105 Shams ol-va'ezin, 'Rowshanfekri-ye dini va jomhuri-ye sevvom', p. 88.

the scope of the Guardian Jurist's institutional and material powers[106] and streamlined the executive branch of government, as the premiership which had been hitherto occupied by Mir-Hosayn Musavi was phased out, leaving a consolidated presidency.[107] The person who took the office of Guardian Jurist, 'Ali Khameneh'i, is also of great significance given his uneasy relationship with several members of the Islamic left. Even though Khomeini's famous statement of the Absolute Guardianship of the Jurist and his prerogative to determine regime expediency was widely regarded to be in favour of the *chap* against the *rast*,[108] it was Khameneh'i who, in his capacity as the newly elected Leader of the Revolution, would actually benefit institutionally from the constitutional amendments which enshrined the principle. As was seen in Chapter 2, at the time of Khomeini's initial enunciation of the Absolute Guardianship of the Jurist, Khameneh'i found himself closer to the traditional right's conception, arguing that the Guardianship of the Jurist was bound by primary Islamic ordinances. Khameneh'i's initial reservations apropos Khomeini's statement of Absolute Guardianship would continue to haunt him and still find themselves used as a basis for polemics by partisan clerics of the Islamic left such as Hadi Ghaffari two decades later.[109]

Recently leaked footage of Khameneh'i's temporary appointment on 4 June 1989 by the Assembly of Experts as Leader, pending the approval of the revised constitution, following Khomeini's death seems to indicate that he was entirely cognisant that his not being a *marja'* or even considered a *mojtahed* among senior 'olama' within the Shi'i clerical establishment would pose a serious, if not altogether crippling, obstacle to the recognition and exercise of his authority. Khameneh'i's reluctance to assume the position of Leader appears to derive from the fact that he was painfully aware that he would lack not

---

[106] For an itemised list of the *vali-ye faqih*'s additional powers, see Akbar Hashemi-Rafsanjani and 'Ali Lahuti, *Karnameh va khaterat-e 1368: bazsazi va sazandegi* (Tehran: Daftar-e nashr-e ma'aref-e enqelab, 1391 [2012]), p. 603.

[107] Moslem, *Factional Politics in Post-Khomeini Iran*, p. 79. Mohsen Milani, 'The Transformation of the *Velayat-e Faqih* Institution: From Khomeini to Khamenei', *The Muslim World* LXXXII, no. 3–4 (1992).

[108] Nehzat-e azadi-ye Iran, 'Tafsil va tahlil-e velayat-e motlaqeh-ye faqih', (Farvardin 1367 [March–April 1988]), p. 14.

[109] 'Towhin-e dowbareh-ye Hadi Ghaffari beh nezam', *Shirazeh* 16 Azar 1393 [7 December 2014].

only the popular charisma but also the religious legitimacy of his predecessor. In fact, in the June session he frankly admits that under such conditions his Leadership would only be a 'formal Leadership (*rahbari-ye suri*), not a real Leadership'. In his words, the proposition of his assuming the Leadership suffered a 'technical problem' (*eshkal-e fani*) and a 'fundamental problem' (*eshkal-e asasi*), given that 'on a religious-jurisprudential (*shar'i*) view, the binding authority (*hoj-jiyyat*) of the Leader is such that the person who wishes to act on the basis of his word considers him a jurist (*faqih*) and authority (*sahebna-zar*) in religious affairs ... now in this very meeting several gentlemen have come and spoken and declared that I am not an authority (*saheb-nazar*)'. Rather than a 'guardianship of the jurist' (*velayat-e faqih*), his appointment would be a 'just guardianship of the faithful' (*velayat-e 'odul-e mo'menin*). In short, his right to rule was not predicated upon his status as a jurist but rather upon his piety and justice.[110] In the absence of the complete transcripts one must exercise caution in ana-lysing the transition between the two Leaders, but what is clear is that Khameneh'i's concerns about the implications of his lacklustre reli-gious credentials for his political authority as Leader were indeed warranted. Since his appointment he has received repeated challenges to his legitimacy in the capacity of Guardian Jurist, the position he would assume on a permanent basis in the aftermath of approval by referendum of the revised constitution. His leadership would be approved by the Assembly on a permanent basis on 6 August 1989 (15 Mordad 1368).

Again, while we do not possess the full transcripts, the issue seems to have been at least formally resolved, since the 'absolute guardianship to command' (Article 57) – albeit without the stipulation of *marja'iyyat* – was enshrined in the revised constitution and Khameneh'i by August had been officially endowed with the highest office in the land. Also, it should not be forgotten that Article 109 stipulates that the Leader should still possess 'the necessary scholarly competency to issue legal rulings (*efta'*) in the different areas of Islamic jurisprudence'. Traditionalists, clerical members of the Islamic left and the one-time heir-designate Ayatollah Montazeri would reiterate time and again that they did not accept the legitimacy of the incumbent Leader's religious

[110] Mohsen Kadivar, 'Sanadi bar tadlis-e maqam-e rahbari va majles-e khebregan', Kadivar.com (19 Dey 1396 [9 January 2018]).

credentials – and by implication his leadership – and therefore would not blindly follow his rulings without question or challenge. Needless to say, Rafsanjani in his role as deputy-chair of the Assembly was masterful and decisive in convincing his fellow clerics of Khameneh'i's bona fides as he chaired the fateful session, not only quoting three instances where Khomeini had reportedly endorsed Khameneh'i as his potential successor but advocating on behalf of his religious credentials, adding that, even if there were shortcomings in Khameneh'i's knowledge of jurisprudence, more senior clerical colleagues could provide appropriate support whenever necessary.[111] In short, the perceived lack of religious credentials on the part of the new Leader arguably deepened pre-existing factional differences and gave further impetus to the Islamic left's political marginalisation.

Shams ol-va'ezin's description of the historic transition and the analogy he drew between the transition from charismatic leadership (i.e., the Prophet and his household/Khomeini) to a staid caliphate (i.e., Umayyad Dynasty/Khameneh'i), so abhorred in traditional Shi'i literature, cannot but grab one's attention and highlight the deep animosity and trepidation with which the new political settlement had been greeted by many in the Islamic left and their allies.

Economic without Political Development

With the end of the war and the election of Akbar Hashemi-Rafsanjani as president of the Islamic Republic, the Islamic left found itself increasingly excluded from the key decision-making institutions of the state. Furthermore, while Rafsanjani's administration had emphasised economic development and attempted to rebuild Iran's relations with some regional and Western states, there were few opportunities for the Islamic left to resume the prominence it had enjoyed in the revolution's first decade. It is under these conditions that the newspaper *Salam*, headed by Musavi-Kho'iniha, became the chief outlet for the Islamic left, along with the monthly *Bayan* overseen by Mohtashamipur,[112] both high-profile clerics in the MRM.

---

[111] Footage of Assembly of Experts 4 June 1989 session, *Youtube*, https://youtu.be /Ey-gydrOj0E.

[112] Mohammad Quchani, *Pedarkhandeh va chap-ha-ye javan: mobarezeh baraye naqd-e qodrat Dey 78 ta Khordad 79* (Nashr-e ney, 1379 [2000]), p. 52.

Crucially, between 1990 and 1994 Kho'iniha and numerous other figures on the Islamic left were active at the Presidential Strategic Research Centre (PSRC),[113] which had several subdivisions but increasingly began to think through and theorise the notion of 'political development' (*towse'eh-ye siyasi*), carefully sifting through and analysing the academic literature on the subject.[114] Kho'iniha was also briefly managing director of the PSRC's periodical *Rahbord*[115] (spring 1992) with important articles by Hajjariyan and Mohsen Kadivar appearing in the pages of the first four issues.[116] By the second issue Kho'iniha had been replaced by future president Hojjat al-Islam Hassan Rowhani; by the third one, Hashemi-Rafsanjani's vice-president for Legal and Parliamentary Affairs (1989–97), Seyyed 'Ataollah Mohajerani, had been named the journal's editor. The shift in the nature and tone of analysis on offer was palpable, and those questions grappling with basic issues of political and theological legitimacy were quietly placed on the back burner.[117]

Hajjariyan – whose writings were absolutely crucial to the theorisation of reformist strategy in the lead-up to, as well as during the tenure of, the first Khatami administration, and who will be interrogated in greater detail in Chapter 7 – was the head of the political section of the Centre during Kho'iniha's tenure and began work there in 1989 (1368).[118] In later years, while working at the PSRC during the mornings, Hajjariyan would, on an almost daily basis, frequent the offices of

---

113   For a critical account, see Jahandar Amiri, *Eslahtalaban-e tajdidnazar-talab va pedarkhandeh-ha* (Tehran: Markaz-e asnad-e enqelab-e eslami, Bahar 1386 [Spring 2007]), p. 141–50. For a more sympathetic account by one of the members of the unit in question, see the interview with 'Ali-Reza 'Alavi-Tabar: Alavi-Tabar and Mirsepassi, 'Alireza Alavi-Tabar and Political Change', p. 132.

114   Sa'id Hajjariyan, 'Tallaqi-ye akademik az towse'eh-ye siyasi', *Rahbord*, no. 1 (Bahar 1371 [Spring 1992]). 'Abbas 'Abdi, 'Jame'eh shenasi-ye tahqqiqat-e ejtema'i dar Iran', ibid.

115   Musavi-Kho'iniha's name appears as *modir-e mas'ul* in the first issue of the journal.

116   Mohsen Kadivar, 'Nazariyyeh-ha-ye dowlat dar feqh-e Shi'eh (1)', *Rahbord*, no. 4 (Paiz 1994 [Autumn 1994]). This essay later comprised part of Kadivar's influential text on theories of government in Shi'i jurisprudence, *Nazariyyeh-ha -ye dowlat dar feqh-e Shi'eh*.

117   See for instance, Sa'id Hajjariyan, 'Negahi beh mas'aleh-ye mashru'iyyat', *Rahbord*, no. 3 (Bahar 1373 [Spring 1994]).

118   Hajjariyan and Baqi, 'Goftogu ba Sa'id Hajjariyan', p. 27; 'Mo'arefi-ye markaz-e tahqqiqat-e esteratezhik', *Rahbord*, no. 3 (Bahar 1373 [Spring 1994]), p. 73.

both *Salam* and *'Asr-e ma*.[119] The centre also funded several of its number, such as Mohsen Mirdamadi, to obtain graduate degrees abroad in the social sciences, some of whom would later become leading members of the Islamic Iran Participation Front in the aftermath of Khatami's presidential victory. While abroad, these men developed their burgeoning ideas and encountered other new critical methods for engaging both the religious and political realities they felt confronted the country and its political system.[120]

Another noteworthy point was that while members of the Islamic left along with their religious intellectual colleagues held the leading positions at the centre, the work of more secular-minded academics was drawn upon, and some were invited to present their research. Hossein Bashiriyeh, who was a political science professor at the University of Tehran, and author of one of the first major books on the Iranian revolution,[121] is perhaps the best known of these scholars. But several other Iranian academics, some of whom were based in Europe or the United States, were also key influences. These included Mohammad-'Ali Homayun Katouzian, Dariyush Ashuri, 'Ezatollah Fuladvand, Dariyush Shayegan, Seyyed Javad Tabataba'i, Sa'id-Amir Arjomand, and Baqer Parham.[122] For example, Fuladvand's 1985 translation of Popper's *The Open Society and Its Enemies* made a major splash in the intellectual life of the Islamic Republic. The dialectic between these various groups and intellectuals and their respective ideas was very intricate, and later chapters will make some effort towards elaborating upon the 'anxiety of influence' which traverses the writings of the Islamic left and *rowshanfekran-e dini*.

Khatami's Resignation and Dashed Hopes for 'Cultural Prosperity'

First headed by Khatami, who had recently returned from Hamburg, the Kayhan Institute provided an opportunity for debate within the

[119] Hajjariyan and Khojasteh-Rahimi, 'Eslahatchi, cheriki nemishavad', p. 45.
[120] 'Alavi-Nik, *8 sal-e bohran afarini-ye eslahtalaban*, p. 189.
[121] Bashiriyeh, *The State and Revolution in Iran, 1962–1982*.
[122] Sa'id Hajjariyan and Hosayn Salimi, 'Suteh delan gerd-e ham amadand: goftogu ba Sa'id Hajjariyan', in *Kalbodshekafi-ye zehniyyat-e eslahgarayan*, ed. Hosayn Salimi (Tehran: Gam-e now, 1384 [2005]), p. 59. Amiri, *Eslahtalaban-e tajdidnazar-talab va pedarkhandeh-ha*, p. 142.

parameters and tacit red lines set down by regime authorities.[123] This
was especially visible in the case of the journal *Kayhan-e farhangi*,
which published the articles of numerous religious intellectuals, including 'Abdolkarim Sorush and Mohammad Mojtahed-Shabestari.[124]
Khatami's initial appointment in November 1980 was on the order of
Khomeini, and Khatami had also been a long-standing friend of
Khomeini's son, Seyyed Ahmad, who similarly endorsed the appointment and Khatami in glowing terms.[125] In the early 1970s Khatami and
Ahmad had both been politically active in Qom as members of a group
called the Society of Combatant Clergy In the Country (*Jame 'eh-ye
rowhaniyyat-e mobarez dakhel-e keshvar*). During these years,
Khatami even wrote a preface for a Xeroxed copy of Jalal Al-e
Ahmad's *Dar khedmat va khiyanat-e rowshanfekran* (On the Service
and Betrayal of the Intellectuals), which was then distributed throughout Qom. It was of course in this posthumously published work that
Al-e Ahmad elaborated upon and elevated the oppositional role of the
clergy in modern Iranian history, claiming they could play a role akin to
Gramsci's 'organic intellectuals' in the struggle against the Shah's
regime and American imperialism, even citing Ayatollah Khomeini
specifically as just such an example.[126] Al-e Ahmad's book even
included an excerpt by none other than Gramsci himself on the formation of intellectuals, which had been translated from French by the

---

[123] According to Hossein Shahidi, the press law became 'the basis for the banning
of most of the 175 publications that were closed down in the first three years of
the Islamic Republic'. Hossein Shahidi, *Journalism in Iran: From Mission to
Profession* (Abingdon & New York: Routledge, 2007), p. 43.

[124] Khatami was appointed as head of *Kayhan* newspaper on the order of
Ayatollah Khomeini on 16 November 1980 (25 Aban 1359) and was approved
by the Majles as Mir-Hosayn Musavi's minister of culture and Islamic guidance
on 9 November 1982 (18 Aban 1361). He was then approved by the Majles
once again in the same post on 25 October 1985 (6 Aban 1364).
On 29 August 1989 (7 Shahrivar 1368) Akbar Hashemi-Rafsanjani presented
Khatami once again as minister of culture, a position which he held
until August–September 1992 (Shahrivar 1371). 'Ali Mohammadpur,
*Dovvom-e Khordad, hamaseh beh yad mandani: farayand-e entekhabat-e
dowreh-ye haftom-e riyasat-e jomhuri az negah-e matbu 'at* (Tehran: Resanesh,
1379 [2000]), p. 315.

[125] See Khomeini's order for Khatami's appointment to the Kayhan Institute and
Ahmad Khomeini's comments praising Khatami in an interview with *Kayhan*
following the appointment on 23 November 1980, ibid., p. 316.

[126] Al-e Ahmad also reproduced Khomeini's well-known speech of 27 October
1964. Jalal Al-e Ahmad, *Dar khedmat va khiyanat-e rowshanfekran* (Tehran:
Majid, 1388 [2009]), pp. 225, 253–60.

socialist intellectual Manuchehr Hezarkhani.[127] Khatami's father, Ayatollah Ruhollah Khatami, was also a respected clergyman on good terms with Khomeini and was appointed by the latter as prayer leader of Yazd in the summer of 1982.[128]

With Khatami's appointment as minister of culture and Islamic guidance in November 1982, Hassan Shahcheraghi took over the Kayhan Institute and initially nurtured *Kayhan-e farhangi* as an 'intellectual and religious centre',[129] the first issue of which was published in the spring of 1984 (Farvardin 1363). Shahcheraghi, who had previously been elected to both the First and Second Majles and had attended the Haqqani School, was killed in the Iran–Iraq War a year later (Esfand 1364). Mostafa Rokhsefat, who would also go on to play an important role in the founding of *Kiyan*, was instrumental to *Kayhan-e farhangi*'s conception, publication, and editorship at the Kayhan Institute along with Hassan Montazer-Qa'em, another early member of the SMEE,[130] and Kamal Hajj Seyyed Javadi.[131] It was in these years that the nucleus of the Kiyan circle, particularly those centrally responsible for its publication, would be formed.

The pressure that was brought to bear on this journal at the end of the 1980s as a result of the inclusion of a number of controversial articles by Sorush – particularly his famous series of articles which were later published in book form under the title of *Qabz va bast-e te'orik-e shari'at* (The Expansion and Contraction of the Theory of the *Shari'ah*)[132] – eventually led to the temporary closure of the journal in 1990 (Khordad 1369) on the orders of Khatami's successor and newly appointed Guardian Jurist Ayatollah Khameneh'i's representative at the Kayhan Institute, Hojjat al-Islam Mohammad Asghari.[133] According to one of the younger participants in the Kiyan circle, Khatami had conveyed to them that Khameneh'i even went so far as

---

[127] Ibid., pp. 82–106.   [128] Mohammadpur, *Dovvom-e Khordad*, p. 312.
[129] Shams ol-va'ezin, 'Gozashteh, hal, ayandeh', p. 11. Amiri, *Eslahtalaban-e tajdidnazar-talab va pedarkhandeh-ha*, p. 142.
[130] Aqajari, Khojasteh-Rahimi, and Bala'i, 'Sharh-e zendegi-ye yek enqelabi-ye naaram', p. 40.
[131] See ' Tali'eh; kalameh-ye avval', *Kayhan-e farhangi* 1, no. 1 (1363 [1984]); Personal correspondence, Arash Naraqi and Eskandar Sadeghi-Boroujerdi, 11 April 2013.
[132] *Kayhan-e farhangi* was at that time under the general management of Mostafa Rokhsefat.
[133] Shams ol-va'ezin, 'Gozashteh, hal, ayandeh', p. 13.

to call an emergency session of the Council for Cultural Revolution in the aftermath of the publication of Sorush's *Qabz va bast*, 'critiquing it for half an hour' because of the danger it supposedly presented.[134]

Khatami's resignation as minister of culture was also a key event in the development of the Islamic left's intellectual evolution, as one of the last prominent personages of the Islamic *chap* with a ministerial portfolio in the executive to be felled. Khatami's exit from office and a broader evacuation of many on the Islamic left from positions of authority in the state apparatus were to have serious repercussions in the coming years. Tajzadeh, for instance, who was deputy for International Affairs at the Ministry of Culture under Khatami at the time, and his comments several years later while political deputy in the Ministry of the Interior under then-President Khatami are worthy of quotation on this score:

After one or two years I did not have any other choice but to study, because with the change of government many of the managers were dismissed. It's interesting that at one time in the Faculty of Law at the University of Tehran we had come together in one faculty along with Messrs Hajjariyan, [Mohsen] Aminzadeh, [Ebrahim] Asgharzadeh, Khosrow Tehrani, Nasiri, Monfared etc. This was surprising for many. They asked what's going on and whether there is a plan underway? On the other hand, the majority of the individuals were doing research alongside Behzad Nabavi, 'Abbas 'Abdi, Armin, Aqajari, and a number of other friends in the Centre for Strategic Research. This Centre did research about the revolution and social and political subjects. At the national level we had political and party activities. The principle centre for the assembly of most of the above friends was the publication *'Asr-e ma*; it was there that individuals such as Messrs Khaniki and Mazru'i gathered together and continued until the presidential election [of Mr. Khatami].[135]

Khatami's resignation was part and parcel of a wider exodus of veteran partisans on the Islamic left, many of whom held positions in state ministries during the 1980s. Many found a new home in institutional and quasi-institutionalised centres revolving around think tanks and publications. This was in certain respects Rafsanjani's attempt at

---

[134] Arash Naraqi and Eskandar Sadeghi-Boroujerdi, 'Interview with Arash Naraqi' (17 March 2013).

[135] Mostafa Tajzadeh, 'Goftogu-ye sarih ba Mostafa Tajzadeh, mo'aven-e vazir-e siyasi-ye keshvar: bozorg-tarin eteham-e ma in ast', *Payam-e emruz*, no. 41, p. 43.

recompense and alleviating factional tensions, after having had an instrumental role in the members of the Islamic left finding themselves either disqualified from running in elections or enduring severe pressure and political isolation – in short, a way of keeping them pre-occupied, in lieu of publicly venting anger at their lot in the post-Khomeini era. Ironically, it was these very circumstances which prepared the ground for their intellectual and political reflection and subsequent theorisation of notions of 'political development' and 'religious democracy', so crucial to both the reformist and religious intellectualist discourses defining the Khatami years.

Returning to Khatami's resignation, some further elaboration is warranted. In his letter of resignation Khatami explicitly spells out his view and belief that Khomeini was an intellectual pathbreaker who insisted Islam keep pace with contemporary exigencies and not fall prey to 'superstition' (*khorafeh*) and 'ignorance' (*jahl*). What is also of note is that even at this early stage Khatami refers to the importance of 'the rule of law' (*hakemiyyat-e qanun*), a term which would act as an ideological linchpin in his presidential campaign several years later.[136] Apart from such principled stances, it appears there were also other motives at work and reasons for the culture minister's resignation. In the letter Khatami tells then-President Rafsanjani that he had sought to resign prior to the Fourth Majles elections being held, in which, as has been mentioned, a raft of the Islamic left's sitting MPs were disqualified from running.[137] The resignation letter is worth quoting at length since it aptly depicts Khatami's world view and the endeavour to reconcile the revolutionary Islamist discourse of Khomeini with a notion of 'cultural prosperity' (*rownaq-e farhangi*),[138] which is a forerunner to many of his later ideas.

It was the epochal openings (*rah gosha'i-ha-ye dowran-saz*) of Imam [Khomeini] which brought with exuberance and hope the just, lettered and

---

[136] Mohsen Kadivar, 'Zekr-e mosibat-e Ayatollah Azari-Qomi', *Rah-e Sabz: JARAS* 27 Esfand 1391 [17 March 2013], p. 3.

[137] Ibid., p. 3.

[138] It is worth noting that *Kiyan* editor Shams ol-va'ezin argued for 'cultural development' in the second issue of the periodical in the fall of 1991. Masha Allah Shams ol-va'ezin, 'Towse'eh-ye farhangi [*Kiyan*, no. 2, Azar 1370 (November–December 1991)],' in *Yaddasht-ha-ye sardabir* (Tehran: Jame'eh-ye Iraniyan, 1379 [2000]), p. 24.

artistic disciples, and especially the educated believers into the arena of struggle and cultural jihad. And it was such, that in all circumstances after the revolution, and even during the imposed war, the cultural face of our revolutionary society directed toward the future, was eminent and radiant, whether inside or outside [the country].

... The creation of stability for thought and the struggle for the rule of law (*hakemiyyat-e qanun*) and building the grounds for the growth of pious and effective forces in this area was not easy, but with God's kindness this auspicious occurrence was realised up to an acceptable point, so that the disciples of thought and culture and art can act within the framework, criteria and law, with a sense of security, which is a condition of creativity. I was and am sure about preparing the ground for a healthy cultural flourishing, the increase of the intellectual capabilities of society and the creation of immunity for a generation which is in the midst of the storms of monstrous atheism, deviance, petrification, and corruption from every direction. It is natural that abetting cultural prosperity has prerequisites and consequences that only the superficial and impatient do not tolerate, even at the price of the suspension of thought and the negation of religiously legitimate (*mashru'*) and legal freedoms. This will produce dreadful and devastating results.

... [I]f in this bedlam (*ashofteh bazar*) the accepted foundations of the regime, such as the views and fatwas of his holiness the Imam, both implicitly and explicitly, are confronted and opposed, even though this rejection and casting of doubt begins with some of the policies relating to art (*siyasat-ha-ye honari*), the basis of that view and firm and specified position is the Imam's [own]. We can be sure that in such an event we will witness the beginning of a dangerous process, the waves of which will shake most of the principles and other foundations. I have said that disagreement with the views of the Imam (whether from well-meaning or malign intentions) on music begins, but will not end there, and let not God bring such a day ...

... On the cusp of the Fourth Majles elections I asked of his Excellency [i.e., President Rafsanjani] on the pretext of the Majles [election] that you accept my resignation. But this demand was not accepted by his Excellency, and despite the expression of kindness and support for this ministry, you emphasised the necessity of endurance and continuing along [the aforementioned] path. Though I did not have much hope for a change in the conditions and circumstances, that would be favourable to thought and culture, I maintained my deference to your view ... I prefer without the distress of executive responsibility, [to work] in freedom and with suitable control, in defence of Islam and the expediency of the system [*maslahat-e nezam*], in the way I recognise and believe, and also confront the rigidity (*jomud*) and petrification (*tahajor*) and reaction (*vapas-gara'i*), which I deem as the biggest scourge of a religious government and regime which has attained power.[139]

Needless to say, the resignation was viewed by *Kiyan* and others with some degree of regret and trepidation, as Khatami was quickly replaced by a conservative layman from an established clerical family in 'Ali Larijani.[140] In his resignation letter Khatami offers an interpretation of Khomeini and his jurisprudential legacy, which takes its point of departure from the latter's well-known rulings pertaining to music and film. At the time, Khomeini's statements, in virtue of his exalted political stature and religious status as a *marja'*, entailed their reception as fatwas, legal opinions that were deemed relatively progressive within the scope of extant clerical views. Khatami's references to 'reaction' and 'petrification' were themselves used on occasion by Khomeini in his periodic invectives against the traditionalist-conservative clergy. It also related to Khomeini's well-known insistence on a dynamic conception of Islamic jurisprudence (*feqh-e puya*), which stressed the need of jurisprudence to take into account the exigencies of time and place (*zaman va makan*).[141] At his farewell ceremony on 26 July 1992 (3 Mordad 1371) Khatami reiterated that 'our revolution is a cultural revolution and a religious one'.[142]

In a letter to Hojjat al-Islam Mohammad-'Ali Ansari on 1 November 1988, less than a year before his death, a letter which is better known as the *Manshur-e baradari* (Proclamation of Fraternity), Khomeini made it clear in the starkest of terms that the burden of Islamic government had made it a duty incumbent on the clergy to voice their rulings on the pressing issues of the day. 'In Islamic government the gate of *ejtehad* must always be open.'[143] While certainly

[139] Kadivar, 'Zekr-e mosibat-e Ayatollah Azari-Qomi', p. 3.
[140] 'Vezarat-e ershad va taghirat-e tazeh', *Kiyan* 2, no. 8 (Mordad va Shahrivar 1371 [July–September 1992]), pp. 45–6.
[141] This is of course not novel amongst Islamic modernists and Salafis in the Arab world and South Asia, as Muhammad Qasim Zaman and others have demonstrated. Muhammad Qasim Zaman, *Modern Islamic Thought in a Radical Age: Religious Authority and Internal Criticism* (Cambridge & New York: Cambridge University Press, 2012), p. 28; Loc 654 of 13053. For the Freedom Movement's analysis of this jurisprudential development, see Nehzat-e azadi-ye Iran, 'Tafsil va tahlil-e velayat-e motlaqeh-ye faqih', p. 7.
[142] 'Vezarat-e ershad va taghirat-e tazeh', p. 46.
[143] Khomeini, 'Manshur-e baradari: maftuh budan-e bab-e ejtehad dar hokumat-e eslami', pp. 176–7.

sensitive to the popular mood, he also sought to mediate between the left and right wings of the ruling clergy, stating that differences of legal opinion should not provoke clergymen to conclude those who disagreed with them had 'acted contrary to truth and in violation of God's religion'.[144] It was only

if differences became substantive (*osuli*) and foundational, that they will cause frailty within the regime. The issue is clear that between the individuals and extant wings (*jenah-ha*) bound to the revolution, if there is disagreement, it is merely political. This is even if a doctrinal form is given to it, because all are united on principle (*osul*), and it is for this reason I confirm them. They are loyal to Islam, the Qur'an and the revolution and they are concerned for the country and the people. All of them have a plan and view for the growth of Islam and service to Muslims, which in their view will bring about salvation (*rastegari*) ... Both currents must not be negligent with respect to the deviousness of these two imperialist demons, and must know that America and the Soviet Union are thirsty for the blood of Islam and their independence ... You have so many common enemies that you must stand against them with all your power, though if you see someone breaching the fundamentals (*osul*), stand decisively against him.[145]

In this proclamation, Khomeini was solely addressing those members of the Shi'i clergy who had accepted the exigency of Islamic government during the Twelfth Imam's Occultation and his own political-religious leadership. He also acknowledges that the clerical factions under his authority are in large part bound together, whether they like it or not, by their many common enemies, surely a recipe for fractiousness once there ceases to be agreement on who their shared enemy happens to be. Khomeini's unwillingness to countenance laymen encroachments on what in his view was exclusively the province of the Shi'i clergy is well known[146] and need not be further elaborated here.

While it appears that Khomeini sought to criticise what he viewed as the *tahajor* of the traditionalist clergy – some of whom, much to his chagrin objected to his famous ruling which sought to justify the abrogation of the primary ordinances of the *shari'ah* in the name of the 'expediency of the system' (*maslahat-e nezam*) – it is unsurprising

---

[144] Ibid., p. 176.   [145] Ibid., p. 178–80.
[146] See *Sahifeh-ye Imam*, 21 vols., vol. 19 (Tehran: Mo'asseseh-ye tanzim va nashr-e asar-e Imam Khomeini, 1378 [1999]), pp. 302–3.

that the Islamic left sought to interpret such statements in their favour and as the revolutionary patriarch's confirmation of their own political views.[147] For example, in another statement on 22 February 1989, *Determining the Strategy of the Regime of the Islamic Republic of Iran: Mission for the Seminaries* or the *Charter for the Clergy* (*Ta'in-e esteratezhi-ye nezam-e jomhuri-ye eslami-ye Iran-resalat-e howzeh-ha-ye 'elmiyyeh-manshur-e rowhaniyyat*), Khomeini in his own inimitable and brusque fashion berated the 'petrified clergy' whom he denounced as 'snakes' and 'purveyors of American Islam'. He stated this while also contending that Salman Rushdie's controversial novel, *The Satanic Verses*, for which Khomeini infamously issued a religious order legitimating the British-Indian writer's execution, was penned 'to strike at the roots of religion and piety, the apex of which is Islam and the clergy. Certainly, if the world-devourers could they would have burned the roots and name of the clergy, but God is always the preserver and guardian of this sacred torch.'[148]

It is on issues such as the privileged, even 'sacred', role of the clergy where fissures, tensions, and theoretical aporias amongst the religious intellectuals and Islamic left would later surface. This was because many of their number, particularly those who had been especially active as members of the leftist faction within the IRP, MRM, and Imam's Line, sought out 'Khomeini' and his blessing, both while he was alive and posthumously. In life, but also in death, he became in many ways the final arbiter of the Islamic Republic's 'regime of truth'. Both his approbation and opprobrium were selected and engineered in a discursive universe of which he was at the centre, so that contestants for power might establish themselves as the rightful heirs to his legacy and the state he established. As can be seen above, Khatami endeavoured to ascribe dynamic and forward-looking cultural values to Khomeini and described accurately Khomeini's throwing down of the

---

[147] The SMEE similarly claims that Khomeini had a 'leftist tendency' and that it was Khomeini's protection which prevented the Islamic left's total exclusion from power. SMEEI, 'Negahi-ye kutah beh barkhi az tayf bandi-ha-ye jadid-e fekri-siyasi-ye jame'eh', pp. 9, 56.

[148] Khomeini, *Sahifeh-ye Imam*, 21, p. 278. Khomeini uses similar terms such as *motahajer* and *vapas-gara* when referring to the Pahlavi regime, which appears to indicate that his use of such terms was far from consistent and was generally invoked when he sought to impugn the credibility of his political and clerical opponents. See Khomeini's letter to Hamid Rowhani, one of the 'official' historians of the revolutionary clerical movement. Ibid., p. 240.

gauntlet to Shi'i traditionalism. As will be demonstrated in later chapters, Khatami and his allies would regularly strive to emphasise the
'popular' elements of Khomeini's politico-religious legacy. By the revolution's third decade a handful of religious intellectuals such as Kadivar
and Ganji,[149] though the style and substance of their criticisms often
differed, publicly extricated themselves from this bind, while others
within the fold of the Islamic left, such as Khatami, have continued
through to the present to wholeheartedly defend their understanding of
Khomeini's mantle.[150]

Intellectual Re-orientation on the Outskirts: Publications, Think Tanks, and Study Groups

To return to the issue of the relationship between the Islamic left and
the *rowshanfekran-e dini*, Sorush himself has spoken of his regular
meetings with Khatami since the latter took up the post of minister of
culture and Islamic guidance, and, as will be shown in Chapter 6, the
former's impact on Khatami's own discourse is palpable, despite the

---

[149] The dates of publication of Kadivar and Ganji's two books reflect two distinct
historical periods in both the Islamic Republic and post-revolutionary religious
intellectualism. Kadivar's *Hokumat-e vela'i* was published in the first years of
the Khatami administration and offered an avowedly Shi'i and jurisprudential
disputation of Khomeini's theory of *velayat-e faqih*, which tried its utmost to
show respect for Khomeini as a *marja' al-taqlid* while throughout the volume
using the honorific of Imam. He was nonetheless arrested and condemned to
jail by the Special Court for the Clergy, which had been formally re-established
to address the case of Hojjat al-Islam Mehdi Hashemi in June 1987. Kadivar,
Hokumat-e vela'i.

  Ganji's *Bud va nomud-e Khomeini: va'deh-ye behesht, barpa'i-ye duzakh*
(The Existence and Appearance of Khomeini: The Promise of Heaven and
Establishment of Hell), by contrast, was written in exile following Ahmadi-
Nezhad's 2009 re-election. It is a polemical text which depicts Khomeini as
a malign and power-hungry despot. It is notable because it breaks almost every
taboo to which the overwhelming majority of the Islamic *chap* and the religious
intellectuals in this study had publicly adhered. Its relevance to the religious
intellectual project is questionable given that by this time Ganji had ceased to
identify himself with the 'religious intellectual' label and had, in principle if not
in practice, claimed to adhere to a more standard creed of Western-style liberal
democracy and secular republicanism. Akbar Ganji, *Bud va nomud-e
Khomeini: va'deh-ye behesht, barpa'i-ye duzakh* (Berlin: Gardun velag, 2011).
[150] Mir-Hosayn Musavi, *Chenin goft Mir-Hosayn majmu'eh-ye sokhanrani-ha,
goftogu-ha, bayaniyyeh-ha, yaddasht-ha, etela'iyyeh-ha va payam-ha-ye Mir-
Hosayn Musavi* (Kanun-e Doktor 'Ali Shari'ati & Kalameh, Khordad 1391
[May–June 2012]), pp. 822–3.

numerous differences which continued to divide them intellectually.[151]
After leaving the Ministry of Culture and Islamic Guidance, Khatami
was appointed head of the National Library. While at the National
Library, Fayzollah 'Arabsorkhi, a central committee member of the
SMEEI, was Khatami's deputy. The two men had first become
acquainted at the prime minister's office in 1982, and it was in the
same year that 'Arabsorkhi was appointed chief of security (*modir-e
koll-e herasat*) for the Ministry of Culture, where he would continue to
act as a loyal subordinate and ally of the future president.[152] Over the
course of these years the future president would conduct research in the
history of Islamic and Western political thought[153] and hold regular
discussions in his office with several of Iran's most prominent intellectuals and academics, Sorush and Seyyed Javad Tabataba'i included.[154]

Amongst the most important events following Khatami's exit from the
Ministry of Culture was that three of the key members of *Kayhan-e
farhangi*'s editorial team, Masha Allah Shams ol-va'ezin, Reza Tehrani,
and Mostafa Rokhsefat, went on to found *Kiyan*, which became the
flagship journal of religious intellectualism in the 1990s.[155] Its first
issue was published in the autumn of 1991 and essentially came
out of the informal discussion sessions gathering together Hajjariyan,

---

[151] Mohammadpur, *Dovvom-e Khordad*, p. 329. Kamal Kharrazi, who would
become foreign minister in Khatami's cabinet, was also a longtime associate of
Sorush and would often attend his lectures at the University of Tehran. Naraqi
and Sadeghi-Boroujerdi, 'Interview with Arash Naraqi'.

[152] Hosayn Dehbashi and Fayzollah 'Arabsorkhi, 'Goftogu-ye Hosayn Dehbashi
ba Fayzollah 'Arabsorkhi', *Khesht-e kham*, no. 31 (15 Mehr 1396 [7 October
2017]).

[153] One of the products of these years of research and discussion was
Mohammad Khatami, *Ayin va andisheh dar dam-e khodkamegi: sayri dar
andisheh-ye siyasi-ye mosalmanan dar faraz va forud-e tamadon* (Tehran:
Tarh-e now, 1378 [1999]).

[154] Naraqi and Sadeghi-Boroujerdi, 'Interview with Arash Naraqi'. After 1989 (1368)
Fayzollah 'Arabsorkhi along with 'Ali Mazru'i, Mohsen Aminzadeh, Mohsen
Armin, Hadi Khaniki and Ahmad Setari began working in the newly established
unit within the Ministry of Culture and Islamic Guidance entitled the Office for
Media Affairs and Propagation (*mo'avenat-e omur-e matbu'at va tabliqati*) until
Khatami's resignation, at which point 'Arabsorkhi accompanied Khatami to the
National Library. 'Ali Mazru'i, 'Yaddasht-e 'Ali Mazru'i dar bareh-ye Fayzollah
'Arabsorkhi: "Fayzollah" dalili ast bar mahkumiyyat-e zendanban', *Ghatreh*.

[155] It should be added that Khatami did not by any means approve of all of *Kayhan-e
farhangi*'s content. Naraqi and Sadeghi-Boroujerdi, 'Interview with Arash
Naraqi'. Seyyed Mostafa Rokhsefat was *Kiyan*'s licence holder, Reza Tehrani the
editorial director, and Masha Allah Shams al-va'ezin the editor-in-chief.

'Alavi-Tabar, Armin, and Tajzadeh, among others.[156] Its name, according to Shams ol-va'ezin, was 'reminiscent of *Kayhan-e farhangi* and through this name, represented the first core of the religious intellectual movement'.[157] Reza Tehrani and Shams ol-va'ezin invited a number of individuals including Arash Naraqi, Akbar Ganji, Hosayn Qaziyan, and Mohammad-Javad Gholam-Reza Kashi to participate as part of an advisory council. The council would meet on a weekly basis and discuss the articles that had been submitted for publication and also issues believed worthy of discussion for future issues of the periodical.[158] Sorush, while always important, increasingly became the centre of these meetings, which broadened out to include other intellectuals and politicians, who would meet every Wednesday afternoon, with someone invited to speak on a chosen subject.[159] The meetings later became known as those of the 'Wednesday companions' (*ashab-e chaharshanbeh*).[160] The importance of Sorush and his intellectual contribution to the intellectual development of members of the Islamic left is undeniable. In the words of Tajzadeh, 'Dr. Sorush did not teach there [i.e., the Faculty of Law and Political Science at the University of Tehran], but we had other meetings outside which is famed as the Kiyan circle ... What is the relation between religion and the world? How can religion and democracy [be reconciled]? How can religion and modernity [be brought together]? In those meetings lots of issues were clarified for me and we utilised Dr. Sorush a lot.'[161]

In addition to Ganji and Sorush, other notable members and participants in the Kiyan circle included Reza Tehrani, Shams ol-va'ezin, Sa'id Hajjariyan, Mohsen Armin, Morteza Mardiha, Arash Naraqi, Ebrahim Soltani, Mohsen Sazgara, Mohammad-Javad Gholam-Reza Kashi, Hosayn Qaziyan, Naser Hadiyan, and Mostafa Tajzadeh.[162] Tajzadeh also regularly chaired the meetings.[163] Other notable individuals who

---

[156] Amin Bozorgiyan and Reza Tehrani, 'Interview with Reza Tehrani' (2006).
[157] Shams ol-va'ezin, 'Gozashteh, hal, ayandeh', p. 10. This was also confirmed by author's interview with a member of the Kiyan circle: Naraqi and Sadeghi-Boroujerdi, 'Interview with Arash Naraqi'.
[158] 'Interview with Arash Naraqi'.   [159] Ibid.   [160] Ibid.
[161] Mostafa Tajzadeh and Hosayn Salimi, 'Nezam ya'ni ma: goftogu ba Mostafa Tajzadeh', in *Kalbodshekafi-ye zehniyyat-e eslahgarayan* (Tehran: Gam-e now, 1384 [2005]), p. 115.
[162] Sorush and Khojasteh-Rahimi, 'Dovvom-e khordad beh ziyan-e Kiyan tamam shod'.
[163] Naraqi and Sadeghi-Boroujerdi, 'Interview with Arash Naraqi'.

worked with the Presidential Strategic Research Centre (PSRC) such as 'Ali-Reza 'Alavi-Tabar and Mohsen Kadivar also frequented the discussions. In addition, 'Arabsorkhi, the longstanding aide to Khatami, and Hamid-Reza Jala'ipur, a former IRGC commander and deputy governor of Iranian Kurdistan, who would become an important Khatami-era editor and journalist and central committee member of the Participation Front, would also occasionally participate. After the meetings had been firmly established, at the suggestion of Ganji and 'Abbas 'Abdi, the group decided to also meet for a monthly dinner at a hotel in Tehran which was serendipitously also named Kiyan.[164] In a move reminiscent, albeit distinct from Habermas' descriptions of the emergent bourgeois public sphere,[165] a salon was reserved in the hotel and a larger and more diverse circle of individuals would attend, albeit still encapsulating a privileged class of persons. These meetings included 'Emad al-Din Baqi, Mohsen Aminzadeh (deputy foreign minister under Khatami and founding member of the Participation Front), 'Arabsorkhi, Ahmad Borqani (reformist journalist, deputy minister for publications in the Ministry of Culture and Islamic Guidance and MP in the reformist-dominated Sixth Majles), and 'Isa Saharkhiz (director of Domestic Media in the Ministry of Culture, 1997–9), amongst others.[166] However, much like Habermas' own figuration of the bourgeois public sphere as critiqued by Nancy Fraser, its claims to genuine 'publicity' and inclusion were severely hampered beyond a limited range of overwhelmingly male political and intellectual allies and associates.[167]

One of *Kiyan*'s founding editors, Reza Tehrani, rejects the characterisation of the Kiyan circle as a well-oiled and meticulously conceived socio-political formation with an explicit mission to capture power. In his words, 'the reality is that we didn't have a circle (*halqeh*) in this sense. It was a number of friends who gathered together and aired their intellectual and social questions, held dialogue, and tried to find

[164] Ibid.
[165] Jürgen Habermas, *The Structural Transformation of the Public Sphere: An Inquiry into a Category of Bourgeois Society*, trans. Thomas Burger and Frederick Lawrence (Oxford: Polity, 1992), pp. 33, 65.
[166] Naraqi and Sadeghi-Boroujerdi, 'Interview with Arash Naraqi'.
[167] Nancy Fraser, 'Rethinking the Public Sphere: A Contribution to the Critique of Actually Existing Democracy', in *Justice Interruptus: Critical Reflections on the Postsocialist Condition* (London & New York: Routledge 1997), Loc 1632.

solutions.'[168] The issue, of course, with Tehrani's characterisation is that it almost entirely abstracts these men's intellectual gatherings and subsequent activities from the social and political context in which they thought and acted. As I have shown, the group which emerged as the Kiyan circle was hardly alone, and was complemented by several other formations where intellectual and political reflection and criticism could occur, the composition of the circle was very much situated within existing social and political networks criss-crossing government ministries, universities, teaching and research institutes, and political organisations but just as importantly personal friendships, alliances, and familial relationships. And while it might have begun as something of an intellectual exercise or avenue for these mutually sympathetic persons receptive to one another's views, possessing a shared understanding of the problems the Islamic Republic faced, their reflections – and their publication and circulation in the public sphere – could not but have had a bearing on the way the political elite came to think about the Islamic state. It was a degree of influence and social capital which more marginal groups, subalterns, and the dissenting intelligentsia could never hope to exercise.

Furthermore, beyond these elite circles, *Kiyan* as a periodical extended its influence and by its final years established a noteworthy readership amongst sections of the educated public. According to a survey undertaken by *Kiyan* in one of its final issues it was concluded that its readership stood at 100,000 strong, since on average five people would read each copy of its 20,000 circulation.[169] The licence to publish and prospect of mass circulation cannot be separated from the access, networks, and goodwill the periodical enjoyed from intellectually disposed elements of the Iranian political class. Similarly, the establishment of *Kiyan* cannot be completely extricated from the desire to exercise intellectual and political influence on a larger scale. In fact, in the very same interview where Tehrani disavows the Kiyan circle was strictly preconceived as a political project, a sentiment which is surely accurate, he admits, '[W]e understood the huge reaction elicited by Dr Sorush's articles in 1988 and 1989, the most important of which was *The Expansion and Contraction of the Theory of the Shari'ah.*

[168] Bozorgiyan and Tehrani, 'Interview with Reza Tehrani'.
[169] Sorush and Khojasteh-Rahimi, 'Dovvom-e khordad beh ziyan-e Kiyan tamam shod'.

We thought of the knots which could be opened with a journal and that it would be greatly welcomed. One of the subjects of discussion at the time was how we could increase its circulation.'[170] In short, it was felt *Kiyan* had the potential to evoke a considerable response amongst an educated readership in the mainstream of Iranian society but that it would also be necessary to ensure its widespread dissemination to reach as many people as possible and effectively impact socio-political and religious consciousness. Furthermore, according to Tehrani, though the impetus for the periodical's founding did not emanate directly from Sorush, his writings were one of the primary axes around which it revolved, and his approbation and close partici-pation in the endeavour was sought out from the very outset.[171]

The other key publication in which the intellectual and political re-orientation of the Islamic left unfolded was the newspaper *Salam*, whose editorial director was Musavi-Kho'iniha and editor-in-chief 'Abbas 'Abdi, both veterans of the hostage crisis. The 'red clergyman' (*rowhani-ye sorkh*), as his detractors often referred to him, having essentially found himself pushed out of the Centre for Strategic Research then under the auspices of the president's office, swiftly brought in other erstwhile members of the Student Followers of the Imam's Line such as Ebrahim Asgharzadeh and Mohsen Mirdamadi. It would come to be known with time, alongside *Bayan*, as one of the chief media platforms for the Association of Combatant Clerics. The newspaper published its first issue on 9 February 1991, at which point it continued to remain steadfast and faithful to its provenance in the Islamic left, unflinchingly denouncing the United States and 'American Islam' alongside reactionary and opulent capitalists the world over.[172] Following the Fourth Majles elections and in subse-quent years, however, it emerged as one of the decisive arenas for critical journalism bringing the government and state officials to account.

The most important exposés which drew the fury of powerful forces within the political class included stories relating to a huge embezzle-ment scandal involving Mohsen Rafiqdust's brother in the mid-1990s. Most controversially, it published on 6 July 1999 a confidential letter from Sa'id Emami, an advisor and one-time deputy of security to the

---

[170] Bozorgiyan and Tehrani, 'Interview with Reza Tehrani'.   [171] Ibid.
[172] Quchani, 'Salam; aqa-ye Kho'iniha', p. 110.

Ministry of Intelligence to Hojjat al-Islam Qorban-'Ali Dorri-Najafabadi, the incumbent minister of intelligence, demanding reform of the press law and a vice-like grip on the 'cultural order', including the establishment of occupational courts specifically for authors, directors, poets, and translators. Even more menacingly, it included the denunciation of the Iranian Writers' Association (_Kanun-e nevisandegan-e Iran_) and named intellectuals and writers, some of whom had lost their lives in a slew of killings for which Emami had been officially cast as the chief perpetrator.[173] The publication of this letter led to _Salam_'s shutdown by the most convoluted of means and sparked one of the decisive crises of the Khatami period. Because Musavi-Kho'iniha was a cleric, the Special Court for Clergy issued an order for the newspaper's closure.[174] The student protests which ensued led to a swift response by the security forces, and several were killed over the course of the following week. It also led to a letter from the Revolutionary Guards addressed to Khatami on 9 July 1999, where the Guards declared their 'patience has come to an end' and threatened to directly intervene if the government did not take immediate action to resolve the situation.

Another relevant institution was the Serat Institute and Press founded in 1988 (1367) by Ganji, Mohsen Sazgara, and Mohammad-Taqi Banki, who was minister of energy in Mir-Hosayn Musavi's second government. Mojtahed-Shabestari and Seyyed Mojtaba Shobayri, son of Grand Ayatollah Seyyed Musa Shobayri-Zanjani (b. 1928), were also members of the institute's governing council (_hay'at-e modireh_). It was initially established to publish and distribute the writings of Sorush and the weekly lectures he delivered at the Aqdasiyyeh mosque in east Tehran, which were also overseen by Ganji. The press would go on to publish the writings of several other prominent religious intellectuals such as Abolqasem Fana'i and Arash Naraqi and even secular intellectuals such as Dariyush Ashuri and Morad Farhadpur. Ganji left Serat in 1997 (1376) – after which Sorush's brother Javad Dabbagh took the reins – and began publishing a periodical entitled _Rah-e now_ (New Path) in the spring of 1998,

173 Babak Dad, _Akharin salam: nagofteh-ha-ye ta'tili-ye ruznameh-ye Salam dar goftogu'i sarih ba Musavi-Kho'iniha_ (Tehran: Sazman-e chap va entesharat-e vezarat-e farhang va ershad-e eslami, 1378 [1999]), p. 33. Hamid Kaviyani, _Dar jostoju-ye mahfel-e jenayatkaran: bazkhani-ye parvandeh-ye qatl-ha-ye siyasi_ (Tehran: Negah-e emruz, 1378 [1999]), p. 117.
174 Dad, _Akharin salam_, p. 57.

which for a short time emerged as another pre-eminent forum for the writings of individuals such as Hajjariyan, Kadivar, and 'Alavi-Tabar, among others.[175]

The Islamic left and several religious intellectuals who were not in their immediate circle gradually coalesced in the first half of the 1990s as a result of their common experiences of opposition to the Shah's regime prior to the revolution, their support of Ayatollah Khomeini and the Islamic Republic's founding,[176] and their later marginalisation by the right (*jenah-e rast*), both modern and traditional. It is their gradual congregation and varied informal alliances that would give rise to the elite-managed discourse of the 2nd of Khordad Front, which of course does not preclude the possibility that their discourse was itself both impacted and in part a response to popular pressures and restiveness from below. In the opening issue of *Kiyan* its editor, the veteran journalist Shams ol-va'ezin, declared in bold terms the journal's hegemonic mission, in the Gramscian sense of intellectual and moral leadership explicated in Chapter 1: 'Schools of thought (*maktab-ha*) must be victorious in the conscience of society (*vojdan-e jame'eh*), not in the minds of ruling cadres.'[177] In this way, these politicised intellectuals and philosophically minded political activists sought to theorise their past experiences of revolution and revolutionary Islamism and provide a diagnoses of 'what had gone awry', leading to the political crisis they now confronted. They also sought to engage new ideas in keeping with the times, while adopting and adapting contemporary methodological approaches in theology, jurisprudence, and political theory.

The SMEEI's journal, *'Asr-e ma*, from its first issue published on 19 October 1994 (27 Mehr 1373) under the editorship of Mohsen Armin, a leading member of the SMEEI and the Kiyan circle and general manager of media at the Ministry of Culture, sought to emphasise that

if we accept the principle of political participation and determination of [the nation's] destiny by the people, one of the most important pillars for building a free, mature and developed society, the activity of political organizations such as the media, will appear to be a natural, necessary, and useful matter . . . We hope our political society will reach such a political development and

[175] Amiri, *Eslahtalaban-e tajdidnazar-talab va pedarkhandeh-ha*, p. 142.
[176] Bozorgiyan and Tehrani, 'Interview with Reza Tehrani'.
[177] Shams ol-va'ezin, 'Gozashteh, hal, ayandeh', p. 14.

maturity that it will construe the diversity of views and political thinking and thus the presence and activities of political parties' activities and publications in the framework of the national interest, as a desirable, necessary and constructive reality.[178]

This discourse was initially hatched at the level of the political and intellectual elite and thereafter progressively simplified, popularised, and made to relate to the more immediate and mundane preoccupations of ordinary Iranians. As evident from Armin's article quoted above, the role of the media was thought to be of central importance to any such endeavour. Mohammad-Reza Khatami, President Khatami's brother, claims that 'we could organise 2–3 million around this idea [i.e., the 2nd Khordad project] ... in the form of an intellectual current (*jaryan-e fekri*)',[179] but there was a need for an 'elite force' (*niru-ye nokhbeh*), which could organise and mobilise a hitherto loose and unorganised ideological-political current of sympathisers towards the end of impacting the future trajectory of the Islamic state.[180]

Mohammad-Reza Khatami describes the gradual congregation of individuals, who would make up this much-needed 'elite force' and attempt to take on this challenge thus:

An opportunity for us was created in the first half of the 1990s. Our intellectual patronage concerned three fields. One was the field of thought imported in the form of translation. In addition to philosophical thought, sociological theories and the experiences of other countries which had traversed the stage of transition (*gozar*). The second field was domestic religious intellectuals. The most influential of those was the Kiyan circle. There were also other individuals who offered new thinking in the field of politics. The third field was the re-reading of national-Iranian thought which did not necessarily have a religious basis ... In 1996–1997 the coming together of these forces resulted in the victory of Mr. Khatami.[181]

Even while this might be something of an exaggeration, it nevertheless shows how they viewed their ideological and political project and its wider significance. As was already mentioned, the Ayin circle was another intellectual hub which contributed to the 2nd of Khordad discourse and was largely composed of those who shared

[178] "Asr-e ma chera?', *'Asr-e ma*, no. 1 (27 Mehr 1373), pp. 1–2.
[179] Khatami and Salimi, 'Tasavvor-e piruzi nemikardim: goftogu ba Mohammad-Reza Khatami', p. 44.
[180] Ibid., p. 43.   [181] Ibid., p. 42.

an intellectual affinity with Khatami. Its members included Hojjat al-Islam Mohammad-Taqi Fazel-Maybodi, Sa'id Hajjariyan, Hadi Khaniki, Mohammad Shari'ati, and [Mohammad-'Ali] Khalili-Ardakani. Mohammad-Reza Khatami describes how this important group of likeminded individuals took shape and some of the repercussions of their activities.

In 1996 (1375) because of my own work or our activities, in 1997 (1376) we started to have close ties with many individuals who in 1996 (1375) we didn't have direct relations. Each person worked in their own field. In 1997 a series of them, in the form of one group, which at that time got the name Ayin, and had regular weekly meetings. They had had experiences in different areas over the years and had had exchanges . . . The series of events and programmes brought these tendencies close together. Someone who worked in the field of religion and new discourses on religion worked with someone in the field of sociology, and new ideas in the world. In this way, they reached one another. I think that the phenomenon which appeared on the 2nd Khordad, was the conflict (*tazarob*) and outcome of the ideas of that group.[182]

Much like the Centre for Strategic Research, preceding the election of 1997, the Ayin circle became an important site of inter-disciplinary collaboration. Several years later, when the actual journal, *Ayin*, began to publish on a regular basis, Mohammad-Reza Khatami would spell out its commitment to the project of 'reform' and its theoretical articulation. The journal sought to be 'a centre for dialogue, critique and innovation, and to deepen the scope of thinking and views through reliance upon the lineage (*tabar*) and ability of all Muslim intellectuals and reformist thinkers (*mottafakeran-e eslahtalab*)'. Furthermore, '*Ayin* sees itself as descending from the legacy of Muslim reformist intellectuals, who always struggled from the movement to revive (*ehya*) religious thought and the Constitutional Movement, till the Islamic Revolution and the Reformist Movement.'[183] At the time of writing this, the individuals involved had tasted electoral success and had several years to formulate an intellectual ambition and lineage for the movement they led. But they were also nearing the end of their tenure where the constitutional and institutional map of the Islamic Republic had only experienced negligible change.

[182] Ibid., pp. 42–3.
[183] Mohammad-Reza Khatami, 'Ayin-e ayiniyan', *Ayin* (Ordibehesht 1385 [April–May 2006]), pp. 2–3.

In the mid-1990s, there was little expectation that their patron would soon become the Islamic Republic's new president – or the chance they would soon be afforded. Instead they had set down the parameters of a long-term group-think through which they could both satisfy their own intellectual curiosity and examine the pressing issues of the day. It provided another safe space by means of which Iranian politicians, social scientists, and theologians could come together and analyse many of the chief problems challenging the Islamic Republic and Iranian society more generally. It was out of a palpable sense of crisis and political lethargy on the margins of state power that a novel counter-hegemonic vision would emerge amongst elements of Iran's political class, a vision and struggle whose fortunes few, if any, of its participants could have foreseen.

Conclusion

Drawing upon the interpretative framework presented in Chapter 1, this chapter has delineated the historical genealogies of the politico-ideological alliances of the Islamic left and the religious intelligentsia in post-revolutionary Iran. Factional rivalry and the contest for power and control over the Iranian state's institutions had real consequences for the Islamic left and its attitudes towards political power. Their ouster and forced retirement from the prominent institutional positions many of them had occupied in the course of the 1980s gave them a new-found appreciation for the problems of unchecked power but also the limita-tions of giving the state free reign to pursue and enact large-scale social transformation with insufficient thought to the consequences. A growing measure of scepticism towards the perceived instrumentalisation of religion and religious rhetoric for political ends and the concentration of power in a few hands was underscored by the fact that the two most powerful offices in the land, that of the Guardian Jurist and the pre-sidency, now resided with the politically able, centre-right (albeit reli-giously undistinguished) Hojjat al-Islams, Khameneh'i and Rafsanjani. Even if one ought to be cautious about overstating factional rifts that would only deepen and sour as years passed by, the seeds of future contests were clearly visible at this time and essential to grasping how and why the 'reformists' emerged within the political class.

In the course of this chapter I have further sought to illustrate how this phenomenon was embedded in a broader network of socio-political and personal relationships and institutions, which shaped its orientation and priorities in several crucial respects. The chapter traced a historically dynamic and emergent network of nodal points occupied by members of the political and intellectual elite, which gave rise to the congregation of like-minded and mutually sympathetic individuals, and the profound confluence of the discourses of religious intellectualism and 'political development' that would form the bedrock of elite-managed reform in the late 1990s. The nodes of this network included *Kayhan-e farhangi* and its editorial team, the SMEEI and its publishing arm *'Asr-e ma*, the Ministry of Culture under Khatami, the Presidential Strategic Research Centre/Centre for Strategic Research, the Kiyan circle, the Ayin circle, the Serat Institute and Press, and *Salam* newspaper, amongst various others. These disparate hubs, each of which enjoyed different degrees of institutionalisation and capital in the post-revolutionary order, would express solidarity and provide mutual support against common ideological and political foes and compete for ideological and moral leadership that went beyond the confines of the IRI's political class. It should therefore be clear that it is exceedingly difficult to demarcate the Islamic left and religious intellectuals in terms of two discrete groups. Their relationships are far more intricate and intertwined than most accounts in the existing literature on religious intellectualism in post-revolutionary Iran are prepared to admit or account for. An appreciation of these relationships is necessary for a more holistic understanding of the context in which Iran's religious intellectuals have thought and intervened in public debate.

The *rowshanfekran-e dini* and the Islamic left were united in part by their opposition to an understanding of 'religion' (*din*) in which the political, albeit conservative, clergy sought a monopoly on religious and political authority at their expense. Indeed, following the death of Khomeini and the introduction of Rafsanjani's first cabinet on 19 August 1989 (28 Mordad 1368), the new order was being described in Islamic left elite circles as a coup d'état. Quite coincidentally, Rafsanjani's cabinet was introduced on the same day as the national government of Prime Minister Mohammad Mosaddeq was overthrown by an MI6- and CIA-orchestrated coup. The Islamic left seized on this in their rhetoric in order to denounce their own political marginalisation, despite their ongoing control of the Third Majles.[184]

---

[184] Hajjariyan and Baqi, 'Goftogu ba Sa'id Hajjariyan', p. 39.

The opposition of the Islamic left and the new religious intellectuals was not, however, merely politically opposed to conservative control of the state's chief institutions but also to an understanding of 'Islam' and political authority,[185] which bestowed unqualified pre-eminence to the clergy and an unyielding conception of Islamic jurisprudence, at the expense of all other conceivable understandings of Islam, its sacred texts, and the nature of religious experience.[186] The Islamic left and *rowshanfekran-e dini* were allied but by no means monolithic or single-minded in their efforts, both politically and intellectually, to pose a challenge to the 'traditional right' (*rast-e sonnati*). The next chapter will examine this ideological transformation in greater detail as it unfolded during the Rafsanjani period and the emergence of what I have called, following Judith N. Shklar, a 'liberalism of fear'.

---

[185] Faisal Devji's comments on how 'Islam' became a proper name without historic precedent in colonial India are provocative on this score. How and when 'Islam' emerged as a seemingly self-explanatory proper name in the Iranian context would require a separate investigation of its own, which we unfortunately cannot undertake here. Faisal Devji, *Muslim Zion: Pakistan as a Political Idea* (London: Hurst & Company, 2013), p. 203.

[186] Tajzadeh and Salimi, 'Nezam ya'ni ma', p. 103.

4 | *Revolution and Its Discontents:*
Ideology and the Death of Utopia

The appeal of Utopianism arises from the failure to realize that we cannot make heaven on earth.[1]

Karl R. Popper

No individual or single institution can claim a monopoly on truth. The truth is the objective property (*melk-e 'ayni*) of all, and everyone must enjoy freedom and the opportunity to search and obtain the truth.[2]

'Abdolkarim Sorush

Out of timber so crooked as that from which man is made nothing entirely straight can be built.[3]

Immanuel Kant

Introduction

While Iran's post-revolutionary religious intellectuals would not have framed it in such terms, one can say that this post-revolutionary ensemble of intellectuals as it developed in the late 1980s and 1990s gradually came to represent a *liberal turn* in Iranian politico-religious thought; i.e., broadly speaking, they held that state power should be limited, the rule of law guaranteed, and civil and human rights protected.[4] This 'liberalism of fear', to use Judith N. Shklar's fortuitous

---

[1] Karl R. Popper, *Conjectures and Refutations: The Growth of Scientific Knowledge* (London: Routledge, 2002), p. 487.

[2] Sorush, 'Arkan-e farhangi-ye demokrasi', p. 270. The lecture was first delivered in Prague in 1991. The relevance of the location of the speech and the world-historical events which had occurred over the preceding two years should not be lost on the reader.

[3] Quoted in Isaiah Berlin, *The Crooked Timber of Humanity: Chapters in the History of Ideas*, Kindle ed. (London: Pimlico, 2003), Loc 44.

[4] This is a very general set of characteristics and essentially negative in character. In this regard many religious intellectuals during the period under study are conceptually closer to certain aspects of the classical liberal tradition. John Gray,

phrase, was borne out of lived experience of precarity, as several of Iran's post-revolutionary religious intellectuals shifted subject position from ideological legitimators of the revolutionary Islamist regime to more ambivalent internal critics on the outskirts of political power and thereby subject to the state apparatus', and its agents', wanton encroachments. For Shklar, the liberalism of fear, while having a content of its own, had abandoned Prometheanism and become explicitly non-utopian in its aspiration, pursuing modest change at an incremental pace.[5] In the words of Shklar, 'liberalism's deepest ground-ing is in place from the first, in the conviction of the earliest defenders of toleration, born of horror, that cruelty is an absolute evil, an offense against God or humanity ... It does not, to be sure, offer a *summum bonum* towards which all political agents should strive, but it certainly does begin with a *summum malum*, which all of us know and would avoid if only we could. That evil is cruelty and the fear it inspires, and the very fear of fear itself.'[6]

It should be stressed that the epithet 'liberal', but also the ideology of liberalism, was still heavily laden with a host of negative connotations on Iran's politico-ideological landscape. At this point, religious intel-lectuals rarely, if ever, referred to themselves as 'liberals' or adherents of liberalism. This would only happen much later. In the Islamic Republic's first decade, 'liberal' had actually been transformed into a derogatory epithet by all factions active under Khomeini's aegis, as well as Marxist-Leninist and Stalinist political groups and organisations.[7] Iran was of course not unique in this regard. As C. A. Bayly notes in his study of the reception and transformation of liberalism in colonial India, 'liberalism' in the minds of many Indian

---

Liberalism, 2nd ed. (Buckingham: Open University Press, 1995), p. 56.
Domenico Losurdo, *Liberalism: A Counter-History*, trans. Gregory Elliott, Kindle ed. (London & New York: Verso, 2011), Loc 1174.

[5] 'Intellectual modesty does not imply that the liberalism of fear has no content, only that it is entirely nonutopian.' Judith N. Shklar, 'The Liberalism of Fear', in *Liberalism and the Moral Life*, ed. Nancy L. Rosenblum (Cambridge & London: Harvard University Press, 1989), p. 26.

[6] Ibid., pp. 23–29.

[7] Khomeini regarded 'liberals' to be Westoxified, beholden to imperial powers, and hostile to the clergy and Islam. For an example of his pejorative use of the term 'liberal', see Khomeini, *Sahifeh-ye Imam*, 21, pp. 284–6. The influence of Marxist-Leninist groups and their great disdain for 'liberals' and 'bourgeois culture' was also palpable, along with the conviction that cultural transformation was part and parcel of political and economic revolution.

intellectuals was associated with the appeasement of colonialism and liberal imperialism's pretension to be engaged in a benevolent 'civilising mission'.[8]

One key political group which was held to be 'liberal' by the pro-Khomeini clergy and their lay allies was the Freedom Movement of Iran (*Nehzat-e azadi-ye Iran*, henceforth NAI), headed by Mehdi Bazargan, Iran's first post-revolutionary prime minister (February 1979–November 1979). This was despite the fact that the NAI had proactively sought to distinguish itself from secular competitors and on the first anniversary of the new constitution's ratification proclaimed itself the first party to have accepted Khomeini's leadership in 1963.[9] Despite such efforts, the Provisional Revolutionary Government (PRG) and the NAI were embattled from the outset, highly dependent on Khomeini's approbation, and out of step with the revolutionary mood that had gripped the country. Bazargan famously referred to his government as 'a knife without a blade'.[10] The hostage crisis initiated on 4 November 1979 by the Muslim Student Followers of the Imam's Line and their mentor, Hojjat al-Islam Mohammad Musavi-Kho'iniha, whom Bazargan once called a 'provocateur from day one', decisively ended the NAI's role in government.[11] The day after the students seized the U.S. embassy on 4 November 1979, Khomeini declared the event 'a revolution that will be greater than the first revolution'.[12]

Subsequently, the uncoordinated act by the radical students quickly came to be touted as 'the second revolution' and brought to

[8] C. A. Bayly, *Recovering Liberties: Indian Thought in the Age of Liberalism and Empire*, Kindle ed., Ideas in Context (Cambridge & New York: Cambridge University Press, 2012), pp. 3, 4, 14.

[9] H. E. Chehabi, *Iranian Politics and Religious Modernism: The Liberation Movement of Iran under the Shah and Khomeini* (London: I. B. Tauris, 1990), p. 287.

Even as late as December 1999, the NAI, under the leadership of former Provisional Revolutionary Government (PRG) foreign minister Ebrahim Yazdi, contended the organisation was 'bound to the principle of *velayat-e faqih* and dissolved in it (*zob shodeh dar an*)'. Nehzat-e azadi-ye Iran, 'Pasokh beh nameh-ye aqa-ye Hamid Ansari' (Tehran, 02/10/1378 [23 December 1999]).

[10] Bakhash, *The Reign of the Ayatollahs: Iran and the Islamic Revolution*, p. 52.

[11] Mehdi Bazargan, *Enqelab-e Iran dar dow harakat* (Tehran: Naraqi, 1363 [1984]), p. 169.

[12] Ruhollah Khomeini, *Sahifeh-ye Imam*, 21 vols., vol. 10 (Tehran: Mo'asseseh-ye tanzim va nashr-e asar-e Imam Khomeini, 1378 [1999]), p. 493.

a premature end the NAI's already highly attenuated role in the post-revolutionary government. In an interview with the Cambridge-educated scholar Hamid Algar a month after the PRG's resignation, a clearly frustrated Bazargan claimed,

I would say, sir, I am also revolutionary, but the negative phase of the revolution is over. The Shah has gone. The positive phase must be methodical. Methodical, insofar, as I have established an advisory minister, an advisory minister for the revolution's programmes, and commissions for agriculture, industry, trade, departments, foreign policy, banks ... all of which would be busy writing up proposals. These men of the Revolutionary Council did not agree and would interfere in everything. Mr. Khomeini, whose spirit had no time whatsoever for [the methodical approach], and most importantly was prone to interfere, did not understand that such interference was damaging ... This didn't at all suit my personality, style of thinking, logic, or the structure of my thought ... I really suffered because of this situation ... He did not accept anyone.[13]

Later in the same interview, Bazargan admits just how out of step his liberal and measured temperament was with the spirit of the times. His clear astonishment at Khomeini's immense charismatic appeal, at one point going so far as to compare it to Hitler's mesmerising grip on the German people in the 1930s, and confoundment at his own failure to connect with the revolutionary *zeitgeist* are patently discernible:

It is strange how an eighty-year-old man's understanding of the youth is far more than, for example, myself, who grew up amongst the youth and the university, and who developed in the revolution and the movement, and to whom I am closer in age. His understanding is ten times that of mine. There is a reciprocal quality and spiritual and intellectual power between him and the revolutionary youth ... I really feel a distance and alienation between myself and those in the revolution, namely, the youth, the seminarians, students, and Revolutionary Guardsmen.[14]

By the late 1980s there were further indications of how much the NAI's star had fallen and the extent to which their 'liberal' orientation had become an object of derision. A letter from Hojjat al-Islam ʿAli-Akbar Mohtashamipur, the minister of the interior and a prominent

13 Mehdi Bazargan, 'Mosahebeh-ye Hamed Algar ba Mohandes Bazargan', in *Enqelab-e eslami-ye Iran, Majmuʿeh-ye asar* (Jamʿ avari, tanzim va tanqih dar bonyad-e farhangi-ye Mohandes Mehdi Bazargan, Aban 1389 [2010]), pp. 201–2.
14 Ibid., p. 205.

figure within the *chap*'s Association of Combatant Clerics, to Khomeini on 8 February 1988 (30 Bahman 1366) on the political activities of the NAI and Khomeini's reply can be held up as one of the more acute illustrations of the fault-lines dividing the so-called liberals and their conception of Islam and the one advocated by the revolutionary clergy.

By way of context, it should be added that the Guardian Council had disqualified members of the NAI from running in the Third Majles election held in April 1988 (17 Farvardin 1367). Despite their disqualification and the fact that they had been refused permission to operate as a legal party by the Ministry of the Interior, the group continued its political activism. The seeming contradiction between the NAI's ongoing political activism and the fact that they still had not been officially recognised as a political party and were disqualified from standing in the Majles elections provoked Mohtashamipur's letter, hoping to resolve the organisation's status once and for all. In his letter to the Guardian Jurist, Mohtashamipur accused the NAI of 'spreading poison' and claimed that, since the resignation of the PRG, the NAI had opposed the Islamic Republic and been responsible for 'confusing minds' (*maghshush kardan-e azhan*).[15] Mohtashamipur took aim at the Freedom Movement for rejecting the 'absolute' (*motlaqeh*) nature of the doctrine of *velayat-e faqih* and endeavouring to weaken the system.[16] Khomeini responded to his acolyte by roundly mocking the Freedom Movement, calling it 'the movement of so-called freedom'

---

[15] Quoted in Shadlu, *Jostari-ye tarikhi piramun-e takasor gara'i dar jaryan-e eslami*, p. 130.

[16] The Freedom Movement has disputed the authenticity of Khomeini's reply to Mohtashamipur and later alleged that Ahmad Khomeini was the real author of the letter. This accusation was in turn rejected by the latter. A long series of court cases ensued, and, after many years and several interregna, on 12 November 1997 [21 Aban 1376] a court gave its final judgement in the case and ruled in favour of the Foundation for the Order and Publication of the Imam's Corpus (*Mo'asseseh-ye tanzim va nashr-e asar-e Imam*), the head of which had been Ahmad Khomeini until his death in 1995. The NAI was also fined by the court (p. 139). Mohtashamipur has claimed that the letter was written in Khomeini's own hand, and its importance was certified by the fact that five copies were distributed to the executive, legislative, judiciary, minister of intelligence, and Mohtashamipur himself. This was despite the letter having been a personal communication between Khomeini and Mohtashamipur. In such instances the protocol had been to send one copy for the recipient, while Khomeini's office retained the original. Ibid., p. 134.

and claiming they were 'serious supporters of Iran's dependence on America'. More importantly, Khomeini spelled out his view that

the movement of so-called freedom is not qualified for any governmental, legislative, or judicial matter and their noxiousness is their pretence to Islam and with this weapon (*harbeh*) they will pervert our dear youth, and also with their frivolous interference in interpreting the noble Qur'an and the honourable hadith and ignorant exegesis, it is possible they will bring about great corruption. [This corruption] is greater than the damage of other groups, even the Hypocrites (*monafeqin* [i.e., the People's Mojahedin]), those dear children of Engineer Bazargan. The Freedom Movement and its people know nothing of Islam and are not familiar with jurisprudential Islam (*Islam-e feqhi*).[17]

As stated in preceding chapters, this book cannot dwell at any length upon the politico-religious thought of Bazargan or other prominent members of the NAI.[18] However, in opening this chapter I should note that one of the great ironies of the Islamic left is that despite its pivotal role in fundamentally undermining and decrying the PRG and Bazargan himself in the first years and decade of the revolution, the 1990s post-revolutionary intellectual scene dominated by the *rowshanfekran-e dini* would be essential to resuscitating the image of individuals like Bazargan as enlightened and unappreciated in their own time and as having constituted a much-lamented missed opportunity.[19] There are many such examples, but the group around *Kiyan* was perhaps one of the first outside of the NAI and its associates to publish the writings of individuals such as Mehdi Bazargan, Ebrahim Yazdi, Gholam-'Abbas Tavassoli, and 'Ezatollah Sahabi in the years following Khomeini's death. In the first half of the 1990s these efforts were complemented by those of 'Ezatollah Sahabi, son of an NAI founding father, Yadollah Sahabi, who took up editorship of the periodical *Iran-e farda* (Tomorrow's Iran), which became the main publication of the so-called 'religious-nationalists' (*melli mazhabi-ha*) until its forcible closure in spring 2000. The extent to which the Kiyan circle was under the direct

[17] Khomeini, 'Arziyabi-ye 'amalkard-e "Nehzat-e azadi"', p. 480.
[18] For such an exposition, see Saeed Barzin, 'Constitutionalism and Democracy in the Religious Ideology of Mehdi Bazargan', *British Journal of Middle Eastern Studies* 21, no. 1 (1994).
[19] See, for example, Mehdi Bazargan, 'Sayr-e andisheh-ye dini-ye mo'aser: goftogu'i ba mohandes Mehdi Bazargan', *Kiyan* 11 (Farvardin–Ordibehesht 1372 [March–April 1993]).

influence of these figures is a far more nebulous question, which cannot be addressed here. Nevertheless, the reappraisal of Bazargan and his legacy also entailed the incorporation of the latter's thinking, as a broadly liberal scepticism of unchecked power became *en vogue*.

Other organisations on the Islamic left, however, in the Khatami era and beyond continued to distinguish themselves from the 'liberals'. For example, in the summer of 1999, the general secretary of the SMEEI, Mohammad Salamati, continued to consider his organisation's ideological persuasion as Islamic or Muslim, in stark contradistinction to 'liberal'.[20] Salamati also pointedly stressed that the Mojahedin did not accept the latter's 'licentious' (*bi-band o bar*) conception of freedom.[21] More to the point, he unambivalently stated that he regarded the Freedom Movement of Iran as *ghayr-e khodi* or outsiders and asserted that, because they do not support the idea that 'Islamic ideology' can rule, 'they do not believe in this system (*nezam*)'.[22] Nonetheless, by 1999, Salamati, a respected personality within the reformist camp, had come to accept that the NAI should be allowed to undertake political activities because they did not aspire to overthrow the revolutionary state.[23]

Even while the NAI had consistently endeavoured to operate within the political and institutional confines of the Islamic Republic and profess its fidelity to the country's constitution and the doctrine of *velayat-e faqih*, in private its members increasingly began to challenge the authoritarian, clerically dominated conception of Islam advocated by Khomeini and his disciples. Indeed, the NAI's *Exposition and Analysis of the Absolute Guardianship of the Jurist* has since been recognised as one of the earlier and more notable intra-religious critiques of the Absolute Guardianship of the Jurist among those forces which had allied themselves with Khomeini during the revolution.[24]

---

[20] Esma'il Azadi, 'Mohammad Salamati: haft goru-ye cheriki, yek sazman-e siyasi', in *Ahzab-e siyasi dar Iran: tabar-shenasi-ye jaryan-ha-ye siyasi va asib-shenasi-ye ahzab dar Iran* (UK & Mardomak: H&S Media, 1390 [2011]), p. 313.
[21] Ibid., p. 314.   [22] Ibid., p. 319.   [23] Ibid., p. 321.
[24] Iran, 'Tafsil va tahlil-e velayat-e motlaqeh-ye faqih'.
Though unstated in the document itself, according to Mehdi Nurbakhsh – Ebrahim Yazdi's son-in-law and today a leading member of the Freedom Movement of Iran – the authors were Mehdi Bazargan, Ebrahim Yazdi, Reza Sadr, and Bazargan's son, Abdol 'Ali Bazargan. Mehdi Nurbakhsh and Eskandar Sadeghi-Boroujerdi, 'Correspondence with Dr. Mehdi Nurbakhsh' (May 2013).

In truth, it is very possible that Mohtashamipur's accusations of the NAI's 'spreading poison' related to this withering critique of the official doctrine for clerical political supremacy. There is not yet any evidence that Khomeini had read the document, but, given the ferociousness of his response, the question certainly poses itself whether he had read, or at least been informed of, the contents of an earlier draft of the tract.

In this trailblazing work, leading members of the NAI not only critique the basis of the Absolute Guardianship of the Jurist but the notion of *velayat-e faqih* itself. They cite clerical luminaries such as Shaykh Morteza Ansari, Akhund Khorasani, and Mohammad-Hosayn Na'ini and their refutation of the arguments of Molla Ahmad Naraqi, often considered the progenitor of *velayat-e faqih* as a political doctrine justifying hierocratic rule. The NAI even adduce Khomeini's own *Kashf al-asrar* where he acknowledges the 'olama''s disputes over the possession or lack thereof of 'guardianship'. Therein Khomeini elaborates that the possession and extent of guardianship (*velayat*) belongs to the domain of secondary or subsidiary (*foru'-e feqhiyyeh*) jurisprudential ordinances and thus can hardly be considered essential to the faith[25] – a rather conventional view, antithetical to his subsequent articulation of the Absolute Guardianship of the Jurist. While the NAI admit of historical precedent for the view that government should take priority over the *shari'ah* and that its secondary ordinances could be changed in the name of expediency (*maslahat*), they insist that one must look to the Umayyad and Abbasid caliphs and Sunni 'olama' for historical examples, not the Shi'i tradition, to which such ideas are alien.[26] The NAI also extensively drew upon the Qur'an to make the case that many of its verses expressly contradict the premises and consequences of the Guardianship of the Jurist, thus demonstrating that it had a negligible basis in the most sacred of sources.[27] If that were not already enough, the NAI declared, 'the recent pronouncements and declarations of the Leader of the Revolution regarding the absolute power of the Guardian Jurist are the absolute negation of the rule of the people over their own destiny'.[28] Given the surfeit criticism of the Islamic Republic's ideological foundations and its Leader's chief intellectual contributions, it is hardly a stretch to fathom why such

---

[25] Iran, 'Tafsil va tahlil-e velayat-e motlaqeh-ye faqih', p. 19.   [26] Ibid., p. 65.
[27] Ibid., p. 58.   [28] Ibid., p. 68.

a tract should provoke the ire and unforgiving animosity of Khomeini and his disciples on the left as well as the right.

Religious intellectuals such as Sorush and Mojtahed-Shabestari not directly affiliated with any political party and laymen of the Islamic left who had been influenced by Shari'ati in their adolescence – himself a founding member of the NAI outside Iran – would ultimately continue along this path and arguably go to even greater lengths to undermine the clerically determined and nomocratic/jurisprudential hermeneutics of Islam.[29] The following two chapters will examine more closely the political thought of 'Abdolkarim Sorush and Mohammad Mojtahed-Shabestari. A deeper examination of the political and intellectual trajectories of these two religious intellectuals and the networks in which they actively participated will not only demonstrate the profound ideological transformation of the Islamic Republic's loyalist intelligentsia but also show how they reshaped Iran's political and religious discourse in important ways that laid the groundwork for a revitalised Islamic left and reformist political project.

Excursus on 'Ideology'

Drawing on the work of Michael Freeden, I will now outline a theoretical framework for the analysis of ideologies, as opposed to 'ideology' writ large. In so doing, I will endeavour to dissect and problematise Sorush's, amongst others, highly influential conception of 'ideology', propagated in the first half of the 1990s, and the latter's affinity with the new political, economic, and ideological orientation of the administration of Akbar Hashemi-Rafsanjani following the end of the Iran–Iraq War and the death of Ayatollah Khomeini. This will permit a more nuanced understanding of the ideological and political milieu and its ongoing permutations in the years preceding the election of Mohammad Khatami in May 1997.

Both during and since the end of the Cold War, 'ideology' has taken on a raft of pejorative connotations.[30] Philosophers and sociologists such as

---

[29] Massoumeh Ebtekar and Fred A. Reed, *Takeover in Tehran: The Inside Story of the 1979 U.S. Embassy Capture* (Vancouver: Talon Books, 2000), p. 49.

[30] Clifford Geertz, The Interpretation of Cultures (New York: Basic Books, 1973), p. 196. Michael Freeden, *Ideologies and Political Theory: A Conceptual Approach* (Oxford: Clarendon, 1996), p. 23.

Karl R. Popper, Raymond Aron,[31] Daniel Bell,[32] Edward Shils, and Leszek Kolakowski[33] have all argued, in different ways, that dogmatism, violence, and irrationality are a necessary outcome of an 'ideological' cast of mind. 'Ideology' and 'Lysenkoism' became idiomatic expressions synonymous with the distortion of 'truth' and 'objectivity' in the political and scientific domains respectively, all justified in the name of rigid and infallible dogmas.[34] This, of course, is merely one highly influential interpretation of ideology and the function it serves and is itself, to a considerable extent, a corollary of the intellectual battle waged by political and ideological elites in the so-called First World against a rival ideological and political bloc ruled by variations of state socialism. This view of 'ideology' and 'utopian' political programmes was further consolidated with the Soviet bloc's eventual collapse and thus, so the argument goes, communism's proven and self-evident historical failure, a development the Islamic left and religious intellectuals could not help but reckon with.[35] In the words of *Kiyan*'s editorial director Reza Tehrani,

the orthodox left tendency in the sense understood everywhere, including here had reached a dead-end; both its religious and non-religious models. Religious leftism in Iran like the People's Mojahedin (*Mojahedin-e khalq*) reached a dead-end. The People's Mojahedin was a flawed fraternal copy of the Marxist left, albeit with the complexion and scent of religion, and Marxism on a global level had reached a dead-end.[36]

31   Raymond Aron, *The Opium of the Intellectuals*, with a new introduction by Harvey C. Mansfield and a foreword by Daniel J. Mahoney and Brian C. Anderson (eds.) (New Brunswick & London: Transaction Publishers, 2001), pp. xxiii, 305.

32   Daniel Bell, *The End of Ideology: On the Exhaustion of Political Ideas in the Fifties* (Cambridge, MA & London: Harvard University Press, 2000), p. 393.

33   Leszek Kolakowski, *Modernity on Endless Trial* (Chicago & London: University of Chicago Press, 1990), p. 232.

34   'Abdolkarim Sorush, *Naqdi va dar amadi bar tazad-e diyalektiki* (Tehran: Mo'asseseh-ye farhang-e serat, 1373 [1994], 1357 [1978]), p. 315. *Idi'olozhi-ye shaytani* (Tehran: Serat, 1373 [1994], 1359 [1980]), p. 23.

35   This interest in Soviet reform started fairly early at *Kayhan-e farhangi* in whose publication Tehrani had a decisive role. See ' Perestroika ya katastroika? dow goftogu ba Alexander Zinoviev', *Kayhan-e farhangi* 7, no. 1 (Farvardin 1369 [March–April 1990]). Sorush would return to the collapse of the Soviet Union many years over the years and also contends that, when he himself visited, the disparity between the official discourse of the Soviet state and its citizens was obviously for all to see. 'Saqf-e azadi (Summer 1377 [1998])', in *Ayin-e shahriyari va dindari* (Tehran: Serat, 1387 [2008]), p. 95.

36   Bozorgiyan and Tehrani, 'Interview with Reza Tehrani'.

While Tehrani points to the People's Mojahedin as an example of a failed leftism, he could not but acknowledge the consequences of what he called orthodox leftism's global demise, for that segment of the Islamic Republic's political class that had self-identified as 'the left'. This included the leftist ideals which informed their revolutionary politics: advocacy of state interventionism in the media, industry, welfare, and social provision, some of which had been assimilated in truncated fashion into the ruling regime's constitution and political institutions.[37] Tehrani candidly acknowledges this when considering the reasons behind the political re-orientation of the Islamic left from the late 1980s through to the summer of 1997. 'The generation of idealistic Muslims [in Iran following the revolution] reached a dead-end in their social experience, and their analyses pursued the question as to why these ideals remained unfulfilled.'[38]

I will by no means provide a survey of the manifold iterations of 'ideology' from Karl Marx to Fredric Jameson. But I shall attempt to adumbrate some of the scholarly debates around the concept, before examining the post-revolutionary religious intellectuals' own critique of 'ideological Islam'. Taking our cue from Clifford Geertz, one might conclude the conception of 'ideology' deployed by Iran's new religious intellectuals is itself ideological.[39] In this ideological figuration of ideology, it is invariably described as indistinguishable from 'bias, oversimplification, emotive language, and adaptation of public prejudice'.[40] Karl Popper, the author of the seminal critique and explication of the origins of authoritarianism in Western political thought *The Open Society and Its Enemies* (1945) and a great source of intellectual inspiration for several of Iran's religious intellectuals,[41] famously argued utopian political projects aim to realise a society that is 'wholly good', without conflict or trade-off.[42] On this reading of ideology there is a promise of finality, the attainment of an

---

[37] For an extensive analysis of the Islamic Republic's welfare institutions and their long-term impact on Iranian society, see Kevan Harris, *A Social Revolution: Politics and the Welfare State in Iran*, Kindle ed. (Oakland: University of California Press, 2017).

[38] Bozorgiyan and Tehrani, 'Interview with Reza Tehrani'.

[39] Geertz, *The Interpretation of Cultures*, p. 193.

[40] Ibid., p. 193. Sorush, *Idi'olozhi-ye shaytani.*, pp. 18–19.

[41] 'Mabani-ye te'orik-e liberalism', p. 135.

[42] Popper, *Conjectures and Refutations*, p. 485. *The Poverty of Historicism* (London & New York: Routledge, 1957), p. 61.

unsurpassable condition in which there is nothing left to correct or improve.[43] Popper, in the context of the Second World War and the beginnings of the Cold War, powerfully argued that utopian ideologies, both implicitly and explicitly, deem violence as necessary, because violence is inseparable from the task of forging earthly paradise.[44] Ideology, or what Popper regularly refers to as 'utopian engineering',[45] provides the blueprint for the realisation of the wholly good society, and, because this ultimate political objective arrogates to itself a sacred status, the utopian blueprint becomes increasingly difficult to change, for fear of undermining its *raison d'être* and the objective to which it aspires.[46] The impact of this line of thinking and approach to the question of 'ideology' on a whole cast of Iranian intellectuals cannot be overstated.

In an interview with Popper conducted for *Kiyan* in 1992 by Hossein Kamaly, the young Iranian translator of *The Logic of Scientific Discovery*, the importance of Popper's critique of the foundations of Marxism and Marxist ideology were noted, as well as their considerable impact inside Iran.[47] It is also worth noting that the latter translation was undertaken and completed with considerable encouragement and oversight by Sorush, who was Kamaly's teacher when he audited classes at the Association of Wisdom and Philosophy (*Anjoman-e hekmat va falsafeh*).[48] In the course of the *Kiyan* interview, Popper explicitly emphasises that 'there is no room left for Marxism, because Marxism makes big promises, and to realize those promises [it] does not possess the slightest hesitation in resorting to oppression (*zolm*) and mercilessness'.[49]

Clifford Geertz has argued the identification of 'ideology' with 'totalitarian ideology' *tout court* is misconceived.[50] Not all ideology

---

[43] Kolakowski, *Modernity on Endless Trial*, p. 132.
[44] Popper, *Conjectures and Refutations*, p. 483.
[45] *The Open Society and Its Enemies* (London: Routledge, 2002), p. 175.
[46] *Conjectures and Refutations*, p. 484.
[47] Karl R. Popper and Hossein Kamaly, 'Goftogu-ye 'Kiyan' ba Karl Popper', *Kiyan*, no. 10 (Azar 1371 [November–December 1992]), p. 5. Eskandar Sadeghi-Boroujerdi and Hossein Kamaly, 'Interview with Hossein Kamaly', (31 October 2016).
[48] Hossein Kamaly, 'Didar ba Sir Karl Popper dar Kenley', *Andisheh-ye puya* 6, no. 46 (Aban 1396 [October–November 2017]), p. 111.
[49] Popper and Kamaly, 'Goftogu-ye "Kiyan" ba Karl Popper', p. 6.
[50] Geertz, *The Interpretation of Cultures*, p. 199.

is totalising dogma harbouring a Manichean view of the world, even if such a form of thinking can be said to exist and often prevail amongst more vituperative and polarising figures. Similarly, a Manichean world view, replete with irredeemable enemies and myriad conspiracies, has also been claimed to be one of the hallmarks of populists and populism, traditionally defined in the academic literature as lacking anything in terms of an identifiably consistent or shared ideology.[51] In a similar vein, Karl Mannheim had distinguished between 'particular' and 'total' conceptions of ideology.[52] While the *particular* conception of ideology is a reflection of an express group's interests, which are not necessarily defined in accordance with strictly economic criteria, the *total* conception, in the words of Daniel Bell, is an 'all-inclusive system of comprehensive reality ... a set of beliefs, infused with passion [which] seeks to transform the whole of a way of life'.[53] As will be shown below, Sorush and a number of other religious intellectuals under the sway of this literature would come to identify 'ideology' as a whole with something approximating the 'total' conception of ideology described by Bell, who, it should be mentioned in passing, was very much at home amongst anti-communist Cold War warriors such as Raymond Aron, Seymour Martin Lipset, and Edward Shils.[54]

Just as the 'ideologized' conception of 'ideology' that emerged in the aftermath of World War II and in the advent of the Cold War was at least in part a reaction to the rise of Nazism, Stalinism, and the horrors unleashed in the course of the Second World War,[55] Iran's generation of post-revolutionary religious intellectuals' understanding of ideology – albeit on a considerably smaller scale – is perhaps best seen as tempered by a particular set of socio-historical circumstances following the Iranian Revolution of 1979 and the ensuing eight-year war with the

---

[51] Ghita Ionescu and Ernest Gellner, 'Introduction', in *Populism: Its Meanings and National Characteristics*, ed. Ghita Ionescu and Ernest Gellner (London: Weidenfield and Nicolson, 1969).

[52] Karl Mannheim, *Ideology and Utopia: An Introduction to the Sociology of Knowledge*, trans. Louis Worth and Edward Shils (Orlando: Harcourt, 1936), pp. 56–7, 64–70.

[53] Bell, *The End of Ideology*, pp. 399–400.

[54] Frances Stonor Saunders, *Who Paid the Piper: The CIA and the Cultural Cold War* (London: Granta Books, 1999), p. 390.

[55] Geertz, *The Interpretation of Cultures*, p. 200.

Ba'thist regime of Saddam Hussein.[56] As I have already mentioned, and as I will discuss in greater detail in the following sections, the *rowshan-fekran-e dini* would draw on some of the critiques of 'ideology' and 'ideological thinking' proposed by an earlier generation of Western critics. For instance, not only was Sorush an avid reader of Popper, but he had also read and adduced Aron's seminal *The Opium of the Intellectuals* in the process of combating the proponents of Iranian Marxism.[57]

According to Freeden, ideologies are consumed by groups and perform a range of services, including legitimation, socialisation, simplification, and action-orientation. It is in this way that ideologies abet the function of societies.[58] Ideologies 'are ubiquitous forms of political thinking, reflecting as they do variegated perceptions, misperceptions, and conceptualizations of existing or imagined social worlds'.[59] Ideologies ultimately succumb to analysis because they are ideational formations, each with their own distinctive morphology consisting of political concepts.[60] Such a conception of ideology is distinct from the one articulated in the course of the Cold War era, which predominantly identified ideology with dogma and closed, abstract 'isms'.[61] According to Freeden, it was only in this limited sense that the 'end of ideology', a phrase coined by Albert Camus in 1946 during an intense period of introspection by the Western European intelligentsia in the immediate aftermath of World War II,[62] was ever realisable. A comparably anachronistic conception of ideology informs the writings of several Iranian religious intellectuals' critiques of political Islamism, 'Islamic ideology', and jurisprudential Islam in the post-revolutionary period. We might therefore suggest that 'ideology' as such has not been surpassed and dispensed with in post-revolutionary Iran. In the agonistic contestation for political and symbolic capital, new political concepts and ideas have been forged and conditioned political, intellectual, and

---

[56] On a side note, the post-revolutionary religious intellectuals' impressions of pro-Soviet currents both prior to and following the revolution were also of some import, even if their mentors such as Motahhari and Shari'ati had borrowed a great deal from Marxist-Leninist rhetoric. I say 'rhetoric' because serious theoretical engagement with the sources of Marxist thought was a rare occurrence. The vulgarity of much Iranian Marxism was often equally at fault, as was the superficial pruning undertaken in the polemics of Iranian Islamists.

[57] Sorush, *Idi'olozhi-ye shaytani*, p. 116.
[58] Freeden, *Ideologies and Political Theory*, p. 22.   [59] Ibid., p. 22.
[60] Ibid., p. 48.   [61] Ibid., p. 23.   [62] Bell, *The End of Ideology*, p. 411.

cultural struggles in turn. More concretely, we can see how during the course of the 1990s Iranian religious reformists sought to stigmatise 'ideology' and 'ideological thinking' and attribute them to their political and intellectual opponents, while simultaneously naturalising their own political and theoretical engagements as fundamentally in harmony with the dictats of reason, rationality, and the good. This point of contention between the so-called proponent of 'ideology' and the ostensible proponent of 'reason', the true intellectual versus the beholden ideologue, would arguably emerge as a confected ideological fault-line in its own right.

According to Freeden, both political philosophy and ideology are forms of political thinking.[63] An important difference which separates them is that ideologies mix rational and emotive debate relatively freely, whereas political philosophy claims to be based on disinterested reason, sober reflection, and critical self-consciousness.[64] What is crucial to grasp is that while every political idea or utterance is not ideological, articulations of political thinking or speech acts include ideological elements.[65] Any one ideology is comprised of particular patterned clusters and configurations of political concepts, which constitute its basic units of meaning.[66] Drawing upon and recasting the categories of Saussurean structural linguistics in order to properly comprehend the form/structure or 'morphology' of ideologies, Freeden suggests we view the terms of political discourse as signifiers and the political concepts to which they refer as the signified.[67] There is thus a direct relationship between political term (word) and political concept (thought). While the morphology of political ideologies is essentially ahistorical (synchronic), the interpretation of political concepts is subject to the vicissitudes of history (diachronic).[68] What is interesting about ideologies, according to Freeden, is their effort to 'cement' the word-concept relationship – i.e., the relationship between political term *qua* signifier and political concept *qua* signified.[69] In such instances, the meaning of a concept is determined and thereby a single meaning is attached to a political term. In this way, ideologies ought to be understood as configurations of *decontested* meanings of political concepts.[70] In this manner an ideology will affix determinate meanings

[63] Freeden, *Ideologies and Political Theory*, p. 27.   [64] Ibid., pp. 30, 41.
[65] Ibid., p. 45.   [66] Ibid., pp. 50, 54.   [67] Ibid., p. 50.   [68] Ibid., p. 52.
[69] Ibid., p. 76.   [70] Ibid., p. 76.

to its own conceptions of justice, liberty, social structure, authority, human nature, and so on. Ideologies are thus groupings of decontested political concepts, and the core of any ideology is comprised of a cluster of such concepts, since ideologies are not, in Freeden's view, exemplified by any one central organising concept.[71] Rather, the reciprocal influences of an ideology's political concepts are determined in accordance with their specific morphological configuration, which establishes their location and relations to one another. The political concepts form a system of internal relations, subject to the influence of bordering concepts, and as a consequence undergo regular permutations.[72]

Ideologies often assert and impute determinate meanings to complex socio-political phenomena – e.g., Islam *is* political or Islam *is* democratic – and this comes about largely as a result of ideology's need to straddle the domains of political thought and action.[73] They have the power to legitimate a single meaning for one signifier in lieu of another, while simultaneously delegitimising other possible meanings. Moreover, because the political sphere is characterised foremost by decision-making, and decision-making is itself a means of decontesting other viable courses of action, while the meanings of political concepts are perpetually contested, the end of the political process is to make decisions which prioritise one course of action over another.[74] In this way, ideologies bridge the gap between contestation and determinacy, allowing for a transition from a plethora of alternatives to certainty and conviction, which is the prerequisite of political decision-making and forms the basis of political identity.[75] Freeden's analysis of ideology is instructive, not merely for the study of so-called 'ideological Islam' but also for an examination of the discourses and political practice of the *rowshanfekran-e dini* and their political allies.

Bazargan, 'Ideology', and 'Jurisprudential Islam'

During the 1990s, two prominent figures whose writings I analyse in this chapter and the next, 'Abdolkarim Sorush and Mohammad Mojtahed-Shabestari, came to identify *Islam-e feqahati* (jurisprudential Islam) as

---

[71] Ibid., p. 84.   [72] Ibid., p. 82.   [73] Ibid., p. 76.   [74] Ibid., p. 76.
[75] Ibid., pp. 76–7.

a form of ideologised religion.[76] *Islam-e feqahati* is Islam understood strictly within the bounds of Shi'i jurisprudence (*feqh*), thereby subjugating or even eliding the many others dimensions which comprise Islamicate civilisation in its totality, comprising mysticism (*tasavvof*), philosophy (*hekmat, falsafeh*), theology (*kalam*), literature, and art.[77] Such an understanding is seen as safeguarding clerical pre-eminence in both the political and spiritual domains, as both the earthly deputies of the Hidden Imam and, thus, the sole legitimate defenders of the authentic Shi'i faith. Mehdi Bazargan, Iran's first post-revolutionary prime minister and a prolific author on religious topics, in his well-known account of the revolution *Enqelab-e Iran dar dow harakat* (Iran's Revolution in Two Movements, 1984) claims the term *Islam-e feqahati* gained currency halfway through the second year of the revolution as it rapidly became clear that Khomeini partisans amongst the clergy were in the process of dominating the still-precarious post-revolutionary political order at the expense of all other political forces comprising the loosely knit coalition which had overthrown the Shah. It was this initial broad-based coalition which Bazargan famously dubbed the 'first movement' of the revolution. It should also be mentioned in passing that Bazargan associates *Islam-e feqahati* with a corresponding interpretation of Islam, *Islam-e motlaq* (absolutist Islam).[78] This world view, identified by Bazargan with the revolutionary clergy and their supporters, held that even those intellectuals who were devout Muslims immersed in the Qur'an and Islamic culture, as laypersons who stood outside the ranks of the clergy, were both 'deviant' (*enherafi*) and 'eclectic' (*elteqati*).[79] Their 'deviance' from the terms of the debate set by the clergy – namely, the parameters of Islamic jurisprudence – was thought dangerous and a serious threat to the revolutionary *rowhaniyyat*'s political leadership.

[76] 'Abdolkarim Sorush, 'Idi'olozhi-ye dini va din-e idi'olozhik [Originally published in *Kiyan*, no. 16, Azar-Dey 1373 (November–December/1995)]', in *Modara va modiriyyat* (Tehran: Serat, 1387 [2008] [1375 (1996)]), p. 149.
Mohammad Mojtahed-Shabestari, '"Qara'at-e rasmi az din" cheguneh payda shod va cheguneh dochar-e bohran gardid?', in *Naqdi bar qara'at-e rasmi az din: bohran-ha, chalesh-ha, rah-e hal-ha* (Tehran: Tarh-e now, 1379 [2000]), p. 31.

[77] Mostafa Malekiyan, 'Goftari dar bab-e kalam-e jadid', in *Moshtaqi va mahjuri: goftogu dar bab-e farhang va siyasat* (Tehran: Nashr-e negah-e mo'aser, 1385 [2006]), pp. 203, 206. For an erudite and wide-ranging account which pursues the enormous question 'what is Islam?' with impressive gusto, see
Shahab Ahmed, *What is Islam?: The Importance of Being Islamic* (Princeton & Oxford: Princeton University Press, 2016).

[78] Bazargan, *Enqelab-e Iran dar dow harakat.*, p. 127.   [79] Ibid., p. 127.

Such individuals would not be suffered gladly and were consequently assured their own ridicule, marginalisation, and even elimination.

In Bazargan's assessment of *Islam-e feqahati*, which he also identifies with *maktabi budan* (being doctrinaire) and its ascendancy since the beginning of the revolution, he quotes Hojjat al-Islam 'Ali Khameneh'i's report and assessment of the three years that had elapsed since the triumph of the revolution. In his assessment, Khameneh'i – who at the time was the incumbent president – candidly divides the Revolutionary Council (*shura-ye enqelab*), which was the consultative body of well-established figures approved by Khomeini to help direct and supervise the revolutionary transition, into two groups: those who argued for the political pre-eminence of *feqahat* or Islamic jurisprudence; and those who, while religious, did not believe in Islamic jurisprudence's political supremacy or at least were reluctant to accept such an eventuality.[80] Khameneh'i went on to elaborate upon this demarcation, now referring explicitly to the PRG of which Bazargan was the head: 'Not being doctrinaire (*ghayr-e maktabi*) does not mean that they [i.e., the Provisional Revolutionary Government] did not accept Islam, perhaps the majority of the members of the Provisional Government were pious and religious, but they did not accept the idea that the basis of the management of society should be based on the jurisprudential rulings of the Qur'an. They did not believe in Islam as a doctrine (*maktab*) that must manage society.'[81] Having drawn the reader's attention to the incumbent president and future Guardian Jurist's politico-ideological distinction, Bazargan probes further what it means to reduce Islam to a doctrine (*maktab*) or ideology, to which all political programmes, goals, and methods must conform. On his reading it is essentially Procrustean and can only understand and order the world through its own limited field of vision. Islam as a doctrine, according to Bazargan, is also characterised by another dimension to which has already been alluded – i.e., Islam as identified explicitly with Islamic jurisprudence and the clerical institution, and that the latter, armed with the former, must rule over law, politics, and culture.[82] In this sense, the correct interpretation of Islam was inseparable from the political and religious prerogatives of the Shi'i clergy.

Continuing his elaboration of the doctrinaire outlook which he viewed as being zealously pursued by the revolutionary clergy,

---

[80] Ibid., p. 127.   [81] Ibid., pp. 127–8.   [82] Ibid., pp. 128–9.

Bazargan argues that it intentionally subordinated 'expertise' (*takhassos*) to 'doctrine' (*maktab*) – a distinction which, as will be shown below, Sorush and Shabestari amongst others would also adopt wholesale in later years. To demonstrate this, he quotes numerous statements and speeches by the late Ayatollah Mohammad Beheshti (1928–81), one of the most important members of Khomeini's inner circle and secretary-general of the Islamic Republic Party. In a statement on 24 November 1980 (3 Azar 1359), Beheshti candidly stated that 'in societies where the divine doctrine (*maktab-e elahi*) determines society's direction in choosing individuals for jobs and tasks, the first question should be their fidelity [to doctrine], and the second question, one of expertise'.[83] In a bid to further illustrate the dogmatism he associates with doctrinaire (*maktabi*) thinking, Bazargan also quotes a speech delivered by the then deceased Mohammad-'Ali Raja'i on 10 September 1980 (19 Shahrivar 1359) while prime minister,[84] stating:

we say that a doctrinaire revolution is one where there exists the guidance of a leader (*rahbar*), who is the most righteous person who can identify the contents of the doctrine (*maktab*). If we accept this revolution and this movement, we must be completely and totally obedient. If someone does not accept this they are not within the bounds of the Imam's line (*khatt-e Imam*) ... The problem is as I have said, if someone does not believe in the Imam's leadership of the *ommat*, this person does not accept completely and entirely the ideology (*idi'olozhi*) of the revolution and this person cannot be a teacher of this revolution's ideology.[85]

In this way, Bazargan sought to demonstrate that 'Islamic ideology' in the post-revolutionary climate had not only become a matter of Islam's politicisation or the sanctification of the clergy's right to executive power but also one of *taqlid* or imitation and total, unthinking obedience to Islamic doctrine as defined by the revolution's leader, Ayatollah Khomeini.[86] Moreover, according to the Ayatollah himself, as quoted by Bazargan immediately afterwards, 'Being doctrinaire means being Islamic, those who mock the doctrinaire (*maktabi*) mock Islam. If he is a believer [and mocks the doctrine] he is an innate apostate (*mortad-e*

---

[83] Ibid., p. 130.
[84] Mohammad-'Ali Raja'i would become president of the Islamic Republic following the impeachment of Abolhasan Bani-Sadr and was assassinated along with Mohammad-Javad Bahonar, the prime minister, by the People's Mojahedin in August 1981.
[85] Ibid., pp. 131–2.   [86] Ibid., p. 132.

fetri) and his wife is illegitimate to him and his property must be given to his child. He himself must also be killed.'[87] Bazargan does not provide a source for this quote, but it does indeed appear in one of Khomeini's speeches to Iranian parliamentarians on 27 May 1981, not long before the fateful clashes between militant devotees of the Imam and IRP on one side and partisans of the People's Mojahedin, People's Fada'iyan (Minority Faction), and President Bani-Sadr on the other.[88] We might speculate that Bazargan's intention was to draw attention to this very identification, which was ongoing at the time of the book's publication: he, who opposed doctrine, opposed Islam itself, and it was Khomeini who, at least in the eyes of his acolytes, defined the contents of doctrine and therefore Islam. Ergo, to break with the Imam was to break with Islam itself and cast oneself in the role of apostate, whose fate left little to the imagination.

As the erstwhile prime minister reminded his readers, there were dangers in such an outlook, whose style of thinking was best exemplified by the slogan 'all those who are not with us are against us'.[89] This style of reasoning and thinking had resulted in the stratification of the polity into 'insiders' (*khodi-ha*) and 'outsiders' (*ghayr-e khodi-ha*), whereby a privileged few monopolise power at the expense of all those who fall outside the bounds of the *maktab* and thus the line determined by Khomeini and his disciples.[90] Though factional infighting has always informed the practical politics of the Islamic Republic, the imagined line separating regime loyalists from its critics – and insiders from outsiders – has continued to pervade and define Iran's political geography to this day. Bazargan's diagnosis describes for his readers the transformation of the revolution from a broad coalition which sought the overthrow of the Shah's despotic rule (*estebdad*), what he calls the first movement, to a situation whereby executive power found itself increasingly concentrated in the hands of the revolutionary clergy, whose doctrinaire ideology called for their complete monopolisation of power to the exclusion of everyone else. This ideology called for the clergy, armed with their knowledge of Islamic jurisprudence, to manage and order society, all under the wise and

[87] Ibid., pp. 132–3.
[88] Ruhollah Khomeini, 'Sokhanrani dar jam'-e namayandegan-e majles-e shura-ye eslami (vazayef-e namayandegan-e majles) [27 May 1981]', in *Sahifeh-ye Imam* (Tehran: Mo'asseseh-ye tanzim va nashr-e asar-e Imam Khomeini, 1378 [1999]), p. 375.
[89] Bazargan, *Enqelab-e Iran dar dow harakat*, p. 134.   [90] Ibid., p. 137.

discerning leadership of Ayatollah Khomeini. Bazargan dubbed this next phase the 'second movement'. At this point in time and while Khomeini was still alive, the Islamic left remained inveterately hostile to such criticisms and viewed the NAI with keen suspicion. It was not until the early 1990s that a handful of intellectuals, who had played an important part in lending ideological legitimacy to the ruling clergy's political takeover, with much circumspection began to articulate criticisms akin to those of Bazargan adumbrated above, while nevertheless continuing to display much reverence for the Imam and his legacy. Bazargan's 1984 critique of 'ideological Islam' and its identification with 'jurisprudential Islam', whether accurate or not, was taken up in later years in a variety of ways and became one of the chief criticisms levelled by the *rowshanfekran-e dini* and elements of the Islamic left against the 'traditional right'.

Sorush and the Cultural Revolution

The importance of 'Islamic ideology' in the writings of (pre-revolutionary) Bazargan,[91] Shari'ati, Taleqani, Motahhari, and the People's Mojahedin Organisation of Iran prior to the revolution,[92] and the ongoing significance of the term for the Islamic left in the 1980s had led to its emergence as something of a lodestar in the revolutionary establishment's political lexicon.[93] Indeed, the Islamic left's *khatt-e imami-ha,* or those who were self-proclaimed followers of

---

[91] But even at this early point, Bazargan's outlook had an identifiable set of 'liberal' preoccupations – e.g., natural rights, democratic governance, respect for the individual. *Be 'sat va idi'olozhi* (Mashhad: Tolu', 1345 [1966]), pp. 120–1.

[92] Lotfollah Maysami, an early member of the People's Mojahedin Organisation of Iran, has described in detail how he attended a meeting prior to the revolution at the home of Freedom Movement of Iran member 'Ali Asghar Hajj Seyyed Javadi, where Jalal al-Din Farsi, the radical pro-Khomeini ideologue, stressed the imperative for an Islamist 'ideology' to the end of analysing social and political phenomena (pp. 156–8). This need (*niyaz*) was taken very seriously by other members of the PMOI such as Taqi Shahram and Torab Haqshenas, both of whom later became Marxist-Leninists and broke with the Islamic faith (pp. 160–2). Maysami, *Az nehzat-e azadi ta mojahedin: khaterat-e Lotfollah Maysami,* 1.

[93] The term 'Islamic ideology' has a far longer history and was first used by the political group the Socialist God-worshippers (*Khodaparastan-e sowsiyalist*) and their leader Mohammad Nakhshab. It also appeared in the political charter of the NAI in spring 1961 (1340). Hassan Yusefi-Eshkevari, *Kherad dar ziyafat-e din* (Tehran: Qasideh, 1379 [2000]), p. 68.

the Imam's line, were also known as the *maktabi-ha*, the doctrinaire. In the 1980s Sorush had not only been an advocate of 'Islamic ideology'[94] but had played a very public role in arguing for its superiority to, in his words, the 'satanic ideologies' of Marxism, Darwinism, and Freudianism.[95] He had also been appointed on 13 June 1980 as a member of the Council for Cultural Revolution (*Setad-e enqelab-e farhangi*, henceforth SEF). The new council was made of up seven individuals: 'Abdolkarim Sorush, Shams Al-e Ahmad (brother of Jalal), Jalal al-Din Farsi, 'Ali Shari'at-madari, Hojjat al-Islam Mohammad-Javad Bahonar, Hassan Habibi, and Hojjat al-Islam Mohammad-Mehdi Rabbani-Amlashi. During this time, he was firmly committed to the Islamicisation of the humanities and the purge of Marxist and so-called 'eclectic' (*elteqati*) thought, often a byword for the People's Mojahedin,[96] from university campuses. Khomeini's decree appointing Sorush along with six other individuals, a few of whom were well-known members of the Islamic Republic Party, called for the council 'to prepare programmes in different fields, to devise educational and cultural policies for the universities on the basis of Islamic culture'.[97]

In an interview with the journal *Daneshgah-e enqelab* (University of the Revolution), the Council for Cultural Revolution's official periodical, published in the autumn of 1981, Sorush distinguished the 'Islamic university' from the 'wicked university' (*daneshgah-e palid*).[98] The council was appointed by Khomeini in order to ensure Islamist hegemony was consolidated in one of the few places which had been a bastion of support for various leftist groups and the People's Mojahedin but also a home for secular-minded professors viewed as ambivalent and deficient in their commitment to the new

[94]   Yusefi-Eshkevari quotes a statement by Sorush made on 31 Shahrivar 1359 (22 September 1980) in the newspaper *Kayhan* defining ideology in terms Sorush would, over a decade later in his essay *Farbehtar az idi'olozhi*, attribute to Shari'ati. This is hardly a surprise given the enthusiasm the young Sorush harboured for Shari'ati. Ibid., p. 80.

[95]   Sorush, *Idi'olozhi-ye shaytani*, p. 40.

[96]   Hashemi-Rafsanjani and Hashemi, *'Obur az bohran*, p. 106.

[97]   Reproduced in Shahrzad Mojab, 'The State and University: The "Islamic Cultural Revolution" in the Institutions of Higher Education of Iran, 1980–87' (University of Illinois at Urbana-Champaign, 1991), p. 287.

[98]   'Abdolkarim Sorush, 'Setad-e enqelab-e farhangi az aghaz ta kanun: mosahebeh ba doktor 'Abdolkarim Sorush', *Daneshgah-e enqelab*, no. 4 (Mehr 1360 [September–October 1981]), p. 8.

order.[99] Because of issues of space it is not possible to address the very complex issue of the Cultural Revolution, but for now it should suffice to note that Sorush accepted Khomeini's appointment and the remit of the SEF set out in the latter's ruling and, following his appointment, concurred with the Imam that 'our universities are greatly behind the revolution'.[100] Those professors who were 'committed' would support the activities of the council, while those professors who proved recalcitrant 'have moved contrary to the direction of this revolution'.[101]

Sorush and other members of the council also met with Khomeini and sought out his support in securing a greater role for the clergy and seminaries in the overhaul of the humanities and the Islamicisation of the 'university environment' (*faza-ye daneshgah*).[102] By Sorush's own contemporary account, high-level members of the clergy, including even the clerical members on the council, such as Hojjat al-Islam Mohammad-Javad Bahonar (a member of the Revolutionary Council and prime minister until his death in 1981) and Hojjat al-Islam Mohammad-Mehdi Rabbani-Amlashi (a close friend of Rafsanjani, later attorney-general and member of the Guardian Council, until his assassination in July 1985), were often preoccupied with other issues.[103] Khomeini suggested Sorush and other members of the SEF contact Ayatollahs Meshkini and Montazeri, to whom they addressed a letter requesting guidance. Ayatollahs Mohammad Beheshti and Musavi-Ardebili were also consulted.[104] In another meeting on 4 October 1983 (12 Mehr 1362) with Ayatollah Khomeini at his

---

[99] Nasser Katouzian, *Az koja amadeh 'am, amadanam bahr-e cheh bud? zendegi-ye man* (Tehran: Sherkat-e sahami-ye enteshar, 1385 [2006]), p. 241.
Nasser Mohajer, 'Enqelab-e farhangi sal-e 1359', in *Gozir-e nagozir: seh revayat-e gozir az jomhuri-ye eslami-ye Iran*, ed. Mihan Rusta et al. (Koln: Noqteh, 1387 [2008]), p. 228.

[100] Sorush, 'Setad-e enqelab-e farhangi az aghaz ta kanun', p. 6.   [101] Ibid., p. 6.

[102] 'We tried to use the clergy in particular in the committees for the humanities and the committees that are relevant to the Islamicisation of the university environment.' Ibid., p. 6. Such statements clearly show that Sorush and the Council for Cultural Revolution's remit was far greater than what he has been prepared to admit in interviews during the 2000s, where he insists that the Council was established merely to 'reopen the universities'. The question that should be posed is 'reopen the universities, but under what conditions?' 'Pasokh-e Sorush beh montaqedanesh dar bareh-ye enqelab-e farhangi: dorosti va doroshti', *E 'temad-e melli* (20/04/1386 [11 July 2007]), p. 11.

[103] 'Setad-e enqelab-e farhangi az aghaz ta kanun', p. 6.   [104] Ibid., p. 59.

residence in Jamaran, at which Sorush was present, along with the incumbent Prime Minister Mir-Hosayn Musavi and Mohammad Khatami, both of whom had been added as members of the council, the *vali-ye faqih* told the council members that 'attention must be heeded after the reopening [of the universities], to never let deviant individuals corrupt our youth with the injection of deviant matters. We greatly need people for the supervision of this matter.'[105]

On Sorush's 1981 account, Hojjat al-Islam Javadi-Amoli actively participated in discussions with the committee relating to the philosophy of the humanities,[106] in addition to the many clerics from Tehran and Qom who were involved in the committee pertaining to the Islamicisation of the universities.[107] Moreover, Sorush states, 'in truth all university resources had been put in the control of the Council for Cultural Revolution', which subsequently founded the so-called University Jihad (*Jihad-e daneshgahi*), which acted as 'our arm and was our child' and which had an active role in monitoring and badgering faculty members at the universities. Naser Katouzian, a prominent law professor at the University of Tehran who was purged during the Cultural Revolution, has recalled in his memoir that the University Jihad assigned students to scrutinise the salaries of faculty members and sign off on them.[108] In certain instances such as the aforementioned, the faculty could resist unwelcome encroachments, while at others it found itself cowed into passive acceptance. The aim of

---

[105] Ruhollah Khomeini, *Sahifeh-ye Imam*, 21 vols., vol. 18 (Tehran: Mo'asseseh-ye tanzim va nashr-e asar-e Imam Khomeini, 1378 [1999]), p. 166.

[106] Sorush, 'Setad-e enqelab-e farhangi az aghaz ta kanun', p. 7.   [107] Ibid., p. 7

[108] Ibid., p. 8. Katouzian, *Az koja amadeh 'am, amadanam bahr-e cheh bud? zendegi-ye man*, p. 241. Naser Katouzian's description has also been confirmed to the author by Professor Hossein Bashiriyeh, who had been newly appointed to the University of Tehran in 1983, following the re-opening of the universities. He states that the *Jihad-e daneshgahi* was responsible for carrying out the rules and regulations set by the Council for Cultural Revolution. Hossein Bashiriyeh and Eskandar Sadeghi-Boroujerdi 'Interview with Hossein Bashiriyeh' (1 June 2013). A Baha'i-born leftist and member of the English literature faculty, Ha'ideh Dar Agahi, has also claimed that Sorush, following a meeting of the Jihad for Cultural Revolution with the faculty at the University of Tehran, told her through one of his guards (*pasdar*) that she should not return to the university 'otherwise it's not clear what they will do with her'. The next day she was formally dismissed. Ha'ideh Dar Agahi, 'An keh beh koshtan-e cheragh amadeh bud', in *Gozir-e nagozir: seh revayat-e gozir az jomhuri-ye eslami-ye Iran*, ed. Mihan Rusta et al. (Koln: Noqteh, 1387 [2008]), p. 70.

such committees, by Sorush's own admission, was 'the production and genesis of the new Islamic humanities'.[109] Moreover, he states, in plain contradiction to many of his later interviews on the issue of the Cultural Revolution, that 'if we cannot reach a satisfactory and palatable programme whereby we feel satisfied by its Islamicness (*eslami budani-ye an*), we prefer that those disciplines remain closed and remain at a standstill until we, God willing, reach a desirable result'.[110]

---

[109] Sorush, 'Setad-e enqelab-e farhangi az aghaz ta kanun', p. 57.

[110] Ibid., p. 59. *Daneshgah-e enqelab* published an article by Sorush in July–August 1981 (Mordad 1360), in which he theorised the Islamicisation of the humanities, which itself is a transcript of a speech delivered at the University of Tehran on the anniversary of the Council for Cultural Revolution's establishment during June 1981. A version of the article was later printed in Sorush's book *Tafarroj-e son '*, which was first published in 1987 (1366), three years after Sorush's exit from the SEF. The book has been reissued a number of times. The reprint of 2000 (1379) cites the speech delivered on 16 June 1981 (26 Khordad 1360). The two articles are not identical, however, and it seems that the original published in *Daneshgah-e enqelab* has been altered in the version reproduced in *Tafarroj-e son '*. For example, the sentence where Sorush declares 'if someone thinks that "thought" is subject to geography or an historical era, he has not recognised thought' does not appear anywhere in the original article published by *Daneshgah-e enqelab*. See ' 'Olum-e ensani dar nezam-e daneshgahi', in *Tafarroj-e son '*: *goftar-ha 'i dar akhlaq va san 'at va 'elm-e ensani* (Tehran: Serat, 1379 [2000]), p. 191, and compare with "'Olum-e ensani dar nezam-e daneshgahi', *Daneshgah-e enqelab*, no. 2 (Mordad 1360 [July/August 1981]), p. 10. In *Tafarroj-e son '* only the speech at the University of Tehran is mentioned. *Daneshgah-e enqelab* published the transcript of the speech some two months after the speech was first delivered. It remains unclear whether the original speech was altered in the later version, albeit attributed to 1981, and published in 1987 (reprinted in 2000). For the moment, we can state confidently that the version of the essay published in 1987 (2000) differs at a number of significant points from the 1981 publication in *Daneshgah-e enqelab*. Several statements which convey a more sceptical attitude to the Islamicisation of the humanities do not appear in the 1981 essay. It is also worthy of note that this essay was published prior to the above cited interview in which Sorush unambiguously declared that any discipline in the universities which cannot be satisfactorily Islamicised will remain closed. In fairness, it should be added that Sorush does contend that the humanities should not be simply dismissed without consideration because of their origin in either the East or West. It is necessary, however, first and foremost to prevent 'Muslim youth and the students of those sciences [i.e., human sciences] departing from the road of guidance (*jadeh-ye hedayat*)'. He then pointedly adds that 'if the society is Islamic, the university must be Islamic', while at the same time arguing that the humanities will bear the 'colour and scent' of the land of their provenance. Ibid., p. 11. The version published in 2000 also differs here and has been noticeably reworked. "'Olum-e ensani dar nezam-e daneshgahi', pp. 192–3. "'Olum-e ensani dar nezam-e daneshgahi', p. 11.

It is difficult to pin down when Sorush finally broke with the drive to Islamicise the humanities in Iran's universities, but he had officially ceased to be a member of the Council for Cultural Revolution in 1984, even if the exact circumstances of his exit remain obscure.[111] By the late 1980s and early 1990s, Sorush had decisively broken with the convictions which led him to accept Khomeini's appointment as a founding member of the SEF. In his essay 'Loftier than Ideology' (*Farbehtar az idi'olozhi*), published in *Kiyan* in August–September 1993 (Shahrivar 1372), he offered his first concerted critique of 'Islamic ideology'. Previous essays, above all *Qabz va bast-e te'orik-e shari'at* (The Theoretical Contraction and Expansion of the *Shari'ah*), had already demonstrated Sorush's firm break with several ideas which had enjoyed immense influence amongst Islamists since the early 1960s, specifically the immutability and timelessness of human beings' understandings of religion as well as the normative political order to which it supposedly gave rise. *Farbehtar az idi'olozhi*, while building on the arguments of *Qabz va bast*, was in many ways distinct because of its explicitly political content and attack on 'ideology', mediated through a highly ambivalent reading of Shari'ati. Sorush sought to pull apart two concepts which had been conjoined in Iran's political-religious nomenclature for over two decades, namely 'Islam' and 'ideology', causing quite a stir and provoking several replies and rebuttals within the Kiyan circle and beyond.[112]

The essay lacks systematic exposition, meanders, and is at times repetitive. It moves from a critique of Shari'ati to an attack on the notion of ideology as deployed in totalitarian states such as the Soviet Union. It then continues by making several criticisms of 'ideology' as he

---

[111]   For one of the best analysis of Sorush's role in the Cultural Revolution, see Ghamari-Tabrizi, *Islam and Dissent in Postrevolutionary Iran: Abdolkarim Soroush, Religious Politics and Democratic Reform*, pp. 105–29. Ghamari-Tabrizi is effective in breaking down Sorush's total lack of compunction and dismissiveness vis-à-vis his role in the Cultural Revolution and failure to come to terms with the significance of his lending ideological legitimacy towards the Islamicisation of the universities and the revolutionary clergy of the IRP against all other political and ideological competitors.

[112]   In a notable essay published in *Kiyan*, Hajjariyan makes the case that ideologies have the capacity to reconstruct traditions and provide order for developing societies undergoing an unsettling period of dislocation. Sa'id Hajjariyan, 'Naqdi bar nazariyyeh-ye "Farbehtar az idi'olozhi" [Originally published in *Kiyan*, no. 15, Mehr-Aban 1372 (September–October 1993)]', in *Az shahed-e qodsi ta shahed-e bazari: 'orfi shodan-e din dar sepehr-e siyasat* (Tehran: Tarh-e now, 1380 [2001]), p. 157.

conceives it, while Shari'ati constantly lingers in the background. He then finally argues why 'ideology' and 'religion' (*din*) are mutually exclusive phenomena and cannot be synthesised without hazardous consequences.

From the Repudiation of 'Satanic Ideology' to the Rejection of 'Ideology'

I do not deny that among an infinite number of acts of violence and folly, some good may have been done. They who destroy everything certainly will remove some grievance.[113]

Edmund Burke

Under the influence of Popper, but also a whole raft of Euro-American critiques of Soviet communism which had been intellectual grist to the mill of the Cold War *Kulturkampf* during the 1950s and 1960s, Sorush attributes a slew of features to what he calls 'ideology', constituting a conception and way of categorising beliefs and attitudes that would perform an important ideological function in the 1990s and 2000s. I will now enumerate and analyse the most important features of his conception below.

1) **Ideology justifies and serves power.** Ironically citing Marx, Sorush avers that ideology serves the function of providing legitimacy to the ruling powers and assuages contradictions at the objective level of society and subjective level of the consciousness of individuals. It was, after all, Marx and Engels who famously declared in *The Communist Manifesto* that 'the ruling ideas of each age have ever been the ideas of its ruling class'.[114] Though Sorush certainly borrows from this well-known figuration of ideology, he completely extracts it from Marx's broader conceptual apparatus detailing the nature of class conflict and its character in the capitalist mode of production.

2) **Ideology is unfalsifiable (*ebtal-napazir*).** The 'falsifiability' of testable hypotheses was Karl Popper's chief criterion for any theory aspiring to the status of science.[115] Many Marxists sought to portray historical

---

[113] Edmund Burke, *Reflections on the Revolution in France* (London & New York: Penguin, 2004), p. 137.

[114] Karl Marx and Frederick Engels, *The Communist Manifesto: A Modern Edition*, Kindle ed. (London & New York: Verso, 2012), Loc 691.

[115] 'Abdolkarim Sorush, 'Idi'olozhi chist?', in *Farbehtar az idi'olozhi* (Tehran: Serat, 1372 [1993]), p. 80.

materialism as 'scientific', and, following suit, Shari'ati on occasion also aspired rather superficially to do the same for 'Islamic ideology'. But he never offered any predictions on the basis of postulated 'historical laws'. Similarly, Khomeini's religious partisans never sought to claim scientific status for their world view, which they argued was above all else sacred and embodied the divine will. They propounded a political theology, not science.

Sorush's eagerness to adapt Popper's critique of historicism and teleology often led him to build straw-men and targets that were incongruous simulacra of the actual objects of his criticism. More vaguely, what he attempts to argue is that ideology is not 'knowledge' but rather a form of sophistry, which is motivated by interests and power as opposed to reasons and truth.[116] How ideology might mask or rationalise material interests or the exercise of power while proving thoroughly dogmatic and incapable of versatility is not dwelled upon, and Sorush subsequently forgoes consideration of the process whereby economic and political interests might evolve and change and the ideology of the group or class in question leavens and adapts over time. Instead, he proclaims that 'ideology' only takes the form of argument but that 'the essence of ideology is a collection of ordinances (*ahkam*), which logically and empirically cannot be proven or falsified'.[117] Thus, Sorush's conception of 'ideology' mirrors his representation of *feqh* and *Islam-e feqahati* as little more than a set of rigid and inert rules. This representation of *feqh*, not uproblematically, dehistoricises Islamic jurisprudence, turning it into nothing more than a formal and constrictive system or set of ordinances, and effectively occludes its evolution and adaptation over time as a living and breathing social and historical tradition and constellation of institutions.

3) **Ideology is monolithic.** While for Shari'ati, ideology and ideologisation were necessary because the former acted as a vehicle for ideals and values and, more crucially, guided praxis in the course of the individual's political and ethical struggle against oppression in the mundane world.[118] For Sorush in the early 1990s, ideology's primary definition was that of an all-encompassing, monolithic, and impenetrable belief system. It determined one's attitude towards everything – philosophy,

---

[116] Ibid., pp. 80–1.   [117] Ibid., p. 82.
[118] 'Farbehtar az idi'olozhi', in *Farbehtar az idi'olozhi* (Tehran: Mo'asseseh-ye farhangi-e Serat, 1372 [1993]), p. 104.

history, anthropology – as well as one's vision of the nature and constitution of the ideal society and ideal human being.[119] It was, by definition, utopian and total.

There would be some pushback against this characterisation from other religious intellectuals. Hojjat al-Islam Hassan Yusefi-Eshkevari, who was generally closer to the NAI and the religious-nationalists around *Iran-e farda*, held that the interpretations of 'religion' and 'ideology' given by Sorush were strictly idiosyncratic to Sorush himself. Yusefi-Eshkevari, by contrast, argued that there was such a thing as 'social Islam' (*Islam-e ejtema'i*) and that it had been essential to the projects of Muslim reformers since at least the nineteenth century that had revived 'the forgotten dimensions of religion'.[120] He also contended that Sorush does not have a clear or adequate conception of ideology, and that he fails to realise that 'ideology' is not essentially good or bad and that it is the content of an ideology which can either promote 'reason' or 'superstition'. On his view, there are different kinds of ideology, not one 'absolute ideology'.[121]

4) Ideology is a weapon and dependent on an enemy for its existence.
Ideology acts as a weapon of war to induce and galvanise action against a clearly defined enemy. Comparable, at a glance, to the *modus operandi* of 'the political' in the work of Carl Schmitt – although there is no evidence Sorush had read the controversial National Socialist jurist at this time – a key difference is that, quite unlike Schmitt, who sees *the political* and its necessary enemies as definitive of sovereignty, Sorush seeks to cast a disapproving normative judgement on ideology and what he sees as its pernicious effects. Sorush also claims that 'ideology', as he narrowly defines it, is invariably transient because it defines itself in relation to its perceived foe, and as soon as the foe in question is defeated, it loses its efficacy.[122] He does not state such directly, but he seems to imply the well-known if rather hackneyed argument that 'ideological regimes' demand a permanent enemy in order to stave off disintegration, obviously ignoring the extent to which Western liberal democracies have also invoked enemies and 'evil empires' to justify and defend controversial foreign and domestic policies, such as the internment of minorities or military interventionism in far-away places. But on this view, ideology perpetually cultivates hatred (*nefrat-varzi*) of

---

[119] Ibid., p. 105.   [120] Yusefi-Eshkevari, *Kherad dar ziyafat-e din*, p. 79.
[121] Ibid., p. 81.   [122] Sorush, 'Farbehtar az idi'olozhi', p. 107.

this enemy in order to guarantee the unity of its own adherents[123] and shows itself fully prepared to trample moral principles under foot for the realisation of its paramount objectives.[124]

5) Ideology must be rigid and dogmatic, Sorush argues, to perform its role as a weapon of ideological-political struggle. As a result, it will inevitably have a selective conception of religion, which completely elides any and all ambivalence and ambiguity.[125] The people are expected to merely imitate and engage in *taqlid*, a not-so-subtle dig at the hierarchy between *mojtahed* and *moqalled* encompassed within the institution of *marja 'iyyat* and especially the latter's politicisation.[126] In opposition to *taqlid*, he posits 'free reasoning', which acts in diametric opposition to 'ideology',[127] since 'untested certainties' are the 'worst enemy' of rationality.[128] While the quest for certainty and knowledge is an important task for humankind, belief in one's absolute certainty crowds out the possibility of rational and critical thinking. Because of a dearth of critical reflexivity, ideological societies are destined to stagnate. In the final analysis, Sorush concludes, 'no ideology is reformable. The only path for the reform of an ideology is its execution (*e 'dam*)'[129] – hardly an inconsequential statement given that Sorush understood many in the Islamic Republic saw the *nezam* as the living embodiment of 'Islamic ideology'.

6) Ideology demands permanent upheaval. Sorush contends that ideology for Shari'ati was a call for movement (*nehzat*) in contradistinction to the institutionalisation/establishment (*esteqrar*) of a new status quo. The upshot of ideology's clarion call for a perpetual state of upheaval and revolution, he insists, was stagnation rather than a flourishing civilisation. He paraphrases Shari'ati's well-known dictum that when the Shi'i were a blameless and oppressed (*mazlum*) minority on the margins of power, Shi'ism acted as a great source of dynamic resistance and remained faithful to the spirit of Karbala and Imam Hosayn's martyrdom. A predicament emerges when the struggle is victorious, the enemy vanquished, and a new order established. As Shari'ati himself argued with much flair, once in power Shi'ism becomes a torpid and reactionary force for conservatism. To avoid such an eventuality, he prescribed a form of popular dictatorship by a conscientious and committed vanguard of

---

[123] Ibid., p. 136.   [124] Ibid., pp. 150–1.   [125] Ibid., p. 107.
[126] Ibid., p. 132.   [127] Ibid., p. 140.   [128] Ibid., p. 145.   [129] Ibid., p. 147.

intellectuals modelled on the example already set by Marxism-Leninism and Third World anti-colonial leaders. He named this political arrangement, as explicated in Chapter 2, 'guided democracy'.

The dilemma as Sorush sees it is that 'permanent revolution' (*enqelab-e modavvem*) is untenable in the long term and eventually a new political order must be founded. But according to his hypostatised understanding of 'ideology', it fails to think through a future state beyond 'movement' and thus advocates the unceasing preponderance of revolution. In making this argument, Sorush seems to have contorted the position of Shariʿati as well as revolutionary socialists such as Leon Trotsky. Trotsky, of course, was famously outmanoeuvred and defeated by Stalin, in part due to his desire to export socialism beyond Russia's borders.[130] But rather than being a capricious whim, Trotsky's advocacy of this policy conformed to the logic of his theory of permanent revolution[131] and the contention that capitalism could not be overthrown on a merely national basis given capital's internationalisation and the inevitable counter-revolutionary backlash to suffocate the nascent stirrings of proletarian revolution. Without lionising Trotsky, who was himself complicit in Bolshevik repression – above all the Kronstandt uprising prior to Lenin's death and his later imposed exile[132] – it is fair to say that Sorush ignores the historical and socio-economic factors which led to the Stalinisation of the Soviet system and thus is at a loss in trying to explain how 'permanent revolution' relates to the USSR's actual historical trajectory of development, if it does at all. Instead, he simply asserts that it is somehow intrinsic to 'ideology' itself.

As intimated above, Sorush declaims that 'ideology' has no programme or plan after the denouement of conflict. '[Ideology] only thinks of roaring, slashing and warring and it does not think that the

---

130 Perry Anderson, 'Trotsky's Interpretation of Stalinism', *New Left Review* I, no. 139 (May–June 1983), p. 50.
131 Isaac Deutscher, *The Prophet: The Life of Leon Trotsky*, Kindle ed. (London & New York: Verso, 2015), chapter 6.
132 Even in exile Trotsky had few scruples about his role in the repression of the Mensheviks and the Kronstadt Revolt, both of which preceded his political defeat and ejection from the Soviet Union. Rather than repudiate the authoritarianism of the Bolshevik Party itself, he merely rejected Stalin as a legitimate representative of 'true Bolshevism' and the proletariat. Leszek Kolakowski, *Main Currents of Marxism: The Founders, The Golden Age, The Breakdown*, trans. P.S. Falla (New York & London: W. W. Norton & Company, 1978), pp. 943–4.

period of war will one day come to an end.'[133] In this caricature, 'ideology', hardened by its blood-lust, gives rise perforce to a battle-worn and inflexible order which cannot help but turn its insatiable appetite for destruction inward and eviscerate the post-bellum polity. Unfortunately, recourse to such an abstract, hypostatised conception of 'ideology' does very little to explain what actually transpired in the Soviet Union or any other authoritarian system born of revolution. Nor does it explain much else about the other features of any such system and why it is able to persist, retain power and evolve, beyond recourse to sheer force and brutality. Instead, it prefers to lump together often vastly different political regimes under the label of 'authoritarianism' eliding their differences and distinctiveness. A more appropriate starting point, amongst several others, might have been to focus on the nature of the Soviet state bureaucracy and its highly centralised structures of decision-making nascent in the 'democratic centralism' of the Bolshevik vanguard itself, for which there is no exact equivalent in the Iranian state. Trotsky himself held that the problem of scarcity under conditions of Russia's undeveloped productive forces was largely to blame for bureaucratic rule.[134] Because Sorush's analysis is fixated on the discursive figure of 'ideology' as an almost mono-causal explicator of the failures of 'revolutionary' regimes, he overlooks this issue as well as the far larger one of rapid state-led modernisation under conditions of underdevelopment and its potential repercussions for democratic participation.[135]

Through his conceptualisation of 'ideology' and reading of Shari'ati, an essentially polemical allegory, however, is not hard to espy. Prior to the revolution the Islamic movement had been an oppressed, dynamic fount of righteous action and moral probity, fighting against an idolatrous dictatorship. Upon assuming power at the helm of an Islamic state, it began to take on a new guise and failed to dispense with the combative rigidity which had formerly acted as a source of strength and whose unyielding intransigence had been so important for its political success. Citing Trotsky's desire to export communist revolution on a global scale, he makes no direct mention of the Islamic Republic's

---

[133] Sorush, 'Farbehtar az idi'olozhi', p. 115.
[134] Anderson, 'Trotsky's Interpretation of Stalinism', p. 53. Leon Trotsky, *The Revolution Betrayed*, trans. Max Eastman (New York: Dover, 2004), p. 17; Loc 283.
[135] Kolakowski, *Main Currents of Marxism*, p. 941.

own efforts in the course of the 1980s to export its revolution throughout regional states, particularly those with significant Shi'i minorities
such as Bahrain, Kuwait, and Saudi Arabia. One can only assume that
his audience, some of whom had been directly involved in and advocated such 'Islamist internationalism', would quite readily make the
connection. Also, given that President Rafsanjani had begun to dispense with such a foreign policy orientation and progressively mend
relations with Saudi Arabia and other members of the Gulf
Cooperation Council, Sorush's sentiments were very much in keeping
with the government's own shift in policy.

7) Ideology requires an 'official class' of interpreters. Sorush also argues –
just as Shabestari would a couple of years later, and from a different
philosophical vantage point – that 'ideology' requires 'a leader or determinate class of official interpreters (*mofaseran-e rasmi*)'.[136] It needs this
class to officiate and guide praxis which is immobilised by a plurality of
different views and opinions. The official interpretation's role is to
prevent such an eventuality and thereby annul any prospect of 'social
discord'.[137] Using the term very liberally, he states that the 'clergy'[138]
(*rowhaniyyat*) and its 'official reading' are fundamentally 'one-
dimensional' and 'inflexible'.[139]

Sorush, Akbar Ganji (at this point very much a disciple of Sorush), and
several other religious intellectuals took their cue from a raft of literature
penned by repentant communists and critically minded dissidents in
Eastern Europe. These included the Yugoslav Milovan Djilas, a one-
time politburo member and close confidant of Tito, whose book
The New Class (1957) provoked a sensation when it argued that the
communist party elites had established a corrupt bureaucracy and lived
a luxurious and privileged lifestyle, despite their vague pretensions to
proletarian solidarity.[140] At a superficial level, there was some degree of

---

[136] Sorush, 'Farbehtar az idi'olozhi', p. 116.   [137] Ibid., p. 117.
[138] Ibid., p. 137.
[139] Ibid., p. 122. 'Idi'olozhi-ye dini va din-e idi'olozhik', *Kiyan*, no. 17 (Azar–Dey
1372 [October 1993–January 1994]), p. 25.
[140] Akbar Ganji, 'Din-e ensani, sowsiyalism-e ensani: negahi beh tajrobeh-ye Nagi,
Dubchek, Gorbachev va Khatami', in *Tallaqi-ye fashisti az din va hokumat:
asib-shenasi-ye gozar beh dowlat-e demokratik-e towse'eh-gara* (Tehran:
Tarh-e now, 1379 [2000]), p. 325. Shari'ati had made a comparable argument
prior to the revolution in his own critique of Marxism. Asef Bayat, 'Shari'ati
and Marx: A Critique of an "Islamic" Critique of Marxism', *Alif: Journal of
Comparative Poetics* (1990), p. 25.

similarity between the biographies of Djilas and prominent Iranian reformists. Both had fought for the establishment of a purportedly radical and redemptive system but had later found themselves increasingly estranged and frustrated by its shortcomings and failure to live up to their ideals. In their estimation, they too had been well-meaning devotees committed to the betterment of their country and society, but it was the system which had let them down.[141] Djilas's *The New Class* and *Conversations with Stalin* had both been translated into Persian by 'Enayatollah Reza, a former communist and member of the Tudeh Party himself, who had lived for close to two decades in the Soviet Union and the People's Republic of China.[142] The second work first appeared in 1984, while the first appeared in the early 1970s but was notably reprinted in 1999, at the height of Khatami's first term and Ganji's journalistic fame. There is thus an unexpected pre-revolutionary lineage for some of the criticisms which would later be resuscitated by the religious intellectuals and reformists: to wit, those intellectuals who broke with the Tudeh Party in 1948 and their subsequent political evolution encompassing a spirited repudiation of Stalinism, and a critique of the Soviet Union more generally, alongside a defence of democratic socialism.[143]

Perhaps the most famous figure in this constellation was Jalal Al-e Ahmad. Al-e Ahmad's controversial and posthumously titled *Safar beh velayat-e 'ezra'il* even highlights some Iranian socialists' attraction to the kibbutz in Israel as a direct response to their rejection of the Stalinist model, while at the same time comparing the similarity of their political journey to none other than Arthur Koestler, author of *Darkness at Noon* and contributor to the much-publicised edited volume *The God That Failed*: 'Like us, when he broke with Stalin, Koestler was drawn to the kibbutz. Why? Because a base had been established there for socializing the means of agricultural production that had been inspired by Russian social democracy, and not by Stalin.'[144] A key difference

---

[141]   Djilas has described this personal experience of estrangement in some detail. See Milovan Djilas, *Conversations with Stalin*, trans. Michael B. Petrovich (London & New York: Penguin, 2014).

[142]   'Abdolhosayn Azarang et al., *Nagofteh-ha: khaterat-e doktor 'Enayatollah Reza* (Tehran: Namak, 1391 [2012]).

[143]   For more on democratic socialism and the critique of Stalinism in Iran, see Homa Katouzian, *Khalil Maleki: The Human Face of Iranian Socialism*, ed. Eskandar Sadeghi-Boroujerdi et al., Radical Histories of the Middle East (London: Oneworld Academic, 2018).

[144]   Jalal Al-e Ahmad, *Safar beh velayat-e 'ezra'il* (Tehran: Majid, 1373), pp. 28–9.

was that the Iranian democratic socialists around Khalil Maleki and their publication *'Elm va zendegi* (Science and Life) were concerned to find an alternative model of socialising the productive forces, whereas, for post-revolutionary religious intellectuals, who were primarily concerned with striking at the right's basis of political rule, the question of political economy and economic organisation dropped entirely out of the picture.

But to return to the arguments of *The New Class*, Djilas held that the communist party cadres and bureaucrats of Eastern Europe and the USSR turned out to be a new exploitative class, having accrued great power through their role in the country's industrialisation. Despite the 'clergy' not formally owning the means of production,[145] Sorush and Ganji saw Iran's own 'official class' as first and foremost concerned with assuring its political supremacy through its monopoly on truth and the prerogative to define Islam and determine the character of sacred ordinances. It was thus primarily a *discursive* imperium with which they were concerned. Djilas had seen the 'new class' as 'totalitarian' in nature and committed to exclude all rival power centres and constantly augment its power throughout society. Both Sorush and Ganji would concur and apply this description to their ideological foes on the traditional right, while remaining reticent vis-à-vis Iran's lack of anything like a central-bureaucratic party of the likes which had existed in the Soviet Union or Nazi Germany.[146] In fact, any such hope

---

[145] Milovan Djilas, *The New Class: An Analysis of the Communist System* (San Diego & New York & London: Harcourt Brace Jovanovich, 1985 [1957]), p. 45.

[146] While the Islamic Republic might share a number of the characteristics of a totalitarian regime as classically enumerated by Juan J. Linz, it crucially does not have a single mass party, nor does it have a single ideology. Instead it has a highly fragmented and internally contested discourse and textual canon revolving around the person of Khomeini and the doctrine of *velayat-e faqih*, a doctrine that was constitutionally enshrined with the founding of the Islamic Republic and so had a dual life. Three decades after the state's founding there are also a whole host of vested institutional interests and patronage networks, in addition to the more traditional familial and clerical networks of the past, which disperse power throughout the system. In accordance with Linz's criteria, the Iranian system can be said to possess mobilisation organisations, with concentrated power in an individual and his collaborators, and *arguably* cannot be dislodged by institutionalised, peaceful means – though this is very much an open question which has been highly politicised in recent years. Nonetheless, the ascription of 'totalitarian' remains highly unconvincing. Juan J. Linz, *Totalitarian and Authoritarian Regimes* (Boulder & London: Lynne Rienner, 2000), p. 67.

had been decisively flouted with the effective dissolution of the Islamic Republic Party in June 1987.[147] Their appraisal, especially that of Sorush, tends to latch onto the 'clergy', a term regularly employed by him to refer to a determinate institution – namely, the Iranian Shiʿite hierocracy straddling the domains of political and religious administrative authority. He especially tends to stress, building upon some of Motahhari's pre-revolutionary writings regarding the potentially negative repercussions of the clergy's financial dependency on the 'plebs' (*ʿavam*),[148] that 'reaching power by means of religion is no different than attaining wealth by means of religion'.[149] In both cases the freedom and integrity of religious thought is hampered and impugned.

The terms *tamamatkhah* (totalitarian) and *fashist* (fascist) were increasingly deployed by religious intellectuals, the Islamic left, and those sympathetic to their cause from the mid-to-late 1990s onwards. This was unheard of in the 1980s, when such epithets might only have been used by oppositionists in exile. Nevertheless, it was hardly unsurprising given the religious intellectuals' heavy debt to Western theorists of 'totalitarianism', whose chief case studies in the 1950s and 1960s were invariably Nazi Germany and the Soviet Union. In truth, it was used to designate domestic political forces with an authoritarian outlook, which were prepared to use violence and the threat of violence against real and imagined adversaries. It would not, despite a few limited resemblances, qualify as 'fascism' in the light of contemporary research, not to mention the palpable absence of the key ingredient of palingenetic ultra-nationalism.[150]

This issue is further complicated on several counts. While not a 'nationalist' regime per se, given the presence of transnational and internationalist Islamist and Shiʿi solidarities, there was certainly a sense in which the discourse surrounding the 'Islamic Revolution' and 'Islamic state' sought to build a new political order following the

---

[147]   H. E. Chehabi, 'Religion and Politics in Iran: How Theocratic Is the Islamic Republic?', *Daedalus* 120, no. 3 (Summer 1991), p. 81.

[148]   It should be noted that Motahhari, even in his famous essay *Moshkel-e asasi dar sazman-e rowhaniyyat* (The Fundamental Problem in the Organisation of the Clergy), still referred to the clergy as 'the sacred institution'.
Morteza Motahhari, 'Moshkel-e asasi dar sazman-e rowhaniyyat', in *Bahsi dar bareh-ye marjaʿiyyat va rowhaniyyat* (Tehran: Sahami, 1962), p. 165.

[149]   ʿAbdolkarim Sorush, 'Horiyyat va rowhaniyyat', in *Modara va modiriyyat* (Tehran: Serat, 1385 [2006]), p. 45.

[150]   See, for instance, Roger Griffin, *A Fascist Century: Essays by Roger Griffin* (New York: Palgrave Macmillan, 2008), xii.

'destruction' of what was held up as a 'dependent' and 'degenerate' regime in the Pahlavi monarchy.[151] The presence of an authoritarian ideology and committed ideological cadres, para-militarism, concerted state propaganda, a centralised economy, and mass mobilisation in the post-revolutionary state's first decade lent themselves to analysis in terms of the totalitarian model. The noted historian Ervand Abrahamian in a classic analysis took something of a different approach and characterised 'Khomeinism' as a third-world authoritarian-populist ideology.[152] The key point in this instance, however, is that Sorush and Ganji were using the epithet of 'fascism' in the 1990s, some years after Khomeini had passed and the existential threat to the new state in the form of the Iran–Iraq War had subsided, while continuing, at least publicly, to regard the latter with reverence.[153] In subsequent years Sorush would lampoon ideological adversaries on the right such as Mesbah-Yazdi with the epithet.[154] Similarly, during the second half of the 1990s, Ganji used it to designate 'rogue elements' in the intelligence services, vigilante 'pressure groups' (*goruh-ha-ye feshar*) which carried out violence against intellectuals, students and dissidents, the 'new left' (based on the '*Asr-e ma* typology) which has since been framed as Iran's own brand of 'neo-conservatism' – again associated with individuals such as Ayatollah Mesbah-Yazdi and Hojjat al-Islam Morteza Aqa-Tehrani. In fairness to Ganji, upon being questioned he does distinguish between 'fascist government' and a 'fascist movement', arguing, somewhat contradictorily, that in Iran the 'fascist movement' has no social base and has been rejected by the Iranian electorate,[155] while at the same time

---

[151] This was a widely held sentiment in the run-up to the revolution, shared by leftist radicals and Islamists alike. See Bahman Nirumand, *Iran: The New Imperialism in Action*, translated by Leonard Mins (New York & London: Monthly Review Press, 1969), chapter 8.

[152] Abrahamian, *Khomeinism: Essays on the Islamic Republic*, chapter 1.

[153] It should be stressed once more that it is highly questionable how useful or clarificatory is any such analysis of the Khomeini decade in terms of 'fascism'. All the more so at the present time when it has the potential to feed Islamophobic rhetoric which attempts to conflate 'Islam' writ large with 'fascism' and seeks to deny that Islam is a religion, insisting that it is nothing more than a 'political ideology'.

[154] 'Abdolkarim Sorush, 'Jaryan-e Mesbah ya'ni fashism', *Baztab-e andisheh*, no. 80 (1384/11/10 [30 January 2006]).

[155] According to Arthur Rosenberg's seminal analysis, the absence of a mobilised social base would mean it ceases to be a 'fascist' movement in any meaningful

applying it to security and vigilante elements either linked directly, or loosely affiliated to, the state or state officialdom.[156]

8) Ideology calls for an unrealisable holistic transformation of state and society. Sorush adapts Popper's arguments in *The Poverty of Historicism* (1957), which objected to holistic social engineering, but also Friedrich Hayek's critique in *The Road to Serfdom* (1944), which viewed centralised socio-economic planning as paving the way for fascism and totalitarianism. Indeed, as Hayek declared in the latter work, 'planning leads to dictatorship because dictatorship is the most effective instrument of coercion and the enforcement of ideals and, as such, essential if central planning on a large scale is to be possible'.[157] No single planner could ever have sufficient knowledge about the actual processes of society to rationally reorder it. Ideology, according to Sorush, with its singular and inflexible programme is fundamentally misguided in believing it can achieve its goal, since the sheer volume of information militates against any possibility of the holistic transformation of society.[158] Similar arguments would become the cornerstone of neoliberal ideology from the late 1970s onwards and gradually came to inform the economic views of many of the centrists around Rafsanjani, as well as would-be reformists from the second half of the 1990s onwards.[159]

The analogy drawn, however, once again proves somewhat strained given that a considerable swathe of the IRI elite – namely, the Society of Combatant Clergy, the Society of Qom Seminary Teachers, and the Islamic Coalition Society – were either directly or circuitously linked to the bazaar and mercantile class or considered it a key base of politico-economic support. Statist-populist policies had in fact been pursued by

---

sense at all. Arthur Rosenberg, 'Fascism as a Mass-Movement (1934)', *Historical Materialism* 20, no. 1 (2012).

[156] Akbar Ganji, 'Shari'ati va fashism: avvalin fashist shaytan ast [Originally published in *Kiyan*, no. 39, Azar–Dey 1376]', in *Tallaqi-ye fashisti az din va hokumat: asib-shenasi-ye gozar beh dowlat demokratik-e towse'eh-gara* (Tehran: Tarh-e now, 1379 [2000]), p. 189. 'Porsesh va pasokh', in *Tallaqi-ye fashisti az din va hokumat: asib-shenasi-ye gozar beh dowlat demokratik-e towse'eh-gara* (Tehran: Tarh-e now, 1379 [2000]), p. 215.

[157] F. A. Hayek, *The Road to Serfdom: Text and Documents, The Definitive Edition*, Kindle ed. (New York & London: Routledge, 2008), p. 110; Loc 2713.

[158] Sorush, 'Farbehtar az idi'olozhi', p. 133.

[159] David Harvey, *A Brief History of Neoliberalism* (Oxford & New York: Oxford University Press, 2005), p. 21.

the Islamic left and, as mentioned in Chapter 3, opposed by the 'traditional right', the very same forces who were often lambasted as 'fascists'. Rafsanjani and his allies had managed to rework the First Five-Year Plan originating in the Musavi government, which was approved by the Majles in January 1990, where it sought to pave the way for widespread privatisation, foreign loans, and foreign direct investment. Even if it remained largely unrealised due to political wrangling, it was a program of action that could hardly diverge further from the command economies found in the former USSR.[160]

Though this comparison and series of analogies were often short on nuance or parity with the composition of the Islamic Republic elite and state apparatus, it served a 'useful' purpose. It was employed by critical religious intellectuals, the Islamic left, and its sympathisers to establish a vivid and emotive connection and chain of intimations between the Western social scientific discourse on Soviet totalitarianism and fascism and the traditional right – and implicitly the incumbent *vali-ye faqih* and his office, even if names were rarely mentioned.[161] The Islamic left and its partisan intelligentsia were not prepared to extend it to the regime in its entirety, nor to its past and the events of the 1980s in which they were often implicated, and restricted its appellation to those political actors possessing both official and unofficial links to state institutions and who were inveterately hostile to their political and intellectual activities.

On another level, the issue of the 'official class' seems to point to a more general issue which was rather straightforward: a critique of dogmatic thinking and world views which assert their own rectitude to the complete exclusion of others. To this extent, Sorush, Mojtahed-Shabestari, and the Islamic left, specifically the Mojahedin Organisation of the Islamic Revolution of Iran, had the traditional and radical Islamic right in mind when formulating their deep reservations vis-à-vis what they perceived as its unyielding antipathy to

---

[160] Anoushiravan Ehteshami, *After Khomeini: The Iranian Second Republic*, Kindle ed. (London & New York: Routledge, 1995), Loc 2325. Pesaran, *Iran's Stuggle for Economic Independence*, pp. 74–5.

[161] Ganji would dub the Ansar-e Hezbollah 'fascist' along with their associated publications such as *Yalasarat* and *Shalamcheh*, the latter being edited by Mas'ud Dehnamaki (a once-infamous 'club wielder' turned film director) as well as *Kayhan* newspaper and the conservative monthly *Sobh*, which he accused of advocating a 'fascist reading of religion'. Ganji, 'Porsesh va pasokh', p. 216.

any alternative views which might challenge its dominance. This is also supported by Sorush's declamation in the course of the essay: 'It is our belief this depiction is not imaginary, but an issue in our time and in our homeland which has had and has many examples.'[162]

The Mutual Exclusivity of Ideology and Religion

At this juncture in his intellectual biography, Sorush wanted to preserve what he believed to be religion's 'mystery' (*raz-alud*), 'wonderment' (*hayrat-afkan*), and elusive ethereal quality.[163] This was intended to assuage, if not fundamentally deny, the prospect of any individual, or class of individuals, declaring an exclusive monopoly on the determination of its truth content. Religion, as he saw it, was not 'ideologisable' (*id'iolozhi shodani*), and Islam writ large could not be professed and confined within a narrow, desiccated Procrustean mould.[164] In his first highly influential series of essays on the 'expansion and contraction of the *shari'ah*', Sorush sought to essentially de-world 'religion', claiming for it a noumenal existence human understanding could never fully apprehend. This haphazard filleting of Kant, and the writings of the late British theologian John Hick (1922–2012), on the one hand was combined with a fast-and-loose rendering of the semantic holism of the French philosopher of science Pierre Duhem (1861–1916), as well as American philosopher Willard van Orman Quine (1908–2000), and adorned with ample allusions to the thirteenth-century poet and mystic Jalal al-Din Rumi. Sorush contended that religious knowledge or human beings' understanding of religion was historically conditioned and interconnected with other bodies of knowledge, such as the natural sciences, so that if the status of human knowledge in such disciplines underwent change and transformation, human beings' understanding of religion and religious issues would as well.[165] In short, he made the question of religious knowledge's historicity central.

Not only did the clergy not possess a monopoly on religious insight, but, if they wished to eschew obsolescence, they would be compelled to familiarise themselves with 'the exigencies of the time' and come to terms with the reality that their own comprehension and methodological approach towards religion and its injunctions were theory-laden

---

[162] Sorush, 'Farbehtar az idi'olozhi', p. 121.   [163] Ibid., p. 126.
[164] Ibid., p. 125.   [165] 'Qabz va bast-e te'orik-e shari'at (1)', pp. 167, 187.

and therefore afflicted by the vagaries of history. 'Religion-in-itself' remains pristine and unscathed by the ravages of time,[166] but human beings' understandings and conceptions were not so fortunate. Sorush never fully explicates how human beings cognitively bridge this onto-logical chasm between our understandings and knowledge of religion and noumenal religion, and their relation is never adequately explained. It was, however, a stinging critique whose portents many conservatively inclined clergymen, including future Chief Justice Hojjat al-Islam Sadeq Larijani, were quick to fathom.[167]

An obvious upshot of Sorush's analysis is that it undercuts any claim to an ahistorical and timeless understanding of religion and its ordi-nances and thus any contention to stand outside the stream of tempor-ality. This would include his own ungrounded positing of the notion of 'religion-in-itself'. Nonetheless, he continues to insist, even if the grounds of his assertion remain opaque, that 'ideology' reflects the needs and goals present within a particular society, whereas 'religion does not target any specific historical society whatsoever'.[168] He neglects the vast literature which has depicted the Prophet Mohammad as a reformer of Arab Bedouin society, of which he was undoubtedly aware, and instead merely asserts that 'mysticism' is indicative of the depth of 'religion', which cannot be ideologised.[169] In this instance, he also overlooks the many acknowledgments in the course of his own oeuvre, as well as that of other Islamic reformers, which contend many of the Prophet's rulings and actions were specific to the culture and time of their occurrence, which meant they might be considered inessential to the world view and obligations of contempor-ary Muslims.[170] It is in this way that his effort to de-world religion becomes unstuck, since if human knowledge of 'religion' is articulated in language, culture, and history and mediated by the state of scientific knowledge, how and on what basis can Sorush then posit it beyond all

---

[166] Ibid., p. 199. Also, see ' Pasokh beh naqd nameh-ye "sobat va taghyir dar andisheh-ye dini"', *Kiyan* 2, no. 7 (Tir 1371 [June–July 1992]), p. 18.

[167] Mohammad-Sadeq Larijani, 'Naqdi bar maqaleh "bast va qabz-e te'orik-e shari'at"', *Kayhan-e farhangi*, no. 55 (Mehr 1367 [September–October 1988]), p. 14.

[168] Sorush, 'Farbehtar az idi'olozhi', p. 127.   [169] Ibid., p. 129.

[170] Some years later, Sorush focused specifically upon the historically contingent elements of prophetic experience. 'Bast-e tajrobeh-ye nabavi [Originally published in *Kiyan*, no. 39, Azar–Dey 1376 (December–January 1997–8)]', in *Bast-e tajrobeh-ye nabavi* (Tehran: Serat, 1378 [1999]).

such mediating relationships? In this way, Sorush is adopting a weak version of social constructivism while abandoning its logical conclusion, where it would 'go all the way down', where nothing essentially precedes its history.[171]

In reply to Sorush, Sa'id Hajjariyan strongly disagreed with the attempt to make an ontological claim for some asocial and ahistorical kernel of religion, arguing instead that there were only disparate interpretations of religion and that 'ideology' was itself eminently important for the deconstruction and reconstruction of beliefs, traditions, and practices for developing societies in periods of transition.[172] Hajjariyan also argued that the ideologisation of religion, while perhaps reproducing and disseminating the sacred in the short term, inevitably acted as a catalyst to secularisation (*'orfi shodan*)[173] – an eventuality which he did not view negatively but rather saw as part of Iran's entry into the modern era.

Sorush's characterisation and criticism of 'ideology' had a huge impact in the 1990s and, despite the fact that it possessed several serious shortcomings, was timely and struck a nerve with many who had grown weary of what, as a result of the war with Iraq, had turned into a decade of conflict and upheaval. On the view of some, the 1980s had turned out to be a dystopian decade of perpetual revolution, war, death, and destruction. Revolution and programs for large-scale social transformation had been discredited. The collapse of the Soviet Union and empirical failure of 'real existing socialism' only compounded such sentiments, and it was in this spirit that *Kiyan* dedicated an issue to the question 'Is Marxism Dead?' The cover bore a pop art silhouette of Marx donning groovy coloured spectacles and had translated several

---

[171]   Richard Rorty, *Contingency, irony, and solidarity*, Kindle ed. (Cambridge & New York: Cambridge University Press, 1989), Loc 92.

[172]   Sa'id Hajjariyan, 'Din-e 'asri dar 'asr-e idi'olozhi [Originally published in *Kiyan*, no. 17, Farvardin–Ordibehesht 1373 (March–April 1994)]', in *Az shahed-e qodsi ta shahed-e bazari: 'orfi shodan-e din dar sepehr-e siyasat* (Tehran: Tarh-e now, 1380 [2001]), p. 161. Ganji, under the pseudonym Hamid Paidar, takes up the question of the use and abuse of 'ideology' as a term, taking aim specifically at Sorush's influential essay, which to this day shapes much public debate on 'ideology' inside Iran. Hamid Paidar, 'Marx, idi'olozhi va din: naqdi bar maqaleh-ye "farbehtar az idi'olozhi"', *Kiyan*, no. 17 (Azar/Dey 1372 [October 1993–January 1994]), p. 17. 'Ezatollah Sahabi was also critical of Sorush's characterisation of ideology. See Sahabi et al., 'Mizgerd-e Kiyan-e dar bareh-ye Jame'eh-ye madani', p. 10.

[173]   Hajjariyan, 'Din-e 'asri dar 'asr-e idi'olozhi', p. 163.

articles by late Soviet thinkers responding to this question at a collo-
quium convened by the USSR Academy of Sciences.[174] The lead article
by an Iranian author alongside the aforementioned pieces was Sorush's
'Religious Ideology and Ideological Religion'.[175] *Kiyan's* editors were
not bashful about drawing connections between their own society and
the Islamic Republic and the 'death of Marxism' at the putative 'end of
history' either:

also, should not our Islamic society, which has behind it the experience of
bestowing objectivity to religious doctrines, with all its bitter and sweet
experiences and its intellectual and social dividends, and the life of religious
thought which is the primary foundation of its historical identity, be subject
to an enlightened rethinking (*baz-andishi-ye rowshan-garaneh*)? And before
questions become crises prepare the possibility for engagement with enliven-
ing theory? The different responses provided by these Soviet philosophers in
this collection of articles might establish comparable models for such
a rethinking.[176]

While the 1980s was characterised by some as a decade of unceasing
'movement', many were divided on whether it had ultimately been for
the better and delivered on the original promissory note of the revolution. The conviction of a considerable part of the political class, now
dominated by the alliance of new and traditional right, held that it
was the time to re-build and establish stability. It was the former
Majles speaker, now president, Akbar Hashemi-Rafsanjani who had
promised he would do just that, under the less-than-self-effacing title
of Commander of the Reconstruction.

Rafsanjani, Technocracy, and Self-Styled 'De-Politicisation'

It is somewhat ironic that it was during Rafsanjani's presidency that
a new period of intellectual ferment for Iran's religious intellectuals
steadily unfurled. This was not purposively willed by the president, but
it was at least in part an outcome of his desire to de-emphasise and
alleviate the heated partisan infighting which had resulted in a slew of

[174] For an English translation of the discussion which was first published in
Pravda, see V. Zh. Kelle et al., 'Is Marxism Dead? Materials from a Discussion',
Soviet Studies in Philosophy 30, no. 2 (1991).

[175] Sorush, 'Idi'olozhi-ye dini va din-e idi'olozhik'.

[176] 'So'al: aya Marxism mordeh ast?', ibid., p. 2.

fraught relationships within the political class, only deteriorating further following Khomeini's death. One way in which factional polarisation took place was the political marginalisation of the Islamic left following the outcome of the Fourth Majles elections which came to an end in May 1992. In that election, several high-profile members of the MRM, such as Mehdi Karrubi, Mohtashamipur, and Hadi Khameneh'i,[177] failed to get re-elected, and many others had found themselves disqualified by the Guardian Council even before the election had been convened. Furthermore, Mohammad Khatami, who was minister of culture and Islamic guidance during Rafsanjani's first term, resigned his post in July 1992 after something of a turbulent stint (see Chapter 3). Nevertheless, it is generally agreed that there was a marked shift away from the political rhetoric which had prevailed in the 1980s.

In stark contrast to the Manichean binaries which often characterised the speeches of Khomeini – to wit, the oppressed and the oppressor, the faithful and the hypocrites, the pious and the Westoxified – Rafsanjani in the aftermath of a debilitating and protracted war with neighbouring Iraq initiated a new reading of the revolution and revolutionary values. Instead of ideological commitment and zealousness for its own sake, he would cite technical expertise and effective management. Rather than laud the virtues of poverty and abstemiousness, he made the case that the credentials of a bona fide revolutionary were not contingent on jettisoning luxury and material affluence.[178] Whether this rhetorical shift reflected a genuine political and economic shift state-wide is disputed and has on occasion been overstated, especially since the president is far from controlling the entirety of the state apparatus;[179] but what is beyond doubt is that during the mid-1990s, because of their extant political capital, Iran's religious intellectuals and the Islamic left had crucial space to think, reflect, and publish their evolving intellectual output. Though it was perhaps originally hoped by Rafsanjani that such research activities would keep 'troublesome' and 'disruptive' elements of the Islamic left

---

[177] Moslem, *Factional Politics in Post-Khomeini Iran*, p. 186.

[178] Mohammad Quchani, *Yaqeh sefid-ha: jame'eh shenasi-ye nehad-ha-ye madani dar Iran-e emruz* (Tehran: Naqsh va negar, 1379 [2000]), p. 128.

[179] For an interesting take on this issue during the Rafsanjani era and its relevance for the IRI's foreign policy, see Maximilian Terhalle, 'Revolutionary Power and Socialization: Explaining the Persistence of Revolutionary Zeal in Iran's Foreign Policy', *Security Studies* 18, no. 3 (2009), pp. 557–86.

preoccupied and pre-empt their perceived 'political mischief-making', its long-term repercussions were to be significant for the political class and Iranian polity overall. The MRM had withdrawn from electoral contestation altogether, while the SMEEI battled on, despite their acknowledgement of the unfair playing field, for the most part unsuccessfully.

Even though many of the religious intellectuals' ideas and recommendations might have been firmly rebuffed by the new ruling establishment,[180] this period in the political wilderness was indispensable to their ability not only to rethink their erstwhile world view and comprehend their political defeat but also disseminate their critical engagement with the past for a broader public. The public in question remained relatively modest but nevertheless provided an opportunity for a fresh political language to gradually enter the public domain. It was a language that to some extent converged with Rafsanjani's new emphasis on technocratic expertise and 'developmentalist' credo but also went further, going beyond the president's ambitions for economic restructuring, privatisation and efficiency, major levels of foreign investment, and the development and expansion of key industries, such as oil and gas.[181] These activists and intellectuals, in virtue of their pivotal cultural, political, and ideological role in the 1980s, were afforded qualified room to manoeuvre, often accompanied by state patronage; indeed, several had held posts in the Ministry of Culture, which neither secular intellectuals, the so-called *digar-andishan* (alternative thinkers), nor the Freedom Movement of Iran (NAI) had the good fortune to enjoy. In fact, the former were actively persecuted and were viewed by a considerable swathe of the IRI political class as perpetrators of a 'cultural onslaught' designed to undermine the *nezam* by means of a soft culture war, an ideological trope that would reach full bloom in the course of the 2000s.[182] Thus, while the

---

[180]   Sahabi goes so far as to assert that he was essentially arrested because of his private critical evaluation of the government's First Five-Year Plan which was sent to Rafsanjani. Sahabi, *Nim-e qarn-e khatereh va tajrobeh*, p. 197.

[181]   Ehteshami, *After Khomeini*, Loc 2304.

[182]   The accusations of 'cultural onslaught' presaged those of 'velvet revolution' which post-2009 were launched against the Islamic left itself. In this earlier formulation domestic secular intellectuals and dissidents were linked to foreign exiles, capital, and governments hell-bent on overthrowing the IRI (p. 19). Mehdi Khaz'ali, the son of the arch-conservative and one-time Guardian Council member Ayatollah Khaz'ali, wrote the publisher's introduction to the

SMEEI was given permission to restart its political activities in the autumn of 1991 as a recognised political party, official recognition of the NAI, as we have seen, was not forthcoming. However, even electoral candidates fielded by the SMEEI found themselves disqualified by the Guardian Council – for example, Behzad Nabavi and Mohsen Armin, in the Fourth and Fifth Majles elections respectively.[183] Nevertheless, they were certainly accorded a series of relative privileges, not only because of their former prominence at the heart of the political system but because, according to Rafsanjani himself, the Islamic left, in particular the MRM, actively supported his segue into the newly restructured executive branch of the presidency in their meetings with Khomeini prior to the latter's death.[184]

In Tehran, the mayoral tenure of Rafsanjani ally Gholam-Hosayn Karbaschi was also significant for several reasons, including the establishment of the municipal newspaper *Hamshahri* (Fellow Townsman), with Mohammad 'Atriyanfar as its editor. While it often championed the president's economic and cultural agendas, it also sought to eschew some of the more overt partisanship and the fiery rhetorical flourishes that had been a mainstay of a national press, which had over the years become heavily factionalised. Established in the winter of 1992, *Hamshahri* dedicated considerable coverage to social and cultural issues while avoiding the minutia and polemics emanating from factional disagreements and personal animosities. For example, in its first run *Hamshahri* published a bold editorial arguing that 'social participation' (*mosharekat-e ejtema'i*) 'is a definite necessity for development and the progress of development programmes'.[185] Development and rational

published transcript of the infamous *Hoviyyat* programme vilifying the so-called *digar-andishan*. There he lambasts the 'alternative thinkers' and 'bad thinkers' (*bad-andishan*) for spreading 'infidelity' (*kofr*) by means of 'culture' and not force of arms. The introduction is especially interesting given Khaz'ali's later imprisonment as an outspoken critic of the Ahmadi-Nezhad administration and defender of the post-2009 Green Movement (p. 5). Mas'ud Khorram, *Hoviyyat* (Tehran: Mo'asseseh-ye farhangi-ye entesharati-ye hayan, 1376 [1997]).

[183]   'Rad-e salahiyyat shodegan az rad-e salahiyyat miguyand', *Payam-e emruz*, no. 11 (Farvardin 1375 [March–April 1996]), p. 12.

[184]   Sadeq Ziba-Kalam, Fereshteh Sadat Etefaqfar, and Akbar Hashemi-Rafsanjani, *Hashemi bedun-e rotush: panj sal-e goftogu ba Hashemi-Rafsanjani* (Tehran: Ruzaneh, 1386 [2007]), p. 122.

[185]   'Yaddasht-e ruz: mosharekat-e ejtema'i-ye mardom', *Hamshahri* (4 Bahman 1371 [24 January 1993]).

management were readily discussed while more contentious issues were quietly placed on the back burner. However, in parallel, newspapers and periodicals such as *Kiyan*, *'Asr-e ma*, and *Salam*, in concert with the research produced by the Presidential Strategic Research Centre, were actively developing their own lines of thinking and gradually reaching the conclusion that 'rational and realistic governance' would prove insufficient to guarantee freedom and prosperity.[186] It was at this point in the early to mid-1990s that an ever-increasing convergence began to emerge between religious intellectuals, who had in recent years distanced themselves from the political fray, and the Islamic left – a coalescence that would reach its denouement with the 2nd Khordad and the movement which emerged around it in subsequent years.

The political commentator Mohammad Quchani identified these efforts by Rafsanjani and his allies with the president's mission for 'depoliticization' and the promotion of technocratic expertise and the administrative state in its stead.[187] This image of 'depoliticization' has been persistent, if not altogether apposite. Rafsanjani had a clear and sweeping programme for the reform of Iran's political economy and foreign policy, even if many of his most ambitious economic policies were left either half-realised or stillborn as a result of unanticipated resistance in the conservative Fourth Majles. These included the privatisation of industry, mines, and other key industries, deregulation of the banking sector and financial services, expansion and modernisation of the Tehran stock exchange, encouragement of direct foreign investment, foreign borrowing, the establishment of free trade zones, devaluation of the currency, the incremental reduction of state subsidies, and the return of exiled capital and expertise[188] – an absolutely huge

---

[186] 'Ezatollah Sahabi has spoken critically in his memoir of the Panglossian view held by many, including the Rafsanjani administration, of the International Monetary Fund and World Bank's 'structural adjustment' programmes at the beginning of the 1990s. Sahabi, *Nim-e qarn-e khatereh va tajrobeh*, p. 194.

[187] This conclusion has been supported in the academic literature by the penetrating work of Kaveh Ehsani. See Kaveh Ehsani, 'The Politics of Property in the Islamic Republic of Iran', in *The Rule of Law, Islam, and Constitutional Politics in Egypt and Iran*, ed. Said Amir Arjomand and Nathan J. Brown (Albany State University of New York 2013), pp. 159–60. 'War and Resentment: Critical Reflections on the Legacies of the Iran–Iraq War', *Middle East Critique* (2016), p. 10.

[188] For further analysis, see Ehteshami, *After Khomeini*, Loc 2335. Asef Bayat, 'Tehran: Paradox City', *New Left Review*, no. 66 (November–December 2010), p. 111.

task which during his tenure floundered along, so that the Commander of the Reconstruction had to content himself with a far more humble, albeit significant, series of achievements – the privatisation of industries associated with the National Iranian Industries Organisation, the unification of the currency, the establishment of free zones, and the expansion of the stock exchange perhaps being amongst the best known.[189]

This platform found a discrete party-political expression in the first months of 1996 with the de facto establishment of a group comprising high-ranking government officials under the name of the 'Servants of the Reconstruction' (*Khedmatgozaran-e sazandegi*), a formation that would later emerge as a fully fledged party organisation called the Executives of Reconstruction Party (*Hezb-e kargozaran-e sazandegi*),[190] and of which Karbaschi went on to become the general secretary.[191] This group, though established at the end of Rafsanjani's presidency, ultimately became a formation to carry forth his legacy and agenda in the form of an organised and sustained political platform. The reasons behind its initial emergence came out of a more immediate political rift, this time within the right itself, as the disagreements surfaced between the Society of Combatant Clergy (JRM), of which Rafsanjani was himself a member, and the Rafsanjani government on the JRM's proposed electoral list on the cusp of the Fifth Majles elections during the final months of 1995. As has been recounted, the Islamic left, comprising the Association of Combatant Clerics (MRM), the Office for Strengthening Unity, and SMEEI, had been decisively routed and marginalised in the aftermath of the Fourth Majles elections. *Salam* went so far as to declaim that 'the right faction are so monopolist (*enhesar-talab*) that they can't even tolerate insiders (*khodi-ha*)' – a belief which no doubt informed the MRM's decision to boycott the approaching elections altogether.[192]

---

[189] Marina Forti, 'Arg-e Jadid: A California Oasis in the Iranian Desert', in *Evil Paradises: Dreamworlds of Neoliberalism*, ed. Mike Davis and David Bertrand Monk (New York & London: The New Press, 2007).

[190] 'Entekhabat: payvast-ha va gosast-ha', *Payam-e emruz*, no. 10 (15 Bahman–15 Esfand 1374 [4 February 1996–5 March 1996]), p. 9.

[191] Quchani, *Yaqeh sefid-ha*, p. 129. Rafsanjani also tried to claim that his own politics – in this instance, the selection and presentation of his first cabinet – had been above partisanship (*fara-jenahi*), and that this had irked the Islamic left and was the reason why the Third Majles, which the latter then dominated, was reluctant to approve his proposed ministers. Ziba-Kalam, Sadat Etefaqfar, and Hashemi-Rafsanjani, *Hashemi bedun-e rotush*, p. 123.

[192] 'Entekhabat: payvast-ha va gosast-ha', p. 15.

The ongoing disagreements between the government on one side and powerful elements within the JRM and Islamic Coalition Society on the other eventually impelled sixteen individuals, ten of whom were ministers and four deputies in the government, to publish a communiqué on 17 January 1996 (27 Dey 1374) announcing their support for the president's political programme.[193] This was an outcome which on the surface Rafsanjani had initially strenuously resisted, asking the former chairman of the Society of Combatant Clergy, Ayatollah Mahdavi-Kani, to intercede, so that a list agreeable to all sides might be decided.[194] In reaction to what he saw as the traditional right's intransigence, former interior minister and prominent MRM member Mohtashamipur declared, 'they [namely, the traditional right] can't even tolerate their likeminded colleagues in the Society of Combatant Clergy like Mr. Hashemi-Rafsanjani and the ministers in the executive entrusted by the same majority in parliament. How can they tolerate the idealistic wing (*jenah-e arman-gara'i*), which fundamentally disagrees with them on political and economic issues?'[195]

The signatories of the communiqué were generally regarded as respected technocrats, often with technical backgrounds and expertise, but also to some extent Rafsanjani loyalists, with critics such as Mohammad-Javad Larijani implying it was little more than a 'political club' and cheerleader for the incumbent president.[196] The group ultimately offered up a separate electoral list for Tehran from that of the Society of Combatant Clergy and, in some way, formalised the faction which had been designated as the modern right. In the broader scheme of things, the rift between the two might be thought symptomatic of the burgeoning antagonism between those clerics on the traditional right and their allies in the bazaar and a rival nascent bourgeoisie with a distinct socio-cultural outlook and economic basis, encouraged under the auspices of Rafsanjani and his technocratic allies.[197]

---

[193] Signatories included government ministers Mohammad 'Ali Najafi, Esma'il Shushtari, Akbar Torkan, Mohammad Gharazi, Gholam-Reza Foruzesh, Mohammad Ne'matzadeh, 'Isa Kalantari, Bizhan Zanganeh, Gholam-Reza Shafe'i, Morteza Mohammad Khan, and deputies 'Ataollah Mohajerani, Mohammad Hashemi, Reza Amrollahi, Mostafa Hashemi-Taba, the head of the Central Bank, Mohsen Nurbakhsh, and Tehran's mayor, Gholam-Hosayn Karbaschi. Ibid., p. 10.

[194] Ibid., p. 9.   [195] Ibid., p. 16.   [196] Ibid., p. 11.

[197] For Ansari's pertinent assessment, see Ansari, *Iran, Islam and Democracy*, chapter 5.

The latter had been pursuing a greater degree of laxity in socio-cultural norms and openings to foreign capital, while the former remained largely hostile to such a prospect. This is despite the fact that the success of Rafsanjani's aspirations to transform Iran's political economy remained seriously constrained and his relations with international financial institutions overstated.[198] As Rafsanjani's programmes came in for growing criticism, and the political vacuum of the absentee *chap* was increasingly felt: the mounting disagreements over approach and outlook exacerbated tensions in the JRM and elsewhere and severely weakened a convenient alliance which had allowed the right to push out their competitors on the left through the targeted deployment of approbatory supervision (*nezarat-e estesvabi*).

Prominent members of the later full-fledged party – namely, the Executives of Reconstruction – included Rafsanjani's long-time legal and parliamentary deputy 'Ataollah Mohajerani, Mohammad-'Ali Najafi, Eshaq Jahangiri, Mohammad 'Atriyanfar, Rafsanjani's brother Mohammad Hashemi, his wife's first cousin Hosayn Mar'ashi, nephew 'Ali Hashemi, and children, Mohsen and Fa'ezeh Hashemi-Bahramani.[199] Quchani, who today is one of Kargozaran's pre-eminent intellectuals and central committee members, extolled the president's project of 'depoliticization' but was hardly a disinterested voice. Nor was his appraisal, for that matter, an accurate description of events, since, as both forces within traditional right and the left understood, Rafsanjani unmistakably possessed his own political vision and hierarchy of values[200] and sought to pursue a specific political trajectory at the expense of others. The president and his partisans made efforts to present their mission statement as beyond partisanship or *fara-jenahi*, and the proto-Kargozaran sought to lend a non-political and 'scientific' air to

[198] Harris, *A Social Revolution*, Loc 3903.
[199] Shadlu, *Etela'ati dar bareh-ye ahzab va jenah-ha-ye siyasi-ye Iran-e emruz*, p. 163. For a partisan and hostile account to their right, see 'Abdollah Shamsi, *Hezb-e kargozaran-e sazandegi* (Qom: Pazhuheshkadeh-ye tahqiqat-e eslami, 1390 [2011]), pp. 66–86.
[200] In 1967, over a decade prior to the 1979 Revolution, Rafsanjani wrote a monograph on Amir Kabir, the Qajar-era prime minister and reformer executed on the order of Naser al-Din Shah in 1852, who has since been the subject of much hagiographical literature and nationalist historiography. In that volume he depicted Amir Kabir as a 'combatant hero against imperialism', whose internal reforms were similarly predicated on the fight against foreign domination of Iran. Akbar Hashemi-Rafsanjani, *Amir Kabir: ya qahreman-e mobarezeh ba este'mar* (Tehran: Mo'asseseh-ye matbu'at-e Farahani, 1346 [1967]).

their policies and thereby place them beyond factional disputes, equating them with Iran's self-evident and identifiable national interest.[201] As illustrated by Cyrus Schayegh, the social capital and strategic deployment of Western science in the formation of modern Iranian society has a long and distinguished lineage in the late nineteenth and twentieth centuries, particularly from the 1920s onwards. Seeing as Rafsanjani and his ministers came of age in the Pahlavi era, they could not but have been affected by this legacy, with its implications for the nature of expert authority and the emergence of a new middle class in many ways predicated on such technical expertise and its mastery. Even though many were openly sceptical of Rafsanjani and his supporters' claims to supra-partisanship or apolitical policymaking, such ways of framing political positions and advocacy undeniably shaped the topography of political debate in the years which ensued.

During the first half of the 1990s, 'Abdolkarim Sorush sought to make the most of Rafsanjani's public and private assurances, as he had known the latter from his days on the Council for Cultural Revolution. On 23 July 1992, Sorush met face to face with Rafsanjani complaining of *Kayhan* newspaper's attacks against him and somewhat patronisingly telling him 'in this regime more attention is given to the culture of the commoners (*'avam*) than the thinkers (*motafakeran*)'. Rafsanjani tried to console Sorush, only to tell him that 'he should expect such attacks regarding some of his statements'[202] – hardly words of reassurance. Nevertheless, Sorush continued to pin his hopes on the moderate elements around the president, hoping they might shield him against a backlash from vigilante forces such as the Ansar-e Hezbollah and the traditional right. The official cultural milieu, however, was far from accommodating or sympathetic, and the appointment as minister of culture of a conservative member of the Islamic Coalition Society in the form of Mostafa Mir-Salim, whom even Rafsanjani had criticised for 'narrow-mindedness' in public,[203] certainly did not help matters.

[201] Cyrus Schayegh, *Who Is Knowledgeable Is Strong: Science, Class, and the Formation of Modern Iranian Society, 1900–1950* (Berkeley, Los Angeles, London: University of California Press, 2009), p. 7.

[202] Akbar Hashemi-Rafsanjani and Hasan Lahuti, *Karnameh va khaterat-e Hashemi-Rafsanjani sal-e 1371: rownaq-e sazandegi* (Tehran: Daftar-e nashr-e ma'aref-e enqelab, 1393 [2014]), p. 233.

[203] Siavush Randjbar-Daemi, *Intra-State Relations in the Islamic Republic of Iran: The Presidency and the Struggle for Political Authority, 1989–2009* (PhD thesis, Royal Holloway, University of London, 2011), pp. 125–6.

A couple of years later, in a series of private and open letters to the president, Sorush protested the public comments made by Ayatollah Naser Makarem-Shirazi comparing him to the historian, intellectual, and uncompromising critic of Shi'i Islam Ahmad Kasravi (1890–1946).[204] As mentioned in Chapter 2, Kasravi was brutally murdered by members of the Fada'iyan-e Islam in 1946. It was therefore a comparison which left little to the imagination and understandably led Sorush to fear for his life. In a private letter to President Rafsanjani in the aftermath of a rowdy disruption and attempted assault at a lecture he delivered in Isfahan on 18 June 1995, Sorush not only said that he found the comparison with Kasravi to be an insult (*tohmat*) but also made the rather poorly judged claim that 'perhaps since the establishment of the Islamic Republic till now, nobody has been insulted and attacked by the media as much as yours truly'.[205] He then pointedly asks the president, 'shouldn't they [i.e., the vigilantes] be shown a better way than this for the defence of the jurisprudential-political theory of *velayat-e faqih* and the encouragement of others to accept it?'[206] In something of a desperate effort to convince the president to take action, while of course selectively forgetting his own active role in the Cultural Revolution and the assault on intellectual-academic freedom, he disingenuously contended that 'as a teacher I can never believe that someone in this country could be rewarded and encouraged to fight with teachers and to scare artists and intellectuals from thinking or writing'.[207]

On 18 July 1995 (27 Tir 1374) a letter was sent to Rafsanjani and was co-signed by a host of prominent members of the Islamic left and religious intellectual circles – to wit, Aqajari, Armin, Baqi, Banki, Ganji, Tajzadeh, Khaniki, 'Arabsorkhi, Hajjariyan, Mazru'i, as well as sympathetic academics and publishers – deploring the disruption of Sorush's Isfahan speech on the anniversary of Shari'ati's death. They insisted Rafsanjani's role as president was that of 'guarding the constitution' and that vigilante groups 'now even targeted the society's

---

[204] 'Abdolkarim Sorush, 'Nameh-ye khosusi beh riyasat-e jomhuri-ye eslami-ye Iran (Aqa-ye Hashemi-Rafsanjani) va riyasat-e qovveh-ye qaza'iyyeh (Aqa-ye Mohammad Yazdi)', in *Siyasat-nameh* (Tehran: Serat, 1378 [1999]), p. 5.
[205] 'Nameh-ye khosusi beh riyasat-e jomhuri-ye eslami-ye Iran (Aqa-ye Hashemi-Rafsanjani) [4 Tir 1374 (25 June 1995)]', in *Siyasat-nameh* (Tehran: Serat, 1378 [1999]), p. 13.
[206] Ibid., p. 17.   [207] Ibid., p. 18.

committed and intellectual Muslims (*mosalmanan-e mota'ahed va andishmand*) with irreverence (*hormatshekani*)'.[208] This was merely one of many similar instances whereby the political and social capital of the Islamic left and other relationships within the political class was deployed in defence of an individual they perceived not merely as an important ally but one of their leading intellectual lights. This is despite the fact that, as was made clear in Chapter 3, Sorush was never a member of the Islamic left or any of its party-political organisations.[209] He did, though, undoubtedly stand as an intellectual leader and mentor for many of their number.

Before writing an open letter to Rafsanjani on 9 May 1996, Sorush insisted that he had remained quiet and not delivered any speeches or accepted any invitations for speaking engagements over the previous eight months out of a desire to 'preserve the interests of the country'.[210] However, as events in subsequent years and the further curtailment of Sorush's public activities would testify, his epistolary indignation and exhortations would fall on deaf ears. As a result of Rafsanjani's perceived inaction, or lack of tangible steps to secure the religious intellectual's security and freedom of expression, on 9 May 1996 Sorush – rather than author another private letter – wrote a public missive to the president, stating that the threats against his person by so-called 'pressure-groups' (*goru-ha-ye feshar*) continued unabated, at one point comparing himself to the Galileo and Giordano Bruno.[211] The latter of course was burned at the stake on account of his alleged heresy, while Galileo was forced to recant his cosmological findings and live out the rest of his days under house arrest. Both found themselves at odds with, and persecuted by, the clerical authorities of the day, only to be vindicated by posterity. Sorush was publicly reading his troubled relationship with elements of the Islamic system he formerly defended through the lens of Western history and the grand confrontation of Renaissance-era science and the Catholic church.

After Sorush's passport was temporarily confiscated at the airport upon returning from a trip abroad, he wrote another letter to the

---

[208] 'Nameh-ye dah-ha shakhsiyyat-e farhangi-ye keshvar beh ra'is-e jomhur', ibid., p. 85.
[209] The letter was also published in issue 25 of *Kiyan*.
[210] Sorush, 'Nameh-ye sar goshadeh beh riyasat-e jomhuri-ye eslami-ye Iran (Aqa-ye Hashemi-Rafsanjani) [20 Ordibehesht 1375/9 May 1996]', p. 33.
[211] Ibid., pp. 32–4.

president imploring him to clarify the situation. Sorush's passport was soon returned, but he was informed that he would be permitted to leave the country only on the condition of ending all 'subversive' activities. He was then in this short period explicitly prohibited from speaking at Hosayniyyeh Ershad for Shari'ati's annual memorial, which he decided to attend in spite of the threats against him. He reiterates in his private letter to Rafsanjani that he had several speaking engagements abroad, including one at St Antony's College, Oxford, and that his inability to attend does not reflect well on the country, complaining, 'till when can I be silent on this issue?'[212] While angered at his treatment, Sorush also invoked his rights as a citizen and thereby sought to perform the role of a liberal subject in an illiberal political and judicial order. His protestations to Rafsanjani remained for the most part private, hoping that the president might be able to restrain those baying for his blood. Though it was ultimately to little avail, and he was forced to miss the conference, it does appear from Sorush's last private letter on 6 July 1997 that Rafsanjani did actually try to intercede on Sorush's behalf, albeit without much by way of tangible success.[213]

---

212 'Nameh-ye khosusi-ye beh riyasat-e jomhuri-ye eslami-ye Iran (Aqa-ye Hashemi Rafsanjani) [7 Tir 1376/28 June 1997]', p. 48.
213 'Nameh-ye khosusi beh riyasat-e jomhuri-ye eslami-ye Iran (Aqa-ye Hashemi-Rafsanjani) [15 Tir 1376/6 July 1997]', p. 53.

5 | Free Faith, Democratic Governance, and the 'Official Reading' of Religion

The democratic state, the true state, does not need religion for its political completion . . . [I]t can discard religion, because in it the human foundation of religion is realized in a secular way. The so-called Christian state, on the other hand, behaves in a political way towards religion and in a religious way towards politics. In the same way as it demeans political forms to appearances, it demeans religion to a mere appearance.[1]

Karl Marx

Never on earth will a utopia and heavenly society be forged. The issue is one of corrupt and less corrupt, bad and worse.[2]

Mohammad Mojtahed-Shabestari

In his diary of 6 April 1981, Hojjat al-Islam Akbar Hashemi-Rafsanjani describes a meeting with the theologian and sitting MP for the East Azerbaijan town of Shabestar, Mohammad Mojtahed-Shabestari. As related by Rafsanjani, Mojtahed-Shabestari had come to discuss and ask him, as a member of the Revolutionary Council and Khomeini's inner circle of trusted advisers, what distinguished the 'essence of the disagreements between us (the Imam's Line) and the liberals [Mr. Bani-Sadr and the Freedom Movement] and he [i.e., Shabestari] wanted an explanation'. Rafsanjani then relays his reply, underlining the analysis of Bazargan, as explicated in the previous chapter: 'I said the issue is with respect to jurisprudential Islam (*Islam-e feqahati*). They do not accept this Islamic jurisprudence, [and] we don't see any other path than the implementation of the same *feqh* (with greater effort and vibrant *ejtehad*). I brought many examples that this was the desire of the Imam [Khomeini] and we defend it.'[3]

---

[1] Karl Marx, 'On the Jewish Question', in *Early Writings* (London & New York: Penguin, 1992), p. 223.

[2] Mohammad Mojtahed-Shabestari, 'Shura-ha va masa'leh-ye 'edalat', in *Naqdi bar qara'at-e rasmi az din: bohran-ha, chalesh-ha, rah-e hal-ha* (Tehran: Tarh-e now, 1381 [2002]), p. 155.

[3] Hashemi-Rafsanjani and Hashemi, *'Obur az bohran*, p. 53.

One can only speculate, but it is certainly curious that Shabestari went to seek Rafsanjani's counsel and clarification to determine the difference between Khomeini's diehard supporters, the Imam's Line, and the so-called 'liberals', encompassing the incumbent president Bani-Sadr and the NAI. The former of course would be impeached and the latter's candidates in due course found themselves disqualified from standing in elections across the board.[4] Though one should be cautious about imputing motives to Shabestari, one can certainly speculate as to whether certain doubts about the path taken by the revolution had not already begun to prey on the then 45-year-old cleric's mind. His virtual abandonment of active politics following the First Majles to focus on intellectual and academic pursuits seems to indicate this may well have been the case.

Nevertheless, less than twenty years later, Shabestari no longer accepted Rafsanjani's assertions regarding ideology and *feqh* and, on the basis of his study of hermeneutics and certain modern trends in Protestant theology, would publicly repudiate, root and branch, *feqh*'s political-executive role in the governance of the modern state.[5] In fact, he would entitle one of his best-known collections of articles and interviews 'the critique of the official reading (*qara'at*) of religion' and in turn identified the 'official reading' with the domination of jurisprudential Islam.[6] Shabestari's writings, along with those of Sorush, were amongst the most important authored by religious intellectuals in arguing against so-called 'ideological Islam', which had been ardently supported by elements of the Islamic left, many of whom continued to act and think in the ideological shadow of Khomeini, Motahhari, Taleqani, and Shari'ati.

Despite his increasingly critical distance from *Islam-e feqahati*, he refused to abandon the 'revolution of Iran', which he argued was regarded as a 'rational movement' by the country's Muslim population. In his estimation, the message of the revolution was decidedly 'rational-humane' and was not by any means exhausted or explained through

---

[4] For a thorough account of the Bani-Sadr presidency and his impeachment in June 1981, see Siavush Randjbar-Daemi, *The Quest for Authority in Iran: A History of the Presidency from Revolution to Rouhani* (London & New York: I. B. Tauris, 2018), chapter 2.

[5] Mojtahed-Shabestari, 'Feqh-e siyasi bastar-e 'oqala'i-ye khod ra az dast dadeh ast', p. 169.

[6] 'Qara'at-e rasmi az din', p. 31.

recourse to Islamic jurisprudence. Furthermore, the 'reading of Islam' advocated by the revolution harboured a political message, which called on Muslims to fight against despotism and imperialism and to establish a political regime predicated on the values of freedom, justice, and independence.[7] However, with the founding of the Islamic Republic, *Islam-e feqahati* became the 'official governmental reading' (*qara'at-e rasmi-ye hokumati*). Affirming much of Bazargan's early analysis, Mojtahed-Shabestari states that those who support the 'official reading' hold that Islam prescribes a 'fixed' and 'eternal' political regime. In the 'official reading' the form of government is putatively derived directly from the Qur'an and hadith, and it is the obligation of the state to implement Islamic ordinances. While Shabestari does not say such, this description bears a great deal of resemblance to the image of the Islamic state envisioned by Ayatollah Khomeini in *Velayat-e faqih, hokumat-e eslami*.

Despite the aforementioned comments of Rafsanjani in 1981 or even the contents of Khomeini's own writings on the nature of Islamic government, Shabestari contends that 'jurisprudential Islam' acquired dominance in the Islamic Republic's second decade.[8] As had been seen in earlier chapters, following Khomeini's death many on the Islamic left argued that there was a concerted effort on the part of the traditional right to monopolise all of the central state institutions by means of the Guardian Council's arrogation of 'approbatory supervision' and domination of the judiciary. As one might expect, the traditional right's conception of jurisprudence was held to be correspondingly 'traditional', if not well-nigh ossified and mired in stasis. The Islamic left, while critical of Rafsanjani, who was seen as the patron of the 'modern right' (*rast-e jadid*), reserved a special venom for the 'traditional right' (*rast-e sonnati*), which was seen as illegitimately dominating many of the state's unelected institutions without popular mandate. Shabestari held a comparable political and theological stance, believing that the 'official reading' in the aftermath of Khomeini's death had led the revolution astray from its 'rational-humane' message of human emancipation. Similar to accounts of the Islamic left pertaining to the 1980s, there is no mention of encroaching political authoritarianism, the mass executions of political prisoners throughout the 1980s culminating in

[7] 'Enqelab-e eslami va qara'at-e ma'qul az din', p. 21.
[8] 'Qara'at-e rasmi az din', p. 31.

the 1988 prison massacres, or the many other infringements on civil liberties and human rights which took place when numerous Islamic leftists had held key posts of authority in the state edifice. While one should certainly try and fathom the immense inexpedience and danger posed by publicly dwelling on such events, it is also worthwhile pointing out this common act of occlusion and omission which has impinged upon the historiography of the revolutionary state and its founding and development as told by the religious intellectuals and especially the Islamic left until fairly recently. In short, liberalism and liberal criteria are taken up as a modality of critique but applied quite selectively to the post-Khomeini period.

The main target of Shabestari's criticism remains the traditional right – namely, the alleged partisans of the 'official reading', who understand basic individual rights laid down in the constitution in accordance with 'traditional jurisprudence'.[9] More controversially, he contends that *velayat-e faqih* was merely one jurisprudential opinion issued by a single *mojtahed* – Khomeini – and upon which no consensus existed but which 'had obtained political legitimacy with the people's votes'.[10] The plurality of views in the seminary is certainly supported by the historical record,[11] as is the conclusion that, except for Khomeini, none of the top-tiered *maraje'* in Iran advocated an executive-governmental conception of *velayat-e faqih* on the eve of the revolution.[12] Unfortunately, in his appraisal Shabestari omits that Khomeini and his clerical disciples (of which he was one) were decisive to the transformation of *velayat-e faqih* from a view advocated by a lone *mojtahed* into an institutionalised structure of rule and political authority in the new constitutional order. The tensions within his political outlook are immediately evident. At once calling for the acknowledgement of individual political and civil rights as codified in the Islamic Republic's constitution, while at the same time pointing to the tenuousness of *velayat-e faqih* as merely one juristic opinion amongst others, which nevertheless also happened to be enshrined within the very same founding document of the post-revolutionary

---

[9] Ibid., p. 30.   [10] Ibid., p. 31.

[11] See Linda S. Walbridge, *The Thread of Mu'awiya: The Making of a Marja' Taqlid* (Bloomington, Ind.: The Ramsay Press, 2014).

[12] Grand Ayatollah Golpayegani only came out publicly in its favour following the revolution. Randjbar-Daemi, 'Building the Islamic State: The Draft Constitution of 1979 Reconsidered', p. 653.

state. Shabestari does to some extent manage to theoretically resolve this tension, as will be seen below. The practical resolution of this contradiction would prove to be quite a different matter, however, and he would have few words of advice on that pressing concern.

According to Shabestari, the defenders of *Islam-e feqahati* contend that the theory of *velayat-e faqih* is beyond criticism. The proponents of the official reading also believe the use of violence is permissible against those who oppose their political programme and pose a threat to its continued rule. In short, it 'theorises violence' in the name of Islam.[13] According to Shabestari, this reading is facing a crisis because it has divested Islam of any 'spiritual message' and argued that the people have no legitimate role in determining their political destiny. This reading has also sought to appropriate the legacy of the revolution for its own purposes, claiming that it occurred for the sole end of establishing an 'eternal' and 'unchangeable' political regime predicated on Islamic law.[14] The question inevitably arises, does not most, if not all, Islamic penal law revolve around the question of the legitimate application, extent, and proportionality of violence and/or retribution when its laws and norms have been trangressed? Is only political jurisprudence concerned with the exercise of violence? What of those kinds of 'legitimate' violence exacted and legitimated through the modern state's juridical channels and carceral forms essential to governmentality in the present? Because Shabestari does not address these questions in any depth or attempt to parse important distinctions, it makes more sense to understand such critiques through a political lens.

One of the main targets in this critique was Ayatollah Mohammad-Taqi Mesbah-Yazdi, head of the Imam Khomeini Educational Research Institute, which some have even speculated was established with the explicit aim of mounting a sustained ideological rebuttal and challenge to Sorush and the nascent religious intellectual project. The two men partook in a private academic discussion in Qom in 1987–8, in which they addressed questions relating to Islamic metaphysics and the epistemology of modern science and for which there exists an unpublished transcript,[15] but

---

[13] Mojtahed-Shabestari, 'Qara'at-e rasmi az din', p. 31.   [14] Ibid., p. 32.
[15] The debate has been confirmed to the author by 'Abdolkarim Sorush himself. Eskandar Sadeghi-Boroujerdi and 'Abdolkarim Sorush, 11 December 2016.

they never debated face-to-face thereafter.[16] By the late 1990s, Mesbah had emerged as one of the most radical defenders of Ayatollah Khameneh'i's 'absolute guardianship', even though many in the traditional seminary had resisted assenting to the latter's *marja 'iyyat* following his accession to the office of Guardian Jurist. Mesbah-Yazdi is not primarily known for being a jurist but rather a teacher of Islamic philosophy, especially Avicenna and Mulla Sadra,[17] and had in 1981 participated alongside Sorush in the ideological debates which aimed to rebuff and discredit the materialism espoused by Marxists Ehsan Tabari and Farrokh Negahdar of the Tudeh Party and the Organisation of the Iranian People's Fada'i Guerrillas, respectively.[18] By the time of the publication of Shabestari's essay, Mesbah had been cast by the Islamic *chap* as the supreme 'theoretician of violence' and accused of issuing fatwas legitimising the extra-judicial assassination of secular writers, journalists, and political activists.[19] Moreover, Khameneh'i's lavish praise of Mesbah-Yazdi during one of the periods of acute backlash against the reformist press and the intelligentsia threw the factional and institutional alignments of the time into clear relief. In a speech at the Base for the Education of the University Basij on 4 September 1999, Khameneh'i reiterated his immense respect for the controversial cleric:

It is almost forty years that I know Mr. Mesbah-Yazdi. It is as a jurist, philosopher, thinker, and authority (*sahebnazar*) on the fundamental issues of Islam that I have heartfelt regard for him. God almighty did not bestow the good fortune to this generation to learn from individuals like 'Allameh Tabataba'i and Martyr Motahhari. But with the grace of God, this dear

---

[16] Mohammad-Taqi Mesbah-Yazdi and 'Abdolkarim Sorush, 'Jalaseh-ye monazereh-ye ostad Mohammad-Taqi Mesbah-Yazdi va Aqa-ye Doktor 'Abdolkarim Sorush' (Unpublished Transcript).

[17] Abolqasem Fana'i and Eskandar Sadeghi-Boroujerdi, 'Interview with Abolqasem Fana'i' (06/08/2012).

[18] Mesbah-Yazdi et al., *Gofteman-e rowshangar dar bareh-ye andisheh-ha-ye bonyadin*. Mesbah's critique of Marxism was later articulated in a small book edited and transcribed by none other than Mostafa Malekiyan. Mohammad-Taqi Mesbah-Yazdi, *Naqdi-ye feshordeh bar osul-e Marxism* (Qom: Mo'asseseh-ye rah-e haqq, 1367 [1988]). For details of Malekiyan's relationship with Mesbah-Yazdi, see Eskandar Sadeghi-Boroujerdi, 'Mostafa Malekian: Spirituality, Siyasat-Zadegi and (A)political Self-Improvement', *Digest of Middle East Studies* 23, no. 2 (2014).

[19] San'ati, *Gofteman-e Mesbah*, p. 370–1.

and greatly valuable person fills the vacuum in our time left by these beloved men.[20]

This was not only a ringing endorsement by the most powerful author-ity in the land but commendation of someone considered by the *chap* and religious intellectuals alike to be a notorious ideologue, a defender of theocratic absolutism, and an advocate of unmitigated violence against critics, not only of the *nezam* but of the Islamic left as well.[21] Whether or not their portrayal was at least partially a caricature,[22] it certainly made clear where the lion's share of the Guardian Jurist's support and his immense networks of patronage resided at the time. This patronage was manifest in tangible material terms given that Mesbah's institute was founded in 1995 (1374) with funds provided directly by the leader's office.[23] Furthermore, the comparison with two titans of Iran's Islamic intellectual life, Motahhari and Tabataba'i, must not only have raised eyebrows but also rubbed ample salt into the wound. This was all the more since several figures on the Islamic left considered themselves the true intellectual heirs to Motahhari, had studied with and struggled alongside him in the decades preceding the revolution, and considered him one of their own number. Today Mesbah's institute constitutes a major research complex in Qom, with several departments covering everything from political theory to psychology, mysticism, and sociology, publishing many journals in a comparable range of disciplines.

For Shabestari, the bankruptcy of the absolutist conception of *velayat-e faqih* and its recourse to violence were two sides of the same coin. On the view of Mesbah-Yazdi and his allies, popular

---

[20] 'Ali Khameneh'i, 'Didar daneshjuyan sherkat konandeh dar ordu-ye amuzeshi-parvareshi-ye Basij-e daneshju'i ba rahbar-e enqelab', *Khamenei.ir* (13/6/1378 [4 September 1999]).

[21] Akbar Ganji, 'Motahhari, ruyaru-ye Khaz'ali, Mahdavi-Kani va Mesbah-Yazdi (Originally published in *Sobh-e emruz*, 8/7/1378 [30 September 1999])', in *Tallaqi-ye fashishti az din va hokumat: asib-shenasi-ye gozar beh dowlat-e demokratik-e towse'eh-gara* (Tehran: Tarh-e now, 1379 [2000]). Mohammad-Taqi Mesbah-Yazdi, *Negahi-ye gozara beh nazariyyeh-ye velayat-e faqih* (Qom: Entesharat-e mo'asseseh-ye amuzeshi va pazhuheshi-ye Imam Khomeini, 1388 [2009]), p. 18.

[22] This article attempts to argue how Mesbah-Yazdi's views have been distorted by his political adversaries. Pezhman Ehsan-Bakhsh, 'Ostad Mesbah va dah te'ori-ye "khoshunat" va "terrorism"', *Ketab-e naqd*, no. 14–15 (1379 [2000]).

[23] San'ati, *Gofteman-e Mesbah*, p. 191.

elections were irrelevant to the legitimacy of the *vali-ye faqih*. The people's votes fundamentally could not bestow legitimacy (*mashru'iyyat*) upon the *vali*.[24] The people could merely demonstrate their acceptance of him, since the only genuine source of legitimacy was divine in nature and essentially negated the notion of popular sovereignty altogether.[25] Shabestari does not mince his words in calling such a view a 'violation of the constitution'. Much like Bazargan before him, he also laments the division of the national polity into 'insiders' and 'outsiders', where, depending on your membership or lack thereof, you either accrue or are deprived of certain privileges.[26] Islam has been instrumentalised by the proponents of the 'official reading', who identify their policies and actions with Islam *in toto* and thus claim any criticism of them beyond the pale.[27] It also takes up the task of remaking cultural practices in its own Procrustean image and imposing its values on the public sphere. Shabestari resolutely states that this is not the role of the state and that it ultimately destroys any chance of democracy coming to fruition.[28] The state should rather ensure that it coordinates its policies with the values and sentiments of 'public culture' (*farhang-e 'omumi*) and should never partake in such cultural reconstruction (*farhang-sazi*). This position taken by Shabestari is not merely a repudiation of 'traditionalist jurisprudence' but goes much deeper, rejecting any role for the state in promoting a specific identity or way of life, and thereby propounds a species of negative freedom, at times advocating a conception of the state which comes perilously close to Robert Nozick's 'night-watchman state'.[29] Shabestari assertively rejects paternalism, arguing that the values and policies adopted by the state must be determined democratically from the bottom up. Following Khatami's election as president, he contended – very much in line with the president's political platform – that if cultural activities are to be undertaken they must be done by non-governmental

---

[24] Mesbah-Yazdi, *Negahi-ye gozara beh nazariyyeh-ye velayat-e faqih*, p. 69. *Nazariyyeh-ye siyasi-ye Islam, jeld-e avval, Majmu'eh-ye asar* (Qom: Entesharat-e mo'asseseh-ye amuzeshi va pazhuheshi-ye Imam Khomeini, 1388 [2009]), p. 308.

[25] Mojtahed-Shabestari, 'Qara'at-e rasmi az din', p. 32.   [26] Ibid., p. 32.

[27] Ibid., p. 33.   [28] Ibid., p. 33.

[29] Robert Nozick, *Anarchy, State, and Utopia* (New York & London: Wiley-Blackwell, 2001).

organisations which occupy civil society, existing independently of the state.[30]

In keeping with his scepticism towards the state's role in *farhang-sazi*, Shabestari further claims that it should not be assumed that it has responsibility for conflating a religious transgression or 'sin' (*gonah*) committed by a private individual with a 'crime' (*jorm*) or breach of the law, so that, even if refusal to wear the hijab might be considered a 'sin', and for Shabestari it is by no means obvious that it constitutes one, the state has no legitimate role in criminalising such a refusal.[31] 'Sins' or religious transgressions are privatised and precluded from the scope of state authority and the coercive enforcement by the state apparatus, which would imply that the role of the state as enforcer of the *shari'ah* and public morality has lost its rationale. This is in stark contradiction to the positions advocated by Navvab Safavi and Ayatollah Khomeini reviewed in Chapter 2, as well as the actual coercive practices of the Islamic Republic and its policing of public morality.

Velayat-e faqih, One View of Many

As was mentioned above, Shabestari is eager to emphasise that the theory of *velayat-e faqih* is only one amongst many others. He adds that the chief reason it received support and was enshrined in the constitution of the Islamic Republic was the popularity and charismatic appeal of Ayatollah Khomeini. 'The extraordinary trust of the people of Iran in the leadership of Imam Khomeini during the revolution and after its victory resulted in a relationship between a large segment of the people and the clergy taking shape, which here we interpret as "political *taqlid*".'[32] Rather than emphasising Khomeini's position as a *marja'*, Shabestari takes care to stress the extraordinary conditions of the revolution itself and Khomeini's charismatic political leadership. He thereby attempts to diminish *velayat-e faqih*'s religious-scriptural basis and to bind and intertwine the theory and institution of *vali-ye faqih* with the specific person of Khomeini and the exceptional circumstances of the revolution. *Velayat-e faqih*'s legitimacy derived from

---

[30] 'Bazgasht beh keramat-e ensani', in *Jame'eh-ye madani, Dovvom-e Khordad, va Khatami: goftogu-ha'i ba andishmandan-e mo'aser-e Iran*, ed. Ma'sud Razavi (Tehran: Farzan-e ruz, 1379 [2000]), p. 54.

[31] 'Mosalmanan bayad hoquq-e bashar ra bepazirand', p. 204.

[32] 'Qara'at-e rasmi az din', p. 34.

popular backing and the people's assent to the charismatic leadership of Khomeini, whereas the 'official reading' has sought to enshrine and sanctify the principle of *velayat-e faqih* in and of itself. Perhaps the most notorious example was that of Ayatollah Ahmad Azari-Qomi, who from Khomeini's death in June 1989 until the winter of 1994 was one of the most senior diehard supporters of the 'absolute guardianship of the Islamic jurist' and Khameneh'i's newfound authority as leader. Prior to his death Azari-Qomi would have a radical change of heart, but during the aforementioned period he went so far as to even assert that 'the *vali-ye faqih* can temporarily suspend monotheism' (*towhid*).[33] What exactly the latter even meant or would entail need not distract us here. Shabestari argues conversely that it was in fact exceptional circumstances which brought about the emergence of *velayat-e faqih* as a particular form of governance.[34] Sorush in a similar vein has called *velayat-e faqih* an 'accidental' in contradistinction to an 'essential' feature of religion, emphasising the institution's historical contingency.[35]

The original act of *taqlid* or 'emulation' which had made *velayat-e faqih* a political reality had ceased to be a viable source of political legitimacy and had given way to the principle of political participation, where the people determine their political destiny through the ballot-box and civic activism.[36] For Shabestari this transition from emulation to participation is indicative of a deeper sea-change in the nature of political legitimacy in Iranian society: 'a state of transition from political legitimacy based on religious beliefs and feelings (political *taqlid*) to political legitimacy predicated on political rationality with the method of trial and error and correction'.[37] In Shabestari's depiction of the profound transformation unfolding within the depths of the

[33] Kadivar, 'Zekr-e mosibat-e Ayatollah Azari-Qomi', *Faraz va forud-e Azari-Qomi: sayri dar tahavvol-e mabani-ye fekri-ye Ayatollah Ahmad Azari-Qomi*, 2., p. 87.

[34] Mojtahed-Shabestari, 'Qara'at-e rasmi az din', p. 36.

[35] Sorush has sought to make a comparable argument. See 'Abdolkarim Sorush, 'Zati va 'arazi dar adiyan (Originally published in *Kiyan*, 42, 1377 [1998]),' in *Bast-e tajrobi-ye nabavi* (Tehran: Serat, 1385 [2006]), p. 68.
Abdulkarim Soroush, 'Essentials and Accidentals in Religion,', in *The Expansion of Prophetic Experience: Essays on Historicity, Contingency and Plurality in Religion*, ed. Forough Jahanbakhsh (Leiden & Boston: Brill, 2009), p. 81. Also see 'Abdolkarim Sorush, 'Velayat-e bateni va velayat-e siyasi', *Kiyan*, no. 44 (Mehr–Aban 1377 [September–October 1998]).

[36] Mojtahed-Shabestari, 'Qara'at-e rasmi az din', p. 35   [37] Ibid., p. 35.

Iranian polity there is a clearly defined shift from passivity to activity, from unreasoned imitation to rational agency, an object becoming a self-determining subject. But beyond that we also observe a clear endorsement of gradualism and technocratic standards of evaluation and assessment.

Shabestari does not restrict his critique to the political domain and concludes that 'political *taqlid* is no different from *taqlid* in the ordinances of religion'.[38] For him both species of *taqlid* rise and fall together. In this regard, he goes far beyond a mere critique of the political order of the Guardianship of the Jurist and effectively undercuts the traditional structure of clerical authority embodied in the *marja'iyyat*, where the believer is expected to emulate a learned *mojtahed* in those matters under the purview of Islamic law. A couple of years later he would reaffirm this conclusion, stating, 'Obedience *(ta'abod)* and political *taqlid* can only find meaning in elementary *(ebteda'i)* societies of the past without scientific *('elmi)* goals and planning.'[39] Sorush in a similar vein pronounced the demise of 'political *taqlid*' with the election of Mohammad Khatami: 'Political *taqlid* is forbidden! Our people have shown in the election of Khordad 1997 that they no longer partake in political *taqlid* and that they are independent.'[40] On this view, the 2nd Khordad represented a neo-Kantian feat of autonomy and self-legislation on a mass scale. But, beyond sloganeering, the international network of institutions which formulate and legitimate technocratic standards and define the metrics of 'development' and under what conditions these processes are undertaken is never considered. Instead, the lexicon of 'good governance' is for the most part taken up uncritically and as a given. What Shabestari does argue in the abstract is that any programme should aim to make society more 'humane' *(ensani)* and 'just' *('adelaneh)*. But rather than resolve debate it merely provokes further contentious disputation over what constitutes the more 'just' way of ordering Iranian society. He does not, for example, even attempt to lay out for the reader a theory of justice à la Rawls or Sen.

Leaving this issue to one side for the moment, since the next chapter will analyse the events surrounding the 2nd of Khordad and the question of political participation in greater detail, I will return to Shabestari's other arguments as to why the 'official reading' is

---

[38] Ibid., p. 36.
[39] ' Siyasat va ta'abod', in *Ta'amolati dar qara'at-e ensani az din* (Tehran: Tarh-e now, 1383 [2004]), p. 209.
[40] Sorush, 'Sokhani ba daneshjuyan-e mazlum: taqlid-e siyasi mamnu'!'.

outmoded and finds itself in crisis. Shabestari enumerates the reasons for the crisis thus:

1. The 'official reading' subjugates all other disciplines and bodies of knowledge to 'religious knowledge'. It establishes a hierarchy in which the humanities and natural sciences must conform to its standards and values. Along similar lines, it cannot accept that there are other sources of knowledge, which are independent of the religious domain.

2. The 'official reading' has an ahistorical and asocial approach to language. It regards its understanding as outside the historical flow of time and space and dis-embeds it from contingent social and political relations.

3. It adheres to the belief that one view or philosophy of history is possible and that history is rationally ordered (*nezam-mand*). This point seems somewhat misplaced, since both the eighteenth-century Enlightenment *philosophes* and the German Idealist tradition, of which G.W.F. Hegel was the foremost exemplar, argued in their respective ways that history had a direction and progressed towards the consummation of reason and rational thought. 'Reason in history' and/or 'order in history' are thus not really amongst the more prominent convictions of tradition-alist religion and its variegated forms, which often rejected any such pretence. A millenarian conception of history and temporality does of course permeate some Shi'i political thought, thereby precluding its reduction to a single common denominator.

4. The 'official reading' is convinced that the meanings of religious texts are directly accessible without mediation and that they har-bour a single meaning. The 'official reading' is impervious to meth-odological innovations in textual hermeneutics. According to Shabestari, these are some of the presuppositions and pre-understandings (*pishfahm-ha*) that lead to the erroneous interpreta-tion of the Qur'an and hadith and the belief that a determinate religious, economic, and legal order can be extracted from textual sources. The proponents of the 'official reading' approach the sources with the various preconceptions, prejudices, and conclu-sions they wish to extract from them. In other words, their reading is pre-determined by the socio-political order they wish to justify and not by some latent normative doctrine they discover therein.[41]

---

[41] Mojtahed-Shabestari, 'Qara'at-e rasmi az din', p. 40.

The reception and interpretation of texts are contingent upon the reader's horizon of understanding and expectations. Under the influence of German hermeneutics, above all Hans-Georg Gadamer's *Truth and Method*,[42] Shabestari contends the reader's pre-understanding of both the world in which he or she is situated and his or her existential comportment towards the Qur'an and hadith are elided by the 'official reading'. These are issues which he addressed in detail in his *Hermenutik, ketab va sonnat* (Hermeneutics, the Book, and Tradition), where he focused on the historicity of scriptural exegesis and its relationship with the time, space, and pre-understandings of the reader engaging the text.[43] For Shabestari, to speak of the 'only possible interpretation (*tafsir*)' is a futile proposition and in fundamental contradiction with the plurality of pre-understandings, life-worlds, and analytical framings which condition exegetes' disparate approaches to scripture.[44] It is thus not merely a question of the 'official reading's' misapprehension of the content of the Qur'an and prophetic traditions, as earlier modernist critics of theocracy such as the Egyptian scholar of the Al-Azhar University 'Ali 'Abd al-Raziq in his volume *Islam and the Foundations of Governance* (1925) had contended when he dismissed wholesale the religious basis of government,[45] but also

---

[42] Mojtahed-Shabestari's acquaintance with the German language preceded the revolution when he replaced Ayatollah Mohammad Beheshti, the Islamic Republic's first chief justice, as director of the Islamic Centre in Hamburg from 1970 to 1978. Future president Mohammad Khatami would also undertake a brief stint in Hamburg.

[43] Mohammad Mojtahed-Shabestari, *Hermenutik, ketab va sonnat: farayand-e tafsir-e vahy* (Tehran: Tarh-e now, 1375 [1996]), p. 163.

[44] 'Qara'at-e rasmi az din', p. 37. 'Modernism va vahy', *Kiyan* 5, no. 29 (March–April 1996), p. 19. Shabestari's approach shares certain similarities with the approach of the late Egyptian scholar of Arab literature and Islamic studies Nasr Hamed Abu Zayd. Mojtahed-Shabestari and Mostafa Malekiyan both played a part in the translation of Abu Zayd's *Mafhum al-nass: dirasah fih 'ulum al-Qur'an* into Persian. Morteza Karimi-Niya translated the text and Malekiyan was one of its editors. Mojtahed-Shabestari acted as an intermediary between Abu Zayd and Karimi-Niya. Nasr Hamed Abu Zayd, *Ma'na-ye matn: pazhuheshi dar 'olum-e qor'an*, trans. Morteza Karimi-Niya (Tehran: Tarh-e now, 1380 [2001]).

[45] 'Abd al-Raziq's argument was taken to be directed against the caliphate, but it was phrased and argued in more general terms targeting Islamic government as a whole. 'Ali 'Abd al-Raziq, 'Message Not Government, Religion Not State', in *Liberal Islam: A Sourcebook*, ed. Charles Kurzman (New York & Oxford: Oxford University Press, 1998), p. 36.

a methodological one pertaining to the very impossibility of deriving a singular and definitive reading from scriptural sources.

5. The presupposition that it is possible by means of 'rational proof' (*esbat-e borhani*) to demonstrate 'a truth' without recourse or reference to philosophical ideas and issues.

6. Contravention ('*odul*) of the methods of philosophers and mystics pertaining to the subject of monotheism (*towhid*). The latter amounts to a critique of what might be called 'methodological monism' – namely, that a single method or broader attitude suffices for comprehending reality in its totality.

Both Shabestari and Sorush, along with several other religious intellectuals, have argued that believers' expectations vis-à-vis Islam, or any religion for that matter, ought to be minimal.[46] Theirs is a species of liberal political theology which seeks not only to completely disentangle 'religion' from state power and state institutions but also to warn against the prospect of 'religion' acting as the basis of normative visions for how state and society ought to be ruled and organised. The 'official reading', on their view, is based upon a 'maximal' understanding of religion which penetrates all aspects of social life. Both injunctions are prescriptive in nature and overlook a significant issue highlighted in the work of anthropologist Saba Mahmood, which points to the actual practice and political rationality of the modern state vis-à-vis religious affairs and institutions – namely, 'its claim to religious neutrality notwithstanding, the modern state has become involved in the regulation and management of religious life to an unprecedented degree, thereby embroiling the state in substantive issues of religious doctrine and practice'.[47] When one views the question of minimalist and maximal religion through the lens of governmentality rather than a formalistic and liberal one, focused strictly on the institutional separation of church and state, the matter proves to be somewhat more complicated. In the words of Mahmood, 'modern governmentality involves the state's intervention and regulation of many aspects of socioreligious life, dissolving the distinction between public and

---

[46] 'Abdolkarim Sorush, 'Din-e aqali va aksari', *Kiyan* 8, no. 41 (Farvardin–Ordibehesht 1377 [March–April 1998]), p. 9. Soroush, 'Maximalist Religion, Minimalist Religion', p. 117.

[47] Saba Mahmood, *Religious Difference in a Secular Age: A Minority Report* (Princeton & Oxford: Princeton University Press, 2016), p. 2.

private', while in practice, the institutionalisation and entrenchment of the distinction entails both 'the regulation of religious life and the construction of religion as a space free from state intervention'.[48]

In any event, Shabestari and Sorush's introduction of historicity into the practice of reading and scriptural exegesis has indubitable social and political implications. Shabestari forcefully argues that the traditionalist or 'official reading' is fundamentally flawed, ignores contemporary developments in both theology and the humanities, and is inadequate to the demands and challenges which face believers towards the close of the twentieth century. On his view, it is a rational technocratic and liberal-democratic political system that is ultimately best suited to the requirements of the present age.

'Democratic Religious Government' and Rights-Centred Discourse

The next chapter will address President Mohammad Khatami's philosophical and political world view and his conception of 'religious democracy'. But before I address Khatami's ideas on the subject in considerable detail, it is necessary to examine the debates regarding the nature of 'democratic religious government' (*hokumat-e demokratik-e dini*), which first began to emerge in the early 1990s, pioneered above all by 'Abdolkarim Sorush in several lectures, most of which were reprinted in *Kiyan*. Some of these articles are deserving of analysis and provoked major debates within the Kiyan circle, even reverberating in wider society. Two of the more prominent interlocutors on the issues of religious government and also ideology were Akbar Ganji and Sa'id Hajjariyan, who wrote under the pseudonyms of Hamid Paidar and Jahangir Salehpur, respectively.[49]

One of the more notable articles authored by Sorush on the issue of 'religious government' was first published in *Kiyan* in March–April 1993 entitled *Hokumat-e demokratik-e dini?* (Religious Democratic Government?)[50] In this essay Sorush lays out the 'problem of religious

---

[48] Ibid., p. 4.
[49] Under their chosen pseudonyms they often took up more radical positions than they were prepared to do publicly given their ongoing relationships with elements throughout the state apparatus.
[50] It should be noted that the article itself is a combination of two speeches. The first was delivered in the course of a seminar on human rights held at the

democratic governments' and states the dilemma they face in ruling to be threefold: 'to reconcile people's satisfaction with God's approval; to strike a balance between the religious and the nonreligious; and to do right by both the people and by God, acknowledging at once the integrity of human beings and of religion'. This essay and a further one, which will be analysed below, were Sorush's attempt to rhetorically distinguish 'liberalism' from 'democracy' and defend a democratic model of governance, which he believed compatible with what he then termed 'religious society'.[51] Sorush takes his point of departure from the assumption that the society from which a religious democratic government springs is itself 'religious' and therefore that the government is a 'reflection of a religious society'.[52] He further states that whether a religious government is democratic depends on two conditions. The first condition is the extent to which the government in question benefits from 'collective reason' (*'aql-e jam'i*). The second is the extent to which human rights are respected.[53] Moreover, on account of what Sorush subsequently called his neo-Mu'tazilitism,[54] which holds that reason, in particular the realm of normativity and moral values, are independent of revelation, he argues that many of the values integral to good governance and statecraft, such as securing the public interest and justice, comprise part of non-religious

Ministry of Foreign Affairs in 1991 (1370), and the second speech was delivered during a seminar in the Middle East Institute based in Hamburg, Germany, in 1992 (1371). 'Abdolkarim Sorush, 'Hokumat-e demokratik-e dini?', *Kiyan* 11 (Farvardin–Ordibehesht 1372 [March–April 1993]). The English translation of the essay has been published in 'Abdolkarim Soroush, 'The Idea of Democratic Religious Government', in *Reason, Freedom, and Democracy in Islam: Essential Writings of 'Abdolkarim Soroush*, ed. Ahmad Sadri and Mahmoud Sadri (Oxford & New York: Oxford University Press, 2000). While I have used the above translation, I have cross-referenced it with the Persian original as printed in *Farbehtar az id'iolozhi* and modified it where deemed appropriate.

51 'Tolerance and Governance: A Discourse on Religion and Democracy', p. 138.
52 'The Idea of Democratic Religious Government', p. 126.   53 Ibid., p. 126.
54 'Abdolkarim Soroush and Matin Ghaffarian, "I'm a Neo-Mu'tazilite: An interview with 'Abdulkarim Soroush," http://www.drsoroush.com/English/ Interviews/E-INT-Neo-Mutazilite_July2008.html. Sorush's conception of revelation-independent reason seems to owe much to Popper and the late twentieth-century advocates of critical rationalism in Anglo-American philosophical circles, as well as elements of historical Mu'tazilitism. Abrahamhov for example has argued that an autonomous conception of reason or purely rationalist theology does not exist in classical Islamic theology and that 'rational tendencies' evident in the latter only pertain to certain theological issues. Binyamin Abrahamov, *Islamic Theology: Traditionalism and Rationalism* (Edinburgh: Edinburgh University Press, 1998), p. 32.

political systems as well. Values such as justice are not derived from religion but rather are themselves the criterion for determining the 'truth' of religion:[55] 'They are inherently (*zatan*) non-religious.'[56] According to Sorush, religions work in the service of values and truth and merely play a role in convincing 'the people'. On his view, it casts deontological values in a language which is both emotive and compelling for the 'common' folk. 'When the common people receive these values from religion, they better believe and use them. The majority of people rely less on their rational judgements.'[57] It is a thoroughly elitist sentiment, in which the religious intellectual for all intents and purposes positions himself as benevolent enlightener. Indeed, Sorush often reproduces a well-nigh Platonic schema where the masses tend to be embroiled in sensuousness, while only an enlightened few are equipped with the capacity to think through and understand rational arguments on their own terms. But, at the same time, he regards it as imperative that the extra-religious nature of values be identified so that religious understanding can be harmonised with them.[58] The agents of such harmonisation are none other than the elite and enlightened religious intellectual class itself, who perform a special role in bridging the gap between normative values, the assent of the masses, and their realisation in practice.

Rights *contra* Duties

It is important to add that in *Hokumat-e demokratik-e dini?* and a significant part of Sorush's work during this period another salient

---

[55] 'Abdolkarim Sorush, 'Tahlil-e mafhum-e hokumat-e dini [Originally published in *Kiyan*, 32 Shahrivar–Mehr 1375]', in *Modara va modiriyyat* (Tehran: Serat, 1387 [2008]), p. 364. It should be added that *'aql* is itself held to be a source (a potential source by some) of Shi'i jurisprudence, and there is a principle which states that whatever is dictated by reason is dictated by religion. It is important to also note that Aristotelian deduction with reference to the Qur'an and *hadith* was one of the main modes of legal reasoning. Hossein Modarressi Tabataba'i, *An Introduction to Shi'i Law: A Bibliographical Study* (London: Ithaca Press, 1984), pp. 3–4, 29.

[56] Sorush, 'Tahlil-e mafhum-e hokumat-e dini', p. 364. 'Bavar-e dini va davar-e dini: mosahebeh ba doktor 'Abdolkarim Sorush', *Ehya*, no. 5 (1370 [1991]), p. 21.

[57] 'Tahlil-e mafhum-e hokumat-e dini', p. 364.

[58] 'Abdolkarim Soroush, 'Tolerance and Governance: A Discourse on Religion and Democracy', in *Reason, Freedom, & Democracy in Islam: Essential Writings of 'Abdolkarim Soroush*, ed. Ahmad Sadri and Mahmoud Sadri (Oxford & New York: Oxford University Press, 2000), p. 132.

objective was to stress that if Islam is to remain relevant, it must come to terms with human rights. This is more asserted than anything else, since he presumes their existence *a priori*. He does not seek Qur'anic justification for this statement or repeat the anachronistic gesture of previous Islamic modernists, who had argued that modern rights and constitutionalism were in fact first formulated and supported in the time of the Prophet Mohammad. Sorush is fully prepared to accept that human rights in their modern guise are the product of Enlightenment thought, which was not merely unsympathetic to religion but often outright hostile towards it.[59] Whether this is entirely accurate or not, he unambiguously states that 'we cannot evade rational, moral, and extra-religious principles and reasoning about human rights, myopically focusing on nothing but the primary texts and maxims of religion in formulating our jurisprudential edicts'.[60] Sorush proceeds negatively and argues that while religion is not the source of human rights and numerous other values, neither is it inherently hostile towards them. In a similar vein, he argues that the faithful cannot afford to concede that 'liberalism' is the sole defender of human rights. 'Islam' must not only come to terms with human rights but must rethink its dispropor-tionate emphasis on duties. As Sorush is fond of saying, 'the language of religion is the language of duty (*taklif*)'.[61] Religious doctrine, he insists, has traditionally shown very little interest in the issue of rights and has instead been steadfast in underscoring human beings' duties to God and obeisance to his revealed law. A shift of priorities and emphasis are demanded by the present. While the *shari'ah* might discuss the laws of inheritance and certain entitlements which accrue to individual persons under specific conditions, they remain a far cry from the modern conception of human rights.

Sorush does not hold modern human rights to be merely a matter of social or cultural convention but claims them to be 'natural' and 'innate'.[62] In this sense, he could be said to follow in the footsteps of early modern European natural rights theorists such as Hugo Grotius

---

[59] Soroush, 'The Idea of Democratic Religious Government', p. 129. This view is supported by Israel in his exhaustive study of the intellectual history of the French Revolution. Jonathan Israel, *Revolutionary Ideas: An Intellectual History of the French Revolution from the Rights of Man to Robespierre* (Oxford & Princeton: Princeton University Press, 2014), p. 479.

[60] Soroush, 'The Idea of Democratic Religious Government', p. 128.

[61] Soroush, 'Tahlil-e mafhum-e hokumat-e dini', p. 362.   [62] Ibid., p. 362.

and John Locke,[63] for whom they are simply taken as a given without much thought to how they emerged historically or became an object of international concern. But as the legal historian Samuel Moyn has argued, the conception of 'human rights' we know today, in terms of an international regime of entitlements transcending the state and national borders, is a relatively recent phenomenon, which only began to permeate the political and diplomatic lexicon of Europe and the United States in the aftermath of the Second World War, and, even at this point, it rarely went beyond declaratory statements of negligible practical import. Not until the late 1970s did the notion enter the global imagination and gain wider currency.[64] In contrast to the late eighteenth century, when rights were primarily associated with revolutionary foundings, in the course of the 1940s advocates of human rights and the dignity of the individual person were largely associated with European conservatives motivated by a deep-seated hostility to communism. According to Moyn, 'conservatism defined rather than destroyed human rights'[65] as 'the idea of human rights had been redeemed only as a concrete Cold War position'.[66] As Moyn persuasively argues, it was only during the 1960s and 1970s, in the context of the great Cold War power rivalry, that Soviet dissidents provided the basis for Western European and American liberals and the anti-communist left to properly embrace and champion the cause of 'human rights'.

On this account, human rights were not only thought to be anti-revolutionary but were ensconced within a project tantamount to nothing less than an 'anti-politics'.[67] It is little coincidence that such views emerged just as revolutionary anti-colonial movements in the Third World had peaked, and many of the idealistic hopes which they had at one time harboured began to dissipate in the face of counter-

---

[63] Both men, however, were grossly hypocritical when it came to the issue of slavery and the slave trade, for which both provided intellectual justifications and in which Locke was financially invested. See Losurdo, *Liberalism: A Counter-History*, Loc 108, 502, 525.

[64] Samuel Moyn, *The Last Utopia: Human Rights in History* (Cambridge, MA & London: Harvard University Press, 2010), Loc 765.

[65] *Christian Human Rights* (Philadelphia: University of Pennsylvania Press, 2015), Introduction. *The Last Utopia: Human Rights in History*, Loc 849.

[66] *The Last Utopia: Human Rights in History*, Loc 911.

[67] *Human Rights and the Uses of History* (London & New York: Verso, 2014), Loc 310.

revolutionary insurgencies and degenerate into either despondency or the hard-headed calculus of survival and realpolitik by postcolonial elites.[68] On such a reading, one can see how Sorush's polemic against 'ideology' covered in the last chapter and his valorisation of rights dovetailed with a broader and deeper international moment, which began its full-fledged ascent in the late 1970s and reached a crescendo following the collapse of the Soviet Union and the proclamation of the 'New World Order'. The new emphasis on rights and the accoutrements of 'good governance' not only sprang from political marginalisation or dissatisfaction with the purported 'democratic deficit'. Many of the alleged shortcomings diagnosed by the religious intellectuals and the Islamic left of the post-revolutionary Iranian state were profoundly inflected by the historic shift in global intellectual and politico-economic discourse and practices, which were in the process of reframing the nature, structures, and imperatives of global governance and international order.

The declining attraction of revolutionary projects of collective emancipation, the faltering order of post-1945 Keynesian 'embedded liberalism', the proliferation of non-governmental organisations and social movements in defence of human rights, and the subsequently short-lived American unipolar moment could not but cast a long, dark shadow over religious intellectualism's political vision and influence the new minimalist, individualist, and ethical turn advocated by the religious intellectuals in the course of the 1990s. This shift was accompanied by a deafening silence on questions of political economy and class politics, which only twenty years earlier had been so pervasive amongst Iranian religious and socialist political currents. By the mid-1990s, the notion of 'human rights' could find itself understood by certain quarters inside Iran as standing above politics and the political fray and, to quote Moyn, be upheld as 'minimal, individual and fundamentally moral; not maximal, collective and potentially bloody'.[69] Without much reflection on the genealogy of human rights discourse or its political contents and context in international law and politics, Sorush states emphatically that rights are not bestowed upon humanity by any religion. It would thus seem that, despite his invocation of 'semantic holism' in *Qabz va bast*, he simply takes certain minimal, individualised rights to be God-given and subsequently

---

[68] Ibid., Loc 1273.   [69] Ibid., Loc 1294.

uncovered by reason.[70] In this way, while the prerogatives of the Guardian Jurist are historicised and made contingent, the rights of individual persons prove to be inviolable. Human rights discourse in this configuration thus becomes primarily an endeavour to constrain the unwanted encroachments of the Islamic state.

Sorush's political outlook in the early to mid-1990s continued to labour under the sway of his appropriation of Popper's political thought. Popper's liberalism, however, advocated a form of negative utilitarianism and the firm conviction that government's duty lay in the alleviation of suffering rather than the guarantee of the greatest happiness. In line with the prejudices of the preceding decade, Sorush still often equates liberalism with a permissive form of relativism, when in reality one of Western liberal thought's founding fathers, John Locke, was anything but a permissive relativist. In his *Two Treatises of Government* (1689), Locke postulated a political 'law of nature' along with man's 'perfect freedom' and equality in the pre-political state of nature,[71] even while justifying the dispossession of Amerindians and the enslavement of black Africans.[72] It does not appear that Sorush's argument for 'natural rights' and Popper's brand of utilitarianism can be easily squared. Popper himself certainly did not attempt to justify rights deontologically and rejects the idea that rights can be intellectually intuited, even if he did not reject the autonomy of the normative sources of morality.[73] For this reason Sorush's arguments are in several ways closer, despite its many occlusions, to Locke's natural law approach with which he was surely familiar. As far as 'democracy' is concerned, Sorush seems more preoccupied with demonstrating that it is not the harbinger of atheism or scientism and that 'democracy' and 'religion' can peacefully cohabitate.

---

[70] It does not seem that such a position can be squared with Popper's views either. Anthony Quinton, 'Karl Popper: Politics Without Essences', in *Contemporary Political Philosophers*, ed. Anthony de Crespigny and Kenneth Minogue (New York: Dodd, Mead & Company, 1975), p. 150. Sorush had actually read this essay as a student in London during the late 1970s.

[71] John Locke, *Two Treatises of Government* (Cambridge: Cambridge University Press, 1988), p. 323.

[72] Losurdo, *Liberalism: A Counter-History*, Loc 527, 703.

[73] Popper expresses his proximity to Kant with respect to questions of morality in the interview he gave to *Kiyan* in 1992. Popper and Kamaly, 'Goftogu-ye 'Kiyan' ba Karl Popper', p. 6.

It is in an essay published a couple of years later, *Tahlil-e mafhum-e 'hokumat-e dini'* (Analysis of the Concept of 'Religious Government', 1996), that Sorush appears to have further honed his views on the issue of religious government. This essay and another one published two years previous, *Modara va modiriyyat-e mo'menan: sokhani dar nesbat-e din va demokrasi* (Toleration & Administration of the Pious: A Talk on the Relation Between Religion & Democracy, 1994),[74] also published in *Kiyan*, are amongst his most important political essays of the 1990s. They address his vision for a distinct political order, surpassing the present constitutional setup in Iran. In both essays he had also more clearly outlined the ultimate and unsurprising target of his critique: in a word, *feqh*. This is especially the case when Islamic jurisprudence is endowed with the executive authority to impose its edicts and rulings on individuals and regulate their behaviour in the context of the modern nation-state and through its apparatuses of control and coercion. In these essays, Sorush also seems to have taken further steps towards propounding his own brand of 'Islamic humanism', which proves itself fundamentally unwilling to discriminate amongst individual citizens on the basis of their religious creed or affiliation. He concedes that society is composed of both 'pious' and 'non-pious' citizens,[75] and rights are not assigned in virtue of citizens' religiosity but rather in their being human beings.[76] This would appear to vitiate the need to refer to any such arrangement as a 'religious democracy', a term coined as a result of either a lack of clarity or strategic obfuscation and ambiguity to eschew the calumny of antagonists. Its rather breathless appropriation by conservative state discourse in recent years, which regularly refers to the Islamic Republic and its constitutional order as a 'religious democracy' (*mardomsalari-ye dini*), highlights a pertinent conundrum.[77]

---

[74] ' Abdolkarim Sorush, 'Modara va modiriyyat-e mo'menan: sokhani dar nesbat-e din va demokrasi', *Kiyan* 21(Shahrivar–Mehr 1373 [September–October 1994]). This article has been reprinted in the following volume: 'Modara va modiriyyat: sokhani dar nesbat-e din va demokrasi', in *Modara va modiriyyat* (Tehran: Serat, 1380 [2001]). It has also been translated into English in the above collection, Soroush, 'Tolerance and Governance: A Discourse on Religion and Democracy'.

[75] Sorush, 'Tahlil-e mafhum-e hokumat-e dini', p. 356.   [76] Ibid., p. 360.

[77] 'Ali Khameneh'i, 'Didar-e kargozaran-e nezam ba rahbar-e enqelab', *Khamenei. ir* (11/08/1382 [2 November 2003]).

While Shabestari's views on human rights are comparable, he has his own distinct approach to the issue. The state, according to Shabestari, is only a source of power (*qodrat*) and not a source of culture.[78] This binary – i.e., state = power vs. society = culture – appears to be largely the product of his antipathy towards the specific interpretation of Islam he believes to have been in political ascendancy since the beginning of the 1990s. It also seems to be the product of a political and social ontology which establishes an antagonistic duality between state and society, where the former is the domain of coercion and the latter the domain of autonomy. Thus, in seeking to evacuate the state or its policies of any cultural foundation or grounding, he articulates a facile and dichotomous conception of power and the state.[79] This is a conception, which his ideological opponents would wholly reject, since they were aware of the immense power of culture and cultural practices and thus the necessity of ensuring the state be empowered to combat the 'cultural onslaught' (*tahajom-e farhangi*) embodied in 'subversive' ideologies and their proponents.[80] Indeed, the state was the embodiment of a religious and cultural mission and had an obligation to shape and impart moral guidance to the people. It amounted to far more than a bundle of institutions merely charged with underwriting contracts between parties or providing basic levels of security and stability. The cultural-religious mission of the Iranian state had long proven close to Ayatollah Khameneh'i's heart, and, following Mohammad Khatami's resignation as minister of culture and throughout the remainder of the decade, cultural policy came to reside largely in conservative hands. The mission of combating the 'cultural onslaught' was specifically stipulated in Khameneh'i's appointment of 'Ali Larijani, son of Ayatollah Mirza Hashem Amoli, as head of Islamic Republic of Iran Broadcasting in the initial months of 1994.[81]

[78] Mojtahed-Shabestari, 'Qara'at-e rasmi az din', p. 34.
[79] This conception slides between being normative and descriptive.
[80] The importance of the notion of 'cultural onslaught' and its centrality to the world view of Ayatollah Khameneh'i is clear from an analysis of his speeches since the early 1990s. 'Ali Khameneh'i, 'Bayanat dar didar-e farmandehan-e gordan-ha-ye 'ashura'', *Khamenei.ir* (22/4/1371 [13 July 1992]). 'Bayanat dar daneshgah-e Tarbiyyat-e Modarress', *Khamenei.ir* (12/6/1377 [3 September 1998]). 'Ali Khameneh'i, 'Bayanat dar didar-e mas'ulan-e sazman-e Seda va Sima', *Khamenei.ir* (11/9/1383 [1 December 2004]).
[81] 'Entesab-e Doktor 'Ali Larijani beh riyasat-e Sazman-e Seda va Sima', *Khamenei.ir* (24/11/1372 [13 February 1994]).

Moreover, in step with Khameneh'i's own pronouncements on the subject, Mesbah-Yazdi would declare, in a volume of the same name, 'Amongst the methods of imperialism and imperiousness, that which is most dangerous, but most hidden, is cultural domination.'[82] Conservative thought in Iran had thus long been aware of the potency and threat posed by 'cultural imperialism' and has as a result sought to address it through the oftentimes obtuse notion of 'cultural engineering'.[83] Meanwhile, reformists have tended to either abandon or repudiate such ideas entirely.

Shabestari, for example, is keen to negate any cultural role for the state. It might initially appear as though Shabestari believes, much in the style of classical liberalism, that the state is expected to act merely as an adjudicator in those instances where the rights of individuals have been infringed by fellow citizens – essentially as an enforcer of J. S. Mill's 'harm principle'. Shabestari fulminates that 'culture in the hands of the government means the execution (*e 'dam*) of culture',[84] but he ignores the fact that neither the state nor civil society are intrinsically proponents of 'progressive' or 'rational' practices and that states also have the capacity to promote 'liberal' as well as 'illiberal' policies. According to Clyde W. Barrow in his analysis of the modern welfare state,

The state has become ... involved in also regulating institutions of civil society that are primarily concerned with the development of personal

---

[82] The notion of *gharbzadegi* (West-struckness or Westoxification) initially propounded by Ahmad Fardid and elaborated upon most famously by Al-e Ahmad in his tract of the same name, which was subsequently adapted by Khomeini and upheld as an affirmation of his own deep-rooted xenophobia, was further theorised by Mesbah-Yazdi and various other ideologues in the 1990s. This discourse was integral to the latter's struggle against secular intellectuals, the so-called *digar-andishan*, but also religious intellectuals who were seen as having fallen afoul of the seductive arguments of a 'decadent' West, which was destined to collapse as a result of its intellectual and moral degeneration. Mohammad-Taqi Mesbah-Yazdi, *Tahajom-e farhangi* (Qom: Entesharat-e mo'asseseh-ye amuzeshi va pazhuheshi-e Imam Khomeini, 1389 [2010]), p. 43. For the definitive work on Ahmad Fardid and the significance of the culturalist, counter-Enlightenment turn undertaken by Ali Mirsepassi, see Ali Mirsepassi, *Political Islam, Iran, and the Enlightenment Philosophies of Hope and Despair* (Cambridge & New York: Cambridge University Press, 2011), chapters 1–2.
[83] Mohamad Tavakoli Targhi, 'Clerico-Engineering: An Introduction', *Iran Nameh* 27, no. 1 (2012), p. 15.
[84] Mojtahed-Shabestari, 'Qara'at-e rasmi az din', p. 34.

identity and normative values, such as the family, education, and the Church. In this social sphere, the welfare state has been more and more directly involved in the regulation and promotion of specific normative values (e.g., abortion and racial integration) and in the maintenance of specific family structures (e.g., through day care, maternity leave, and family allowances).[85]

Shabestari simply denies the role of the state, including the liberal capitalist state, as a structuring force, which plays a vital role in organising the terrain of civil society and regulating the forms of ideological and cultural production individuals consume and reproduce in turn.

In the words of Stuart Hall, the state harbours a kind of 'double-sidedness'. It is rarely, if ever, simply coercive. Rather, it 'is also educative: It enlarges social and cultural possibilities; it enables people to enter new terrains.'[86] State and civil society thus almost never have the kind of antipodal dynamics delineated by Shabestari – and sometimes found in cliché-ridden Western media reporting – which pits a secular, modern, and young society, constantly in rebellion, against an oppressive, dogmatic, and fundamentalist state. If we take Shabestari's point to be a more concrete one aimed directly at the Iranian state, then it might be understood as a commentary on the inherently destructive effects of the Islamic Republic's cultural agenda and purported desire to defend and inculcate 'Islamic' values. His critique can thus be understood as an attack upon the authoritarian state which seeks to deprive the organisations and institutions of cultural production of any autonomy whatsoever and thereby make them dependent, economically and ideologically, on the state alone. In the Iranian context, it thus remains an important critique of major import for how we conceive of the relations between state and society and between politics and culture.[87] But it nonetheless amounts to a rather one-dimensional appraisal of not only the cultural politics of the Islamic Republic but also the significant impact of the Iranian state's developmentalist agenda in the areas of health care and education and the kind of normative values and social forms it has fostered and promoted.[88]

[85] Clyde W. Barrow, *Critical Theories of the State: Marxist, Neo-Marxist, Post-Marxist* (Madison, WI: University of Wisconsin Press, 1993), p. 7.
[86] Hall, *Cultural Studies 1983: A Theoretical History*, Loc 3164.
[87] Anderson, 'The Antinomies of Antonio Gramsci', p. 36.
[88] See Kevan Harris, 'A Martyrs' Welfare State and Its Contradictions: Regime Resilience and Limits through the Lens of Social Policy in Iran', in *Middle East Authoritarianisms: Governance, Contestation and Regime Resilience in Syria*

In another article Shabestari paradoxically claims a 'realistic' approach towards the question of human rights in Muslim societies would entail the 'actual freedoms' found in Western and Muslim societies continue to be distinct.[89] In seeming contradiction with what he has said elsewhere, he claims that those freedoms which are not compatible with 'Islamic culture' can be limited on the premise that doing such is 'devoid of political malevolence' and harbours 'useful effects'.[90] He cites gay rights as an example, claiming that this is not an issue of contention between 'democrats and autocrats' inside Iran.[91] Shabestari then moves to assure his readers that 'liberty' and 'licentiousness' are not one and the same, appearing to equate gay rights with the latter.[92] Shabestari is careful to stipulate that irrespective of the issue of 'compatibility with Islamic culture' – an area of considerable contention – certain basic rights such as freedom of expression, association, political participation, and religion ought not to be violated. He does not consider that gay rights might also be linked to basic rights such as freedom of expression and association. His argument contends, rather, that 'the boundaries of legal freedoms' ought to evolve as cultural-religious norms are critiqued and reconstructed.[93] He thus offers a historically attuned, gradualist, and selective approach from the subject-position of a believer within a Muslim-majority society, which is not without problems of its own. But in his mind, such an approach permits for the incremental and smoother incorporation of various liberal freedoms into the intricate and variegated web of Iranians' socio-cultural lives and, one would assume, the legal system of the country. The views and arguments he puts forth clearly result in some provocative conclusions, given the context in which he was writing.

Quintessential Piety and Free Faith

Both Sorush and Shabestari contend that religious duties are not duties which the state should take upon itself to enforce. They are 'non-governmental' (*ghayr-e hokumati*) in nature, and pious

and Iran, ed. Steven Heydemann and Reinoud Leenders (Stanford, CA: Stanford University Press, 2013).
[89] Mojtahed-Shabestari, 'Mosalmanan bayad hoquq-e bashar ra bepazirand', p. 206.
[90] Ibid., p. 207.   [91] Ibid., p. 207.   [92] Ibid., p. 207.   [93] Ibid., p. 206.

individuals must take it upon themselves to perform them.[94] They are thus freely self-imposed *qua* religious obligations, and their performance is the outcome of the believer's autonomous and uncoerced choice. By this time, the notion of freely choosing to be religious had become crucial for Sorush, since, much like Mojtahed-Shabestari, he argues that 'faith' cannot be imposed by force of law or threat of punitive sanction.[95]

As was seen in the case of two of the Islamist ideologues examined in Chapter 2, 'faith' and its cultivation were secondary considerations, if they appeared at all. In these cases, faith was simply assumed in contradistinction to infidelity (*kofr*). The overriding ambition was rather the capture of the state to the end of executing a specific conception of the *shari'ah*. By the mid-1990s both Sorush and Mojtahed-Shabestari began to publicly enunciate the very impossibility of such a venture and regard it as doomed to failure. For example, Mojtahed-Shabestari, in his essay *Iman, siyasat va hokumat* (Faith, Politics, and Government, 1376 [1997]), insists that it is 'faith' which compels the religious to seek out political and social regimes where they are 'better able to consciously and freely cultivate faith'[96] and that it is 'a choice with all of one's being'.[97] Their favoured political order is not only anti-paternalist and thus contrary to one of the main threads running through the political thought of Khomeini, particularly in his middle period; it also constitutes a rupture with classical Muslim philosophers such as al-Farabi and a major swathe of Western political thought, which held that 'felicity can be forced on human beings'.[98] As is well known, Farabi's elevation of the philosopher-imam and the derivation of his right to rule were heavily influenced by Plato's *The Republic* and the notion of the Philosopher-King. Khomeini was certainly familiar with Farabi's thought, and his own theological orientation had been influenced by both Farabi and Ibn 'Arabi and

---

[94] Locke made a similar argument in his much-feted *A Letter Concerning Toleration*. John Locke, *A Letter Concerning Toleration* (Indianapolis: Hackett Publishing, 1983), pp. 26–7.

[95] Mojtahed-Shabestari, 'Mosalmanan bayad hoquq-e bashar ra bepazirand', p. 281.

[96] 'Iman, siyasat va hokumat', in *Iman va azadi* (Tehran: Tarh-e now, 1376 [1997]), p. 79.

[97] Ibid., p. 76.

[98] Lenn E. Goodman, *Islamic Humanism* (Oxford & New York: Oxford University Press, 2003), p. 9.

their confidence that man's philosophical-rational and mystical ascension to sainthood and perfectibility were not merely desirable but possible.[99] Both Mojtahed-Shabestari and Sorush, on the contrary, make a case that the government's only role is to provide conditions whereby individuals can freely pursue the decision to be religious. Both men thus fall on the side of 'negative liberty', and Sorush was indeed apprised of Isaiah Berlin's famed distinction.[100] In this way, variegated threads of anti-utopianism and anti-paternalism are closely interwoven in the work of both men.

Furthermore, it appears that both Sorush and Mojtahed-Shabestari are trying to navigate between what they regard as two extremes. One is embodied by the political regime of velayat-e faqih, which holds clerical rule and supervision are necessary for the implementation of the shari'ah in the absence of the Hidden Imam, and the other is manifested in regimes which impose secularism autocratically and are inherently hostile towards the influence of religious institutions and religious appurtenances in public–political space, often referred to in Persian as nezam-ha-ye la'ic, originating in the French term laïcité. Regularly adduced examples of such a regime are the authoritarian and modernising states of Mustafa Kemal Atatürk and Reza Shah in Turkey and Iran respectively.[101] The latter, in particular, had been a repeated target of derision in post-revolutionary historiography and beyond because of his sartorial reforms and banning of the veil (see Chapter 2), which has since been depicted on many an occasion as the obverse of compulsory veiling under the Islamic Republic.

Feqh versus Faith

For Sorush, 'rational criteria' and harmony between reason ('aql) and the shari'ah are of primary importance. He states that the 'disregard of rational criteria and of the necessity for the harmony of religious understanding and rational findings is a breach of religious

---

[99] Martin, Creating an Islamic State, p. 34.
[100] Sorush mentions the distinction in a speech he gave at Shahid Beheshti University in 1990. Sorush, "Aql va azadi', p. 236. In the later essays pertaining to the nature of religious government, Sorush holds the middle ground. While highly critical of paternalism, he holds the conviction that individuals' basic needs such as security, shelter, and sustenance must be guaranteed by the state and are indeed a precondition for intellectual pursuits.
[101] Soroush, 'Three Cultures', p. 160.

responsibility'.[102] In this way, religion (*din*) merely confirms or corro-
borates the norms and principles which govern statecraft and ethics,
which are discovered by rational inquiry. He makes it abundantly clear
that neither 'religion' nor 'revelation' (*vahy*) are the sources of such
norms and principles. Here Sorush breaks with the views of Khomeini
and the standard Osuli position more generally, since he does not take
ejtehad to be the exclusive province of any specific group, nor reason to
comprise merely one component in the apparatus of the more comprehensive endeavour of Islamic jurisprudence.

Just as he had done with 'ideology', Sorush differentiates 'religion'
and *feqh* in emphatic and stark terms. He contends that a non-religious
society could implement a governmental system in accordance with the
precepts of orthodox Islamic jurisprudence, on the premise that such
a regime could hypothetically yield greater social utility. Such a policy
would not, however, qualify the society in question as a 'religious' one.
This is because, according to Sorush, *feqh* is merely a technique or craft
(*fan*).[103] According to him, it fails to distil, isolate, or capture what is
fundamentally sacred and constitutive of true piety. *Feqh* does not
touch on issues of belief and faith, which are addressed by theology
and mysticism – merely external behaviours. *Feqh* focuses on practical
religious obligations and religious government cannot ultimately rest
on such a foundation. Its foundation must be predicated on individually chosen and autonomously self-imposed faith. In this respect the
argument is homologous to that of Kant's description of the self-
imposed character of rational-normative maxims cum universalisable
laws in the form of the categorical imperative. Sorush thus concludes
that 'religious government is other than jurisprudential government . . .
religious government in the respect that it is religious, in principle, is
a government of faith, which means a government which the faithful
establish because they are human beings, righteous and pious'.[104]
'Faith' (*iman*) can only be defined as such when it is freely chosen and
is therefore by definition antithetical to heteronomy. This point has
been argued for by virtually all members of the post-revolutionary
rowshanfekri-ye dini collective and had been forcefully defended by
Bazargan from at least the mid-1960s.[105] In the history of Western

---

[102] 'The Idea of Democratic Religious Government', p. 127.
[103] Sorush, 'Tahlil-e mafhum-e hokumat-e dini', p. 355.   [104] Ibid., p. 355.
[105] Bazargan, *Be'sat va idi'olozhi*, pp. 122–7.

political and religious thought it was perhaps most famously argued for by Locke in his *A Letter Concerning Toleration* (1689), where he associated 'faith' with 'inward sincerity'.[106] Sorush holds this position for much the same reason:

[R]eligion is a species of love ... [F]aith cannot enter the hearts of human beings with force. If we accept this, in that case, religious government will be a government commensurate with the people's free faith and its duty will consist in guarding the people's free faith ... meaning, that the societal climate will be one favourable to the conscious and free choice of religion.[107]

In this way Sorush creates a hierarchy of value, with 'faith' at its apogee;[108] 'ethics' (*akhlaq*) and then one's deeds (*a'mal*) follow.[109] It is on this basis that Sorush concludes 'hypocrisy' (*riyakari*) is far worse and antithetical to religiosity than either drinking wine or gambling. *Feqh*, he contends, is incapable of distinguishing between 'external action' and 'the habits of the heart'.[110] *Feqh* is of no use for identifying 'hypocrisy': it can only categorise and label actions as lawful, unlawful, permissible, or objectionable. In addition, much like implacable 'ideology', as soon as the 'jurisprudential view' (*binesh-e feqhi*) acquires the reins of power it immediately strives to impose a rigid and legalistic structure upon society, in the form of mandatory veiling or religiously sanctioned blood money for crimes committed.[111] Perhaps of greater interest is Sorush's attribution of primacy to the interiority of 'true' religion and assigning only a secondary value to orthopraxy and public observance – a move that would find itself deeply problematised by scholars such as Talal Asad and Saba Mahmood, who might regard it as a surreptitious stipulation of what religion 'ought' to be, replete with normative assumptions, which in key respects mimics a Protestant Christian conception of religion as a set of propositions within a belief system to

---

[106] Locke, *A Letter Concerning Toleration*, p. 38.
[107] Sorush, 'Tahlil-e mafhum-e hokumat-e dini', p. 356. Sorush alludes to the famous ayah of the Qur'an in the surah *The Cow*, which states that 'there is no compulsion in religion'. The Qur'an, trans. M. A. S. Abdel Haleem (Oxford & New York: Oxford University Press, 2004), p. 29; 2:256.
[108] Shabestari similarly states 'faith is the crux of being a Muslim'. Mojtahed-Shabestari, 'Mosalmanan bayad hoquq-e bashar ra bepazirand', p. 281.
[109] Sorush, 'Tahlil-e mafhum-e hokumat-e dini', p. 357.   [110] Ibid., p. 357.
[111] Ibid., p. 357.

which the believer gives their assent.[112] Such a normative conception is foremost interior and privatised, while its 'authenticity' is assayed in the individual act of volition. Given Sorush's own invocation of the 'Protestant reformation' as a model for emulation, as well as the considerable impact of Protestant theologians such as Paul Tillich and Karl Barth on Shabestari, this should come as little surprise, even if their reception of such ideas and thinkers are at times more nuanced than this line of critique, in its cruder variations, might be prepared to admit.

Shabestari argues that the equation of religion and *feqh* is fundamentally destructive to 'the spirit of religion' and 'brittles the roots' of feeling and experience, so crucial to the faith perspective.[113] Shabestari contends that religion's main purpose is to facilitate the attainment of meaning for believers: 'the bestowal of meaning is the primary function (*karkerd*) of religion'.[114] This bequeathment emerges in the process by which the existential questions posed by the individual receive intelligible answers and explanations.[115] Religion has the capacity to open new horizons of meaning, and humankind is effectively engaged in the perpetual interpretation of the manifold incarnations of the deity.[116] This is not an instrumental relationship but one that is genuinely preoccupied with a human impulse for spiritual transcendence.[117] Only insofar as it fulfils such a function in the modern world can it be assured longevity going into the future.[118] Only thus can 'tradition' undergo expansion and new horizons be opened. It is here that Shabestari can be clearly seen as borrowing from Gadamer and the latter's notion of a dialogical relationship with 'tradition'.[119] In the aftermath of the collapse of theological authority, only a dynamic

---

[112] Saba Mahmood, 'Religious Reason and Secular Affect: An Incommensurable Divide?', in *Is Critique Secular? Blasphemy, Injury, and Free Speech* (New York: Fordham University Press, 2013), Loc 1274. 'Secularism, Hermeneutics, and Empire: The Politics of Islamic Reformation, *Public Culture*, no. 2 (2006), p. 329. Talal Asad, *Genealogies of Religion: Discipline and Reasons of Power in Christianity and Islam* (Baltimore & London: Johns Hopkins University Press, 1993), pp. 28, 46.

[113] Mojtahed-Shabestari, 'Qara'at-e rasmi az din', p. 50.

[114] Ibid., p. 50. Religion performs a role much like the one Malekiyan would claim for *ma'naviyyat*, bestowing meaning to man's existence. See Sadeghi-Boroujerdi, 'Mostafa Malekian: Spirituality, Siyasat-Zadegi and (A)political Self-Improvement'.

[115] Mojtahed-Shabestari, 'Qara'at-e rasmi az din', p. 51.   [116] Ibid., p. 52.

[117] Ibid., p. 52.   [118] Ibid., pp. 52–3.   [119] Ibid., p. 53.

and innovative relationship with tradition can provide faith with an anchored set of coordinates and orientation out of which to speak.[120] In the words of Shabestari, 'Life does not have a framework and yet someone must impart a framework to it. Under such conditions all the authorities upon which man has depended have collapsed.'[121] Acceptance of religion for Shabestari does not occur by means of critical rationality but through its speaking to an existential and practical desire for transcendence and meaning in the world. In this respect his approach to faith is not a deistic one. Critical rationality is not dispensed with, however. It plays an essential role insofar as it staves off the possibility of a final or ultimate interpretation of transcendence. Instrumental rationality's only role is one of ordering and managing worldly affairs. Neither critical nor instrumental rationality effects the acceptance of a specific spiritual way of life and its accompanying values. It is instead the result of what Shabestari calls an 'existential harmony' (hamahangi-ye vojudi), which is itself assayed in experience.[122]

Sorush, by contrast, rehashes the timeworn metaphysical distinction between the individual's soul/heart and body/external appearance. This distinction has had many different variations in the Islamic tradition, the best-known of which is the distinction between *zaher* and *baten*, and it has a long and rich history in Islamic philosophy and mystical literature. For Sorush, because of the real possibility of incommensurability between one's apparent and public disposition and behaviour (*zaher*) and inner nature (*baten*), and *feqh*'s sole preoccupation with the former, a jurisprudential government is capable of committing a far more heinous 'sin' than any individual transgression. In short, it can produce a plentiful supply of 'hypocrites', who have not come to a position of faith through their own volition, but rather have been compelled to live in accordance with a set of imposed norms which structure their behaviour in public space under threat of sanction. Though clearly a rousing critique, which could not but resonate with a great many of his readers, whose lived experience chimed with the violent bifurcation of public and private life, it is, nevertheless, one which stands along a continuum as opposed to reposing in a static

---

[120] 'Seh guneh-ye qara'at az sonnat dar 'asr-e moderniteh', in *Sonnat va sekularism: goftar-ha'i az 'Abdolkarim Sorush, Mohammad Mojtahed-Shabestari, Mostafa Malekiyan, Mohsen Kadivar* (Tehran: Serat, 1381 [2002]), p. 219.

[121] Ibid., p. 217.   [122] 'Qara'at-e rasmi az din', pp. 52–3.

condition. Since beyond the naked power of state enforcement, society has always provided sanctions regulating public conduct and behaviours and their transgression, in the spirit of what Durkheim once called the *conscience collective*. The difference between late-twentieth-century Iran and earlier periods, of course, is the vast capacity for coercion afforded by the mechanisms of social control and surveillance concentrated in the hands of the modern state and the technologies it has harnessed to perpetually extend its reach.

Traditionally, external observance and inner sincerity were viewed as being intertwined and indissociable. External observance and abidance by the precepts of the *shari'ah* were held to be a necessary, if not sufficient, condition for moral conduct but also spiritual ascendance and mindfulness of the godhead. However, Sorush insists that *feqh* is purely a 'worldly' (*donyavi*) concern that can do little for the lot of the faithful in the other world, nor can it perform the role of moral compass and guide. He is also anxious to make clear that 'jurisprudential Islam (*Islam-e feqhi*) is not necessarily real Islam (*Islam-e vaqe'i*)'.[123] Only 'heartfelt faith' (*iman-e qalbi*) can address humanity's fate in the hereafter. In this highly anti-nomocratic stance, the relationship between an individual's actions in the mundane world and the hereafter are refined, though not severed, while external affectations of piety, if not ritual in its entirety, become altogether irrelevant to soteriological questions.[124]

Religious Intellectuals and the 'Woman Question'

As I noted in Chapter 1, the so-called 'woman question' was not a subject to which the religious intellectuals devoted much-focused attention. There were manifold reasons for this, as I suggested: some political and philosophical, others personal. The boundaries between the two were carefully differentiated and kept at a distance. It was a lacuna that was acknowledged very openly and highlighted in the popular periodical *Zanan*, edited by Shahla Sherkat and Roza Eftekhari. Indeed, according to Eftekhari, when confronted by Sorush's seeming reluctance to give an interview to the periodical, *Zanan*, forthrightly presented the eminent philosopher of 'religious

---

[123] Sorush, 'Tahlil-e mafhum-e hokumat-e dini', p. 368.
[124] In this respect Sorush's views at this point bear a strong resemblance to the later ideas of Mehdi Bazargan. See Bazargan, *Akherat va khoda: hadaf-e resalat-e anbiyya'*, p. 37.

democracy' with an ultimatum: he would either give them an interview or they would print that he had declined to do so and let their readers decide for themselves why he had been less than forthcoming.[125] Published some two years into the Khatami presidency, in his interview Sorush would once more reiterate the mantra that Islamic jurisprudence and its role within society was irrelevant to the question of its 'religiosity', as well as well-worn bromides such as 'when ethical values are realised, society will be just'.[126]

In the course of the ensuing discussion, Sorush argues that relations between men and women are conditioned by social, cultural, and economic factors but ought to be predicated upon 'ethical values': 'in the relations between women and men some important ethical values must be preserved and for the preservation of these values, ordinances have been weighed. These ordinances are provisional, and depend on the social, economic and cultural period. Though ethical values are more enduring and permanent. It can be said perhaps that some of these values are eternal and ahistorical.' But when asked to give an example of such values, Sorush quickly appears to commit to a more traditional form of gender essentialism. In his view, 'one of the most important values in the relations between men and women is that *women be women and men be men* . . . [T]his belief is amongst the most important values ruling relations between women and men and determining feminine ethics (*akhlaq-e zananeh*) and masculine ethics (*akhlaq-e mardaneh*). Relations between women and men must not violate the fulfilment of masculinity (*mardanegi*) and femininity (*zananegi*) or remove woman from the sphere of femininity.'[127] In this formulation, *sex* appears to neatly map onto *gender* and we observe a stark binary dividing, with women and 'femininity' on one side, and men and 'masculinity' on the other. Needless to say, these equations and dichotomies have been deeply problematised by poststructuralist theoreticians of gender and sexuality such as Judith Butler and Iranian historians of gender and sexuality such as Afsaneh Najmabadi.[128] Sorush does qualify this statement by saying that our

---

[125] Eskandar Sadeghi-Boroujerdi, interview with Roza Eftekhari, 27/02/2018.
[126] Sorush, 'Qabz va bast-e hoquq-e zanan', p. 32.
[127] Italics added. Ibid., p. 32.
[128] Judith Butler, *Gender Trouble: Feminism and the Subversion of Identity* (New York & London: Routledge, 1990), chapter 1. Afsaneh Najmabadi, *Professing Selves: Transsexuality and Same-Sex Desire in Contemporary Iran* (Durham & London: Duke University Press, 2014).

definitions of femininity and masculinity are subject to culture and history and are therefore liable to change, even if an irreducible substance or kernel remains. Predictably, and as one might expect, Sorush takes aim at Islamic jurisprudence: 'I personally believe that the general interpretation of the schools of old thinking, especially the religious schools, regarding women is alloyed with myth (*ostureh*). This judgement is true for almost all of the Islamic ordinances (*ahkam-e shar'i*), including those germane to women.' Just as he did in several other areas, Sorush declared Islamic jurisprudential rulings formulated to the end of 'preserving women's honour and virtue (*'effat*)' to be 'accidental' (*'arazi*) in nature and therefore historically contingent and in need of demystification.[129] Questions of inheritance, court testimony, blood money, and polygamy are not addressed directly, but one can assume that they would also be encompassed by the quintessential historicity he believes to characterise Islamic ordinances.

Shabestari, who had also given an interview in a previous issue of *Zanan*, similarly distinguished between those jurists who contended women were endowed with certain natural God-given capacities and roles, such as childbirth and childrearing, and more recent views which saw gender roles as historically conditioned and constructed. Much like Sorush, Shabestari held that, if assessment of women's rights and place in society was guided foremost by values of justice, it would be possible to undertake reform and achieve a more equitable arrangement between men and women in society.[130] In support of his argument he recounts the story of his encounter with Ayatollah Seyyed Mohammad-Baqer al-Sadr (d. 1980) during a visit to Iraq in the mid-1970s. According to Shabestari, al-Sadr was of the opinion that religious ordinances pertaining to women were outmoded and enmeshed within premodern social relations.[131] Al-Sadr believed that in contemporary times, when women were regarded as a 'life partner' (*sharik-e*

---

[129] Sorush, 'Qabz va bast-e hoquq-e zanan', p. 34.
[130] Mohammad Mojtahed-Shabestari, 'Zanan, ketab va sonnat', *Zanan*, no. 57 (Aban 1378 [October–November 1999]), p. 20.
[131] This view has been further substantiated at length in the critical work of scholars such as Leila Ahmed and Kecia Ali. Leila Ahmed, *Women and Gender in Islam: Historical Roots of a Modern Debate* (New Haven & London: Yale University Press, 1992). Kecia Ali, 'Progressive Muslims and Islamic Jurisprudence: The Necessity for Critical Engagement with Marriage and Divorce Law', in *Progressive Muslims: On Justice, Gender and Pluralism*, ed. Omid Safi (Oxford: Oneworld, 2003).

zendegi) of comparable standing and stature to their male counterparts, their rights should change accordingly:

> [al-Sadr] gave the example of leadership (*riyasat*) in the family, and said that this leadership is on the condition that the man of the family take upon himself all of the burden of the family. But if the family burden (*bar*) is divided between the man and woman, the man cannot lead alone. He believed that if women are shoulder to shoulder with men in the general development of society ... they must enjoy rights appropriate to this role.[132]

Shabestari continues by reiterating a familiar argument for the reform of women's rights, which avers that the Prophet Mohammad had sought to improve the lot of women in his own society and therefore we ought to abide by the spirit of his actions[133] rather than cleave to archaic and myopic literalism.[134] 'The Prophet changed several oppressive rules and norms in that time that were germane to women. He entrained the oppression (*zolm*) of the time regarding women, toward a more just (*'adl*) age. He formally recognised women's right to property, limited unrestrained polygamy, and believed in adjustments to inheritance provisions. In short, he changed those gross inequalities which existed against women in accord with the understanding and perception of the "justice" of the day.'[135]

Sorush held the view that the ancient Greeks, Islamic philosophers, and European philosophers were all of the view that women had a 'lower status' until the dawn of the Enlightenment, a linear and not unproblematic view which itself has been subject to serious criticism in the work of feminist historian Joan Wallach Scott,[136] among others. But, elaborating upon these enduring patriarchal tropes found in pre-modern thinkers, he continues:

> [A]lso emotionally they thought of women as beings that don't have control of their emotions and not only do they tempt others, but they do not even use themselves for good. This is in the Islamic hadith and it appears in Ghazali's *Revival of the Religious Sciences* that women are half of Satan's army, and with their help, Satan can realise his objectives (*maqased*) in religious

---

132 Mojtahed-Shabestari, 'Zanan, ketab va sonnat', p. 21.

133 Amina Wadud, *Inside the Gender Jihad: Women's Reform in Islam* (London: Oneworld, 2006), chapter 6.

134 Mojtahed-Shabestari, 'Zanan, ketab va sonnat', p. 21.   135 Ibid., p. 22.

136 Joan Wallach Scott, *Sex and Secularism* (Princeton & Oxford: Princeton University Press, 2018), Introduction.

society ... [T]hese narratives which are most likely fabricated, are instructive from a phenomenological perspective. They show how religious society thought; how a religious scholar of Ghazali's calibre thought ... [S]uch thinking was very common, and it is for this same reason that many of these narrations and ordinances were nowhere protested in religious society.

Rights, including those pertaining to women, thus had to be updated and made consonant with 'the custom (*'orf*) and psychology of the time'.[137] He adds, 'the new perception (*tallaqi*) of woman is incompatible with the antiquated rights of women. We must analyse the religious ordinances and see from exactly which anthropological sources they arose ... In my opinion, true values (*arzesh-ha-ye asil*), in the service of justice, must be extracted from religious and rational sources, and it should be seen that the preservatory and temporary husks which protect those values have no sanctity in and of themselves. In this way, with a change of circumstances, a fresh husk (*pusteh-ye tazeh*) must be readied for safeguarding those same genuine values.'[138] As should be clear, Sorush is essentially applying the theory he propounded in *Qabz va bast-e te'orik-e shari'at*, which encompasses all 'religious knowledge', including that pertaining to women's rights. When probed about his insistence on some variation of gender essentialism and what he means by 'the sphere of femininity' (*madar-e zananegi*), Sorush struggles to provide a cogent answer. Rather than dismiss the distinction, he admits that it is indeed very difficult to provide a coherent answer and instead flees once more into the more abstract and general category of 'humanity': 'the difficulty of defining "humanity" in this regard can be seen from the many definitions of the human [the philosophers] have offered. They have said that the human being is the animal endowed with speech (*hayvan-e nateq*); the ethical animal (*hayvan-e akhlaqi*); the tool maker (*abzar-saz*); is an artist etc. Providing a cogent definition of woman and man is very difficult.' Despite such difficulties, Sorush once more acknowledges that the role of women in Iranian society at the opening of the twenty-first century has irrevocably changed and that 'contemporary society necessitates that those [antiquated] values [regarding women] change. Naturally, such change transforms our perception and definition of honour and virtue (*'effat*), modesty (*haya*), and all those facets that in the past were extraordinarily mystified ... [W]omen have shown that they are different beings and

---

[137] Sorush, 'Qabz va bast-e hoquq-e zanan', p. 34. [138] Ibid., p. 35.

have broken with the historical past.'[139] In this regard, Sorush appears to be suggesting that, rather than dispense with the notion of modesty altogether, it might be possible to revise our understanding of its entailments in a way that remains pertinent in the present.

In Sorush's reading of history, by means of which he believes it possible to reach broader conclusions and generalisations, he argues that 'we cannot simply say that women were oppressed for all of history, and because they were oppressed, they were unable to show their nature (*gowhar*) in the way they might have [otherwise] ... If we begin from such claims, we must conclude that women were entirely prone to accept oppression; and if this was the case until now, it will be the same in the future. Unless women wash their hands of being women ... we must understand the biological-psychological makeup of women, and study their historical role.'[140] Sorush thus appears to completely avoid serious engagement with the complex role of patriarchy and its manifold historical manifestations, with its focus on the specific nature of women's oppression, and the way it has manifested and shaped gender and gender relations during the course of human history, and Iran's modern history in particular.[141] In fact, he brackets women's oppression entirely, stating that he does not want to comment on whether or not it has historically been the case or existed: 'with this explanation predicated on oppression (*zolm*) the issue is not solved'. Rather, he claims he is interested in 'why it turned out this way'. In this manner, he is able to admit of evidence for a history of patriarchal systems without recognising it as a kind of 'oppression'. In other words, he is prepared to think about women's historically subordinate position in society, and even the possible reasons why such a situation came to pass, without undertaking a systematic and structural analysis under the name of patriarchy whose objective would be to understand the myriad historical forms and processes of women's oppression and discrimination.[142] His seeming unwillingness to admit of women's oppression and how the discursive operations of power and their generative effects have constituted gender and gender relations appears to stem from a qualified reiteration of gender essentialism and above all the

---

[139] Ibid., p. 35.   [140] Ibid., p. 36.

[141] Minoo Moallem, *Between Warrior Brother and Veiled Sister: Islamic Fundamentalism and the Politics of Patriarchy in Iran* (Berkeley & London: University of California Press, 2005), Loc 1992.

[142] Sorush, 'Qabz va bast-e hoquq-e zanan', p. 37.

presumed link between gender and biological sex, which very clearly inform his views on the subject: 'rights and obligations should not be approved which [men and women's] historical, biological and psychological existence make unrealisable (*nashodani*), undesirable and disagreeable ... If the body and biological makeup of women or men was such, that it rejected certain religious ordinances, those ordinances will too be proclaimed abrogated (*laghv*) ... We do not have any obligation (*taklif*) which exceeds our ability and personal forbearance.' These problematic claims notwithstanding, Sorush acknowledges once more that his conclusions are temporary and belong to our specific historical juncture: 'our words are for our own time and those which come after us will have to speak in their own time for themselves'.[143]

How to Govern in lieu of the *Right* to Govern

While procedurally speaking – namely, how citizens elect their representatives – the political regime envisioned by Sorush can be termed democratic, it harbours a basic difference with regimes which espouse laicism: 'The society of the religious (*dindaran*) choose their leaders and they have the right to demand from rulers that they continuously keep the space of religious experience and the free cultivation of faith, in society and observe the rights of the religious'.[144] 'Religious democracies, unlike their laicist counterparts, are obliged to furnish conditions amenable for freely chosen religiosity. What this would entail in actual policy terms is left characteristically vague, and Sorush does not entertain or give much thought to the possibility that individually religious members of Iranian society might elect a government because of its economic policies – e.g., better healthcare or less regressive taxation – as opposed to the promotion of conditions amenable to 'heartfelt faith'. Nor does he ponder how, for instance, one of the perennial arguments of American political life – to wit, reproductive rights – might be balanced with the rights of the religious and their objection to a woman's right to terminate an unwanted pregnancy. Would the observance of reproductive rights by the state be considered an affront to the rights of the religious? And if observed, would a democracy consequently be considered 'irreligious', even if it granted freedom of religious expression predicated on the harm principle?

---

[143] Ibid., p. 37.   [144] 'Tahlil-e mafhum-e hokumat-e dini', p. 357.

This is not a mere piece of abstract theorising. Sorush speaks explicitly of the Islamic Republic's institutions but sets the scene by first recalling the classical question of political theory asked by Plato in *The Republic*: 'who has the right to rule?' Sorush, without explicitly citing Popper, replaces the question of who has the right to rule with the question 'how must one rule?'[145] Unlike Plato, who posited the ideal of the Philosopher-King, or Khomeini, who similarly argued on behalf of the entitlement and duty of the just *faqih* to rule, Sorush, closely following Popper, is concerned with the procedural question 'how must one rule?'[146] Popper was primarily preoccupied with procedural questions of how political power can be limited and the possibility of dictatorship and wayward authority be thwarted. As a result, democracy in Popper's estimation was first and foremost a matter of ensuring people could defend themselves against the threat of dictatorship.[147] For Popper, it was the ability to depose a leader or government without bloodshed that was the crux of democratic governance.[148] Pursuing this line of thought, Sorush refers to the role of the Assembly of Experts

---

145   Ibid., p. 358.   146   Ibid., p. 358.

147   Kadivar also affirms this position in Mohsen Kadivar, 'Azadi dar hokumat-e dini', in *Daghdagheh-ha-ye hokumat-e dini* (Tehran: Nashr-e ney, 1379 [2000]), p. 420. This article was a speech delivered at the Economics Faculty at the University of Tehran on 12 November 1996 (22 Aban 1375). It was subsequently published in *Salam*, amongst other publications, in three parts on 2, 12, 19 Dey 1375 [December–January 1996–7]. Mojtahed-Shabestari also takes a comparable position, albeit some years later. Mojtahed-Shabestari, 'Demokrasi va dindari', p. 108. In this essay, which was first published in Tehran municipality's newspaper, several years after Sorush's well-known essays on religious democracy, Mojtahed-Shabestari speaks of democracy's importance as a form of government which permits the people to peacefully remove those in authority from political power and replace them with another government.

148   Karl R. Popper, *The Lesson of This Century: With Two Talks on Freedom and the Democratic State*, trans. Patrick Camiller (London & New York: Routledge, 1997), p. 70–1. This very same volume by Popper was translated into Persian, and Mohammad Khatami suggested that his cabinet read it upon taking office. 'Abdolkarim Sorush, 'Critical Rationalism and Religious and Political Reform in Iran', in *Sir Karl Popper Memorial Lecture, London School of Economic and Political Science* (15 March 2012). Sorush's comments in this particular essay, however, appear to largely rely on Popper's debate with Herbert Marcuse, whose publication long preceded that of *The Lesson of This Century* in both English and Persian. See Herbert Marcuse and Karl R. Popper, *Revolution or Reform? A Confrontation*, trans. Michael Aylward and A. T. Ferguson (Chicago: Precedent Publishing; New University Press, 1976), p. 78. The latter had been translated into Persian prior to the revolution. 'Ali Paya

(*Majles-e khebregan*) in the Islamic Republic's political system and constitution and states that its responsibility is to depose the leader (*rahbar*) if he ceases to fulfil the criteria of a just leader.[149] The criteria of 'justice' is not specified or fleshed out, but, given his aforementioned positions, it could not be determined by the methods of Islamic jurisprudence, which, of course, raises the question of why refer to the Assembly of Experts at all, given it is a body composed solely of jurists. It could be another strategic proposition, perhaps, taking leave of the actual institutions constitutive of the constitutional and political process. In any event, he continues, surmising that by means of the Assembly of Experts we observe 'indirect supervision of the state by the people'.[150]

Sorush then moves to focus on the fallibility of the human ruler (*hakem*) because 'the temptation of power and wealth ... is not a small temptation and can cause anyone to err'[151] – arguably another instance of Sorush's embrace of Popper's epistemological fallibilism or perhaps the Actonian dictum convinced that unchecked power is invariably corrupting.[152] Popper did not hold 'objectivity' to be the property of a single individual or specific class but rather a 'social product' and the product of critical discussion.[153] Therefore no single individual could ultimately claim to be in possession of the truth to the exclusion of others. For Popper, but also for Sorush, such an eventuality is an *a priori* impossibility, whether it be the proletariat claiming to be the universal subject of history or the *foqaha'* contending to be the sole guardians of the *shari'ah*. Continuing this line of argument, Sorush argues that if all the state's institutions ultimately receive legitimacy from the *vali-ye faqih*, as some ideologues à la Mesbah-Yazdi in the Islamic Republic are wont to claim, then the Assembly of Experts'

and Mohammad Amin Ghaneirad, 'The Philosopher and the Revolutionary State: How Karl Popper's Ideas Shaped the Views of Iranian Intellectuals', *International Studies in the Philosophy of Science* 20, no. 2 (July 2006), p. 186. This view was also advocated by critically disposed clerics such as Hojjat al-Islam Mehdi Ha'eri-Yazdi (d. 1999) throughout the 1990s. See Mehdi Ha'eri-Yazdi, 'Hokumat dar mafhum-e vekalat-e shahrvandan', in *Siyasat-gari va siyasat-andishi: zendegi va fekri-ye siyasi-ye Mehdi Ha'eri-Yazdi*, ed. Mas'ud Razavi (Tehran: 'Elm, 1387 [2008]), p. 92.

[149] Sorush, 'Tahlil-e mafhum-e hokumat-e dini', p. 359.   [150] Ibid., p. 359.
[151] Ibid., p. 359.   [152] Ibid., p. 359.
[153] Jeremy Shearmur, *The Political Thought of Karl Popper* (London & New York: Routledge, 1996), p. 111.

supervisory role is effectively nullified. Legitimacy cannot be bestowed entirely from on high but must come from an alternative source: in this instance, popular election. If the people are endowed with the right of indirect supervision of the leader, Sorush concludes that they are also entitled to rule. Following Popper almost verbatim, he argues that 'the right of deposition takes precedence over the right of appointment'.[154] Emphasis is therefore placed just as it is in Popper on the 'how of rule' and the ease of deposition rather than the procedure of selection and right to rule.

Such an approach essentially abandons any attempt to understand sovereignty as 'constituent power': namely, the power to found and establish a political community on a different basis to the one which preceded it, a revolutionary founding which institutes and 'instaures' a new political and legal order. Sorush's procedural approach to governance under the sway of Popper, prioritising the power to depose, pointedly rejects the idea of sovereignty as constituent power, which it decries as a recipe for arbitrary violence and the wayward abuse of political power. Because it views such power through a strictly negative lens and as inherently repressive and to be constrained, it completely neglects its capacity to perform a positive, creative function that might give rise to novel forms of socio-political life and organisation. In the words of Andreas Kalyvas, 'the sovereign constituent subject is not a repressive force, but a productive agency', where 'the mission of the sovereign is not to exercise power, but to design the higher legal norms and procedural rules that will regulate this exercise of power'.[155] In this sense, sovereign constituent power is both external and antecedent to any established system of positive laws. Sorush's ideal political regime, which valorises the right of deposition, appears thus incapable of understanding the conditions of its own collective generation, where under exceptional conditions of crisis this political vision may indeed be advanced and find itself enshrined in a new constitutional order. Just as it is incapable of conceiving popular and collective challenges extraneous to its own limited terms, which might set out to challenge a perceived democratic deficit and overturn it in favour of another political and constitutional arrangement, its understandable focus on

---

[154] Sorush, 'Tahlil-e mafhum-e hokumat-e dini', p. 361.
[155] Andreas Kalyvas, 'Popular Sovereignty, Democracy, and the Constituent Power', *Constellations* 12, no. 2 (2005), p. 226.

deposing the powerful leads it to occlude consideration of popular sovereignty as constituent power, which amounts to a novel restatement of the older and more recognisable notion of self-determination and self-rule whereby people author the laws which govern them.

By the summer of 2004, the influence of Popper's thought was such that even Ayatollah Khameneh'i felt it necessary to express his disapproval of the Austrian-born philosopher by name along with his Iranian partisans, in direct connection with what he took to be the threat of 'cultural onslaught'.

When I say cultural onslaught (*tahajom-e farhangi*) some imagine I mean some boy with long hair. They think I disapprove of long hair. This is not the issue of cultural onslaught. Of course, licentiousness and corruption are one of the branches of cultural onslaught, but it is greater than this. Over a protracted number of years, they injected into the brains and beliefs of Iranians that "you can't, you must follow the West and Europe" ... The same way the faithful believe in the Qur'an, the word of God and divine revelation, to the same degree, they believe in the theories of such and such European scholar. What is interesting is that these theories become antiquated and obsolete (*mansukh*), and are replaced by new theories. But these people hold up the same theories of fifty years ago as a sacred text and a religion (*din*). For decades, the bases of Popper's political and social theories have been dated and outmoded, and tens of books in Europe have been written against them. But in recent years, there are people who claim to have an understanding of philosophy that have started disseminating the theories of Popper! ... These people have two issues: the first is that they are imitative followers (*moqalled*), and the second, they are uninformed of new developments ... Our country commends philosophy, but for understanding philosophy refer to others![156]

In the course of making this intervention, the decisive contributions of 'Abdolkarim Sorush and their import for Iranian intellectual life could not have been far from the Leader's mind. What is notable is that just as religious reformists had implicitly and explicitly taken the institution of *marja'iyyat* to task for formalising the structures of religious authority which enjoined the lay classes to imitate and partake in *taqlid*, Ayatollah Khameneh'i disparagingly invoked the purportedly uncritical *taqlid* of Popper by religious intellectuals. Apart from finding fault with their deference to an ostensibly passé philosopher, it was a matter

---

[156] 'Ali Khameneh'i, 'Bayanat dar didar-e daneshjuyan va asatid-e daneshgah-ha-ye ostan-e Hamedan' (*Khamenei.ir*, 17/04/1383 [7 July 2004]).

of blindly imitating Western theories and drawing on them to understand Iranian society as well as to prescribe the norms and rules by
which it ought to be governed. Though crucially distinct in tenor and
configuration, appeals of this kind were redolent of the more acerbic
taunts in Jalal Al-e Ahmad's *Gharbzadegi* and the infamous bon mots
of Ahmad Fardid, stridently bemoaning Iranians' ineluctable surrender
to Western cultural and intellectual hegemony. The fear of the cultural
onslaught went far beyond the realm of the sartorial or even certain
lifestyle choices as Khameneh'i himself makes clear. Ultimately, it was
a question of the political metaphysics through which Iranian society
should be ordered and understood.

Concluding Remarks

For many of the *rowshanfekran-e dini* the question of 'governance'
was synonymous with the absence of politics, and to this extent it
fitted well with the broader political context of the 1990s and the
outlook of the Kargozaran, which attempted to amplify the idea that
governance was ultimately a 'technical' and 'scientific' question
rather than a political one.[157] 'Non-ideological' technical and scientific know-how, as well as trial and error, were the best means of
governing. Revelation, on this view, was of limited use to the open-
ended challenge of running a modern state and the myriad challenges
it faced in the domestic and international arenas. It might serve as
a source of personal consolation and moral exhortation, but beyond
the purview of the private sphere its utility was far from self-evident.
'Ideology' was dangerous and political *feqh* could not offer any solutions to the complex questions facing the modern state.[158] 'Ideology'
had been tarnished by what many intellectuals held to be an 'excess of
politics'. While it does not entirely coincide – indeed, Rafsanjani
showed little interest in taking the advice of the religious intellectuals
and their allies calling for political development[159] or in the harassment they received at the hands of vigilante 'pressure groups' – the
conviction that governance was first and foremost a technocratic
question under the purview of experts with a specified division of

[157] Sorush, 'Tahlil-e mafhum-e hokumat-e dini', p. 363.
[158] Mojtahed-Shabestari, 'Qara'at-e rasmi az din', p. 36.
[159] Hajjariyan and Khojasteh-Rahimi, 'Eslahatchi, cheriki nemishavad', p. 45.

labour who engineer the domains under their jurisdiction found broad support in principle, even if it was not always reflected in practice, with nepotism, bribery, and other forms of corruption continuing to afflict the country in all manner of ways. The dalliance with neoliberal tropes under the auspices of the apolitical rule of experts and the engagement with Cold War liberal and neoliberal critiques of the bloated, authoritarian state certainly made a powerful impression on reformist discourse and the intellectual horizons of Iran's political debates more generally. On another level, however, it is undeniable that the *rowshanfekran-e dini* were mounting a concerted assault on the ideological underpinnings of the Islamic state, taking inspiration from the cataclysmic fall of the Soviet Union and the end of the Cold War. The 'end of ideology' and 'end of history' were taken up with far more eagerness by some than others, but nevertheless these tropes made an indelible mark on Iran's intellectual landscape and would profoundly shape its character.

Furthermore, the great emphasis Popper had laid on piecemeal social engineering in contradistinction to revolutionary transformation was imbibed by several *rowshanfekran-e dini*, who had not only lived the revolution but had played the part of committed revolutionaries. In many instances, they creatively entertained this paradigm even though Popper certainly never had anything like a constitutional hierocratic order in mind when he first penned his theory. Nevertheless, distinct forms of *epistemological fallibilism* and demands for *gradualist and piecemeal social change* found themselves theoretically married in the thought of Sorush, Mojtahed-Shabestari, Ganji, Kadivar, and many others who would openly advocate incremental political reform after the electoral victory of Mohammad Khatami inaugurated the 'epoch of reforms' (*dowran-e eslahat*) and find its associated keywords disseminated and popularised through intellectual networks which had taken shape and evolved over the course of the first half of the 1990s. The objective was first and foremost to limit and condition wayward power and interference in the individual's personal autonomy and liberty, rather than to revolutionise and overhaul social relations in their entirety. Who was best suited to manage the process of gradualist reforms and how it ought to be realised were themselves the subject of serious contention and, as the following chapters will show, could not be easily resolved, as intra- and inter-factional jockeying showed little prospect of abatement.

By the mid-1990s, Sorush and Mojtahed-Shabestari, through their various critiques of jurisprudential Islam, were not only undermining the theocratic bastions of the Islamic Republic but the very raison d'être of the clergy itself. These views were not uniformly shared by either religious intellectuals or members of the Islamic left, many of whom theorised in more overtly practical terms and were better apprised of the institutional and constitutional challenges confronting transformative political action. This was especially the case for organisations such as the Association of Combatant Clerics or the Mojahedin Organisation of the Islamic Revolution. The following two chapters will address some of the intellectual and strategic fault-lines within the so-called 'reformist camp', as it developed in the years after 1997. Teasing out the disagreements and debates over the semantics, pace, and scope of reform, and how it it ought to be strategically realised, helps us to understand some of the intellectual and political rifts which afflicted the reformist coalition itself.

6 | Khatami, the 2nd Khordad Front, and the Pedagogics of Pluralism

Will Khatami compromise?

And Khatami went to the Majles to defend his policies.
One group believed: Khatami mustn't compromise.
Another group believed: Khatami must compromise.
The third group were saying: But didn't Khatami compromise?
The fourth group were saying: But Khatami compromised?
Khatami once again defended the politics which he supported and all of
   which he had cast aside in 2000 (1379).
The people were saying: now that nothing will be done, the least we can do
   is talk about it.[1]

Ebrahim Nabavi, *Dar sal 79*
etefaq oftad (Something happened in the year 2000)

Introduction

The first two years of Hojjat al-Islam Mohammad Khatami's tenure
were ones of hope and vibrancy, not merely on the country's intellectual scene but also for journalism. While many of the discursive keywords of the reformist lexicon had been coined and theorised prior to
Khatami's electoral victory, following the 1997 presidential election
which brought the 'Smiling Seyyed' (*seyyed-e khandan*) to office, they
were now able to reach a far broader audience than hitherto and extend
their reach far beyond the elite networks of think tanks, academic and
informal study groups, and specialist periodicals. While newspapers
such as *Salam* – overseen by political veteran and former attorney-
general Hojjat al-Islam Mohammad Musavi-Kho'iniha – had been

---

[1] Ebrahim Nabavi and Nikahang Kowsar, *Dar sal-e 79 etefaq oftad* (Tehran:
   Rowzanah, 1380 [2001]), p. 216.

active since February 1991 and had acted as the most important media podium of the Islamic left during the 1990s, after the election a whole raft of newspapers were founded by various members and affiliates of the Islamic left and those sympathetic to Khatami's electoral platform.

During Khatami's first term, allies of the president and stalwart members of the Islamic *chap*, along with those linked to religious intellectual circles, saw the media as one of the chief avenues through which they might consolidate their capture of the executive and thereby disseminate their ideas for a wider public. It was in this way that a new 'common sense' and public understanding of politics and the role of religion in the public sphere would be fostered. Gramsci famously defined 'common sense' as 'the folklore of "philosophy"' standing 'midway between real "folklore" . . . and the philosophy, the science, the economics of the scholars'. It is neither 'rigid' nor 'static'; rather, 'it changes continuously, enriched by scientific notions and philosophical opinions which have entered into common usage'.[2] According to Stuart Hall, 'common sense is not coherent; it is usually "disjointed and episodic," fragmentary and contradictory', and its importance resides in the fact that 'it is the terrain of conceptions and categories on which the practical consciousness of the masses of the people is actually formed. It is the already formed and "taken-for-granted" ground on which more coherent ideologies and philosophies must contend for mastery, the ground which new conceptions of the world must contest and even transform, if they are to shape the conceptions of the world of the masses and in that way become historically effective.'[3]

Very much in this vein, it would be partisan newspapers edited by members and devotees of the Islamic left and those sympathetic to the 'religious intellectual' project that would become a pre-eminent vehicle for the articulation and dissemination of the keywords and idioms of reform and their entry into the quotidian everyday conversations of the reading public. In accord with this ambition, several popular news-papers became associated with both prominent members of the Islamic left and their intellectual allies. Thus, Hamid-Reza Jala'ipur and Mohsen Sazgara founded *Jame'eh* (Society) with Masha Allah Shams ol-va'ezin as editor in February 1998. From the outset the newspaper

---

[2] Antonio Gramsci, *Prison Notebooks*, trans. Joseph A. Buttigieg and Antonio Callari, vol. 1 (New York: Columbia University Press, 1992), p. 173.
[3] Hall, *Cultural Studies 1983: A Theoretical History*, Loc 3196.

was firmly committed to Khatami's political programme, announcing itself 'the first newspaper of Iranian civil society'.[4] In billing it thus, they sought to firmly distinguish themselves from official and state-owned news outlets. They tacitly pledged to offer an alternative narrative to that of the latter, while at the same time receiving encouragement from the Khatami administration and the Ministry of Culture, with which some of these new journalists and editors had been associated or collaborated at one time or another.[5] Prior to *Jame'eh*'s publication, 'Abdolkarim Sorush was intimately involved in the details of the newspaper's founding in May–June 1997, and even advised Shams ol-va 'ezin, who regarded himself as the former's student and disciple, to accept editorship in the new venture.[6] The theoretical journal *Kiyan* was still active publishing during this time under the guidance of Ebrahim Soltani and Reza Tehrani, but it was regarded as for the most part restricted to a small and well-educated middle-class audience.[7] 'It seemed Dr. Sorush wished to reproduce the success of *Kiyan* on a larger scale', recalled Shams ol-va'ezin in a retrospective interview published in early 2013. With *Jame'eh*, 'Religious intellectualism possessed a far-reaching media-outlet,' and its initial daily circulation exceeded *Kiyan*'s bimonthly print-run five-fold.[8] Shams ol-va 'ezin and Sazgara had even at one point pondered founding a party bearing the name of 'religious intellectualism' in a bid to capitalise on the opportunity afforded by the Islamic left's unexpected victory.[9] The Kiyan circle as a whole did not endorse the move, as several of them believed their role was best served in an exclusively theoretical capacity. The idea was, however, stillborn when the Ministry of the Interior refused to provide the group with a licence to undertake political activities.[10]

The Mojahedin Organisation of the Islamic Revolution of Iran's (SMEEI's) journal *'Asr-e ma* also continued to be active and was

---

[4] Masha Allah Shams ol-va'ezin, 'Osul-e 10 ganeh-ye Jame'eh [*Jame'eh*, no. 1, 16 Bahman 1376 (5 February 1998)]', in *Yaddasht-ha-ye sardabir* (Tehran: Jame'eh-ye Iraniyan, Bahar 1380 [Spring 2001]), p. 105.

[5] Masha Allah Shams ol-va'ezin, 'Halqeh-ye Kiyan mokhalef bud: goftogu ba Masha Allah Shams ol-va'ezin', *Mehrnameh*, no. 27 (Bahman 1391 [January–February 2013]), p. 197.

[6] Ibid., p. 195–6. [7] Ibid., p. 195–6. [8] Ibid., p. 196.

[9] Mohsen Sazgara and Eskandar Sadeghi-Boroujerdi, 'Interview with Mohsen Sazgara' (13 May 2013).

[10] Ibid.

perhaps the main outlet for Sa'id Hajjariyan's strategic-political analyses until it was banned in the spring of 2002, while its editor, Mohsen
Armin, would enter the Sixth Majles and become a deputy speaker.
During this initial flurry of activity, the writings of none other than
Akbar Ganji came to typify a new chapter in engaged journalism.[11]
In addition to exposing the many misdeeds of the Islamic Republic's
intelligence services and 'rogue' elements therein, he edited the fort-
nightly periodical *Rah-e now* (New Path), which emerged as another
prodigious outlet for religious intellectuals and the more theoretically
disposed elements of the Islamic left. Meanwhile, Hajjariyan began
publication of *Sobh-e emruz* (This Morning), edited by his one-time
colleague at the Presidential Strategic Research Centre, 'Ali-Reza
'Alavi-Tabar. Hojjat al-Islam 'Abdollah Nuri of the Assembly of
Combatant Clerics (MRM) founded *Khordad*, edited by 'Ali
Hekmat, and a one-time seminarian, IRGC member, and religious
reformist intellectual, 'Emad al-Din Baqi, emerged as a controversial
editor of *Fath* (Victory).[12] All in all, these activities were indicative of
the very real impact of the religious intellectual discourse amongst the
Islamic left elite and their desire to propagate it in a more public and
accessible format, furthering their political programme in the process.

Morteza Mardiha – an erstwhile Islamist student activist-turned
liberal academic, who was a participant in the Kiyan circle and also
a prominent commentator for the newspaper *'Asr-e azadegan* (Age of
the Free-Thinkers, which was later edited by Shams ol-va'ezin) – pointedly stated in one of his articles on the cusp of the Sixth Majles election
that 'the press is the epitome and essence (*'osareh*) of 2nd of Khordad
[23 May 1997, the date of Khatami's election] and it is for this reason
that a legion of outstanding intellectual, cultural, and political elements
gathered together in this domain'. Mardiha compared the burgeoning
reformist press corps to Iran's Islamic Revolutionary Guard Corps in
the first years of the revolution, stating that

---

[11] The most famous example is, of course, Akbar Ganji, *'Alijenab-e sorkhpush va
      'alijenab-e khakestari: asib-shenasi-ye gozar beh dowlat-e demokratik-e
      towse'eh-gara* (Tehran: Tarh-e now, 1378 [1999]).

[12] It was largely in *Fath* that Baqi, like Ganji (who was also on the editorial board
      of the paper), worked tirelessly to expose the murder of secular intellectuals and
      dissidents by 'rogue elements' in the intelligence services. See 'Emad al-Din Baqi,
      Terazhedi-ye demokrasi dar Iran: bazkhani-ye qatl-ha-ye zanjireh'i, 2 vols., vol.
      1 (Tehran: Nashr-e ney, 1378 [1999]).

at that time a considerable part of the educated and cognoscenti entered the Revolutionary Guards because the activities and institutions of the revolution and country had not yet been split apart and in their absence the Revolutionary Guards were considered the essence (*'osareh*) of the revolution.[13]

In hindsight, it is a suggestive analogy, given that Jala'ipur, Sazgara, Baqi, and 'Alavi-Tabar had all served in the paramilitary force during the Iran–Iraq War,[14] and 'Abdollah Nuri had briefly served as Khomeini's representative to the organisation. Many would begin to pursue graduate studies, often state-sponsored, at both home and abroad, following the war. In any case, this group of individuals, bound by their robust opposition to Khomeini's challengers and the protracted brutality of the conflict with Saddam Hussein's Iraq, had gradually come to adopt a very different outlook to the one which they had previously so staunchly advocated.[15] Instead of conducting hot wars they now chose to spar with the traditional right in print and in the lecture hall. Rather than allusions to *The Wretched of the Earth* and the necessity of anti-colonial purgative violence, Habermasian invitations to dialogical reasoning and communicative consensus became the touchstones of considered debate.

As the prominent journalist and writer Mas'ud Behnud observed, 'following the 2nd Khordad, the role and share of the Iranian media in the civic movement became clear',[16] and, in many instances, it would be members of the loose, sprawling network of the Islamic left, religious intellectuals, and their associates who would be leading the charge. The press was touted as the 'fourth pillar' (*rokn-e chahrom*) or 'fourth estate' of democratic society, and similarly a free, critical press was thought indispensable for unmasking the abuses of political

---

[13] Morteza Mardiha, 'Andisheh-ha-ye now dar 'arseh-ye entekhabat-e sheshom', in *Amniyyat dar eghma: negahi beh jelveh-ha-ye surrealism-ye siyasi dar Iran* (Tehran: Naqsh va negar, 1379 [2000]), p. 21.

[14] One of Farideh Farhi's interviewees, a former field commander, makes the interesting observation that the origins of the 'reformist' reading of Islam can be traced back to the war front during the Iran–Iraq War. Farideh Farhi, 'The Antinomies of Iran's War Generation', in *Iran, Iraq, and the Legacies of War*, ed. Lawrence G. Potter and Gary G. Sick (New York: Palgrave Macmillan, 2004), p. 109.

[15] Gramsci, *Selections from the Prison Notebooks of Antonio Gramsci*, p. 52–3.

[16] Mas'ud Behnud, 'Dow Dovvom-e Khordad, yek goru va yek matbu'at', in *Goluleh bad ast: maqalat-e Jame'eh, Tus, Neshat va Adineh* (Tehran: 'Elm, 1378 [1999]), p. 307.

power and the propagation of a critical consciousness throughout the country.[17] There was an almost naïve faith in the power of 'civil society' and the 'public sphere', populated by an independent press, myriad NGOs, and conscientious individuals. Extricated from geo-politics, economic relations, and capital flows, and by virtue of their very existence, they were able to hold wayward state institutions to account and inevitably compel their peaceful and gradualist reform in a liberal democratic direction.[18] Nonetheless, there were genuine exchanges unfolding through the press, and as a result the expression of its readers' demands and expectations. *Salam,* for example, received reams of letters from readers addressing the foremost issues of the day and would publish those they regarded to be the 'best' in columns entitled 'Political Letters' and 'Political Public Opinion'. Internally, the newspaper analysed the subjects most spoken about by readers and tabulated them, drawing on them as an informal barometer of public opinion.[19]

This chapter and the following will not and cannot offer a panoramic view of the Khatami era. Rather, it will provide a detailed exposition of Mohammad Khatami's political and religious world view based on his politico-ideological writings of the early 1990s and thereafter his speeches delivered during his first term in office. It will thereby try to situate him in relation to other post-revolutionary religious intellectual currents, of which, as has been shown in previous chapters, he was apprised and with which he was in regular contact. It will examine his views and conceptualisation of 'law', 'guardianship', and 'legitimacy' and evaluate the extent to which their articulation shaped his politics and relationships with other reformist currents. The following chapter will focus on the writings of Sa'id Hajjariyan, the so-called 'brain of reform' (*maghz-e eslahat*), elucidating his positions on the issues of 'sovereignty' and 'political development' and how they pertained to

---

[17] Shams ol-va'ezin uses this very term in *Jame'eh*'s ten-point manifesto. Shams ol-va'ezin, 'Osul-e 10 ganeh-ye *Jame'eh*', p. 106. 'Emad al-Din Baqi, 'Matbu'at va towse'eh-ye siyasi', in *Bahar-e rokn-e chaharom: moruri bar jonbesh-e matbu'at-e eslah-talab (1376–1379)* (Tehran: Nashr-e sara'i, 1381 [2002]), pp. 76–7.

[18] Asef Bayat has analysed this long-term structural and discursive shift in the context of the MENA region. Asef Bayat, 'Revolution in Bad Times', *New Left Review* (March–April 2013), p. 56.

[19] Karim Arghandehpur, *Dowran-e Salam* (Tehran: Nashr-e negah-e emruz, 1380), p. 89.

reformist strategy in the late 1990s and early 2000s. In this way, the two chapters together aim to glean some of the Islamic left's and religious intellectual complex's unresolved theoretical and political aporias, as well as the intellectual resources they brought to bear in their struggle for ideological and political hegemony. Getting a handle on the intellectual disagreements dividing Iran's reformists provides a deeper appreciation of the ideological landscape of the Khatami period and shows how post-revolutionary Iranian reformism was itself internally differentiated and a spectrum of opinion which was far from monolithic. It also demonstrates that there were alternative analyses and strategies available to the Khatami administration but that the president's conception of politics and his role in the polity prevented him from pursuing them. Whether a more audacious strategy would have succeeded in providing the breakthrough many of his supporters had hoped for will remain a counter-factual left to posterity to answer.

Khatami and the 2nd Khordad Front

I should begin by stating that the relationship between the political thought of Khatami and other well-known religious intellectuals such as Sorush, Mojtahed-Shabestari, and Kadivar was by no means straightforward. Chapter 3 detailed how prior to Khatami's electoral victory he had emphasised the necessity for cultural development, while several other centres of intellectual ferment with ties to the political elite gradually began to stress the imperative of 'political development' – often a euphemism for 'democratisation' – and their own ideological and moral leadership, predicting that Rafsanjani's contentment with 'economic development' would ultimately come unstuck and culminate in a veritable cul-de-sac.

Khatami's discourse by all accounts offered a refreshing alternative to his conservative rival and the incumbent parliamentary speaker, Hojjat al-Islam 'Ali-Akbar Nateq-Nuri,[20] and was in two obvious and uncontroversial respects under the sway of 1990s-era religious intellectualism and its accompanying network. First, Khatami's acknowledgement of multiple *qara'at-ha* or readings of religion, in tandem with an insistence on mutual toleration, was unmistakably

---

[20] Babak Dad, *Sad ruz ba Khatami* (Tehran: Entesharat-e vezarat-e farhang va ershad eslami, 1377 [1998]), pp. 128–30.

influenced by the work of Shabestari, Sorush, and others, even if he still remained considerably more conservative in his conclusions than the latter.[21] Second, at the same time his insistence on electoral participation as a vehicle for political development was inspired by his colleagues in the Ayin circle, which included his younger brother Mohammad-Reza, and also members of the SMEEI, who had had good relations with Khatami throughout the 1990s. The journal *Ayin* would only begin publication in the summer of 2004 and was thoroughly committed to theorising the project of 'reform' in the political, religious, and legal spheres[22]; however, the interpersonal relationships and points of intellectual exchange had long been in place. Apart from his younger brother, Fayzollah 'Arabsorkhi, an SMEEI central committee member, had essentially acted as Khatami's 'right-hand man' while the former culture minister headed the National Library. The influence of these channels of communication and formal and informal networks of individuals, reading groups, research centres, and publications cannot be underestimated in terms of their impact upon Khatami's public platform as well as many of the policies he would propound during his presidency. This does not mean that, upon reaching office, Khatami was always able or even willing to actualise the objectives of this influential group of intellectuals and politicos, as we shall see in due course. In fact, it was his at times seeming impotence and ineffectuality while in office which not only emboldened the conservative establishment but also led more radical reformists to increasingly slide into apathy and declare that they had 'surpassed Khatami' and left his limited aspirations behind.[23]

---

21 His lecture 'The Official Reading of Islam', delivered on 22 June 1998 (which I will analyse in greater detail below), is one such example. Though it is not clear whether Khatami is alluding to Shabestari's critique of the 'official reading of religion', it echoes in a simplified fashion many of the tropes and ideas found in the latter's oeuvre. It is also worth noting that Khatami and Shabestari share the same publisher. Mohammad Khatami, 'Tafsir-e rasmi az Islam (1/4/1377 [22/6/ 1998]),' in *Islam, rowhaniyyat va enqelab-e eslami* (Tehran: Tarh-e now, 1379 [2000]).
22 Khatami, 'Ayin-e ayiniyan', pp. 2–3.
23 In a collection of essays entitled *Surpassing Khatami*, Hossein Bashiriyeh, who was by no means a member of the Islamic left even if he had had a significant impact on several of its prominent members, was most frank in plainly stating that almost four years later the 'reformist project' was flagging and had lost much of its initial impetus. Hossein Bashiriyeh, 'Payan-e yek perozheh', in *'Obur az Khatami*, ed. Amir-Reza Sotudeh (Tehran: Zekr, 1379 [2000]), p. 40.

The next pages will analyse some of the chief features of Khatami's own world view and the key words around which his discourse revolved, both prior to, and in the years following, his ascendance to head of the executive. It has been assumed on occasion that Khatami came to the presidency with a programme of sweeping reform as an Iranian Gorbachev in the making.[24] Apart from the obvious differences between their respective offices' standing and powers within the hierarchy of the state power structure – e.g., the Iranian president is not the highest-ranking official in the country, nor is he head of the armed forces – the reality proved far more complicated. Antagonists of the Islamic left such as long-time Foreign Minister 'Ali-Akbar Velayati (1981–97) and Khatami's defeated rival Hojjat al-Islam Nateq-Nuri tried to conflate Khatami and Gorbachev and thereby depict the former as an existential threat to the *nezam* – the beginnings of a slippery slope on the road to disintegration and eventual collapse.[25] All the while, partisans such as Akbar Ganji with equal vigour repudiated the analogy, despite at several other junctures borrowing heavily from the rhetoric of Soviet and Eastern bloc reformers:[26] 'Khatami is not the Iranian Gorbachev. Khatami is the symbol of compassionate and humane Islam. Khatami is the man of security, law and civil society,' Ganji proclaimed.

Nevertheless, in a lecture delivered at Sharif University in December 1998, Ganji explicitly turned his attention to Soviet and Eastern bloc reformers such as Nikita Khrushchev and the process of 'de-Stalinisation' (which he initiated), Hungary's Imre Nagy,

---

Publicly articulated disillusion with the reformist project under Khatami's leadership was more uncompromisingly stated by those who were prepared to break with elite political circles in the Islamic Republic and face prison and exile. This usually occurred after formerly committed intellectuals of the Islamic *chap* directly experienced brutalisation, torture, and imprisonment. The best example is undoubtedly Akbar Ganji and his *Republican Manifesto*, which he smuggled out of Evin prison for publication in 2002. Akbar Ganji, *Manifest-e jomhuri-khahi: jomhuri khahi dar barabar-e mashruteh-khahi, modeli baraye khoruj az bonbast-e siyasi* (PDF published online, 1381 [2002]).

[24] Zhand Shakibi has given an excellent dissection of this problematic analogy, which often obscures more than it enlightens. See Zhand Shakibi, *Khatami and Gorbachev: Politics of Change in the Islamic Republic of Iran and the USSR* (London & New York: I. B. Tauris, 2010), esp. chapter 6.

[25] Ganji, 'Din-e ensani, sowsiyalism-e ensani: negahi beh tajrobeh-ye Nagi, Dubchek, Gorbachev va Khatami', pp. 324–5.

[26] Ibid., p. 325.

Czechoslovakia's Alexander Dubček, and the last general secretary of the Communist Party of the Soviet Union, Mikhail Gorbachev. Ganji attempted to show how the experience of Soviet reformers might illuminate the dilemmas confronting Iran's *eslahtalaban* and how the emotive accounts of disillusioned ex-communists demonstrated that all 'totalitarianisms' and the ideologies which they upheld were morally indefensible. Also noteworthy, as evidenced by Ganji's footnotes, is the ample literature authored by Soviet and Eastern bloc reformers, which had been translated into Persian, including Gorbachev's *Perestroika*, Khrushchev's memoirs, and Dubček's autobiography, *Hope Dies Last*. As was briefly analysed in Chapter 4, disillusioned ex-communists such as André Gide and Arthur Koestler were also taken up with alacrity. Gide's *Return from the Soviet Union* (1936),[27] which was translated by none other than Jalal Al-e Ahmad in the early 1950s in the years following his acrimonious break with the Tudeh Party, and Koestler's *Darkness At Noon* were now being quoted profusely. As had become common in much liberal discourse during the 1980s and 1990s, fascism and communism were depicted as twin totalitarianisms and evils anti-thetical to the 'democratic systems' now populating the so-called 'free world'.[28] As noted in Chapter 4, there is thus something of an unexpected intellectual continuity between the men of Third Force Party who broke with the Tudeh Party and the post-revolutionary reformist intellectuals who believed themselves to be announcing a break with a very different kind of orthodoxy.[29]

Curiously, Ganji deploys this literature to vindicate a position he attributes to Friedrich Hayek, claiming that those schools of thought which have promised 'social justice' and an end to 'exploitation'

---

[27] 'Rowshanfekran va dadgah-ha-ye farmayeshi [Originally published in *Payam-e now*, no. 13, 23/4/1380]', in *Majma' al-jazayer-e zendan-guneh* (Tehran: Tarh-e now, 1381 [2002]), p. 78.

[28] Ibid., p. 78–80. Joseph Massad shows how the literature on 'totalitarianism' which emerged out of the Cold War has since been appropriated and used by scholars such as Huntington and Lewis, amongst others, to effectively label 'Islam' a totalitarian religion. Joseph A. Massad, *Islam in Liberalism* (Chicago & London: University of Chicago Press, 2015), p. 305.

[29] Arguably it is the work of Homa Katouzian which stands as the missing intellectual link between the two political movements and intellectual traditions of Third Force and post-revolutionary reformism. It would be inaccurate to assimilate Katouzian's own scholarly contribution to either tradition, just as it would be deeply problematic to overlook the extensive differences in terms of historical and political context, as well as ideological content dividing the two.

(*estesmar*) have in practice paved the 'the road to serfdom' (*rah-e bardegi*) and the gulag.[30] The cross-pollination of anti-Soviet polemics, the rhetorics of *glasnost* and *perestroika*, and the articulation of reformist politics were thus a double-edged sword. They could be recalibrated to polemicise against the traditional right and elements in the judiciary and security apparatus. The Soviet Union in many ways became an allegory and convenient foil which Iranian reformists such as Ganji could criticise in unrestrained fashion and as a result jettison the caution normally reserved for when talking about the Iranian state itself. In many ways, it allowed tacit red lines to be crossed with less risk, even if both the authors and the audience knew full well that the object of criticism was the powerful and unaccountable institutions in the Iranian state. However, the analogy could also be used by critics to argue that the logic of reform was tantamount to calls for the dissolution of the regime as a whole. In subsequent years, the security apparatus's own ideological cadres would use the notion of 'soft war' (*jang-e narm*), an adaptation of Joseph S. Nye's notion of 'soft power' diplomacy, interchangeably with the threat of 'velvet revolution' to categorise the objectives of more radical reformists and the dangers of cultural-ideological subversion of the *nezam* from within its own ranks.[31] In this way, more radical reformists' recourse to Eastern European dissident literature and the security state's characterisation of the former as proponents of 'soft' subversion arguably reinforced one another.

Khatami was not the first choice of the Islamic left, the chief groups of which were the Coalition of the Imam's Line, the Hezbollah Association of Combatant Clerics in the Majles, the Office for Strengthening Unity, and the Association of Combatant Clerics which, following the Fourth Majles elections, had suspended all electoral activism. The initial preference of these groups and the SMEEI,[32] lobbying for which gained pace in the autumn of 1996, was Mir-Hosayn Musavi, prime minister from 1981 to 1989.[33] Musavi's stellar revolutionary credentials as

---

[30] Ganji, 'Idi'olozhi-ye khoshunat va bohran-e mashru'iyyat', p. 262.
[31] For further exposition of this notion, see Annabelle Sreberny and Massoumeh Torfeh, *Persian Service: The BBC and British Interests in Iran*, Kindle ed. (London & New York: I. B. Tauris, 2014), Loc 408.
[32] Shadlu, *Jostari-ye tarikhi piramun-e takasor gara'i dar jaryan-e eslami*, p. 387.
[33] Mohammad-Javad Gholam-Reza Kashi, *Jadu-ye goftar: zehniyyat-e farhangi va nezam-e ma'ni dar entekhabat Dovvom Khordad* (Tehran: Mo'asseseh-ye farhangi-ye ayandeh-ye puya, 1379 [2000]), pp. 89–90.

Khomeini's prime minister of eight years and his prominent role during the Iran–Iraq War made him a most fitting candidate for the Islamic *chap* and their hopes to regain a robust foothold in the regime's power structure. Only after Musavi categorically declared that he would not stand on 28 October 1996 (7 Aban 1375), and other prospective candidates also refused, was Khatami's candidacy finally resolved upon.

The Islamic left's strategy for their proposed candidate was also telling. Following Khatami's agreement to stand, it was widely held that he would not win but that he would be able to garner a respectable number of votes, in the region of 4–5 million.[34] This would expedite the Islamic left's fully fledged return to the political fray and perform the role of an opening salvo in a longer-term strategy to build their support base in preparation for the next round of electoral contestation. Khatami's landslide victory over the 'traditional' and more 'radical' elements of the right came as a surprise not only to the latter but to the Islamic *chap* itself, with even the president's brother admitting that 'we did not have a programme for matters like decreasing tensions (*tanesh-zoda'i*) [i.e., internationally], which is a simple matter and only broached as an idea, let alone issues like limiting *velayat-e faqih* or the role of religion in politics which are very complicated'.[35] Indeed, Mohammad-Reza Khatami was so sure that his elder brother would not be named victor that he left for a conference in Australia even before the results had been announced.[36] If electoral victory was unimaginable, this held *a fortiori* for the margin of the victory and the 20 million votes – some 70% of the popular vote – Khatami ultimately received.[37]

The Islamic left's initial ambivalence towards Khatami's candidacy, in concert with unresolved differences of intellectual and political outlook

---

[34] 'Emad al-Din Baqi, 'Mavane'-e asli-ye jonbesh-e eslahat [Originally published in *Asharq Alawsat*, 5 August 2000]', in *Jonbesh-e eslahat-e demokratik-e Iran: enqelab ya eslah* (Tehran: Sara'i, 1382 [2003]), p. 324.

[35] Khatami and Salimi, 'Tasavvor-e piruzi nemikardim: goftogu ba Mohammad-Reza Khatami', p. 47.

[36] Ibid., p. 47. Armin has also testified to the unforeseen nature of the victory. Mohsen Armin, ''Elat-yabi-ye moshkelat-e Khatami', *Rah-e now* 1, no. 1 (5 Ordibehesht 1377 [April–May 1998]).

[37] The reformists were not the only ones surprised by the result. Rafsanjani is also on record stating that the final tally was unexpected. Sayfollah Bani-Asadi, 'Naqdi bar maqaleh-ye "Jebheh-ye mosharekat, chap-ravi va Hashemi-Rafsanjani" neveshteh-ye Sadeq Ziba-Kalam' [Originally published in *'Asr-e azadegan*, no. 45, 10 Azar 1378 (1 December 1999)]', in *Hashemi va Dovvom-e Khordad* (Tehran: Rowzaneh, 1380 [2001]), p. 47.

which continued to distinguish the latter from more critically minded religious-reformist intellectuals and intellectually engaged members of the Islamic left, meant that, despite the euphoria following his victory, the risk of misplaced expectations on all sides was high. Rather than explore the alleged 'failure' of the reform movement or its lack of success in achieving its purported political objectives as a number of scholars have already,[38] the following two chapters will focus their attention on the political-theological writings and pronouncements of two individuals who have held prominent positions within elite institutions and organisations of the movement. This is so as to convey the parlous nature of the 2nd Khordad Front as a historical bloc and the lack of consensus on its ultimate objectives, as well as the forms of political contestation and struggle it ought to employ. There were therefore real disagreements regarding not only the *means* but also the *ends* of reformist politics during this period.

In naming it thus the 2nd Khordad Front sought to equate Khatami's election with the revitalisation of the national will and thereby emplot that fateful day as a watershed moment in the nation's trans-historical quest for self-determination. Despite notable differences, the Khatami government and those forces associated with it would, on more than one occasion, summon the spectre of Mohammad Mosaddeq's National Front of Iran (*Jebheh-ye melli-ye Iran*) during the height of the oil crisis of 1951–3. The 2nd Khordad Front was putatively conceived as an umbrella under which disparate political organisations and personalities, which accepted the framework of the IRI constitution and Khatami's leadership, might partake in political and civic activism. The National Front was first established in 1949 and convened its first and only national congress in the early 1960s, bringing manifold parties and personalities across a fairly broad spectrum of political opinion under its imprimatur. In the case of the 2nd Khordad Front, this endeavour was largely managed or overseen from above by members of the Islamic left elite. Nevertheless, intra-factional differences and disputes continued to make themselves apparent. The main

---

[38] See, for example, Kazem Alamdari, *Chera eslahat shekast khord: naqdi bar 'amalkard-e hasht saleh-ye eslahtalaban dar Iran, 1376–1384* (Woodland Hills, CA: Sayeh, 1387 [2008]). For an excellent and rigorous assessment of the reformist coalition and the immense challenges it faced from a social movement theory perspective see, Mohammad Ali Kadivar, Alliances and Perception Profiles in the Iranian Reform Movement, 1997 to 2005, *American Sociological Review*, Vol 78, Issue 6, 2013.

point to grasp is that, despite the new sense of hope and unity of purpose following Khatami's surprise win, a fair amount of variety regarding the lexicon and semantics of 'reform' and its ambit quickly began to emerge.

Kalam-e Jadid and Religious Intellectualism

Prior to 1997, as both minister of culture and Islamic guidance and head of the National Library, Khatami came into regular contact with religious intellectuals and a section of the broader intelligentsia and artistic community. During this time, particularly after setting aside his ministerial portfolio, he authored several articles and books, perhaps the best-known of which was *Bim-e mowj* (Fear of the Wave), published in 1993. This collection of articles is essential for understanding Khatami's world view between his exit from the Rafsanjani cabinet and his election as president. Khatami makes it clear that he sees himself as following in the footsteps of Ayatollahs Motahhari and Khomeini and their theological and political legacies. Accordingly, he views himself as an exponent of *kalam-e jadid* or the new theology, which emphasises the dynamic relationship between reason and revelation and theology's necessary engagement with modern ideologies and scientific disciplines.[39]

It is also worth drawing the reader's attention to Khatami's self-professed proximity to Motahhari, rather than Shari'ati, since it was the former who was most strident in his efforts to refute not only Marxism and materialism but, more importantly, the so-called *elteqati* or 'eclectic' thought of the People's Mojahedin, which following the revolution was denounced by the clerisy as the *monafeqin* (hypocrites).[40] In the early 1990s Khatami credited Motahhari with

---

[39] Mohammad Khatami, *Bim-e mowj* (Tehran: Sima-ye javan, Bahar 1372 [Spring 1993]), p. 80.

[40] Khomeini used the term *monafeqin* (though he had used it prior to this date) interchangeably to designate the People's Mojahedin following the Revolutionary Guards' outright conflict with the organisation beginning on 19 June 1981 (30 Khordad 1360). In a speech two days prior to the bloody repression of the Mojahedin on the 30 Khordad, Khomeini launched into a scathing attack against the organisation which he simply referred to as the *monafeqin*, in addition to the National Front and the National Democratic Front, calling on the Revolutionary Guards and Basij to counter any and all 'threats' to the revolution. Ruhollah Khomeini, *Sahifeh-ye Imam*, 21 vols., vol. 14 (Tehran: Mo'asseseh-ye tanzim va nashr-e asar-e Imam Khomeini, 1378 [1999]), p. 475. The term is regularly deployed in the Qur'an to refer to

exposing the People's Mojahedin's 'inner apostasy (*baten-e elhadi*) under the pretence of Islam'.[41]

Despite having cordial ties with several members of the People's Mojahedin, Shari'ati, who would of course not live to see the revolution and its aftermath, remained a source of great inspiration for young men and women who would later consider themselves amongst Khomeini's most impassioned devotees. Motahhari's increasingly embittered and hostile relationship with Shari'ati from around 1970 until the latter's death, however, made it difficult for clergymen on the left to be overzealous in their praise of the unorthodox Islamic ideologue.[42] In recent decades this has been assuaged somewhat due to Khameneh'i's personal friendship with Shari'ati in their shared hometown of Mashhad before the revolution and his sporadic interventions in Shari'ati's favour regarding the dispute with Motahhari.[43] Nevertheless, a certain ambivalence regarding his legacy and positions on the clergy continued to linger, especially

individuals who pretend to be Muslim when they are in reality insincere in their belief in Islam and the prophethood of Mohammad. Al-Munafiqun is a Medinan surah and the 63rd *surah* in the Qur'an, and the passage is certainly worthwhile citing since it demonstrates the real weight and severity of the term and the seriousness of Khomeini's deployment of it against a political rival: 'God knows that you truly are His Messenger and He bears witness that the hypocrites are liars – they use their oaths as a cover and so bar others from God's way: what they have been doing is truly evil – because they professed faith and then rejected it ... God will not forgive them: God does not guide such treacherous people.' *The Qur'an*, p. 374.

41 Khatami, *Bim-e mowj*, p. 81.

42 Regarding the reasons and beginnings of disagreements between Motahhari and Shari'ati, see Rahnema, *An Islamic Utopian*, pp. 252–3. Khatami actually quotes a passage from Motahhari in which he alludes derisively to Shari'ati's text *Religion against Religion* (*Mazhab 'alayeh mazhab*), even though this particular section of *Bim-e mowj* is referring to Motahhari's refutation of 'materialism' and the 'eclecticism' of the *monafeqin*. Such instances do highlight how Khatami's intellectual orientation might, in certain respects, differ from that of the SMEEI, for example. Khatami, *Bim-e mowj*, p. 83.

43 'Akharin nazarat-e rahbar-e enqelab dar bareh-ye Shari'ati: ou donbal-e farib-e rezhim bud, qezavat-ha-ye Shahid Motahhari mobalegheh-amiz bud', *Entekhab* 29 (Khordad 1390 [19 June 2011]). Khameneh'i claims that he was amongst the first to receive news of Shari'ati's death and personally offer his condolences to Mohammad-Taqi Shari'ati, the father of the deceased. The Supreme Leader's biographer claims that he oversaw the funeral ceremony in Mashhad as well, the city from where both men originally hailed. Hedayatollah Behbudi, *Sharh-e esm: zendegi nameh-ye Ayatollah Seyyed 'Ali Hosayni-Khameneh'i* (Tehran: Mo'asseseh-ye motale'at va pazhuhesh-ha-ye siyasi, 1391 [2012]), p. 562.

as regards two of his more infamous formulas: 'Islam minus the clergy' and 'Islamic Protestantism'.

Many clergymen understood well the implications of these aspects of Shari'ati's oeuvre and responded accordingly. Islamist laymen and women, including members of the Muslim Student Followers of the Imam's Line and the reconstituted Mojahedin Organisation of the Islamic Revolution of Iran, had admired Shari'ati in their youth but – because of their encounters with the People's Mojahedin and the conversion to Marxism of a considerable swathe of its membership in 1975 inside Pahlavi-era jails[44] – had become close adherents and defenders of the revolutionary clergy. The intellectual and conceptual tensions between 'Islamic government' versus 'clerical republic' (*jomhuri-ye akhundi*), and even the dangers of a 'despotism of the jurists' (*estebdad-e foqaha*), had surfaced in intra-religious debates before the foundation of the Islamic Republic. This is evidenced by a nationally televised interview Motahhari gave in March 1979 to 'Ali Paya, who would go on to become a notable contributor to *Kiyan* as well as a close philosophical ally of Sorush.[45] Unsurprisingly, Motahhari strove to allay any such fears and provide various counter-arguments, but it is nonetheless significant that such objections were clearly posed and articulated mere months after Khomeini's return from exile and that it was correspondingly felt that a cogent intellectual response was in order. Motahhari would arguably become a victim of this very real ideological bone of contention when he was assassinated by the fervently anti-clerical group *Forqan* less than two months later.

Following the death of Khomeini – who, in the estimation of these lay followers, was not merely a charismatic and exceptional leader but unmatched within the ranks of the Shi'i clergy – an increasingly mundane view of the clerical institution began to emerge. Living under 'real existing hierocracy' had imbued once taboo elements of Shari'ati's

---

[44] I am referring to the 'Statement Announcing the Change of Ideological Positions' (autumn 1975) which was largely written by central committee member Taqi Shahram, who would be executed by the clerically led regime in July 1980, apparently as revenge for Shahram's murder of Majid Sharif-Vaqefi, who had opposed the Mojahedin's turn to Marxism. For more information, see Torab Haqshenas, 'Ahzab va sazman-ha-ye jonbesh-e komunisti-ye Iran', *Noqteh* 3, no. 7 (Bahar 1376 [1997]), pp. 11–12.

[45] Morteza Motahhari and 'Ali Paya, 'Mosahebeh dar sima-ye jomhuri-ye eslami piramun-e jomhuri-ye eslami', in *Piramun-e jomhuri-ye eslami* (Qom: Sadra, 1362 [1983]), pp. 85–6.

thought with a new lease of life and resonance for this segment of the Islamic left, as they came to view the clergy as they would any other social institution. In other words, living and working alongside clergy-men in an institutional setting had dispelled much of the forbidding aura and mystique which had at one time been one of the prominent features of Khomeini and his *bayt*.[46]

The reason for recounting such differences of intellectual filiation is that they help to explain intellectual divisions and distinct ideological positions within the Islamic *chap* itself and how different actors envisaged the depth and scope of the reformist project, especially its relationship with the questions of constitutional and religious reform and the political duties and functions of the Shi'i clergy. Both Motahhari and Shari'ati were seen as part of the 'religious intellectual' mission and *kalam-e jadid*, and Sorush had had close ties with Motahhari preceding the revolution until the cleric's assassination.[47] Moreover, like most laymen of the Islamic left, such as Hajjariyan and Aqajari, Sorush had also been a devotee of Shari'ati's writings, being among the first to visit Southampton (he was still in England at the time) following Shari'ati's premature death in June 1977.[48] Khatami, by contrast, saw himself as treading a middle path between 'eclecticism' (*elteqat*) and 'petrification' (*tahajor*), between the likes of the Mojahedin and the unyielding dogmatism of the traditional right, all the while placing ample emphasis on the necessity for intellectual reflection and thinking in the religious sphere.[49]

Law, *Estebdad,* and *Mashrutiyyat*

During his presidential campaign Khatami did not announce himself a reformist intent on overhauling the power structure of the Islamic system, nor did he contend that he would rewrite its constitution, let alone trigger its collapse. However, like Gorbachev he believed his programme would reinvigorate and breathe new life into the political

[46] See Alviri's memoir and account of his first meeting with Khomeini for an example. Alviri, *Khaterat-e Morteza Alviri*, p. 63.
[47] See Sorush's interview with Motahhari: Morteza Motahhari, 'Mosahebeh-ye Doktor Sorush ba Ostad Shahid piramun-e jomhuri-ye eslami', in *Piramun-e enqelab-e eslami* (Qom: Sadra, 1362 [1983]), p. 126.
[48] Rahnema, *An Islamic Utopian*, p. 368.
[49] 'Vizheh-nameh-ye Salam: farda-ye behtar baraye Iran-e eslami', *Salam* (Farvardin 1376 [March–April 1997]), p. 6.

regime of which he had been a part since its founding.[50] He was sure to emphasise his loyalty to the theocratic basis of the system, declaring during the campaign that 'the guardianship of the jurist is the basis of the regime and the source of far-reaching intellectual, political and social movement'[51] – while also insisting that 'I am not the representative of a single guild (*senf*) on the electoral scene' (in other words, the clergy).[52] In fact, Khatami sought to stress that he was not privileged as a candidate by virtue of his clerical garb, nor should he expect votes on such grounds. In this regard at least, Khatami's attitudes towards the basis of electoral competition conformed with the archetype of the 'post-Islamist' laid out by Asef Bayat.[53] His political capital, at least in principle, should not stem from his Islamic credentials but rather his ability to meaningfully respond to voters' political, social, and cultural demands.

Further indications of Khatami's reservations about playing the role of epochal reformer, which some were swift to mark out for him, included his explicit seeking out of Khameneh'i's approval before announcing his candidacy, as well as sparse use of the term 'reform' in his campaign literature and in his speeches over the next few years following election. He would often use the term *eslah-gari* (reformism) and *ehya-gari* (revivalism) in the same breath and in reference to Ayatollah Khomeini's political-religious thought and his indispensable role in founding the Islamic Republic.[54] Khomeini was held up as one of the great reformers of the Islamic world and the Islamic Republic; he was the restorer of 'dignity' (*'ezat*) to a once oppressed and subjugated people.[55] Khatami, moreover, did not explicitly campaign on the basis of a call to constitutional reform. If he had, it is unlikely he would have made it past the Guardian Council, but at this stage it is highly doubtful

---

[50] Zdenek Mlynar and Mikhail Gorbachev, *Conversations with Gorbachev: On Perestroika, the Prague Spring, and the Crossroads of Socialism*, trans. George Shriver, Kindle ed. (New York: Columbia University Press, 2002), p. 66; Loc 1473.

[51] Dad, *Sad ruz ba Khatami*, p. 129.

[52] 'Vizheh-nameh-ye *Salam*: farda-ye behtar baraye Iran-e eslami', p. 7.

[53] Asef Bayat, 'The Coming of a Post-Islamist Society', *Critique: Critical Middle Eastern Studies* 5, no. 9 (Fall 1996), p. 45.

[54] Khatami, 'Imam Khomeini va hokumat-e dini (11/3/1377 [1/6/1998])', p. 147. Khatami speaks of Prophet Mohammad as both a reformist and a revivalist in the preceding paragraph. Ibid., p. 146.

[55] 'Din va siyasat (29/10/1376 [19/1/1998])', p. 43.

that he even had the intent to pursue such a line. Indeed, according to the president's brother, Mohammad-Reza,

the discourse which existed at that time [i.e., prior to the election] was not reform. All [members of the coalition backing Khatami] emphasised legality, civil society etc. The term "reform" was aired six months to a year later. The first newspapers which came out like *Jame'eh* put reform forward. Reform (*eslahat*) was not part of Khatami's language or the forces which followed him, it wasn't on the agenda at all. The return to the implementation of the constitution and law-orientedness were primarily being discussed.[56]

As will be shown, Khatami's initial intellectual ambit was less one of constitutional politics per se but rather one demanding 'law-orientedness' and 'legality'. It stressed adherence and implementation of the extant constitutional order,[57] addressing state officials and citizens alike. Furthermore, rather than articulate a partisan programme, Khatami sought to position himself as a consensus figure. In his own words, he reassured rivals in the establishment that 'I will take into consideration the shared principles of all the groups of the *nezam*, even though I am a member of the Association of Combatant Clerics'[58] – a move in which he was somewhat successful, receiving the endorsement of the Executives of Reconstruction, as well as the stalwart organisations and factional alignments within the Islamic left.[59]

Khatami used a vocabulary that had little currency in official circles and an endearing demeanour that distinguished him from the many drab and austere officials to whom Iranians had become accustomed. Rather than 'reform' or *eslahat*, the keywords of Khatami's nomenclature were 'law' (*qanun*), 'legality' or 'law-orientedness' (*qanun-gara'i*), 'civil society' (*jame'eh-ye madani*), and, to a lesser extent, 'political development' (*towse'eh-ye siyasi*), because, on his view, the latter basically encompassed all of the above. The issues of law and legality were of especial importance and ran through a great many of his speeches during his initial years in office. It was not particularly novel, however. In the years preceding the 1997 presidential contest, the Islamic left's media enclave, *Salam*, foremost the editorials of

---

[56] Khatami and Salimi, 'Tasavvor-e piruzi nemikardim: goftogu ba Mohammad-Reza Khatami', p. 45.
[57] 'Vizheh-nameh-ye *Salam*: farda-ye behtar baraye Iran-e eslami', p. 5.
[58] Ibid., p. 6.   [59] Ibid., p. 57.

'Abbas 'Abdi, had repeatedly advocated the inextricable and profound connection between law-orientedness or legality and civil society, and so it already had some purchase in the public imagination.[60] Khatami's great achievement was to give this rhetoric a national profile it had not previously enjoyed hitherto and ensure its large-scale diffusion into everyday political parlance. In this sense, Khatami was not merely responding and reacting to grievances and political claims made upon him but also framing them in terms of simple and distilled formulae in which he and others in the political elite had increasingly come to think.

Furthermore, Khatami was well-apprised of the fact that such commitments would tie him to a distinguished lineage of Iranian intellectuals, statesman, and movements, both preceding and since the Constitutional Revolution (1905–11), in which the issue of law (*qanun*) was regarded as paramount. It was envisaged as an almost magical panacea and the source of European progress, while its absence *ipso facto* destined the Islamic world to 'backwardness' and otherwise inexplicable decline.[61] Perhaps the two best examples which influenced Iranian constitutionalists in the first decade of the twentieth century, and many more since, are Mirza Yusef Khan Mostashar al-Dowleh Tabrizi's *Yek kalameh* (One Word), the one word in question being nothing other than 'law', and Mirza Malkam Khan's call for the rule of law and the imperative to restrain the seemingly unbridled personalised power of the monarch in the pages of his London-based periodical *Qanun*.[62] Khatami's vocabulary would thus be immediately recognisable to the historically informed and educated members of his audience. While Khatami's own thinking borrows much from what I will henceforth refer to as the Iranian 'legalist' tradition, it also has its own set of peculiarities in combining elements of Khomeini's legacy and the

[60] 'Abbas 'Abdi, 'Beh kodam jahat miravim, qanunmandi ya khodmadari (*Salam*, 7/6/1374 [29/08/1995])', in *Qanun, qodrat, farhang: yaddasht-ha-ye siyasi-ye ruznameh-ye Salam* (Tehran: Tarh-e now, 1379 [2000]), p. 71.

[61] Mirza Yusuf Khan Mustashar ad-Dowla Tabrizi, *One Word – Yak Kaleme: 19th-Century Persian Treatise Introducing Western Codified Law*, with an introduction and annotated translation by A. A. Seyed-Gohrab and S. McGlinn, ed. (Leiden: Leiden University Press, 2010), p. 9.

[62] See *Majmu'eh-ye asar-e Mirza Malkam Khan*, Tehran 1327 (1948) ed. Mohammad Mohit Tabataba'i (Berlin: Gardun, 2010), p. 26. Mirza Malkum Khan, 'The Law', in *Modernist Islam, 1840–1940: A Sourcebook*, ed. Charles Kurzman (Oxford & New York: Oxford University Press, 2002), p. 114. Ervand Abrahamian, *Iran Between Two Revolutions* (Princeton, NJ: Princeton University Press, 1982), pp. 68–9.

political-theological heritage of the clerical wing of the constitutional movement.

Like his forebears in this tradition, Khatami's vision sought to remedy a long-standing lack of reciprocity between rulers and ruled. He held that the Iranian Revolution of 1979, which he invariably refers to as the 'Islamic Revolution', strove to rectify this dire problem, and argued that Khomeini's legacy offered the relevant nostrums for ending the cycle of despotism and chaos which had afflicted Iranian history since time immemorial. It was not Khomeini's political philosophy or the constitution that was at fault but rather disregard or misapplication of constitutional principles. It was a question of correct implementation rather than substantive disagreement. As Khatami declared in a speech on 23 September 1997 before clergymen in Ardebil province, 'Now, the law is both popular (*mardomi*) and religious.'[63] It was on this score, Khatami insisted, that the Islamic Republic had succeeded where other Iranian regimes have failed. Much like the nativist discourse he had been steeped in as a young seminarian, Khatami diagnoses one of the key deficiencies and shortfalls of the Pahlavi monarchy to have been its blind imitation of Western-style modernisation and dismissal of religion and spirituality[64] – though it should be acknowledged that this rather clichéd view of late Pahlavi-era cultural initiatives has been seriously challenged in recent scholarship by Ali Mirsepassi and others.[65] But according to Khatami, this not only led the *ancien régime* down an undemocratic path but also left it alienated and uncomprehending of Iranians' deepest-held religious beliefs and attachments. The great strength of the Islamic Republic was its 'religious democracy' (*mardom-salari-ye dini*), with its 'beautiful and novel combination' of

---

[63] Khatami, 'Rowhaniyyat va hal-e mo'zelat-e jame'eh (1/7/1376 [23/9/1997])', p. 107.

[64] Khatami cites Shari'ati and Al-e Ahmad explicitly. Khatami, *Bim-e mowj*, p. 200.

[65] Mirsepassi effectively demonstrates the idea that the late Pahlavi state blithely dismissed 'Islam' or jettisoned appeals to nativism and/or 'spirituality' in the name of 'Western modernisation' to be a crude oversimplification. Ali Mirsepassi, *Transnationalism in Iranian Political Thought: The Life and Times of Ahmad Fardid* (New York & London: Cambridge University Press, 2017). Ali Mirsepassi and Mehdi Faraji, 'De-politicizing Westoxification: The Case of Bonyad Monthly', *British Journal of Middle Eastern Studies* (2016).

eslamiyyat (Islamicness) and *jomhuriyyat* (republicanism).[66] It was the balance of these two elements that was crucial to the Islamic Republic's identity and superiority over its ideological rivals, both domestically and internationally. Any attempt to weaken either element was 'contrary to the road chosen by the Imam [Khomeini]'.[67] Needless to say, Khatami does not categorise the political order of the Islamic Republic as either 'electoral authoritarian' or 'competitive authoritarian', as contemporary Anglo-American political science might be inclined.[68] Instead, he offers a picture of the Islamic Republic's constitutional order as a harmonious marriage between the two putatively cardinal features of the revolution of 1979 – i.e., Islam and republicanism. The coercive apparatus of the modern state does not feature in such a depiction. Rather what we observe in Khatami's understanding and casting is a strictly constitutional arrangement incorporating distinct, though necessary, sources of political legitimacy: the popular and the divine. It was a dichotomy which came to be known in certain reformist circles as the predicament of 'dual sovereignty'.

Clerical Constitutionalism(s)

Before the establishment of the Pahlavi dynasty in 1925, constitutional-era clerics such as the radical preacher Seyyed Jamal al-Din Esfahani had argued law abidance was part and parcel of religious observance.[69]

---

[66] Khatami, 'Imam Khomeini va hokumat-e dini (11/3/1377 [1/6/1998])', p. 150.
[67] Ibid., p. 150.
[68] See Andreas Schedler, 'The Logic of Electoral Authoritarianism', in *Electoral Authoritarianism: The Dynamics of Unfree Competition*, ed. Andreas Schedler (Boulder & London: Lynne Rienner, 2006), p. 3. I would caution further reflection on the question of whether the Islamic Republic reaches the 'procedural minimum' of a competitive authoritarian state. The Islamic Republic more readily approximates electoral authoritarianism instead of a competitive authoritarian one, for several reasons which due to limitations of space cannot be addressed here. But it should be noted, if only in passing, that there are manifold problems with this genre of political science literature and its shortcomings when it comes to capturing both the institutional complexity and historical specificity of the post-revolutionary Iranian political system and the multivalent political rationalities and forms of governmentality which traverse it. Steven Levitsky and Lucan A. Way, *Competitive Authoritarianism: Hybrid Regimes After the Cold War* (Cambridge & New York: Cambridge University Press, 2010), p. 12.
[69] 'Observing religion means law, religion means law, Islam, the Qur'an, mean God's law ... [T]he ruler is law alone, and no one's rule is valid but that of law.'

Even more prominently at the time, leading clergymen of the *'atabat* such as the pre-eminent *marja' al-taqlid*, Akhund Molla Mohammad-Kazem Khorasani, and his student Mirza Mohammad-Hosayn Na'ini not only defended a particular conception of constitutionalism on religious grounds but actively lobbied for the movement's success.[70] Khatami in a different vein not only focuses on law abidance, even if it is one of his chief pre-occupations, but also its popular basis, which stems from the revolution and resulting regime's legacy of populism and mass mobilisation. His conviction that the overwhelming majority of Iranians are deeply religious and therefore entitled to a religious regime with religious law is also implicit in a great many of his statements. In the above-mentioned televised interview, Motahhari had argued in a similar vein just prior to his untimely death that 'the religious right (*haqq-e shar'i*) of the Imam (Khomeini) derived from the people's attachment (*vabastegi*) to Islam as a doctrine (*maktab*). The people approve him as worthy of the station to identify persons to undertake Islamic duties. In truth, the religious right (*haqq-e shar'i*) and legislative guardianship (*velayat-e shar'i*), means the ideological stamp of the people, and the customary ('*orfi*) right is the rule of the people, who must choose an individual approved by the leader (*rahbar*), and give him a vote of confidence.'[71] Khatami could thus be interpreted as reprising a well-established mantra for the 'popular' basis of Islamic rule.

Khatami was essentially trying to both manage and balance several distinct priorities. He wanted to engender and encourage respect and reverence for the law, while admitting that it had at least two alternative sources of legitimacy enshrined and institutionalised within the constitutional order and the agglomeration of state institutions:

Seyyed Jamal al-Din Esfahani, quoted in Homa Katouzian, 'European Liberalisms and Modern Concepts of Liberty', in *Iranian History and Politics: The Dialectic of State and Society* (London & New York: Routledge, 2003), p. 85.

[70] None other than Mohsen Kadivar had been instrumental in reviving the political and intellectual legacy of Akhund Khorasani. Mohsen Kadivar, *Siyasat-nameh-ye Khorasani: qata'at-e siyasi dar asar-e Akhund Molla Mohammad-Kazem Khorasani* (Tehran: Ghazal, 1385 [2006]), Introduction. For a biography of Akhund Khorasani and his role in the Constitutional Revolution in English, see Mateo Mohammad Farzaneh, *The Iranian Constitutional Revolution and the Clerical Leadership of Khurasani*, Kindle ed. (Syracuse, NY: Syracuse University Press, 2015).

[71] Motahhari and Paya, 'Mosahebeh dar sima-ye jomhuri-ye eslami piramun-e jomhuri-ye eslami', p. 86.

namely, 'popular' and 'religious'. Thus, while the constitution does safeguard certain civil liberties such as freedom of association (article 26) and freedom of assembly (article 27), they are not interpreted as unconditional or inviolable rights but legitimate only insofar as the action in question is not determined to be in violation of the basic principles of Islam.[72] In this way, what is held up as a violation of the bounds of acceptability becomes a matter of contentious interpretation, whose final arbiters lack sound or cut-and-dried criteria.

The dilemma of balancing rival sources of legitimacy was also prominent in the debate between the 'olama' of the constitutional era, even if the primary objective of the constitutionalists was to end arbitrary and despotic rule. While the issue of popular representation was surely a consideration, the chief aim was limiting government by conditioning it with law,[73] further attested to by the fact that suffrage was limited by the 1906 Electoral Law to the Qajar tribe, 'olama', merchants, landowners, and guilds.[74] Nevertheless, the question of diremption between the 'popular' and 'sacred' sources of law was already acutely felt by leading clergymen during this turbulent period. Even between the constitutionalist forces there were notable differences of opinion. The *mojtaheds* of the Moderate Party (*e'tedaliyun*), the most prominent of which were Seyyed 'Abdollah Behbahani and Seyyed Mohammad Tabataba'i, predicated their support on the assurance that the laws passed by the Majles would be consonant with Islamic law and the preservation of their judicial prerogatives.[75] By contrast,

[72] Article 4 of the constitution holds that all laws must be based on Islamic criteria.
[73] Homa Katouzian, *The Persians: Ancient, Mediaeval and Modern Iran* (New Haven & London: Yale University Press, 2009), p. 180. Said Amir Arjomand, 'Ideological Revolution in Shi'ism', in *Authority and Political Culture in Shi'ism*, ed. Said Amir Arjomand (Albany: State University of New York, 1988), p. 178–9.
[74] Bashiriyeh, *The State and Revolution in Iran, 1962–1982*, p. 9.
[75] More recent scholarship also supports this fairly robust distinction between the clerical and lay wings of the constitutional movement (p. 336). The clerics' initial call for a House of Justice still did not entail constitutionalism – i.e., limiting the Shah's power – by the summer of 1906 (p. 342). The House of Justice simply embodied the demand for the redress of grievances and injustices against wayward officials. Nader Sohrabi, *Revolution and Constitutionalism in the Ottoman Empire and Iran* (Cambridge & New York: Cambridge University Press, 2011). Janet Afary, Armenian Social Democrats, the Democrat Party of Iran, and *Iran-i Naw*: A Secret Camaraderie, in *Reformers and Revolutionaries in Modern Iran: New Perspectives on the Iranian Left*, ed. Stephanie Cronin (London & New York: Routledge, 2004), p. 75.

Seyyed Hassan Taqizadeh, a former seminarian and prominent member of the Democratic Party, had initially contended that the law should apply to all in equal measure, controversially arguing that the law should hold equally for Muslims and non-Muslims alike.[76] Ultimately, it was the clerical view that carried the day.

On the other side of the constitutionalist battle, the anti-constitutionalist *mojtahed*, Shaykh Fazlollah Nuri, was depicted as justifying royal absolutism with an Islamic veneer,[77] especially following Mohammad-ʿAli Shah Qajar's bombardment of the Majles in July 1908.[78] The reality was in fact more complex, as Nuri was also antagonistic towards parliamentary democracy and judicial reform because of the perceived threat they posed to the clergy's monopoly over the interpretation of the *shariʿa*.[79] Besides the pivotal issue of whether the ruler could legitimately claim absolute and unfettered authority, another difference separating the pro- and anti-constitutionalist clergymen was the issue of whether the political order could be religiously legitimate in the absence of the Hidden Imam. The answer of pro-constitutionalist clerics was a resounding 'no',[80] though as deputies of the Hidden Imam[81] they believed they

---

[76] Edward Granville Browne, *The Persian Revolution of 1905–1909* (London: Cambridge University Press, 1910), p. 146–7. Vanessa Martin, 'Shaikh Fazlallah Nuri and the Iranian Revolution 1905–09', *Middle Eastern Studies* 23, no. 1 (January 1987), p. 43. Curiously, at one point in his writings Sorush does actually mention Nuri's repudiation of equality between Muslims and non-Muslims, contending that those constitutionalists in favour of legal equality were 'the children of the school of liberalism'. It is an interesting historical sleight of hand and erasure in the light of the fact that many of those constitutionalists who advocated for religious equality before the law were self-described social democrats and socialists. Sorush, 'Mabani-ye teʾorik-e liberalism', p. 132.

[77] Browne, *The Persian Revolution of 1905–1909*, p. 242.

[78] Martin, 'Shaikh Fazlallah Nuri and the Iranian Revolution 1905–09', p. 46.

[79] Arjomand, 'Ideological Revolution in Shiʿism', p. 181; Vanessa Martin, 'The Anti-Constitutionalist Arguments of Shaikh Fazlallah Nuri', *Middle Eastern Studies* 22 (April 1986), p. 183.

[80] Masha Allah Ajudani, *Mashruteh-ye Irani* (Tehran: Akhtaran, 1382 [2003]), p. 36.

[81] It should be noted that not all clergymen of the constitutional era accepted that the 'deputyship of the Hidden Imam' during his absence devolved to the clergy. Shaykh Asadollah Mamaqani, for instance, held that matters which concerned *hisbah* devolved upon 'the just believers' and not the clergy. Of even greater significance was that one of the most pre-eminent clerics of the nineteenth century, Shaykh Morteza Ansari (d. 1864), argued that the basis of the clergy's 'general deputyship' (*niyabat-e ʿam*) was not based on the sturdiest of foundations.

were designated with the responsibility of supervising matters relating to *hisbah* or the public moral order.[82] A further issue relating to the necessity of conditioning the ruler's power was the pro-constitutionalists' belief that a 'conditioned monarchy' (*saltanat-e moqayyad* or *saltanat-e mashruteh*) would by definition be less prone to corruption and oppression than an 'absolute monarchy' (*saltanat-e motlaq*)[83] and that a constitutional regime would be less susceptible to dependence upon foreign non-Muslim powers.[84] There was, in fact, little serious disagreement over the pre-eminence of Islamic law, even if there were notable differences over the extent of clerical guardianship.[85] The primary area of disagreement resided in the central and divisive issue of whether monarchical rule ought to be 'conditioned' or not.[86] Akhund Khorasani certainly held that it should be, while continuing to reserve a role for clerical oversight in the legislative domain,[87] at one point even declaring Taqizadeh's political beliefs to be 'corrupt' and un-Islamic, demanding that he be expelled from the Majles.[88]

Over a decade earlier, during the Tobacco Protests of 1891–2, Malkam Khan had similarly intoned in the pages of *Qanun*, 'Our desire is that our learned people and the chiefs of our religion may meet together and have the laws of our God carried out in a proper

Arjomand, 'Ideological Revolution in Shi'ism', p. 184. Another interesting stance held by Ansari was his disapproval of Friday prayer congregations during the absence of the Hidden Imam. Seeking to broach a compromise with the Osuli position, he said that Friday prayers could be held if they obtained the ruler's approval. Amanat, *Apocalyptic Islam and Iranian Shi'ism*, p. 167.

[82] This was also Grand Ayatollah Seyyed Abolqasem Khu'i's view, which Kadivar sought to bring to public attention within Iran. Abolqasem Khu'i, 'Barressi-ye velayat-e motlaqeh-ye faqih', in *Daghdagheh-ha-ye hokumat-e dini*, ed. Mohsen Kadivar (Tehran: Nashr-e ney, 1376 [1997]), p. 103.

[83] Ajudani, *Mashruteh-ye Irani.*, p. 36.

[84] Amirhassan Boozari, *Shi'i Jurisprudence and Constitution: Revolution in Iran*, Kindle ed. (New York: Palgrave Macmillan, 2011), Loc 1797. Hadi Enayat, *Law, State, and Society in Modern Iran: Constitutionalism, Autocracy, and Legal Reform, 1906–1941* (New York: Palgrave Macmillan, 2013), p. 63; Loc 1790.

[85] Said Amir Arjomand, 'The Ulama's Traditionalist Opposition to Parliamentarianism: 1907–1909', *Middle Eastern Studies* 17, no. 2 (April 1981), p. 180. Mohsen Kadivar, 'The Innovative Political Ideas and Influence of Mulla Muhammad Kazim Khurasani', Kadivar.com.

[86] Also see *Siyasat-nameh-ye Khorasani*, p. 13.

[87] 'The Innovative Political Ideas and Influence of Mulla Muhammad Kazim Khurasani'.

[88] Enayat, *Law, State, and Society in Modern Iran*, p. 85; Loc 2362.

way.'[89] Thus both in the decades preceding and during the Constitutionalist Revolution, clerical oversight of the law's interpretation and implementation was deemed indispensable, including by many modernist intellectuals, if for no other reason than to elicit clerical and popular support for the movement's broader aims.[90] Khatami's own position is comparable in certain respects, but it also has its own peculiarities in virtue of his acceptance of the executive-political role of *velayat-e faqih*, which is quite alien to the legacy of Khorasani and other early twentieth-century supporters of constitutionalism in Iran.

Constitutionalist Guardians of the *Shari'ah*?

The preceding sketch of the debates between the constitutional-era 'olama' and laymen in the context of an exposition of Khatami's political thought helps to show how the intellectual tensions and contradictions in which Khatami's thinking was embroiled, while hardly new, have become more acute with the founding of the constitutional order of the Islamic Republic. This is because two antipodal sources of legality, one derived ostensibly from the Qur'an and hadith and another from positive law (the latter at least in principle underwritten by a popularly-elected assembly), while institutionalised and functioning also regularly produced deadlock, which on more than one occasion halted the legislature's initiatives in its tracks. Sorush was able to theoretically resolve this tension by siding with popular legitimacy – i.e. religious government – with its legitimacy first and foremost emanating from the ballot box. But Khatami's vision and practice of governance continued to be riven by competing frames of legitimation: to wit, the *shari'ah* and popular legitimacy. His proffered solution was recourse to the constitution, but this would only temporarily defer conflict because of how rival sources of legitimacy have been embedded within the constitution itself and subsequently gave rise to querulous and politicised interpretations of key articles subject to dispute between and within the executive, the

---

[89] Nikki R. Keddie, *Religion and Rebellion in Iran: The Iranian Tobacco Protest of 1891–1892* (Oxford & New York: Routledge, 1966), p. 54.

[90] Hossein Kamaly, *God and Man in Tehran: Contending Visions of the Divine from the Qajars to the Islamic Republic* (New York: Columbia University Press, 2018), Loc 603.

Majles, the Guardian Council, and the judiciary, among others.[91] In the eyes of the conflicting parties, the two competing sources of legitimacy regularly proved irreducible to one another, and the mechanism for resolving their disagreements time and again was shown to be inadequate to the task. The following pages will try to demonstrate how these two antipodal sources of legitimacy were embodied in Khatami's world view and public pronouncements.

In line with the distinguished lineage outlined above, Khatami presented 'law' and 'chaos' (*harj-o-marj*) as antithetical social states.[92] Freedom without law was held to be a recipe for licence. This notion is also one common to ancient and modern Western political thought. Perhaps the best-known modern example can be found in the social contract theory of Thomas Hobbes. Immanuel Kant would internalise this notion and define freedom as acting in accordance with the moral law. In short, 'freedom' was firmly distinguished from 'licence' or licentiousness by Hobbes and Locke, as well as nineteenth-century Iranian statesmen-intellectuals such as Malkam Khan or Mostashar al-Dowleh. 'Freedom' was not libertinism but ought to be bounded by law. As had already been intimated, Khatami's approach was similar to that of the pro-constitutionalist clergy insofar as he contended that law ought to have a religious basis or at the very least not contravene Islamic law.[93] His views are also comparable in that he supported

[91] Long after Khatami left the presidential palace in 2012, Sorush, now living in exile, would lay the blame for prevailing injustices at the door of the Islamic Republic's lack of a 'strong', 'independent' judiciary. He basically repeats a number of the basic themes of the Iranian 'legalist' discourse laid out above, without acknowledging this long-standing tradition. Only an independent judiciary is viewed as capable of protecting citizens' rights and enforcing the law, free from political interference and therefore checking arbitrary rule. He does go one step further, no doubt influenced by his time in exile, by suggesting that judicial officials might be elected. See 'Abdolkarim Sorush, 'The Crust and the Core of Rule by the People', www.drsoroush.com, http://www.drsoroush.com /English/By_DrSoroush/E-CMB-20111201-The%20Crust%20and%20the%2 0Core%20of%20Rule%20by%20the%20People.html

[92] Khatami, 'Rowhaniyyat, bayad-ha va nabayad-ha (1/7/1376 [23/9/1997])', p. 143. 'Qanun va eqtedar (6/10/1376 [27/10/1997])', in *Gozideh-ye sokhanrani-ha-ye ra'is-e jomhur dar bareh-ye towse'eh-ye siyasi, towse'eh-ye eqtesadi va amniyyat* (Tehran: Tarh-e now, 1379 [2000]), p. 57.

[93] Hadi Enayat argues that, during the constitutional-era debates, talk of the 'rule of law' was more or less interchangeable with the call for the 'proper implementation of the shari'a'. Enayat, *Law, State, and Society in Modern Iran*, p. 76; Loc 2159.

clerical supervision of the legislative process in the form of the Guardian Council (*Shura-ye negahban*).[94]

In the course of a speech at another clerical gathering on 23 September 1997 in Khuzestan, he contended that 'in our regime juridical matters (*amr-e qaza*) must be Islamic and a judge must be a *mojtahed*'.[95] A key difference distinguishing Khatami from the pro-constitutionalist clerics of the first decades of the twentieth century was his revolutionary and Khomeinist inheritance, which cast government as a fundamental principle of the Islamic religion. As was detailed in Chapter 2, Khomeini broke with Shi'i orthodoxy when he arrogated executive authority for the 'olama''s 'guardianship', thereby claiming hierocratic government to be not merely desirable but necessary in the Hidden Imam's absence. Khatami accepted this premise wholesale, as I will show further in the following sections. However, he does elaborate his own vision of its implications for the Islamic state in a language heavily influenced by the discourse of religious intellectualism.

For Khatami the constraint on freedom and source of law is the Islamic Republic's constitution. Many of his statements upon election in 1997 also indicate that he wholeheartedly accepted not only the constitution but also the place and status of the six *foqaha* appointed to the Guardian Council by the *vali-ye faqih*, whose role was to determine the compatibility of the laws passed by the Majles with the *shari'ah* and interpret the constitution in accordance with the same criteria. 'We are defenders of order in the framework of the law ... The law is assessed and goes to the Guardian Council. Six grandees (*bozorgan*) sit and vote on the compliance of this law with the *shar'*,' he insisted.[96] Freedom bound by law, specifically Islamic law, is integral to Khatami's outlook and of course extends to freedom of speech: 'In our system the limits of freedom of speech are insofar as they are not contrary to the principles (*mabani*) of Islam.' Similarly, he fully recognised the prerogative of the Guardian Council to veto legislation in the Majles, a power that would itself come to haunt Khatami's administration time and again. 'In our regime, bills of the Majles are not implementable unless six Islamic jurists (*faqihan*), who are the appointees of the Leader, announce the compatibility of these

---

[94] Khatami, 'Rowhaniyyat, bayad-ha va nabayad-ha (1/7/1376 [23/9/1997])', p. 143.
[95] Ibid., p. 138.   [96] Ibid., p. 143.

bills with the *shari'ah*.[97] This subject, particularly the Guardian Council's arrogation of the prerogative to supervise elections and vet candidates, was a thoroughly partisan issue, as I have sought to show in previous chapters, and one which, perhaps more than any other, provoked the ire of politicians and public intellectuals associated with the Islamic left.[98] Furthermore, this issue returns to a more fundamental one, which sets Khatami apart from several prominent religious intellectuals, such as Sorush, Shabestari, Kadivar, and Mostafa Malekiyan, and even politicians of the Islamic left, such as 'Abdollah Nuri or Mostafa Tajzadeh, who might be described as 'post-Islamist', as defined by Bayat:

Spearheaded by pious Muslims, post-Islamism attempts to undo Islamism as a political project by fusing faith and freedom, a secular democratic state and a religious society. It wants to marry Islam with individual choice and liberties, with democracy and modernity, to generate what some have called an "alternative modernity."[99]

As we saw in the previous chapter, neither Sorush nor Shabestari held that the political order or even the moral-ethical values underwriting it were exclusive to Islam or derived from holy writ. Following his impeachment as interior minister at the hands of the conservative-dominated Fifth Majles, 'Abdollah Nuri was also willing to go so far as to claim that the Guardian Council was emblematic of the spectre of paternalism (*pedar-salari*), which had haunted Iranian society for hundreds of years. On this account, the order of the electoral and legislative process as supervised by the Guardian Council subjugated the independence and autonomy of 'the people' to an omnipotent father figure who thought himself the only power capable of identifying the people's true interests.[100] This was not Khatami's publicly stated view, however – quite far from it. At one point, Bayat attributes post-Islamism to the Khatami government itself,[101] despite having previously exercised greater scepticism in this regard. But it should start to become clear that this attribution was premature as the fundamental tension

---

[97]   Ibid., pp. 137–8.
[98]   'Abdollah Nuri and Akbar Ganji, *Naqdi baraye tamam-e fosul: goftogu-ye Akbar Ganji ba 'Abdollah Nuri* (Tehran: Tarh-e now, 1378 [1999]), p. 89.
[99]   Asef Bayat, *Life as Politics: How Ordinary People Change the Middle East*, Kindle ed. (Stanford, CA: Stanford University Press, 2010, 2013), p. 16.
[100]   Nuri and Ganji, *Naqdi baraye tamam-e fosul*, p. 88–9.
[101]   Bayat, *Life as Politics*, p. 16.

between the two sources of legality was never adequately resolved by the president, and this important wedge issue has persisted until the present. Khatami plainly insisted in a speech at Khomeini's mausoleum on 19 January 1998, 'Religion and politics are linked together':

> If you refer to the Qur'an you see that most of the social ordinances (*ahkam*) and even individual ordinances are not executable without the existence of a social order compatible with the teachings of the Qur'an. If it is intended to make use of these ordinances, we must have a religious government, religious society and religious politics and if not a considerable amount of the lessons of the Qur'an remain inactive.[102]

The responsibility of the clergy is made even more onerous by the fact that the fate of the clergy is inextricable from the fate of the revolution[103] and that the 'success' of the Islamic Republic is held to be the 'biggest publicity boon' there can be for religion.[104] The repudiation of the Guardian Council's prerogative to veto electoral candidates was not only a question of defending the democratic will of the people: it was also a thoroughly partisan one. The deeper tension between the *shari'ah* as interpreted by the Guardian Council, and the will of the Majles, remained unscathed in Khatami's early pronouncements. He accepted not only the necessity of the Guardian Council but also the prerequisite and imperative of an Islamic state if the ordinances of the *shari'ah* were not going to fall into abeyance. If there was an objection, it was not at the institutional and procedural level but rather about the ideological orientation of the occupants of these tutelary bodies and their jurisprudential hermeneutics.

Khatami cannot be straightforwardly viewed as post-Islamist, because of his continued insistence on the irreducibility of the *shari'ah* qua legislation to positive law, and the need for the clergy to ensure the *shari'ah* is both observed and implemented. This, however, does not imply stasis, since the latter is party to reinterpretation in the light of the ongoing challenges and crises confronting the Islamic system. But Khatami's emphasis on law and rights sets him apart from many of his clerical peers in both state institutions and the seminaries and indicates that he had taken up Khomeini's own statement of *feqh-e puya* with utmost seriousness, while also combining it with the well-known discourse of legal-orientedness by defending the existence of rights

---

[102]   Khatami, 'Din va siyasat (29/10/1376 [19/1/1998])', p. 36.
[103]   'Rowhaniyyat va jahan-e jadid (1/8/1376 [23/10/1997])', p. 113.
[104]   'Rowhaniyyat va nezam-e jomhuri-ye eslami (13/4/1377 [4/7/1998])', p. 167.

independently of the will and caprice of any single individual.[105] In other words, it applies to and binds all citizens. Also, the fact that he speaks of *qanun* instead of simply the *shari'ah* implies a much broader under-standing of the multivalent nature of law and its numerous sources. In this way, he attempts to advocate an escape from what has often been cast as the perennial malady of arbitrary rule marring Iranian political life. He does not cite the classical hadith collections when he argues that human beings are endowed with the right to determine their own destiny, but rather the advent of contemporary times.[106] *Feqh* had long sought to balance its ability to straddle contemporary exigencies and historical precedent, but now the state had to take the lead in tilting the balance in favour of acknowledging the former and the challenges confronting it at the end of the twentieth century. That is why Khatami often insisted that the clergy must become familiar with the times (*zaman-shenas*) in which they live.

The Semantic Ambivalence of *Velayat* and *Vekalat*

As has been mentioned, Khatami follows Khomeini, accepting the lat-ter's challenge to traditional Osulism which had accepted that clerical guardianship ought to be restricted to *hisbah*: namely, those matters falling under the purview of the *shari'ah*, including the rather sweeping maxim of forbidding evil and enjoining the good, without extending to executive-governmental authority *per se*.[107] In this tradition, the

---

[105] It should be noted that constitutionalist-era clerics had already set such a precedent and had also distinguished between the 'changeable ordinances' (*ahkam-e motaghayyer*) and 'unchangeable ordinances' (*ahkam-e sabet*) of the *shari'ah*. While the latter could not be changed, the prominent constitutionalist Mirza Mohammad-Hosayn Na'ini contended that 'changeable ordinances' were subject to temporal exigencies and the interests of the country and could therefore be changed when and if necessary. Mohammad-Hosayn Na'ini, *Tanbih al-ommeh va tanzih al-melleh* (Qom: Bustan-e ketab, 1382 [2003]), pp. 137–8.

[106] Khatami, 'Haqq va taklif (14/12/1376 [3/3/1998])', p. 85.

[107] Though Fazlollah Nuri is often portrayed as a precursor to Khomeini, he was far more conventional and restrictive in his delineation of the clergy's powers. In his 'Book of Admonition to the Heedless and Guidance for the Ignorant' (*Ketab-e tazakorat al-qafel va ershad al-jahel*), Nuri goes so far as to claim that it is beyond the scope of the authority of the *maraje'* to bind their *moqalledin* to endorse constitutionalism, because it illegitimately interferes with the dominion of the ruler. Fadl Allah Nuri and 'Abd al-'Azim 'Imad al-'Ulama' Khalkhali, 'Two Clerical Tracts on Constitutionalism', in *Authority and*

'olama''s 'guardianship' had been conceived as first and foremost legal and juridical in nature, and a de facto division of labour between the sphere of Islamic law and custom (*'orf*) overseen by the mundane authority determined the terms of coexistence and reciprocity between the clergy and the latter. Khomeini overturned this tacit age-old agreement between the clergy and worldly rulers by claiming government to be a fundamental precept or primary ordinance of the Islamic faith. Khatami unsurprisingly follows suit and asserts that government (*hokumat*) is a principle of religion (*osul-e din*), as would be expected given that it is not only a basic premise of Khomeini's seminal *Velayat-e faqih, hokumat-e eslami* but of the Islamic Republic's constitution. Moreover, within that system 'the centrality (*mehvariyyat*) of *velayat-e faqih* and the leadership (*rahbari*)'[108] is also legally binding since its enshrinement in law has ceased to be the mere opinion of one jurist amongst others.

The pivot and axis of our system is *velayat-e faqih. Velayat-e faqih* is the theory of his Excellency Imam [Khomeini]. Of course, it is possible that jurists and clergymen may not agree with this theory of the Imam, but when this theory enters the constitution it ceases to be one jurisprudential theory amongst others. Disagreement with it is not disagreement with one jurisprudential theory, but is disagreement with the principle (*osul*) and basis (*asas*) of the system (*nezam*). It is clear that no system permits attacks on its principle and foundation. Of course, this point is not tantamount to a prohibition of scientific debates in their own place. God willing, all of us will coordinate our desires and tastes with the law.[109]

In this way, early in his tenure Khatami had already placed fundamental political objections to the principle of *velayat-e faqih* beyond the pale.[110] Given the context of enunciation and his role as president, it

Political Culture in Shi'ism, ed. Said Amir Arjomand (Albany: State University of New York, 1988), pp. 360–1. Also, see Boozari, *Shi'i Jurisprudence and Constitution*, Loc 1956.

108 Khatami, 'Rowhaniyyat, bayad-ha va nabayad-ha (1/7/1376 [23/9/1997])', p. 137.

109 'Rowhaniyyat va nezam-e jomhuri-ye eslami (13/4/1377 [4/7/1998])', p. 170.

110 In a special issue produced by *Salam* following the announcement of his candidacy in a section specifically addressing the question of *velayat-e faqih*, Khatami refers to it as a 'fundamental pillar of the Islamic Republic'. The interview was conducted prior to his electoral victory. He continues, however, that the doctrine must be interpreted in such a way that it gains the assent of the majority of citizens, not only Shi'i but also Sunnis and other religious minorities. 'Vizheh-nameh-ye *Salam*: farda-ye behtar baraye Iran-e eslami', p. 12.

may well have been misplaced to expect anything else, at least by way of his public pronouncements. Moreover, while limited pluralism would be accepted, ultimately 'the system (*nezam*) was above tendencies and tastes ... [A]ll tastes (*saliqeh-ha*) and tendencies (*gerayesh-ha*) must struggle for the preservation and strengthening of the system and the preservation of the sanctity (*hormat*) of the leadership and the preservation of the pillars of the system.'[111] Debate was thus permissible insofar as it did not undermine the foundations of the system itself, and diversity was welcomed insofar as it proved advantageous to the political order as a whole. This position is somewhat different from Mojtahed-Shabestari's view, adumbrated in the previous chapter, where he argued the rule of the jurist was merely one view amongst others but enjoyed legal status by virtue of its constitutional enshrinement. For Khatami, it would have understandably been counterintuitive to attack the very constitution he had sworn to uphold and enforce, elevating the pre-eminence of the rule of law while simultaneously undercutting it. But it was with reference to such pertinent statements made during Khatami's first years in office that clear differences between the discourses and political objectives articulated within the Islamic *chap*/reformist camp began to emerge. The ideological and theoretical differences will become more apparent in the next chapter, though for now it will suffice to state once again that Khatami's chief priorities were stability and ensuring the poly-cephalous state would act within the bounds of the law and thus not without coordination or in an arbitrary fashion. In itself this was no mean feat.

There was also arguably a deeper scheme at work, since, while the discourse of legalism certainly had an 'Islamic-jurisprudential' complexion and basis, it was also thought that if exhortations to law-abidance gained traction the much-feted notion of 'civil society' would also finally be able to take root and allow for an associational space not dominated by the state or para-statal organisations.[112] This sphere of private interests and associational activity would allow for independent expression and the articulation of societal demands within the parameters of the constitution, strengthening the degree of

---

[111] 'Rowhaniyyat va nezam-e jomhuri-ye eslami (13/4/1377 [4/7/1998])', p. 167.
[112] 'Payam-ha va payamad-ha-ye Dovvom-e Khordad (2/3/1377 [23/5/1998]),' in *Gozideh-ye sokhanrani-ha-ye ra 'is-e jomhur dar bareh-ye towse 'esh-ye siyasi, towse 'eh-ye eqtesadi va amniyyat* (Tehran: Tarh-e now, 1379 [2000]), p. 117.

reciprocity between the rulers and ruled.[113] The activities of a less cowed civil society could be capitalised upon to make further limited gains, the ultimate logic of which could not be foreseen by either the Khatami administration or its opponents. The primary issue was one of constraining the waywardness of official and quasi-official bodies not under executive control rather than opening up the political system to the contestation of unfamiliar political and social forces. There was no expectation that either 'outsiders' or organised labour would find themselves empowered, an absence that was coupled with a very real scepticism of popular mobilisation and democratic forms of life and expression that circumvented or failed to conform to the mediation and control of recognised institutional configurations. This programme would rather elicit and consolidate support for the system's constitutional and legal framework, complementing coercion with a form of active consent and 'hegemony'. It was part and parcel of the ongoing negotiation of the nature of the Islamic Republic's social contract with its citizenry. It also had a broadly liberal tenor, since, to quote Ellen Meiksins Wood, it often appeared to regard the 'history, progress and evolution of freedom' in the 'contradiction between individual and state' and overlooked class antagonism and social relations of exploitation, even while such a vision uneasily co-existed with a more positive one entailing the responsibilities and obligations of the Islamic state to cultivate and shape the ethos and moral dispositions of its citizenry.[114]

Underwriting and providing guarantees for legally sanctioned public spaces in which citizens might congregate appealed to Khatami's electoral base, replete with newly eligible voters, students, women, and religious and ethnic minorities. They would permit the varied elements of this electoral base to engage in civic activism and create a routinised pattern of interpersonal interactions, by means of which they could articulate their demands and relay them via institutionalised channels to government.[115] By 1996–7 the demographic reality of, for instance, 1.2 million students in higher education, with their hopes and

---

[113] Gramsci, *Selections from the Prison Notebooks of Antonio Gramsci*, p. 259.
[114] Ellen Meiksins Wood, 'The Uses and Abuses of "Civil Society"', *Socialist Register* 26 (1990), p. 68.
[115] Individuals coming together in what are known as 'voluntary associations' are a staple of the civil society and democratisation literature. Alexander Tocqueville praised such associations in *Democracy in America* exactly because he saw them as evidence of citizens defending and attempting to procure their interests instead of the state taking on the role. The Iranian system

aspirations for advancement and prosperity, could not help but make itself felt.[116] Khatami was certainly aware of the problems facing modern Iranian society, and they weighed heavily on his mind. Legality and abidance by the constitution were again held up as the only way forward for the cultivation of civil society and eschewal of the parlous estrangement between *dowlat* and *mellat*:[117] 'the most important condition for the establishment of civil society is acceptance of the constitution *(qanun-e asasi)*'.[118] Khatami appears to reject the crass paternalism of certain political interpretations of clerical guardianship which effectively reduce the population to the status of the mentally challenged and orphans.[119] 'Despotism' *(estebdad)* or 'arbitrary rule' has merely only ever thought of human beings as duty-bound subjects.[120] In such an equation they do not possess anything which might be thought of as inviolable rights or the ability to determine their own destinies.

There was, however, another component to the advocacy for stronger civil associations – namely, the demand for smaller government. This would be pointedly stressed in a Khatami government report published by the National Organization for Management and Planning *(Sazmam-e modiriyyat va barnameh-rizi-ye keshvar)* in early

is still to provide strong guarantees for the right of voluntary associations to assemble and express themselves, even if they are underwritten in the country's constitution. They nevertheless do continue to exist and remain active, albeit in a zone of insecurity. Jeffrey C. Alexander, *The Civil Sphere* (Oxford & New York: Oxford University Press, 2006), p. 96. Khatami was clear in his acknowledgement of the support he received from students and educated quarters of Iranian society. Khatami, 'Payam-ha va payamad-ha-ye Dovvom-e Khordad (2/3/1377 [23/5/1998])', p. 113.

116   Said Amir Arjomand, *After Khomeini: Iran Under His Successors*, Kindle ed. (Oxford & New York: Oxford University Press, 2009), Loc 1292.

117   The profound influence of the work of Homa Katouzian should be noted, in particular his early volume: Mohammad-'Ali Homayun Katouzian, *Eqtesad-e siyasi-ye Iran: az mashrutiyyat ta payan-e selseleh-ye Pahlavi*, trans. Mohammad-Reza Nafisi and Kambiz 'Azizi (Tehran: Nashr-e markaz, 1366, 1367 [1987, 1988]; 14th printing 1387 [2008]). 'Ali-Reza 'Alavi-Tabar has acknowledged explicitly the impact of Katouzian's work on members of the Islamic left based at the Presidential Strategic Research Centre during the 1990s. Alavi-Tabar and Mirsepassi, 'Alireza Alavi-Tabar and Political Change', p. 132.

118   Khatami, 'Payam-ha va payamad-ha-ye Dovvom-e Khordad (2/3/1377 [23/5/1998])', p. 119

119   Amanat, *Apocalyptic Islam and Iranian Shi'ism*, p. 190.

120   Khatami, 'Haqq va taklif (14/12/1376 [3/3/1998])', p. 86.

2001, entitled *The Transformations of the Country and Government Policy: The President's Report to the People* (*Tahavvolat-e keshvar va 'amalkard-e dowlat: gozaresh-e ra'is-e jomhur beh mardom*). According to the report, 'Government in our country is very swollen (*motavvarem*), and there is no other way but to reduce it. But importantly, without civil institutions (*nehad-ha-ye madani*) to guarantee the people's participation and preserve individual rights ... it (i.e. the reduction of government) will not be realised.'[121] Though expressed at the level of aspiration, it is clear that the government report regards 'big government' in a negative light, as something to be reformed and diminished. State and society are pitted against one another and viewed in terms of a zero-sum game. Moreover, civil institutions and voluntary associations are ostensibly tasked with acting as the guarantor of individuals' participation in public life as well as protecting their rights. The sphere of civic participation and individual rights, as well as their protection, should to some extent be vacated from the responsibilities of government and find themselves devolved to the non-governmental domain.

Reminiscent of Alexis de Tocqueville's writings on New England and the idealised town hall meeting, which had become a *locus classicus* and key reference point outlining the virtues of civic participation, self-reliance, and republican self-rule for several of Iran's leading reformist intellectuals, this valorisation of civil society and NGOs and their decisive role in the ushering-in of more democratic forms of governance also took place against the backdrop of the demise of the Soviet Union, the Solidarity Movement in Poland, the 'Velvet Revolution', which overran Prague in 1989, and the U.S.'s more explicit turn to 'democracy promotion' as a vehicle of foreign policy.[122] In the case of Prague's 'Velvet Revolution', according to John Ehrenberg, it was pervasively argued that what was being witnessed was a 'a revolt of civil society against the state':[123] a characterisation of state-society relations which has not unproblematically also greatly influenced much of the academic and journalistic literature on post-revolutionary Iran. In this discourse 'civil society' became first and foremost a means of limiting and checking

---

[121] *Tahavvolat-e keshvar va 'amalkard-e dowlat*, p. 8.
[122] John Ehrenberg, *Civil Society: The Critical History of an Idea*, 2nd ed. (New York: New York University Press, 2017), Loc 3515.
[123] Ibid., Loc 3661.

the state and its exertion of power; in short, the two are framed in strictly antipodal terms, as the economy tends to fall out of the picture altogether and finds itself detached from democratic demands and processes writ large, and the state is thought of solely in oppressive terms, not as a social relation.

When the National Organization for Management and Planning report moves to clarify which civil institutions and organisations it has in mind, it becomes clear that the strict demarcation between 'swollen government' and civil society is somewhat confused. While the report calls for supporting a free press to the end of government accountability, it also outlines a prominent role for city and village councils and political parties, which cannot really be determined to stand outside the realm of government, its attendant regulations, and the state more broadly speaking.[124] Particularly in the case of the city and village councils, it would appear that what was really meant was responsive and vibrant local government rather than the government's absence altogether. It is worth noting that this also had a factional component, insofar as self-avowed reformists considered local elections as one of the few arenas with a more level playing field, which they could better contest and where they might potentially triumph. Meanwhile, the 'state' was often associated with political adversaries controlling appointed and more opaque institutions. Cultural, scientific, artistic, and professional societies are also mentioned in passing and certainly contribute to social life in vital ways, but how they are expected to take up the roles to be abandoned by 'big government' is left unspecified.

Indeed, more critical approaches to the almost Panglossian genre of literature extolling the virtues of 'civil society' in the aftermath of the Berlin Wall's collapse have concluded that 'civil society can just as easily impede democracy as advance it'.[125] It is just as often utilised by states to further their interests at home and abroad, as much as it has embodied the now rather clichéd dictum of 'speaking truth to power'. As Ehrenberg forcefully argues, 'any civil society can be created, supported, manipulated, or repressed by any state, and it is profoundly misleading to try to conceptualize it apart from political power'.[126] This is not to deny that organisations and social formations ensconced within civil society can play a decisive role in critiquing political power

---

[124] *Tahavvolat-e keshvar va 'amalkard-e dowlat*, pp. 9–10.
[125] Ehrenberg, *Civil Society*, Loc 5138.   [126] Ibid., Loc 5191.

and its *modus operandi* but that such a conceptualisation is far from sufficient and obscures much in the process, such as the nature of such organisations' relationships to capital and the market, the pull of private interests, or the role of government itself in shaping civil society and political subjectivities. This ambivalence and ambiguity comes out in the Khatami government's own confused articulation and framing of the idea of civil society.[127]

While Sorush held that religion had typically been articulated in the language of duties, Khatami was keen to argue that the dearth of attention to rights was not the fault of religion per se but rather of political systems acting in the name of religion and the dark chapter in the history of Islam which began with the Umayyad dynasty following the assassination of Imam ʿAli.[128] In Khatami's mind this was an aberration, despite casting a shadow over much of Islamic history: 'Islamic government has no conflict with [the right of human beings to determine their destiny].'[129] These systems of arbitrary rule came to power through force of arms and enforced hereditary kingships which continued to cast people as subservient subjects rather than persons with rights and legitimate expectations of government.

Though the president is directly elected, Khatami argued that the *vali-ye faqih* was also decided through popular election, albeit indirectly by means of the election of the Assembly of Experts, a clerical body with approximately eighty-six members.[130] For Khatami both institutions are in different ways embodiments of the popular will. In stark contrast to other prominent members of the Islamic *chap*, neither prior to nor in the years immediately following his election did Khatami publicly object to the Guardian Council's arrogated

---

[127] The political and organisational activities of political parties might certainly be considered within the domain of civil society, but to see legally recognised and institutionalised political parties as antithetical to the state and state power would be somewhat quixotic, if understandable given modern Iranian states' common hostility to independent political organising. It is worth noting that political activities of political parties are guaranteed by Article 26 of the constitution alongside those of associations, trade unions, and the minority organisations – a distinction that reinforces the strict distinction between state and society, placing political parties firmly in the sphere of the latter. 'The Constitution of the Islamic Republic of Iran (1989 Edition)', *Iranian Studies* 47, no. 1 (2014), p. 170.

[128] Khatami, 'Haqq va taklif (14/12/1376 [3/3/1998])', p. 86.   [129] Ibid., p. 87.

[130] The number of *foqaha* has varied since the body was first constituted.

powers to veto candidates deemed inappropriate for high office. Nonetheless, even on such an understanding of *velayat-e faqih* there is still some difficulty presented by the fact that the notion of political representation is not well-established in Shiʻi *feqh*. The concept of *vekalat* does have historical precedent even if it was totally disconnected from modern notions of representation and popular will advocated by social contract theory and later notions of republicanism and representative parliamentary democracy[131] and might be thought of as a kind of advocacy or agency.[132] With the Constitutional Revolution the term acquired greater currency and was used when referring to the function of parliamentarians and the assembly of which they were members. It was also argued at the time by the prominent cleric Mirza Mohammad-Hosayn Naʼini, whose pro-constitutional tract *Tanbih al-ommeh va tanzih al-melleh* (1909) made the case that *vekalat* was not intrinsically religious in nature and could be applied in the context of a constitutional assembly.[133]

The notion of *velayat* designated in terms of 'guardianship' harboured undeniably almost by definition paternalistic implications and was, at least in the present moment, widely held to be the exclusive possession of the clergy.[134] The distinction and the muddying of waters between the semantics of *vekalat* and *velayat* in the post-revolutionary constitutional order have posed, and continue to pose, a dilemma for

---

[131] When the Shiʻi Imams were still alive, a *vakil* was an agent of the Imam who would collect alms from members of the Imami community on his behalf. This role, along with its authority and scope, developed in the course of both the Lesser and Greater Occultation as the Imami community found itself forced to address the very real absence of the Imam. Jassim M. Hussain, *The Occultation of the Twelfth Imam* (Muhammadi Trust, 1982), chapter 4.

[132] The Tunisian reformist Islamic thinker and statesman Rashid al-Ghannushi also draws on the notion of *wakil*, seeing the ruler as an 'agent' of the ummah, though important differences continue to distinguish his theory from that of Naʼini. Andrew F. March, 'Genealogies of Sovereignty in Islamic Political Theology', *Social Research: An International Quarterly* 80, no. 1 (2013), p. 311.

[133] Naʼini, *Tanbih al-ommeh va tanzih al-melleh*, pp. 114–15.

[134] This was insofar as it extended the presupposition that those over whom it was granted guardianship were *saghir* or minors who had yet to reach puberty. This conclusion is also recognised and criticised by Kadivar. Mohsen Kadivar, 'Mosahebeh ba ruznameh-ye Khordad', in *Baha-ye azadi: defaʼiyyat-e Mohsen Kadivar dar dadgah-e vizheh-ye rowhaniyyat*, ed. Zahra Rudi Kadivar (Tehran: Nashr-e ney, 1378 [1999]), p. 160.

'religious democracy' as defined by Khatami and like-minded allies. The preponderance of the dichotomy between 'representation' (very loosely speaking, *vekalat*) and 'guardianship' is exacerbated by the lack of justification for how the people's *vokala*' or representatives can legislate on a national scale and on matters pertaining to the *shari'ah* without a clerical body whose mandate does not derive from democratic election but from their religious status as deputies of the Hidden Imam supervising the legislation of the *shari'ah*.[135] This problem was often solved through the explicit or implicit assumption that any legislative body would count a substantial number of qualified clerics amongst its number or that there would be a clerical body evaluating any laws passed by the legislature. It is this issue which, by Khatami's own admission, necessitates a body along the lines of the Guardian Council. As early as the summer of 1993, Akbar Ganji had argued by means of an exposition of Na'ini's famous tract that 'government is nothing other than guardianship (*velayat*) bestowed by the people as a trust (*amanat*)', which if violated could be recalled.[136] He thus undermined the idea that 'guardianship' was the self-evident right of the clergy, contending instead that it was given by the people on a temporary basis and could be revoked if the clerical leadership ceased to maintain their confidence.

In the constitutional era, the much-vaunted article 2 of the Fundamental Laws, proposed in its initial form by Shaykh Fazlollah Nuri,[137] stipulated that a council of five *mojtaheds* should ensure that all legislation remain concordant with the *shari'ah* and thus in one important respect sought to perform a comparable function. Unlike the Guardian Council, however, this five-member council did not have the power to interpret the constitution as it saw fit or veto electoral candidates on the basis of such interpretations. This issue simply remains unresolved in Khatami's thought and writings, and its status as something of Gordian knot recurred on several occasions during his two terms as president. Even while Khatami sought to imbue *velayat-e faqih* with democratic overtones by stressing the Leader's indirect election,

---

135   For the dispute between Na'ini and Nuri on this score, see Martin, 'The Anti-Constitutionalist Arguments of Shaikh Fazlallah Nuri', p. 191.

136   Akbar Ganji, 'Mashru'iyyat, velayat, vekalat', *Kiyan* 3, no. 13 (Tir–Mordad 1372 [June–July 1993]), p. 23.

137   Article 2 was modified and was not codified into the constitution the way Nuri had envisaged.

he simply never confronted the issue of whether, in the final analysis, majority vote could trump the sacred precepts as delineated by the 'olama'. In a similar vein, he never sought to fashion an argument making the case that *velayat* might be bestowed solely through recourse to a democratic vote, since a precondition of consideration was that the candidate in question be a *mojtahed* and thus endowed with the authority accompanying 'general deputyship'.[138] In short, he lacked a theory where perhaps he needed one the most, preferring instead to remain ambiguous to the defenders of both theocracy and democracy and keep them guessing as to where he actually stood.

Khatami's Readings (*qara'at-ha*) and the Pedagogy of Tolerance

But is it not of equal importance to ask what Khatami's objectives were in forging a religious society and politics? His stated objective at several junctures is that of fashioning a 'Qur'anic human' (*ensan-e qur'ani*) whose 'ethics, thought, manners, behaviour, sentiments and reason are formed on the basis of the criteria that God communicated in the Qur'an'.[139] In certain respects this positive conception set on actualising its model or archetypal citizen might be thought to warrant comparison (though not conflation) with the German notion of *Bildung*, meaning 'education' or 'cultivation', most prominently developed by the Jena Romantics in the early nineteenth century.[140] *Bildung* could be meant in terms of both *process* and *result*, to form, to shape, to fashion, and finally to cultivate.[141] An important dimension of its meaning was first captured by Jean-Jacques Rousseau in his *Emile or On Education* (1762), the proto-typical Bildungsroman which laid the template of an educational system, which aimed to fashion the ideal citizen unscathed by worldly corruption.[142] In the twentieth century, Hans-Georg

---

138   This very step was eventually taken by Grand Ayatollah Hosayn-'Ali Montazeri, but it did not become part of the mainstream debate in official circles. See Hosayn-'Ali Montazeri, *Hokumat-e dini va hoquq-e ensan* (Tehran: Sera'i, 1387 [2008]), pp. 16–17.
139   Khatami, 'Din va siyasat (29/10/1376 [19/1/1998])', p. 36.
140   Philippe Lacoue-Labarthe, *Heidegger, Art and Politics: The Fiction of the Political* (Oxford: Blackwell, [1990], p. 53.
141   Michael Inwood, *A Hegel Dictionary* (Oxford: Blackwell, 1992), p. 68.
142   Han-Georg Gadamer speaks of *Bildung*'s contemporary association with culture as a condition of human flourishing and best cultivating human beings' natural talents and capacities. Hans-Georg Gadamer, *Truth and Method*,

Gadamer would understand the hermeneutic experience itself in terms of *Bildung* and education, whereby understanding was renewed, enriched, and enlarged through a process of mediation between the familiar and that which was alien and other. In the words of Georgia Warnke,

Bildung describes the process through which individuals and cultures enter a more and more widely defined community. The "cultured" individual is one who can place his or her life and concerns within a larger perspective or, to use Gadamer's term, "horizon." That is, he or she is the person who is not only familiar with but interested in issues, problems and ways of life that may be quite distant from his or her own and by being distant put the individual life into perspective.[143]

Without desiring to wantonly overextend this comparison, it should also be acknowledged that in an earlier work, *Discourse on Political Economy* (1755), Rousseau insisted that both legislators and citizens alike should feel themselves duty-bound by the law. Furthermore, this sense of duty ought to emanate from a sense of respect and reverence for the law inculcated by means of public education.[144] We might say that Khatami, by way of his speeches and public appearances, sought to compensate for the constraints on his office by embarking on an elite-led process of education and counsel (*nasihat*), which spoke of the virtues of law and legality, rights, and mutual toleration. This endeavour understood that reform could not be willed and brought into being by fiat but was premised on the notion that both parties to the social contract feel themselves obliged by the laws which govern them and thus refuse to opt out when the opportunity and disparities of power permit.

There is a further dimension to this issue of public education and cultivation which is perhaps the crux of his unsevered continuity with the revolutionary Islamism of 1979 and the 1980s. Insofar as Khatami remains firmly within the ideological school which aspired with the revolution to forge or at least engender the conditions for the formation

trans. Joel Weinsheimer and Donald G. Marshall (London & New York: Bloomsbury, 2004), p. 10.

143 Georgia Warnke, *Gadamer: Hermeneutics, Tradition and Reason* (Cambridge & Oxford: Polity, 1987), p. 173.

144 Jean-Jacques Rousseau, *Discourse on Political Economy and the Social Contract*, trans. Christopher Betts (Oxford & New York: Oxford University Press, 1994), p. 23.

and cultivation of the 'Qur'anic human', two conceptions of freedom emerge which uneasily co-existed alongside one another. One is bound by law, more specifically the Islamic Republic's constitution, and the other 'positive' conception demands the fashioning of the 'Qur'anic human', the latter appearing to be along similar lines to Ibn 'Arabi's own *ensan-e kamel*, to which Khomeini also subscribed.[145] A third possibility is that the normative content of the law is supposed to produce 'Qur'anic human beings', though he never directly enunciates such a view. More likely, Khatami saw cultivation, education, and law as mutually complementary and as integral to the production of upstanding, moral, and law-abiding citizens.

Where the gamut of the Kiyan circle had quite clearly devolved religiosity to the level of the abstract subject and an individualised act of volition in their efforts to echo an amalgam of Kant, Locke, and Luther, Khatami continued to adamantly believe that government must be 'religious' and play a constructive role in the religious and ethical formation of its citizenry. His view of the educative role of the state and its prominent place in the arena of cultural production is quite different and, perhaps, closer to the actual *modus operandi* of the state and its regulation and management of the cultural life of its citizens than that of Shabestari, who sought to reduce the state to a minimal guarantor of basic abstract rights.

A dichotomy evident at a deeper level of Khatami's thought is one with which all theologians are familiar – namely, the acknowledgement of man's 'autonomy' and 'will'[146] and its necessary coexistence with 'servitude to God' (*bandegi-ye khoda*), which he argues was epitomised in the ideal Islamic community under the auspices of the Prophet Mohammad.[147] While asserting the perfect co-existence of 'autonomy' and 'obedience' to God, Khatami applauds Khomeini's revolt against humanism and the belief, which began to steadily gain ascendance from the Renaissance, that man is the measure of all things.[148] He does not accept that a repudiation of humanism entails the denigration of man and, quite typical of religious apologetics, associates a raft of value-laden signifiers – to wit, humane, compassionate, upright, enlightening, justice, freedom, etc. – with 'Islam' or 'monotheism', while dismissing

---

[145] Khatami, 'Din va siyasat (29/10/1376 [19/1/1998])', p. 35.   [146] Ibid., p. 35.
[147] 'Imam Khomeini va hokumat-e dini (11/3/1377 [1/6/1998])', p. 146.
[148] Ibid., p. 147.

any failures to measure up to such criteria as 'deviations'.[149] 'Independence, freedom, progress, reconstruction (*sazandegi*) exist in the heart of monotheism and prepare the ground for the growth of all humans and justice.'[150] In this way, Khatami identifies the keywords of the Islamic Republic's rhetorical arsenal and perhaps even the preceding Rafsanjani administration (*sazandegi*) with the kernel of monotheism itself. At a rhetorical level, these for the most part normative concepts remain capacious and unencumbered by more determinate stipulations and policy prescriptions and an evaluation of their political and social consequences.

Nevertheless, in keeping with this public exercise in pedagogy as reflected in his homiletic style, the theologian-president holds that 'Iranian culture' has proven to be historically hostile towards the law (*qanun-setiz*).[151] The problem of antipathy to the law or insufficient reverence for the law is thus deemed to be a long-established feature of Iranian political culture.[152] The arbitrary state does not stand alone and isolated in polar opposition to a beleaguered society but rather finds its provenance in a society beholden to entrenched practices of *qanun-setizi*. It is Khatami's desire, but also that of the very same society which endorsed his election, to elevate law-orientedness to the status of a 'national and religious value'.[153]

There was more to Khatami's homiletics than his call for law-bound citizenry. They also entailed a genuine effort to augment respect for pluralism and toleration, not only within the polity at large but within the political elite itself, including even the Islamic Revolutionary Guard

---

[149] 'Tafsir-e rasmi az Islam (1/4/1377 [22/6/1998])', p. 80. Houchang E. Chehabi, when analysing the ideology of the NAI, refers to its approach as that of the 'rhetoric of apologetic thought' (p. 73). Islamic modernism not only dismisses alternatives in order to argue that 'Islam' is the superior system but also often misrepresents the objects of its criticism such as comparing an 'historical' Christianity with an 'idealised' Islam (p. 80). Chehabi's description has been slightly adapted, but it certainly holds for Khatami's discourse. Chehabi, *Iranian Politics and Religious Modernism*.

[150] Khatami, 'Tafsir-e rasmi az Islam (1/4/1377 [22/6/1998])', p. 81.

[151] 'Rowhaniyyat va hal-e mo'zelat-e jame'eh (1/7/1376 [23/9/1997])', p. 107.

[152] Homa Katouzian, whose scholarly contributions had a discernable impact on the intellectual discourses of 'reform', is perhaps best known for his theorisation of this insight and notion of 'arbitrary rule'. Katouzian, *The Persians*, Introduction.

[153] Khatami, 'Rowhaniyyat va hal-e mo'zelat-e jame'eh (1/7/1376 [23/9/1997])', p. 107.

332   *Khatami, the 2nd Khordad Front, and the Pedagogics of Pluralism*

Corps. While his idea of pluralism was constrained by the bounds of the constitution which has several discriminatory regulations and directives embedded within it, in a speech entitled 'The Official Interpretation of Islam', delivered before members of the IRGC on 23 September 1997, Khatami attempted to draw upon the travails of the Shi'i and their history of marginalisation as a minority within the Islamic world and thereby valorise respect for the meek and seemingly heterodox.

In accordance with the narrative of established orthodox Shi'i historiography, the Imams were said to have toiled in the shadow of gruesome and unjust caliphs during both the Umayyad and Abbasid dynasties. According to this traditional narrative the Imams were not only disempowered and deprived of their legitimate claim to the Prophet's mantle but were also systematically persecuted, each one meeting with a dark and grisly demise. Behind such familiar sermonising would have been a desire to spell out for his audience that the most sacred personages of the Shi'i faith not only suffered injustices: their *ahadis*, which are taken for granted as the epitome of truth, righteousness, and piety, were scorned and disdained in their own time by the ruling estate. By commenting that 'alongside official Islam [the Imams] introduced another Islam',[154] the implication was hard to miss. Thus, 'alongside the official Islam which holds power, there is another Islam which has another view of the world and humanity'.[155] This recognition of the possibility for rectitude and the capacity for truthfulness in the subaltern and ostracised is again part and parcel of what might be called Khatami's pedagogy of tolerance. This entails not only the acknowledgement that the deity created abundance and variety in the world and that diversity and abundance accord with the 'natural' order but also that power and righteousness are basically distinct and not to be conflated. Moreover, like other religious intellectuals, Khatami links tolerance to fallibility. Because of our perpetual capacity to err we must act conscientiously in our judgements and accept differences within the bounds of the law.

Beyond this point also lies an epistemological one, again pertaining to the issue of fallibility, which contends that truth potentially lies with the marginalised and not the state's imprimatur alone or exclusively – by all accounts, a significant admission. The infallible Imams were the

[154] 'Tafsir-e rasmi az Islam (1/4/1377 [22/6/1998])', p. 78.   [155] Ibid., p. 78.

first 'truthful' interpreters of the Qur'an and, over the course of several generations, 'taught us the correct understanding and interpretation of revelation'.[156] As seen above, it was paradoxically through invoking the example of the infallible Imams that Khatami embraced the centrality of fallibilism to post-revolutionary religious thought, which grew from strength to strength from the late 1980s onwards: 'Do not forget that we are in an era when an infallible is not amongst us and error and mistakes can be made by all of us.'[157] In this way, the 'official Islam' and 'righteous Islam' fall apart at the seams, and discerning rectitude and piety becomes an exercise in patience and forbearance.

Just as Khomeini had exalted the supremely 'innocent' and 'tyrannised' (*mazlumiyyat*) Imam Hosayn and his destruction at the hands of the Umayyad Caliph Yazid so as to tap into the stream of Iranian cultural memory and thereby galvanise resistance to the rule of the Pahlavi regime, Khatami sought to engender a sense of empathy for those readings and narratives excluded by the *tafsir-e rasmi*,[158] which by definition harbours the power to draw the boundary between the orthodox and its Other. Whether it has the power to enforce and constantly police such a manufactured boundary is another issue. As Khatami says, even the venerated Safavid-era philosopher Mulla Sadra Shirazi was persecuted in his own time and, by some accounts, excommunicated.[159] This point should be considered in the light of the fact that Khomeini but also a raft of leading 'olama' – such as 'Allameh Tabataba'i (d. 1981), Mesbah-Yazdi, Mohammad-Taqi Bahjat-Fumani (d. 2009), Hassan Hassanzadeh-Amoli and Ja'far Sobhani – have either written marginalia, furnished exegeses, taught or studied Mulla Sadra's *Asfar al-arba'eh* and Sadrian philosophy before the establishment of the Islamic Republic, and it is in large part due to

---

[156] Ibid., p. 77.   [157] Ibid., p. 83.

[158] The critique of 'official' interpretations of religion was also a key theme in Sorush's well-known essay on pluralism. 'Abdolkarim Sorush, 'Serat-ha-ye mostaqim: sokhani dar peluralism-e dini; mosbat va manfi', in *Serat-ha-ye mostaqim* (Tehran: Serat, 1378 [1999]), p. 6. Other intellectually disposed politicians like Tajzadeh would also regularly echo the notion of 'official Islam' delineated by Mojtahed-Shabestari, Sorush, and Khatami to describe their conservative rivals. See Mostafa Tajzadeh, 'Gofteman-e rasmi, gofteman-e mardomi [Originally published in *Nowruz*, 28/12/1380 (19 March 2002)]', in *Siyasat, kakh va zendan* (Tehran: Zekr, 1381 [2002]), p. 208.

[159] Khatami, 'Rowhaniyyat, bayad-ha va nabayad-ha (1/7/1376 [23/9/1997])', p. 141.

their efforts that it has since emerged as the dominant philosophical school in the Qom seminary.[160] Indeed, 'Allameh Tabataba'i, perhaps best known for his voluminous exegesis of the Qur'an, *Tafsir al-mizan*, famously received a message from Grand Ayatollah Hosayn Borujerdi, the pre-eminent Shi'i *marja' al-taqlid* at the time, advising him against the instruction of philosophy in Qom – an exhortation which, despite its heavy price, 'Allameh Tabataba'i chose to defy.[161] Today, by contrast he is almost universally admired and the subject of a veritable outpouring of hagiographic literature. Khatami thus presents another example of the historicity and fluidity of orthodoxy, its shifting normative bounds, and how dominant and officially sanctioned doxa can fall prey to the vicissitudes of history and contingency.

Because of the many unelected and unaccountable institutions and organisations which operate under the imprimatur of the state – not to mention the myriad informal clerical patron-client networks and the impotence of the executive in controlling or even bringing them to account – it was not so much Khatami's acknowledgement of a plurality of multiple readings of Islam and its sacred texts that was important as it was his effort to cultivate an atmosphere of mutual respect and empathy whereby the proponents of different religious interpretations within the Iranian polity might come to recognise and respect the irreducible existence of one another. Sincere dialogue and engagement would be the next logical step along this path, but the question of recognition and the acceptance of plurality were at the forefront of this effort. If such an atmosphere could take root then the groups and institutions Khatami might have had in mind, such as the Ansar-e Hezbollah vigilantes and their ilk, might refrain from taking it upon themselves to extra-legally impose their perceptions of orthodoxy on others.[162]

---

[160]   Hamid Algar, "Allama Sayyid Muḥammad Husayn Ṭabataba'i: Philosopher, Exegete, and Gnostic', *Journal of Islamic Studies* 17, no. 3 (2006), p. 333. Sajjad H. Rizvi, '"Only the Imam Knows Best": The Maktab-e Tafkik's Attack on the Legitimacy of Philosophy in Iran', *Journal of the Royal Asiatic Society* 22, no. 3–4 (October 2012), p. 487.

[161]   For an analysis of this important incident in the intellectual history of the modern *howzeh*, see Dabashi, *Theology of Discontent: The Ideological Foundation of the Islamic Revolution in Iran*, pp. 282–3.

[162]   An account of the *modus operandi* of such groups has been provided in the following slim volume. Michael Rubin, *Into the Shadows: Radical Vigilantes in Khatami's Iran* (Washington: The Washington Institute for Near East Policy, (2001), esp. chapter 3.

In the mid-1990s the head of the Guardian Council, Ayatollah Ahmad Jannati, during Friday prayers had even quoted Khomeini's last will and testament – a seminal document which high-school and university students have often been compelled to study – in support of a form of vigilantism, asserting that the Imam's will takes precedence over the law.[163] In that document Khomeini had spoken of the necessity of thwarting what he called 'destructive freedoms' (*azadi-ha-ye mokhareb*) which are 'forbidden by the Islamic law' and 'contrary to the dignity of the Islamic Republic'. It continues, '[I]f the people and *Hezbollahi* youth are confronted with the aforesaid issue, refer to the relevant institutions and if they lack the wherewithal, [the people and *Hezbollahi* youth] are obliged to thwart [such destructive freedoms] themselves.'[164] Despite Khomeini's *Hokumat-e eslami* delineating a juridical Leviathan in which all authority would be unified in the singular power of *velayat-e faqih*, the reality of the state-building process and the Imam's own final political will and testament went to ensure the preponderance of competing mandates and agonistic struggles between official, quasi-official, and unofficial organisations and groups. Such agonism was especially pronounced over issues of who had the right to regulate and impose their conception of the moral order upon public space and how those held responsible for its perceived abasement and infringement should be countered.[165] One upshot has been that Khomeini's sundry epigones have constantly moved to obstruct and combat one another on the basis of their perception of the state's best interests, what they held up as righteous and moral conduct in the public domain, or what they consider to constitute the sacred law.

Given the plurality of readings and the routine weakness of the executive in enforcing the law, let alone a single interpretation of the

---

[163] 'Abdi, 'Beh kodam jahat miravim', p. 72.

[164] Ruhollah Khomeini, 'Matn-e kamel-e vasiyyat-nameh-ye elahi-ye siyasi-ye Imam Khomeini' (*Khamenei.ir*, 5 June 1989 [15 Khordad 1367]). Accessed 11/08/2013. Khatami also says that 'we do not regard the [Western] conception of freedom as complete, nor an instance of freedom which bestows happiness'. Khatami, *Bim-e mowj*, p. 191.

[165] Shahram Khosravi's ethnography of the Julfa quarter and the coffee shop culture in Isfahan is a fascinating illustration of this difficult process of spatial negotiation, broaching as it does issues of religious and moral claims on public space, as well as class stratification revolving around consumption. Shahram Khosravi, *Precarious Lives: Waiting and Hope in Iran*, Kindle ed. (Philadelphia: University of Pennsylvania Press, 2017), Loc 2948.

faith, a condition of arbitrariness and disorder continued to afflict the polity. It should be noted that this condition was by no means exclusive to Iran and that the image of the state's putative 'monopoly on violence' has always been a fragile reality that could easily break apart and fracture given the right circumstances. But with that important caveat in mind, vigilantes – epitomised by groups such as the Ansar-e Hezbollah – took it upon themselves to act in accordance with their religious understanding rather than obey the writ of the law (which was often sufficiently opaque in any case).[166] It is under such circumstances that Khatami insisted that 'we should accept that God created human beings differently and we must tolerate one another'.[167] In his earlier work *Bim-e mowj*, he rejects radical forms of religious pluralism that would accept multiple interpretations of the Godhead as equally 'real' or 'valid' – what Sorush, following John Hick, terms 'positive' pluralism. At most, he accepts a form of 'negative' pluralism, acknowledging diverse interpretations of the divine reality as manifold views on a single transcendent reality.[168] But Khatami's comments are perhaps best thought of as serving the political objective of mutual co-existence given the social fact of pluralism in Iranian society,[169] rather than an ontological proposition attesting to the veracity of multiple incommensurable divine realities or even a strand of Perennialism.

As has been mentioned, Khatami's chief objective with such speeches and their dissemination was to strengthen the government's hand by appealing to as broad and variegated a constituency as possible, promoting inclusivity within the bounds of the elite-defined, albeit contested, cultural-political order, while fostering the public's respect for

---

166 This is 'Abdi's own conclusion, since, as he realised, if members of such groups were given free rein by senior Ayatollahs – in this particular instance, Guardian Council chairman Ahmad Jannati – to take it upon themselves to obstruct or attack anything or anyone they might deem an affront to the *nezam*, then the outcome would be 'chaos' or *harj-o-marj*. It was, therefore, crucial for all to submit to the law and institutionalised legal channels. 'Abdi, 'Beh kodam jahat miravim', p. 73.
167 Khatami, 'Rowhaniyyat, bayad-ha va nabayad-ha (1/7/1376 [23/9/1997])', p. 142.
168 Khatami, *Bim-e mowj*, p. 184; Sorush, 'Serat-ha-ye mostaqim', p. 14.
169 An issue which had of course been dealt with at length by the liberal philosopher John Rawls under the rubric of the 'fact of pluralism'. See Will Kymlicka, 'Two Models of Pluralism and Tolerance', *Analyse & Kritik* 13 (1992).

lawfulness, peaceful co-existence, and security in the face of plurality and diversity. While at times speaking in withering terms vis-à-vis secular intellectuals – in *Bim-e mowj*, for instance, going so far as to call them an 'insidious and destructive pain' throughout the course of modern Iranian history[170] – he not only acknowledged their existence but also their 'right to disagree' so long as such expressions of disagreement fell within the bounds of the law: 'Even an infidel that is not a combatant[171] (*mohareb*) falls within the domain of Islam.'[172] While certainly not a flattering portrayal, such a concession was of inestimable importance since it afforded secular intellectuals and critics the prospect of expressing their views under the enveloping shadow of the Islamic state without fear of violent reprisal.[173] These efforts to open up a limited space in which subaltern groups could speak and publish in the open also boosted the Khatami administration's attempts to consolidate a hegemonic front and a broader base and claim to representation.

But once again it proved to be the polycephalous nature of the Iranian state which prevented Khatami from actually realising such a policy, most vividly illustrated by the infamous 'chain murders', which saw 'rogue elements' within the Ministry of Intelligence prosecute the extra-judicial executions of several 'outsider' secular intellectuals and political activists throughout the 1990s, reaching its

---

[170] Khatami, *Bim-e mowj*, p. 197.

[171] *Mohareb* can have various meanings depending on context. It is often translated as 'crusader against God' or 'combatant against the state'. Historically, the *Mohareb* tribe were hostile towards the Prophet Mohammad and his self-proclaimed prophetic mission. There were a number of raids and counter-raids between the *Mohareb* and the Muslim forces following Mohammad's relocation to Medina known as the hijra. G. Levi Della Vida, 'Muḥārib', in *Encyclopaedia of Islam*, ed. P. Bearman et al. (Brill Online).

[172] Khatami, 'Rowhaniyyat va nezam-e jomhuri-ye eslami (13/4/1377 [4/7/1998])', p. 167.

[173] It should be made clear that in an earlier work, *Bim-e mowj*, Khatami makes comments vis-à-vis secular intellectuals which are in most respects indistinguishable from the incendiary rhetoric of the traditional or radical right: 'Irreligious intellectuals whether they want to or not and whether they know or not, provide fodder for the enemy, an enemy which is against our independence ... [T]hey are a channel into society for the penetration of [the enemy].' In this way, one might conclude that Khatami was himself complicit in contributing to an atmosphere in which state violence against secular intellectuals had become acceptable. Khatami, *Bim-e mowj*, p. 200.

denouement in the autumn of 1998. The list included figures such as 'Ali-Akbar Sa'idi-Sirjani, Majid Sharif, Mohammad-Ja'far Puyandeh, Mohammad Mokhtari, Dariyush Foruhar, and his wife, Parvaneh Eskandari. It was with the help of key insiders such as Hajjariyan that the murders' alleged source was exposed to the media,[174] perhaps most forcefully in *Sobh-e emruz*, of which he was the managing director, and *'Asr-e ayandegan*, edited by Shams ol-va'ezin.

In fact, it was Hajjariyan's critical part in exposing the role of Ministry of Intelligence officials in the murders which some have since contended to be the chief motivation behind the unsuccessful assassination attempt against him. Meanwhile, the fierce and unrelenting journalism of Akbar Ganji covering this grim chapter in the history of the Islamic Republic transformed him into a well-nigh legendary figure amongst students and avid readers alike. During this turbulent period, Ganji churned out article after article replete with codenames for those figures of the state apparatus few dared name, as well as sordid details many in the political elite, while disapproving, would rather not be spoken about in the public domain, given fears about the broader reaction they might provoke. It was in the late 1990s and early 2000s that Ganji outpaced and distanced himself from the methods and prescriptions of the Islamic left as he rapidly came to emerge as a full-blown political dissident. For many of his readers and political supporters, he embodied and symbolised so much of what the reformist liberal turn was about and how it had conceived itself – to wit, the ability of the courageous and principled journalist and/or intellectual to single-handedly hold the actions of a wayward and unaccountable state to account from the nurturing bosom of civil society.

But beyond the state itself – first and foremost, the Ministry of Intelligence and the judiciary – Ganji's intrepid campaign also had a personal dimension. Few individuals were as instrumental as Ganji in not only attacking the legacy of Hashemi-Rafsanjani but also implicating the latter in the violence and repression which had unfolded at home and abroad during his tenure as president.[175]

---

174   'Ali-Asghar Ramezanpur and Eskandar Sadeghi-Boroujerdi, 'Interview with 'Ali-Asghar Ramezanpur, former deputy minister for culture in the Ministry of Culture and Islamic Guidance, 2000–2003; former editor at *Sobh-e emruz* and former editor-in-chief of *Aftab-e emruz* newspapers' (8 April 2012).
175   Ganji, *'Alijenab-e sorkhpush va 'alijenab-e khakestari*, p. 56.

Ganji, both at the time and subsequently, would be criticised for his near-obsessive focus on Rafsanjani, who more sober voices have argued may well have been brought over to support moderate reforms if only he had not become such a figure of revilement in the 2nd Khordad press[176] – yet another counter-factual without an easy or definitive answer.

[176] Following the Green Movement and before the election of Hasan Rowhani, Ganji would reexamine his former hostility to Rafsanjani, now hailing him as the 'Green Eminence' (*'alijenab sabzpush*) *in potentia*, who had ceased to be the same Rafsanjani of past years. The new Rafsanjani in the year 2013 stood as a possible ally of the reform agenda. Ganji, 'Az "'alijenab-e sorkhpush" ta "'alijenab sabzpush"'.

7 | Sa'id Hajjariyan and Reformist Strategy: Sovereign Disenchantment and the Politics of Participation

The fate of our times is characterised by rationalization and intellectualization and, above all, by the "disenchantment of the world".[1]

Max Weber

[T]he subaltern classes always suffer the initiative of the dominant class, even when they rebel.[2]

Antonio Gramsci

Sa'id Hajjariyan cuts an exceptional figure for several reasons, but his transition from intelligence officer to theoretician of democratic transition and popular sovereignty surely counts amongst them. Hajjariyan contributed much to the reformists' basic rethinking of the Islamic Republic's political theology, but, apart from his penchant for ideas, he stands out as perhaps *the* grand strategist of the reform movement in the second half of the 1990s. In this chapter I will focus above all on his theorising of the concepts of political development and participation, legitimacy and sovereignty, and how they relate more broadly to the Islamic left's manifold articulations of 'reform', as well as its ambit and scope. I will further tease out the intellectual and political fault lines, as well as commonalities which defined the Islamic left at the end of the twentieth century, and thereby convey a more nuanced picture of the reformists' theoretical and political positions while in office. In this way, it will highlight some of the more notable ideological debates within a faction of the Islamic Republic's political and ideological-intellectual elite, which reconceived the nature and limits of political agency and change with distinct vigour from the mid-1990s onwards.

---

[1] Max Weber, 'Science as a Vocation', in *From Max Weber: Essays in Sociology*, ed. H. H. Gerth and C. Wright Mills (Cornwall: Routledge, 1991), p. 155.
[2] Massimo Modonesi, *Subalternity, Antagonism, Autonomy: Constructing the Political Subject*, trans. Adriana V. Rendon Garrido and Philip Roberts, Kindle ed. (London: Pluto Press, 2014), Loc 535.

To everyone's surprise, including their own, reformist-aligned candidates managed to clinch the executive, the legislature and the overwhelming majority of local councils in the space of a mere three years following Khatami's election. This in turn sparked something of a backlash from the right, even while it took the latter time to absorb the magnitude and significance of their defeat. Similarly, comprising a spectrum of political positions and forces, it would in due course recast itself as the ideological counterpoint of the reformists in the form of the Principalist (*Osulgara*) camp, backed by opaque and unaccountable elements within the security, intelligence, and judicial apparatuses. The 'chain murders' alluded to in the previous chapter were merely one incident of many in which these forces sought to curb the perceived threat emanating from the reformists and their efforts, channelling effervescent popular support to recapture and ultimately repurpose state institutions.

As was remarked upon in Chapter 3, Hajjariyan had an important role in the founding of the Intelligence Ministry during the course of the First Majles in 1984 (1363).[3] Prior to the ministry's establishment he had worked in the intelligence office for counter-espionage and research under Prime Minister Mohammad-'Ali Raja'i (d. 1981). Like many other members of the Islamic left he hailed from the less privileged neighbourhoods of southern Tehran, and after achieving impressive results in the standardised national examinations, the so-called *konkur*, he was admitted to study electrical engineering at the University of Tehran in 1972 (1351). As a youth, he had been an avid reader of 'Ali Shari'ati and attended the latter's classes at the Hosayniyyeh Ershad.[4] By the early 1990s, and some years after having left the Intelligence Ministry, Hajjariyan had also been a participant in the Kiyan and Ayin circles. The latter, as previously relayed, focused predominantly on issues in political theory and development. More importantly, he was appointed head of the political bureau within the newly established Presidential Strategic Research Centre (PSRC) in 1989 at the outset of the Rafsanjani presidency.

The PSRC was headed by Hojjat al-Islam Mohammad Musavi-Kho 'iniha, who had left his position as attorney-general and was perhaps equally notorious for his role as mentor to the Muslim Student Followers of the Imam's Line, which had taken the U.S. embassy staff

---

[3] Hajjariyan and Baqi, 'Goftogu ba Sa'id Hajjariyan', p. 20.   [4] Ibid., p. 53–5.

hostage for 444 days in November 1979.[5] Kho'iniha, Hajjariyan, 'Abbas 'Abdi, and Behzad Nabavi, amongst others, all began working at the centre at the same time, with Hajjariyan effectively acting as Kho'iniha's deputy. It was during this time that Hajjariyan left the science of engineering behind once and for all and began formal studies in political science at the University of Tehran. It was from this institution of higher learning that he obtained both a master's degree and a doctorate under the supervision of the UK-trained academic Hossein Bashiriyeh,[6] arguably Iran's pre-eminent political scientist at the time. Bashiriyeh's own writings have focused on a large range of issues, but his work on political transitions to democracy and authoritarian regimes had a considerable impact within academic and non-academic circles inside the country.[7] He also published influential translations of Thomas Hobbes' *Leviathan* and Barrington Moore's *Social Origins of Dictatorship and Democracy*. As I mentioned above, Hajjariyan headed the political section at the centre, and this is where he first began to elaborate the notion of 'political development' (*towse'eh-ye siyasi*)[8] that would in due course become one of the Islamic *chap*'s favourite keywords, eventually becoming central to the reformist vision of state–society relations. For Raymond Williams, *keywords* 'are significant, binding words in certain activities and their interpretation; they are significant, indicative words in certain forms of thought. Certain uses bound together certain ways of seeing culture and society ... [They are] the elements of an active vocabulary – a way of recording, investigating and presenting problems of meaning in the area in which the meanings of *culture* and *society* have formed.'[9] Hajjariyan and his fellow think-tankers in this way strived to forge a new vocabulary in a clear bid to both investigate and 'present the problems and meanings' of the Iranian Revolution and the political order they had helped establish, as well as the often problematic manner of its institutionalisation. More critically, keywords were developed to the end of changing the Islamic state's present course, while preserving what they took to be the worthy

---

[5] Ibid., p. 45.
[6] For Bashiriyeh's biography, see Hossein Bashiriyeh and 'Ali Mirsepassi, 'Goftogu-ye 'Ali Mirsepassi ba Hossein Bashiriyeh', Iranian Studies Initiative NYU (12 October 2017).
[7] Bashiriyeh and Sadeghi-Boroujerdi, 'Interview with Hossein Bashiriyeh'.
[8] Hajjariyan, 'Tallaqi-ye akademik az towse'eh-ye siyasi', p. 39–41.
[9] Williams, *Keywords: A Vocabulary of Culture and Society*, Loc 243.

gains of the revolutionary process they had supported and to which they had dedicated their lives.

Hajjariyan's political bureau had an additional five sub-divisions: the 'Islamic revolution group', 'the government group' (which worked on the nature of government in Iran), the political behaviour group, political culture group, and finally the political renewal group.[10] Hajjariyan and Kho'iniha met with Rafsanjani during his presidency and explained the notion of political development, since he was widely considered to have put much stock in the prospects of economic development and reintegrating Iran into the global economy, as well as strengthening the country's lines of credit with the American-dominated network of global financial institutions such as the International Monetary Fund and World Bank.[11] In the course of the meeting, a bemused Rafsanjani admitted to never having previously encountered the term 'political development' and initially supposed that it was Hajjariyan's own coinage and adaptation of the concept of 'economic development'. When Hajjariyan outlined the meaning of the term and contended that it should be postulated as one of the preconditions of Rafsanjani's own programme of economic liberalisation, 'he didn't really welcome this project'.[12]

After Khatami's election, Hajjariyan increasingly came to be known as the architect or chief strategist of the reform movement. He was credited with the landslide victory of the Islamic left in the council elections of 1999 and Sixth Majles elections of 2000. In an interview in May 1999, after being elected with the second highest number of votes to the Tehran City Council and at the height of his powers, he

---

[10] See Hajjariyan and Khojasteh-Rahimi, 'Eslahatchi, cheriki nemishavad', p. 44. It seems that the remit of the research groups changed upon Rowhani's assuming charge at the Centre for Strategic Research. Markaz-e tahqiqat-e esteratezhik, 'Mo'arefi-ye markaz-e tahqiqat-e esteratezhik', *Rahbord*, no. 3 (Bahar 1373 [Spring 1994]), p. 230–2.

[11] Bahman Ahmadi-Amu'i, *Eqtesad-e siyasi-ye jomhuri-ye eslami* (Tehran: Gam-e now, 1382 [2003]), p. 210.

[12] ' Emad al-Din Baqi, *Baraye tarikh: goftogu ba Sa'id Hajjariyan* (Tehran: Nashr-e ney, 1379 [2000]), p. 46. Ansari summarises many of the key principles which would guide the reformists after 1997, and most, if not all, are visibly present in the writings of Hajjariyan in *'Asr-e ma*. This is not to suggest that he was the sole architect of the reformist project by any means. In fact, the key arguments of this book run counter to any such proposition. Hajjariyan's role as both a theorist and organiser, however, should not be underestimated. Ansari, *Iran, Islam and Democracy*, pp. 114–16.

forthrightly criticised both Rafsanjani and former Tehran mayor Gholam-Hosayn Karbaschi for their 'elitist tendencies', adding that they were 'not particularly concerned with the public and the masses'.[13] In another important extended interview published in 2005, Hajjariyan would go so far as to claim that '[Rafsanjani] doesn't believe in politics and democracy in the slightest [*ou yek shahi beh siyasat va demokrasi e'teqad nadarad*]';[14] a widely held view amongst the younger, lay elements of the Islamic left prior to 2005.[15]

With Khatami's election, Hajjariyan became the focus of ire and anger by hard-line forces and elements of the intelligence services who accused him of engaging in 'psychological warfare' during the first presidential campaign,[16] so much so that he later became the target of an assassination attempt which left him paralysed in March 2000. 'Emad al-Din Baqi described the assassination attempt as nothing less than 'an excuse to dissolve the Khatami government and eliminate the 2nd Khordad and reform front'.[17] Ganji also regarded the desire to eliminate 'the brain of reform' (*maghz-e eslahat*) to be 'the most important event after the Sixth Majles election', demonstrating rightist forces within the elite were prepared to resort to violence to forestall their eclipse from power through legitimate electoral channels.[18] As much as the reformists insisted that the constitution act as a 'national pact' (*misaq-e melli*), touchstone, and framework through which competing political organisations and forces methodically

---

13 Sa'id Hajjarian and Kaveh Ehsani, '"Existing Political Vessels Cannot Contain the Reform Movement": A Conversation with Sa'id Hajjarian', *Middle East Report*, no. 212 (Autumn 1999), p. 42. Ehsani has provided an important account of how Karbaschi fostered a real estate boom which benefited the well-heeled and connected during the 1990s. Ehsani, 'The Politics of Property in the Islamic Republic of Iran'.

14 Hajjariyan and Salimi, 'Suteh delan gerd-e ham amadand', p. 66.

15 Akbar Ganji, 'Rowshanfekran va gofteman-e 'alijenab [Originally published in 'Asr-e azadegan, no. 92, 9 Bahman 1378 (29/01/2000)]', in *Hashemi-Rafsanjani va Dovvom-e Khordad* (Tehran: Rowzaneh, 1380 [2001]), p. 59.

16 Mohammad-Hosayn Ravanbakhsh and Ahmad Madadi-Ta'emeh, *Andisheh va aqayan-e khoshunat* (Tehran: Mo'alefan, 1379 [2000]), p. 31.

17 'Emad al-Din Baqi, 'Hadaf-e tarahan-e terur barchidan-e dowlat-e Khatami va hazf-e jebheh-ye Dovvom-e Khordad bud [Aftab-e emruz, 16 Farvardin 1379 (4/4/2000)]', in *Baraye tarikh: goftogu ba Sa'id Hajjariyan* (Tehran: Nashr-e ney, 1379 [2000]), p. 113.

18 Akbar Ganji et al., 'Matn-e sokhanrani-ha-ye ruz-e avval', in *Konforans-e Berlin; khedmat ya khiyanat*, ed. Mohammad-'Ali Zakariya'i (Tehran: Tarh-e now, 1379 [2000]), p. 73.

resolve their disagreements,[19] elements in the right and in the national security state were comfortable resorting to the courts and extra-legal violence when deemed necessary to obstruct various initiatives by the reformist coalition.

I will now turn to analyse in greater detail several of the key themes and ideas found in Hajjariyan's writings throughout the 1990s and early 2000s, which regularly appeared in the leading publications of the Islamic left in a fluid and ongoing conversation with fellow religious intellectuals linked to the political class – such as the SMEEI's *'Asr-e ma, Kiyan, Ayin,* and the organ of the Islamic Iran Participation Front, *Mosharekat,* founded in 1998. Unlike prominent religious intellectuals such as 'Abdolkarim Sorush who have arguably gone through several philosophically incommensurable periods, Hajjariyan's analyses and theoretical outlook possess, for the most part, a fair amount of consistency. Firstly, I will set the context by examining some of Hajjariyan's pre-2nd Khordad writings which were first published in *Kiyan* under the pseudonym Jahangir Salehpur. The chapter will then proceed to explore his conception of political development in greater depth and its concrete expression in the Participation Front of Islamic Iran (*Jebheh-ye mosharekat-e Iran-e eslami*), its relationship with the Khatami administration, and some of the political challenges it faced between 1998 and 2005.

Disenchanting Sovereignty

We reinterpret the views of Imam Khomeini in such a way that they are compatible with democracy. Imam Khomeini is not amongst us, but our understanding and exegesis of his texts are.[20]

Akbar Ganji

As is often the case in revolutionary states with charismatic founders, long after their passing a contested legacy remains, over which successors scramble to acquire legitimacy for their political programs and policies. Hajjariyan's reading of Khomeini's political thought is certainly one of the more innovative and radical of the Islamic *chap* and

---

[19] Kaviyani, *Pishgaman-e eslahat,* p. 45. 'Bayad ba jediyyat pasdar-e arzesh-ha-ye qanun-e asasi bashim', *Sobh-e emruz* (23/3/1378 [13 June 1999]).

[20] Akbar Ganji, *Kimiya-ye azadi: defa'iyyat-e Akbar Ganji dar dadgah-e konforans-e Berlin* (Tehran: Tarh-e now, 1380 [2001]), p. 83.

sheds light on his own aspirations for political reform within the Islamic Republic. His analysis is also significantly more dynamic and prone to thinking in terms of social and historical processes, a trait so often absent from the work of other religious intellectuals who tend to have an idealistic – i.e., that ideas determine the nature of historical transformations – and Whiggish view of Western history – namely, that 'modernity' was the progressive unfurling of critical rationality, humanism and enlightenment – which they then hold up as a bench-mark to appraise Iran's own historical trajectory. This is not to deny their acknowledgement of historicity, which both Sorush and Shabestari invoke in ironically abstract ways, but their propensity to disaggregate the historical nature of texts and ideas from broader social, political, and economic transformations, which ultimately receive little serious attention. On a related note, there is also a strong tendency amongst the Islamic left to have a Whiggish view of its own historical trajectory and efface not only the highly authoritarian and paternalistic strands running through Khomeini's views on political authority and rule but also their very real complicity in the bloody internal battles and repression which followed the revolution. While Hajjariyan is by no means free of such issues, he is by far the most sophisticated and theoretically adept of the Islamic left.

In an essay entitled 'The Process of Shi'i Jurisprudence's Secularisation' (*Farayand-e 'orfi shodan-e feqh-e Shi'eh*), first pub-lished in *Kiyan* in April–May 1995, instead of proclaiming *feqh* mere artifice produced by a mundane-historical institution – to wit, the clergy – he takes the view that Khomeini had in fact secularised Shi'i *feqh* by sacrificing it on the altar of the prerogatives and exigencies of the nation-state.[21] He argued that because the Guardian Jurist (*vali-ye faqih*) had been endowed by Khomeini with 'absolute guardianship' which conferred the powers of the Prophet and Imams as regards the power to legislate (*amr-e tashri'*) and pass laws at the state and national level, such legislation must be recognised by the 'olama' as a whole.[22] The age-old problem in which temporal authority was deemed reli-giously illegitimate, usurping the rightful place of the Hidden Imam, had been dissolved, and the religious authority's rivalry and strained co-existence with temporal power – namely, the state – neutralised. More fundamentally, the long-established and basic dichotomy of

[21] Hajjariyan, 'Farayand-e 'orfi shodan-e feqh-e Shi'eh', p. 84.   [22] Ibid., p. 83.

customary law (*'orf*) and the sacred law (*shari'ah*) had been effectively obliterated. This occurrence – while lamented by some scholars who have viewed it as nothing more than the destruction of the *shari'ah* and its epistemic community[23] – and its transformation into positive law was overtly welcomed by Hajjarian.

Hajjariyan describes this in analogous terms to the process outlined in Perry Anderson's seminal *Lineages of the Absolutist State*, in which Western Europe underwent the historical transition from what he terms 'parcellized sovereignty' under feudalism to powerful centralised monarchies, accompanied by huge bureaucracies and standing armies, bestowing these social formations with a degree of autonomy they had not hitherto possessed.[24] On this reading, Khomeini had succeeded where kings since the Safavids had failed as he was able to unify the two distinct spheres of legislative legitimacy under the imprimatur of the nation-state, which as it happened was indistinguishable from the fittingly vague 'interests of Islam'.[25] While Khomeini's political thought had an undeniable internationalist bent,[26] with the founding of the Islamic Republic it has been irrevocably territorialised in the Iranian nation-state. Khomeini's famous fatwa of January 1988, which decreed it permissible for the state to suspend even matters of ritual

---

23 Hallaq, *An Introduction to Islamic Law,* p. 169. 'Can the Shari'a Be Restored?', in *Islamic Law and the Challenges of Modernity,* ed. Yvonne Yazbeck Haddad and Barbara Freyer Stowasser (Lanham, MD & Oxford: Altamira Press, 2004), p. 40.

24 Perry Anderson, *Lineages of the Absolutist State,* Kindle ed., World History Series (London & New York: Verso, 2013 [1974]), p. 17; Loc 165. It still is not entirely clear whether Hajjariyan had read Perry Anderson's classic book on the subject or not at this point. He does not cite Anderson or his work directly even while repeatedly speaking of the 'absolute state'. Hajjariyan does, however, allude to *Lineages of the Absolutist State* in a later article published in 2003, but he expresses a preference for what he calls the Weberian approach. It is clear from his analysis that he was not inclined to the method of historical materialism, foremost the analysis and role of class conflict, in defining the nature of political power. Nor is it apparent that he had a deep appreciation of Anderson's work on this score. Sa'id Hajjariyan, 'Mashruteh-talabi', in *Eslahat dar barabar-e eslahat: goftogu'i-ye enteqadi* (Tehran: Tarh-e now, 1382 [2003]), p. 122.

25 Hajjariyan is quoting Khomeini's historic fatwa of January 1988. 'Farayand-e 'orfi shodan-e feqh-e Shi'eh', p. 83.

26 Arshin Adib-Moghaddam, *Iran in World Politics: The Question of the Islamic Republic* (London & New York: Hurst, 2008), p. 56. A Critical Introduction to Khomeini (Cambridge & New York: Cambridge University Press, 2014), Introduction.

practice ('ebadat), was an invasive step of unprecedented proportions and to some extent derived directly from Iran's numerous disputes with the Saudi kingdom, in addition to the many challenges facing the new state.

Despite Hajjariyan's originally formulated hypothesis, traditional authority, as he would acknowledge himself, had proven to be far more resilient than he had anticipated. Upon 'Ali Khameneh'i's taking up the office of the Guardian Jurist, it had been thought necessary to promote his retroactive transformation from a mid-ranking Hojjat al-Islam to the rank of Ayatollah overnight. This step was taken, at least in part, to placate the traditionalist clergy and *marja'iyyat* and was recognition of the fact that political acumen alone could not suffice to lend the institution credibility to perform the role of Leviathan both Khomeini and Hajjariyan, in their distinct ways, envisaged. Ever since his appointment by the Assembly of Experts in the summer of 1989, Khameneh'i's office repeatedly campaigned to promote his status as a *marja'-e taqlid* – a claim that riled the feathers of many senior 'olama' and has been met with a chorus of dissenting voices, the most truculent of whom was an initially staunch defender of Khameneh'i's 'absolute' authority as *vali-ye faqih*, Ayatollah Ahmad Azari-Qomi.[27] Despite Hajjariyan's positive recasting on the unforeseen consequences of the Absolute Mandate of the Jurist, it can and has been interpreted in a manner directly antithetical to Hajjariyan's reading – namely, as a justification of theocratic absolutism and a total negation of the popular basis of sovereignty. Even if he conveniently omits that Khomeini had predominantly spoken of 'the expediency of the system' (*maslahat-e nezam*), Hajjariyan had hoped the political credo of 'expediency' *qua* public good would take centre stage and be understood by the Islamic state as identical with the interests of the nation (*mellat*) rather than limited to the preservation of a specific political 'system' or 'regime'. It was on such a basis that he consequently made the leap to assert that, because of the centrality of the public good, the *faqih*'s power and authority derived from the social compact he had concluded with the people. Just as Hobbes replaced the divine covenant with the social contract, thereby establishing modern politics and the nation-

---

[27] Wilfried Buchta, *Who Rules Iran? The Structure of Power in the Islamic Republic* (Washington: Washington Institute for Near East Policy and the Konrad Adenauer Stiftung, 2000), pp. 52–3.

state on the basis of human volition,[28] Hajjariyan follows suit in his efforts to read the very same transition into the political and theological revolutions enacted by Khomeini. The *faqih*'s legitimacy was thus thought to derive from below, with him contracted as a representative of the popular will. It is questionable whether this is in fact the case following the constitutional revisions of July 1988, since the stipulation in article 5 of the constitution which stated that 'the majority of the people recognise and accept [the *vali-ye faqih*] as leader' was scratched.[29] Moreover, as Hajjariyan knew well, the relationship of the traditional *faqih* and *marja*' with his followers was for the most part informal, where even by the second half of the twentieth century it could still be said to enjoy a low-level institutionalisation through the presence and activities of his household, *vokala*', as well as any charitable endowments the latter might support across the world. It was not in theory or practice confined to the territoriality of the nation-state, the state apparatus, or formed on a contractual basis that was in any sense legally binding. Such a theorisation also makes hardly inconsequential assumptions about the religious homogeneity of the aforesaid state. Moreover, only in a very loose and imprecise sense could the institution of *marja 'iyyat* be said to be 'democratic' insofar as it assumes that the leading *marja*' *al-taqlid* will attract the most followers and receive religious taxes therefrom.[30] There is no formal procedure of election akin to the Papacy, and it is its traditional *informality* which had arguably allowed the *howzeh* to survive and adapt under different political regimes and trying circumstances.

Hajjariyan saw Khomeini as a '*faqih* of transition' capable of devolving the prerogative to identify the public interest from the jurist to the nation-state with its foundation in popular republicanism.[31] In this regard he casts Khomeini as a force majeure of raw and unmediated populist energy, corroding the grip of traditionalist jurisprudence while

---

28 Paul W. Kahn, *Political Theology: Four New Chapters on the Concept of Sovereignty* (New York: Columbia University Press, 2011), p. 1.

29 Shams, *Qanun-e asasi: az farman-e mashrutiyyat ta emruz*, p. 105.

30 Some of these issues are adeptly tackled in Elvire Corboz, *Guardians of Shi'ism: Sacred Authority and Transnational Family Networks* (Edinburgh: Edinburgh University Press, 2015).

31 Sa'id Hajjariyan, 'Imam Khomeini, faqih-e dowran-e gozar: az feqh-e javaheri ta feqh al-maslahat [Originally published in *Kiyan*, no. 46, Farvardin–Ordibehesht 1378 (March–April 1999)]', in *Az shahed-e qodsi ta shahed-e bazari: 'orfi shodan-e din dar sepehr-e siyasat* (Tehran: Tarh-e now, 1380 [2001]), p. 92.

new forms of authority and legitimacy gained verve and appeal. Unsurprisingly, Hajjariyan's professed theoretical sources of inspiration were Hobbes and Jean Bodin, with their advocacy of centralised and indivisible authority in the locus of the state Leviathan, even adducing the phrase 'earthly God' (*khoda-ye zamini*).[32] 'The *vali-ye faqih* is the representative and symbol of "national sovereignty" (*hakemiyyat-e melli*) and is bound to defend the "public interest" and "national interest".'[33] He is 'the *vakil* of a people who in accord with a "compact" elected him to this position' and 'his legitimacy is a consequence of the rights of the nation'.[34] This popular republican dimension is, it should be noted, quite distinct from the Hobbesian social contract, which first and foremost sought to constitute 'a common power' to end the 'warre of every man against every man' and provide a basis for social peace and security, because 'where there is no common Power, there is no Law: where no Law, no Injustice'.[35]

On Hajjariyan's rendering, after vanquishing traditional religious authority and the establishment of the public interest's primacy as determined by the republic, the state's religious basis was supposed to steadily slide into obscurity and segue into the civilianisation of political power. The supervision and security of civil transactions (*mo'amelat*) would be underwritten by the state and not the clergy, while the domain of religion and the authority of the traditional institutions of organised religion would withdraw into the private sphere in the form of religious worship (*'ebadat*) – a somewhat conventional, though now rather dated, version of the secularisation thesis. Rituals address the immutable dimension of religion but also have the ability to contribute to social stability. The role of *feqh*, insofar as it has one, would be restricted to *'ebadat*, while public issues of jurisprudence would be regulated by the state, which is their sole guarantor.[36] 'In the same way that today Muslims as a result of the progress of knowledge have cast aside immense volumes of texts (*nosus*) relating to the jurisprudence of medical practice, they may accordingly secularise the

---

[32] 'Farayand-e 'orfi shodan-e feqh-e Shi'eh', pp. 84–5.   [33] Ibid., p. 84.
[34] Ibid., p. 85. He claims that his reading is supported by article 56 of the constitution.
[35] Thomas Hobbes, *Leviathan*, Kindle ed., Cambridge Texts in the History of Political Thought (Cambridge & New York: Cambridge University Press, 1996), p. 71; Loc 3355.
[36] Hajjariyan, 'Farayand-e 'orfi shodan-e feqh-e Shi'eh', p. 88.

jurisprudence of commerce, inheritance and the judiciary.'[37] All of these juridical categories, which have been the traditional prerogative of the *shari'ah* and thus the 'olama', would be subsumed under the remit of state law, leaving change and reform to be undertaken by the state and its organs as exigency demands. He echoes Anderson's description of the early modern absolutist states' adaptation of Roman law, which was reformulated in accordance with the times and 'corrupted [in] its pristine form and cleansed ... of its particularist contents'. It was a process that 'paradoxically "universalized" it, by removing the large portions of Roman civil law that were strictly related to the historical conditions of Antiquity'.[38] In similar fashion, Khomeini's jurisprudential revolution had paradoxically engendered the conditions for the endogenous secularisation of Iran's legal system and cleansed it of its anachronistic and irrelevant vestiges.[39]

Playing on Max Weber's famous account of the process of 'disenchantment' which had been irrevocably provoked with the inception of the European Enlightenment,[40] Hajjariyan argues that the subordination of religious injunctions to the state by Khomeini may well have triggered the 're-enchantment' (*baz-afsuni*) of the political order in the short term, but that ultimately this act had and will spur the process of Shi'i *feqh*'s secularisation onwards.[41] His conclusions are thus very different from those of Khatami, who held that, without an Islamic state, many important religious ordinances would remain in abeyance. For Khatami the Islamic state in concert with the clergy retain their mandate and must jointly continue as guarantors of the *shari'ah* and its implementation.

While reason (*'aql*) is an established source of law in Shi'i *feqh*, Hajjariyan argues the Shi'i juristic conception of reason differs from its modern counterpart in several important respects.[42] As one of the four sources by means of which religious ordinances are derived, alongside consensus (*ejma '*), the Qur'an, and Traditions, 'reason' came to be

---

[37] Ibid., p. 82.   [38] Anderson, *Lineages of the Absolutist State*, p. 24; Loc 267.

[39] Hajjariyan speaks of 'modernity' as an 'endogenous' process, in contrast to what he terms 'exogenous' forms of 'modernization'. Sa'id Hajjariyan, 'Enqelab-e eslami; moderniyyat 'alayheh modernizasiyun [Originally published in *Mosharekat*, No. 2–3, Bahman 1377 (January–February 1999]', in *Az shahed-e qodsi ta shahed-e bazari: din dar sepehr-e siyasat* (Tehran: Tarh-e now, 1380 [2001]), p. 243.

[40] Weber, 'Science as a Vocation', p. 155.

[41] Hajjariyan, 'Farayand-e 'orfi shodan-e feqh-e Shi'eh', p. 83.   [42] Ibid., p. 94.

understood, for all intents and purposes, as the mere sum of practical rules for the derivation of such rulings – in short, a series of ossified and unreflexive procedures. These practical rules include 'presuming the continuance of the *status quo*' (*esteshab*), 'exemption' (*bara'at*), and 'option' (*takhyir*) and have historically set the parameters of legal reasoning (*ejtehad*) in Shi'i jurisprudence.[43] Hajjariyan also claims that 'reason', as a source of religious rulings, came to be practically overshadowed by the other three sources of Shi'i jurisprudence – namely, consensus, the Qur'an, and the Traditions. The prohibition on *qiyas* or reasoning by analogy, in stark contrast to the Sunni schools of jurisprudence, he argues, was another reason for the intellectual torpor plaguing the legal methodology of the guardians of the *shari'ah*. It was for these reasons that only a revolutionary transformation and the charismatic appeal of Khomeini could have overcome such obstacles on the road to modern forms of reasoning and institution-building and subsequently propel *maslahat* to the forefront of the process of law-making in the Shi'i state.[44] The obvious question, as already implied above, is why this should have continued to hold, following the charismatic leader's death and the subsiding of revolutionary fervour, and thereby prevent legal parallelism – the dichotomy between traditional and rational-legal state authority, resurfacing in another form? The reader is not provided with a clear answer.

While Khatami in a number of respects continued to cede ground to the longstanding distinction between the *shari'ah* and positive law manifest in the modus operandi of the Guardian Council and the Majles, Hajjariyan highlights the role of the Council for the Discernment of Regime Expediency (*Majma'-e tashkhis-e maslahat-e nezam*), established by Khomeini in February 1988 to mediate thorny disagreements between the Guardian Council and Majles. Given Khomeini's much-vaunted emphasis on the 'preservation of the system' (*hefz-e nezam*) as the obligation which supersedes all others (*owjab-e vajebat*), he contended that in principle the institution harboured the potential for ushering in a new era of popular sovereignty.[45] Another

---

43 Ibid., p. 94. For more details see Modarressi Tabataba'i, *An Introduction to Shi'i Law*, p. 10.
44 Hajjariyan, 'Farayand-e 'orfi shodan-e feqh-e Shi'eh', p. 94.
45 Ibid., p. 85. Interestingly enough, in May 1993 a controversy between the Guardian Council and Expediency Council would see the former attempt to restrict the powers of the Expediency Council and circumscribe its powers

argument made by Hajjariyan[46] was that Islamic government's entwinement with the everyday preoccupations of running the affairs of a modern state and overseeing a civilian bureaucracy in keeping with the imperatives of means–end or goal-oriented rationality (*'aqlaniyyat-e hadaf vasileh*) progressively eroded the ideological dogmas once held to be unassailable and sacrosanct, as the mundane exigencies of state administration take priority.[47]

Re-Imagining the Sultan

Arguably what had not been adequately accounted for by Hajjariyan was the prospect that the Absolute Guardianship of the Jurisconsult would refuse to discard its pretence to sanctity and religiosity and instead locate the very fount of its legitimacy in a divinely bestowed mandate without intermediary (*mashru'iyyat-e elahi-ye bela vaseteh*). On this reading, in the final analysis, 'legitimacy' (*mashru'iyyat*) derives not from the will of the people but only from God. It would be left to clergymen on the far right of the ruling ideological spectrum to elaborate and theorise the Absolute Guardianship of the Jurist in a way that was conducive to something approximating pure theocracy. Ayatollah Mesbah-Yazdi, for example, substituted popular legitimacy with the notion of acceptability (*maqbuliyyat*) – i.e., the regime should be acceptable to the people, but they cannot furnish it with any legitimacy, which is the prerogative of God alone.[48] Mesbah-Yazdi was hardly alone in holding this view. Another erstwhile critic of the reformists, 'Ali Motahhari, son of none other than Ayatollah Morteza Motahhari, in his book-length jeremiad against 'reformism' published in 2000 similarly rejected the idea that the people's vote

within the limits of the secondary injunctions, as opposed to the primary injunctions of the *shari'ah*, as had been previously assumed on the basis of Khomeini's famous decree analysed above. See Yasuyuki Matsunaga, 'The Secularization of a Faqih-Headed Revolutionary Islamic State of Iran: Its Mechanisms, Processes, and Prospects', *Comparative Studies of South Asia, Africa and the Middle East* 29, no. 3 (2009), p. 477.

46 Mohsen Kadivar also repeats this argument verbatim in his interview with *Khordad*. The interview was amongst the chief reasons for his arrest and conviction by the Special Court for Clerics. Kadivar, 'Mosahebeh ba ruznameh-ye Khordad', p. 162.

47 Hajjariyan, 'Farayand-e 'orfi shodan-e feqh-e Shi'eh', p. 95.

48 Mesbah-Yazdi, *Negahi-ye gozara beh nazariyyeh-ye velayat-e faqih*, p. 53.

could furnish the legitimacy of the Guardianship of the Jurist: 'from the
Principalists' (*Osulgarayan*) perspective, the vote of the people is a sign
of the Islamic system's acceptability (*maqbuliyyat*) and places an obligation on the Guardian Jurist to establish an Islamic system ...
The reformists want absolute democracy without condition and the
Principalists want conditioned democracy within the framework of
doctrine (*maktab*).'[49] The procedure for quantifying or discerning
such 'acceptability' is rarely fleshed out in any depth, but the specific
doctrine Motahhari has in mind is clearly *velayat-e faqih* and Iranian
society's regulation by the *shari'ah*. In later years Motahhari's views
would considerably evolve and change, in a way in which his father's
views were never able, namely from within the context of the established political class and post-revolutionary Islamic system itself.
Needless to say, such a position expressed in these terms was rejected
by Hajjariyan.[50]

The logic of the inversion of Hajjariyan's thesis meant that, instead
of the secularisation of religious authority and its subsumption in the
democratic process, the Absolute Guardianship of the Jurist turned
into the equation of the interests of the ruling regime and the person of
the Guardian Jurist with the Divine Will itself. In the eyes of several
right-wing ideologues, defiance of the system (*nezam*) and its helms-
man, the Guardian Jurist, was tantamount to defiance of God himself.
Additionally, one ought not to forget the crucial material resources
and institutional leverage at the disposal of the *vali-ye faqih*'s office,
which, apart from directly appointing six of the Guardian Council's

---

[49] 'Ali Motahhari, *Eslahtalabi* (Tehran: Sadra, 1379 [2000]), p. 17.
    Motahhari's views would evolve and find themselves considerably
    complicated following the 2009 presidential contest and the appearance of
    the Green Movement.

[50] See Mohammad-Taqi Mesbah-Yazdi, 'Hokumat va mashru'iyyat', *Ketab-e
    naqd* 2, no. 7 (1377 [1998]), p. 52. San'ati, *Gofteman-e Mesbah*, pp. 539–93.
    Sa'id Hajjariyan, 'Falsafeh-ye entekhabat [Originally published in *'Asr-e ma*,
    no. 90, 1376/12/06 (25/02/1998)]', in *Jomhuriyyat; afsun zoda'i az qodrat*
    (Tehran: Tarh-e now, 1389 [2000]), p. 539. He wrote an explicit critique of
    Mesbah-Yazdi in *'Asr-e ma* in August 1998 referring to him as 'Hojjat al-Islam'
    (p. 640) and not Ayatollah. He compares Mesbah's political thought
    unfavourably with that of Motahhari and Beheshti, depicting him as
    a retrograde apologist for absolutism and even slavery (p. 643). 'Mesbah-Yazdi
    dar kakh-e zojaji [Originally published in *'Asr-e ma*, no. 101, 21/05/1377 (12/
    08/1998)]', in *Jomhuriyyat; afsun zoda'i az qodrat* (Tehran: Tarh-e now, 1379
    [2000]).

twelve members, also appoints the Chief Justice, the full thirty-one members of the Expediency Council, the Head of State Radio and Television, the Commander of the Islamic Revolutionary Guard Corps,[51] the Commander of the Regular Military, the Chief of the General Staff of the Armed Forces, and the Commander of the Law Enforcement Forces,[52] as well as Friday prayer leaders across the country. There are also myriad quasi-official channels through which the Guardian Jurist can exert influence upon the political and economic fate of persons and events, such as the Revolutionary Foundations (*bonyad-ha*).[53]

It was on this point that Hajjariyan and later Ganji would draw on Weber's theory of sultanism as laid out in the latter's magnum opus, *Economy and Society*.[54] There Weber defined sultanism as an 'extreme case' of patrimonialism, where 'traditional domination develops an administration and military force which are purely personal instruments of the master ... Where domination is primarily traditional, even though it is exercised by virtue of the ruler's personal autonomy, it will be called *patrimonial authority*; where indeed it operates primarily on the basis of discretion, it will be called *sultanism*.'[55] While

---

[51] Kevan Harris has made a persuasive case why the IRGC's economic operations should not be viewed in monolithic terms. See Kevan Harris, 'The Rise of the Subcontractor State: Politics of Pseudo-Privatization in the Islamic Republic of Iran', *International Journal of Middle East Studies*, no. 45 (2013).

[52] Buchta, *Who Rules Iran? The Structure of Power in the Islamic Republic*, p. 8.

[53] Ali-Asghar Saeidi, 'The Accountability of Para-governmental Organizations (Bonyads): The Case of Iranian Foundations', *Iranian Studies* 37, no. 3 (2004).

[54] Hajjariyan was amongst the earliest to introduce the theory, which then became fodder for many future analyses of the Iranian political system. Sa'id Hajjariyan, 'Sakht-e eqtedar-e soltani, asibpazir-ha va badil-ha', *Etela'at-e siyasi-eqtesadi*, no. 2 (1374 [1995]).

[55] Weber quoted in H. E. Chehabi and Juan J. Linz, 'A Theory of Sultanism 1: A Type of Nondemocratic Rule', in *Sultanistic Regimes*, ed. Juan J. Linz and H. E. Chehabi (Baltimore & London: John Hopkins University Press, 1998), p. 4. It is still not clear to what extent this really is an accurate analogy as far as Khameneh'i's style of statecraft is concerned, simply because we still do not have an accurate picture of the modus operandi of the *bayt*'s bureaucracy, much of which has been predicated on hearsay transmitted to the foreign-based Persian-language press. There are occasional indications as to its modus operandi in the domestic press as a result of leaks in the midst of factional infighting. One such instance was Karrubi's open letter to Khameneh'i, alleging that the latter's son, Mojtaba, had openly interfered in the 2005 presidential race and backed a rival candidate, namely Ahmadinejad, though he is not mentioned by name. But again, this hardly suffices for a serious or rigorous assessment. Mehdi Karrubi,

Hajjariyan was often cautious in his deployment of the term, he not only played a vital part in introducing the theory to Iranian audiences in the mid-1990s but also on many occasions held that elements of the theory, such as the personalisation of power, were serious obstacles confronting both the Islamic *chap* and the future of political development.[56] Even after the failed assassination attempt, Hajjariyan was hardly reticent in arguing that 'after the death of Imam [Khomeini] we have gradually returned to the previous governmental structure [i.e., the Pahlavi monarchy]'.[57] Ganji would be even less circumspect in later years and insisted in numerous articles published in Persian and English that the Islamic Republic was a full-blown

'Matn-e kamel-e nameh-ye Mehdi Karrubi beh rahbar-e jomhuri-ye eslami', BBC Persian, http://www.bbc.co.uk/persian/iran/story/2005/06/050619_kar oubi-objection.shtml
  A further glimpse into the economic power which undergirds the *bayt* has more recently been provided by a Reuters special report on the financial operations of an organisation called the Headquarters for Executing the Order of the Imam (*Setad-e ejra'i-ye farman-e hazrat-e Imam*), which is not only under the ultimate control of Khameneh'i's office but also devoid of parliamentary scrutiny. It has been estimated to control assets in the region of $95 billion, much of which has been accumulated as a result of asset seizures.
  Steve Stecklow, Babak Dehghanpisheh, and Yeganeh Torbati, 'Khamenei controls massive financial empire built on property seizures', *Reuters* (11 November 2013).
  Though the analyses provided by the Islamic left in this regard can prove insightful and accurate in part, they all completely ignore the personalised clerical and familial networks which informed Khomeini's style of rule. Though Khomeini no doubt exhibited several characteristics of the Weberian archetype of the 'charismatic leader', empirical reality rarely, if ever fully approximates such idealisations. The role of Khomeini's *bayt* or household and of his son, Ahmad, in particular, and how they defined his style of statecraft demand further research; there is of course no denying that during Khameneh'i's time as Leader that his *bayt* has massively expanded its bureaucracy and on some accounts has become a state within a state. Nevertheless, the role of personalised, familial, and clerical networks under Khomeini is undeniable. Mehdi Ha'eri-Yazdi in his memoir quite clearly says that it was nearly impossible to speak to Khomeini directly without going through Ahmad or being in Ahmad's presence. Mehdi Ha'eri-Yazdi and Ziya Sedqi, 'Mehdi Ha'eri-Yazdi' (Iranian Oral History Collection, Harvard University, 28 January, 4 February 1989 and 29 April 1992), Tape 4; p. 18.
56 In this essay first published in 'Asr-e ma, Hajjariyan highlights both the personalisation of power and its transformation into a question of proximity to and familial ties with the 'sultan'. Hajjariyan, 'Nahveh-ye baz towlid-e saltanat dar andisheh-ye khelafat va velayat [First published in 'Asr-e ma, no. 95, 30/02/ 1377 (20/05/1998)]', pp. 581–3.
57 'Mashruteh-talabi', p. 123.

sultanistic system.[58] While there was certainly some truth to the analogy given the Leader's office's control of a vast network of institutions, appointments, and endowments, in the Islamic *chap*'s lexicon it performed the role of a polemical catchword used by them and their sympathisers to undermine the agents and persons they held to be the chief obstacle to their contestation of popular institutions. An unalloyed sultanistic system predicated on traditional forms of authority and familial ties is quite clearly not an accurate representation of the Islamic Republic's political system in its entirety for numerous reasons, but more importantly it stood in an uneasy relationship to the 2nd Khordad Front's own claim to stand as the embodiment of the national will. The more cautious amongst them were thus careful not to overextend the metaphor in too unqualified or crude a fashion, since they recognised that several other institutional mechanisms of control and forms of authority were simultaneously at work. The discourse of sultanism did, however, serve the purpose of *personalising* and focusing the disparate origins of their frustrations on a single individual. The portrayal of a decrepit sultanistic system also fed into the Islamic *chap*'s narrative of degeneration, which contended that, following the loss of the incomparably charismatic leader, the republic had regressed into a traditionalist, wayward, and personal fiefdom in which they had only limited room to manoeuvre and which, by implication, only they could restore to glory.[59] On this view, there has been a temporal

[58] Several years later, in exile in the United States, Ganji undertook a frontal assault against Khameneh'i and what he saw as the former's personalisation of political rule. In this article Ganji proclaimed, 'Formally or not, the executive, legislative, and judicial branches of government all operate under the absolute sovereignty of the supreme leader; Khamenei is the head of state, the commander in chief, and the top ideologue' (p. 45). He was also adamant that Khamenei 'has secured a complete stranglehold on power in Iran' (p. 49). Akbar Ganji, 'The Latter-Day Sultan: Power and Politics in Iran', *Foreign Affairs* 87, no. 6 (2008), p. 45. This approach has rightly been criticised as a sort of latter-day Kremlinology. Arang Keshavarzian, 'The Iran Deal as Social Contract', *Middle East Research and Information Project* 45, no. 277 (2015). A much earlier comment by Kadivar, which provoked the ire of the Special Court for Clerics, was where he averred that 'in the method and nature of some it is observed that their interpretation of Islamic government bears no difference with a monarchical regime'. Kadivar, 'Mosahebeh ba ruznameh-ye Khordad', p. 157.

[59] In 2009, following the controversial re-election of Mahmud Ahmadi-Nezhad, a wheelchair-using Hajjariyan was hauled before the Islamic Revolutionary Court, to repudiate (allegedly under duress) the theory of sultanism and state that it bore no relation to the doctrine and political order of *velayat-e faqih*. He also

reversal in lieu of progress. In its worst incarnations, the application of the theory became not only an inaccurate and misleading characterisation of the Islamic Republic's political system but also a flawed exercise in self-Orientalisation.

In keeping with such an outlook, Hajjariyan was sure to emphasise that Khatami's victory was the convergence of the chief objectives of the Constitutional Revolution (*mashrutiyyat*) and the 1979 Revolution (*jomhuriyyat*).[60] *Mashrutiyyat* of course stood for the limitation of state power, namely the personal power of the shah, while *jomhuriyyat* was the embodiment of the people's will in popular institutions: 'the people are not the property or children of the government ... [T]he government is a product of [the people's] will and it does not have an identity independent of them.'[61] Hajjariyan was thus eager to claim that the election of Khatami symbolised an essentially political movement with a political set of demands; it was 'a completely political phenomenon', he contended.[62] At the same time he argued that 'we are going through a phase of patrimonialism, where no polity yet exists, and where politics is interpreted as a purely personal matter'.[63] In his eyes, somewhat paradoxically, it was necessary for a political act to

resigned from the Mosharekat Party in what many reputable observers have compared to 'Stalinist-style show trials'. In the course of his 'confession', he was quoted as stating that the works of Max Weber, Jürgen Habermas, and Talcott Parsons were responsible for jeopardising the country's national security. 'Hajjariyan: bekhater-e enherafat va khesarat-ha'i keh beh mardom zadim az hezb-e Mosharekat este'fa mikonam', *Fars News Agency* 03/06/1388 [25 August 2009].

Hajjariyan's 'confession' is symptomatic of a deep-seated hostility to critical social theory, which dates back at least to the early 1990s when the programme *Hoviyyat* (Identity) was broadcast on national television and systematically attempted to depict secular and even some religious intellectuals who drew on critical methods in the social sciences as subversive and dangerous. The program even used material originating in confessions extracted under duress when political prisoners such as 'Ezatollah Sahabi had been imprisoned years previously. Sahabi claims he was interrogated by Hosayn Shari'at-madari, the incumbent editor of *Kayhan* newspaper, while the latter was still working in the service of the Ministry of Intelligence. Sahabi, *Nim-e qarn-e khatereh va tajrobeh*, pp. 209–12.

[60] Hajjariyan, 'Dovvom-e Khordad: omid-ha va bim-ha: payam-ha va cheshm andaz-ha', p. 17.
[61] 'Falsafeh-ye entekhabat', p. 538.
[62] 'Dovvom-e Khordad: omid-ha va bim-ha: payam-ha va cheshm andaz-ha', p. 17.
[63] Hajjarian and Ehsani, 'A Conversation with Sa'id Hajjarian', p. 41.

limit the *vali-ye faqih*'s power by law so that a polity might be forged. This in turn would lead to what he called the rationalisation and depersonalisation of politics, as established bureaucratic, impersonal, and meritocratic (*shayesteh-salar*) procedures were incrementally absorbed and institutionalised in the country's political institutions.[64] In this way, the Islamic Republic in Weberian terminology, which by Hajjariyan's own account is his key point of reference,[65] would have traversed the phases of charismatic authority and unmediated populism (Khomeini) to patrimonialism (Khameneh'i) transitioning into popular-democratic legitimacy and rational-legal bureaucratic authority and management (Hajjariyan and the Mosharekat Front's avowed political objective).[66] The Islamic *chap*'s victory on the 2nd Khordad had been an initial step in this direction and had introduced what Hajjariyan would term 'dual sovereignty' (*hakemiyyat-e dowganeh*), whereby patrimonialism would govern alongside institutions predicated on elections and popular sovereignty,[67] even if the latter continued to harbour numerous shortcomings. Hajjariyan observes that the clergy itself had proven incapable of bringing about 'dual sovereignty' in the form of patrimonialism in parallel with a form of 'clerical aristocracy', by which he appears to mean the enduring institution of *marja'iyyat* and the continued influence of leading clerical families and their networks in Qom.[68] Following the death of Grand Ayatollah Seyyed Mohammad-Reza Golpayegani in 1993, the last to pass of the four most prominent Iran-based *maraje'* at the time of Khomeini's return from exile, the clergy instead found itself incorporated within the Islamic state's bureaucracy.[69] Notably, it was none other than Golpayegani who had been resoundingly defeated by Khameneh'i, 60 to 14, in the Assembly of Experts election, elevating Khameneh'i to the leadership in the first place. Rafsanjani's diaries of 1989 claim that, in the debates leading up to the famous election, Khameneh'i had disagreed with the notion of an individual clergyman succeeding Khomeini as *vali-ye faqih* and instead expressed his preference for the

---

[64] Hajjariyan, 'Falsafeh-ye entekhabat', p. 539.   [65] 'Mashruteh-talabi', p. 122.
[66] '"Velayat-e motlaqeh-ye faqih" va "qanun-e asasi" (1) [Originally published in *'Asr-e ma*, no. 61, 1375/11/19 (07/02/1997)]', p. 265.
[67] 'Mashruteh-talabi', p. 126.
[68] For details, see Linda S. Walbridge, ed. *The Most Learned of the Shi'a: The Institution of the Marja' Taqlid* (Oxford & New York: Oxford University Press, 2001), Introduction and chapter 13.
[69] Hajjariyan, 'Mashruteh-talabi', p. 123.

formation of a council, a view which in later years was commonly attributed to Rafsanjani as well and would also appear to be confirmed in leaked video footage of the Assembly of Experts' vote on the issue discussed in Chapter 3.[70]

Managed Participation Confronts Entrenched Unaccountability

While Hajjariyan had always been practical-minded and capable in administrative and managerial tasks, Khatami's victory provided impetus to thinking through how the political platform of the executive and Islamic left might in fact be realised given the many constitutional and institutional obstacles it now faced. Two key issues occupied him during Khatami's first term, both of which in limited fashion were addressed by the incumbent administration. The first that will be briefly touched upon was restraining the Guardian Council and its ability not only to strike down legislation, which it regarded as violating Islamic law, but also to veto prospective electoral candidates for the presidency, parliament, and Assembly of Experts.[71] The second was the problem of increasing and ensuring high levels of political participation through institutionalised electoral channels, since it was held that high participation would by default lead to the victory of the Islamic *chap*, while a low turnout due to apathy would inevitably be to their detriment.

Returning to the first issue, Hajjariyan came up with some pertinent arguments on how to introduce a constitutional court (*dadgah-e qanun-e asasi*), which might perform the role of judicial review and thus act as a body to which citizens could lodge complaints if they felt their rights had been infringed or violated by other organs of the state. In this way, their rights would be independently protected and not have to rely upon the caprice of the executive or judicial branch alone. It would also re-establish a de facto separation of powers, by which the Guardian Council could be checked since this principle had been 'tarnished', according to Hajjariyan.[72] This body would also examine those instances whereby laws passed by the Majles or Expediency Council

---

[70] Hashemi-Rafsanjani and Lahuti, *Karnameh va khaterat-e 1368: bazsazi va sazandegi*, pp. 149–51.

[71] Ravabet-e 'omumi-ye daftar-e tahkim-e vahdat, ed. *Nezarat-e estesvabi* (Tehran: Nashr-e afkar, 1378 [1999]), p. 92.

[72] Hajjariyan, 'Pasdari az qanun-e asasi', p. 483.

were held to have infringed upon individual citizens' rights. The content of such rights would not be determined in terms of their consonance with a traditionalist conception of the *shari'ah*[73] and can be interpreted as an important dividend of the religious intellectuals' efforts to justify rights independently of either *feqh* or scriptural authority. Such basic entitlements were the rightful endowment of citizens independent of the rulings or purview of Islamic jurists. Moreover, candidates disqualified by the Guardian Council would hypothetically possess a body to which they could turn and potentially overturn the rulings of the Guardian Council.

The Guardian Council is not answerable to any authority regarding its decisions (the rejection of laws approved by the Majles, interpretation of the Constitution and the determination of the competency of candidates) and complaints against them go unheard. Perhaps the duty of a constitutional court could be the scrutiny of complaints against the Guardian Council.[74]

This proposal was also linked for Hajjariyan to the question of keeping electoral participation high, since if reformist candidates were not permitted to stand for elected bodies in the first place there would be little chance of inducing large turnouts and governments with popular mandates for substantive change. This innovative proposal, first aired in *'Asr-e ma* in December 1997, was never realised, but it was putatively intended to follow on from Khatami's appointment of a Commission for the Implementation and Supervision of the Constitution at the end of November.[75] With the appointment of this commission consisting of five jurists, Khatami invoked the relevant presidential prerogative as stipulated in article 113 of the constitution, which Hajjariyan mentions explicitly.[76] It was also thought by invoking article 13 of the 1986 Law of Delimitation of the Functions, Powers, and Responsibilities of the President that Khatami would be empowered to rebuke branches of government in the instance of

---

[73] The issue of the Guardian Jurist's power of 'executive order' or *hokm-e hokumati*, which could putatively override the *shari'ah* in the name of the 'preservation of the Islamic system', acted as an effective veto on unwelcome legislation and was used on occasion by Khameneh'i, most notably against a proposed press law in August 2000, still seems not to have presented itself as a serious problem.

[74] Hajjariyan, 'Pasdari az qanun-e asasi', p. 485.

[75] Hosayn Mehrpur, *Ra'is-e jomhur va ma'suliyyat-e ejra'i-ye qanun-e asasi*, 2 vols., vol. 1 (Tehran: Etela'at, 2001), pp. 13–15.

[76] More on this issue below. Hajjariyan, 'Pasdari az qanun-e asasi', p. 479.

a constitutional violation.[77] Hajjariyan, spotting the obvious weaknesses of article 13 of the 1986 Law, tried to call for something like an independent judicial review with real teeth. The proposition, however, never managed to get off the ground.

Another maxim the reformist camp took up with alacrity was that of 'realising the hidden capacity (zarfiyyat)'[78] of the constitution and implementing those constitutional articles which 'have not reached the stage of actuality (fe 'liyyat) in practice'.[79] The main constitutional articles that he had in mind and saw as pivotal to increasing the leverage of popular institutions against appointed ones were article 113, which gave the president responsibility for supervising the implementation of the constitution, and articles 100–106, elaborating the functions and responsibilities of directly elected city, township, and village councils. As mentioned above, Khatami actually appointed a Commission for the Implementation and Supervision of the Constitution, citing article 113, in the hope that it might permit the president to counter the prerogative of the Guardian Council to interpret the constitution as stipulated in article 98. In his own analysis, Hajjariyan neglects to mention the second clause of article 113, which permits the president to undertake the constitution's execution 'except in matters directly concerned with the office of the Leadership'. This would make the issue a lot more nebulous than Hajjariyan had arguably been prepared to admit, especially given the same article also states that the president is second to the Leader in the regime power structure.[80]

On a related note, article 57 of the constitution which stipulated the Leader's 'supervision' (nezarat) of the three branches of government (the actual wording of the article is zir-e nazar-e velayat-e motlaqeh-ye amr, under the view of the Absolute Guardianship to Rule) was another point of contention between Hajjariyan and Khatami. Hajjariyan sought to interpret it merely at the level of the Leader's being informed (etela'i), whereas since at least 1992 article 57 had predominantly been interpreted

---

[77] Arjomand, After Khomeini, Loc 2055.
[78] Sa'id Hajjariyan, 'Sharhi bar maram-nameh-ye jebheh-ye mosharekat-e Iran-e eslami', Mosharekat, no. 27 (18 Shahrivar 1378 [9 September 1999]).
[79] 'Pasdari az qanun-e asasi', p. 479.
[80] It also ignores ample legislation dating back to the early 1980s where the Guardian Council's prerogative to supervise elections had been codified. Daftar-e tahkim-e vahdat, Nezarat-e estesvabi, pp. 92–3.

as 'approbatory' (*estesvabi*). This second reading, which had been in the ascent after Khomeini's death, was one of the bases of the judiciary's and the Guardian Council's ability to stonewall the executive.[81]

Khomeini's massive popular following had allowed him to simply override the Guardian Council if he sensed its views were out of step with the popular mood and revolutionary atmosphere, without any significant consequences; and in several instances where this occurred, the Imam had ruled in favour of the Islamic left. In his absence, they could no longer beseech the patriarch to intervene on their behalf and so were compelled to constrain the Guardian Council by an alternative reading of the revised constitution. As should be clear from the exposition of Khatami's pronouncements on the issue in the previous chapter, the president was unable to make the leap, which had been made by the more radical wing of the Islamic *chap*, and it is because of the failure to clarify his position on article 57 that Khatami's relationship with Hajjariyan began to suffer.[82] Most on the more radical wing of the left saw the issue of the Guardian Council's powers over elections as Ganji did, even if they sought to be more circumspect in their expression: 'approbatory supervision (*nezarat-e estesvabi*) was approved by the right (*rast*) to give a legal veneer to the elimination of their rivals in the political arena'.[83] Rather than mere arbitrary violence, however, such practices were evidence of a reliance upon and deployment of the law and legal mechanisms against political adversaries. *Sobh-e emruz* regularly carried Mosharekat's party political positions, which took direct aim at the Guardian Council. One communiqué published on 1 June 1999 expressed their analysis with utmost clarity and candour:

The basic philosophy of supervision (*nezarat*) is that a few people can discern the essence of Islamic government, and they have a view that anyone in disagreement with that interpretation, should be prevented from entering parliament. This matter has led them to believe in their wardship (*qaymuniyyat*) over the people. The Participation Front at present holds the approbatory supervision (*nezarat-e estesvabi*) of the Guardian Council is establishing a wrong approach. Any person in a position of power who gives himself permission to

---

[81] Hajjariyan and Salimi, 'Suteh delan gerd-e ham amadand', p. 64.
[82] Ibid., p. 65.
[83] Akbar Ganji, 'Tavan-e sangin-e poruzheh-ye towse'eh-ye siyasi (Originally published in *Sobh-e emruz*, 15/6/1378 [6 September 1999])', in *Tarikkhaneh-ye ashbah: asib-shenasi-ye gozar beh dowlat-e demokratik towse'eh-gara* (Tehran: Tarh-e now, 1379 [2000]), p. 385.

express an opinion and decide upon the competence of individuals and their rights [to stand for election] ... experience has shown that it eliminates political activists and results in the promotion of marginal figures (*afrad-e hashiyyeh 'i*). Because of these individuals' rootlessness (*bi-risheh*) [within the system], in cases it results in cases where the system and revolution are struck at ... Such behaviour is certainly an insult to the revolutionary society of Iran.[84]

Without getting into the minutiae, the debates surrounding articles 113 and 99 drove Khatami's introduction of the so-called 'Twin Bills' (*lavayeh-ye dowqolu*) in September 2002, to both expand his own powers and limit the Guardian Council's approbatory supervision of elections. Their predictable rejection at the hands of the Guardian Council and their humiliating withdrawal by Khatami in April 2004 at the end of his second term was arguably made all the more inevitable by the president's failure to clarify his position in just the way demanded by Hajjariyan.[85] Admittedly, it is equally conceivable that a more adversarial Khatami, one who was prepared to challenge the scope and extent of the Leader's authority, would have provoked a violent backlash by the appointed organs under the latter's control, which in any event effectively came to pass a mere two years into the president's first term. Again, this was a symptom of the fundamental challenge I mentioned in Chapter 1, which speaks to the limitations of an ideological hegemony largely excluded from meaningful control over the means of violence and coercion.

The founding of the Participation Front for Islamic Iran (*Hezb-e jebheh-ye mosharekat-e Iran-e eslami*) in 1998, a year after Mohammad Khatami's electoral victory, was largely the outcome of the efforts of those individuals and groups of the Islamic *chap*, which, prior to the 2nd Khordad, had reached the conclusion that the fate of 'political development' was intertwined with that of 'political participation'.[86] Mosharekat's official stance in keeping with the arguments of both Hajjariyan and Bashiriyeh was to see 'political

---

84 'Nezarat-e shura-ye negahban amri mosallam ast, ama ghayd-e estesvabi nadarad,' *Sobh-e emruz* (11/3/1378 [1 June 1999]).

85 'Nameh-ye Mohammad Khatami beh Mehdi Karrubi', *BBC Persian* (13 April 2004).

86 Hossein Bashiriyeh's writings on this score were an important point of departure, and the fact that he acted as a doctoral supervisor to some of Iran's main 'reformist' strategists (e.g., Sa'id Hajjariyan and Mostafa Tajzadeh) is by no means a coincidence. See Hossein Bashiriyeh, 'Mosharekat-e siyasi, reqabat-e siyasi va towse'eh-ye siyasi', in *'Aql dar siyasat* (Tehran: Negah-e mo'aser, 1382 [2003]), p. 581.

participation' (*mosharekat-e siyasi*) as a cornerstone of their political programme. In line with a noted current in Anglo-American political science, which had since been taken up by several Iranian academics, it was held that the greater the levels of political participation, the 'more developed' the political order.[87] In several respects, the Participation Front was an experiment to realise this principle in practice, since participation was considered a necessary, if not sufficient condition for democratic development. Theories and ideas are rarely put into practice as their originators had intended, and the Participation Front preoccupied itself with harnessing socio-political forces which could encompass and mobilise a broader cross-section of Iranian society, reaching out to women and ethnic and religious minorities, many of whom had had an ambivalent relationship to political activism and civic engagement following the revolution. This effort was epitomised in the Front's slogan 'Iran for all Iranians', emitting a seductive aura of inclusivity and consciously challenging the nomenclature of 'insider' (*khodi*) and 'outsider' (*ghayr-e khodi*), which divided Iran's citizenry into two camps: those who were historically invested in the Islamic system's (*nezam*) establishment and its preservation; and everyone else.[88]

The elections for provincial councils held in February 1999 were part and parcel of the desire to boost and maintain high electoral turnout while ensuring that the seemingly amorphous populism, which had been characteristic of the revolution's first decade, would be channelled and regulated through an electoral process bestowing some form of popular legitimacy.[89] The municipal and village councils were an especially fortuitous forum to test-run the principles of mass participation and popular mobilisation, given that there was no stipulation in the constitution investing the Guardian Council with the power to veto prospective candidates, not to mention the sheer number of them. Mostafa Tajzadeh as political deputy of the interior minister was responsible for organising the council elections and thereby extending

---

[87] Ibid., p. 581. A later volume edited by Bashiriyeh is also instructive in this regard. *Gozar beh demokrasi* (Tehran: Negah-e now, 1384 [2005]).

[88] This effort to appeal to a broader demographic can also be seen in Mosharekat's use of the nationalist anthem *Ey Iran* or the selective invocation and recollection of the memory of the popular nationalist premier Dr Mohammad Mosaddeq. See Ansari, *Iran, Islam and Democracy*, p. 206.

[89] Hajjariyan, 'Falsafeh-ye entekhabat', p. 539.

electoral participation to villages throughout the country.[90] Over half a million candidates competed for seats in 900 municipal councils and 35,000 villages and saw reformists win 80% of the popular vote.[91] Mohammad Na'imipur, a member of the Mosharekat Front's central committee, contended that 47% of those elected were Mosharekat candidates.[92] On all accounts, it could be considered a triumph. Participation was prioritised above increasing political pluralism and the broader competitiveness of elections, since in the Islamic *chap*'s estimation it was naturally the first priority that their own candidates get past the Guardian Council and be permitted to stand.[93] As Hajjariyan would state in his analysis of Mosharekat's charter, 'we thought that with the establishment of the Islamic Iran Participation Front we could draw on our own share to create variety and plurality and lawful and institutionalised competition'.[94] The chief objective for Hajjariyan was to establish the precedent of electoral competition in which 'at least two "firms"' would accept elections, and not extra-legal means and violence, as the only legitimate basis of political contention.[95] Candidates of the Freedom Movement and Religious Nationalists which had long been considered the 'loyal opposition',[96] despite having had their candidates systematically disqualified since at least the Third Majles in 1988, was next on the list but hardly a high priority. No other groups were ever seriously considered.

This was in contrast to academic political scientists who had directly impacted Hajjariyan, Tajzadeh, and other members of Mosharekat but whose professional lives and ideological-orientation were extraneous to the factional wranglings of the *nezam*, of which Bashiriyeh is the most prominent example. In the case of the latter, ideological competition and the rotation of elites were held as central for political

---

[90] For a detailed account of the right's partisan attack on Tajzadeh's management of the Sixth Majles elections, as well as the judicial pressure that was brought to bear against him, see Mostafa Tajzadeh and Babak Dad, *Ra'i-ye mardom: mohakemeh va defa'iyyat-e Seyyed Mostafa Tajzadeh* (Tehran: Tarh-e now, 1380 [2001]).

[91] Arjomand, *After Khomeini*, Loc 2035.

[92] '47 dar sad-e montakhabin-e shura-ha az kandida-ha-ye jebheh-ye mosharekat hastand', *Sobh-e emruz* (29/01/1378 [18 April 1999]).

[93] Hajjariyan, 'Sharhi bar maram-nameh-ye jebheh-ye mosharekat-e Iran-e eslami'.

[94] Ibid.   [95] Hajjarian and Ehsani, 'A Conversation with Sa'id Hajjarian', p. 41.

[96] See Chehabi, *Iranian Politics and Religious Modernism*, chapter 8.

development to prosper and remain viable.[97] To be fair to Hajjariyan, he did indeed acknowledge this deficiency, but such acknowledgements were a rare occurrence.[98] Such an objective did not seem practicable or even desirable to either Mosharekat or any other groups of the Islamic left at the time, and with good reason, since they were hard-pressed to stay in the race themselves.

Mosharekat's first chairman was President Khatami's brother, Mohammad-Reza Khatami (1998–2005), a physician by training, who had himself been amongst the students that seized the U.S. embassy in November 1979. Other prominent members like Hajjariyan held mass participation in elections to be crucial to expanding the democratic capacity of the Islamic Republic's political system and had also collaborated with Khatami in the intellectual networks of the early 1990s. Other prominent figures such Mohsen Mirdamadi, Mostafa Tajzadeh, Rajab-'Ali Mazru'i, Hadi Khaniki, 'Abbas 'Abdi, and 'Ali-Reza 'Alavi-Tabar had also been well-known participants in these networks encompassing the Kiyan and Ayin circles, the Centre for Strategic Research, and the Mojahedin Organisation of the Islamic Revolution of Iran (SMEEI), as well as newspapers such as *Salam*. This group of individuals, while undoubtedly comprising part of the Islamic left, were younger laypersons and, to a large extent, were more radically disposed towards restructuring state power than their clerical allies in the Association for Combatant Clerics. Despite their best efforts to persuade the president, the older Khatami refused to join the party and expressly told Hajjariyan that he did not want to be a leader of the opposition but of the country as a whole, quickly casting aside any hope that he might become 'the leader of a social movement'.[99]

The Participation Front's charter opened by declaring that 'the epic of the 2nd of Khordad was another manifestation of the 22nd of Bahman [i.e. the day the *ancien régime* fell], which added to the clarity (*shafafiyyat*) of the revolution's values and hastened the people's

---

[97] Hossein Bashiriyeh, 'Mosharekat-e siyasi va towse'eh-ye siyasi', *Rah-e now* 1, no. 1 (5 Ordibehesht 1388 [April–May 1998]), pp. 6–7. 'Mosharekat-e siyasi, reqabat-e siyasi va towse'eh-ye siyasi', p. 587.

[98] I have come across one such instance thus far in my reading of Hajjariyan's voluminous writings. Sa'id Hajjariyan, 'Bohran-e dowganegi dar qodrat', in *'Obur az Khatami*, ed. Amir-Reza Sotudeh (Tehran: Zekr, 1379 [2000]), p. 108.

[99] Hajjariyan and Salimi, 'Suteh delan gerd-e ham amadand', p. 65.

movement towards a just and wise society. The 2nd of Khordad was another manifestation of the unity and alliance between the enlightened clergy and pious intellectuals.'[100] After acknowledging the role of religious intellectuals, the charter goes on to incorporate a welter of tropes from the canon of post-revolutionary religious intellectualism such as respect for disparate interpretations of religion, opposition to 'ideology',[101] rational and peaceful dialogue, religious democracy, rational governance, respect for enshrined legal rights, incremental change and the benefits of accumulated experience,[102] acknowledgement of political and religious pluralism within the framework of the constitution, and, lastly, political development.[103] Quixotic as it might sound, in his analysis of Mosharekat's charter in the eponymously named party organ Hajjariyan insisted that political parties with an ideology normally reflect 'dogmatism' (*jazmiyyat*) in their public manifestos. This is something he claims Mosharekat had sought to avoid. Such statements can best be explained by taking into consideration the recoil against anything which smacked of the idiosyncratic conception of 'ideology' advocated by religious intellectuals, foremost Sorush, from the early 1990s and their aggrandisement of putatively 'apolitical' technocratic standards and competencies. Such pretence sat uneasily with the Front's bolder political stances on constitutional politics, the Khatami government, and the future of the Iranian economy.

Hajjariyan argued that it was imperative to use Mosharekat as a party vehicle for the transference of an identity and bounded set of experiences to a new generation of Iranian youth, which had not directly experienced the revolution.[104] It is in this way that the Islamic *chap* sought to impart their views and narrative of the

---

[100] Shadlu, *Ettela'ati dar bareh-ye ahzab va jenah-ha-ye siyasi-ye Iran-e emruz*, p. 370.

[101] Hajjariyan, 'Sharhi bar maram-nameh-ye jebheh-ye mosharekat-e Iran-e eslami'.

[102] Ibid.

[103] Abbas Shadlu, 'Hezb-e jebheh-ye mosharekat-e Iran-e eslami', in *Etela'ati dar bareh-ye ahzab va jenah-ha-ye siyasi-ye Iran-e emruz* (Tehran: Nashr-e vozara, 1387 [2008]), p. 380.

[104] Hajjariyan, 'Sharhi bar maram-nameh-ye jebheh-ye mosharekat-e Iran-e eslami'. Another example of such efforts to forge group solidarity and socialisation would be during Moharram, when Mosharekat supporters and politically aligned clerics would congregate in designated mosques to mourn the death of Imam Hosayn. 'Marasem-e sowgvari-ye salar-e shahidan dar jebheh-ye mosharekat', *Sobh-e emruz* 4/2/1378 [24 April 1999].

revolution and its aftermath – in short, their own ideology and politicised historiography – to succeeding generations and thus expand their social base while carefully regulating newly inducted cadres. In other words, it would have to be a controlled process of harnessing a broader range of social forces, which were not already themselves in possession of an organisation and a hierarchical political structure of their own. By speaking in putatively universal terms, namely the discourse of abstract rights and equality before the law, this elite group sought to conserve and possibly extend the active consent of subaltern groups and what Bayat has called nonmovements to their leadership.[105] Moreover, they would endeavour to exercise a considerable degree of control over them and finally mobilise subaltern classes against their political rivals in the context of civil and electoral contestation – in short, establish a fragile hegemony and historical bloc to give necessary impetus to their program.

Despite such outreach, its limitations were also strongly felt throughout the Iranian intelligentsia. Secular intellectuals such as the sociologist Changiz Pahlavan continued to speak boldly of the continued existence of 'second class citizens' – namely, those individuals considered suspect and disloyal by the political system. Individuals not connected to anyone of the ruling factions in the political class and therefore deprived of any of the latter's associated privileges.[106] In the words of Pahlavan, 'this [second-class] citizen is not only ostracised by the state, but also by the "official" opposition ... In the publication '*Asr-e ma* the individuals of society were divided into three categories: (1) supporters of the system, (2) legal opposition, and (3) those who wage war against (*mohareb*) and seek to overthrow the system (*barandaz*). The first are considered insiders (*khodi*) and the second and third are outsiders (*ghayr-e khodi*). Apart from this there is another division, the first and the second are categorised as legal and the third illegal.'[107] Pahlavan

---

[105] This does, of course, not mean that such social non-movements simply brought to a halt their 'quiet encroachment of the ordinary'. Everyday resistances would continue regardless. Bayat, *Life as Politics*, p. 28.

[106] Changiz Pahlavan, 'Dovvom-e khordad 1376 va bohran-e gozar (1)', *Rah-e now* 1, no. 4 (26 Ordibehesht 1377 [16 May 1998]), p. 10. Pahlavan's speech during the Berlin conference is also illuminating in this regard. 'Matn-e sokhanrani-ha-ye ruz sevvom', in *Konforans-e berlin; khedmat ya khiyanat*, ed. Mohammad-'Ali Zakariya'i (Tehran: Tarh-e now, 1379 [2000]), pp. 168–75.

[107] 'Dovvom-e khordad 1376 va bohran-e gozar (1)', p. 10.

appeared to imply that not only were the reformists implicated in the exclusion of non-insider intellectuals and political forces but that they substantively benefited from it as well.

In the final years of the Khatami government, Hajjariyan, too, was prepared to admit the ultimately 'elitist' nature of the Islamic *chap*'s reform agenda.[108] A predictable cycle of electoral mobilisation, followed by demobilisation when the excitement of the electoral season had subsided, and the reformist political class had found itself voted into power, seemed to have established itself. He could also be unapologetic and patronising, especially of Iranian youth who were for their part expected to stand by and deferentially heed the exhortations of elder statesmen, who continued to excuse their own youthful indiscretions: 'the youth mustn't be allowed to head in the direction of an alternative [i.e., to Islamic *chap*-led reform]. [We] must propagate (*tabliq*) against other paths. The difference between our young friends and others is that the younger they are the more revolutionary they become.'[109] In making this statement the brutally repressed student protests of July 1999 and their aftermath could not have been far from Hajjariyan's mind.

Both the reformist press and Mosharekat enjoyed considerable student support. Moreover, it would be remiss not to mention that the incident which sparked the student protests of July 1999 was the closure of none other than *Salam* newspaper. Mosharekat fiercely objected not only to the closure of this stalwart paper of the left but also to the violent crackdown meted out to students following their protestations.[110] In a communiqué published on 11 July 1999, they not only demanded the immediate firing of the chief of Law Enforcement but also that the commanders overseeing police operations during the crackdown be charged and convicted. Unsurprisingly, the Mosharekatis also sought to defuse a situation, taking refuge in the law, advising restraint, since they were extremely concerned about the violence spiralling out of all control and

---

[108]   Hajjariyan and Salimi, 'Suteh delan gerd-e ham amadand', p. 63.
[109]   Ibid., p. 66.
[110]   Mosharekat Front, to a considerable extent, emerged out of these networks of personalities, organisations, and publications, and this is clearly in evidence in the way it reacted to the closure of *Salam* newspaper, which it deemed illegal. 'Bayaniyeh-ye jebheh-ye mosharekat-e Iran-e eslami dar bareh-ye towqif-e ruznameh-ye salam', *Sobh-e emruz* 19/04/1378 [10 July 1999].

providing a pretext for additional crackdowns: 'at this stage the fundamental priorities of any political action are the observance of vigilance, awareness, equanimity and good judgement in the face of this portentous event and restraint from any kind of extremism, violence or law-breaking'.[111]

Despite such rhetoric, the Islamic *chap* struggled to form a front which could genuinely and systematically incorporate social forces beyond its own inner sanctum. Even amongst 'insiders', Mosharekat and the more established SMEEI found it difficult to engage in constructive collaboration and fully succeed in the process of *kadr-sazi* or cadre-building they had envisaged, let alone democratically incorporate a broader array of social forces cutting across Iranian society.[112] This was despite the fact that Mosharekat had members who were also prominent figures in the SMEEI. Hajjariyan, for instance, recounted how Front members had concluded that a mass party was necessary if the programme of political development was to be realised. To this end, Hajjariyan and the other founders of Mosharekat had decided to explore the prospect of joining the SMEEI. In response, Mohammad Salamati, the party's chairman, stated that it would take a year until its charter could be changed, permitting new members to join the organisation. As a result, Hajjariyan later described the Mojahedin as 'a minibus and it did not have room'.[113] Aqajari echoed this statement, adding that the SMEEI was also explicitly founded as a political 'cadre' and never intended to be a mass political organisation.[114] Ultimately, it did not even prove feasible to incorporate the 120 founding signatories of the Mosharekat Party, let alone a mass party with a countrywide membership penetrating deep into the provinces.[115]

---

[111] 'Bayaniyyeh-ye jebheh-ye mosharekat-e Iran-e eslami beh monasebat-e havades-e akhir-e ku-ye daneshgah-e Tehran', *Sobh-e emruz* 20/04/1378 [11 July 1999].

[112] This term is explicitly used by Hajjariyan vis-à-vis Mosharekat. Hajjariyan, 'Sharhi bar maram-nameh-ye jebheh-ye mosharekat-e Iran-e eslami'.

[113] Hajjariyan and Khojasteh-Rahimi, 'Eslahatchi, cheriki nemishavad', p. 45.

[114] Hashem Aqajari, Reza Khojasteh-Rahimi, and Amir-Hosayn Bala'i, 'Sharh-e zendegi-ye yek enqelabi-ye naaram: goftogu ba Hashem Aqajari', *Andisheh-ye puya* 2, no. 11 (Mehr–Aban 1392 [October–November 2013]), p. 42.

[115] Sa'id Hajjariyan and Reza Khojasteh-Rahimi, 'Eslahatchi, cheriki nemishavad: sharh-e yek zendegi-ye siyasi-fekri', *Andisheh-ye puya* (Tir–Mordad 1391 [July–August 2012]), p. 45.

From the 2nd Khordad Front to the Green Movement

While previously revolutionary clerics had been preoccupied with ensuring mass mobilisation to support a programme that was, in the final analysis, often orchestrated by a small elite circle, Hajjariyan and the other members of Mosharekat had hoped that by increasing the number of regular elections not only would the Islamic *chap*'s democratic legitimacy be consolidated but the results would better reflect citizens' actual political and ideological preferences. The articulation of political preferences had previously been allowed insofar as they were given vent and expression in the street rally or Friday prayer sermon in support of the clerical leadership and against an anathematised Other. But by holding more elections with the robust presence of the Islamic *chap*, it was speculated that even those individuals who did not necessarily view the reformist candidate as their ideal representative would nevertheless vote for the candidate which they perceived as most proximate to them on the political spectrum.[116]

It was participation that would help realise Hajjariyan's mantra of 'pressure from below, bargaining from above', because he held political development impeded by 'political obstructions' (*ensedad-ha-ye siyasi*) could only be overcome on the basis of a dialectical synthesis between the two great revolutions which had transformed Iranian society in their own distinct ways. Hajjariyan believed that while the 1979 Revolution had been one of unadulterated popular mobilisation which culminated in a revolutionary outcome because of the Shah's unyielding absolutism, the Constitutional Revolution had primarily entailed a process of strategic bargaining within the political elite.[117] If the Islamic Republic was to avoid the catastrophic fate of the Pahlavi monarchy, the unaccountable organs of the state would have to incrementally come to terms with certain constraints on their exercise of power. It would, however, be naïve to think that such groups and institutions would willingly concede their accumulated privileges

---

[116] Hajjarian and Ehsani, 'A Conversation with Sa'id Hajjarian', p. 41.

[117] Baqi, *Baraye tarikh: goftogu ba Sa'id Hajjariyan*, p. 25. Needless to say, his characterisation of the Constitutional Revolution is highly contestable, especially in the light of the illuminating research of Janet Afary, amongst others. See Janet Afary, *The Iranian Constitutional Revolution: Grassroots Democracy, Social Democracy, and the Origins of Feminism* (New York: Columbia University Press, 1996).

without concerted pressure.[118] Participation and popular mobilisation through legally sanctioned elections in concert with voluntary and pro-active organisations in civil society were essential to leveraging unaccountable state organs into bowing to the policies pursued by the Khatami government and later reformist-dominated Sixth Majles. Though Khatami had called for an enlivened civil society and social life independent of the state, he was wary, if not timorous, vis-à-vis actually mobilising his supporters behind his policies. He instead preferred to rely on persuasion and cajoling his opponents out of the public eye. There was no mention or thought about seriously drawing on organised or unionised labour, and, despite Mosharekat's pretence to extend throughout the reaches of the country, the party hierarchy and upper echelons were frequently dominated by well-known figures of the Islamic left and their extended families. Hajjariyan in later years would be frank in his criticism, 'the elite thought that they could solve all their problems in closed circles (*halqeh-ha*), bargaining (*chaneh zani*) without pressure and the support of their social base'.[119] This glaring weakness and elitism was perhaps best illustrated, when preceding the Seventh Majles elections in early 2004, 131 sitting reformist MPs went on strike after 80 of their number had been disqualified by the Guardian Council and there was little by way of popular reaction.

Ironically, the extensive social mobilisation envisioned by Hajjariyan would only emerge on the streets of several Iranian cities in the summer of 2009 in the form of the Green Movement (*jonbesh-e sabz*), when the Islamic *chap* were no longer in power but instead had been vying for it in the presidential run-off between the incumbent Mahmud Ahmadi-Nezhad and the former prime minister and veteran of the Islamic left Mir-Hosayn Musavi. The Green Movement undoubtedly owed much of its intellectual and political maturity to the 2nd Khordad Front and entwined strains of religious intellectualism, which preceded it, and took many of the propositions that featured in the latter platforms to their logical conclusion. But, in several respects, it went further. It not only demanded free and fair elections, the rule of law, social justice, and constitutional reform, and spoke eloquently on the subjects of religious pluralism, tolerance and

---

[118] Pressure would initially come from 'public opinion', which would be least likely to provoke a backlash. Ibid., p. 26.

[119] Hajjariyan and Salimi, 'Suteh delan gerd-e ham amadand', p. 63.

inclusive citizenship, the dangers of intemperate ideology, self-criticism and open-ended dialogue: in a historic manifesto, it declared itself first and foremost a social movement, without a central leadership.[120] Such claims were partly rhetorical, partly substantive, but also in response to a *fait accompli*, given that many of the leading figures of Mosharekat, SMEEI, and the National Trust Party were arrested on the night of Ahmadi-Nezhad's fateful re-election or soon thereafter. Nevertheless, the claim of a leaderless movement not only made the Green Movement both a remarkable and novel occurrence in contemporary Iranian political history but also acted as a source of strength and weakness, arguably contributing to its inability to realise its demands in the short-to-medium term.[121]

Following the 2009 post-electoral tumult in which Tehran saw peaceful mass protests on a scale unprecedented since the revolution, intra-elite bargaining was incapable of convincing the Leadership or Guardian Council to reach a strategic compromise. For that to come to pass the reformists arguably had to wait until the 2013 presidential election and back a compromise candidate, Hojjat al-Islam Hassan Rowhani, who had ironically been instrumental in shutting down the political development project at the Presidential Strategic Research Centre in the first half of the 1990s.[122] The debt which many of Rowhani's campaign pledges and its slogan of 'Prudence and Hope' (*tadbir va omid*) owed to the legacy of President Khatami and the 2nd Khordad Front was certainly not lost on many reformists, who qualifiedly supported the centrist candidate while continuing to harbour tempered expectations of a propitious change in their fortunes.[123]

---

[120] 'Matn-e kamel-e virast-e dovvom-e manshur-e sabz', *Kalameh* 3 Esfand 1389 [22 February 2011].

[121] It is not my aim here to provide a comprehensive analysis of the Green Movement. For further analysis of this important moment in the history of Iranian social movements, see Hamid Dabashi, *Iran, the Green Movement and the USA: The Fox and the Paradox* (London & New York: Zed Books, 2010). Negin Nabavi, ed. *Iran: From Theocracy to the Green Movement* (New York: Palgrave Macmillan, 2012). Nader Hashemi and Danny Postel, eds., *The People Reloaded: The Green Movement and the Struggle for Iran's Future* (Brooklyn: Melville House, 2010).

[122] Hajjariyan and Salimi, 'Suteh delan gerd-e ham amadand', p. 61.

[123] Mojtaba Hosayni, 'Fayzollah 'Arabsorkhi dar goftogu ba "E'temad": rah-e eslahat rah-e Khatami ast', *E'temad* 26/05/1393 [17 August 2014].

Conclusion

Historically, revolutions have been factories of utopias; they have forged new imaginaries and new ideas, and have aroused expectancies and hopes ... [T]he twenty-first century is born as a time shaped by a general eclipse of utopias.[1]

Enzo Traverso

On 28 December 2018, protests broke out in the north-eastern city of Mashhad. Initially, chants were heard of 'death of Rouhani', the centrist president who had been overwhelmingly supported by leading reformists in two successive presidential elections. The protestors decried a still-stagnant economy and the Rouhani government's alleged negligence of the poorer segments of Iranian society in the aftermath of the nuclear accord with the P5+1, known in official circles as the Joint Comprehensive Plan of Action. But then something quite unexpected happened. This relatively modest protest rapidly gave way to a larger one of a far more unwieldly variety, and its demands quickly broke with the tacit rules defining Iran's factional tit-for-tat. Swiftly the protests began to mushroom throughout the country, eventually reaching over seventy provincial towns and villages. In terms of geographical scope, it was in certain respects unprecedented, and many areas saw demonstrations of this kind for the first time since the revolution, if ever. While some demands expressed anger at economic hardship, corruption, and lack of opportunities, as the protests persevered many of the chants became increasingly radical, lambasting not only the Supreme Leader but the *nezam* in its entirety. Perhaps even more surprising were chants in cities such as Qom, home to Iran's preeminent religious seminaries, in favour of the deposed Pahlavi Shahs. The protests were by and large peaceful in nature, but there were outbreaks of violence, both by the state and by the protestors with

---

[1] Enzo Traverso, *Left-Wing Melancholia: Marxism, History, and Memory* (New York: Columbia University Press, 2016), pp. 3–5.

meagre resources at their disposal, all captured on smart phones and circulated via social media throughout the country and the world.

But rather than embrace the protestors, some prominent reformists greeted them with trepidation and a fair degree of scepticism, with one of the grand theorists of the reformist project, Saʿid Hajjariyan, even appearing to equate much of what he witnessed to 'hooliganism' and 'vandalism'.[2] Despite a recognition of the economic and political drivers of the unrest, reformists were adamant in their insistence that protestors refrain from violence, looting, or the damage of public property.[3] While hardly unique to Iran's reformists there was a pattern of sorts – a decided fear of popular mobilisations which failed to correspond to pre-determined institutionalised forms of contestation. This hesitancy stemmed not merely from a clear preference for 'institutionalized conflicts', because, in the words of James C. Scott, 'Opposition institutions with names, office bearers, constitutions, banners, and their own internal governmental routines favor, naturally enough, institutionalized conflict, at which they are specialists.'[4] There were also deep-seated historical and ideological reasons, which led Iran's erstwhile Islamist revolutionaries to harbour grave concern towards non-institutionalised forms of popular mobilisation, 'disruptive power' and revolutionary transformation.[5] Indeed, the hostility of many prominent reformists, even if there continued to be diversity of opinion, to more radical challenges and non-institutional forms of political contestation had become so overwhelming that it had almost found itself turned into an eternal and inviolable imperative. This was perhaps best summed up in an interview with one-time guerrilla revolutionary cum reformist elder statesman Behzad Nabavi, who, in the aftermath of the seemingly leaderless protests that rocked the nation,

---

[2] Saʿid Hajjariyan, 'Fattiyan, luti-ha va khodsar-ha', *Sharq* 27 Dey 1396 [17 January 2018].

[3] A comment piece by Hajjariyan penned a week after the article of 27 Dey was more considered and nuanced and took both the drivers and complex composition of the protests more seriously. 'Pas az Rowhani', *E'temad* 4 Bahman 1396 [24 January 2018].

[4] James C. Scott, *Two Cheers for Anarchism: Six Easy Pieces on Autonomy, Dignity, and Meaningful Work and Play* (Princeton & Oxford: Princeton University Press, 2012), Loc 168.

[5] Frances Fox Piven, *Who's Afraid of Frances Fox Piven? The Essential Writings of the Professor Glenn Beck Loves to Hate* (New York & London: The New Press, 2011), p. 210.

reiterated his resolute opposition to the very notion of revolution and all it entailed: 'In prison I became anti-revolution, all revolutions! From the French Revolution to the Arab Spring. In my view, all revolutions have fundamental problems.'[6] There were good reasons to be fearful in the face of a belligerent Trump administration and the civil wars and conflicts that wracked several of Iran's neighbours. But the seeming inability to recognise, understand and meaningfully reach out to the protestors, if only to co-opt and calm them, in stark contrast to the historic election of 1997, threw into stark relief the limitations of the brand of reformism espoused by many of these distinguished politicians and intellectuals. And in the vocal denunciations of factionalism and the entirety of the political elite, we might well be witnessing not only a historic low point but what Gramsci famously termed an 'organic crisis', where 'the old is dying and the new cannot be born' in the two-decade-old articulation of reformism still cleaved to by a significant portion of the Iranian political class.[7]

While the semantics of 'reform' remained contested within the reformist apparatus cum hegemonic formation, I have tried to argue that its manifold valences emerged out of a specific historical trajectory and set of political traditions, which nevertheless drew inspiration across national and temporal boundaries. Though in many respects an elite-led and carefully managed process, it often harboured unpredictable results and reactions which the participants could hardly have foreseen. During their many political and ideological skirmishes, more radical religious intellectuals and members of the Islamic left took clerical guardianship and even Islamic jurisprudence to task and came to regard them as obstructions, not only to Iran's democratisation but to the democratisation of 'Islam' itself. This was, however, by no means a universal conclusion within the Islamic left or amongst the *rowshan-fekran-e dini*, but it is one which increasingly found itself with a receptive constituency. There were others who, while refusing such conclusions, were politically aligned and worked in step with the reform agenda for the rule of law, more vibrant electoral participation, and deepened civic engagement.

---

[6] Mashid Sotudeh, 'Behzad Nabavi dar goftogu ba *Vaqaye'-e etefaqiyeh*: Rowhani dar 9 sa'at yek bohran darad', *Vaqaye'-e etefaqiyeh* 3 Bahman 1396 [23 January 2018].

[7] Gramsci, *Selections From the Prison Notebooks*, p. 276.

In this book I have shown that – rather than some inevitable neo-Hegelian historico-rational unfolding of the self-consciousness of freedom – these individual and collective transformations were forged through conflict, bloodshed, unspeakable violence, irrecuperable loss, and myriad struggles to rebuild. To paraphrase Susan Buck-Morss, we cannot simply recount the tale of Iranian reformism as a coherent narrative of human freedom and its triumphant realisation.[8] The aim of the preceding chapters has been to try and problematise the depiction of 'religious intellectualism' as a cosmic battle between the forces of light and darkness, reason and unreason, or even the terminus of a rational-historical process, as some its exponents have been wont to claim. Nor was religious intellectualism and the crafting of 'reformism' a disembodied feat of grandiose intellection unscathed by more immediate political interests, personal and institutional rivalries, and jockeying, in which they were oftentimes embroiled. As I have argued, the advocates and exponents of reform within and tangential to the political class traversed a network of reading groups, periodicals, think tanks, government ministries, university faculties, connected families and interpersonal relationships, and mass-circulation newspapers; they consciously endeavoured to disseminate and propagate not only their critical views but in many respects their own moral leadership and symbolic capital. As a result, oftentimes the amorphous and internally differentiated discourse of 'religious intellectualism', like the political constellation of 'reform', came to define and shape the terms of political debate in important ways and was shaped by the balance and asymmetry of political forces in turn. It forged a new 'common sense' and hegemonic formation, which helped define the terrain and set the terms of ideological and political contestation, even after it ceased to occupy the executive or dominate the legislature.

Drawing a strict line demarcating 'religious intellectuals' on one side and the 'Islamic left' or 'reformist statesmen' on the other – as has often been the case in scholarship and, more importantly, the pronouncements of the actors themselves – should be greeted with scepticism, given their profound intertwinement. Over the last three decades, members of this sprawling network have *performed* the part of intellectual/internal critic and political entrepreneur and mobiliser. When a member of this constellation has found him- or herself under threat or

---

[8] Susan Buck-Morss, 'Hegel and Haiti', *Critical Inquiry* 26, no. 4 (2000), p. 822.

in precarious circumstances, such putative 'roles' and 'functions' have proven immaterial, as expressions of intra-elite solidarity across the political–intellectual divide asserted themselves and as the collective defence of the 'reformist' project and its stake in the 'original promise' of the revolution and the system it established came to the fore. These conclusions are not drawn to diminish their achievements but rather exhibit why the contours of this discursive formation have taken the form they have, as well as elicit some of the presuppositions which have taken for granted and been occluded in the re-presentation of their own activities as embedded public intellectuals and activists with informal and formal ties to the extant political order and its manifold institutions and personnel.

In Chapter 2 I explored the immense appeal of the image of the newly forged nation-state for Shi'i Islamism, which in important respects dispensed with the salvific millenarianism of the past and in its stead envisioned the state as a vehicle for the construction of a paradisiacal atemporal nomocracy, free of tension, doubt, or ambiguity. Both clergymen and laymen imagined this order coming into being, and both participated in a revolution awash with hopes of great transformation and definitive solutions.[9] However, following the bloody battles and repression for control of the state, the promissory declarations of future perfection with the assumption of power came up against unforeseen constraints, both domestic and international, which instigated a reconsideration of revolutionary voluntarism and the claim to enact God's will through the enforcement of the 'sacred' law. Many Iranian men and women, but for our purposes even those deeply committed young radicals such as Hashem Aqajari, Sa'id Hajjariyan, Ma'sumeh Ebtekar, Mostafa Tajzadeh, 'Emad al-Din Baqi, Zahra Rahnavard, Jamileh Kadivar, and Akbar Ganji, struggled to make sense of what had happened and the immensity of the rift between slogans and the reality of ignoble defeat, stasis, and lethargy. The repetitive experience of ideals coming up against brutal and recalcitrant realities increasingly came to be perceived as impugning not only the viability but the veracity of those same ideals. Cold War liberalism and anti-

---

[9] This political metaphysics of 'total change' has been most rigorously and powerfully critiqued in the work of Ali Mirsepassi. See Ali Mirsepassi, *Democracy in Modern Iran: Islam, Culture, and Political Change* (New York & London: New York University Press, 2010), Introduction. *Political Islam, Iran, and the Enlightenment Philosophies of Hope and Despair*, chapter 4.

communist polemics would provide much ideological ballast in rethinking the Islamic state anew.

Moreover, in reaction to their post-war and post-Khomeini political marginalisation by intra-elite competitors, the 'practical utility'[10] and efficacy of such discourses and signifiers as 'the end of ideology', enshrined God-given natural rights, constitutionalism, the critique of Oriental despotism and sultanism, and the rule of law became all the more tangible and palpable. Sometimes the strategic, polemical, and selective deployment of these concepts proved effective and at other times less so, while at the same time creating new blind-spots and dilemmas of their own. It was never simply a matter of North to South diffusion or imposition but rather uptake by Iranian actors in response to their own concrete struggles both within and without the state. As Dipesh Chakrabarty has observed in the case of South Asia, post-colonial intellectuals have worked tirelessly translating and mis-translating Western socio-political ideas and concepts in an effort to understand their own predicament and thereby grasp where they stand in relation to 'European Enlightenment' and 'modernity'.[11] Iranian intellectuals' efforts have similarly been characterised by periodic bouts of enchantment, repulsion, and confusion and the compulsion to dwell in a state of inept and more or less incongruous translations. This came about through a process of recognition and misrecognition of socio-political and religious parallels with salient images of Euro-Atlantic as well as Russian political and religious development, and the selective application and misapplication of the accompanying socio-political concepts putatively mirrored in Iran's own political and his-torical experiences. Such efforts regularly fell short of capturing the distinct dynamics which confronted these men (and they have predo-minantly been men) and women, and it is in this way that skewed prognostications and misleading diagnoses came to pass. It was a dynamic that could prove exceedingly creative but also crippling. Indeed, the staid binary of 'tradition versus modernity' which cast such a heavy shadow over Iranian intellectual debates in the 1990s and 2000s is just one corollary of these sorts of engagements.

---

[10] Dipesh Chakrabarty, 'Radical Histories and Question of Enlightenment Rationalism: Some Recent Critiques of Subaltern Studies', in *Mapping Subaltern Studies and the Postcolonial*, ed. Vinayak Chaturvedi (London & New York: Verso, 2000), Loc 6723.

[11] Ibid., Loc 6630. *Provincializing Europe*, p. 7; Loc 419.

But there were also numerous moments when the strategic deployment of such concepts appeared to closely map onto the country's institutional cartography, the power structure, and the adversaries in their polemics, leading them to profoundly resonate and thus find themselves redeployed and replicated time and again. In this way, they forcefully contributed to the refashioning of the political lexicon and the keywords used by intellectuals and statesmen to understand, explain, and make social and political reality intelligible. In the case of Iran, the religious intellectuals – and they were by no means an exception in this regard – have invoked their own specific translations, often culled from Euro-American philosophers and scholars, because of their apparent applicability and practical utility in the context of more local, concrete ideological struggles.

The *rowshanfekran-e dini* played a formidable role in subjecting the ruling political theology of *velayat-e faqih* and clerical guardianship to sustained criticism. Thus, as has been shown throughout the preceding chapters, in contradistinction to guardianship they argued for autonomy; rather than present a scriptural basis for morality and political agency they valorised extra-religious rational-normative criteria; and, in opposition to the personalised rule of God's intermediary, they demanded rationalised bureaucracy, technical expertise, and popular sovereignty expressed through free and fair elections. But religious intellectualism's focus on the question of religious authority meant that its challenge was first and foremost directed against the *discursive imperium* of the governing establishment, which sought to anchor its legitimacy in the scriptural sources of revelation and sacred verities. In this regard, many of the religious intellectuals' engagements can be viewed as largely abstracted from concrete socio-economic processes and how the latter might be understood, explained, and shaped. The focus of their critiques tended to reside with competing religious discourses and the hermeneutics which governed their construction as well as the sources of normativity and their desired model of social change, instead of the material forces which defined social reality and imbued it with content. With the notable exception of perhaps Sa'id Hajjariyan and a handful of others, concrete praxis and the means of realising their normative socio-political vision, and the relationship between the two, often proved less of a concern than the values by which it ought to abide. But it should be acknowledged that their critiques had the capacity to be both personal and political, directed against the persons who occupied appointed and deeply entrenched power centres and the political theology upon which their occupancy and powers were justified.

In the course of this book, I have also sought to show how the story of 'reform' in Iran is inextricable from a much larger global history. The end of the Cold War and the collapse of the Soviet Union, not to mention the effusion of unapologetic trans-Atlantic triumphalism which came on the heels of the Reagan Revolution and the First Gulf War,[12] catalysed 'the end of ideology' thesis and technocratic anti-politics in key respects popularised by ʿAbdolkarim Sorush, among others. This epochal shift reinforced the almost complete recession of any sustained consideration of imperial domination, human and cultural alienation, class struggle, social inequality, and economic exploitation – issues which had been of unparalleled significance for a pre-revolutionary generation of Iranian intellectuals.[13] This occurred in part because of the marginalisation and elimination of the Marxist left following the revolution, but perhaps more importantly because it was believed that much of this terrain had come to be occupied and monopolised by entrenched conservative elites against whom the reformists increasingly came to define themselves. It was also the result of their discursive preoccupation with the question of religious authority and its dovetailing with the seemingly implacable intellectual Euro-American neoliberal hegemony in the wake of 1989, where it was taken for granted, in the words of Francis Fukuyama, that world history had finally witnessed 'the total exhaustion of viable systematic alternatives to Western liberalism'.[14] Rather than perpetuate the historicist analogy of 'Islamic Reformation' and its tacit teleological assumptions implying that Iranian religious reformism was, and is little more than, an Islamic iteration of the earlier Protestant one, we should consider the extent to which Iranian reformism was, at least in part, the outcome of the historical interregnum out of which it emerged, and in response to the apparent paucity of alternatives to 'Western liberalism', which of course included Iran's very own ruling ideology of the Guardianship of the Jurist.

---

[12] Perry Anderson, *The Origins of Postmodernity* (London & New York: Verso, 1998), pp. 32, 91.

[13] This has since been acknowledged by individuals such as Mostafa Tajzadeh. See Tajzadeh and Dehbashi, 'Goftogu ba Mostafa Tajzadeh'.

[14] Fukuyama, 'The End of History?', p. 1.

Specific historical conjunctures, dynamics of symbolic and economic capital accumulation, and the perceived verisimilitude of critical concepts and notions in the context of politico-ideological struggles fostered the circulation and reproduction of certain nomenclatures and keywords instead of others. In the course of this process, discernible critical vocabularies flourished, while others found themselves condemned to decline and disappearance. Whereas 'dependency theory' and Andre Gunder Frank had been de rigueur in the era of Jalal Al-e Ahmad, when Mohammad-Reza Pahlavi was seen as the quintessential U.S. client-autocrat, it was Popper, Berlin, and Hayek, with their critiques of Nazi Fascism and Soviet Communism, who were very much in vogue by the 1990s. Liberalism, the valorisation of the minimal state and free markets, and the politics of compassion and humanitarianism supplanted the politics of resistance and anti-colonial struggle.[15] Moreover, human rights, in the words of Samuel Moyn, emerged as 'the last utopia ... one that became powerful and prominent because other visions imploded'.[16] This is merely one example, of course, and does not claim to exhaust the post-revolutionary intellectual field in its entirety. But it illustrates a broader shift in paradigm and ethos which has not merely been witnessed inside Iran but elsewhere in both the Global North and Global South.

While their conclusions were often ambivalent and mediated by the political environment and the dominant discourses in which they were embedded, Iran's post-revolutionary religious intellectuals have sought, with varying degrees of success, to vernacularise, define, and determine their own uneven experience of the experiment of the Islamic Republic and its relationship with an ethereal, though putatively universalisable, image of 'modernity'.[17] They decided to embrace disenchantment and the 'iron cage' out of genuine conviction but also as a gambit to challenge and transform the domestic status quo and balance of power, without much thought to what might follow in its aftermath.[18] Apart from the perceived inexorability of history, they

---

[15] Enzo Traverso, 'Marx, History, and Historians: A Relationship in Need of Reinvention', *Actuel Marx*, no. 50 (2011/2), vi.

[16] Moyn, *The Last Utopia: Human Rights in History*, Loc 59.

[17] Partha Chatterjee, 'Our Modernity', in *Empire and Nation: Selected Essays* (New York: Columbia University Press, 2010), p. 141; Loc 3060. More recently, see Anievas and Nisancioglu, *How the West Came to Rule*.

[18] This is of course Talcott Parson's disputed translation of Weber's phrase, *stahlhartes Gehäuse*, more recently translated as the 'shell as hard as steel',

were convinced that the future did not belong to misplaced nostalgia or nativist revanchism; the present needed to be reformed to save the future.

As Partha Chatterjee has remarked, 'There is no promised land of modernity outside the network of power ... [O]ne cannot be for or against modernity; one can only devise strategies for coping with it.'[19] The paradox and accompanying difficulties of trying to express agency, the power of critique, and autonomy within the interstices of the language of Western historical development and philosophy – and so many 'invented traditions',[20] symbols, myths, and customs – is one with which the Islamic Republic's intellectual and political elite and grass-roots democratic movements will continue to wrestle, albeit without any prospect of final resolution. The discourse of 'reform' and its ambient concepts in their current form are arguably unprepared for such a task, even while they mark an important landmark in the *longue dureé* of modern Iran's manifold struggles for 'emancipation' in and through the repudiation of much that preceded them.

symbolising the rationalisation of modern life under industrial capitalism, which finds itself increasingly encroached upon by hitherto unanticipated mechanisms of control, rational calculation, and bureaucratisation. See Max Weber, *The Protestant Ethic and the "Spirit" of Capitalism and Other Writings*, Kindle ed. (New York & London: Penguin Books, 2002), p. 121; Loc 3722.

19 Chatterjee, 'Our Modernity', p. 150; Loc 3232.
20 Eric Hobsbawm, 'Introduction: Inventing Traditions', in *The Invention of Tradition*, ed. Eric Hobsbawm and Terence Ranger (Cambridge & New York: Cambridge University Press, 1983), p. 9; Loc 217.

Appendix

	Kiyan	PSRC	SMEEI	Ershad	Mosharekat	Ayin	Khatt-e Imam	MRM	Serat	NAI	Salam	SFMMI
A. Sorush	x	x		x					x			
S. Hajjariyan	x	x	x (P)		x	x	x					
M. Tajzadeh	x		x	x	x	x (P)						
M. Mojtahed-Shabestari	x (P)								x			
Fazel Maybodi	x (P)					x						
M. Kadivar	x	x				x						
M. Khatami				x		x		x				
M. R. Khatami	x	x	x (P)		x	x	x					
A. R. 'Alavi-Tabar	x	x	x (P)		x	x (P)						
M. Malekiyan	x (P)				x (P)	x (P)			x (P)			
M. Musavi-Kho'iniha		x					x	x			x	
M. Aminzadeh	x			x	x	x (P)						
M. Shams ol-va'ezin	x											

	Kiyan	PSRC	SMEEI	Ershad	Mosharekat	Ayin	Khatt-e Imam	MRM	Serat	NAI	Salam	SFMMI
Behzad Nabavi		x	x			x (P)						
Hadi Khaniki	x (P)	x			x	x						
Arash Naraqi	x								x			
A. Ganji	x		x (P)						x			
Mohsen Armin	x	x	x	x								
Hashem Aqajari		x	x	x								
'Abbas 'Abdi	x	x			x	x	x				x	
R. A. Mazru'i				x		x						
H. R. Jala'ipur	x	x (P)			x	x			x			
M. Mirdamadi		x			x		x				x	
F. 'Arabsorkhi	x		x	x								

E. Baqi	x								
M. Bazargan	x (P)					x			
E. Sahabi	x (P)								x

Kiyan — Kiyan Circle
Ayin — Ayin Circle
SMEEI — Mojahedin Organisation of the Islamic Revolution of Iran
NAI — Freedom Movement of Iran
MRM — Association of Combatant Clerics
PSRC — Presidential Strategic Research Centre
Ershad — Ministry of Culture and Islamic Guidance
SFMMI — Council of National-Religious Activists of Iran
HJMIE — Participation Front for Islamic Iran
SFMMI — Council of National-Religious Activists of Iran
Khatt-e Imam — Though often used more broadly, here it designates the Muslim Student Followers of the Imam's Line and those affiliated with them.
Serat — Serat Institute and Publisher
(P) — Signifies individuals who were not amongst the formal or regular members of the group or circle in question but contributed intermittently to either its periodical or publications.

It must be noted that the above table does not indicate frequency of attendance, and this varies considerably between individuals. [1]

* Sorush was not a formal member of the PSRC, but he did attend the Centre on occasion.[1]

μ Sorush was on the Supreme Book Council at the Ministry of Culture and Islamic Guidance. Other members included Gholam-'Ali Haddad-'Adel, Reza Davari-Ardakani, Nasrollah Purjavadi, and the clerics Mohi al-Din Fazel-Harandi, Ahmad Jannati, and Rasuli Mahallati.[2]

∞ Hajjariyan was not a formal member of the SMEEI, but he did write regularly for their periodical 'Asr-e ma. He also was not formally a member of the Muslim Student Followers of the Imam's Line but delivered lectures at the U.S. embassy in the course of the hostage crisis.

Fig. 1 – Religious Intellectuals and Politicos of the Islamic Left: Past and Present Affiliations and Relationships

1 Alavi-Tabar and Mirsepassi, 'Alireza Alavi-Tabar and Political Change', p. 139.
2 Aqajari, Khojasteh-Rahimi, and Bala'i, 'Sharh-e zendegi-ye yek enqelabi-ye naaram', p. 42.

Glossary

Afsun zoda'i – Demystification, de-mythologisation
'Aql – Reason
'Aql-e enteqadi – Critical reason
Chap – Left
Din-e aqali – Minimal religion
Din-e askari – Maximal religion
Elteqati – Eclectic
Eslah talaban – Reformists
Eslah talabi – Reformism
Hakemiyyat-e qanun – Rule of law
Islam-e feqahati – Jurisprudential Islam
Jame'eh-ye madani – Civil society
Maktab – Doctrine
Maktabi – Doctrinaire
Mardom salari-ye dini – Religious democracy
Maqam-e mo'azzam-e rahbari – Office of Supreme Leadership
Mashru'iyyat – Legitimacy
Mashrutiyyat – Constitutionality
Mosharekat – Participation
Qabuliyyat – Acceptability
Qanun-e asasi – Constitution, Fundamental Law
Qanun gara'i – Law-orientedness
Qanun mandi – Legality
Qara'at-e rasmi-ye din – Official reading of religion
Rahbar – Leader
Rast-e jadid – New Right
Rast-e sonnati – Traditional Right
Rowhaniyyat – Clergy
Rowshanfekran-e dini – Religious intellectuals
Rowshangari – Enlightenment
Tahajom-e farhangi – Cultural onslaught
Taqlid – Emulation, imitation
Towse'eh-ye siyasi – Political development

Velayat-e faqih – Guardianship of the Jurist
Velayat-e motlaqeh-ye faqih – Absolute Guardianship of the Jurist
Vali-ye faqih – Guardian Jurist

Select Bibliography

Persian Primary Sources

'Abdi, 'Abbas. 'Beh kodam jahat miravim, qanunmandi ya khodmadari' (*Salam*, 7/6/1374 [29/8/1995]). In *Qanun, qodrat, farhang: yaddasht-ha-ye siyasi-ye ruznameh-ye Salam*. Tehran: Tarh-e now, 1379 (2000).

'Abdi, 'Abbas. 'Jame'eh shenasi-ye tahqiqat-e ejtema'i dar Iran'. *Rahbord*, no. 1 (Bahar 1371 [Spring 1992]).

Abu Zayd, Nasr Hamed. *Ma'na-ye matn: pazhuheshi dar 'olum-e qor'an*. Translated by Morteza Karimi Niya. Tehran: Tarh-e now, 1380 (2001).

Ahmadi-Amu'i, Bahman. *Eqtesad-e siyasi-ye jomhuri-ye eslami*. Tehran: Gam-e now, 1382 (2003).

Al-e Ahmad, Jalal. *Dar khedmat va khiyanat-e rowshanfekran*. Tehran: Majid, 1388 (2009).

Alviri, Morteza. *Khaterat-e Morteza Alviri*. Tehran: Daftar-e adabiyyat-e enqelab-e eslami, 1375 (1996).

Amjadi, Jalil. Tajzadeh, Mostafa, and Hosayn Dehbashi. 'Goftogu ba Mostafa Tajzadeh'. *Tarikh Online* (3 Bahman 1395 [22 January 2017]).

Aqajari, Hashem. 'Doktor Shari'ati va porozheh-ye porotestantism-ye eslami'. In *Aqajari*. Tehran: Jameh daran, 1382 (2003).

Aqajari, Hashem. 'Jonbesh-e eslahtalabi, chalesh-e dow farhang-e siyasi va hamelan-e an'. In *Hokumat-e dini va hokumat-e demokratik*. Tehran: Zekr, 1381 (2002).

Aqajari, Hashem, Reza Khojasteh-Rahimi, and Amir-Hosayn Bala'i. 'Sharh-e zendegi-ye yek enqelabi-ye naaram: goftogu ba Hashem Aqajari'. *Andisheh-ye puya* 2, no. 11 (Mehr–Aban 1392 [October–November 2013]).

'Araqi, Mehdi. *Nagofteh-ha: khaterat-e Shahid Hajj Mehdi 'Araqi, Paris-Pa'iz 1357*. Tehran: Mo'asseseh-ye khadamat-e farhang-e rasa, 1370 (1991).

Arghandehpur, Karim. *Dowran-e Salam*. Tehran: Nashr-e negah-e emruz, 1380 (2001).

Armin, Mohsen. ''Elat yabi-ye moshkelat-e Khatami'. *Rah-e now* 1, no. 1 (5 Ordibehesht 1377 [April–May 1998]).

Arman-e mostaz'afin. 'Nazar-e shoma dar bareh-ye rowhaniyyat chist?' Iran: Entesharat-e mostaz'afin, Summer 1355 (1976).

'Asgarowladi, Habibollah. *Khaterat-e Habibollah 'Asgarowladi*. Tehran: Markaz-e asnad-e enqelab-e eslami, 1391 (2012).

Azadi, Esma'il. 'Mohammad Salamati: haft goru-ye cheriki, yek sazman-e siyasi'. In *Ahzab-e siyasi dar Iran: tabar shenasi-ye jaryan-ha-ye siyasi va asib shenasi-ye ahzab dar Iran*. UK: Mardomak & H&S Media, 1390 (2011).

Badamchiyan, Asadollah. *Ashena'i ba jam'iyyat-e mo'talafeh-ye eslami*. Tehran: Andisheh-ye nab, 1385 (2006).

Bani-Asadi, Sayfollah. 'Naqdi bar maqaleh-ye "Jebheh-ye mosharekat, chap ravi va Hashemi-Rafsanjani" neveshteh-ye Sadeq Ziba-Kalam [Originally published 'Asr-e azadegan, no. 45, 10 Azar 1378 (1 December 1999]'. In *Hashemi va Dovvom-e Khordad*. Tehran: Rowzaneh, 1380 (2001).

Baqi, 'Emad al-Din. *Baraye tarikh: goftogu ba Sa'id Hajjariyan*. Tehran: Nashr-e ney, 1379 (2000).

Baqi, 'Emad al-Din. *Dar shenakht-e hezb-e qa'edin-e zaman*. Tehran: Nashr-e danesh-e eslami, Esfand 1362 (February–March 1984).

Baqi, 'Emad al-Din. 'Hadaf-e tarahan-e terur barchidan-e dowlat-e Khatami va hazf-e jebheh-ye Dovvom-e Khordad bud [*Aftab-e emruz*, 16 Farvardin 1379 (04/04/2000)]'. In *Baraye tarikh: goftogu ba Sa'id Hajjariyan*. Tehran: Nashr-e ney, 1379 (2000).

Baqi, 'Emad al-Din. 'Matbu'at va towse'eh-ye siyasi'. In *Bahar-e rokn-e chaharom: moruri bar jonbesh-e matbu'at-e eslah talab (1376–1379)*. Tehran: Nashr-e sara'i, 1381 (2002).

Baqi, 'Emad al-Din. 'Mavane'-e asli-ye jonbesh-e eslahat [Originally published in *Asharq Alawsat*, 5 August 2000]'. In *Jonbesh-e eslahat-e demokratik-e Iran: enqelab ya eslah*. Tehran: Sara'i, 1382 (2003).

Baqi, 'Emad al-Din. *Terazhedi-ye demokrasi dar Iran: bazkhani-ye qatl-ha-ye zanjireh'i*. 2 vols., vol. 1. Tehran: Nashr-e ney, 1378 (1999).

Bashiriyeh, Hossein, ed. *Gozar beh demokrasi*. Tehran: Negah-e now, 1384 (2005).

Bashiriyeh, Hossein. 'Mosharekat-e siyasi va towse'eh-ye siyasi'. *Rah-e now* 1, no. 1 (5 Ordibehesht 1388 [April–May 1998]).

Bashiriyeh, Hossein. 'Mosharekat-e siyasi, reqabat-e siyasi va towse'eh-ye siyasi'. In *'Aql dar siyasat*. Tehran: Negah-e mo'aser, 1382 (2003).

Bashiriyeh, Hossein. 'Payan-e yek porozheh'. In *'Obur az Khatami*, edited by Amir-Reza Sotudeh. Tehran: Zekr, 1379 (2000).

Bazargan, Mehdi. ''Akherat va khoda: hadaf-e be'sat-e anbiyya''. *Kiyan* 5, no. 28 (Azar–Bahman 1374 [November 1995–January 1996]).

Bazargan, Mehdi. *Akherat va khoda: hadaf-e resalat-e anbiyya'*. Tehran: Mo'asseseh-ye khadamat-e farhangi-ye rasa, 1377 (1998).

Bazargan, Mehdi. *Be'sat va idi'olozhi*. Mashhad: Tolu', 1345 (1966).

Bazargan, Mehdi. *Enqelab-e Iran dar dow harakat*. Tehran: Naraqi, 1363 (1984).

Bazargan, Mehdi. 'Sayr-e andisheh-ye dini-ye mo'aser: goftogu'i ba mohandes Mehdi Bazargan'. *Kiyan* 11 (Farvardin–Ordibehesht 1372 [March–April 1993]): 2–11.

Bazargan, Mehdi. 'Mosahebeh-ye Hamed Algar ba Mohandes Bazargan'. In *Enqelab-e eslami-ye Iran. Majmu'eh-ye asar*: Jam' avari, tanzim va tanqih dar bonyad-e farhangi-ye Mohandes Mehdi Bazargan, Aban 1389 (2010).

Behbudi, Hedayatollah. *Sharh-e esm: zendegi nameh-ye Ayatollah Seyyed 'Ali Hosayni Khameneh'i*. Tehran: Mo'asseseh-ye motale'at va pazhuhesh-ha-ye siyasi, 1391 (2012).

Behnud, Mas'ud. 'Dow Dovvom-e Khordad, yek goru va yek matbu'at'. In *Goluleh bad ast: maqalat-e Jame'eh, Tus, Neshat va Adineh*. Tehran: 'Elm, 1378 (1999).

Dad, Babak. *Akharin salam: nagofteh-ha-ye ta'tili-ye ruznameh-ye Salam dar goftogu'i sarih ba Musavi-Kho'iniha*. Tehran: Sazman-e chap va entesharat-e vezarat-e farhang va ershad-e eslami, 1378 (1999).

Dad, Babak. *Sad ruz ba Khatami*. Tehran: Entesharat-e vezarat-e farhang va ershad eslami, 1377 (1998).

Dar Agahi, Ha'ideh. 'An keh beh koshtan-e cheragh amadeh bud'. In *Gozir-e nagozir: seh revayat-e gozir az jomhuri-ye eslami-ye Iran*, edited by Mihan Rusta, Mahnaz Matin, Nasser Mohajer, and Sirus Javidi. Koln: Noqteh, 1387 (2008).

Do'a'i, Mahmud. *Gusheh'i az khaterat-e Hojjat al-Islam va al-Moslamin Seyyed Mahmud Do'a'i*. Tehran: Mo'asseseh-ye tanzim va nashr-e asar-e Imam Khomeini, 1387 (2009).

Ehsan-Bakhsh, Pezhman. 'Ostad Mesbah va dah te'ori-ye "khoshunat" va "terrorism"'. *Ketab-e naqd* no. 14–15 (1379 [2000]).

Ehtesham-Razavi, Nayyereh Sadat, and Hojjatollah Taheri. *Khaterat-e Nayyereh Sadat Ehtesham-e Razavi*. Tehran: Markaz-e asnad-e enqelab-e eslami, 1383 (2004).

Ehtesham-Razavi, Nayyereh al-Sadat. 'Ostureh-ye mehr: goft va shenudi ba "Nayyereh al-Sadat Navvab-e Ehtesham" Hamsar-e Shahid Navvab-e Safavi'. *Shahed-e yaran* no. 2 (Dey 1384 [December–January 2005]).

Fallahi, Akbar. *Tarikh-e shafahi-ye zendegi va mobarezat-e Imam Khomeini dar Najaf*. Tehran: Markaz-e asnad-e enqelab-e eslami, 1390 (2011)

Ganji, Akbar. '*Alijenab-e sorkhpush va 'alijenab-e khakestari: asib-shenasi-ye gozar beh dowlat-e demokratik-e towse'eh gara*. Tehran: Tarh-e now, 1378 (1999).

Ganji, Akbar. *Bud va nomud-e Khomeini: va'deh-ye behesht, barpa'i-ye duzakh*. Berlin: Gardun velag, 2011.

Ganji, Akbar. 'Din-e ensani, sowsiyalism-e ensani: negahi beh tajrobeh-ye Nagi, Dubchek, Gorbachev va Khatami'. In *Tallaqi-ye fashisti az din va hokumat: asib shenasi-ye gozar beh dowlat-e demokratik-e towse'eh gara*. Tehran: Tarh-e now, 1379 (2000).

Ganji, Akbar. 'Idi'olozhi-ye khoshunat va bohran-e mashru'iyyat [Originally published in *Rah-e now*, 5/2/1377 (25 April 1998)]'. In *Tallaqi-ye fashisti az din va hokumat: asib shenasi-ye gozar beh dowlat-e demokratik-e towse'eh gara*. Tehran: Tarh-e now, 1379 (2000).

Ganji, Akbar. 'Jang-e Iran va 'araq; dorughgu'i va siyasat bazi'. *Radio Zamaneh*, 24 Shahrivar 1392 (15 September 2013).

Ganji, Akbar. *Manifest-e jomhuri khahi: jomhuri khahi dar barabar-e mashruteh khahi, modeli baraye khoruj az bonbast-e siyasi*. PDF published online, 1381 (2002).

Ganji, Akbar. 'Motahhari, ruyaru-ye Khaz'ali, Mahdavi-Kani va Mesbah-Yazdi [Originally published in *Sobh-e emruz*, 8/7/1378 (30 September 1999)]'. In *Tallaqi-ye fashishti az din va hokumat: asib shenasi-ye gozar beh dowlat-e demokratik-e towse'eh gara*. Tehran: Tarh-e now, 1379 (2000).

Ganji, Akbar. 'Porsesh va pasokh'. In *Tallaqi-ye fashisti az din va hokumat: asib shenasi-ye gozar beh dowlat demokratik-e towse'eh gara*. Tehran: Tarh-e now, 1379 (2000).

Ganji, Akbar. 'Rowshanfekran va gofteman-e 'alijenab [Originally published in '*Asr-e azadegan*, no. 92, 9 Bahman 1378 (29 January 2000)]'. In *Hashemi-Rafsanjani va Dovvom-e Khordad*. Tehran: Rowzaneh, 1380 (2001).

Ganji, Akbar. 'Shari'ati va fashism: avvalin fashist shaytan ast [Originally published in *Kiyan*, no. 39, Azar–Dey 1376]'. In *Tallaqi-ye fashisti az din va hokumat: asib shenasi-ye gozar beh dowlat demokratik-e towse'eh gara*. Tehran: Tarh-e now, 1379 (2000).

Ganji, Akbar, et al. 'Matn-e sokhanrani-ha-ye ruz-e avval'. In *Konforans-e Berlin; khedmat ya khiyanat*, edited by Mohammad 'Ali Zakariya'i. Tehran: Tarh-e now, 1379 (2000).

Ha'eri-Yazdi, Mehdi, and Ziya Sedghi. *Khaterat-e Mehdi Ha'eri-Yazdi, faqih va ostad-e falsafeh-ye eslami. Majmu'eh-ye tarikh-e shafahi-ye Iran*, edited by Habib Lajevardi. Bethesda, MD: Center for Middle Eastern Studies of Harvard University, 2001.

Ha'eri-Yazdi, Mehdi. 'Hokumat dar mafhum-e vekalat-e shahrvandan'. In *Siyasat gari va siyasat andishi: zendegi va fekri-ye siyasi-ye Mehdi Ha'eri-Yazdi*, edited by Mas'ud Razavi. Tehran: 'Elm, 1387 (2008).

Ha'eri-Yazdi, Mehdi, and Ziya Sedqi. 'Mehdi Ha'eri-Yazdi'. Iranian Oral History Collection, Harvard University, 28 January, 4 February 1989 and 29 April 1992.

Hajjariyan, Sa'id. 'Bohran-e dowganegi dar qodrat'. In *'Obur az Khatami*, edited by Amir-Reza Sotudeh. Tehran: Zekr, 1379 (2000).

Hajjariyan, Sa'id. 'Din-e 'asri dar 'asr-e idi'olozhi [Originally published in *Kiyan*, no. 17, Farvardin–Ordibehesht 1373 (March–April 1994)]'. In *Az shahed-e qodsi ta shahed-e bazari: 'orfi shodan-e din dar sepehr-e siyasat*. Tehran: Tarh-e now, 1380 (2001).

Hajjariyan, Sa'id. 'Dovvom-e Khordad: omid-ha va bim-ha: payam-ha va cheshm andaz-ha'. *Rah-e now* no. 5 (2 Khordad 1377 [23 May 1998]).

Hajjariyan, Sa'id. 'Enqelab-e eslami; moderniyyat 'alayheh modernizasiyun [Originally published in *Mosharekat*, no. 2–3, Bahman 1377 (January–February 1999)]'. In *Az shahed-e qodsi ta shahed-e bazari: din dar sepehr-e siyasat*. Tehran: Tarh-e now, 1380 (2001).

Hajjariyan, Sa'id. 'Falsafeh-ye entekhabat [Originally published in *'Asr-e ma*, no. 90, 1376/12/6 (25 February 1998)]'. In *Jomhuriyyat; afsun zoda'i az qodrat*. Tehran: Tarh-e now, 1389 [2000].

Hajjariyan, Sa'id. 'Farayand-e 'orfi shodan-e feqh-e Shi'eh [Originally published in *Kiyan*, no. 24, Farvardin–Ordibehesht 1374 (April–May 1995)]'. In *Az shahed-e qodsi ta shahed-e bazari: 'orfi shodan-e din dar sepehr-e siyasat*. Tehran: Tarh-e now, 1380 (2001).

Hajjariyan, Sa'id. 'Imam Khomeini, faqih-ye dowran-e gozar: az feqh-e javaheri ta feqh al-maslahat [Originally published in *Kiyan*, no. 46, Farvardin–Ordibehesht 1378 (March–April 1999)]'. In *Az shahed-e qodsi ta shahed-e bazari: 'orfi shodan-e din dar sepehr-e siyasat*. Tehran: Tarh-e now, 1380 (2001).

Hajjariyan, Sa'id. 'Mashruteh-talabi'. In *Eslahat dar barabar-e eslahat: goftogu'i-ye enteqadi*. Tehran: Tarh-e now, 1382 (2003).

Hajjariyan, Sa'id. 'Mesbah Yazdi dar kakh-e zojaji [Originally published in *'Asr-e ma*, no. 101, 21/ 5/1377 (12 August 1998)]'. In *Jomhuriyyat; afsun zoda'i az qodrat*. Tehran: Tarh-e now, 1379 (2000).

Hajjariyan, Sa'id. 'Nahveh-ye baz towlid-e saltanat dar andisheh-ye khelafat va velayat [Originally published in *'Asr-e ma*, no. 95, 30/2/1377 (20 May 1998)]'. In *Jomhuriyyat; afsun zoda'i az qodrat*. Tehran: Tarh-e now, 1379 (2000).

Hajjariyan, Sa'id. 'Naqdi bar nazariyyeh-ye "Farbehtar az idi'olozhi" [Originally published in *Kiyan*, no. 15, Mehr–Aban 1372 (September–

October 1993)]'. In *Az shahed-e qodsi ta shahed-e bazari: 'orfi shodan-e din dar sepehr-e siyasat*. Tehran: Tarh-e now, 1380 (2001).

Hajjariyan, Sa'id. 'Negahi beh mas'aleh-ye mashru'iyyat'. *Rahbord*, no. 3 (Bahar 1373 [Spring 1994]).

Hajjariyan, Sa'id. 'Pasdari az qanun-e asasi, rahi baraye nowsazi-ye siyasi [Originally published in *'Asr-e ma*, no. 85, 26/9/1376 (17 December 1997)]'. In *Jomhuriyyat; afsun zoda'i az qodrat*. Tehran: Tarh-e now, 1379 (2000).

Hajjariyan, Sa'id. 'Sakht-e eqtedar-e soltani, asib pazir-ha va badil-ha'. *Etela'at-e siyasi-eqtesadi*, no. 2 (1374 [1995]).

Hajjariyan, Sa'id. 'Sharhi bar maramnameh-ye jebheh-ye mosharekat-e Iran-e eslami'. *Mosharekat*, no. 27 (18 Shahrivar 1378 [9 September 1999]).

Hajjariyan, Sa'id. 'Tallaqi-ye akademik az towse'eh-ye siyasi'. *Rahbord*, no. 1 (Bahar 1371 [Spring 1992]).

Hajjariyan, Sa'id. '"Velayat-e motlaqeh-ye faqih" va "qanun-e asasi" (1) [Originally published in *'Asr-e ma*, no. 61, 19/11/1375 (7 February 1997)]'. In *Jomhuriyyat; afsun zoda'i az qodrat*. Tehran: Tarh-e now, 1389 (2000).

Hajjariyan, Sa'id, and 'Emad al-Din Baqi. 'Goftogu ba Sa'id Hajjariyan'. In *Baraye tarikh: goftogu ba Sa'id Hajjariyan*. Tehran: Nashr-e ney, 1379 (2000).

Hajjariyan, Sa'id, and Reza Khojasteh-Rahimi. 'Eslahatchi, cheriki nemishavad: sharh-e yek zendegi-ye siyasi-fekri'. *Andisheh-ye puya* (Tir–Mordad 1391 [July–August 2012]).

Hajjariyan, Sa'id, and Hosayn Salimi. 'Suteh delan gerd-e ham amadand: goftogu ba Sa'id Hajjariyan'. In *Kalbodshekafi-ye zehniyyat-e eslahgarayan*, edited by Hossein Salimi. Tehran: Gam-e now, 1384 (2005).

'Hajjariyan: bekhater-e enherafat va khesarat-ha'i keh beh mardom zadim az hezb-e Mosharekat este'fa mikonam.' *Fars News Agency*, 3/6/1388 (25 August 2009).

Hajjariyan, Sa'id (S. S.). 'Mashru'iyyat, mashrutiyyat, jomhuriyyat'. *'Asr-e ma*, no. 14 (13 Ordibehesht 1374 [3 May 1995]).

Haqshenas, Torab. 'Ahzab va sazman-ha-ye jonbesh-e komunisti-ye Iran.' *Noqteh* 3, no. 7 (Bahar 1376 [1997]).

Hashemi, Mohsen, and Habibollah Hamidi. *Majara-ye Makfarlin: forush-e selah, azadi-ye gerugan-ha*. Tehran: Daftar-e nashr-e ma'aref-e enqelab, 1388 (2009).

Hashemi-Rafsanjani, Akbar. *Amir Kabir: ya qahreman-e mobarezeh ba este'mar*. Tehran: Mo'asseseh-ye matbu'at-e Farahani, 1346 (1967).

Hashemi-Rafsanjani, Akbar. *Dowran-e mobarezeh: khaterat, tasvir-ha, gah shomar.* 2 vols., vol. 1, Tehran: Nashr-e ma'aref-e enqelab, 1386 (2007).

Hashemi-Rafsanjani, Akbar. 'Nagofteh-ha-ye Hashemi-Rafsanjani az 'azl-e Ayatollah Montazeri'. *Tarikh-e Irani,* www.tarikhirani.ir

Hashemi-Rafsanjani, Akbar, and 'Ali-Reza Hashemi. *Karnameh va khaterat-e 1366: defa' va siyasat.* Tehran: Daftar-e nashr-e ma'aref-e enqelab, 1389 (2010).

Hashemi-Rafsanjani, Akbar, and Yaser Hashemi. *'Obur az bohran: karnameh va khaterat-e sal-e 1360 Hashemi-Rafsanjani.* Tehran: Daftar-e nashr-e ma'aref-e enqelab, 1378 (1999).

Hashemi-Rafsanjani, Akbar, and 'Ali Lahuti. *Karnameh va khaterat-e 1368: bazsazi va sazandegi.* Tehran: Daftar-e nashr-e ma'aref-e enqelab, 1391 (2012).

Hashemi-Rafsanjani, Akbar, and Hasan Lahuti. *Karnameh va khaterat-e Hashemi-Rafsanjani sal-e 1371: rownaq-e sazandegi.* Tehran: Daftar-e nashr-e ma'aref-e enqelab, 1393 (2014).

Hassanifar, 'Abdolrahman, ed. *Fada'iyan-e Islam dar kalam-e yaran.* Tehran: Markaz-e asnad-e enqelab-e eslami, 1389 (2010).

Hill, Christopher, and Sa'id Hajjariyan. 'Seh khoda dar enqelab-e engelestan'. *Rah-e now* 1, no. 1 (5 Ordibehesht 1377 [April–May 1998]).

Ja'fari, Mohammad. *Taqabol-e dow khatt ya kudeta-ye Khordad 1360.* Frankfurt: Barzavand, 1386 (2007).

Jazani, Bizhan. *Tarh-e jame'eh shenasi va mabani-ye esteratezhi-ye jonbesh-e enqelabi-ye khalq-e Iran (tarikh-e si saleh-ye siyasi-ye Iran).* Tehran: Entesharat-e Maziyar, 1357 (1978).

Judaki, Mahbubeh. *Hosayniyyeh-ye ershad beh revayat-e asnad.* Tehran: Markaz-e asnad-e enqelab-e eslami, 1388 (2009).

Kadivar, Mohsen. 'Azadi dar hokumat-e dini'. In *Daghdagheh-ha-ye hokumat-e dini.* Tehran: Nashr-e ney, 1379 (2000).

Kadivar, Mohsen. *Enqelab va nezam dar buteh-ye naqd-e akhlaqi: Ayatollah Seyyed Mohammad Rowhani, mobaheteh va marja'iyyat. Movajeheh-ye jomhuri-ye eslami ba 'olama-ye montaqed.* Vol. 3, www.kadivar.co m: Mohsen Kadivar: Official Website, 1394 (2015).

Kadivar, Mohsen. *Faraz va forud-e Azari Qomi: sayri dar tahavvol-e mabani-ye fekri-ye Ayatollah Ahmad Azari-Qomi. Movajeheh-ye jomhuri-ye eslami ba 'olama-ye montaqed.* Vol. 2, www.kadivar.com: Mohsen Kadivar: Official Website 1392 (2013).

Kadivar, Mohsen. *Hokumat-e vela'i. Andisheh-ye siyasi dar Islam (2).* Tehran: Nashr-e ney, 1377 (1998).

Kadivar, Mohsen. 'Mosahebeh ba ruznameh-ye Khordad'. In *Baha-ye azadi: defa'iyyat-e Mohsen Kadivar dar dadgah-e vizheh-ye rowhaniyyat*, edited by Zahra Rudi Kadivar. Tehran: Nashr-e ney, 1378 (1999).

Kadivar, Mohsen. *Nazariyyeh-ha-ye dowlat dar feqh-e Shi'eh*. Tehran: Nashr-e ney, 1376 (1997).

Kadivar, Mohsen. 'Nazariyyeh-ha-ye dowlat dar feqh-e Shi'eh (1)'. *Rahbord*, no. 4 (Paiz 1994 [Autumn 1994]).

Kadivar, Mohsen. *Ostad az shekashteh shodan-e namus-e enqelab: negahi beh sal-ha-ye payani-ye zendegi-ye Ayatollah Seyyed Kazem Shari'atmadari. Movajeheh-ye jomhuri-ye eslami ba 'olama-ye montaqed*. Vol. 1, www.kadivar.com: Mohsen Kadivar: Official Website 1394 (2015).

Kadivar, Mohsen. *Siyasat nameh-ye Khorasani: qata'at-e siyasi dar asar-e Akhund Molla Mohammad-Kazem Khorasani*. Tehran: Ghazal, 1385 (2006).

Karrubi, Mehdi, Hamid Rowhani, and Mehdi Imam-Jamarani. 'Nameh-ye aqayan-e Karrubi, Jamarani va Rowhani beh mo'azam lah'. In *Khaterat-e faqih va marja'-e 'aliqadr hazrat Ayatollah Hosayn-'Ali Montazeri* [1379 (2000)]: www.amontazeri.com, 29 Bahman 1367 (18 February 1989).

Kashi, Mohammad-Javad Gholam-Reza. *Jadu-ye goftar: zehniyyat-e farhangi va nezam-e ma'ni dar entekhabat Dovvom Khordad*. Tehran: Mo'asseseh-ye farhangi-ye ayandeh-ye puya, 1379 (2000).

Katouzian, Naser. *Az koja amadeh'am, amadanam bahr-e cheh bud? zendegi-ye man*. Tehran: Sherkat-e sahami-ye enteshar, 1385 (2006).

Kaviyani, Hamid. *Dar jostoju-ye mahfel-e jenayatkaran: bazkhani-ye parvandeh-ye qatl-ha-ye siyasi*. Tehran: Negah-e emruz, 1378 (1999).

Kaviyani, Hamid. *Pishgaman-e eslahat: naqsh-e sazman-e mojahedin-e enqelab-e eslami-ye Iran dar tahavvolat-e siyasi-ye daheh-ye 70* Tehran: Salam, 1379 (2000).

Khalkhali, Sadeq. *Khaterat-e Ayatollah Khalkhali: az ayyam-e talabegi ta dowran-e hakem-e shar'-e dadgah-ha-ye enqelabi-ye eslami*. Tehran: Nashr-e sayeh, 1379 (2000).

Khameneh'i, 'Ali. 'Bayanat dar daneshgah-e Tarbiyyat-e Modarress'. www.khamenei.ir (12/6/1377 (3 September 1998]).

Khameneh'i, 'Ali. 'Bayanat dar didar-e daneshjuyan va asatid-e daneshgah-ha-ye ostan-e Hamedan'. www.khamenei.ir (17/4/1383 [7 July 2004]).

Khameneh'i, 'Ali. 'Bayanat dar didar-e farmandehan-e gordan-ha-ye 'ashura''. www.khamenei.ir, (22/4/1371 [13 July 1992]).

Khameneh'i, 'Ali. 'Bayanat dar didar-e mas'ulan-e sazman-e Seda va Sima'. www.khamenei.ir, (11/9/1383 [1 December 2004]).

Khameneh'i, 'Ali. 'Didar-e kargozaran-e nezam ba rahbar-e enqelab'. www.khamenei.ir (11/8/1382 [2 November 2003]).

Khameneh'i, 'Ali. 'Didar daneshjuyan sherkat konandeh dar ordu-ye amuzeshi-parvareshi-ye Basij-e daneshju'i ba rahbar-e enqelab'. www .khamenei.ir (13/6/1378 [4 September 1999]).

Khameneh'i, 'Ali, 'Entesab-e Doktor 'Ali Larijani beh riyasat-e Sazman-e Seda va Sima'. www.khamenei.ir (24/11/1372 [13 February 1994]).

Khameneh'i, 'Ali, 'Khaterat-e Ayatollah Khameneh'i az avvalin didar ba Navvab-e Safavi'. *Khabar Online* (27 Dey 1389 [17 January 2011]).

Khatami, Mohammad. *Ayin va andisheh dar dam-e khodkamegi: sayri dar andisheh-ye siyasi-ye mosalmanan dar faraz va forud-e tamadon.* Tehran: Tarh-e now, 1378 (1999).

Khatami, Mohammad. *Bim-e mowj.* Tehran: Sima-ye javan, Bahar 1372 (Spring 1993).

Khatami, Mohammad. 'Din va siyasat [29/10/1376 (19 January 1998)]'. In *Islam, rowhaniyyat va enqelab-e eslami.* Tehran: Tarh-e now, 1379 (2000).

Khatami, Mohammad. 'Haqq va taklif [14/12/1376 (3 March 1998)]'. In *Gozideh-ye sokhanrani-ha-ye ra'is-e jomhur dar bareh-ye towse'eh-ye siyasi, towse'eh-ye eqtesadi va amniyyat.* Tehran: Tarh-e now, 1379 (2000).

Khatami, Mohammad. 'Imam Khomeini va hokumat-e dini [11/3/1377 (1 June 1998)]'. In *Islam, rowhaniyyat va enqelab-e eslami.* Tehran: Tarh-e now, 1379 (2000).

Khatami, Mohammad. 'Payam-ha va payamad-ha-ye Dovvom-e Khordad [2/3/1377 (23 May 1998)]'. In *Gozideh-ye sokhanrani-ha-ye ra'is-e jomhur dar bareh-ye towse'eh-ye siyasi, towse'eh-ye eqtesadi va amniyyat.* Tehran: Tarh-e now, 1379 (2000).

Khatami, Mohammad. 'Qanun va eqtedar [6/10/1376 (27/10/1997)]'. In *Gozideh-ye sokhanrani-ha-ye ra'is-e jomhur dar bareh-ye towse'eh-ye siyasi, towse'eh-ye eqtesadi va amniyyat.* Tehran: Tarh-e now, 1379 (2000).

Khatami, Mohammad. 'Rowhaniyyat va hal-e mo'zelat-e jame'eh [1/7/1376 (23 September 1997)]'. In *Islam, rowhaniyyat va enqelab-e eslami.* Tehran: Tarh-e now, 1379 (2000).

Khatami, Mohammad. 'Rowhaniyyat va jahan-e jadid [1/8/1376 (23 October 1997)]'. In *Islam, rowhaniyyat va enqelab-e eslami.* Tehran: Tarh-e now, 1379 (2000).

Khatami, Mohammad. 'Rowhaniyyat va nezam-e jomhuri-ye eslami [13/4/ 1377 (4 July 1998)]'. In *Islam, rowhaniyyat va enqelab-e eslami.* Tehran: Tarh-e now, 1379 (2000).

Khatami, Mohammad. 'Rowhaniyyat, bayad-ha va nabayad-ha [1/7/1376 (23 September 1997)]'. In *Islam, rowhaniyyat va enqelab-e eslami.* Tehran: Tarh-e now, 1379 (2000).

Khatami, Mohammad. 'Tafsir-e rasmi az Islam (1/4/1377 [22 June 1998])'. In *Islam, rowhaniyyat va enqelab-e eslami*. Tehran: Tarh-e now, 1379 (2000).

Khatami, Mohammad-Reza. 'Ayin-e ayiniyan'. *Ayin* (Ordibehesht 1385 [April–May 2006]).

Khatami, Mohammad-Reza, and Hosayn Salimi. 'Tasavvor-e piruzi nemikardim: goftogu ba Mohammad-Reza Khatami'. In *Kalbodshekafi-ye zehniyyat-e eslahgarayan*. Tehran: Gam-e now, 1384 (2005).

Khomeini, Ruhollah. ''Adam-e salahiyyat baraye tasadi-ye rahbari-ye nezam-e jomhuri-ye eslami'. In *Sahifeh-ye Imam*. Tehran: Mo'asseseh-ye tanzim va nashr-e asar-e Imam Khomeini, 1378 (1999).

Khomeini, Ruhollah. 'Arziyabi-ye 'amalkard-e "Nehzat-e azadi"'. In *Sahifeh-ye Imam*. Tehran: Mo'asseseh-ye tanzim va nashr-e asar-e Imam, 1378 (1999).

Khomeini, Ruhollah. 'Ebraz-e 'allaqeh va ta'kid bar 'adam-e hemayat az Seyyed Mehdi Hashemi va hoshdar dar mored-e dasiseh-ha-ye ou'. In *Sahifeh-ye Imam*. Tehran: Mo'asseseh-ye tanzim va nashr-e asar-e Imam Khomeini, 1999.

Khomeini, Ruhollah. *Kashf al-asrar*. Tehran: 1943.

Khomeini, Ruhollah. 'Lozum-e barkhord-e qate' ba afrad-e zed-e enqelab va monharefin vabasteh beh Mehdi Hashemi'. In *Sahifeh-ye Imam*. Tehran: Mo'asseseh-ye tanzim va nashr-e asar-e Imam Khomeini, 1378 (1999).

Khomeini, Ruhollah. 'Manshur-e baradari: maftuh budan-e bab-e ejtehad dar hokumat-e eslami'. In *Sahifeh-ye Imam*. Tehran: Mo'asseseh-ye tanzim va nashr-e asar-e Imam Khomeini, 1378 (1999).

Khomeini, Ruhollah. 'Matn-e kamel-e vasiyyat nameh-ye elahi-ye siyasi-ye Imam Khomeini'. www.khamenei.ir (15 Khordad 1367 [5 June 1989]).

Khomeini, Ruhollah. *Misbah al-hidaya ila al-khilafa wa al-wilaya*. Translated by Hosayn Mostowfi. Dual Text ed. Tehran: Nashr-e 'aruj, 1389 (2010).

Khomeini, Ruhollah. *Sahifeh-ye Imam*. 21 vols., vol. 14. Tehran: Mo'asseseh-ye tanzim va nashr-e asar-e Imam Khomeini, 1378 (1999).

Khomeini, Ruhollah. *Sahifeh-ye Imam*. 21 vols., vol. 20. Tehran: Mo'asseseh-ye tanzim va nashr-e asar-e Imam Khomeini, 1378 (1999).

Khomeini, Ruhollah. *Sahifeh-ye Imam*. 21 vols., vol. 18. Tehran: Mo'asseseh-ye tanzim va nashr-e asar-e Imam Khomeini, 1378 (1999).

Khomeini, Ruhollah. *Sahifeh-ye Imam*. 21 vols., vol. 10. Tehran: Mo'asseseh-ye tanzim va nashr-e asar-e Imam Khomeini, 1378 (1999).

Khomeini, Ruhollah. *Sahifeh-ye Imam*. 21 vols., vol. 21. Tehran: Mo'asseseh-ye tanzim va nashr-e asar-e Imam Khomeini, 1378 (1999).

Khomeini, Ruhollah. *Sahifeh-ye Imam*. 21 vols., vol. 15. Tehran: Mo'asseseh-ye tanzim va nashr-e asar-e Imam Khomeini, 1378 (1999).

Khomeini, Ruhollah. *Sahifeh-ye Imam*. 21 vols., vol. 9. Tehran: Mo'asseseh-ye tanzim va nashr-e asar-e Imam Khomeini, 1378 (1999).

Khomeini, Ruhollah. *Sahifeh-ye Imam* 21 vols., vol. 19. Tehran: Mo'asseseh-ye tanzim va nashr-e asar-e Imam Khomeini, 1378 (1999).

Khomeini, Ruhollah. 'Vazayef-e siyasi-ye hajj'. In *Sahifeh-ye Imam*. Tehran: Mo'asseseh-ye tanzim va nashr-e asar-e Imam, 1378 (1999).

Khomeini, Ruhollah. *Velayat-e faqih va jehad-e akbar*. Tehran: Seyyed Jamal Hedayat.

Khomeini, Ruhollah. *Velayat-e faqih, hukumat-e eslami*, 1357 (1978).

Khorram, Mas'ud. *Hoviyyat*. Tehran: Mo'asseseh-ye farhangi-ye entesharati-ye hayan, 1376 (1997).

Khosrowshahi, Hadi. *Zendegi va mobarezeh-ye Navvab Safavi*. Tehran: Ettela'at, 1386 (2007).

Khosrowshahi, Hadi. *Fada'iyan-e Islam: tarikh, 'amalkard, andisheh*. Tehran: Ettela'at, 1379 (2000).

Khu'i, Abolqasem. 'Barressi-ye velayat-e motlaqeh-ye faqih'. In *Daghdagheh-ha-ye hokumat-e dini*, edited by Mohsen Kadivar. Tehran: Nashr-e ney, 1376 (1997).

Kordi, 'Ali. *Jame'eh-ye rowhaniyyat-e mobarez az sheklgiri ta enshe'ab*. Tehran: Markaz-e asnad-e enqelab-e eslami, 1386 (2007).

Larijani, Sadeq. 'Naqdi bar maqaleh "bast va qabz-e te'orik-e shari'at"'. *Kayhan-e farhangi*, no. 55 (Mehr 1367 [September–October 1988]).

Mahallati, Fazlollah. *Khaterat va mobarezat-e Shahid Mahallati*. Tehran: Markaz-e asnad-e enqelab-e eslami, 1376 (1997).

Mahdavi-Kani, Mohammad-Reza, and Gholam-Reza Khajeh-Sarvi, eds. *Khaterat-e Ayatollah Mahdavi-Kani*. Tehran: Markaz-e asnad-e enqelab-e eslami, 1385 (2006).

Malekiyan, Mostafa. 'Goftari dar bab-e kalam-e jadid'. In *Moshtaqi va mahjuri: goftogu dar bab-e farhang va siyasat*. Tehran: Nashr-e negah-e mo'aser, 1385 (2006).

Mardiha, Morteza. 'Andisheh-ha-ye now dar 'arseh-ye entekhabat-e sheshom'. In *Amniyyat dar eghma: negahi beh jelveh-ha-ye surrealism-ye siyasi dar Iran*. Tehran: Naqsh va negar, 1379 (2000).

Maysami, Lotfollah. *Az nehzat-e azadi ta mojahedin: khaterat-e Lotfollah Maysami*. Vol. 1, Tehran: Nashr-e samadiyyeh, 1383 (2004).

Mehrpur, Hosayn. *Ra'is-e jomhur va ma'suliyyat-e ejra'i-ye qanun-e asasi*. 2 vols., vol. 1, Tehran: Etela'at, 2001.

Mesbah-Yazdi, Mohammad-Taqi. *Enteqam: nashriyyeh-ye makhfi-ye tolab-e howzeh-ye 'elmiyyeh-ye Qom, 1342–44*. Tehran: Markaz-e asnad-e enqelab-e eslami, 1389 (2010).

Mesbah-Yazdi, Mohammad-Taqi. 'Hokumat va mashru'iyyat'. *Ketab-e naqd* 2, no. 7 (1377 [1998]): 42–77.

Mesbah-Yazdi, Mohammad-Taqi. *Naqdi-ye feshordeh bar osul-e Marxism.* Qom: Mo'asseseh-ye rah-e haqq, 1367 (1988).

Mesbah-Yazdi, Mohammad-Taqi. *Nazariyyeh-ye siyasi-ye Islam, jeld-e avval. Majmu'eh-ye asar.* Qom: Entesharat-e mo'asseseh-ye amuzeshi va pazhuheshi-ye Imam Khomeini, 1388 (2009).

Mesbah-Yazdi, Mohammad-Taqi. *Negahi-ye gozara beh nazariyyeh-ye velayat-e faqih.* Qom: Entesharat-e mo'asseseh-ye amuzeshi va pazhuheshi-ye Imam Khomeini, 1388 (2009).

Mesbah-Yazdi, Mohammad-Taqi. *Tahajom-e farhangi.* Qom: Entesharat-e mo'asseseh-ye amuzeshi va pazhuheshi-e Imam Khomeini, 1389 (2010).

Mesbah-Yazdi, Mohammad-Taqi, and 'Abdolkarim Sorush. 'Jalaseh-ye monazereh-ye ostad Mohammad-Taqi Mesbah-Yazdi va Aqa-ye Doktor 'Abdolkarim Sorush'. Unpublished Transcript.

Mesbah-Yazdi, Mohammad-Taqi, 'Abdolkarim Sorush, Farrokh Negahdar, Ehsan Tabari, and 'Ali Zinati. *Gofteman-e rowshangar dar bareh-ye andisheh-ha-ye bonyadin: monazereh-ye aqayan-e Ehsan Tabari, 'Abdolkarim Sorush, Farrokh Negahdar, Mohammad-Taqi Mesbah-Yazdi.* Qom: Mo'asseseh-ye amuzeshi va pazhuheshi-ye Imam Khomeini, 1385 (2006).

Mohammadi, Majid. 'Mavane'-e roshd-e jame'eh-ye madani dar Iran'. *Kiyan* 6, no. 33 (November–December 1996).

Mohit-Tabataba'i, Mohammad, ed. *Majmu'eh-ye asar-e Mirza Malkam Khan.* Tehran 1327 (1948). Berlin: Gardun, 2010.

Mohtashamipur, 'Ali-Akbar. *Chand seda'i dar jame'eh va rowhaniyyat.* Tehran: Andisheh-ye javan, 1379 (2000).

Mojtahed-Shabestari, Mohammad. 'Bazgasht beh keramat-e ensani'. In *Jame'eh-ye madani, Dovvom-e Khordad, va Khatami: goftogu-ha'i ba andishmandan-e mo'aser-e Iran,* edited by Ma'sud Razavi. Tehran: Farzan-e ruz, 1379 (2000).

Mojtahed-Shabestari, Mohammad. 'Demokrasi va dindari'. In *Naqdi bar qara'at-e rasmi az din: bohran-ha, chalesh-ha, rah-e hal-ha.* Tehran: Tarh-e now, 1379 (2000).

Mojtahed-Shabestari, Mohammad. 'Enqelab-e eslami va qara'at-e ma'qul az din'. In *Naqdi bar qara'at-e rasmi az din: bohran-ha, chalesh-ha, rah-e hal-ha.* Tehran: Tarh-e now, 1379 (2000).

Mojtahed-Shabestari, Mohammad. 'Feqh-ye siyasi bastar-e 'oqala'i-ye khod ra az dast dadeh ast'. In *Naqdi bar qara'at-e rasmi az din: bohran-ha, chalesh-ha, rah-e hal-ha.* Tehran: Tarh-e now, 1379 (2000).

Mojtahed-Shabestari, Mohammad. *Hermenutik, ketab va sonnat: farayand-e tafsir-e vahy.* Tehran: Tarh-e now, 1375 (1996).

Mojtahed-Shabestari, Mohammad. 'Iman, siyasat va hokumat'. In *Iman va azadi*. Tehran: Tarh-e now, 1376 (1997).

Mojtahed-Shabestari, Mohammad. 'Modernism va vahy'. *Kiyan 5*, no. 29 (March–April 1996).

Mojtahed-Shabestari, Mohammad. 'Mosalmanan bayad hoquq-e bashar ra bepazirand'. In *Naqdi bar qara'at-e rasmi az din: bohran-ha, chalesh-ha, rah-e hal-ha*. Tehran: Tarh-e now, 1379 (2000).

Mojtahed-Shabestari, Mohammad. '"Qara'at-e rasmi az din" cheguneh payda shod va cheguneh dochar-e bohran gardid?'. In *Naqdi bar qara'at-e rasmi az din: bohran-ha, chalesh-ha, rah-e hal-ha*. Tehran: Tarh-e now, 1379 (2000).

Mojtahed-Shabestari, Mohammad. 'Seh guneh-ye qara'at az sonnat dar 'asr-e moderniteh'. In *Sonnat va sekularism: goftar-ha'i az 'Abdolkarim Sorush, Mohammad Mojtahed-Shabestari, Mostafa Malekiyan, Mohsen Kadivar*. Tehran: Serat, 1381 (2002).

Mojtahed-Shabestari, Mohammad. 'Siyasat va ta'abod'. In *Ta'amolati dar qara'at-e ensani az din*. Tehran: Tarh-e now, 1383 (2004).

Mola'i-Tavani, 'Ali-Reza. *Zendegi nameh-ye siyasi-ye Ayatollah Taleqani*. Tehran: Nashr-e ney, 1388 (2009).

Montazeri, Hosayn-'Ali. *Hokumat-e dini va hoquq-e ensan*. Tehran: Sera'i, 1387 (2008).

Montazeri, Hosayn-'Ali. *Khaterat-e faqih va marja'-e 'aliqadr hazrat Ayatollah Hosayn-'Ali Montazeri*. www.amontazeri.com (1379 [2000]).

Montazeri, Hosayn-'Ali, and Sa'id Montazeri. *Enteqad az khod: 'ebrat va vasiyyat*. Qom: www.amontazeri.com, 1387 (2008).

Motahhari, Morteza. 'Mosahebeh-ye Doktor Sorush ba Ostad Shahid piramun-e jomhuri-ye eslami'. In *Piramun-e enqelab-e eslami*. Qom: Sadra, 1362 (1983).

Motahhari, Morteza. 'Moshkel-e asasi dar sazman-e rowhaniyyat'. In *Bahsi dar bareh-ye marja'iyyat va rowhaniyyat*. Tehran: Sahami, 1962.

Musavi, Mir-Hosayn. *Chenin goft Mir-Hosayn majmu'eh-ye sokhanrani-ha, goftogu-ha, bayaniyyeh-ha, yaddasht-ha, etela'iyyeh-ha va payam-ha-ye Mir-Hosayn Musavi*. Kanun-e Doktor 'Ali Shari'ati & Kalameh, Khordad 1390 (2012).

Nabavi, Behzad, and Hosayn Salimi. 'Eslahat piruz shodeh; goftogu ba Behzad Nabavi'. In *Kalbodshekafi-ye zehniyyat-e eslahgarayan*. Tehran: Gam-e now, 1384 (2005).

Nabavi, Ebrahim, and Nikahang Kowsar. *Dar sal-e 79 etefaq oftad*. Tehran: Rowzanah, 1380 (2001).

Na'ini, Mohammad-Hosayn. *Tanbih al-ommeh va tanzih al-melleh*. Qom: Bustan-e ketab, 1382 (2003).

Naraqi, Ahmad. 'Baznegari-ye rabeteh-ye morid-moradi dar 'erfan'. *Kiyan*, no. 2 (Azar 1370 [November–December 1991]).

Nasr, Seyyed Hosayn, and Hosayn Dehbashi. *Hekmat va siyasat: goftogu ba Doktor Seyyed Hosayn Nasr*. Majmu'eh-ye tarikh-e shafahi va tasviri-ye Iran-e mo'aser. Vol. 1, Tehran: Sazman-e asnad va ketabkhaneh-ye melli-ye jomhuri-ye eslami, 1393 (2014).

Nateq-Nuri, 'Ali-Akbar, and Morteza Mirdar. *Khaterat-e Hojjat al-Islam 'Ali-Akbar Nateq-Nuri*. Vol. 2. Tehran: Markaz-e asnad-e enqelab-i eslami, Autumn 1384 (2005).

Nehzat-e azadi-ye Iran. 'Tafsil va tahlil-e velayat-e motlaqeh-ye faqih'. Farvardin 1367 [March–April 1988].

Nuri, 'Abdollah, and Akbar Ganji. *Naqdi baraye tamam-e fosul: goftogu-ye Akbar Ganji ba 'Abdollah Nuri*. Tehran: Tarh-e now, 1378 (1999).

Paidar, Hamid. 'Marx, idi'olozhi va din: naqdi bar maqaleh-ye "farbehtar az idi'olozhi"'. *Kiyan* no. 17 (Azar–Dey 1372 [October 1993–January 1994]).

Puyan, Amir-Parviz, and Mas'ud Ahmadzadeh. *Mobarezeh-ye mosalahaneh – ham esteratezhi, ham taktik; zarurat-e mobarezeh-ye musalahaneh va rad-e te'uri-ye baqa'*. London: Cherikha-ye fada'i-ye khalq-e Iran, 1379 (2000).

Quchani, Mohammad. 'Farzand-e maktab-e Khorasan: pazhuheshi dar risheh-ha-ye fekri-ye Anjoman-e Hojjatiyyeh: az mobarezeh ba falsafeh ta talash baraye enhelal-e hezb-e Tudeh'. *Mehrnameh*, no. 25 (Mehr 1391 [September–October 2012]).

Quchani, Mohammad. *Nazi-abadi-ha*. Tehran: Nashr-e sara'i, 1383 (2004).

Quchani, Mohammad. 'Salam; aqa-ye Kho'iniha'. In *Jomhuri-ye moqaddas: boresh-ha'i az tarikh-e jomhuri-ye eslami*. Tehran: Naqsh va negar, 1381 (2002).

Quchani, Mohammad. *Yaqeh sefid-ha: jame'eh shenasi-ye nehad-ha-ye madani dar Iran-e emruz*. Tehran: Naqsh va negar, 1379 (2000).

Quchani, Mohammad. *Pedarkhandeh va chap-ha-ye javan: mobarezeh baraye naqd-e qodrat Dey 78 ta Khordad 79*. Nashr-e ney, 1379 (2000).

Ravabet-e 'omumi-ye daftar-e tahkim-e vahdat, ed. *Nezarat-e estesvabi*. Tehran: Nashr-e afkar, 1378 (1999).

Rayshahri, Mohammad. *Khaterat-e siyasi*. Tehran: Mo'assesseh-ye motale'at va pazhuhesh-ha-ye siyasi, 1369 (1990).

Rayshahri, Mohammad. *Khatereh-ha*. Vol. 1. Tehran: Markaz-e asnad-e enqelab-e eslami, 1383 (2004).

Reza'i, Ahmad. *Tahlili az nehzat-e Hosayni* (Sazman-e mojahedin-e khalq). Springfield, MO, 1975.

Reza'i, 'Ali. 'Zohur va takamol-e jame'eh-ye madani'. *Kiyan* 6, no. 33 (November–December 1996).

Safavi, Mojtaba Navvab. *Barnameh-ye hokumati-ye Fada'iyan-e Islam.* Tehran: Bonyad-e be'sat, 1386 (2007).

Sahabi, 'Ezatollah. *Nim-e qarn-e khatereh va tajrobeh: khaterat-e mohandes 'Ezatollah Sahabi; sal-ha-ye 1357 ta 1379.* Paris: Khavaran, 2013.

Sahabi, 'Ezatollah, 'Ali-Reza 'Alavi-Tabar, Morad Farhadpur, and Musa Ghani-Nezhad. 'Mizgerd-e Kiyan-e dar bareh-ye Jame'eh-ye madani'. *Kiyan* 6, no. 33 (Aban–Azar 1375 [November–December 1996]).

Salamati, Mohammad. 'Didgah-ha-ye sazman-e mojahedin-e enqelab-e eslami-ye Iran dar bareh-ye tahazob va fa'aliyyat-ha-ye tashkilati'. *'Asr-e ma*, no. 1 (27 Mehr 1373 [15 October 1994]).

Sazman-e mojahedin enqelab-e eslami-ye Iran. 'Negahi-ye kutah beh barkhi az tayf bandi-ha-ye jadid-e fekri-siyasi-ye jame'eh'. *'Asr-e ma* (7 Dey 1373–10 Khordad 1374 ([28 December 1994–31 May 1995]).

Shams, 'Abdollah. *Qanun-e asasi: az farman-e mashrutiyyat ta emruz.* Tehran: Dark, 1386 (2007).

Shams ol-va'ezin, Masha Allah. 'Halqeh-ye Kiyan mokhalef bud: goftogu ba Masha Allah Shams ol-va'ezin'. *Mehrnameh*, no. 27 (Bahman 1391 [January–February 2013]).

Shams ol-va'ezin, Masha Allah. 'Towse'eh-ye farhangi [*Kiyan*, no. 2, Azar 1370 (November–December 1991)]'. In *Yaddasht-ha-ye sardabir*. Tehran: Jame'eh-ye Iraniyan, 1379 (2000).

Shams ol-va'ezin, Masha Allah. 'Gozashteh, hal, ayandeh [Originally published in *Kiyan*, no. 1, Aban 1370 (October–November 1991)]'. In *Yaddasht-ha-ye sardabir*. Tehran: Jame'eh-ye Iraniyan, Bahar 1380 (Spring 2001).

Shams ol-va'ezin, Masha Allah. 'Osul-e 10 ganeh-ye *Jame'eh* [*Jame'eh*, no. 1, 16 Bahman 1376 (5 February 1998)]'. In *Yaddasht-ha-ye sardabir*. Tehran: Jame'eh-ye Iraniyan, Bahar 1380 (Spring 2001).

Shams ol-va'ezin, Masha Allah. 'Rowshanfekri-ye dini va jomhuri-ye sevvom [Original article published in *Kiyan*, Khordad–Tir 1376, 37 (June–July 1997)]'. In *Yaddasht-ha-ye sardabir*. Tehran: Jame'eh-ye Iraniyan, Bahar 1380 (Spring 2001).

Shari'ati, 'Ali. *Bazgasht.* Tehran: Elham, 1384 (2005).

Shari'ati, 'Ali. *Jahatgiri-ye tabaqati-ye eslami.* Tehran: Qalam, 1388 (2009).

Shari'ati, 'Ali. "Ommat va emamat." In *'Ali.* Tehran: Nashr-e amun, 1386 (2007).

Shari'ati, 'Ali. "Shi'eh yek hezb-e tamam." In *Shi'eh.* Tehran: Elham, 1362 (1983).

Shari'ati, 'Ali. *Tashayo'-e 'alavi va tashayo'-e safavi.* Tehran: Entesharat-e chapkhash va bonyad-e farhangi-e Doktor 'Ali Shari'ati, 1388 (2009).

Shari'ati, 'Ali. 'Ta'arif-e din'. In *Ensan-e bikhod.* Tehran: Qalam, 1389 (2010).

Sazman-e mojahedin-e enqelab-e eslami. 'E'lam-e mavaze'-e sazman-e mojahedin-e enqelab-e eslami'. In *Majmu'eh-ye bayaniyyeh-ha va etela'iyyeh-ha*. Tehran: Entesharat-e sazman-e mojahedin-e enqelab-e eslami, 16 Farvardin 1358 (5 April 1979).

Sazman-e mojahedin-e enqelab-e eslami. 'E'lam-e mowjudiyyat'. In *Majmu'eh-ye bayaniyyeh-ha va etela'iyyeh-ha*. Tehran: Entesharat-e sazman-e mojahedin-e enqelab-e eslami, 7 Farvardin 1358 (27 March 1979).

'So'al: aya Marxism mordeh ast?'. *Kiyan*, no. 17 (Azar–Dey 1372 [October 1993–January 1994]).

Sorush, 'Abdolkarim. ''Aql va azadi'. In *Farbehtar az idi'olozhi*. Tehran: Serat, 1372 (1993).

Sorush, 'Abdolkarim. 'Arkan-e farhangi-ye demokrasi'. In *Farbehtar az id'iolozhi*. Tehran: Serat, 1372 (1993).

Sorush, 'Abdolkarim. *Bani-Sadr, sazman-e mojahedin va hegelism*. Rome: Markaz-e farhangi-ye eslami-ye orupa, 1362 (1983).

Sorush, 'Abdolkarim. 'Bast-e tajrobeh-ye nabavi [Originally published in *Kiyan*, no. 39, Azar–Dey 1376 (December–January 1997–8)]'. In *Bast-e tajrobeh-ye nabavi*. Tehran: Serat, 1378 (1999).

Sorush, 'Abdolkarim. 'Bavar-e dini va davar-e dini: mosahebeh ba doktor 'Abdolkarim Sorush'. *Ehya*, no. 5 (1370 [1991]).

Sorush, 'Abdolkarim. 'Din-e aqali va aksari'. *Kiyan* 8, no. 41 (Farvardin–Ordibehesht [March–April 1998]).

Sorush, 'Abdolkarim. 'Farbehtar az idi'olozhi'. In *Farbehtar az idi'olozhi*. Tehran: Mo'asseseh-ye farhangi-e Serat, 1372 (1993).

Sorush, 'Abdolkarim. 'Hokumat-e demokratik-e dini?' *Kiyan* 11 (Farvardin–Ordibehesht 1372 [March–April 1993]).

Sorush, 'Abdolkarim. 'Horiyyat va rowhaniyyat'. In *Modara va modiriyyat*. Tehran: Serat, 1385 (2006).

Sorush, 'Abdolkarim. 'Idi'olozhi-ye dini va din-e idi'olozhik'. *Kiyan*, no. 17 (Azar–Dey 1372 [October 1993–January 1994]).

Sorush, 'Abdolkarim. 'Idi'olozhi-ye dini va din-e idi'olozhik [Originally published in *Kiyan*, no. 16, Azar–Dey 1373 (November–December 1995)]'. In *Modara va modiriyyat*. Tehran: Serat, 1387 (2008) [1375 (1996)].

Sorush, 'Abdolkarim. *Idi'olozhi-ye shaytani*. Tehran: Serat, 1373 (1994) [1359 (1980)].

Sorush, 'Abdolkarim. 'Idi'olozhi chist?'. In *Farbehtar az idi'olozhi*. Tehran: Serat, 1372 (1993).

Sorush, 'Abdolkarim 'Jaryan-e Mesbah ya'ni fashism'. *Baztab-e andisheh*, no. 80 (1384/11/10 [30 January 2006]).

Sorush, 'Abdolkarim. 'Mabani-ye te'orik-e liberalism'. In *Razdani va rowshanfekri va dindari*. Tehran: Serat, 1377 (1998).

Sorush, 'Abdolkarim. 'Modara va modiriyyat-e mo'menan: sokhani dar nesbat-e din va demokrasi'. *Kiyan* 21 (Shahrivar–Mehr 1373 [September–October 1994]).

Sorush, 'Abdolkarim. 'Modara va modiriyyat: sokhani dar nesbat-e din va demokrasi'. In *Modara va modiriyyat*. Tehran: Serat, 1380 (2001).

Sorush, 'Abdolkarim. 'Nameh-ye khosusi-ye beh riyasat-e jomhuri-ye eslami-ye Iran (Aqa-ye Hashemi-Rafsanjani) [7 Tir 1376 (28 June 1997)]'. In *Siyasat nameh*. Tehran: Serat, 1378 (1999).

Sorush, 'Abdolkarim. 'Nameh-ye khosusi beh riyasat-e jomhuri-ye eslami-ye Iran (Aqa-ye Hashemi-Rafsanjani [4 Tir 1374 (25 June 1995)]'. In *Siyasat nameh*. Tehran: Serat, 1378 (1999).

Sorush, 'Abdolkarim. 'Nameh-ye khosusi beh riyasat-e jomhuri-ye eslami-ye Iran (Aqa-ye Hashemi-Rafsanjani) [15 Tir 1376 (6 July 1997)]'. In *Siyasat nameh*. Tehran: Serat, 1378 (1999).

Sorush, 'Abdolkarim. 'Nameh-ye khosusi beh riyasat-e jomhuri-ye eslami-ye Iran (Aqa-ye Hashemi Rafsanjani) va riyasat-e qoveh-ye qaza'iyeh (Aqa-ye Mohammad Yazdi)'. In *Siyasat nameh*. Tehran: Serat, 1378 (1999).

Sorush, 'Abdolkarim. 'Nameh-ye sar goshadeh beh riyasat-e jomhuri-ye eslami-ye Iran (Aqa-ye Hashemi-Rafsanjani) [20 Ordibehesht 1375 (9 May 1996)]'. In *Siyasat nameh*. Tehran: Serat, 1378 (1999).

Sorush, 'Abdolkarim. *Naqdi va dar amadi bar tazad-e diyalektiki*. Tehran: Mo'asseseh-ye farhang-e serat, 1373 (1994) (1357 [1978]).

Sorush, 'Abdolkarim. 'Nazarat-e yeki az nazdikan-e Dr. Sorush dar mored-e dargiri-ye daneshgah-ye fani-ye Daneshgah-e Tehran [Originally published in *Salam*, 29/7/1374 (21 October 1995)]'. In *Siyasat nameh*. Tehran: Serat, 1378 [1999].

Sorush, 'Abdolkarim. ''Olum-e ensani dar nezam-e daneshgahi'. *Daneshgah-e enqelab*, no. 2 (Mordad 1360 [July–August 1981]).

Sorush, 'Abdolkarim. ''Olum-e ensani dar nezam-e daneshgahi'. In *Tafarroj-e son': goftar-ha'i dar akhlaq va san'at va 'elm-e ensani*. Tehran: Serat, 1379 (2000).

Sorush, 'Abdolkarim. 'Pasokh beh naqd nameh-ye "sobat va taghyir dar andisheh-ye dini"'. *Kiyan* 2, no. 7 (Tir 1371 [June–July 1992]).

Sorush, 'Abdolkarim. 'Qabz va bast-e te'orik-e shari'at (1) [Originally published in *Kayhan-e farhangi*, 5, no. 2, Ordibehesht 1367 (April–May 1988)]'. In *Qabz va bast-e te'orik-e shari'at: nazariyyeh-ye kamel-e ma'refat-e dini*. Tehran: Serat, 1374 (1995).

Sorush, 'Abdolkarim. 'Saqf-e azadi [Summer 1377 (1998)]'. In *Ayin-e shahriyari va dindari*. Tehran: Serat, 1387 (2008).

Sorush, 'Abdolkarim. 'Serat-ha-ye mostaqim: sokhani dar peluralism-e dini; mosbat va manfi'. In *Serat-ha-ye mostaqim*. Tehran: Serat, 1378 (1999).

Sorush, 'Abdolkarim. 'Setad-e enqelab-e farhangi az aghaz ta kanun: mosahebeh ba doktor 'Abdolkarim Sorush'. *Daneshgah-e enqelab*, no. 4 (Mehr 1360 [September–October 1981]).

Sorush, 'Abdolkarim. 'Shari'ati va porotestanism'. *Madreseh* (Tir 1384 [June–July 2005]).

Sorush, 'Abdolkarim. 'Sokhani ba daneshjuyan-e mazlum: taqlid-e siyasi mamnu'! (Originally published in *Bahar*, 20/4/1379 [10 July 2000])'. In *Ayin-e shahriyari va dindari*. Tehran: Serat, 1387 (2008).

Sorush, 'Abdolkarim. "Tahlil-e mafhum-e hokumat-e dini [Originally published in *Kiyan*, 32 Shahrivar-Mehr 1375]." In *Modara va modiriyyat*. Tehran: Serat, 1387 [2008].

Sorush, 'Abdolkarim. 'Zati va 'arazi dar adiyan (Originally published in *Kiyan*, 42, 1377 [1998])'. In *Bast-e tajrobi-ye nabavi*. Tehran: Serat, 1385 (2006).

Sorush, 'Abdolkarim, and Reza Khojasteh-Rahimi. 'Dovvom-e khordad beh ziyan-e Kiyan tamam shod: halqeh-ye Kiyan dar goftogu ba doktor 'Abdolkarim Sorush'. www.drsoroush.com/Persian/Interviews/P-INT-Kian.html

Tajzadeh, Mostafa. *Dar defa' az entekhabat-e azad va 'adelaneh*. Tehran: Farhang va andisheh, 1381 (2002).

Tajzadeh, Mostafa. 'Gofteman-e rasmi, gofteman-e mardomi [Originally published in *Nowruz*, 28/ 12/1380 (19 March 2002)]'. In *Siyasat, kakh va zendan*. Tehran: Zekr, 1381 (2002).

Tajzadeh, Mostafa. 'Goftogu-ye sarih ba Mostafa Tajzadeh, mo'aven-e vazir-e siyasi-ye keshvar: bozorgtarin eteham-e ma in ast'. *Payam-e emruz*, no. 41.

Tajzadeh, Mostafa, and Babak Dad. *Ra'i-ye mardom: mohakemeh va defa'iyyat-e Seyyed Mostafa Tajzadeh*. Tehran: Tarh-e now, 1380 (2001).

Tajzadeh, Mostafa, and Hosayn Salimi. 'Nezam ya'ni ma: goftogu ba Mostafa Tajzadeh'. In *Kalbodshekafi-ye zehniyyat-e eslahgarayan*. Tehran: Gam-e now, 1384 (2005).

Tarikh-e shafahi-ye masjed-e hedayat. Tehran: Markaz-e asnad-e enqelab-e eslami, 1387 (2008).

Vahedi, Seyyed Mohammad, and Mahnaz Mizbani, eds. *Khaterat-e Shahid Seyyed Mohammad Vahedi*. Tehran: Markaz-e asnad-e enqelab-e eslami, 1381 (2002).

'Vizheh-nameh-ye *Salam*: farda-ye behtar baraye Iran-e eslami'. *Salam* (Farvardin 1376 [March–April 1997]).

Yusefi-Eshkevari, Hassan. *Kherad dar ziyafat-e din*. Tehran: Qasideh, 1379 [2000].

Yusefi-Eshkevari, Hassan. 'Tarhi az oumanism-e eslami'. *Baztab-e andisheh*, no. 40 (Mordad 1382 [July–August 2003]).

Ziba-Kalam, Sadeq, Fereshteh Sadat Etefaqfar, and Akbar Hashemi-Rafsanjani. *Hashemi bedun-e rotush: panj sal-e goftogu ba Hashemi-Rafsanjani*. Tehran: Ruzaneh, 1386 (2007).

Persian Secondary Sources

Ajudani, Masha Allah. *Mashruteh-ye Irani*. Tehran: Akhtaran, 1382 (2003).

Alamdari, Kazem. *Chera eslahat shekast khord: naqdi bar 'amalkard-e hasht saleh-ye eslahtalaban dar Iran, 1376–1384*. Woodland Hills, CA: Sayeh, 1387 (2008).

'Alavi-Nik, Salman. *8 sal-e bohran afarini-ye eslahtalaban*. Tehran: Markaz-e asnad-e enqelab-e eslami, 1389 (2010).

Amiri, Jahandar. *Eslahtalaban-e tajdidnazar talab va pedarkhandeh-ha*. Tehran: Markaz-e asnad-e enqelab-e eslami, Bahar 1386 (Spring 2007).

Ja'fariyan, Rasul. *Jaryan-ha va sazman-ha-ye mazhabi-siyasi-e Iran: az ruy kar amadan-e Mohammad-Reza Shah ta piruzi-ye enqelab-e eslami*. Tehran: Khaneh-ye ketab, 1387 (2008).

Katouzian, Mohammad-'Ali Homayun. *Eqtesad-e siyasi-ye Iran: az mashrutiyyat ta payan-e selseleh-ye Pahlavi*. Translated by Mohammad-Reza Nafisi and Kambiz 'Azizi. Tehran: Nashr-e markaz, 1366, 1367 [1987, 1988]; 14th printing 1387 (2008).

Mohajer, Nasser. 'Enqelab-e farhangi sal-e 1359'. In *Gozir-e nagozir: seh revayat-e gozir az jomhuri-ye eslami-ye Iran*, edited by Mihan Rusta, Mahnaz Matin, Nasser Mohajer, and Sirus Javidi. Koln: Noqteh, 1387 (2008).

Mohajer, Nasser. 'Kard ajin kardan-e doktor Berjis'. *Baran*, no. 19–20 (1387 [2008]).

Mohajer, Nasser, and Mahnaz Matin. 'Koshtar 67, pardeh-ye dovvom-e Khordad-e 60'. *'Asr-e now* (8 November 2006).

Mohajer, Nasser, and Mahnaz Matin. 'Negah-ha-ye gunagun beh si va panj sal-e koshtar'. *Arash*, no. 110 (Bahman 1392 [February 2014]).

Mohammadpur, 'Ali. *Dovvom-e Khordad, hamaseh beh yad mandani: farayand-e entekhabat-e dowreh-ye haftom-e riyasat-e jomhuri az negah-e matbu'at*. Tehran: Resanesh, 1379 (2000).

Rahnema, 'Ali. *Niru-ha-ye mazhabi bar bastar-e harakat-e nehzat-e melli.* Tehran: Gam-e now, 1384 (2005).

Ravanbakhsh, Mohammad-Hosayn, and Ahmad Madadi-Ta'emeh. *Andisheh va aqayan-e khoshunat.* Tehran: Mo'alefan, 1379 (2000).

Sa'idi, Mehdi. *Sazman-e mojahedin-e enqelab-e eslami; az ta'sis ta enhelal 1358–1365.* Tehran: Markaz-e asnad-e enqelab-e eslami, 1385 (2006).

San'ati, Reza. *Gofteman-e Mesbah: gozareshi az zendegani va mavaze'-e 'elmi-siyasi-ye Ayatollah Mesbah-Yazdi.* Tehran: Markaz-e asnad-e enqelab-e eslami, 1387 (2008).

Sazman-e mojahedin-e khalq: payda'i ta farjam (1344–1386). Vol. 1. Tehran: Mo'asseseh-ye motale'at va pazhuhesh-ha-ye siyasi, 1388 (2009).

Shadlu, 'Abbas. *Ettela'ati dar bareh-ye ahzab va jenah-ha-ye siyasi-ye Iran-e emruz.* Tehran: Nashr-e vozara', 1387 (2008).

Shadlu, 'Abbas. *Jostari-ye tarikhi piramun-e takasor gara'i dar jaryan-e eslami va paydayesh-e jenah-e rast va chap-e mazhabi.* Tehran: Vozara', 1381 (2002).

Shamsi, 'Abdollah. *Hezb-e kargozaran-e sazandegi.* Qom: Pazhuheshkadeh-ye tahqiqat-e eslami, 1390 (2011).

English Primary & Secondary Sources

'Abd al-Raziq, 'Ali. 'Message Not Government, Religion Not State'. In *Liberal Islam: A Sourcebook*, edited by Charles Kurzman. New York & Oxford: Oxford University Press, 1998.

Abrahamian, Ervand. *The Coup: 1953, the CIA, and the Roots of Modern U. S.–Iranian Relations.* New York & London: The New Press, 2013.

Abrahamian, Ervand. *Iran Between Two Revolutions.* Princeton, NJ: Princeton University Press, 1982.

Abrahamian, Ervand. *Khomeinism: Essays on the Islamic Republic.* Berkeley & London: University of California Press, 1993.

Abrahamian, Ervand. *Radical Islam: The Iranian Mojahedin.* London: I. B. Tauris, 1989.

Abrahamian, Ervand. *Tortured Confessions: Prisons and Public Recantations in Modern Iran.* Kindle ed. Berkeley: University of California Press, 1999.

Abrahamov, Binyamin. *Islamic Theology: Traditionalism and Rationalism.* Edinburgh: Edinburgh University Press, 1998.

Adib-Moghaddam, Arshin, ed. *A Critical Introduction to Khomeini.* Cambridge & New York: Cambridge University Press, 2014.

Adib-Moghaddam, Arshin. *Iran in World Politics: The Question of the Islamic Republic.* London & New York: Hurst, 2008.

Agamben, Giorgio. *What Is an Apparatus? and Other Essays.* Translated by David Kishik and David Pedatella, eds. Kindle ed. Stanford, CA: Stanford University Press.

Aghaie, Kamran Scot. 'Islamist Historiography in Post-Revolutionary Iran'. In *Iran in the 20th Century: Historiography and Political Culture,* edited by Touraj Atabaki. London & New York: I. B. Tauris, 2009.

Ahmed, Shahab. *What Is Islam?: The Importance of Being Islamic.* Princeton & Oxford: Princeton University Press, 2016.

Akhavi, Shahrough. *Religion and Politics in Contemporary Iran: Clergy–State Relations in the Pahlavi Period.* Albany: State University of New York Press, 1980.

al-Sarhan, Saud. 'The Saudis as Managers of the Hajj'. In *The Hajj: Pilgrimage in Islam,* edited by Eric Tagliacozzo and Shawkat M. Toorawa. New York: Cambridge University Press, 2016.

Alatas, Syed Farid. *Applying Ibn Khaldun: The Recovery of a Lost Tradition in Sociology.* London & New York: Routledge, 2014.

Alavi-Tabar, Alireza, and Ali Mirsepassi. 'Alireza Alavi-Tabar and Political Change'. In *Modern Democracy in Iran: Islam, Culture, and Political Change.* New York & London: New York University Press, 2010.

Alexander, Jeffrey C. *The Civil Sphere.* Oxford & New York: Oxford University Press, 2006.

Algar, Hamid. '"Allama Sayyid Muhammad Husayn Tabataba'i: Philosopher, Exegete, and Gnostic'. *Journal of Islamic Studies* 17, no. 3 (2006).

Algar, Hamid. 'Imam Khomeini, 1902–62: The Pre-Revolutionary Years'. In *Islam, Politics and Social Movements,* edited by Ira Lapidus and Edmund Burke. Berkeley & London: University of California Press, 1988.

Allen, Graham. *Intertextuality.* London & New York: Routledge, 2000.

Amanat, Abbas. *Apocalyptic Islam and Iranian Shi'ism.* London: I. B. Tauris, 2009.

Amin, Camron Michael. *The Making of the Modern Iranian Woman: Gender, State Policy, and Popular Culture 1865–1946.* Gainesville: University Press of Florida, 2002.

Amir-Moezzi, Mohammad Ali. *The Divine Guide in Early Shi'ism: The Sources of Esotericism in Islam.* Translated by David Streight. Albany: State University of New York Press, 1994.

Amirpur, Katajun. 'The Expansion of the Prophetic Experience: 'Abdolkarim Sorush's New Approach to Qur'anic Revelation'. *Die Welt des Islams,* no. 51 (2011).

Anderson, Perry. 'The Antinomies of Antonio Gramsci'. *New Left Review* 1, no. 100 (November–December 1979).

Anderson, Perry. "Heirs to Gramsci." *New Left Review*, no. 100 (July–August 2016).

Anderson, Perry. *Lineages of the Absolutist State*. World History Series. Kindle ed. London & New York: Verso, 2013 (1974).

Anderson, Perry. *The Origins of Postmodernity*. London & New York: Verso, 1998.

Anderson, Perry. 'Trotsky's Interpretation of Stalinism'. *New Left Review* I, no. 139 (May–June 1983).

Anievas, Alexander, and Kerem Nisancioglu. *How the West Came to Rule: The Geopolitical Origins of Capitalism*. Kindle ed. London: Pluto Press, 2015.

Ansari, Ali M. *Iran, Islam and Democracy: The Politics of Managing Change*. 2nd ed. London: Chatham House, Royal Institute of International Affairs, 2006.

Ansari, Ali M. 'The Myth of the White Revolution: Mohammad Reza Shah, "Modernization" and the Consolidation of Power'. *Middle Eastern Studies* 37, no. 3 (July 2001).

Ansari, Ali M. *The Politics of Nationalism in Modern Iran*. Kindle ed. Cambridge & New York: Cambridge University Press, 2012.

Anzali, Ata. *"Mysticism" in Iran: The Safavid Roots of a Modern Concept*. Columbia, SC: University of South Carolina Press, 2017.

Arjomand, Said Amir. *After Khomeini: Iran Under His Successors*. Kindle ed. Oxford & New York: Oxford University Press, 2009.

Arjomand, Said Amir. 'Ideological Revolution in Shi'ism'. In *Authority and Political Culture in Shi'ism*, edited by Said Amir Arjomand. Albany: State University of New York, 1988.

Arjomand, Said Amir. 'The State and Khomeini's Islamic Order'. *Iranian Studies* 13, no. 1 (1980): 147–64.

Arjomand, Said Amir. *The Turban for the Crown: The Islamic Revolution in Iran*. Oxford & New York: Oxford University Press, 1988.

Arjomand, Said Amir. 'The Ulama's Traditionalist Opposition to Parliamentarianism: 1907–1909'. *Middle Eastern Studies* 17, no. 2 (April 1981).

Atabaki, Touraj. 'From 'Amaleh (Labor) to Kargar (Worker): Recruitment, Work Discipline and Making of the Working Class in the Persian/Iranian Oil Industry'. *International Labor and Working-Class History*, no. 84 (2013).

Aron, Raymond. *The Opium of the Intellectuals*. Introduction by Harvey C. Mansfield, foreword by Daniel J. Mahoney and Brian C. Anderson, eds. New Brunswick & London: Transaction Publishers, 2001.

Ashraf, Ahmad. 'EDUCATION vii. GENERAL SURVEY OF MODERN EDUCATION'. *Encyclopaedia Iranica* VIII (2011).

Azimi, Fakhreddin. 'Khomeini and the "White Revolution"'. In *A Critical Introduction to Khomeini*, edited by Arshin Adib-Moghaddam. New York: Cambridge University Press, 2014.

Azimi, Fakhreddin. *The Quest for Democracy in Iran: A Century of Struggle against Authoritarian Rule*. Cambridge, MA & London: Harvard University Press, 2008.

Bakhash, Shaul. *The Reign of the Ayatollahs: Iran and the Islamic Revolution*. New York: Basic Books, 1984.

Baktiari, Bahman. *Parliamentary Politics in Revolutionary Iran: The Institutionalization of Factional Politics*. Gainesville, Tallahassee, Tampa: University Press of Florida, 1996.

Bani-Sadr, Abol Hassan. *My Turn to Speak: Iran, the Revolution & Secret Deals with the U.S.* Foreword by Ambassador L. Bruce Laingen, ed. Washington & New York: Brassey's (US), Inc., A Macmillan Publishing Company, 1991.

Banisadr, Masoud. *Masoud: Memoirs of an Iranian Rebel*. London: Saqi, 2004.

Barzin, Saeed. 'Constitutionalism and Democracy in the Religious Ideology of Mehdi Bazargan'. *British Journal of Middle Eastern Studies* 21, no. 1 (1994).

Bayat, Asef. 'The Coming of a Post-Islamist Society'. *Critique: Critical Middle Eastern Studies* 5, no. 9 (Fall 1996).

Bayat, Asef. 'Revolution in Bad Times'. *New Left Review* (March–April 2013).

Bayat, Asef. 'Shari'ati and Marx: A Critique of an "Islamic" Critique of Marxism'. *Alif: Journal of Comparative Poetics* (1990).

Bayat, Asef. *Life as Politics: How Ordinary People Change the Middle East*. Kindle ed. Stanford, CA: Stanford University Press, 2010, 2013.

Bayat, Asef. 'Tehran: Paradox City'. *New Left Review*, no. 66 (November–December 2010).

Bayly, C. A. *Recovering Liberties: Indian Thought in the Age of Liberalism and Empire*. Ideas in Context. Kindle ed. Cambridge & New York: Cambridge University Press, 2012.

Behdad, Sohrab. 'Islamic Utopia in Pre-Revolutionary Iran: Navvab Safavi and the Fada'ian-e Eslam'. *Middle Eastern Studies* 33, no. 1 (1997).

Bell, Daniel. *The End of Ideology: On the Exhaustion of Political Ideas in the Fifties*. Cambridge, MA & London: Harvard University Press, 2000.

Benjamin, Walter. 'On the Critique of Violence'. Translated by J. A. Underwood. In *One-way Street and Other Writings*. London & New York: Penguin, 2009.

Berlin, Isaiah. *The Crooked Timber of Humanity: Chapters in the History of Ideas*. Kindle ed. London: Pimlico, 2003.

Boozari, Amirhassan. *Shi'i Jurisprudence and Constitution: Revolution in Iran*. Kindle ed. New York: Palgrave Macmillan, 2011.

Boroujerdi, Mehrzad. *Iranian Intellectuals and the West: The Tormented Triumph of Nativism*. Mohamed El-Hindi series on Arab culture and Islamic civilization. Syracuse, NY: Syracuse University Press, 1996.

Boroujerdi, Mehrzad, and Kourosh Rahimkhani. 'The Office of the Supreme Leader: Epicenter of a Theocracy'. In *Power and Change in Iran: Politics of Contention and Conciliation*, edited by Daniel Brumberg and Farideh Farhi. Bloomington & Indianapolis: Indiana University Press, 2016.

Bosworth, C. E., E. van Donzel, W. P. Heinrichs, and Ch. Pellat, eds. *Encyclopaedia of Islam*. Vol. 7. Leiden & New York: E. J. Brill, 1993.

Bottomore, Tom. *Elites and Society*. Kindle; Second ed. London & New York: Routledge, 1993.

Bourdieu, Pierre. 'The Forms of Capital'. In *The RoutledgeFalmer Reader in Sociology of Education*, edited by Stephen J. Ball. London & New York: RoutledgeFalmer, 2004.

Bourdieu, Pierre. *Language and Symbolic Power*. Translated by Gino Raymond and Matthew Adamson. Cambridge: Polity Press, 1991.

Bourdieu, Pierre. *Outline of a Theory of Practice*. Translated by Richard Nice. Kindle ed. Cambridge & New York: Cambridge University Press, 1977.

Bourdieu, Pierre, and Terry Eagleton. 'Doxa and Common Life: An Interview'. In *Mapping Ideology*, edited by Slavoj Zizek. London & New York: Verso, 1994, 2012.

Bourdieu, Pierre, and Loic J. D. Wacquant. *Invitation to Reflexive Sociology*. Oxford: Polity, 1992.

Brumberg, Daniel. *Reinventing Khomeini: The Struggle for Reform in Iran*. Chicago & London: University of Chicago Press, 2001.

Buchta, Wilfried. *Who Rules Iran? The Structure of Power in the Islamic Republic*. Washington: Washington Institute for Near East Policy and the Konrad Adenauer Stiftung, 2000.

Butler, Judith. *Excitable Speech: A Politics of the Performative*. London & New York: Routledge, 1999.

Byrne, Malcolm. *Iran–Contra: Reagan's Scandal and the Unchecked Abuse of Presidential Power*. Lawrence, KS: University Press of Kansas, 2014.

Browne, Edward Granville. *The Persian Revolution of 1905–1909*. London: Cambridge University Press, 1910.

Calhoun, Craig. 'Civil Society and the Public Sphere'. In *The Oxford Handbook of Civil Society*, edited by Michael Edwards. Oxford & New York: Oxford University Press, 2011.

Camus, Albert. *The Rebel: An Essay on Man in Revolt*. Foreword by Sir Herbert Read, ed. New York: Vintage, 1991.

Carlyle, Thomas. *On Heroes, Hero-Worship and the Heroic in History, Rethinking* the Western Tradition. Kindle ed. New Haven & London: Yale University Press, 2013.

Chakrabarty, Dipesh. *Provincializing Europe: Postcolonial Thought and Historical Difference*. Kindle ed. Princeton & Oxford: Princeton University Press, 2000.

Chakrabarty, Dipesh. 'Radical Histories and Question of Enlightenment Rationalism: Some Recent Critiques of Subaltern Studies'. In *Mapping Subaltern Studies and the Postcolonial*, edited by Vinayak Chaturvedi. London & New York: Verso, 2000.

Chatterjee, Partha. '*Our Modernity*'. In *Empire and Nation: Selected Essays*. New York: Columbia University Press, 2010.

Chehabi, H. E. *Iranian Politics and Religious Modernism: The Liberation Movement of Iran under the Shah and Khomeini*. London: I. B. Tauris, 1990.

Chehabi, H. E. 'Religion and Politics in Iran: How Theocratic Is the Islamic Republic?' *Daedalus* 120, no. 3 (Summer 1991).

Chehabi, H. E., and Juan J. Linz. 'A Theory of Sultanism 1: A Type of Nondemocratic Rule'. In *Sultanistic Regimes*, edited by Juan J. Linz and H. E. Chehabi. Baltimore & London: John Hopkins University Press, 1998.

Chehabi, Houchang E. 'Staging the Emperor's New Clothes: Dress Codes and Nation-Building under Reza Shah'. *Iranian Studies* 26, no. 3/4 (1993).

Chibber, Vivek. *Postcolonial Theory and the Specter of Capital*. Kindle ed. London & New York: Verso, 2013.

Cole, Juan. *Sacred Space and Holy War: The Politics, Culture and History of Shi'ite Islam*. London & New York: I. B. Tauris, 2002.

Corboz, Elvire. *Guardians of Shi'ism: Sacred Authority and Transnational Family Networks*. Edinburgh: Edinburgh University Press, 2015.

Crist, David. *The Twilight War: The Secret History of America's Thirty-Year Conflict with Iran*. Kindle ed. New York: Penguin Press, 2012.

Cronin, Stephanie. *The Army and the Creation of the Pahlavi State in Iran, 1910–1926*. London & New York: Tauris Academic Studies, 1997.

Cronin, Stephanie. *Soldiers, Shahs and Subalterns in Iran: Opposition, Protest and Revolt, 1921–1941*. Basingstoke & New York: Palgrave Macmillan, 2010.

Dabashi, Hamid. 'Mulla Ahmad Naraqi and the Question of the Guardianship of the Jurisconsult (Wilayat-e Faqih)'. In *Expectation of the Millennium: Shi'ism in History*, edited by Seyyed Hossein Nasr, Hamid Dabashi, and Seyyed Vali Reza Nasr. Albany: State University of New York Press, 1989.

Dabashi, Hamid. *Shi'ism: A Religion of Protest*. Cambridge & London: Harvard University Press, 2011.

Dabashi, Hamid. *Theology of Discontent: The Ideological Foundation of the Islamic Revolution in Iran*. New Brunswick, NJ: Transaction Publishers, 2006.

Dahlén, Ashk P. *Islamic Law, Epistemology and Modernity: Legal Philosophy in Contemporary Iran*. Middle East Studies: History, Politics, and Law, edited by Shahrough Akhavi. New York & London: Routledge, 2003.

Dailami, Pezhmann. 'The First Congress of Peoples of the East and the Iranian Soviet Republic of Gilan, 1920–21'. In *Reformers and Revolutionaries in Modern Iran: New Perspectives on the Iranian Left*, edited by Stephanie Cronin. London & New York: RoutledgeCurzon, 2004.

Deutscher, Isaac. *The Prophet: The Life of Leon Trotsky*. Kindle ed. London & New York: Verso, 2015.

Devji, Faisal. *Muslim Zion: Pakistan as a Political Idea*. London: Hurst & Company, 2013.

Djilas, Milovan. *The New Class: An Analysis of the Communist System*. San Diego, New York, London: Harcourt Brace Jovanovich, 1985 (1957).

Donohue, John J., and John L. Esposito. *Islam in Transition: Muslim Perspectives*. 2nd ed. New York & Oxford: Oxford University Press, 2007.

Ebtekar, Massoumeh, and Fred A. Reed. *Takeover in Tehran: The Inside Story of the 1979 U.S. Embassy Capture*. Vancouver: Talon Books, 2000.

Ehsani, Kaveh. 'The Politics of Property in the Islamic Republic of Iran'. In *The Rule of Law, Islam, and Constitutional Politics in Egypt and Iran*, edited by Said Amir Arjomand and Nathan J. Brown. Albany State University of New York, 2013.

Ehsani, Kaveh. 'The Urban Provincial Periphery in Iran: Revolution and War in Ramhormoz'. In *Contemporary Iran: Economy, Society, Politics*, edited by Ali Gheissari. Oxford & New York: Oxford University Press, 2009.

Ehsani, Kaveh. 'War and Resentment: Critical Reflections on the Legacies of the Iran–Iraq War'. *Middle East Critique* (2016).

Ehteshami, Anoushiravan. *After Khomeini: The Iranian Second Republic.* Kindle ed. London & New York: Routledge, 1995.

Ehteshami, Anoushiravan, and Mahjoob Zweiri. *Iran and the Rise of Its Neoconservatives: The Politics of Tehran's Silent Revolution.* London: I. B. Tauris, 2007.

Elden, Stuart. *Foucault's Last Decade.* Kindle ed. Cambridge: Polity, 2016.

Enayat, Hadi. *Law, State, and Society in Modern Iran: Constitutionalism, Autocracy, and Legal Reform, 1906–1941.* New York: Palgrave Macmillan, 2013.

Enayat, Hamid. 'Iran: Khumayni's Concept of the "Guardianship of the Jurisconsult"', In *Islam in the Political Process*, edited by James P. Piscatori. Cambridge: Press Syndicate of the University of Cambridge, 1983.

Fairclough, Norman. *Analysing Discourse: Textual Analysis for Social Research.* London & New York: Routledge, 2003.

Farsoun, Samih K., and Mehrdad Mashayekhi. *Iran: Political Culture in the Islamic Republic.* London & New York: Routledge, 1992.

Farzaneh, Mateo Mohammad. *The Iranian Constitutional Revolution and the Clerical Leadership of Khurasani.* Kindle ed. Syracuse, NY: Syracuse University Press, 2015.

Fathi, Nazila. 'Iran: Another Death Sentence Is Lifted'. *New York Times*, February 15, 2003.

Femia, Joseph V. *Gramsci's Political Thought.* Oxford: Oxford University Press, 1981.

Fischer, Michael M. J. 'Imam Khomeini: Four Levels of Understanding'. In *Voices of Resurgent Islam*, edited by John L. Esposito. New York & Oxford: Oxford University Press, 1983.

Floor, Willem. *Guilds, Merchants, & Ulama in Nineteenth-Century Iran.* Washington: Mage Publishers, 2009.

Forti, Marina. 'Arg-e Jadid: A California Oasis in the Iranian Desert'. In *Evil Paradises: Dreamworlds of Neoliberalism*, edited by Mike Davis and David Bertrand Monk. New York & London: The New Press, 2007.

Foucault, Michel. 'The Political Function of the Intellectual'. *Radical Philosophy*, no. 17 (1977).

Foucault, Michel. *Society Must Be Defended: Lectures at the Collège de France 1975–76.* Translated by David Macey, edited by Arnold I. Davidson. London & New York: Allen Lane, 2003.

Foucault, Michel. *On the Government of the Living: Lectures at the Collège de France, 1979–1980.* Translated by Graham Burchell, edited by Arnold I. Davidson. Kindle ed. Basingstoke & New York: Palgrave Macmillan, 2014.

Foucault, Michel. *Power/Knowledge: Selected Interviews and Other Writings 1972–1977*. Translated by Colin Gordon, Leo Marshall, John Mepham, and Kate Soper, edited by Colin Gordon. New York: Pantheon Books, 1980.

Freeden, Michael. *Ideologies and Political Theory: A Conceptual Approach*. Oxford: Clarendon, 1996.

Fukuyama, Francis. *The Origins of Political Order: From Prehuman Times to the French Revolution*. Kindle ed. London: Profile Books, 2011.

Gadamer, Hans-Georg. *Truth and Method*. Translated by Joel Weinsheimer and Donald G. Marshall. London & New York: Bloomsbury, 2004.

Ganji, Akbar. 'The Latter-Day Sultan: Power and Politics in Iran'. *Foreign Affairs* 87, no. 6 (2008).

Geertz, Clifford. *The Interpretation of Cultures*. New York: Basic Books, 1973.

Ghamari-Tabrizi, Behrooz. *Islam and Dissent in Postrevolutionary Iran: Abdolkarim Soroush, Religious Politics and Democratic Reform*. London & New York: I. B. Tauris, 2008.

Gheissari, Ali. *Iranian Intellectuals in the 20th Century*. 1st ed. Austin: University of Texas Press, 1998.

Goodman, Lenn E. *Islamic Humanism*. Oxford & New York: Oxford University Press, 2003.

Gramsci, Antonio. *Prison Notebooks*. Vol. 3. New York: Columbia University Press, 2007.

Gramsci, Antonio. *Prison Notebooks*. Translated by Joseph A. Buttigieg and Antonio Callari. Vol. 1. New York: Columbia University Press, 1992.

Gramsci, Antonio. *Selections from the Prison Notebooks of Antonio Gramsci*. Edited by Quintin Hoare and Geoffrey Nowell-Smith. Midsomer. Norton & Bath: Lawrence and Wishart, 1971.

Gray, John. *Liberalism*. 2nd ed. Buckingham: Open University Press, 1995.

Gray, John. *Two Faces of Liberalism*. Oxford: Polity, 2000.

Griffin, Roger. *A Fascist Century: Essays by Roger Griffin*. New York: Palgrave Macmillan, 2008.

Guha, Ranajit. *Dominance without Hegemony: History and Power in Colonial India. Convergences*: Inventories of the Present. Edited by Edward W. Said. Cambridge, MA, London: Harvard University Press, 1997.

Guha, Ranajit. 'Gramsci in India: Homage to a Teacher'. In *The Small Voice of History: Collected Essays*, edited by Partha Chatterjee. Hyderabad: Permanent Black, 2012.

Habermas, Jürgen. *The Structural Transformation of the Public Sphere: An Inquiry into a Category of Bourgeois Society.* Translated by Thomas Burger and Frederick Lawrence. Oxford: Polity, 1992.

Haider, Najam. *Shi'i Islam: An Introduction.* New York: Cambridge University Press, 2014.

Hajjarian, Sa'id, and Kaveh Ehsani. '"Existing Political Vessels Cannot Contain the Reform Movement": A Conversation with Sa'id Hajjarian'. *Middle East Report*, no. 212 (Autumn 1999).

Hall, Stuart. *Cultural Studies 1983: A Theoretical History.* Durham & London: Duke University Press, 2016.

Haraway, Donna. 'Situated Knowledges: The Science Question in Feminism and the Privilege of Partial Perspective'. *Feminist Studies* 13, no. 3 (Autumn 1988).

Harris, Kevan. 'The Rise of the Subcontractor State: Politics of Pseudo-Privatization in the Islamic Republic of Iran'. *International Journal of Middle East Studies*, no. 45 (2013).

Harris, Kevan. 'Social Welfare Policies and the Dynamics of Elite and Popular Contention'. In *Power and Change in Iran: Politics of Contention and Conciliation*, edited by Daniel Brumberg and Farideh Farhi. Bloomington, IN: Indiana University Press, 2016.

Harvey, David. *A Brief History of Neoliberalism.* Oxford & New York: Oxford University Press, 2005.

Hayek, F. A. *The Road to Serfdom: Text and Documents, The Definitive Edition.* Kindle ed. New York & London: Routledge, 2008.

Heern, Zackery M. *The Emergence of Modern Shi'ism: Islamic Reform in Iraq and Iran.* London: Oneworld Publications, 2015.

Hill, Christopher. *Puritanism and Revolution: Studies in Interpretation of the English Revolution of the 17th Century.* Kindle ed. London: Pimlico, 2001.

Hobbes, Thomas. *Leviathan.* Cambridge Texts in the History of Political Thought. Kindle ed. Cambridge & New York: Cambridge University Press, 1996.

Hobsbawm, Eric. 'Introduction: Inventing Traditions'. In *The Invention of Tradition*, edited by Eric Hobsbawm and Terence Ranger. Cambridge & New York: Cambridge University Press, 1983.

Hodgson, Marshall G. S. 'How Did the Early Shi'a become Sectarian?' *Journal of the American Oriental Society* 75, no. 1 (1955).

Hussain, Jassim M. *The Occultation of the Twelfth Imam.* Muhammadi Trust, 1982.

Inwood, Michael. *A Hegel Dictionary.* Oxford: Blackwell, 1992.

Ionescu, Ghita, and Ernest Gellner. 'Introduction', In *Populism: Its Meanings and National Characteristics*, edited by Ghita Ionescu and Ernest Gellner. London: Weidenfield and Nicolson, 1969.

Israel, Jonathan. *Revolutionary Ideas: An Intellectual History of the French Revolution from The Rights of Man to Robespierre*. Oxford & Princeton: Princeton University Press, 2014.

Jahanbakhsh, Forough. *Islam, Democracy and Religious Modernism in Iran, 1953–2000: From Bazargan to Soroush*. Social, Economic, and Political Studies of the Middle East and Asia. Leiden & Boston: Brill, 2001.

Jayawardena, Kumari. *Feminism and Nationalism in the Third World*. Kindle ed. London & New York: Verso, 2016.

Jazani, Bizhan. *Capitalism and Revolution in Iran*. Translated by Iran Committee. London: Zed, 1980.

Jones, Steven. *Antonio Gramsci*. London and New York: Routledge, 2006.

Kadivar, Mohsen. 'The Innovative Political Ideas and Influence of Mulla Muhammad Kazim Khurasani'. www.kadivar.com

Kadushin, Charles. *Understanding Social Networks: Theories, Concepts, and Findings*. Kindle ed. Oxford & New York: Oxford University Press, 2012.

Kahn, Paul W. *Political Theology: Four New Chapters on the Concept of Sovereignty*. New York: Columbia University Press, 2011.

Kahn, Victoria. 'Political Theology and Liberal Culture: Strauss, Schmitt, Spinoza, and Arendt'. In *Political Theology and Early Modernity*, edited by Graham Hammill and Julia Reinhard Lupton. Chicago & London: University of Chicago Press, 2012.

Kamali, Mohammad Hashim. *Shari'ah Law: An Introduction*. Oxford: Oneworld Publications, 2008.

Kant, Immanuel. 'An Answer to the Question: "What Is Enlightenment?"'. Translated by H. B. Nisbet. In *Kant: Political Writings*, edited by Hans Reiss. Cambridge & New York: Cambridge University Press, 1991.

Katouzian, Homa. 'European Liberalisms and Modern Concepts of Liberty'. In *Iranian History and Politics: The Dialectic of State and Society*. London & New York: Routledge, 2003.

Katouzian, Homa. *The Persians: Ancient, Mediaeval and Modern Iran*. New Haven & London: Yale University Press, 2009.

Katouzian, Homa. *Sadeq Hedayat: The Life and Literature of an Iranian Writer*. London & New York: I. B. Tauris, 2002.

Katouzian, Homa. 'Seyyed Hasan Taqizadeh: Three Lives in a Lifetime'. *Comparative Studies of South Asia, Africa and the Middle East* 32, no. 1 (2012).

Katouzian, Homa. *State and Society in Iran: The Eclipse of the Qajars and the Emergence of the Pahlavis*. Library of modern Middle East studies. London: I. B. Tauris, 2006.

Kazemi-Moussavi, Ahmad. 'The Establishment of the Position of Marja'iyyt-i Taqlid in the Twelver-Shi'i Community'. *Iranian Studies* 18, no. 1 (1985).

Kazemi-Moussavi, Ahmad. *Religious Authority in Shi'ite Islam: From the Office of Mufti to the Institution of Marja'*. Kuala Lumpur: International Institute of Islamic Thought and Civilization, 1996.

Kazemi, Farhad. 'The Fada'iyan-e Islam: Fanaticism, Politics and Terror'. In *From Nationalism to Revolutionary Islam*, edited by Said Amir Arjomand. Albany: State University of New York, 1984.

Keddie, Nikki R., and Yann Richard. *Modern Iran: Roots and Results of Revolution*. Updated ed. New Haven, CT: Yale University Press, 2006.

Kelle, V. Zh., V. I. Tolstykh, V. S. Stepin, E. Iu. Solov'ev, A. I. Guseniov, F. T. Gel'man, V. M. Mikhailov, V. M. Mezhuev, and K. Kh. Momdzhian. 'Is Marxism Dead? Materials from a Discussion'. *Soviet Studies in Philosophy* 30, no. 2 (1991).

Keshavarzian, Arang. 'The Iran Deal as Social Contract'. *Middle East Research and Information Project* 45, no. 277 (2015).

Keshavarzian, Arang. 'Regime Loyalty and Bazari Representation under the Islamic Republic of Iran: Dilemmas of the Society of Islamic Coalition'. *International Journal of Middle East Studies* 41 (2009).

Khan, Mirza Malkum. 'The Law'. In *Modernist Islam, 1840–1940: A Sourcebook*, edited by Charles Kurzman. Oxford & New York: Oxford University Press, 2002.

Kholdi, Shahram. 'The Politics of Memory in the Islamic Republic of Iran: Memoirs and the Historiography of the Iranian Revolution of 1979'. PhD, University of Manchester, 2011.

Khomeini, Ruhollah. 'Islamic Government'. In *Islam and Revolution I : Writings and Declarations of Imam Khomeini (1941–1980)*, edited by Hamid Algar. Berkeley: Mizan Press, 1981.

Khomeini, Ruholah. 'Lectures on Surat al-Fatiha'. Translated by Hamid Algar. In *Islam and Revolution I: Writings and Declarations of Imam Khomeini (1941–1980)*, edited by Hamid Algar. Berkeley: Mizan Press, 1981.

Khosrokhavar, Farhad, and Mohammad Amin Ghaneirad. 'Iranian Women's Participation in the Academic World'. *Iranian Studies* 43, no. 2 (2010).

Knysh, Alexander. 'Irfan Revisted: Khomeini and the Legacy of Islamic Mystical Philosophy'. *Middle East Journal* 46, no. 4 (Autumn 1992).

Kohlberg, Etan. 'Imam and Community in the Pre-Ghayba Period'. In *Authority and Political Culture in Shi'ism*, edited by Said Amir Arjomand. Albany: State University of New York Press, 1988.

Kolakowski, Leszek. *Main Currents of Marxism: The Founders, The Golden Age, The Breakdown.* Translated by P. S. Falla. New York & London: W. W. Norton & Company, 1978.

Kolakowski, Leszek. *Modernity on Endless Trial.* Chicago & London: University of Chicago Press, 1990.

Kurzman, Charles, and Lynn Owens. 'The Sociology of Intellectuals'. *Annual Review of Sociology* 28 (2002).

Laclau, Ernesto, and Chantal Mouffe. *Hegemony and Socialist Strategy: Towards a Radical Democratic Politics.* London & New York: Versi, 1985.

Lacoue-Labarthe, Philippe. *Heidegger, Art and Politics: The Fiction of the Political.* Oxford: Blackwell, 1990.

'Lebanese Paper on Hashemi, McFarlane Issues, Al-Shira', 3 November 1986'. *FBIS* VIII.

Lenin, V. I. *Essential Works of Lenin: 'What Is to Be Done?' and Other Writings.* Kindle ed. New York: Dover, 1987 (1966).

Lenin, V. I. *State and Revolution.* Kindle ed. London & New York: Penguin Books, 1992.

Levi Della Vida, G. 'Muharib'. In *Encyclopaedia of Islam*, edited by P. Bearman, Th. Bianquis, C. E. Bosworth, E. van Donzel, and W. P. Heinrichs: Brill Online.

Levitsky, Steven, and Lucan A. Way. *Competitive Authoritarianism: Hybrid Regimes After the Cold War.* Cambridge & New York: Cambridge University Press, 2010.

Linz, Juan J. *Totalitarian and Authoritarian Regimes.* Boulder & London: Lynne Rienner, 2000.

Litvak, Meir. *Shi'i scholars of nineteenth-century Iraq: 'ulama' of Najaf and Karbala.* Cambridge: Cambridge University Press, 1998.

Locke, John. *A Letter Concerning Toleration.* Indianapolis: Hackett Publishing, 1983.

Locke, John. *Two Treatises of Government.* Cambridge: Cambridge University Press, 1988.

Losurdo, Domenico. *Liberalism: A Counter-History.* Translated by Gregory Elliott. Kindle ed. London & New York: Verso, 2011.

Mallat, Chibli. *The Renewal of Islamic Law: Muhammad Baqer as-Sadr, Najaf and the Shi'i International.* Kindle ed. Cambridge & New York: Cambridge University Press, 1993.

Mannheim, Karl. *Ideology and Utopia: An Introduction to the Sociology of Knowledge.* Translated by Louis Worth and Edward Shils. Orlando: Harcourt, 1936.

Marcuse, Herbert, and Karl R. Popper. *Revolution or Reform? A Confrontation*. Translated by Michael Aylward and A. T. Ferguson. Chicago: Precedent Publishing & New University Press, 1976.

Martin, Vanessa. 'The Anti-Constitutionalist Arguments of Shaikh Fazlallah Nuri', *Middle Eastern Studies* 22 (April 1986).

Martin, Vanessa. 'Aqa Najafi, Haj Aqa Nurullah, and the Emergence of Islamism in Isfahan 1889–1908'. *Iranian Studies* 41, no. 2 (2008).

Martin, Vanessa. *Creating an Islamic State: Khomeini and the Making of a New Iran*. London: I. B. Tauris, 2003.

Martin, Vanessa. 'Religion and State in Khumaini's "Kashf al-asrar"'. *Bulletin of the School of Oriental and African Studies, University of London* 56, no. 1 (1993).

Martin, Vanessa. 'Shaikh Fazlallah Nuri and the Iranian Revolution 1905–09'. *Middle Eastern Studies* 23, no. 1 (January 1987).

Marx, Karl. *Capital: A Critique of Political Economy*. Translated by Ben Fowkes. Kindle ed. Vol. I, London & New York: Penguin Books, 1976.

Marx, Karl. 'On the Jewish Question'. Translated by Rodney Livingstone and Gregor Benton. In *Early Writings*. London & New York: Penguin, 1992.

Marx, Karl. 'Theses on Feuerbach'. In *Karl Marx: Selected Writings*, edited by David McLellan. New York: Oxford University Press, 2000.

Marx, Karl, and Frederick Engels. *The Communist Manifesto: A Modern Edition*. Kindle ed. London & New York: Verso, 2012.

Matin-asgari, Afshin. *Iranian Student Opposition to the Shah*. Cost Mesa, CA: Mazda, 2002.

Matin, Kamran. *Recasting Iranian Modernity: International Relations and Social Change*. Iranian Studies. Edited by Homa Katouzian and Mohamad Tavakoli Targhi. London & New York: Routledge, 2013.

Matsunaga, Yasuyuki. 'The Secularization of a Faqih-Headed Revolutionary Islamic State of Iran: Its Mechanisms, Processes, and Prospects'. *Comparative Studies of South Asia, Africa and the Middle East* 29, no. 3 (2009).

Matthiesen, Toby. *The Other Saudis: Shiism Dissent and Sectarianism*. Kindle ed. New York: Cambridge University Press, 2015.

Meiksins Wood, Ellen. *Citizens to Lords: A Social History of Western Political Thought From Antiquity to the Middle Ages*. London & New York: Verso, 2008.

Milani, Abbas. *Eminent Persians: The Men and Women Who Made Modern Iran, 1941–1979*. 1st ed., 2 vols. Syracuse, NY & New York, NY: Syracuse University Press & Persian World Press, 2008.

Milani, Abbas. *The Shah*. Kindle ed. New York: Palgrave Macmillan, 2011.

Mirsepassi, Ali. *Democracy in Modern Iran: Islam, Culture, and Political Change.* New York & London: New York University Press, 2010.

Mirsepassi, Ali. *Political Islam, Iran, and the Enlightenment Philosophies of Hope and Despair.* Cambridge & New York: Cambridge University Press, 2011.

Mlynar, Zdenek, and Mikhail Gorbachev. *Conversations with Gorbachev: On Perestroika, the Prague Spring, and the Crossroads of Socialism.* Translated by George Shriver. Kindle ed. New York: Columbia University Press, 2002.

Modarressi Tabataba'i, Hossein. *An Introduction to Shi'i Law: A Bibliographical Study.* London: Ithaca Press, 1984.

Modonesi, Massimo. *Subalternity, Antagonism, Autonomy: Constructing the Political Subject.* Translated by Adriana V. Rendon Garrido and Philip Roberts. Kindle ed. London: Pluto Press, 2014.

Moin, Baqer. *Khomeini: Life of the Ayatollah.* London: I. B. Tauris, 1999.

Mojab, Shahrzad. 'The State and University: The "Islamic Cultural Revolution" in the Institutions of Higher Education of Iran, 1980–87'. University of Illinois at Urbana-Champaign, 1991.

Morton, Adam David. *Unravelling Gramsci: Hegemony and Passive Revolution in the Global Political Economy.* Kindle ed. London: Pluto, 2007.

Moslem, Mehdi. *Factional Politics in Post-Khomeini Iran.* Syracuse: Syracuse University Press, 2002.

Mottahedeh, Roy. *The Mantle of the Prophet: Religion and Politics in Iran.* Boston: Oneworld Publications, 1985, 2000.

Mottahedeh, Roy P. 'Shi'ite Political Thought and the Destiny of the Iranian Revolution'. In *Iran and the Gulf: A Search for Stability,* edited by Jamal S. Al-Suwaidi. Abu Dhabi, London, New York: The Emirates Center for Strategic Studies and Research, 1996.

Mourad, Suleiman, and Perry Anderson. *The Mosaic of Islam: A Conversation with Perry Anderson.* Kindle ed. London & New York: Verso, 2016.

Moyn, Samuel. *The Last Utopia: Human Rights in History.* Cambridge, MA & London: Harvard University Press, 2010.

Mustashar ad-Dowla Tabrizi, Mirza Yusuf Khan. *One Word – Yak Kaleme: 19th-Century Persian Treatise Introducing Western Codified Law.* With an introduction and annotated translation by A. A. Seyed-Gohrab and S. McGlinn, ed. Leiden: Leiden University Press, 2010.

Mutahhari, Murtaza. *Fundamentals of Islamic Thought: God, Man and the Universe.* Translated by R. Campbell, edited by Hamid Algar. Berkeley: Mizan Press, 1985.

Najmabadi, Afsaneh. *Women with Mustaches and Men without Beards: Gender and Sexual Anxieties of Iranian Modernity*. Kindle ed. Berkeley & Los Angeles: University of California Press, 2005.

Nuri, Fadl Allah, and 'Abd al-'Azim 'Imad al-'Ulama' Khalkhali. 'Two Clerical Tracts on Constitutionalism'. Translated by Hamid Dabashi. In *Authority and Political Culture in Shi'ism*, edited by Said Amir Arjomand. Albany: State University of New York, 1988.

Paya, 'Ali, and Mohammad-Amin Ghaneirad. 'The Philosopher and the Revolutionary State: How Karl Popper's Ideas Shaped the Views of Iranian Intellectuals'. *International Studies in the Philosophy of Science* 20, no. 2 (July 2006).

Pesaran, Evaleila. *Iran's Struggle for Economic Independence: Reform and Counter-reform in the Post-revolutionary Era*. London & New York: Routledge, 2011.

Piscatori, James P. 'Religion and Realpolitik: Islamic Responses to the Gulf War'. In *Islamic Fundamentalism and the Gulf Crisis*, edited by James P. Piscatori. Chicago: American Academy of Arts and Sciences, 1991.

Pocock, J. G. A. *Political Thought and History: Essays on Theory and Method*. Cambridge: Cambridge University Press, 2009.

Popper, Karl R. *Conjectures and Refutations: The Growth of Scientific Knowledge*. London: Routledge, 2002.

Popper, Karl R. *The Lesson of This Century: With Two Talks on Freedom and the Democratic State*. Translated by Patrick Camiller. London & New York: Routledge, 1997.

Popper, Karl R. *The Open Society and Its Enemies*. London: Routledge, 2002.

Popper, Karl R. *The Poverty of Historicism*. London & New York: Routledge, 1957.

Poulantzas, Nicos. 'Preliminaries to the Study of Hegemony in the State'. In *The Poulantzas Reader: Marxism, Law, and the State*, edited by James Martin. London & New York. Verso, 2008.

Prashad, Vijay. *The Darker Nations: A People's History of the Third World*. Kindle ed. New York & London: The New Press, 2007.

Quinton, Anthony. 'Karl Popper: Politics Without Essences'. In *Contemporary Political Philosophers*, edited by Anthony de Crespigny and Kenneth Minogue. New York: Dodd, Mead & Company, 1975.

Qutb, Sayyid. *Milestones*. New Delhi: Islamic Book Service, 2001.

Rahnema, Ali. *An Islamic Utopian: A Political Biography of Ali Shari'ati*. London: I. B. Tauris, 1998.

Rahnema, Ali. *Pioneers of Islamic Revival*. New York: Zed Books, 2005.

Rahnema, Ali. *Shi'i Reformation in Iran: The Life and Theology of Shari'at Sangelaji*. Kindle ed. London & New York: Routledge, 2016.

Rahnema, Ali. *Superstition as Ideology in Iranian Politics: From Majlesi to Ahmadinejad*. Cambridge & New York: Cambridge University Press, 2011.

Randjbar-Daemi, Siavush. 'Building the Islamic State: The Draft Constitution of 1979 Reconsidered'. *Iranian Studies* 46, no. 3 (2013).

Richard, Yann. 'Shariʿat Sangalaji: A Reformist Theologian of the Riḍa Shah Period'. Translated by Kathryn Arjomand. In *Authority and Political Culture in Shiʿism*, edited by Said Amir Arjomand. New York: State University of New York Press, 1988.

Rizvi, Sajjad H. '"Only the Imam Knows Best": The Maktab-e Tafkik's Attack on the Legitimacy of Philosophy in Iran'. *Journal of the Royal Asiatic Society* 22, no. 3–4 (October 2012).

Rizvi, Sajjad H. '"Seeking the Face of God": The Safawid Hikmat Tradition's Conceptualisation of Walaya Takwiniyya'. In *The Study of Shiʿi Islam: History, Theology and Law*, edited by Farhad Daftary and Gurdofarid Miskinzoda. London & New York: I. B. Tauris Publishers, 2014.

Rodinson, Maxime. *Mohammed*. Translated by Anne Carter. Harmondsworth: Penguin Books, 1971.

Rorty, Richard. *Contingency, Irony, and Solidarity*. Kindle ed. Cambridge & New York: Cambridge University Press, 1989.

Rostam-Kolayi, Jasamin, and Afshin Matin-asgari. 'Unveiling Ambiguities: Revisiting 1930s Iran's *kashf-i hijab* Campaign'. In *Anti-Veiling Campaigns in the Muslim World: Gender, Modernism and the Politics of Dress*, edited by Stephanie Cronin. London & New York: Routledge, 2014.

Rousseau, Jean-Jacques. *Discourse on Political Economy and The Social Contract*. Translated by Christopher Betts. Oxford & New York: Oxford University Press, 1994.

Rubin, Michael. *Into the Shadows: Radical Vigilantes in Khatami's Iran*. Washington: The Washington Institute for Near East Policy, 2001.

Sadeghi-Boroujerdi, Eskandar. 'Mostafa Malekian: Spirituality, Siyasat-Zadegi and (A)political Self-Improvement'. *Digest of Middle East Studies* 23, no. 2 (2014).

Saeidi, Ali Asghar. 'The Accountability of Para-governmental Organizations (Bonyads): The Case of Iranian Foundations'. *Iranian Studies* 37, no. 3 (2004).

Saffari, Said. 'The Legitimation of the Clergy's Right to Rule in the Iranian Constitution of 1979'. *British Journal of Middle Eastern Studies* 20, no. 1 (1993).

Said, Edward W. *Representations of the Intellectual: The Reith Lectures*. New York: Pantheon Books, 1994.

Salehi-Isfahani, Djavad. 'Human Resources in Iran: Potentials and Challenges'. *Iranian Studies* 38, no. 1 (2005).

Schayegh, Cyrus. '"Seeing like a State": An Essay on the Historiography of Modern Iran'. *International Journal of Middle East Studies* 42 (2010).

Schayegh, Cyrus. *Who Is Knowledgeable Is Strong: Science, Class, and the Formation of Modern Iranian Society, 1900–1950*. Berkeley, Los Angeles, London: University of California Press, 2009.

Schedler, Andreas. 'The Logic of Electoral Authoritarianism'. In *Electoral Authoritarianism: The Dynamics of Unfree Competition*, edited by Andreas Schedler. Boulder & London: Lynne Rienner, 2006.

Schmitt, Carl. *Concept of the Political*. Translated by George Schwab. Introduction by Tracy B. Strong ed. Chicago & London: University of Chicago Press, 2007.

Schmitt, Carl. *Political Theology: Four Chapters on the Concept of Sovereignty*. Translated by George Schwab. Foreword by Tracy B. Strong ed. Chicago & London: University of Chicago Press, 2005.

Service, Robert. *Lenin: A Biography*. Kindle ed. London: Pan Books, 2002 [2000].

Shahidi, Hossein. *Journalism in Iran: From Mission to Profession*. Abingdon & New York: Routledge, 2007.

Shakibi, Zhand. *Khatami and Gorbachev: Politics of Change in the Islamic Republic of Iran and the USSR*. London & New York: I. B. Tauris, 2010.

Shearmur, Jeremy. *The Political Thought of Karl Popper*. London & New York: Routledge, 1996.

Shklar, Judith N. 'The Liberalism of Fear'. In *Liberalism and the Moral Life*, edited by Nancy L. Rosenblum. Cambridge & London: Harvard University Press, 1989.

Siegel, Evan. 'The Case of Mehdi Hashemi'. Iranian Studies: Evan Siegel's Personal Website, http://iran.qlineorientalist.com/Articles/MehdiHashemi/MehdiHashemi.html

Skinner, Quentin. *Visions of Politics: Volume 1: Regarding Method*. Cambridge & New York: Cambridge University Press, 2002.

Slobodian, Quinn. *Foreign Front: Third World Politics in Sixties West Germany*. Durham & London: Duke University Press: 2012.

Sohrabi, Nader. *Revolution and Constitutionalism in the Ottoman Empire and Iran*. Cambridge & New York: Cambridge University Press, 2011.

Soroush, 'Abdolkarim. 'The Crust and the Core of Rule by the People' www.drsoroush.com, http://www.drsoroush.com/English/By_DrSoroush/E-CMB-20111201-The%20Crust%20and%20the%20Core%20of%20Rule%20by%20the%20People.html

Soroush, 'Abdolkarim. 'The Idea of Democratic Religious Government'. In *Reason, Freedom, and Democracy in Islam: Essential Writings of 'Abdolkarim Soroush*, edited by Ahmad Sadri and Mahmoud Sadri. Oxford & New York: Oxford University Press, 2000.

Soroush, 'Abdolkarim. 'Three Cultures'. In *Reason, Freedom, and Democracy in Islam: Essential Writings of 'Abdolkarim Soroush*, edited by Ahmad Sadri and Mahmoud Sadri. Oxford & New York: Oxford University Press, 2000.

Soroush, 'Abdolkarim. 'Tolerance and Governance: A Discourse on Religion and Democracy'. In *Reason, Freedom, and Democracy in Islam: Essential Writings of 'Abdolkarim Soroush*, edited by Ahmad Sadri and Mahmoud Sadri. Oxford & New York: Oxford University Press, 2000.

Soroush, 'Abdolkarim. 'Tolerance and Governance: A Discourse on Religion and Democracy'. In *Reason, Freedom, & Democracy in Islam: Essential Writings of 'Abdolkarim Soroush*, edited by Ahmad Sadri and Mahmoud Sadri. Oxford & New York: Oxford University Press, 2000.

Soroush, 'Abdolkarim, and Matin Ghaffarian. 'I'm a Neo-Mu'tazilite: An interview with 'Abdulkarim Soroush'. www.drsoroush.com/English/Interviews/E-INT-Neo-Mutazilite_July2008.html

Soroush, Abdulkarim. 'Essentials and Accidentals in Religion'. Translated by Nilou Mobasser. In *The Expansion of Prophetic Experience: Essays on Historicity, Contingency and Plurality in Religion*, edited by Forough Jahanbakhsh. Leiden & Boston: Brill, 2009.

Soroush, Abdulkarim. 'Maximalist Religion, Minimalist Religion'. Translated by Nilou Mobasser. In *The Expansion of Prophetic Experience: Essays on Historicity, Contingency and Plurality in Religion*, edited by Forough Jahanbakhsh. Leiden & Boston: Brill, 2009.

Soroush, 'Abdolkarim. 'Critical Rationalism and Religious and Political Reform in Iran'. In Sir Karl Popper Memorial Lecture, London School of Economic and Political Science, 15 March 2012.

Sreberny, Annabelle, and Massoumeh Torfeh. *Persian Service: The BBC and British Interests in Iran*. Kindle ed. London & New York: I. B. Tauris, 2014.

Stecklow, Steve, Babak Dehghanpisheh, and Yeganeh Torbati. 'Khamenei controls massive financial empire built on property seizures'. *Reuters*, 11 November 2013.

Swartz, David. *Symbolic Power, Politics, and Intellectuals: The Political Sociology of Pierre Bourdieu*. Kindle ed. Chicago: University of Chicago Press, 2013.

Tabataba'i, Sayyid Muhammad Husayn. *The Return to Being: A Translation of Risalat al-Walayah*. Translated by Fazel Asadi Amjad and Mahdi Dasht Bozorgi. Introduced and annotated by S. K. Toussi, ed. London: ICAS Press, 2009.

Talebi, Shahla. *Ghosts of Revolution: Rekindled Memories of Imprisonment in Iran*. Kindle ed. Stanford, CA: Stanford University Press, 2011.

Taylor, Charles. *Modern Social Imaginaries*. Durham, NC: Duke University Press; Chesham: Combined Academic, 2004.

Tazmini, Ghoncheh. *Khatami's Iran: The Islamic Republic and the Turbulent Path to Reform*. London & New York: I. B. Tauris, 2009.

Terhalle, Maximilian. 'Revolutionary Power and Socialization: Explaining the Persistence of Revolutionary Zeal in Iran's Foreign Policy'. *Security Studies* 18, no. 3 (2009).

The Qur'an. Translated by M.A.S. Abdel Haleem. Oxford & New York: Oxford University Press, 2004.

Thompson, E. P. 'The Peculiarities of the English'. In *The Poverty of Theory & Other Essays*. London: Montly Review Press, 1978.

Thompson, E. P. 'The Poverty of Theory or an Orrey of Errors'. In *The Poverty of Theory & Other Essays*. London: Montly Review Press, 1978.

Thompson, Martyn P. 'Reception Theory and the Interpretation of Historical Meaning'. *History and Theory* 32, no. 3 (October 1993).

Tilly, Charles. *Coercion, Capital, and European States, AD 990–1992*. Cambridge, MA: Blackwell, 1992.

Traverso, Enzo. *Left-Wing Melancholia: Marxism, History, and Memory*. New York: Columbia University Press, 2016.

Trotsky, Leon. *The Revolution Betrayed*. Translated by Max Eastman. New York: Dover, 2004.

Vahabzadeh, Peyman. *A Guerrilla Odyssey: Modernization, Secularism, Democracy, and the Fadai Period of National Liberation in Iran, 1971–1979*. Kindle ed. New York: Syracuse University Press, 2010.

Vahdat, Farzin. *God and Juggernaut: Iran's Intellectual Encounter with Modernity*. 1st ed. Syracuse: Syracuse University Press, 2002.

Voll, John O. 'Renewal and Reform in Islamic History: Tajdid and Islah'. In *Voices of Resurgent Islam*, edited by John L. Esposito. Oxford University Press, 1983.

Von Schwerin, Ulrich. *The Dissident Mullah: Ayatollah Montazeri and the Struggle for Reform in Revolutionary Iran*. London & New York: I. B. Tauris, 2015.

Wacquant, Loic J. D. 'Sociology as Socioanalysis: Tales of "Homo Academicus" [By Pierre Bourdieu]'. *Sociological Forum* 5, no. 4 (December 1990).

Walbridge, Linda S., ed. *The Most Learned of the Shi'a: The Institution of the Marja' Taqlid.* Oxford & New York: Oxford University Press, 2001.

Walbridge, Linda S. *The Thread of Mu'awiya: The Making of a Marja' Taqlid.* Bloomington, IN: The Ramsay Press, 2014.

Weber, Max. 'The Prophet'. In *On Charisma and Institution Building,* edited b y S. N. Eisenstadt. Chicago & London: University of Chicago Press, 1968.

Weber, Max. *The Protestant Ethic and the 'Spirit' of Capitalism and Other Writings.* Kindle ed. New York & London: Penguin Books, 2002.

Weber, Max. 'Science as a Vocation'. In *From Max Weber: Essays in Sociology,* edited by H. H. Gerth and C. Wright Mills. Cornwall: Routledge, 1991.

Westad, Odd Arne. *The Global Cold War: Third World Interventions and the Making of Our Times.* Kindle ed. Cambridge & New York: Cambridge University Press, 2007.

Williams, Raymond. *Keywords: A Vocabulary of Culture and Society.* Kindle ed. London & New York: HarperCollins, 1976.

Wittgenstein, Ludwig. *Culture and Value.* Oxford: Blackwell Publishers, 1998.

Wolin, Sheldon D. *Politics and Vision: Continuity and Innovation in Western Political Thought Expanded Edition,* 2nd ed. Kindle ed. Princeton & Oxford: Princeton University Press, 2004.

Zaman, Muhammad Qasim. *Modern Islamic Thought in a Radical Age: Religious Authority and Internal Criticism.* Cambridge & New York: Cambridge University Press, 2012.

Persian-Language Periodicals (Published inside Iran)

Daneshgah-e enqelab
Kayhan-e farhangi
Naqd va nazar
Kiyan
Rah-e now
Shahrvand-e emruz
Bayan
Andisheh-ye puya
Shahed-e yaran

Ketab-e naqd
Rahbord
Mosharekat
Ayin
Mehrnameh
Ehya
Madreseh
Baztab-e andisheh
'Asr-e ma
Payam-e emruz
Zanan

Persian-Language Periodicals (Published outside Iran)

Baran
Noqteh
Arash

Newspapers

Nabard-e Islam
Paykar
Hamshahri
Neshat
Khordad
'Asr-e azadegan
Aftab-e emruz
Jomhuri-ye eslami
Sharq
Salam
Nowruz
Sobh-e emruz
Jame'eh
E'temad
Mosharekat
Nowruz
Fath

Websites

www.ghatreh.com/
http://madresehaghani.ir/
www.drsoroush.com
http://kadivar.com/
www.farsnews.com/
www.radiofarda.com/
www.khabaronline.ir/
http://gooya.com/
www.radiofarda.com/
www.entekhab.ir/
http://farsi.khamenei.ir/
www.rahesabz.net/
www.kaleme.com/
www.asre-nou.net/
www.amontazeri.com
www.tarikhirani.ir
http://tarikhonline.com

Interviews and Correspondence

Abolqasem Fana'i
Mohsen Kadivar
'Abdolkarim Sorush
Arash Naraqi
Mohsen Sazegara
'Ali-Asghar Ramezanpur
Mehdi Nurbakhsh
Sorush Dabbagh
Hossein Kamaly
Hossein Bashiriyeh
'Ali-Akbar Musavi-Kho'ini
Roza Eftekhari

Index

Abadan, 5, 91
Abbasid Caliphate, 194, 332
'Abdi, 'Abbas, 30, 46, 168, 177, 179,
    306, 342, 367
Abraham (prophet), 120
Abrahamian, Ervand, 223
Abu Zarr, 129
Ahmadi-Nezhad, Mahmud, 373, 374
Ahmadi-Rowhani, Hosayn, 118
'Ala', Hosayn, 82
a 'lamiyyat,102, 103, 111
'Alavi-Tabar, 'Ali-Reza, 31, 176, 177,
    181, 290, 291, 367
Al-e Ahmad, Jalal, 166, 220, 284, 296,
    383
Al-e Ahmad, Shams al-Din, 208
al-Farabi, Abu Nasr Mohammad, 100,
    267
Algar, Hamid, 190
Algerian War of Independence, 127
al-Ghazali, Abu Hamid Mohammad,
    99
al-Hakim, Mohsen, 105
'Ali's Shi'ism, 120, 121
al-Najafi Kashef al-Ghita', Shaykh
    Ja'far, 93
al-Sadr, Mohammad-Baqer, 115
al-Tusi, Nasir al-Din, 88
Alviri, Morteza, 105, 119, 148
Amanat, Abbas, 107
Amanollah Khan, 68
Amini, 'Ali, 126
Aminzadeh, Mohsen, 46, 168, 177
Amoli, Mirza Hashem, 263
Anderson, Perry, 347, 351
Andisheh-ye puya (publication), 60
Anglo-Iranian Oil Company, 91
Ansar-e Hezbollah, 237, 334, 336
Ansari, Mohammad-'Ali, 171
Ansari, Morteza, 103, 194

apparatus, 13, 21, 39, 377
approbatory supervision, 144, 146,
    236, 243, 363
Aqajari, Hashem, 1, 2, 4, 5, 6, 7, 31,
    126, 149, 159, 238, 371
Aqa-Tehrani, Morteza, 223
'Arabsorkhi, Fayzollah, 148, 149, 150,
    175, 177, 238, 294
Arak, 81
'Araqi, Mehdi, 74, 78, 91, 149
Arjomand, Sa'id-Amir, 89, 165
Armin, Mohsen, 30, 148, 149, 150,
    168, 176, 181, 182, 232,
    238, 290
Aron, Raymond, 15, 40, 196, 200
Arya Mehr University of Technology,
    114
Asad, Talal, 270
Asad-Abadi, Seyyed Jamal al-Din, 46
'Asgarowladi, Habibollah, 139
Asghari, Mohammad, 167
Asgharzadeh, Ebrahim, 147,
    168, 179
Ashuri, Dariyush, 165, 180
'Asr-e ayandegan (publication), 338
'Asr-e ma (publication), 42, 44, 48,
    150, 165, 168, 181, 233, 388
Assembly of Experts, 144, 151, 161,
    280, 281, 348, 359
Association of Combatant Clerics, 138,
    179, 191, 234, 286, 297, 305
Association of Wisdom and Philosophy,
    198
Atatürk, Mustafa Kemal, 67, 77, 268
'Atriyanfar, Mohammad, 232, 236
Austin, J.L., 23, 24
Avicenna, 246
Ayin circle, 46, 47, 182, 183, 185, 294,
    341, 367
Azari-Qomi, Ahmad, 250

433